Laura J. Downing and Annie Rialland (Eds.)
Intonation in African Tone Languages

Phonology and Phonetics

Editor
Aditi Lahiri

Volume 24

Intonation in African Tone Languages

Edited by
Laura J. Downing and Annie Rialland

DE GRUYTER
MOUTON

ISBN 978-3-11-061071-0
e-ISBN (PDF) 978-3-11-050352-4
e-ISBN (EPUB) 978-3-11-049907-0
ISSN 1861-4191

Library of Congress Cataloging-in-Publication Data
A CIP catalog record for this book has been applied for at the Library of Congress.

Bibliographic information published by the Deutsche Nationalbibliothek
The Deutsche Nationalbibliothek lists this publication in the Deutsche Nationalbibliografie; detailed bibliographic data are available on the Internet at http://dnb.dnb.de.

© 2018 Walter de Gruyter GmbH, Berlin/Boston
This volume is text- and page-identical with the hardback published in 2017.
Typesetting: RoyalStandard, Hong Kong
Printing and binding: CPI books GmbH, Leck

♾ Printed on acid-free paper
Printed in Germany

www.degruyter.com

Table of contents

Laura J. Downing and Annie Rialland
Introduction —— 1

I Northern Africa

Sharon Rose and Page Piccinini
Intonation in the Thetogovela dialect of Moro —— 19

II Western Africa

Michael Cahill
Kɔnni intonation —— 53

Frank Kügler
Tone and intonation in Akan —— 89

Bruce Connell
Tone and intonation in Mambila —— 131

Emmanuel-Moselly Makasso, Fatima Hamlaoui and Seunghun J. Lee
Aspects of the intonational phonology of Bàsàá —— 167

Annie Rialland and Martial Embanga Aborobongui
How intonations interact with tones in Embosi (Bantu C25), a two-tone language without downdrift —— 195

III Eastern Africa

Charles W. Kisseberth
Chimiini intonation —— 225

Cédric Patin
Tone and intonation in Shingazidja —— 285

IV Eastern Central and Southern Africa

Nancy C. Kula and Silke Hamann
Intonation in Bemba —— 323

Laura J. Downing
Tone and intonation in Chichewa and Tumbuka —— 365

Sabine Zerbian
Sentence intonation in Tswana (Sotho-Tswana group) —— 393

Notes on contributors —— 435
Index —— 439

Laura J. Downing and Annie Rialland
Introduction

1 Organization of the book

The twelve languages investigated in the studies in this volume represent different language families and are spoken in disparate regions of the African continent. The chapters are organized geographically, moving from north to south and west to east. The first chapter is thus on Moro (Kordofanian), spoken in the Nuba Mountains region of Sudan. The next five chapters discuss languages spoken in western Africa: both non-Bantu – Kɔnni (Gur, Ghana), Akan (Kwa, Ghana) and Mambila (Bantoid, Cameroon) – and Bantu – Basaa (A43, Cameroon) and Embosi (C25, Congo-Brazzaville). We move then roughly due east in the next two chapters, which discuss closely related eastern Bantu languages (with quite different prosodic systems): Chimiini (G42, formerly spoken in Somalia); and Shingazidja (G44a, Comoros Islands), both considered varieties of Swahili. The final three chapters discuss east central and southern Bantu languages: Bemba (M42, Zambia), Chichewa (N31) and Tumbuka (N21), both spoken in Malawi, and Tswana (S31, South Africa). Two of the languages – Chimiini and Moro – are endangered, and documenting their prosody is especially urgent. The selection of languages also represents a variety of prosodic systems, from highly tonal Mambila (with four level tone contrasts) to the restricted tone or tonal accent systems of Chimiini, Shingazidja and Tumbuka.

Each chapter contains a discussion of the complete prosodic system of the language(s) under investigation: tone and intonation and the interaction between the two. The authors were asked to investigate the prosody of particular constructions (declaratives, polar and content questions and focus constructions), and, if possible, dislocations and complex sentences. In analysing their data, the authors were asked to be attentive to register effects like downstep or pitch raising, to boundary tones and to evidence for different levels of prosodic phrasing. Within these guidelines, the authors were left free to take a more or less quantitative approach, though all were asked to provide pitch tracks of representative constructions. Sound files for the pitch tracks in each chapter can be found at the following link: http://dx.doi.org/10.1515/9783110503524.suppl. The authors were also left free to concentrate on the topics related to intonation that turned out to be most interesting for their particular language.

Laura Downing, University of Gothenburg
Annie Rialland, Laboratory of Phonetics and Phonology, (CNRS) Paris

2 Realization of intonation in tone languages

The contributions aim not only to broaden the descriptive base for intonation typology but also to test proposals about the way intonation can be realized in tone languages. Current textbooks on tone and/or intonation – like Cruttenden (1997), Yip (2002) and Ladd (2008) – survey the expected range of phonetic means for expressing intonation in tone languages, based on the scant existing literature. The consensus is that tonal languages can make use of: 1- pitch register raising or lowering (Cruttenden 1997, Yip 2002); 2- downdrift (downstep) and the suspension of downdrift (Cruttenden 1997, Yip 2002); 3- expansion or narrowing of the pitch range (Cruttenden 1997, Ladd 2008 and Yip 2002); 4- some kind of modification of the final tone of the utterance (Cruttenden 1997); or 5- boundary tones at domain edges or on the closest head (Yip 2002, Ladd 2008). The studies in this volume make particular contributions to our knowledge of the role of "downtrends" (i.e., downdrift, downstep, declination and final lowering), changes in register, and boundary tones, especially final boundary tones, in the intonation of tone languages.

2.1 Downtrends

Within the field of prosody, the study of downtrends is almost a field in itself. Many articles have been devoted to downtrends, as well as lengthy book chapters (Ladd 1996, Gussenhoven 2004). While pioneering approaches analyzed downtrends as overall slopes (Cohen & t'Hart 1967, Delattre 1966, Gårding 1982, for example), the field has made progress by decomposing the downtrends, differentiating the processes at work and providing a better characterization of them. Currently, the following processes are generally recognized as participating in the make up of downtrends:

1) *Declination* is a gradual downsloping of the fundamental frequency. Declination is more easily detectable in sequences of like tones (sequences of High as well as sequences of Low). Declination is generally considered as not being under phonological control.
2) *Downdrift* (or "automatic downstep") is a progressive lowering of tone realisation in alternating High and Low tone sequences. It differs from declination, as it is not gradual. Since the seminal work of Liberman & Pierrehumbert (1984), it has been shown that its general shape is that of a decaying exponential to a non-zero asymptote. Phonetic studies have confirmed this shape

for downdrift in many languages, including African languages such as: Igbo (Liberman et al. 1993), Dschang Bamileke (Bird 1994), Yoruba (Laniran & Clements 2003), Chichewa (Myers 1996), and Dagara (Rialland & Some 2011). Downdrift is often modeled with hierarchical structures, encoding the progression of the step-by-step lowering (Clements 1979, 1981; Ladd 1990).

3) *Downstep* (or "non-automatic downstep") is a downward register shift of a tone, which extends also to the realisation of the following tones. Realisations of "automatic downsteps" (downdrift) and downstep can be similar or not within a given language; see Rialland & Some (2011) for a case study and an overview. Downstep can be triggered by a floating Low tone, or not. In some systems, downstep separates two adjacent High tones and is triggered by the OCP (Obligatory Contour Principle; see, e.g., Odden 1986; Yip 1988 for discussion).

4) *Final lowering* is an additional lowering at the end of an utterance (or a prosodic constituent). This final lowering can be partial or total (lowering of a High tone to the level of a Low). Its domain varies depending upon languages, from a single syllable to a phonological phrase.

5) *Register compression/expansion or register lowering/raising* are register modifications of the tonal realisations. They can have linguistic or paralinguistic functions. If they apply locally, as in register compression of the post-focus parts of an utterance, for example, they can modify the shape of the downtrend.

Understanding downtrends in a given language involves trying to find answers to questions such as the following: do the observed downtrends involve downdrift or declination? To what extent does the downtrend depend upon the sequences of tones involved? Is there final lowering? What is its nature and its extent? If there are downsteps, are they due to floating Low tones, or are they introduced to separate two consecutive High tones (as a consequence of an OCP effect)? Is downdrift realised similarly to downstep?

In the chapters of the present book, downtrends are examined in detail, and the processes involved are analysed and discussed. The table in (1) lists the processes involved in the downtrends of assertive utterances found in the various languages investigated in this volume. (F0 trends in questions are discussed in a separate section of the Introduction, below.)

(1) Downtrends

	Tones	Downdrift	Downstep	Final lowering
Akan	H/L	– (but "phonologized declination")	+	+ (Neutralisation of final L and H)
Basaa	H/L	+	+	–
Bemba	H/ø	+	+ due to OCP	+ (2 types of FL)
Chichewa	H/ø	+	–	+
Chimiini	H/ø	+	–	+
Embosi	H/L	–	–	+
Kɔnni	H/L	+	+	–
Mambila	T1, T2, T3, T4	+ (optional downdrift in T2, T3 alternating sequences)	–	+ (only with the lowest tone, T4)
Moro	H/ø	+	+ due to OCP	+
Shingazidja	H/ø	+	–	+
Tumbuka	H/ø	–	–	+
Tswana	H/ø	+	+ due to OCP	+ (only with final L)

The table in (1) reveals a great deal of diversity. Note that there are languages both with and without downdrift. Two languages (Embosi and Tumbuka) have no downdrift, but they still exhibit a form of downtrend as they have final lowering. To our knowledge, these descriptions are the first ones of a language with this type of prosodic organisation, that is, with final lowering but without downdrift. Note also that in the chapter on Akan, downdrift is reanalysed as "phonologised declination," based on the fact that the downdrift slope shares similarities with the declination found in non-alternating High and Low tone sequences. Various types of downstep are illustrated, including three cases of downstep separating adjacent H tones (in Bemba, Moro and Tswana), motivated by the OCP.

The data and discussion concerning final lowering are particularly rich in this book. Final lowering can be identified in most of the languages: Akan, Bemba, Chichewa, Chimwiini, Embosi, Mambila, Moro, Shingazidja, Tumbuka, Tumbuka, and Tswana. Note that in two languages (Mambila and Tswana), only the Low tone or the lowest tones are affected. In Bemba two forms of Final lowering are found depending upon their domain: a final lowering on one syllable, triggering a sharp drop, and a final lowering stretching over several tone bearing units, forming a smoother fall. Many of the chapters bring interesting new information about the process of final lowering, showing its variety in terms of domains and phonetic implementation. Final lowering can be total, leading to the neutralisation of High and Low tones, as in Akan. It can be realized as a low register plateau, as in Chichewa or in Bemba (for the long stretched one), or as a gradual fall, as in Embosi, or as a sharp fall, as in Bemba (for the one syllable one). Its domain can be short (one syllable) or rather long (a stretch of tone bearing units).

2.2 Boundary tones

As mentioned above, boundary tones are not restricted to non-tonal languages. Rather, they have also been identified as components of the intonation system of tone languages. Some languages seem to have no boundary tone, such as Yoruba, a three tone language (Ladd 1996: 142). As suggested by Hyman & Monaka (2011), languages with complex tonal systems and many tone contrasts are probably most likely to grant a limited role to intonation, in general, and to boundary tones, in particular. Actually, the present book confirms this intuition, as the detailed study of Mambila, a four-tone language, demonstrates that it has no boundary tones.

Other languages in the present book do provide evidence for boundary tones (or some forms of tones associated to boundaries). One of the first difficulties encountered in analysing intonation in tone languages is: how to distinguish lexical tones and boundary tones. A corollary issue is: how do lexical tones and boundary tones interact? Do they simply follow each other, with boundary tones realized linearly before or after the lexical tones? Are their realisations simultaneous, superimposed? Do they cancel each other out? Are there special affinities or antagonisms between lexical tones and boundary tones?

Hyman & Monaka (2011) propose a three-way typology of the possible interactions between lexical tone and boundary tones. Languages can exhibit *accommodation*: both tone and intonation are realized, perhaps on different syllables or with intonation superimposed on lexical tone to give different pitch levels or pitch ranges. Or one can find *submission*: lexical tone is overridden by intonation. A third possibility is *avoidance*: intonation is minimized.

The main result of the chapters in this volume is to illustrate cross-linguistic variety in types of accommodation. Pitch register changes; boundary tone melodies realized alongside lexical tones; boundary tones attracted to particular tones are all attested as ways to allow intonation to be realized without compromising lexical tone contrasts. As noted, only one language totally avoids intonation (Mambila), though others show partial or complete avoidance of certain intonation patterns in some tonal contexts. The extent of submission of lexical tone to intonation is harder to evaluate in these studies. Perhaps final lowering (discussed in more detail above) could be considered a form of submission, as it can lead to the neutralization of (some) tone contrasts in domain final position. These studies raise issues concerning how one should interpret Hyman & Monaka's proposal that require further investigation.

One of the topics which is examined in particular detail in the chapters in this volume is the superimposition of boundary tones and lexical tones. This superimposition can be manifested either by register lowering (for a L% or a L-) or register raising (for a H% or a H-). Superimposition can be local or it can cover a domain defined in terms of prosodic constituents or stretches of tones. Extensive discussion of superimposition can be found in the chapters on Bemba, Embosi, and Shindgazidja. The findings reported demonstrate an attraction or repulsion between certain lexical tones and boundary tones, particularly between H tones and H% boundary tones. This can be found, for example, in Embosi and Shindgazidja.

Another central issue related to boundary tones concerns their use: what do they mark? How are they involved in the marking of modalities such as assertions or questions? How do they participate in the signalling of subdivisions, either syntactical or informational? We will turn to these issues in sections 3 and 4, below.

To sum up this section, the contributions to this volume show that we have to split apart the various types of downtrends into distinct categories to arrive at a better typology. More complexity is also needed in the study of the variety of the effects of boundary tones. The contributions also illustrate less well-studied types of intonation, such as re-phrasing and penult lengthening (or its absence), and draw attention to the need for more work on phenomena like final lengthening or devoicing to signal boundaries. In contrast, the expansion or narrowing of pitch range is not systematically documented in these studies. Further research is needed to test what role pitch range manipulation plays in intonation (as opposed to paralinguistic use).

3 The role of prosody in the grammar

The investigations of intonation in the volume contribute to our understanding of the typical cross-linguistic roles that prosody can play in the grammar (Zerbian 2010): 1- to express focus, 2- to distinguish sentence types (e.g. assertions and questions), and 3- to demarcate syntactic constituent edges. We take up each of these topics in turn.

3.1 The expression of focus

It is commonly assumed that all languages prosodically highlight focused elements, either through culminativity (i.e., stressing or otherwise making the focused word prominent) or through demarcation (i.e., placing a juncture before or after the focused word). (See, e.g., Downing & Pompino-Marschall 2013, Zubizarreta 2010 for discussion.) However, recent surveys of information structure in African (and other non-European) languages, like Downing & Pompino-Marschall (2013) and Güldemann et al. (2015), call into question how widespread the prosodic marking of focus is.

The papers in this collection contribute to this typological investigation. Several languages discussed in the book do not appear to have any focus prosody. Of those that do, only two (Akan, Shingazidja) use demarcative means – rephrasing – to highlight focused elements. None of the languages use culminativity or prominence assignment. On the contrary, we find pitch lowering of focused elements in some languages (Akan, Bemba), and, in others, typologically unusual means of marking out-of-focus constituents, such as default accent assignment (Chimiini). The range of expressions of focus – and lack of focus prosody – illustrated by the languages in this volume is summarized in the table in (2):

(2) Focus prosody

	Focus prosody?	If so, type of marking
Akan	yes	phrasing; pitch lowering
Basaa	no	
Bemba	yes	pre-focus pitch raising; pitch compression from the focussed word
Chichewa	no	
Chimiini	yes	suspension of downstep; accent placement
Embosi	no	
Kɔnni	no	
Mambila	no	
Moro	no	
Shingazidja	yes	phrasing
Tumbuka	no	
Tswana	no	

3.2 Distinguishing assertions and questions: the intonation of polar questions

Downtrends are typical of assertions in all the languages investigated in the book, except for Mambila (where downtrend is restricted to T4 sequences). In all of the languages documented in this collection, content questions have a similar intonation to assertions, or at least a similar overall intonational profile. (As noted in work since Bolinger 1978, this is cross-linguistically very common.)

In contrast, it has been shown that polar question intonations are quite diverse in Africa; see Rialland (2007) for a typology. This diversity is also exemplified in the set of languages investigated in the present book. The table in (3) surveys the prosodic markers found by the authors of the various chapters:

(3) Polar question prosody

	Tones	Falling intonation	Downdrift suppression	V length	Raising of first or last H(s)	Register raising/ expansion
Akan	H/L	L%	–	lengthening	–	+
Basaa	H/L	– (but -ɛ̀ in some contexts)	–	lengthening in some contexts	–	+
Bemba	H/ø	L%	+	–	–	+
Chichewa	H/ø	L H L%	+	–	–	irregular
Chimiini	H/ø	L%	–	–	+ last H (optional)	+
Embosi	H/L	L%	–	–	+ last H	+
Kɔnni	H/L	ꜜH, L, HꜜH	–	lengthening	–	+
Mambila	T1, T2, T3, T4	–	–	–	–	–
Moro	H/ø	L% -à (optional)	–	–	+ first H(s) or all H(s)	+
Shingazidja	H/ø	L%	+	–	+ penultimate supra-high	+
Tumbuka	H/ø	L H L%	–	–	+ last H(s)	+
Tswana	H/ø	L% only in all L sequences à (optional)	–	Suppression of penultimate lengthening	–	+

At first glance, the striking point of this list is the absence of languages with a H%, that is with a rising final intonation, even though intonation surveys like Bolinger (1978) observe that a rising terminal is a cross-linguistically dominant pattern for polar questions. All of the languages in this list instead have a falling intonation or no special intonation in polar questions. However, many of the languages do have the pitch raising or register expansion or suspension of downstep in polar questions that work like Gussenhoven (2004) suggests is a strong cross-linguistic tendency. Moro, the only Kordofanian language studied in the book, is also the only one to optionally display targeted raising of High tones towards the beginning (rather than just at the end) of a polar question.

Two languages (Basaa and Mambila) have no boundary tones in polar questions. Basaa has global register raising, while Mambila demonstrates no intonational marking of questions at all. It is noteworthy that both of these languages have a question particle: ɛ/ɛ̀ in Basaa and wā in Mambila.

"Lax question prosody," as defined in Rialland (2009), can be recognized in Akan and Kɔnni. Both have falling intonations (quite diversified in Kɔnni) and a vowel lengthening, which are two characteristics of the lax prosody. These characteristics are combined with register raising, forming a hybrid form of the lax prosody. Note that these two languages are spoken in the Sudanic Belt, where lax prosody is an areal feature (Clements & Rialland 2008). Basaa, spoken at the margins of the Sudanic belt, could also be a candidate to be integrated in the group of languages with lax prosody, due to its final vowel lengthening (even if it is only in some contexts) and its toneless or L tone question particle. It can also be remarked that Moro, a Kordofanian language spoken in the Sudanic belt, has two features which are reminiscent of lax prosody markers: the final L% and a marker –à (which is optional).

As for the non-Bantoid Bantu languages, all except Basaa have a L% and some form of high-pitch marker. The list of Bantu languages sharing these two features is: Bemba, Chichewa, Chimiini, Embosi, Shingazidja, Tumbuka and Tswana. The high-pitched markers involved are: suspension of downdrift (Bemba, Chichewa, Shingazidja), raising of first or last H tone(s) (Chimiini, Embosi, Shingazidja, Tumbuka), and register raising for all of them. Tswana fits only partially in this characterisation, as its L% boundary tone in questions is found only in very restricted contexts. Its main marker of polar question seems to be the suppression of penultimate lengthening. (See, too, Hyman & Monaka 2011 for discussion of the role of penultimate lengthening in the intonation of a closely related language.)

3.3 Providing cues to syntactic constituent edges

A final important function of intonation is to demarcate certain syntactic constituent edges. (See, e.g., Nespor & Vogel 1986; Selkirk 1986; Truckenbrodt 2005; Watson & Gibson 2004.) In particular, fronted and other topicalized constituents are often set off by intonational markers, such as pause or a boundary tone (Frascarelli 2000), as are the edges of embedded or conjoined clauses in a complex sentence (Truckenbrodt 2005). Several of the papers in this collection examine the prosody of these two types of constructions. As shown in the table in (4), these constructions are, indeed, often set off by distinctive prosody. (Note that not all of the papers discuss the prosody of these constructions.) There are interesting exceptions to this trend, however. The edges of fronted constituents and complex clauses are not systematically marked in Embosi. In Tswana, fronted constituents are not set off from what follows if they are immediately preverbal:

(4) Constituent edge marking

	Fronted constituent	Embedded clause
Akan	pause; partial pitch reset	pause; partial pitch reset
Basaa	–	–
Bemba	H% for non-clausal topic; L% for clausal topic (right dislocations are compressed)	H% or L% (depending on subordinate clause type)
Chichewa	optional pause, phrase boundary, H%	optional pause, phrase boundary, H%
Chimiini	phrasing (right dislocations are compressed)	phrasing; accent placement
Embosi	no special prosody (though right dislocations are preceded by L%)	no special prosody
Kɔnni	pause not followed by downdrift	pause; register lowering; pitch range reduction
Mambila	–	–
Moro	H% following fronted cleft	H%; vowel lengthening following subordinate construction
Shingazidja	H% (and other boundary tones)	H%
Tumbuka	optional pause, H%	optional pause, H%
Tswana	pause, partial reset (if fronted non-subject is not immediately preverbal)	partial reset; boundary tones

We can make some generalizations about types of non-final prosody based on this sample. Pauses, continuation rises (H%) and (partial) pitch resets are common markers of sentence-internal Intonation Phrase edges in these languages, as they are cross-linguistically. (See, e.g., Gussenhoven 2004; Nespor & Vogel 1986; Truckenbrodt 2005.) However, other types of prosody are also attested, showing that these constructions deserve further cross-linguistic research.

4 Prosodic domains and the phonology-syntax interface

Prosodic phenomena in African languages, and most notably Bantu languages, have played an important role in the development of theories of the phonology-syntax interface since the mid-1970s. A central question for interface theories is, as Chen (1990) so neatly puts it, "What must phonology know about syntax?" One finds two leading approaches, which provide two very different answers to this question. *Indirect reference theories* propose that phonology is not directly conditioned by syntactic information. Rather, the interface is mediated by phrasal prosodic constituents, which need not match any syntactic constituent. Only very limited syntactic parameters can be referred to in defining the prosodic constituents. In current indirect reference theories (e.g. Itô & Mester 2012, 2013; Selkirk 2011; Truckenbrodt 2005), only two levels of phrasal constituents are available: Phonological Phrase, which correlates with a syntactic XP, and Intonational Phrase, which correlates with a clause.[1] *Direct reference theories*, in contrast, argue that phrasal prosodic constituents are superfluous, as phonology can – indeed, must – refer directly to syntactic structure. (See Cheng & Downing (2016) and Downing (2013) for more detailed recent overviews.) The papers in this volume that explicitly discuss phrasing take the indirect reference approach, assuming that prosodic parsing algorithms are only informed by where the edges – right and/or left – of major constituents – XP or clause – are located in the string.

From the earliest work on the phonology-syntax interface in African languages it has become clear that we can identify two broad types of phrasing. In some languages, the entire sentence up to the left or right edge of a clause is

---

[1] Confusingly, these same prosodic domains are used in approaches to intonation which do not assume that prosodic domains like Intonation Phrase map to syntactic constituents. See Bennett (2015) for critical discussion.

the domain for some prosodic processes. Languages with this pattern include Haya (Byarushengo et al. 1976, Hyman & Byarushengo 1984). That is, in these languages, one only appears to find Intonation Phrases. In other languages, we find evidence for smaller prosodic chunks, as every DP (XP) conditions a prosodic domain. Languages with this pattern include Chimiini (Kisseberth & Abasheikh 1974; Selkirk 1986). That is, in these languages, the basic unit of phrasing is the Phonological Phrase. Few previous studies of prosodic phrasing in African languages have been concerned with motivating more than one level of phrasing. (Kanerva 1990 is a noteworthy exception.)

The papers in this volume contribute to our knowledge of how many levels of phrasing we expect to find in a particular language, and the types of motivations for proposing distinct levels of phrasing. As we can see in the table in (5), most of the languages in this volume provide evidence for both a Phonological Phrase and an Intonational Phrase level.

(5) Levels of phrasing

	Phonological Phrase (XP)	Intonational Phrase (clause)
Akan	✓ (recursive)	✓ (recursive)
Basaa	✓	✓
Bemba	✓	✓ (recursive)
Chichewa	✗	✓ (recursive)
Chimiini	✓ (recursive)	?
Embosi	✗	✓
Kɔnni	?	✓
Mambila	✗	✓
Moro	?	?
Shingazidja	✓	✓
Tumbuka	✓	✓
Tswana	✓	✓

Some of these results represent changes from previous research on the language concerned. Kanerva (1990) argues for two levels of phrasing, in Chichewa whereas the chapter on Chichewa in this volume proposes that the phrasing is best analysed by appealing to only one level, the Intonational Phrase. The issue of number of levels is complicated for the papers that assume prosodic phrasing can be recursive, following work from Ladd (1986) through, more recently, the papers in Selkirk & Lee (2015). It is a matter for future research on prosodic domains to investigate whether languages like Bemba or Chichewa, for example, with recursive Intonational Phrase is best analyzed as having one level of prosodic phrasing or two. In this volume, Embosi and Mambila provide the clearest evidence that in some languages just one level of phrasing – the Intonation

Phrase – is relevant for the prosody. Finally, the chapter on Tswana illustrates that one can find variation in the number of levels even between closely related languages like Tswana (S.31) and No. Sotho (S.32), both members of the Sotho-Tswana group. Zerbian (2006, 2007) analyzes No. Sotho with only one level of phrasing, the Intonational Phrase, while Tswana provides prosodic evidence for both the Phonological Phrase and the Intonational Phrase.

5 Conclusion and perspectives for future research

To sum up, the chapters in this volume make typological contributions to a number of issues related to intonation in tone languages, from the means of realizing intonation to the functions of intonation to the phonology-syntax interface. There is still far too little research on intonation in African tone languages, and it is hoped that this volume will inspire more phonetically- and phonologically informed studies in the future.

Acknowledgements

We would like to thank Aditi Lahiri for encouraging us to edit this volume and for good advice and encouragement all along the way. The unfailing helpfulness of the editorial staff at Mouton made the practical part of putting the work together go smoothly. A number of external reviewers helped us set high standards for the papers in the volume – and also thoughtfully respected our deadlines, in spite of their busy schedules: Yiya Chen, Elisabeth Delais-Roussarie, Gorka Elordieta, Caroline Féry, Sonia Frota, Martine Grice, Carlos Gussenhoven, Larry Hyman, Shinichiro Ishihara, Sara Myrberg, and Pilar Prieto. We thank all of you.

Annie Rialland's work on this volume was partially supported by a public grant overseen by the French National Research Agency (ANR) as part of the program "Investissements d'Avenir" (reference: ANR-10-LABX-0083).

References

Bennett, Ryan. 2015. Review of: Sun-Ah Jun (ed.), *Prosodic typology II: the phonology of intonation and phrasing. Phonology* 32: 337–350.

Bird, Steven. 1994. Automated tone transcription. In Steven Bird (ed.), *Proceedings of the First Meeting of the ACL Special Interest Group in Computational Phonology*. Las Cruces, NM. http://www.aclweb.org/anthology/W94-0201

Bolinger, Dwight. 1978. Intonation across languages. In Joseph H. Greenberg (ed.), *Universals of Human Language. vol. 2: Phonology*. Stanford: Stanford University Press, 471–524.

Bostoen, Koen. 2003. *Introduction à l'intonation du cilubà*. Ghent University: RECALL.

Byarushengo, Ernest Rugwa, Larry M. Hyman & Sarah Tenenbaum. 1976. Tone, accent, and assertion in Haya. In Larry M. Hyman (ed.), *Studies in Bantu Tonology. SCOPIL* 3, 185–205.

Chen, Matthew Y. 1990. What must phonology know about syntax? In Sharon Inkelas & Draga Zec (eds.), *The Phonology-Syntax Connection*. Chicago: CSLI, 19–46.

Cheng, Lisa L.-S. & Laura J. Downing. 2016. Phasal syntax = phrasal phonology? *Syntax* 19 (2), 159–191.

Clements, G. N. 1979. The description of terraced-level tone languages. *Language* 55: 536–558.

Clements, G. N. 1981. A hierarchical model of tone. In W. U. Dressler, O. E. Pfeiffer, & J. Rennison (eds.), *Phonologica 1980*. (Innsbrucker Beiträge zur Sprachwissenschaft, vol. 36), 69–75.

Clements, G. N. 1990. The Status of Register in Intonation Theory: Comments on the Papers by Ladd and by Inkelas and Leben. In J. Kingston & M. Beckman (eds.), *Papers in Laboratory Phonology I: Between the Grammar and the Physics of Speech*. Cambridge: Cambridge University Press, 58–72.

Clements, G. N. & Annie Rialland. 2008. Africa as a phonological area. In Bernd Heine & Derek Nurse (eds.), *A Linguistic Geography of Africa*. Cambridge: Cambridge University Press, 36–85.

Cohen, A. & J. t'Hart. 1967. On the anatomy of intonation. *Lingua* 19: 177–192.

Connell, Bruce & D. Robert Ladd. 1990. Aspects of pitch realisation in Yoruba. *Phonology* 7: 1–29.

Cruttenden, Alan. 1997. *Intonation*. 2nd edition. Cambridge: Cambridge University Press.

Delattre, Pierre. 1966. Les dix intonations de base du français. *French Review* 40: 1–14.

Downing, Laura J. 2013. Issues in the phonology-syntax interface in African languages. *Selected Proceedings of the 43rd Annual Conference on African Languages*. Somerville, MA: Cascadilla Proceedings Project, 26–38.

Downing, Laura J. & Bernd Pompino-Marschall. 2013. The focus prosody of Chichewa and the Stress-Focus constraint: a response to Samek-Lodovici (2005). *Natural Language and Linguistic Theory* 31: 647–681.

Frascarelli, Mara. 2000. *The Syntax-Phonology Interface in Focus and Topic Constructions in Italian*. Dordrecht: Foris.

Gårding, Eva. 1982. Swedish prosody: summary of a project. *Phonetica* 39: 288–301.

Güldemann, Tom, Sabine Zerbian & Malter Zimmermann. 2015. Variation in Information Structure with special reference to Africa. *Annual Linguistics Review* 1: 55–78.

Gussenhoven, Carlos. 2004. *The Phonology of Tone and Intonation*. Cambridge: Cambridge University Press.

Gussenhoven, Carlos and Tomas Riad (eds.), *Tones and Tunes: Studies in Word and Sentence Prosody*, Berlin: Mouton de Gruyter.

Herman, Rebecca. 1996. Final lowering in KiPare. *Phonology* 13: 171–193.

Hirst, Daniel & Albert di Cristo. 1999. *Intonation Systems: A Survey of Twenty Languages*. Cambridge: Cambridge University Press.

Hyman, Larry M. & Ernest Rugwa Byarushengo. 1984. A model of Haya tonology. In G. N. Clements & John Goldsmith (eds.), 53–103.

Hyman, Larry M. & Kemmonye C. Monaka. 2011. Tonal and non-tonal intonation in Shekgalagari. In Sonia Frota, Gorka Elordieta & Pilar Prieto (eds), *Prosodic categories: production, perception and comprehension*, 267–290. Dordrecht: Springer Verlag.

Itô, Junko and Armin Mester. 2012. Recursive prosodic phrasing in Japanese. In T. Borowsky, S. Kawahara, T. Shinya and M. Sugahara (eds.), *Prosody Matters*. Sheffield: Equinox Publishing, 280–303.

Itô, Junko and Armin Mester. 2013. Prosodic subcategories in Japanese. *Lingua* 124, 20–40.

Jun, Sun-Ah (ed.). 2005. *Prosodic Typology: The Phonology of Intonation and Phrasing*. Oxford: OUP.

Jun, Sun-Ah (ed.). 2014. *Prosodic Typology II: The Phonology of Intonation and Phrasing*. Oxford: OUP.

Kanerva, Jonni M. 1990. *Focus and Phrasing in Chichewa Phonology*. New York: Garland.

Kisseberth, Charles W. & Mohammad Imam Abasheikh. 1974. Vowel length in Chi-mwi:ni – a case study of the role of grammar in phonology. *CLS Papers from the Parasession on Natural Phonology*, 193–209.

Ladd, D. Robert. 1986. Intonational phrasing: the case for recursive prosodic structure. *Phonology Yearbook* 3: 311–340.

Ladd, D. Robert. 1990. Metrical representation of pitch register. In J. Kingston and M. Beckman (eds.), *Papers in Laboratory Phonology I: Between the Grammar and Physics of Speech*, 35–57. Cambridge: Cambridge University Press.

Ladd, D. Robert. 1996. *Intonational Phonology*, 1st edition. Cambridge: Cambridge University Press.

Ladd, D. Robert. 2008. *Intonational Phonology*. 2nd edition. Cambridge: Cambridge University Press.

Laniran, Yetunde O. 1992. Intonation in tone languages: the phonetic implementation of tones in Yoruba. Ph.D. dissertation, Cornell University.

Laniran, Yetunde O. & G. N. Clements. 2003. Downstep and high raising: interacting factors in Yoruba tone production. *Journal of Phonetics* 31: 203–250.

Leben, Will E. 1989. Intonation in Chadic: an overview. In Zygmunt Frajzyngier (ed.), *Current Progress in Chadic Linguistics*. Amsterdam: John Benjamins, 199–217.

Liberman, Mark & Janet Pierrehumbert. 1984. Intonational invariance under changes in pitch range and length. In Mark Aronoff & R. T. Oehrle (eds.), *Language and sound structure*. Cambridge, MA: The MIT Press, 157–233.

Liberman, Mark, J. Michael Schultz, Soonhyun Hong & Vincent Okeke. 1993. The phonetic interpretation of tone in Igbo. *Phonetica* 50: 147–160.

Maw, Joan & John Kelly. 1975. *Intonation in Swahili*. London: SOAS.

Myers, Scott. 1996. Boundary tones and the phonetic implementation of tone in Chichewa. *Studies in African Linguistics* 25: 29–60.

Myers, Scott. 1999a. Downdrift and pitch range in Chichewa intonation. *Proceedings of ICPhS99*: 1981–1984.

Myers, Scott. 1999b. Tone association and f_0 timing in Chichewa. *Studies in African Linguistics* 28: 215–239.

Nespor, Marina & Irene Vogel. 1986. *Prosodic Phonology*. Dordrecht: Foris.

Odden, David. 1986. On the role of the Obligatory Contour Principle in phonological theory. *Language* 62: 353–383.

Rialland, Annie. 2007. Question prosody: an African perspective. In *Tones and Tunes: Studies in Word and Sentence Prosody*, C. Gussenhoven and T. Riad (eds.), Berlin: Mouton de Gruyter, 35–62.

Rialland, Annie. 2009. The African lax question prosody: Its realisation and geographical distribution. *Lingua* 119: 928–949.

Rialland, Annie & Achille P. Somé. 2011. Downstep and linguistic scaling in Dagara-Wulé. In J. Goldsmith, E. Hume & L. Wetzels (eds.), *Tones and features: phonetic and phonological perspectives*. Berlin: Mouton de Gruyter, 108–136.
Selkirk, Elisabeth. 1986. On derived domains in sentence phonology. *Phonology Yearbook* 3, 371–405.
Selkirk, Elisabeth O. 2011. The syntax-phonology interface. In: J. Goldsmith, J. Riggle & A. Yu (eds.), *The Handbook of Phonological Theory*, 2nd edition. Oxford: Wiley-Blackwell, 435–484.
Selkirk, Elisabeth O. & Seunghun J. Lee (eds.). 2015. Constituent structure in sentence phonology. Special issue of *Phonology* 32, 1.
Truckenbrodt, Hubert. 2005. A short report on Intonation Phrase boundaries in German. *Linguistische Berichte* 203: 273–296.
Watson, Duane & Edward Gibson. 2004. The relationship between intonational phrasing and syntactic structure in language production. *Language and Cognitive Processes* 19: 713–755.
Yip, Moira. 1988. The Obligatory Contour Principle and phonological rules: a loss of identity. *Linguistic Inquiry*: 65–100.
Yip, Moira. 2002. *Tone*. Cambridge: Cambridge University Press.
Zerbian, Sabine. 2006. Expression of Information Structure in the Bantu Language Northern Sotho. Doctoral dissertation. Humboldt-University Berlin.
Zerbian, Sabine. 2007. Phonological phrasing in Northern Sotho. *The Linguistic Review* 24: 233–262.
Zerbian, Sabine. 2010. Developments in the study of intonational typology. *Language and Linguistics Compass* 4: 874–889.
Zubizarreta, Maria Luisa. 2010. The syntax and prosody of focus: the Bantu-Italian connection. *Iberia* 2: 131–168.

I **Northern Africa**

Sharon Rose and Page Piccinini
Intonation in the Thetogovela dialect of Moro

Abstract: This chapter describes and analyzes the intonation patterns of assertive declaratives, polar questions, wh-questions, clefts and continuations in the Thetogovela dialect of Moro, a Kordofanian language of Sudan. Declaratives and polar questions are marked by a L%, but polar questions are differentiated from declaratives through F0 pitch range expansion in the early part of the sentence followed by F0 compression. Wh-in-situ non-subject questions show a similar F0 contour to declaratives, but are articulated with an F0 range in between polar questions and declaratives. Wh-ex-situ questions use a cleft construction in which the question word is fronted, and marked with a H prominence on the final syllable of the cleft. Moro uses clefts to express focus constructions, and they show the same intonation pattern as wh-ex-situ questions. Narrative subordinate structures and list continuations show evidence for H% boundary tones and phrase-final lengthening of vowels.

Keywords: Moro, polar questions, pitch range, downstep, pitch compression, F0 raising, boundary tones, wh-questions, clefts, phrase-final lengthening

1 Introduction

Moro is a Kordofanian (Niger-Congo) language spoken in the Nuba Mountains region in South Kordofan State in the Republic of Sudan. In this chapter, we describe and analyze the basic intonation patterns of declarative, neutral assertion sentences and information seeking questions in the Thetogovela dialect, including both polar (yes/no) questions and wh- (content) questions. We also briefly address the intonation patterns of clefts and continuations. The chapter provides both description and some quantitative analysis, and is structured as follows. In section 2, we briefly introduce the language and the dialect under consideration. In 3, we present an overview of the basic lexical tones of the language, along with a description of tone patterns, tone spreading, downstep and

---

Sharon Rose, University of California San Diego
Page Piccinini, École Normale Supérieure

DOI 10.1515/9783110503524-002

tonal stability. In section 4, we discuss the distinction between simple declarative sentences and polar questions. We assess how intonation interacts with the lexical tone, and show that Moro signals polar questions by pitch range adjustment. In section 5, we present simple wh-questions and clefts and discuss their intonation patterns. In section 6, we address continuations, and in section 7, we conclude.

2 Moro language

Moro belongs to the Heiban branch of Kordofanian (Schadeberg 1981), and is divided into seven dialects. There is a standard written form used in pedagogical and religious materials, primarily based on the Werria dialect. The native name for Moro is Ðəmwĕđənia (as written in the standard dialect). The dialect studied in this chapter is Thetogovela [ðətogovəlá], also identified as Toberelda in Ethnologue and as Tobaɾəlda in Blench (2005). The exact number of Moro speakers is unknown. Thousands have been displaced internal to Sudan or to other countries due to ongoing war in the Nuba Mountains.

3 Tone

Moro has two contrastive tones, a high (H) tone, marked with an accent diacritic, and a low (L) tone, unmarked, as shown by the following disyllabic minimal pairs. This opposition can be construed as a H/Ø contrast (Jenks & Rose 2011), as tone rules reference H tone.

(1) a. HH ðólóŋ   'iron nail'   LH ðolóŋ 'eel'
    b. LL ŋata   'dirtiness'   LH ŋatá   'very little'
    c. HL káw:a   's/he is urinating' LH kaw:á 's/he is persuading'
    d. LL ðəra   'tree sp.'   HH ðə́rá   'vine of gourd'

Tone bearing units are usually vowels, but high tone can also appear on nasals and [r].

In the nominal system, all combinations of H and L tones occur, with the restriction that two high tones separated by one or more low tones cannot occur within a single root (including noun class markers): *HLH, *HLHL, *LHLH,

*HLLH. Exceptions are reduplications, such as ləɲáləɲá 'sandstone' or compound words. Adjacent sequences of H tone are widely attested, and the restriction can therefore be analyzed as a restriction of one single autosegmental H tone per word, assuming that tone sequences consist of a single H tone that is spread to other vowels (Jenks & Rose 2011).

Rightward tone spreading is attested in nouns with two affixes. The instrumental/comitative suffix /-Ca/ copies the tone of the final syllable of the noun. We assume this is accomplished through spreading. C indicates noun class concord.

(2) Instrumental –Ca

a.	LH-H	ʌðú-já	'breast'	LL-L	eða-ga	'meat'
b.	LHH-H	ðəbárá-ðá	'cotton'	HL-L	ðóṭoŋ-ða	'agama lizard'

The locative prefix /é-/ spreads high tone rightwards. Either the high tone may spread once to the following tone bearing unit, or it may spread to the end of the noun stem (excluding other suffixes), as shown below. In both cases, if the noun contains a LH sequence, H tone spreading halts one syllable away to avoid placing two H tones adjacent to each other, ex. ðəŋəlá → é-ðəŋəlá.

(3) Locative é-

	Noun	locative		noun	locative	
a.	ðaba	é-ðábá	cloud	ðəŋəlá	é-ðəŋəlá	tongue
b.	ŋəðəmáná	é-ŋəðəmán	beans	ðáɲala	é-ðáɲala	sheep
c.	ðəbárá	é-ðəbárá	cotton	ləŋɡʌ́l:əme	é-ləŋɡʌ́l:əme	pen

Rightward tone spreading is also observed between words. When a verb ends in a single H tone, this tone extends to the first tone-bearing unit of the following object, as long as it is not H-tone bearing itself. In the following examples, the word lugi 'trees' is low-toned, but receives a H tone in (4b) due to the final single H tone on the verb. There is no spreading in (4a) as the H tone originates on the verb root and has already spread onto the final verb suffix -a[1]

---

[1] Glossing abbreviations used: CAUS: causative, CL: noun class, CLF: cleft, COMP: complementizer, DEM: demonstrative, DPC: dependent clause; IMPV: imperfective, INF: infinitive, OC: objective case, OM: object marker, PFV: perfective, PL: plural, QP: question particle; RTC: root clause, SG: singular, SM: subject marker

(4) a. l-a-pə́g-á lugi loaɲa
SM.CLl-RTC-uproot-IMPV CLl.tree CLl.many
'They are uprooting a lot of trees.'

b. l-a-pəg-ó lúgi loaɲa
SM.CLl-RTC-uproot-PFV CLl.tree CLl.many
'They uprooted a lot of trees.'

Downstep, or the lowering of a H tone adjacent to another H tone, is observed at some word and stem boundaries in Moro. H tones do not delete, but they can undergo lowering. The High tone spreading rule shown in (4b) does not apply if the following noun begins with a high tone, as in (5). In these cases, the high toned-object can undergo downstep, indicated with ↓, because the preceding word ends in a High tone.

(5) a. l-a-pəg-ó ↓nə́deə́ noaɲa
SM.CLl-RTC-uproot-PFV CLn.doleib palm CLn.many
'They uprooted a lot of doleib palm trees.'

b. ŋerá ŋalagó ↓ŋwóréðá
CLŋ.girl SM.CLŋ-RTC-plant-PFV CLŋ.sesame seed
'The girl planted sesame seeds.'

Downstep can be seen in the following pitch track in Figure 1 of sentence (5b). The HHH object [ŋwóréðá] shows a drop of the H tones to a mid F0 range following the final H of the verb, but not as low as the low tones of the verb [ŋalagó] preceding it. The final syllable of the sentence shows a falling tone, indicative of a low boundary tone L%. This will be discussed further in section 4.

The other environments for downstep occur within the verb stem itself. See Jenks & Rose (2015) for details.

Moro shows tonal stability. If a vowel bearing a single H tone is deleted, the H tone appears on a neighbouring vowel or sonorant. Tonal stability occurs when vowels are juxtaposed across morphemes or word-boundaries, and the first vowel deletes. Compare the forms in (6a) and (6b). In the latter, the subject relative clause marker /é-/ is deleted due to the following vowel-initial root, but its high tone appears on the root. In (6d), the object marker /ɲé-/ loses its vowel, and the high tone is recuperated on the preceding vowel rather than the following, a pattern which is unique to high-toned object markers.

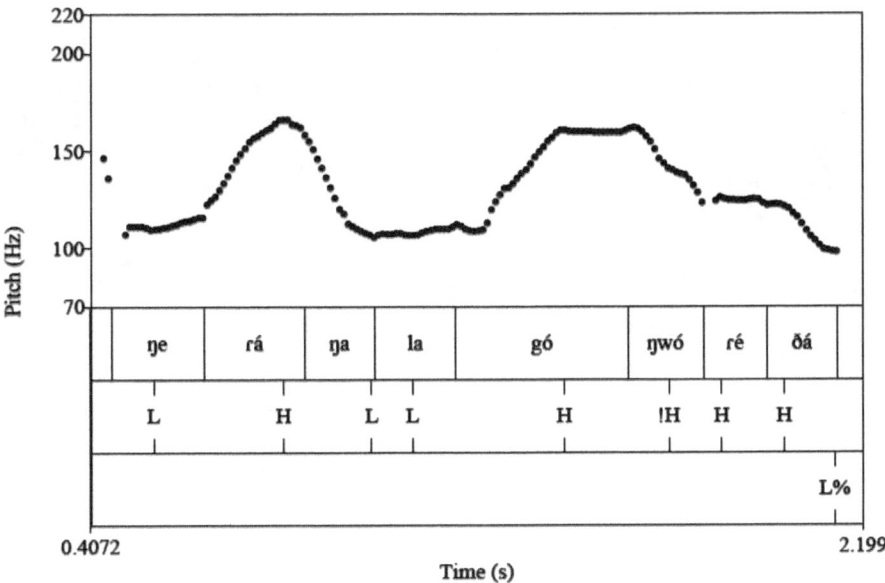

Figure 1: ŋerá ŋalagó ↓ŋwóréðá 'the girl planted sesame seeds' (Speaker AN)

(6) a. g-a-ogət̪-ó [kogət̪ó] 's/he jumped'
    b. g-é-ogət̪-ó [kógət̪ó] '... who (sg.) jumped'
    c. g-ʌ-ʌwút̪-ʌ [kʌwút̪ʌ] 'he is about to drop something'
    d. g-ʌ-ɲé-ʌwut̪-ʌ [kʌ́ɲʌwut̪ʌ] 'he is about to drop me'

In running speech, the same effect is observed across word boundaries:

(7) [lapəgúgi]
    l-a-pəg-ó   ugi
    SM.CL1-RTC-uproot-PFV   CLg.tree
    'They uprooted a tree.'

4 Simple declarative utterances and polar questions

We now consider the basic structure and intonation patterns of simple subject-verb-object declarative assertive utterances and corresponding polar questions. Polar questions can be morphologically distinguished from declarative sentences in Thetogovela Moro by a low-toned question particle /-a/ ([ʌ] under vowel harmony), attached to the last word in the question as in (8b). Use of a low-toned low vowel question particle is widely attested in African languages in the Sudanic belt (Rialland 2007, 2009). However, this particle is optional in Moro, and there are no word order changes to signal a polar question. The responses to positive polar questions are typically *aa* 'yes' or *ndo* 'no', but can also include the verb and its complement (8c–d).

(8) a. k-a-vǝ́l-á   áŋǝ́-p↓ǝ́g-á   ŋwóréðá   úlʌlítu̠
       SM.CLg-RTC-go-IMPV   3SGSM-pick-INF   CLŋ.sesame seed   tomorrow
       'He/she is going to pick sesame tomorrow.'

   b. a-g-a-vǝ́l-á   a-pǝ́g-á   ŋwóréðá   úlʌlítu̠-ʌ?
      2SGSM-CLg-RTC-go-IMPV   2SGSM-pick-INF   CLŋ.sesame seed   tomorrow-QP
      'Are you going to pick sesame tomorrow?'

   c. aa   é-g-a-vǝ́l-á   e-pǝ́g-á   ŋwóréðá
      yes 1SGSM-CLg-RTC-go-IMPV   1SGSM-pick-INF   CLŋ.sesame seed
      'Yes, I'm going to pick sesame.'

   d. ndo é-g-a-vǝ́l-á   e-pǝ́g-á   lájá
      no   1SGSM-CLg-RTC-go-IMPV   1SGSM-pick-INF   CLl.honey
      'No, I'm going to collect honey.'

The question particle often fails to appear after words ending in vowels, and there is no discernible long vowel if the final word of the question ends in [a].

In order to determine the overall prosodic pattern of declaratives and polar questions, and to ascertain the effect of intonation on lexical tone, an experiment was conducted in which speakers produced assertive declarative sentences and matching polar questions.

4.1 Experiment 1 – Polar questions and declaratives

4.1.1 Materials

A set of ten sentences of the form subject-verb-object or subject-verb-adverb was constructed in which the tone patterns and word length varied. All words except one subject were vowel-final – see the Appendix for a list of stimuli. The vowel-final pattern reflects Moro word structure, as most nouns and all verbs are vowel-final. Materials were presented in Moro orthography, which uses the

Roman alphabet with some IPA symbols such as ŋ and ə. Tone is not indicated. The polar question particle was written as -a attached to the final word. Three of the ten questions were marked with the question particle, following words that ended in [i], [o] and [u]. All other questions ended in [a] or [eə] and did not contain a question particle. Although the question particle is often omitted after vowels, the speakers preferred to include it in the written materials. This also enabled us to have data both with the particle and without.

4.1.2 Speakers

Two male speakers of Thetogovela Moro participated in the study, EJ and AN.[2] They are above the age of 40 and currently reside outside the main Moro-speaking area, EJ in the United States, and AN in Omdurman, Sudan. Both participants also speak Arabic and English. The results for each speaker were analyzed separately as preliminary analyses found that speakers exhibited some different patterns.

4.1.3 Procedures

Recordings took place in a sound proof booth in the Phonetics Lab at UC San Diego or in a private home, depending on speaker preference and availability. Stimuli were elicited in two blocks. In the first block, speakers produced the neutral assertion declarative sentences. In the second block, speakers produced (corresponding) polar questions, and the experimenter answered *aa* 'yes' after each question so the questions were not produced in isolation. The speakers each produced five repetitions of each sentence.

4.1.4 Annotation and statistical analysis

All annotations were conducted in Praat using the TextGrid facility. The lexical tone target of each syllable was marked, the maximum F0 peak for H and the minimum valley for L. Although it may be the case that there is no phonological L tone in Moro, we still needed to determine F0 values for those syllables, and so they are annotated as L in all the pitch tracks. F0 values were then pulled from those points for data analysis. Undefined values due to creaky voice were

---

[2] Both speakers gave permission for their names to be identifed in the study. EJ is Elyasir Julima, and AN is Angelo Naser.

not included. Linear mixed effects models for all analyses were run in R (R Core Team, 2014), using the lme4 package version 1.1-7 (Bates et al 2014).

4.1.5 Results

To test for significant effects, linear mixed-effects models (LMEMs) were run. The dependent variable was F0 in Hertz taken at the tone target for each tone in the sentence. The fixed effects were context of the sentence (declarative and polar question), syllable number (to assess declination effects), and tone (H and L).[3]

Both speakers had a significant effect of context, with polar questions being produced with a higher F0 than declaratives [EJ: β = 9.23, SE = 1.96, $\chi^2(1)$ = 11.84, p < 0.001; AN: β = 43.55, SE = 5.84, $\chi^2(1)$ = 18.94, p < 0.001]. Both speakers also had a significant effect of syllable number, with a drop in F0 throughout the sentence [EJ: β = −3.73, SE = 0.52, $\chi^2(1)$ = 17.91, p < 0.001; AN: β = −5.38, SE = 1.37, $\chi^2(1)$ = 9.24, p < 0.01]. Both speakers had a significant effect of tone, with L tones having a lower F0 than H tones [EJ: β = −22.10, SE = 1.80, $\chi^2(1)$ = 27.72, p < 0.001; AN: β = −58.91, SE = 3.97, $\chi^2(1)$ = 31.83, p < 0.001]. EJ had a trending interaction of context and syllable number [β = −1.17, SE = 0.62, $\chi^2(1)$ = 3.05, p = 0.08]; the interaction was not significant for AN.

4.2 Discussion

The statistical models show that both speakers have higher F0 for polar questions than for declaratives. Raised F0 occurs in the earlier part of the question but drops towards the end. As both utterance types show an F0 drop phrase-finally, this suggests that there is a L% boundary tone in both cases. Marking polar questions with a final L% is a property shared by many of the languages discussed in this book: Akan, Bemba, Chimiini, Embosi, Shingazidja and Tswana. The questions are therefore not distinguished from the declaratives by a final rise or fall, but by higher F0 earlier in the utterance. AN shows an expanded pitch range with prominent F0 concentrated on the H tone of the subject or verb, whereas EJ tends to exhibit overall raised F0. In addition, polar questions can show pitch compression on the object/adverb following the raised F0.

---

[3] Context and syllable number were included as an interaction. All categorical fixed effects were coded with contrast coding. Sentence was included as a random slope by context, syllable number, and tone with context and syllable number included as an interaction. This was the maximal, uncorrelated random-effects structure that converged. Significance of fixed effects was assessed using model comparison. Alpha was set at p < 0.05.

Example pitch tracks of the sentence in (9) are provided in Figure 2 and Figure 3.

(9) ləvaja   l-a-mán-á   ŋaɲa
    CL1.poor people SM.CL1-RTC-cook-IPFV   CLŋ.grass
    'The poor people are cooking grass.'/'Are the poor people cooking grass?'

Figure 2 provides an example pitch track of a declarative utterance, whereas Figure 3 shows a corresponding polar question. In the latter, the lexical tone pattern of the utterance is maintained, but the overall F0 is higher, and there is considerable raising of the H tones of the verb. The final object with a LL tone pattern has higher F0 in the question than declarative, but F0 converges in the final syllable. The F0 raising can be accommodated in ToBI annotation with a %q-raised annotation at the beginning of the question, as proposed for Mandarin (Peng et al 2005). This notation signals an overall higher pitch setting. In addition, a lexical H tone that is considerably raised is marked with a %-prom notation. If there is compression, it is indicated with %-compression. These notations are useful for lexical tone languages, which may exhibit overall pitch range expansion or compression in certain utterances.

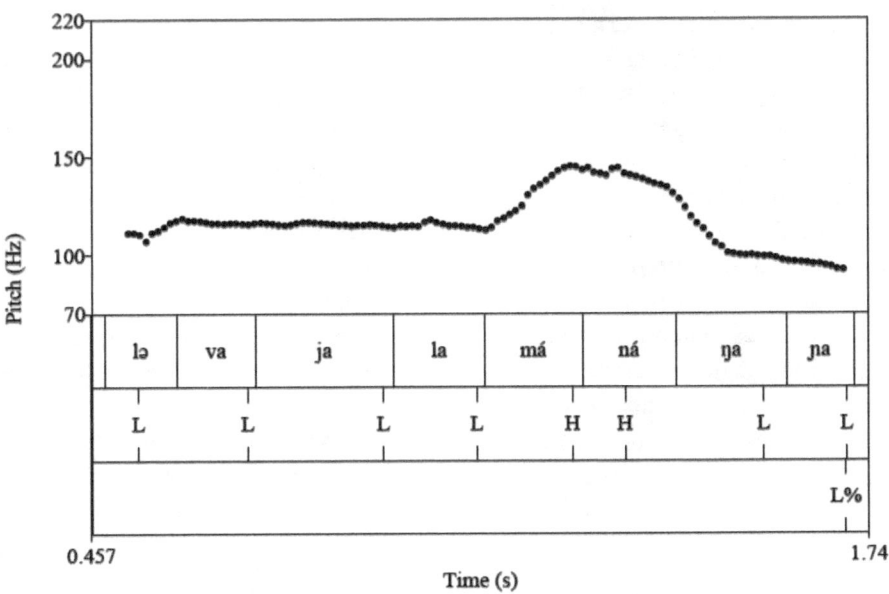

Figure 2: Pitch track for declarative sentence *ləvaja lamáná ŋaɲa* 'The poor people are eating grass.' (AN)

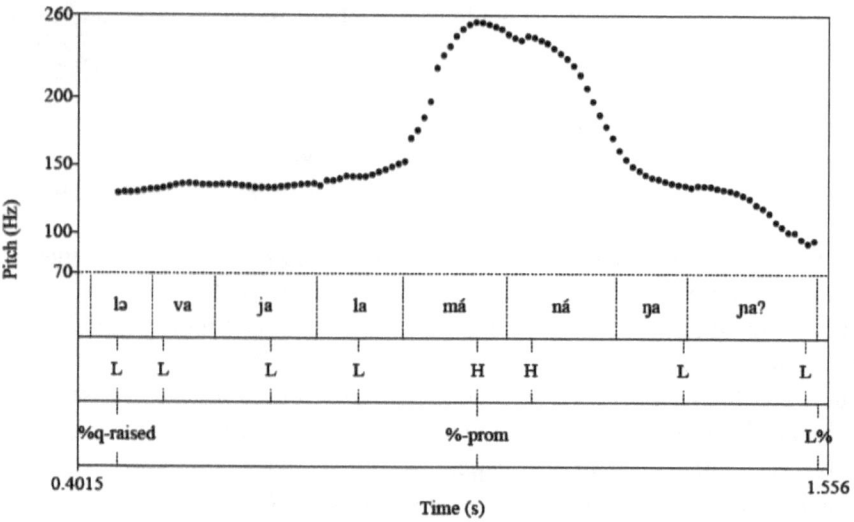

Figure 3: Pitch track for polar question *ləvaja lamáná ŋaɲa?* 'Are the poor people eating grass?' (AN)

If the tone of the object is HHH, LHH or HH, the H tones are not higher in questions, but have comparable or even lower F0 compared to the same object in declaratives. In the example pitch track in Figure 4, *ɲerá ɲalagó ꜜŋwórèðá*, the speaker (EJ) speaks slowly in the declarative, so there are breaks between words. The final HHH word undergoes downstep due to the preceding H tone. This is the same sentence glossed in (5b) and provided in Figure 1 uttered by a different speaker. In the polar question, there is slight raising in the early part of the utterance, but the strongest indication of a polar question is pitch compression starting at the lexical H tone of the last syllable of the verb. There is no indication of downstep as the trigger H tone is already lowered. The final object is produced at a lower pitch than it is in the declarative.

A composite graph in Figure 6 of all the F0 measurement points for the five repetitions of the declarative and polar question for this sentence (speaker EJ) clearly shows the compression effect in questions.

If the final word ends in a single H tone, such as LH or LLH words, there is a different pattern. Consider the following example sentences.

(10) a. um:iə   g-a-mám-a   ŋombəgó
        CLg.boy SM.CLg-RTC-lead-IPFV   CLŋ.baby goat
        'The boy is leading the baby goat.'/'Is the boy leading the baby goat?'

   b. um:iə   g-a-mám-a   ŋombəgó-a
      CLg.boy SM.CLg-RTC-lead-IPFV   CLŋ.baby goat-QP
      'Is the boy leading the baby goat?'

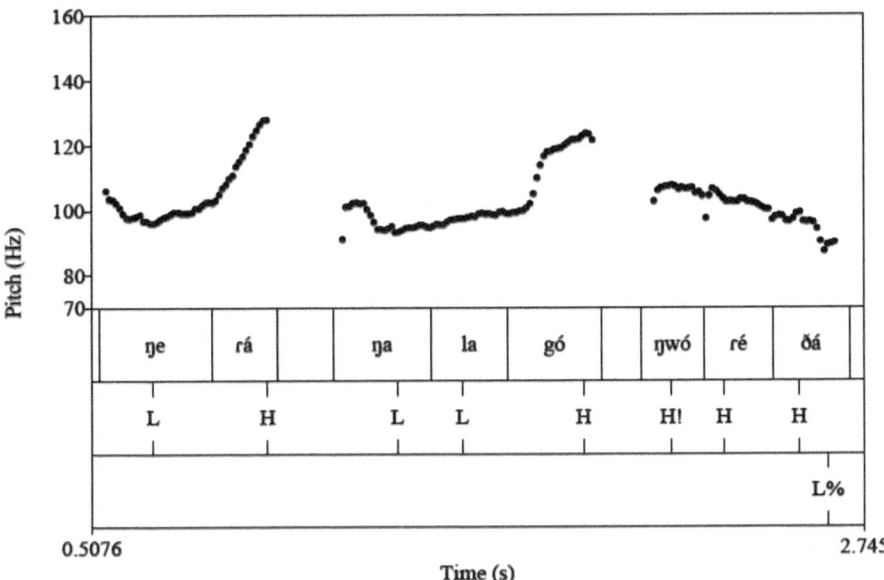

Figure 4: Declarative ŋerá ŋalagó ↓ŋwóréðá 'The girl planted the sesame seeds.' (EJ)

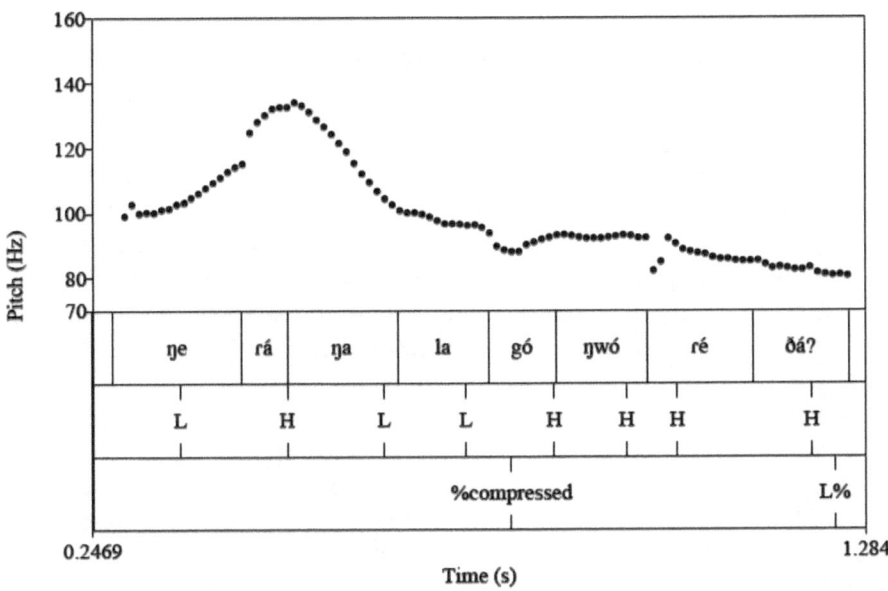

Figure 5: Polar question ŋerá ŋalagó ŋwóréðá? 'Did the girl plant the sesame seeds?' (EJ)

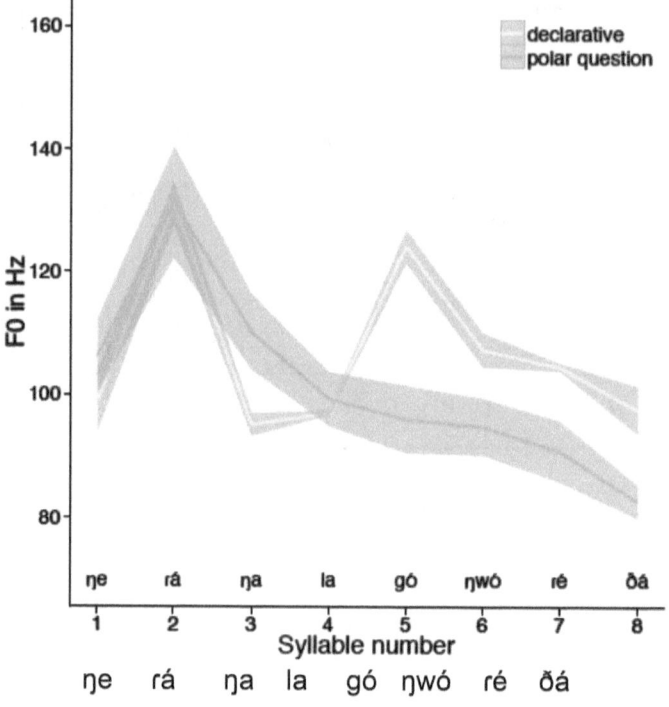

Figure 6: Average productions of *ŋerá ŋalagó ŋwóréðá?* tone targets (EJ)

Declaratives show a rise to the final H target tone before descending again slightly due to the L% (Figure 7), but polar questions show no clear H target as distinguished from the previous L tones (Figure 8). In this example, there is a final low-toned question particle -a in the question, which results in a strong fall.

In conclusion, the main distinction between declaratives and polar questions in Moro is higher F0 in the early part of the polar question. See Chung et al (2016) for replication of this pattern using carrier phrase style sentences with identical subject and verb, but different final objects. This can be rendered as either global F0 register raising or targeted raising of the H lexical tones. Both utterances show overall declination and a fall phrase finally, an indication of a L% boundary tone. While the tone distinctions between objects/adverbs are well differentiated in declarative utterances, there is some pitch compression of objects/adverbs in polar questions, which results in H tones being pronounced with lowered F0.

Intonation in the Thetogovela dialect of Moro — 31

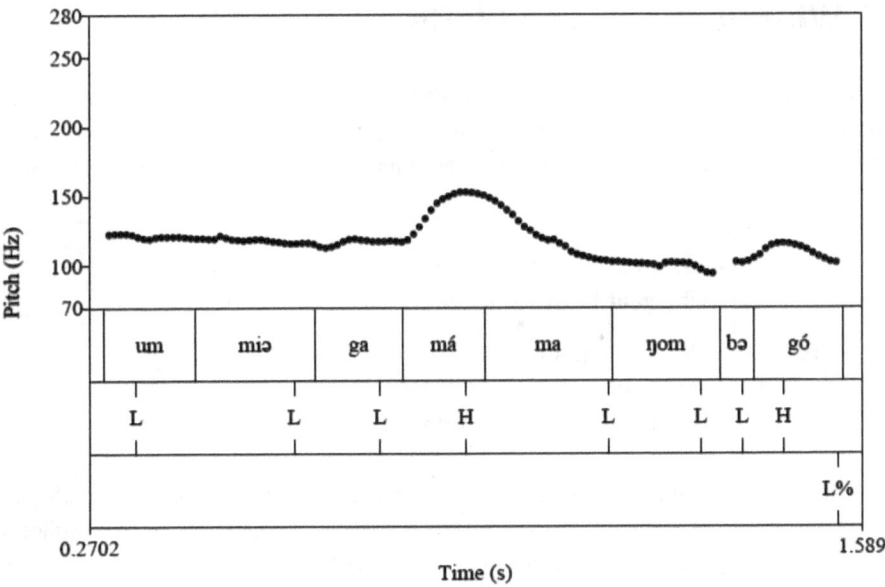

Figure 7: *ummiə gamáma ŋombəgó* 'The boy is leading the baby goat.' (AN)

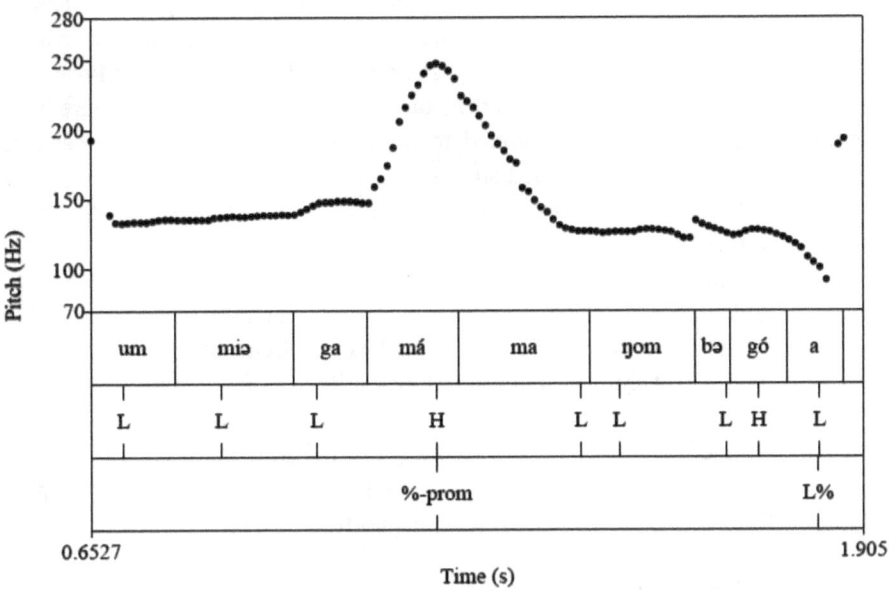

Figure 8: *ummiə gamáma ŋombəgóa?* 'Is the boy leading the baby goat?' (AN)

5 Wh-questions and Clefts

Moro has both in-situ and ex-situ wh-questions (Rose et al 2014). In-situ questions occur only with non-subjects; an example of an object in-situ question is given in (11b). The wh-word replaces the object in the same canonical position:

(11) a. ŋəməná   ŋ-a-mə́nw-á   ŋgárá
        CLŋ.baby goat SM.CLŋ-RTC-lick-IMPV CLŋ.salt
        'The baby goat is about to lick the salt.'

    b. ŋəməná   ŋ-a-mə́nw-á   wánde?
        CLŋ.baby goat SM.CLŋ-RTC-lick-IMPV CLg.what
        'What is the baby goat about to lick?'

Ex-situ questions, on the other hand, involve a wh-cleft strategy and different verb morphology. Subject questions are always ex-situ, whereas non-subjects may employ either the in-situ strategy as in (11) or the ex-situ strategy. In each case, the wh-word occurs in the initial position of the question with a cleft prefix ŋwə́- and a suffix -*iC:i*, a demonstrative that functions as a relative pronoun (the C refers to the noun class agreement consonant; for 'what' and 'who', this is -*ík:i* (singular) or -*íl:i* (plural). Subject questions are marked with the prefix *é-* instead of *a-* on the verb (12a), whereas non-subject questions are marked with *ə́-* instead (12b). These prefixes also mark other types of dependent clauses – see Rose et al (2014), Jenks & Rose (to appear). In the non-subject question in (12b), there is an optional complementizer *nə́-* prefixed to the subject and to the verb. Because wh-ex-situ questions employ a cleft structure, they closely resemble cleft sentences as seen in (12c,d). Clefts are also marked with ŋwə́- and -*iC:i*, and show the same verbal prefixes.

(12) a. ŋwʌ́ndə́k:i   ŋ-é-mə́nw-á   ŋgárá?
        CLF.what.CLg.DEM   SM.CLŋ-DPC1-lick-IMPV CLŋ.salt
        'What (is it that) is about to lick the salt?'

    b. ŋwʌ́ndə́k:i   (nə́-)ŋəməná   (nə́-)ŋ-ə́-mə́nw-á?
        CLF.what.CLg.DEM (COMP-)baby goat   (COMP-)SM.CLŋ-DPC2-lick-IMPV
        'What (is it that) the baby goat is about to lick?'

    c. ŋwə́-ŋəmənʌ́-ŋ:i   ŋ-é-mə́nw-á   ŋgárá.
        CLF-baby goat-CLŋ.DEM SM.CLŋ-DPC1-lick-IMPV CLŋ.salt
        'It is the baby goat that is about to lick the salt.'

d. ŋwə́-ŋgárʌ́-ŋ:i (nə́-)ŋəməná (nə́-)ŋ-ə́-mə́nw-á?
   CLF-salt-CLŋ.DEM (COMP-)baby goat (COMP-)SM.CLŋ-DPC2-lick-IMPV
   'It is the salt that the baby goat is about to eat.'

Answers to both in-situ and ex-situ wh-questions may consist of a nominal marked with -íC:i (*ŋgárʌ́-ŋ:i* 'salt' or *ŋəmənʌ́-ŋ:i* 'goat'), a full sentence as in (11a), or a cleft sentence as in (12c,d).

5.1 Experiment 2

Wh-in-situ and wh-ex-situ versions of the ten sentences in Experiment 1 were produced by the same speakers, with three repetitions. While these sentences are not directly comparable to the declaratives and polar questions due to the wh-structure and changes in the tone patterns of verbs, intonational effects are still observable.

5.1.1 Wh-in-situ questions

We compared the overall intonation contour of wh-in-situ questions to declarative utterances and polar questions for the ten sentences.

5.1.1.1 Results

To test for significant effects linear mixed effects models (LMEM) were run on the measurements for syllables in the subject and verb of the sentences, as the final wh-word has a different tone pattern than the final word in the declaratives and questions. F0 at the target of the syllable was the dependent variable. Fixed effects were context (declarative, polar question, and wh-question) and syllable number included as an interaction.[4]

For both speakers there was a significant effect of context with wh-questions having a higher F0 than declaratives [EJ: $\beta = 10.28$, $SE = 3.13$, $\chi^2(1) = 8.11$, $p < 0.01$; AN: $\beta = 23.12$, $SE = 4.78$, $\chi^2(1) = 16.66$, $p < 0.001$]. For AN the effect of context with polar questions having a higher F0 than wh-questions was significant, but for EJ it was only trending [AN: $\beta = 31.63$, $SE = 6.61$, $\chi^2(1) = 13.65$, $p < 0.001$; EJ: $\beta = 5.15$, $SE = 2.91$, $\chi^2(1) = 2.90$, $p = 0.09$]. For EJ F0 significantly decreased throughout the utterances (effect of syllable number), but for AN

---

4 Since context had three levels it was included as two fixed effects, declarative vs. wh-question and wh-question vs. polar question. Tone (L, H) was included as a covariate. All variables were coded with contrast coding, except syllable number which was included as a continuous variable. Sentence was included as a random slope by context, syllable number, and tone. This was the maximal, uncorrelated random effects structure that would converge.

the effect was only trending [EJ: $\beta = -2.05$, $SE = 0.47$, $\chi^2(1) = 10.03$, $p < 0.01$; AN: $\beta = -2.73$, $SE = 1.41$, $\chi^2(1) = 3.17$, $p = 0.07$]. Both speakers had a significant effect of tone, with H tones having higher F0 than L tones [EJ: $\beta = 26.67$, $SE = 0.90$, $\chi^2(1) = 55.16$, $p < 0.001$; AN: $\beta = 60.99$, $SE = 2.37$, $\chi^2(1) = 42.47$, $p < 0.001$]. For AN both interactions of context and syllable number were significant [declarative vs. wh-question x syllable number: $\beta = 6.65$, $SE = 1.12$, $\chi^2(1) = 33.92$, $p < 0.001$; wh-question vs. polar question x syllable number: $\beta = 9.43$, $SE = 1.14$, $\chi^2(1) = 65.29$, $p < 0.001$]. Follow-up simple regressions found that syllable number was only significant for polar questions, with an increase in F0 over time [$\beta = 7.35$, $SE = 1.81$, $r = 0.23$, $p < 0.001$]. While the other two contexts did not have a significant effect of syllable number, the coefficients show that F0 marginally decreased with syllable number for declaratives but increased for wh-questions. The interactions were not significant for EJ. The following boxplots illustrate the average F0 for the subject-verb portion of all ten sentences:

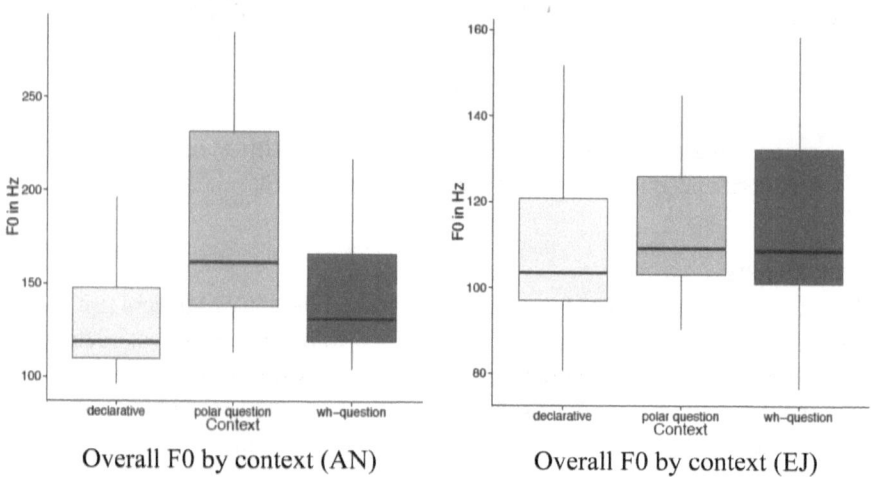

Overall F0 by context (AN)   Overall F0 by context (EJ)

Figure 9: Overall F0 for subject-verb of ten sentences by context for declaratives, polar questions and wh-in-situ questions

5.1.1.2 Discussion

For both speakers, wh-questions were significantly different than declaratives, being produced with higher F0 overall. EJ showed high variability in the production of wh-questions, and while they were significantly different than declaratives, they were not significantly different than polar questions. For AN, on the other hand, wh-questions were significantly different than both declaratives and polar questions; their overall F0 was intermediate between the two other utterance types, but showed a closer match to declaratives. Polar questions showed a significant increase in F0 across the utterance, but wh-questions did not. This correlates with the prominently raised target H tones in polar questions for AN.

The statistical model only tracks the earlier part of the utterance, but pitch tracks show that, like declaratives and polar questions, wh-in-situ questions also have a final L%. Illustrative pitch tracks from AN are provided for the following three utterances:

(13) a. lʌm:iə   l-a-lág-á   ŋwala
        CL1.boy   SM.CL1-RTC-plant-IPFV CLŋ.sorghum seeds
        'The boys are planting sorghum seeds.'

   b. lʌm:iə   l-a-lág-á   ŋwala?
        CL1.boy   SM.CL1-RTC-plant-IPFV CLŋ.sorghum seeds
        'Are the boys planting sorghum seeds?'

   c. lʌm:iə   l-a-lág-á   lánde?
        CL1.boy   SM.CL1-RTC-plant-IPFV CL1.what(plural)
        'What (all) are the boys planting?'

The wh-question (Figure 11) shows a similar F0 shape to the declarative (Figure 10), despite the lexical tone patterns of the objects being different. Note that the H tones in the verb are higher in the wh-question. The polar question (Figure 12), on the other hand, shows considerably raised F0 in the verb, with a sharper drop to a flatter F0 for the object.

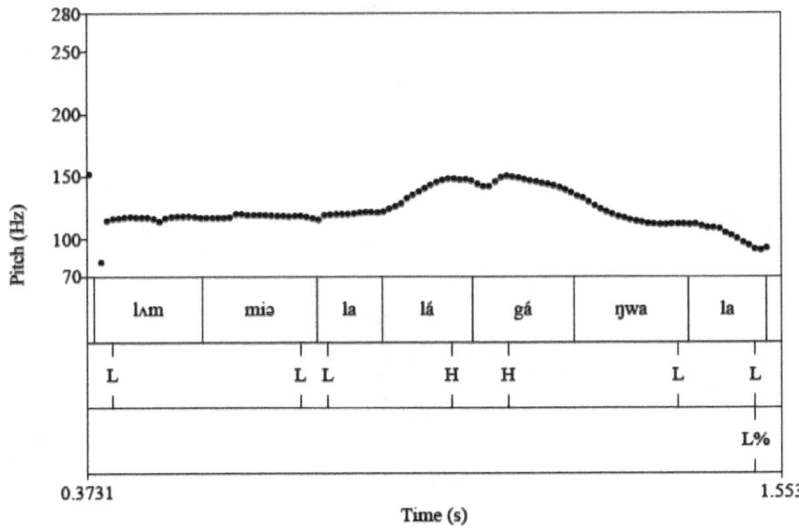

Figure 10: Declarative sentence lʌmmiə lalágá ŋwala 'The boys are planting sorghum seeds.' (AN)

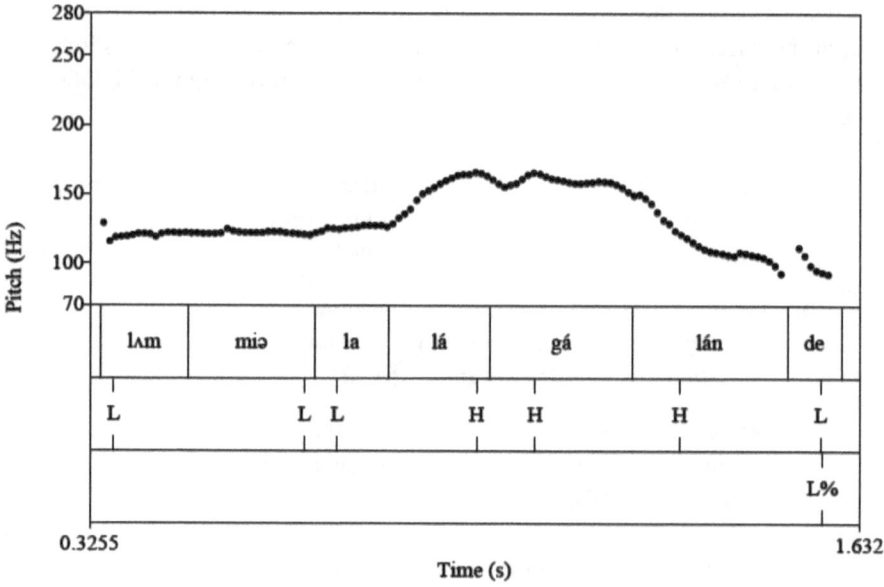

Figure 11: Wh-question *lʌmmiə lalágá lánde?* 'What are the boys planting?' (AN)

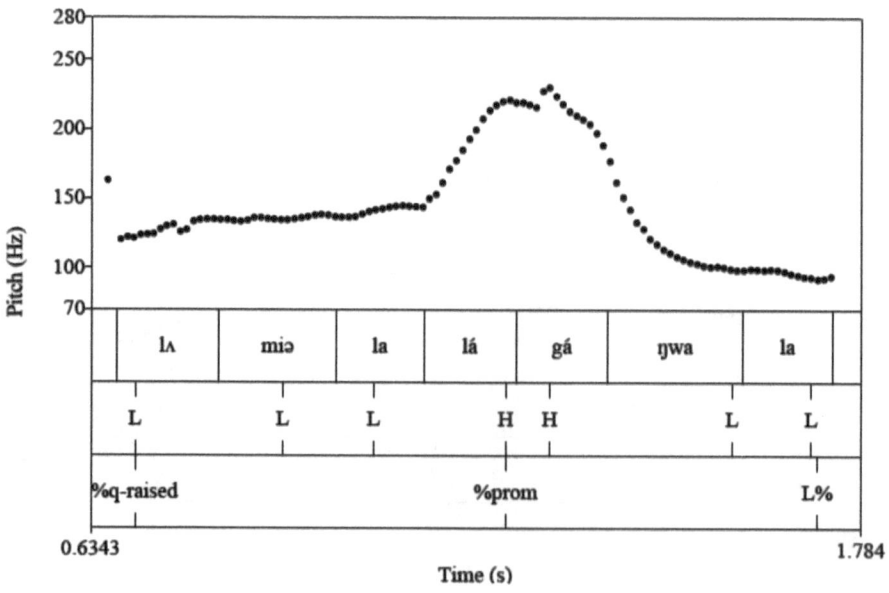

Figure 12: Polar question *lʌmmiə lalágá ŋwala?* 'Are the boys planting sorghum seeds?' (AN)

In conclusion, there is some raised F0 for wh-in-situ questions, but in this example not as pronounced as that of a polar question.

5.1.2 Wh-ex-situ questions

As wh-ex-situ questions show a number of structural differences from declaratives, polar questions and wh-in-situ questions, it is not possible to quantify their intonational differences. In this section, we rely on pitch tracks to illustrate the differences.

Wh-ex-situ questions also show a phrase-final L% boundary tone. There is also evidence of added H tone in the early part of the sentence The demonstrative -íC:i ends in a low tone when used as a demonstrative (ex. /ləvaja+íl:i/ → [ləvajÁl:i] 'those poor people'), but in wh-ex-situ questions where it functions as a relative pronoun, it ends in a H tone. The H tone spreads to the first syllable of a low-toned subject. Consider the following wh-ex-situ object question:

(14)   ŋwÁndə́l:i   ləvaja   l-ə́-mán-á-lo?
       CLF.what.CL1.DEM   CL1.poor people   SM.CL1-DPC2-cook-IMPV-3PLO
       'What all (is it that) are the poor people about to eat?'

The added H tone that appears at the end of the question cleft extends onto the all low-toned subject, raising the F0 of the first syllable [lə]. This is annotated with H → H to indicate the spreading.

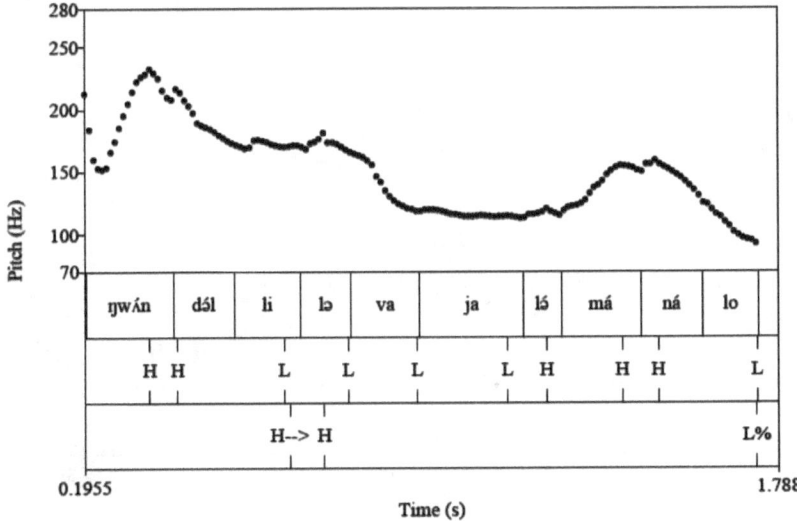

Figure 13: Wh-ex-situ object question *ŋwÁndə́l:i ləvaja lə́mánálo?* 'What all are the poor people about to eat?' (AN)

Although it might be tempting to treat the additional H tone as a boundary tone, marking the boundary between the cleft and the dependent clause, the fact that the H spreads rightwards suggests it is not a phrasal boundary tone. Boundary tones may spread, but within the phrase they mark (Gussenhoven 2000).

Wh-ex-situ subject questions also show the same H tone at the end of the wh-word, but no H spreading effect is observed. This is because the following verb always begins with a H tone due to the clause marking prefix é- (15a).

(15) a. ŋwʌ́dʒə́k:i   g-é-gəɲ-ó   lárá?
CLF.who.CLk.DEM   CLg-DPC1-kill-PFV   CLl.chicken
'Who killed the chickens?'

b. ləŋg-áɲ   g-a-gəɲ-ó   lárá
CLL.mother-1SGPOSS   CLg-RTC-kill-PFV   CLl.chicken
'My mother killed the chickens.'

The pitch track for sentence (15a) in Figure 14 shows this effect. One could construe the higher F0 on the syllable [ki] as interpolation between the preceding H tone and the next H tone, which is slightly lower due to declination. However, L tones intervening between two Hs usually show a dip, as observed in the verb *géɡəɲó*.

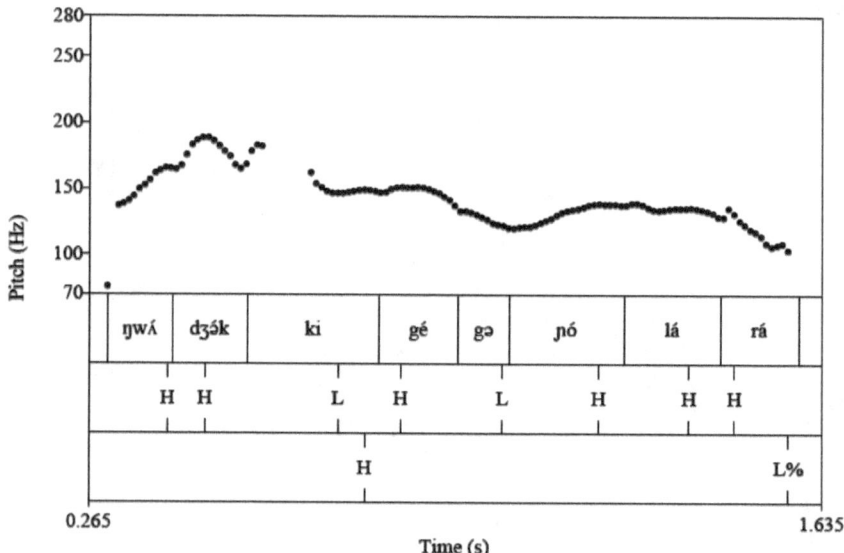

Figure 14: Wh-ex-situ subject question *ŋwʌ́dʒə́k:i géɡəɲó lárá?* 'Who killed the chickens?'[5] (AN)

---

[5] A H toned object usually shows downstep following a perfective verb form, but there is no downstep observed in this example.

The pitch track in Figure 14 can be compared with the answer to the wh-question (15b) in Figure 15. A similar intonational contour is observed despite the lexical tone differences, although the declarative is articulated at a lower pitch.

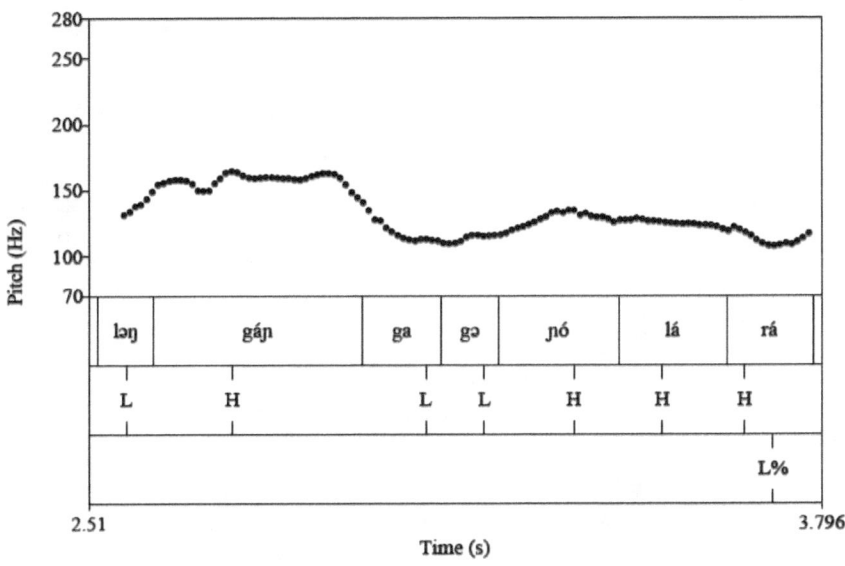

Figure 15: *ləŋgáɲ gagəɲó lárá* 'My mother killed the chickens.' (AN)

5.2 Clefts

Moro does not use intonation to convey focus. Instead, focus is signalled by use of a cleft construction as in (12c,d) and the examples in (16). The cleft marker ŋwə́- fuses with the following word, shifting its H tone (and labialization) onto the first syllable of the noun /ŋwə́-ŋgá../ → [ŋŋ́gwá] and /ŋwə́-ɲe../ → [ŋwɲé]. The suffix *-íŋ:i* also fuses with the vowel of the noun, so that /..a+íŋ:i/ → [ʌ́ŋ:i].

(16) **Object cleft**
 a. [ŋŋ́gwárʌ́ŋ:i nə́ŋə́mə́ná ŋə́↓mə́nwá]
  ŋwə́-ŋgárá-ŋ:i   nə́-ŋə́mə́ná   ŋ-ə́-mə́nw-á
  CLF.CLŋ.salt-CLŋ.DEM   COMP-CLŋ.baby goat   SM.CLŋ-DPC2-lick-IMPV
  'It's salt that the baby goat is licking.'

Subject cleft

b. [ŋwŋérʌ́ŋːi ŋélagó ŋwóréðá]
  ŋwə́-ŋerá-ŋːi   ŋ-e-lag-ó   ŋwóréðá
  CLF.CLŋ.girl-CLŋ.DEM   CLŋ-DPC1-plant-PFV   CLŋ.sesame seed
  'It's the girl who planted the sesame seeds.'

The pitch track for the object cleft in (16a) is given in Figure 16. Note the same H tone on the final syllable of the relative pronoun [ŋːi] that was noted in pitch tracks of wh-ex-situ questions.

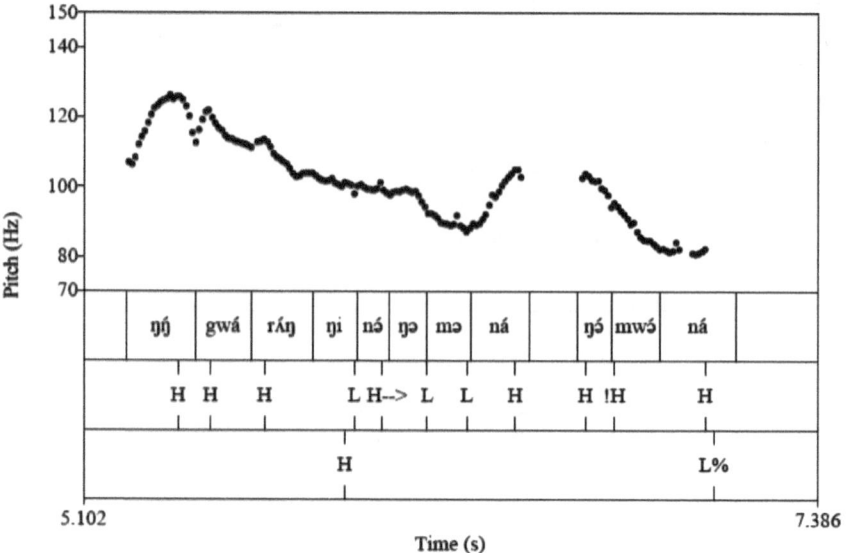

Figure 16: Object cleft: *ŋŋ́gwárʌ́ŋːi nə́ŋəməná ŋə́ˇmə́nwá* 'It is salt that the baby goat is licking.' (EJ)

Although this H tone is lower than preceding H tones of the focused object (this occurs due to declination), it is at the same level as the following H-toned complementizer *nə́-*. In addition, the complementizer *nə́-* appears to spread its H tone rightwards onto the following noun. The F0 dips in the subject *ŋəməná*, but only at the second syllable, not the first, which is lexically low.

The pitch track for the subject cleft in (16b) is given in Figure 17. In this case, the H tone at the end of the cleft shows rising F0.

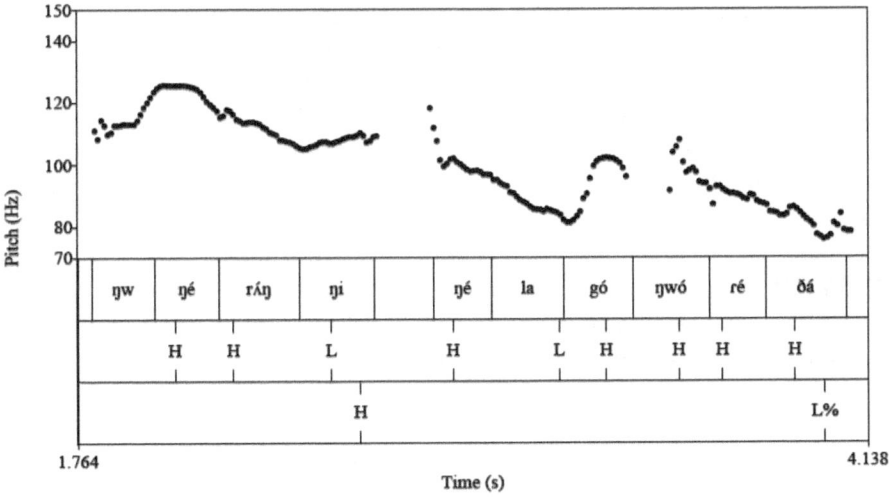

Figure 17: Subject cleft: *ŋwŋérʌŋ:i ŋélagó ŋwóréðá* 'It is the girl who planted the sesame seeds.' (EJ)

Overall, wh-questions exhibit two characteristic properties. Wh-in-situ questions have the same overall intonation profile as declaratives, but with raised F0. Their overall F0 range is similar to or lower than polar questions. Like polar questions, wh-in-situ questions show a final lowering rather than a final rise, an indication of a L%. Wh-ex-situ questions employ a wh-cleft structure. There is an additional H tone at the end of the cleft on the relative pronoun which may spread to a following low-toned subject in object wh-ex-situ questions. Cleft sentences show similar syntactic structure and intonation to wh-ex-situ questions.

6 Continuations

In this section, we examine two kinds of continuations. The first are subordinate phrases in narrative structures and the second are lists. Continuations provide evidence for a H% boundary tone and vowel lengthening.

6.1 Narrative subordinate phrases

A common structure in Moro narrative stories is for the first verb to be in a main clause aspectual form, with subsequent verbs in the subordinate consecutive or infinitive form, often preceded by a complementizer or conjunction. The main clause verb has a subject marking paradigm that includes noun class agreement for 3rd person, the root clause prefix *a-* and a final aspectual suffix, whereas subordinate verbs have a different subject marking paradigm with no noun class agreement, no clause marking prefix, and a different final suffix (Rose 2013). These subordinate phrases are signalled as continuations of the story by three mechanisms: absence of a phrase final L% boundary tone, final vowel lengthening, and/or a H% boundary tone.

Consider the following continuation from a story about a wedding told by EJ. In this story, the first main clause verb is followed by a long series of some twenty-five phrases with subordinate verbs, including the two in (17). Phrasing is indicated with parentheses.

(17) [(nipi   ndálánóŋ   ṭiá:)
       .. n-i-p-i   ndá-lá-ánóŋ   ṭiá
       .. COMP-1SGSM-beat-INF   CLl-head-CLl.INST-PART   like that
       '... I worked hard (lit. 'I hit with my head against') until

      (nenádʒəð   ðoálá:)]
       n-e-nátʃ-əð-e   ðoálá
       COMP-1SGSM-give-DIST-INF   CLð.money
       I could pay the money...'

The pitch track (Figure 18) shows the H tones of the HH object *ðoálá* 'money' being produced with higher F0 than the preceding H tones. There is no clear evidence for an extra rise conditioned by a H%. Instead, both H lexical tone targets are reached, and the final syllable [lá] is lengthened. There is a slight F0 dip at the end of the phrase, but nothing like the effect of the L% seen at the end of declaratives and clefts. In declaratives and clefts, final objects with lexical high tones (cf. Figures 1, 4, 15, 17) show declination and a phrase-final fall to a low F0 (for EJ in the range of 80Hz or below). Furthermore, the conjunction *ṭiə* in this example is phrased with the first phrase and produced with a very long vowel.

From the same narrative, the following phrase shows the effects of a H% on a low-toned word.

(18) [(neŋómáṭega)
       n-e-ŋó-m:-áṭ-e   ega
       COMP-1SGSM-3SGOM-take-LOC.APPL-INF   CLg.house
       '... I married her (lit. 'I took her to the house')

      (rəmwa náŋʌnṭi ŋéné)..]
       rəmwa   n-ə́ŋ-ʌnṭ-i   ŋéné
       CLl.god COMP-3SGSM-enter-INF CLŋ.word
       and God blessed the marriage (lit. God entered the word)'

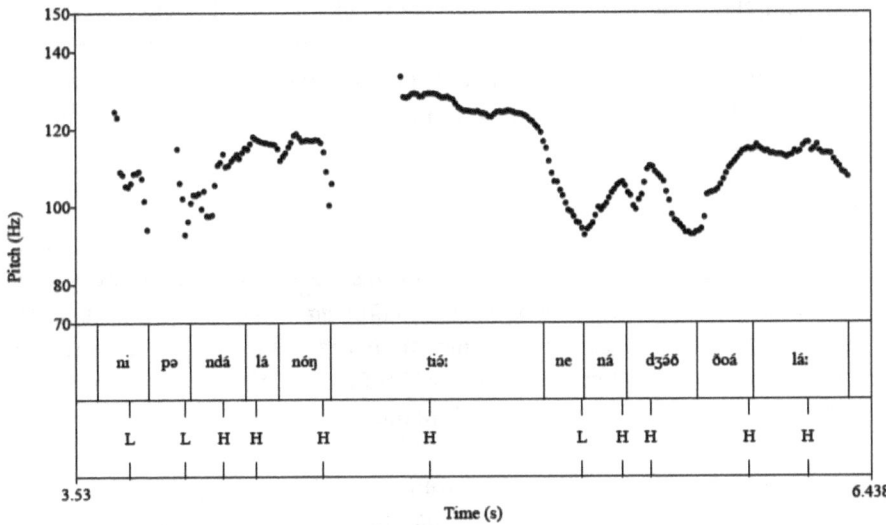

Figure 18: *(nipi ndálánóŋ ṭiə̀:) (nenádʒə̀ð ðoálá:)* 'I worked hard until I could pay the money' (EJ)

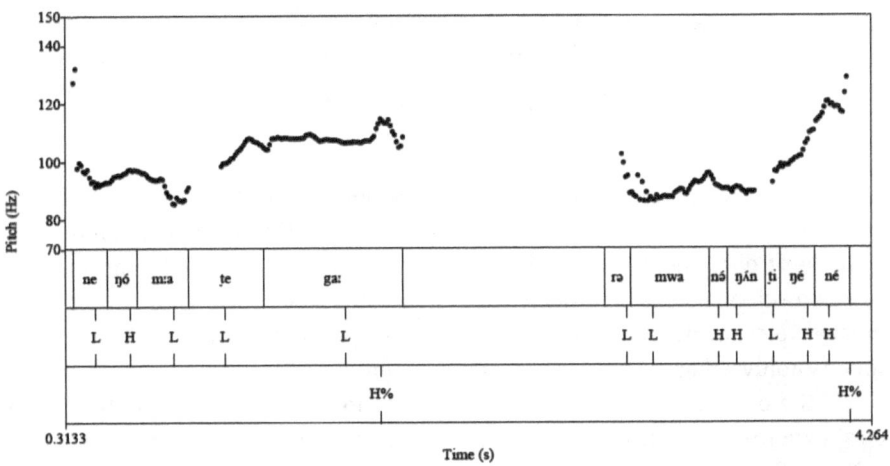

Figure 19: *neŋómáṭega rəmwa nə̀ɲʌ́nṭi ŋéné* 'I married her and God blessed the marriage' (EJ)

In Figure 19, the word *ega* 'house' is low-toned, but shows overall raised F0. We take this as evidence of a H%, which may have spread leftwards within the word. In addition, the final syllable [ga] is considerably lengthened. The word *ŋéné* 'word' at the end of the second phrase is H-toned and the final syllable shows considerable final raising but no lengthening, another indication of a H%.

In sum, these narrative continuations show evidence for H% and final lengthening, two patterns that were not observed in simple declarative phrases, clefts and questions. It is not clear under what circumstances each of these patterns is employed. In these examples, they occur both alone and in combination.

6.2 Lists

Turning to coordinated list structures, Moro has several ways to express a list of nominals. One method uses the conjunction *na* or *nə* 'and' preceding the second and following objects (19a), while another method uses the instrumental/comitative marker -Ca (C denotes noun class) suffixed to the second and following objects (19b). Phrasing is indicated with parentheses.

(19) a. [(ígʌsʌtʃóða:) (na ɲiðəniá na ŋgwón)]
í-g-ʌ-sʌtʃ-ú   oða   na ɲiðəniá   na ŋgwón
1SGSM-CLg-RTC-see-PFV CLg.deer and CLɲ.rabbit and CLɲ.squirrel
'I saw a deer, a rabbit and a squirrel.'

     [(égas:éða:) (átʃəvángá:) (ŋəðəmanaŋa)]
b. é-g-a-s:-ó   eða   átʃəván-gá   ŋəðəmana-ŋa
1SGSM-CLg-RTC-eat-PFV CLg.meat CLg.porridge-CLg.INST CLɲ.bean-CLɲ.INST
'I ate meat, porridge and beans.'

In the example pitch track in Figure 20 corresponding to (19a), the final H-toned syllable of the verb is deleted due to hiatus, and the H tone appears on the first syllable of *oða*. There is an additional F0 rise on the final syllable of *oða*. The final vowel of *oða* is lengthened and the latter portion is pronounced with creaky voice, which causes the perturbation in the pitch track. This extra H tone is analysed as H% marking a continuation.

If the order of the objects is switched, the low-toned *oða* has no high tone, as shown in Figure 21. The final H tone of the verb spreads to the first syllable of *ɲiðəniá*, the standard tone spreading rule discussed in section 3 for sentence (4b). There is likely a H% on the final syllable of *ɲiðəniá* in this example, as that syllable has the highest F0 in the sentence.

The following pitch track illustrates the pattern with the instrumental/comitative suffix -Ca as in (19b). The first noun *eða* receives H tone on its first syllable from the deleted suffix *-ó* of the verb. It receives H tone on the second syllable from the H%, and also undergoes lengthening in this position. The second noun is marked with the suffix *-ga*. This syllable receives H tone via

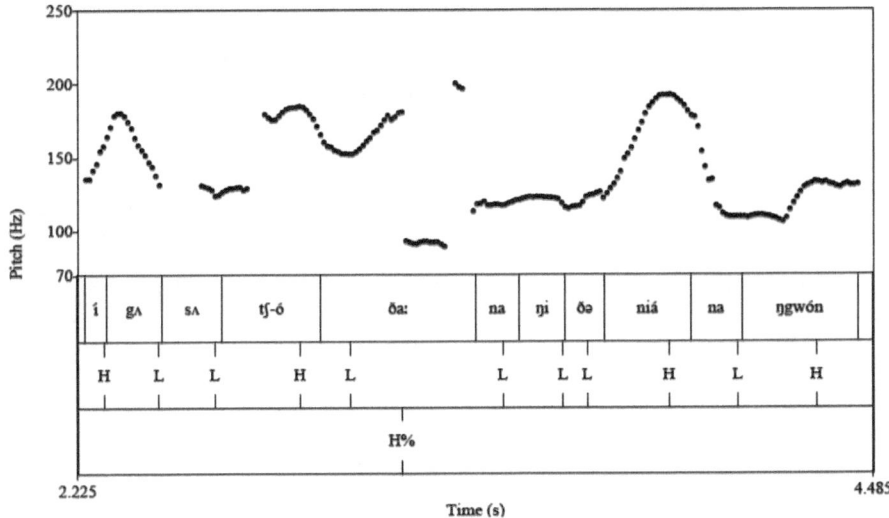

Figure 20: *(ígʌsʌtʃ-óða:) (na ɲiðaniá na ŋgwón)* 'I saw a deer, a rabbit and a squirrel.' (AN)

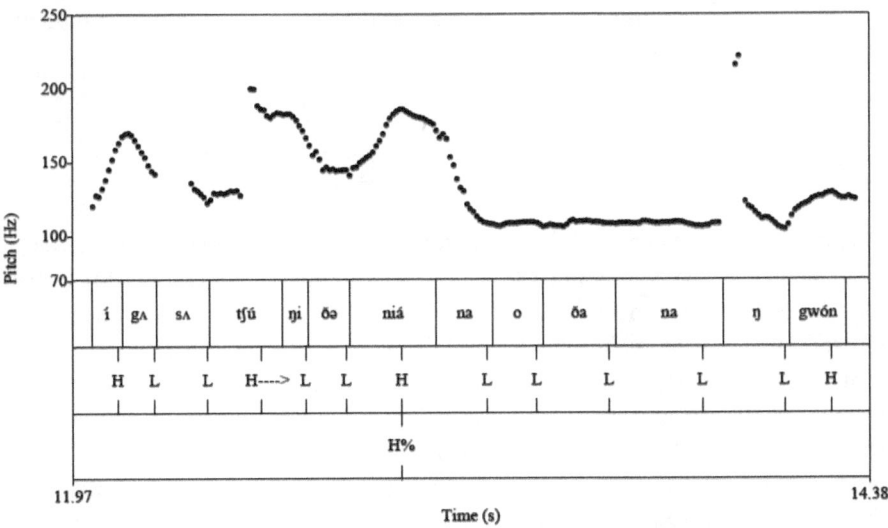

Figure 21: *(ígʌsʌtʃú ɲiðaniá) (na oða na ŋgwón)* 'I saw a rabbit, a deer and a squirrel.' (AN)

spreading from the preceding syllable, but it is also lengthened and realized higher than the preceding H tones due to the H%. These are both indications of a continuation and separate phrasing. The final word is all low toned, and shows steep declination from the preceding H%.

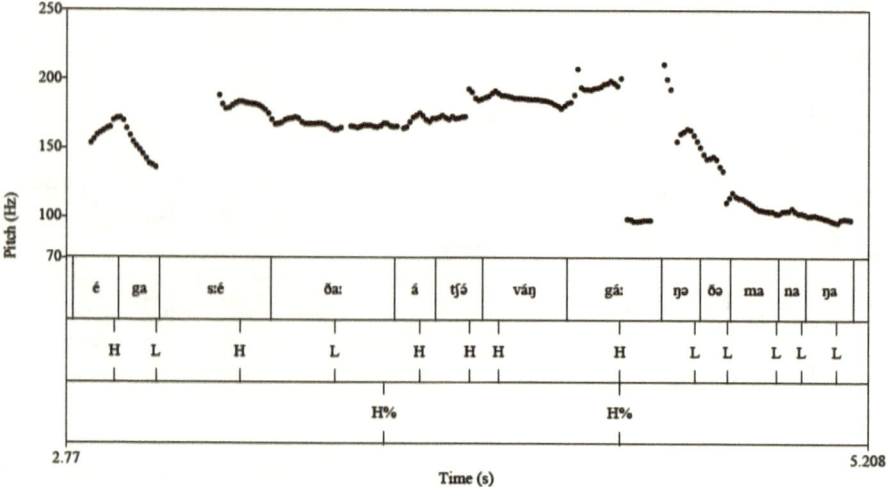

Figure 22: (égas:éða:) (átʃəváŋga:) (ŋəðəmanaŋa) 'I ate meat, porridge and beans.' (AN)

The lists of nominals discussed in this section provide further examples of how Moro employs both final lengthening and H% boundary tones to indicate continuation of the utterance.

7 Conclusion

This is the first detailed study of intonation in a Kordofanian language. As Moro has lexical tone, it is important to assess how intonation interacts with lexical tone in the production of basic sentences. Declarative assertive sentences are marked by tonal declination and a final fall. Polar questions may be differentiated from declaratives by use of an utterance final polar question marker /-a/, but this marker is optional, and has a tendency to be employed following consonant-final words, but not vowel-final words. Polar questions are differentiated from declaratives primarily through raised F0 in the early part of the sentence compared to declaratives; the F0 drops off in the final word, and in some cases even shows lower F0 than that of declaratives. These effects are modelled using %q-raised and %compressed annotation. Typologically, Moro resembles many other African languages in the use of a low vowel sentence-final question particle and/or final pitch compression to indicate distinctions between polar questions and declaratives (Rialland 2007, 2009). However, it also uses pitch raising or expansion in the earlier part of the question. Moro has wh-in-situ non-subject questions and both wh-ex-situ subject and wh-ex-situ non-subject questions. Wh-in-situ non-subject questions show a similar F0 contour to declaratives, but are articulated with an F0 range in between polar questions and declaratives. Wh-ex-situ questions use a cleft construction in which the question word is fronted. These questions also resemble declaratives in overall pitch, but the wh-ex-situ object question is marked with a H prominence on the final syllable of the cleft. Moro does not employ intonation to mark focus, but instead uses clefts. Clefts resemble wh-ex-situ questions in both structure and intonation. Finally, narrative subordinate structures and list continuations were examined. These showed evidence for H% boundary tones and phrase-final lengthening of vowels. This study is preliminary in that, apart from the narrative continuations, it primarily uses constructed and elicited sentences to establish the basic intonation patterns, and carefully controlled environments to determine the effect on lexical tone. While this has allowed certain patterns to be observed, it has obvious drawbacks due to the unnaturalness of the 'laboratory' situation. Further studies should focus on longer utterances and natural conversations.

Acknowledgements

We sincerely thank Elyasir Julima and Angelo Naser for contributing the data. Thank you to the reviewers and editors for comments that greatly improved this chapter. We also benefited from feedback and discussion at UC San Diego, UCLA, and Leiden University, especially with Yiya Chen. This research is part of the Moro Language Project (moro.ucsd.edu) and was supported by the National Science Foundation under Grant No. 0745973.

References

Bates, Douglas, Martin Maechle, Ben Bolker & Steven Walker. 2014. *lme4: Linear mixed-effects models using Eigen and S4*. R package version 1.1-7, http://CRAN.R-project.org/package=lme4.

Blench, Roger. 2005. A dictionary of the Moro language of the Nuba hills, Sudan. Ms., Kay Williamson Foundation.

Chung, Younah, Page Piccinini & Sharon Rose. 2016. The interaction of polar question and declarative intonation with lexical tone in Moro. *Proc. Speech Prosody 2016*, 615–619.

Gussenhoven, Carlos. 2000. The boundary tones are coming: on the nonperipheral realization of boundary tones. In M.B. Broe & J.B. Pierrhumbert (eds.) *Papers in Laboratory Phonology V: Acquisition and the Lexicon*, 132–151. Cambridge: Cambridge University Press.

Jenks, Peter and Sharon Rose. to appear. Documenting control and raising in Moro. In J. Kandybowicz & H. Torrence (eds.) *Africa's Endangered Languages: Documentary and Theoretical Approaches.* Oxford University Press.

Jenks, Peter & Sharon Rose. 2011. High Tone in Moro: Effects of Prosodic Categories and Morphological Domains. *Natural Language and Linguistic Theory* 29, 211–250.

Jenks, Peter & Sharon Rose. 2015. Mobile Object Markers in Moro: The Role of Tone. *Language.*

Ladd, D. Robert. 2008. *Intonational Phonology.* 2nd edition. Cambridge Studies in Linguistics 119. New York: Cambridge University Press.

Peng, Shu-hui, Marjorie K.M. Chan, Chiu-yu Tseng, Tsan Huang, Ok Joo Lee, & Mary Beckman. 2005. Towards a Pan-Mandarin System for Prosodic Transcription. In S.-A. Jun (ed.) *Prosodic Typology – The Phonology of Intonation and Phrasing.*

R Core Team. 2014. R: A language and environment for statistical computing. R Foundation for Statistical Computing, Vienna, Austria. URL http://www.R-project.org/.

Rialland, Annie. 2007. Question prosody: an African perspective. In Gussenhoven, Carlos, and Tomas Riad (eds.), *Tunes and Tones, Volume 1: Typological Studies in Word and Sentence Prosody.* Berlin: Mouton deGruyter, pp. 35–62.

Rialland, Annie. 2009. The African lax question prosody: Its realisation and geographical distribution. *Lingua* 119.6: 928–949.

Rose, Sharon. 2013. The morphological structure of the Moro verb. In T. Schadeberg & R. Blench (eds.) *Nuba Mountain Language Studies,* 25–56. Cologne: Rüdiger Köppe.

Rose, Sharon, Farrell Ackerman, George Gibbard, Peter Jenks, Laura Kertz, Hannah Rohde. 2014. In-situ and ex-situ wh-question constructions in Moro. *Journal of African Languages and Linguistics* 35.1, 91–125.

Schadeberg, Thilo. 1981. *A survey of Kordofanian. Volume 1: The Heiban Group.* Hamburg: Helmut Buske.

Appendix

Sentences used in Experiment 1

Declaratives

1. ŋəməná ŋamə́nwá ŋgárá 'The baby goat is about to lick the salt'
2. lʌm:iə lalágá ŋwala 'The boys are planting sorghum seeds.'
3. ŋerá ŋalagó ŋwóréðá 'The girl planted sesame seeds.'
4. ogómá gʌmə́rniniə lóvárá 'The thief is acting like a guinea fowl.'
5. lə́w:áná lan:ó oleə 'The porcupine heard the sound.'
6. ləvaja lamáná ŋaɲa 'The poor people are cooking grass.'
7. ŋwʌlíə ɲʌníniə úlə́ŋí 'The hyena is prowling at night.'
8. um:iə gamáma ŋombəgó 'The boy is leading the calf.'
9. lárá lagə́ɲá ləðwʌ́ 'The chickens are killing the worms.'
10. ləŋgáɲ gagəŋó lárá 'My mother killed chickens.'

Polar questions

1. ŋəməná ŋamə́nwá ŋgárá?   'Is the baby goat about to lick the salt?'
2. lʌm:iə lalágá ŋwala?   'Are the boys planting sorghum seeds?'
3. ŋerá ŋalagó ŋwóréðá?   'Did the girl plant sesame seeds?'
4. ogómá gʌmə́rniniə lóvárá?   'Is the thief acting like a guinea fowl?'
5. lə́w:áná lan:ó oleə?   'Did the porcupine hear the sound?'
6. ləvaja lamáná ŋaɲa?   'Are poor people cooking grass?'
7. ŋwʌlíə ɲʌníniə úlə́ŋgíʌ   'Is the hyena prowling at night?'
8. um:iə gamáma ŋombəgóa   'Is the boy leading the calf?'
9. lárá lagə́ɲá ləðúʌ   'Are the chickens killing the worms?'
10. ləŋgáɲ gagəɲó lárá   'Did my mother kill chickens?'

Sentences used in Experiment 2

Wh-in-situ non-subject questions

1. ŋəməná ŋamə́nwá lánde?   'What (all) is the baby goat about to lick?'
2. lʌm:iə lalágá lánde?   'What (all) are the boys planting?'
3. ŋerá ŋalagó lánde?   'What (all) did the girl plant?'
4. ogómá gʌmə́rniniə wánde?   'What is the thief acting like?'
5. lə́w:ana lan:ó wánde?   'What did the porcupine hear?'
6. ləvaja lamáná lánde?   'What (all) are the poor people cooking?'
7. ŋwʌlíə ɲʌníniə ndóŋ?   'When is the hyena prowling?'
8. um:iə gamám:a wánde?   'What is the boy leading?'
9. lárá lagə́ɲá wánde?   'What are the chickens killing?'
10. ləŋgáɲ gagəɲó lánde?   'What (all) did my mother kill?'

Wh-ex-situ subject questions

1. ŋwʌ́dʒʌ́k:i gímə́nwá ŋgárá?   'Who is about to lick the salt?'
2. ŋwʌ́dʒʌ́k:i gélágá ŋwala?   'Who is planting sorghum seeds?'
3. ŋwʌ́dʒʌ́k:i gélagó ŋwóréðá?   'Who planted sesame seeds?'
4. ŋwʌ́dʒʌ́k:i gímə́rniniə lóvárá?   'Who is acting like a guinea fowl?'
5. ŋwʌ́dʒʌ́k:i gén:ó oleə?   'Who heard the sound?'
6. ŋwʌ́dʒʌ́k:i gémáná ŋaɲa?   'Who is cooking grass?'
7. ŋwʌ́dʒʌ́k:i gíníniə úlə́ŋgí?   'Who is prowling at night?'
8. ŋwʌ́dʒʌ́k:i gémáma ŋombəgó?   'Who is leading the calf?'
9. ŋwʌ́dʒʌ́k:i gégə́ɲá ləðwʌ́?   'Who is killing the worms?'
10. ŋwʌ́dʒʌ́k:i gégəɲó lárá?   'Who killed chickens?'

Wh-ex-situ non-subject questions

1. ŋwʌ́ndə́kːi ŋəməná ŋə́mə́nwá? 'What is the goat about to lick?'
2. ŋwʌ́ndə́lːi lʌmːiə lə́lágálo? 'What (all) are the boys planting?'
3. ŋwʌ́ndə́lːi ŋerá ŋə́lágálo? 'What (all) did the girl plant?'
4. ŋwʌ́ndə́kːi ogómá gə́mə́rniniə? 'What is the thief acting like?'
5. ŋwʌ́ndə́kːi lə́wːáná lə́nːó 'What did the porcupine hear?'
6. ŋwʌ́ndə́lːi ləvaja lə́mánálo 'What (all) are the poor people cooking?'
7. ŋwə́ndóŋ ŋwʌlíə ŋə́níniə? 'When is the hyena prowling?'
8. ŋwʌ́ndə́kːi umːiə gə́mámːa? 'What is the boy leading?'
9. ŋwʌ́ndə́kːi lárá lə́gə́ɲá? 'What are the chickens killing?'
10. ŋwʌ́ndə́kːi ləŋgáɲ gə́gəɲó? 'What did my mother kill?'

II **Western Africa**

Michael Cahill
Kɔnni Intonation

Abstract: Kɔnni [kom] is a Gur language of northern Ghana, with a combination of normal and unusual prosodic characteristics. Downstep is the manifestation of a floating Low tone, and the associative construction is marked by a floating High tone. The OCP is shown to be inactive with regard to both High and Low tones. Kɔnni exhibits true tonal polarity on one nominal suffix, not the commonly analyzed tone dissimilation. The intonation portion of this study presents pitch patterns of basic, compound, and complex sentences. Direct and indirect quotations are examined in complex sentences, along with elements fronted for emphasis. Kɔnni has an unusual pattern for polar questions, with at least three distinct tonal strategies evident. The paralinguistic intonation patterns relating to several emotional states are presented and related to cross-linguistic studies. Unlike most of the languages in this volume, with the limits of the present data, no boundary tones are evident.

Keywords: Tone polarity, polarity, OCP, paralinguistic, emotions, duration, syllable as TBU, downstep, floating tones, associative tone, tone spreading, declarative sentence, compound sentence, quotes, direct quotes, indirect quotes, fronting, paragraphs, content questions, polar questions (or "yes/no questions"), lax question intonation, anger, surprise, bored, emphasis, contemptuous, discourse

1 Introduction

This chapter[1] aims at providing a beginning look at some aspects of intonation in Kɔnni [kma], a Gur language spoken in the north of Ghana. It is not a large language compared to other Ghanaian languages, with Ethnologue listing the population at about 3800 (Lewis, Simons, and Fennig 2016) from a 2003 report, but a more recent estimate being about 8,000 (Konlan Kpeebi, pc). It is bordered by the more populous Mampruli, Buli, and Sisaala languages. Naden (1986), on

---

[1] Abbreviations used here include 1SG = first person singular, 3SG = third person singular, ATR = advanced tongue root, FUT = future tense, LOC = locative marker, NEG = negative, PAST = past tense, PERF = perfective aspect, POSS = possessive, and TBU = tone-bearing unit.

Michael Cahill, SIL International

the basis of a limited survey trip, produced the first sketch of Kɔnni phonology, morphosyntax, and vocabulary. For specific tonal phenomena, Cahill (2000, 2004) provides analysis of the Kɔnni tonal associative morpheme and tonal polarity, and the most thorough presentation of all aspects of Kɔnni phonology and morphology, including tone, is Cahill (2007). The only previous publications on Kɔnni intonation are a brief mention of polar question intonation in Cahill (2007), a more detailed examination of this topic in Cahill (2012), and a conference presentation on Kɔnni emotions and intonation in Cahill (to appear).

A particular instance of intonation can be classified as either *structural* (phonological, indicating linguistic boundaries or functions) or *paralinguistic* (e.g. indicating emotions and attitudes, which have gradient values of pitch) (Gussenhoven 2004, Ladd, Sherer, and Silverman 1986, Ladd 2008). Examples of each of these are examined for Kɔnni. Structural intonation, being phonological, adds or replaces specific tones. We will see this especially in Kɔnni polar question intonation. Paralinguistic intonation is most evident when discussing emotions in Kɔnni, but also appears in other contexts.

A broad question is how intonation can function in a tone language, since both affect pitch. Cruttenden (1997: 9–10) writes that tone languages may still use "superimposed intonation" in four ways:
- the pitch level of the whole utterance may be raised or lowered
- the range of pitch may be narrower or wider
- the final tone of the utterance may be modified
- the normal downdrift of a sentence may be suspended

All except the third bullet would be cases of paralinguistic intonation patterns. More recent studies, including several in this volume, would modify this to include not only utterance-final modifications, but phrasal boundaries. In Kɔnni, we will see cases of all these except the last.

Thus far the term "intonation" has been used in the common way, to refer to variations in pitch that contribute meaning to an utterance. However, this is not universal; a broader view is that intensity and duration are also included in "intonation," as Ladd (2008: 4) specifically notes. Hirst and DiCristo (1998: 3–8) have a detailed discussion of the oft-confusing terminology of prosody, intonation, etc., concluding that intonation proper does include the physical properties of duration and other characteristics. This chapter includes measures of duration as well as of fundamental frequency. We will see duration coming into play in polar question intonation, as well as in the paralinguistic aspects of intonation related to emotional expression in Kɔnni.

Since intonation interacts with tone, I first present the broad patterns of tonal inventory and phenomena for Kɔnni in Section 2, including some patterns which are cross-linguistically unusual. Section 3 begins the presentation of intonation with an examination of declarative sentences, beginning first with simple sentences, then compound sentences, complex sentences which encode direct and indirect quotes, and finally sentences with fronted elements. It will be seen that there is no clear evidence for boundary tones thus far in Kɔnni. Also, phonological phrasing, significant in some of the other chapters in this volume, is likely relevant in Kɔnni, but is not evident from the data currently at hand, and will not be discussed in this chapter. Section 4 presents patterns of question intonation, briefly covering content questions (which have a pattern identical to declarative sentences), but with the bulk of the section concentrating on polar questions. These have some resemblance to Rialland's (2007, 2009) typological patterns, but in Kɔnni they are quite distinct in having not one, but three patterns. Section 5 examines the paralinguistic intonation patterns produced by several different emotional states, and compare with scholars' findings in other languages. Section 6 offers some concluding observations, and directions for future research.

2 Basic patterns of tone in Kɔnni

The patterns in this section[2] are condensed from Cahill (2007), in which the interested reader can find more data and argumentation, as well as detailed analysis from an Optimality Theory perspective.

2.1 Tonal inventory and the tone-bearing unit

Kɔnni has two underlying tones, High (H) and Low (L). These combine as rising (LH) and falling (HL) contours on single syllables, as well as a High-downstepped High (H!H) on a single syllable as a second type of falling tone. The tone-bearing unit is the syllable, to which one or two autosegmental tones may associate. A sample of contrasts is given below. Tones are marked on every vowel in this chapter, even if, as in the case of *chííŋ* below, there would be only one autosegment associated with the entire syllable.[3]

---

[2] I follow the common conventions of marking a High tone with acute accent (á), a Low tone with grave accent (à), rising tone as (ǎ), falling tone as (â), and downstepped High with superscripted exclamation point (!á). Transcriptions are IPA, except that orthographic <r> is IPA [ɾ], <ch> is IPA [tʃ], <j> is IPA [dʒ], and <y> is IPA [j]. Some phonetic detail, such as centralization of front vowels before [ŋ], is omitted.
[3] There are no all-Low nouns in Kɔnni; a High is required. If a High is not present underlyingly, one will be inserted.

(1) Monosyllabic
   L͡H vs. H   kòáŋ   'back'   kúáŋ   'farm'
   L͡H vs. H⁼H   jìíŋ   'spitting cobra'   jí¹íŋ   'tree (sp.)'
   H vs. H⁼H   chííŋ 'moon, month'   chí¹íŋ 'squirrel'
   H͡L vs. L͡H   chîàŋ 'chair'   chǐàŋ   'bottom, waist'
   H͡L vs. H⁼H   yîì   'blind person'   yí¹íŋ   'nail, arrow'
   H͡L vs. H   táà   'sister'   tá   'and (joining clauses)'

(2) Disyllabic
   L.H vs. H.H   ɲùùrí   'the tree (sp.)'   ɲúúrí   'the chest'
   L.H vs. H.¹H   hààríŋ   'tree (sp.)'   háá¹ríŋ 'boat'
   L.L͡H vs. H.H   nànjǔǔŋ 'pepper'   nánjúúŋ 'fly'

African languages have been variously claimed to have either the syllable or the mora as the tone-bearing unit (TBU) (Odden 1995). For Kɔnni, distribution and alternations both support the syllable as TBU. Surface syllable types are V, N, CV, CVC, CVN, CVV, and CVVN. Only the last three stand as independent words. Kɔnni allows either one or two associated tones per syllable; this distribution is shown in (1) and (2). If the mora were the TBU, one expected pattern would be three distinct tones on a trimoraic word CVVN, e.g. *gàáŋ. However, such a pattern is unattested.

A more complex line of evidence pertaining to the TBU is the behavior of words such as *kààní* 'one' with respect to spreading of High tone. As discussed in greater detail in Section 2.4, a HLH underlying tone is realized as H¹HH on the surface. Thus in *zàsíŋ* 'fish' and *ŋ̀ wó ¹zásíŋ* 'I lack fish', when the High-toned verb *wó* precedes the LH of the noun *zàsíŋ*, this creates an underlying HLH sequence which surfaces as H¹HH. However, if two Low-toned TBUs intervene between the High tones, the underlying HLLH is unchanged, as in *ŋ̀ wó dàmpàlá* 'I lack bench'. The question, then, is whether the first two moras of *kààní* [kaa] act like two TBUs, with two instances of Low, or one.

If *kààní* is preceded by a Low tone on the head noun, the two first moras [kaa] are on the same Low pitch and the second syllable [nɪ] is High-toned, as in *kàgbà kààní* 'one hat'. However, if the preceding noun ends in a High tone, both syllables of *kaanɪ* are pronounced on the same pitch, as a downstepped High tone, as in *zàsíŋ ¹káání* 'one fish'. The long vowel in *kaanɪ* acts as if it were a single TBU with a single Low tone, as in *zàsíŋ* rather than *dàmpàlá* in the preceding paragraph.

Therefore the long vowel in *kààní* and other words can be represented with a configuration something like the following (omitting a moraic tier):

(3)   L   H
       | |
       σ   σ
      /|\   /|
      C V V C V
      | |/ | |
      k a   n ɪ

For brevity's sake, however, I will use

(4)   L H
      | |
      kaanɪ

as a shorthand representation for (3) above, with the L tone to be regarded as being linked to the whole syllable kaa. All vowel sequences in the same word, such as [ɪa] or [ie], are likewise in the same syllable, and thus in the same TBU.

The usual default tone inserted on an unspecified vowel is Low, with three exceptions. The first is when an epenthetic vowel occurs between two High-toned syllables, in which case the vowel shows a High tone. The second exception is that when a noun is underlyingly toneless, a High tone is inserted on the last syllable, with the preceding syllables being Low, e.g. hɔ̀gʊ́ 'woman,' shown to be toneless by other paradigms.[4] The third exception is tonal polarity in the Noun Class 1 plural suffix, discussed in Section 2.3.

2.2 Downstep

The downstepped H is a phonetic implementation of a floating Low tone. In this conceptualization, a word like kpá'áŋ 'guinea fowl' is represented as having a /HLH/ tone pattern, with the Low floating and causing downstep. Note that the two H autosegments are the only ones associated to the single syllable in (5).

(5)   H L H
       \ /
      kp a a ŋ

---

[4] This includes forms like ʊ̀ hɔ́gʊ̀ 'his wife/woman', where the High on hɔ́gʊ̀ is from the tonal associative morpheme discussed in Section 2.5, and hɔ̀gʊ̀-kpí'ŋ́ 'big woman', in which hɔ̀gʊ̀ has no High at all. The cognate for 'woman' in the related Gur languages Moore (Kenstowicz, Nikiema & Ourso 1988) and Dagaare (Antilla & Bodomo 1996), has also been independently analyzed as underlyingly toneless.

The source of the floating Low can be specifically determined in many instances. For example, when the plural definite suffix of Noun Class 1 (High-toned -*há*) is added to a plural noun ending in Low, a downstep results.

(6) ɲʊ́rà   'chests'
    ɲʊ́ˈráhá   'the chests'

This is represented straightforwardly in autosegmental notation as in (7). The process is discussed more fully in Section 2.4.

(7)   H L   H L H
       | | | / |
       ɲʊ ra   ɲʊ ra ha

In some languages, a sequence of two adjacent High tones creates a downstep between them, e.g. Supyire (Carlson 1983) and KiShambaa (Odden 1982), among others, including Bemba, Moro, and Tswana in this volume. This is demonstrably not the case in Kɔnni, as seen in individual words such as *tígíŋ* /tíg-ŋ́/, where the stem and the suffix both are High (also see discussion in 2.6 vis-à-vis the OCP).

As with many West African languages, Kɔnni has "automatic downstep," often called "downdrift," where a High after overt phonetic Lows is lowered. It also has what has been referred to as "non-automatic downstep", that has been discussed in this section. The combination of automatic and non-automatic downstep in a single sentence results in a tone pattern that continually declines, as in (8), extracted from a dramatic telling of a local event. The high tones toward the end of the sentence are actually lower than the low tones at the beginning.

(8) *sʊ̀kʊ́rʊ̀ gè ó háá jìè fʊ̀ wó ɲín'tí gárá kʊ́ˈáŋ* 'This morning he woke up seeing you lack things going to farm.' (speaking of a watchman and a thief)

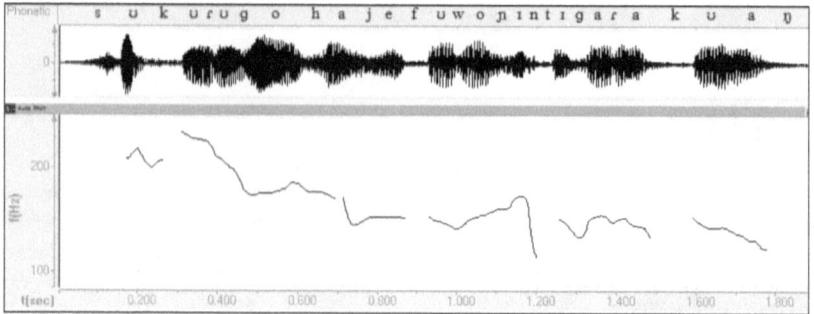

2.3 High-toned nominal suffixes and tonal polarity

The table below contains a selection of various tone patterns by noun class.[5] The most striking generalization to be noted is that an overwhelming majority of nouns, whether singulars or plurals, definite or not, end with a High tone, whether a downstepped High or non-downstepped High. The generalization is that all the suffixes (with the systematic exception of the plurals [-a/-e] in Noun Class 1) are High-toned. Singulars in Class 5 lack a suffix and vary in final tone.[6]

(9)

Nouns	Singular	Sg.+ Art.	Plural	Pl.+ Art.
Noun Class 1	/-ŋ́/	/-rÍ/	/-A/	/-A-hÁ/
stone	tăŋ	tànní	tàná	tànáhá
chest	ɲʊ́ʊ́ŋ	ɲʊ́ʊ́rí	ɲʊ́ʊ́rà	ɲʊ́ʊ́ˈráhá
bee	síébíŋ	síébírí	síébíè	síébíéˈhé
breast	bììsíŋ	bììsìrí	bììsá	bììsáhá
Noun Class 2	/-ŋ́/	/-kÚ/	/-tÍ/	/-tÍ-tÍ/
courtyard	gbààŋ	gbààkʊ́	gbààtí	gbààtítí
monitor lizard	yúóŋ	yúókú	yúótí	yúótítí
hawk	kpíˈlíŋ	kpíˈlíkʊ́	kpíˈlítí	kpíˈlítítí
Noun Class 3	/-ŋ́/	/-kÁ/	/-sÍ/	/-sÍ-sÍ/
person	vúóŋ	vúóké	vúósí	vúósísí
dawadawa tree	dʊ̀ʊ̀ŋ	dʊ̀ʊ̀ká	dʊ̀ʊ̀sí	dʊ̀ʊ̀sísí
fly	nánjʊ́ŋ	nánjʊ́ká	nánjʊ́sí	nánjʊ́sísí
man	dèmbíŋ	dèmbìké	dèmbìsí	dèmbìsísí
Noun Class 4	/-ŋ́/	/-bÚ/	/-tÍ/	/-tÍ-tÍ/
water	ɲááŋ	ɲáábʊ́	ɲáátí	ɲáátítí
meat	nɔ̆ŋ	nɔ̀mbʊ́	nɔ̀ntí	nɔ̀ntítí
sleep	gbíˈíŋ	gbíˈbʊ́	gbíˈtí	gbíˈtítí
peanut	sìŋkpááŋ	sìŋkpáábʊ́	sìŋkpáátí	sìŋkpáátítí
Noun Class 5	/-Ø/	/-wÁ/	irreg.	irreg.
child	bʊ̀á	bʊ̀àwá	bàllí	bàllílí
woman	hɔ̀gʊ́	hɔ̀wwá	hʊ̀àŋ	hʊ̀àbá
sister	táà	tááˈwá	tááˈlíŋ	táálíˈbá

Note that since every noun ending in -ŋ also ends in a High tone, the singular suffix -ŋ has a High tone in underlying representation.

---

[5] Noun classes here are numbered arbitrarily.
[6] Capital letters here represent vowels unspecified for ATR, e.g /-kÚ/ surfaces as either -kú or -kʊ́.

As noted, the plural suffix of Noun Class 1 [-a/-e] (depending on ATR vowel harmony) is exceptional in Kɔnni morphology by consistently surfacing with a tone opposite to the previous stem tone. Again, the singular /-ŋ́/ suffix is what contributes the final High tone in the singular. Stripping off this High reveals the root tone.

(10)

Singular	Plural	Root tone	Pl. suffix tone	gloss
tăŋ	tàn-á	L	H	'stone/s'
wíŋ	wí-è	H	L	'face mark/s'
bìisíŋ	bìis-á	L	H	'breast/s'
tígíŋ	tíg-è	H	L	'house/s'
tàŋbáŋ	tàŋbán-à	LH	L	'land god/s'

The suffix /-A/ is toneless and a polar tone is inserted. This is shown to be true tonal polarity rather than dissimilation by means of more complex data and analysis in Cahill (2004, 2007).

2.4 High-tone spreading

The Low that is present and associated in ɲʊ́rà 'chests' is still present but floating when the definite suffix is added in ɲʊ́ˈráhá 'the chests'. This is a result of a common and pervasive spreading process in which the second H of a HLH sequence spreads one TBU leftward, resulting in surface HˈHH, often termed plateauing. This process is illustrated in (11).

(11) a. H L H   H L H   b. H L H   H L H
        | | | → | / | | | | → | / |
        σ σ σ   σ σ σ   ɲʊ ra + ha   ɲʊ ra ha

The leftward spread is pervasive, spreading within words, as above, or between words, as in jɔ́rɔ́ŋ ˈkáánɪ́ 'one ladder.'

(12) H H L H   H H L H
      | | | | → | | / |
      jɔrɔŋ kaanɪ   jɔrɔŋ kaanɪ

Not all grammatical contexts have been investigated; known cases of an unusual phonetic [HLH] are shown in (14) and (21).

There are two cases of rightward H-spread in Kɔnni. In the first, when there are a series of pre-verbal particles, and the first is High-toned, this High spreads one syllable to the right. This is shown below with the High-toned *tín* followed by the Low-toned *yà*.

(13) a. ʊ̀   **yà**   bɔ̀bá   mìŋ   's/he is still tying'

     b. ʊ̀   tín   **yá**   ꜝbɔ́bá   mìŋ   's/he was still tying'
       3s   PAST   still   tying   AFF

The High tone which has spread from the left in the preceding examples spreads only one particle (TBU) to the right. This is shown when two Low-toned particles follow the High-toned *tín*. In these cases, there is a free variation in pronunciation.

(14) a. ʊ̀   tín   **ŋáán**   yè   díꜝgé   mìŋ   's/he had been still cooking'

     b. ʊ̀   tín   **ŋáán**   ꜝyé   díꜝgé   mìŋ
       3s   PAST   had.been   still   cooking   AFF

Note that (14a) shows a rare case of a phonetic [HLH], created by the H-spreading.

The second case of rightward High spreading is in the specific morphological context of a noun-adjective complex as in (15).

(15) H-spread from noun into adjectival suffix

```
    H L H          H L H
    /|  |  |   →   /|\  |
    tigi-yɛɛlıŋ    tigi-yɛɛlıŋ    tígí-yééꜝlíŋ    'white house'
                                  cf. jà-yèèlíŋ   'white thing'
```

2.5 The floating associative morpheme

At least one morpheme consists of a single floating tone: a High tone signifying association or possession. In third person possession (where the possessor is either pronoun or noun), the possessed noun always starts with a High tone, even if Low in citation form, as in (16).

(16) a. tăŋ   ʊ̀ **tá˥ŋ**⁷   (cf. ǹ tăŋ 'my stone')
         stone   'his/her stone'

   b. bʊ̀àwá   dààŋ   bʊ̀àwá **dá˥áŋ**
       child.the stick   'child's stick'

   c. kʊ́rʊ́bâ   chìăŋ   kʊ́rʊ́bá **˥chí˥áŋ**
       bowl   bottom   'bowl's bottom'

This process for (16a) and the more complex (c) can be visualized as below.

(17) a. L   H   L H   L   H L H
         | \ / → | \ /   ʊ̀ tá˥ŋ
         ʊ   POSS taŋ   ʊ   taŋ

   b. H H H L   H   L H   H H H L   H L H
       | | | /   \/   → | | | \ /   kʊ́rʊ́bá ˥chí˥áŋ
       kʊrʊba   POSS chɪaŋ   kʊrʊba   chɪaŋ

The floating associative tone is not an uncommon phenomenon in West African languages. A cross-linguistic survey focusing on the directionality of H-docking is found in Cahill (2000).

2.6 The absence of the OCP in Kɔnni

In many languages, when morphology or syntax concatenates two identical tones, they either merge, or one dissimilates, or a downstep (possibly a floating Low) is inserted between them. The uniting principle in these phenomena is the Obligatory Contour Principle (OCP), which forbids sequences of two identical tones. This constraint is so common (it is alluded to in this volume specifically for Embosi, Shingazidja, Bemba, Tswana, and Moro) that its presence in an African tone language may be looked on as almost a default assumption. However, in Kɔnni, the OCP is not active with regards to tones, either LL or HH. Both of these are allowed.

---

[7] Note that both possessed forms in (8) illustrate a H˥H contour on a *single* tone-bearing unit, a rare but attested phenomenon, e.g. Essien (1990: 55) for Ibibio and Casali (1995, fn. 22) for Nawuri. As previously noted, the TBU in Kɔnni is the syllable, and both *tá˥ŋ* and *dá˥áŋ*, with CVN and CVVN syllable structures, exemplify this.

For High tone, consider *jág-â* 'shades' and *mǔg-à* 'rivers'. Both have the tonally polar plural suffix *-A*, discussed in Section 2.3, which in both of these words inserts a Low tone. The question is how to explain the difference between the final Low tone of *mǔgà* in contrast to the final HL falling tone in *jágâ*. This fall cannot be the result of a spreading process, since it does not occur in the structurally identical *mǔgà*. The proposed solution is that *jágâ* has two adjacent High tones in underlying representation, while *mǔgà* has only one, as in (18).

(18) H H L   H L
      | | / | |
      ja ga   mʊ ga

For Low tones, two Low autosegments may be distinguished from a single Low associated to two TBUs. The word *dàmpàlá* 'bench' (lit. 'logs'), contrasted with *bʊ̀rɪ̀mɪ́ŋ* 'oryx' illustrates this. Each of these words has two initial TBUs which bear surface Low tones. However, in a context in which *dàmpàlá* and *bʊ̀rɪ̀mɪ́ŋ* have a High-toned word preceding them, they exhibit different tonal behavior:

(19) dàmpàlá   ŋ́ wó dàmpàlá   'bench, I lack bench'
      bʊ̀rɪ̀mɪ́ŋ   ŋ́ wó ˈbʊ́rɪ́mɪ́ŋ   'oryx, I lack oryx'

As previously mentioned, a HLH underlying tone is realized as HˈHH on the surface. A single Low between Highs is unassociated, resulting in downstep. However, if more than one Low is present between Highs, then these distinct Lows are associated and pronounced as Low. The difference in tonal behavior between 'bench' and 'donkey' is explained as the result of the presence of two lexical Low tones versus one.

(20) a. underlying representations

              L L H   L H[8]
              | | | | |
              dampala   bʊrɪmɪŋ

      b. in the "I lack X" frame

              H L L H   H L H
              | | | | | /|\
              wo dampala   wo bʊrɪmɪŋ

Two distinct Low tones, then, may also be adjacent.

---

[8] In *bʊ̀rɪ̀mɪ́ŋ*, the stem has a single L lexically, while the High has its origin in the suffix *-ŋ*.

3 Kɔnni declarative intonation

The data for this and the following intonation sections was gathered by Mr. Konlan Kpeebi of the Ghana Institute of Linguistics, Literacy, and Bible Translation (GILLBT), since I was not able to personally travel to Ghana during the window of time available for this volume. I supplied the English translations of the data to ask for, based on my prior knowledge of what Kɔnni syntax allows, and Kpeebi recorded native Kɔnni speakers Mr. Naaza Solomon Dintigi and Mr. Mumuni Salifu Barnabas in a recording studio in Tamale, Ghana. I am very grateful for their assistance in this project; obviously, it would not have happened without their assistance. Specifics of the recording equipment are not available, but the recordings, sent partly by email and partly through Dropbox, are good quality, clear, with no background noise, such as the roosters and other outside noises so frequently encountered in field recording situations. The recording quality was quite adequate for pitch and duration analysis.

A few question intonation sentences had been recorded by me in previous years with different speakers, and these are noted when appropriate.

3.1 Basic declarative sentences

The pitch trace in (21) illustrates a normal intonational pattern of a declarative sentence and also the methodology of measuring frequency in this study. All recordings were analyzed using SIL's Speech Analyzer program.[9]

(21)   ǹ   tím   bá   ń   nàwá   ¹jááŋ[10]
       1SG   PAST   want   1SG   pick   thing   'I intended to get something'

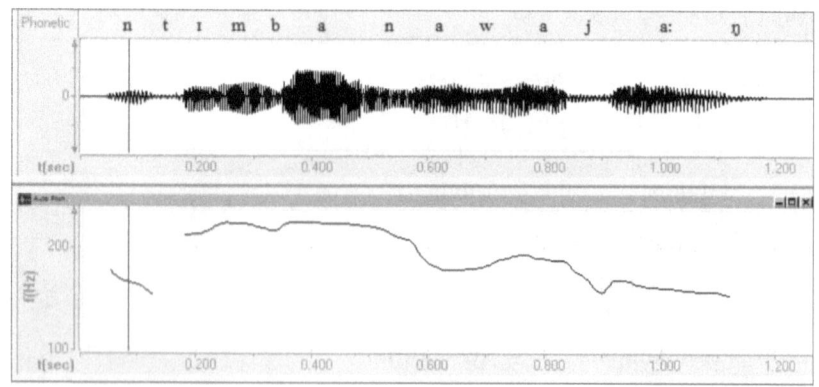

---

[9] Available as free download at. http://www.sil.org/resources/software_fonts/speech-analyzer.
[10] The second *n* is high due to H-spread from the preceding *bá*, creating an unusual HLH phonetic sequence.

This sentence exemplifies the phonetic downdrift so common in African languages (Yip 2002: 147–149, Odden 1995: 454, Clements 2000: 158), in which the second H of a sequence HLH is phonetically lower than the first H. This was also illustrated in the longer sentence in (8). The phonetics in the pitch trace above is schematized, along with the actual F0 measurements, in (22).

(22) ǹ   tím   bá   ń   nàwá   ꜜjááŋ
      _   ‾   ‾   ‾   _ ‾   ꜜ‾
      159 236 235 229 173–185   152   Hz

Note the downstepped High on the last word. The difference in pitch of the HꜜH sequence is not as great as the pitch difference for the HL sequence, in this example, 33 Hz for HꜜH vs. 56 Hz for HL.

Tones are measured by placement of the cursor as in (21) above where the cursor line is placed in the middle of the /ǹ/, and the frequency, here 159 Hz, is displayed directly in a part of the Speech Analyzer window not shown here. Frequency was measured either in the middle of the syllable, as here, or in the most stable part of the syllable toward the end.

A methodological question was how to compare both the pitch height of a sentence (how high is the sentence) and the pitch range (what is the difference between High and Low tones). For purposes of this study, the measure of the initial Low (general a pronoun) and the first High in the sentence (generally a verb or verbal particle) are taken to be a measure of the height and pitch range of the sentence, relevant for comparing the height of clauses in Section 3.2, as well as the paralinguistic measures of various emotions in Section 5. Since the number of syllables in the sentences varies, and thus the final F0 of the sentence will vary considerably due to the downdrift exemplified in (8), measurement of sentence-final tones were judged to be not useful. These two measures, at the beginning of the sentence, give a more consistent result across utterances.

An issue that arises in a volume like this which explicitly compares languages is the existence of boundary tones, whether at the phrase, clause, or utterance level. In (21), the final downstepped High remains fairly level for the duration of its pronunciation, with no final lowering. We see no evidence for an utterance-final L% boundary tone which occurs in all the other languages in this volume except Basaa.

3.2 Compound sentences

For this study, I focused on three compound sentences, with the coordinating conjunction being either *ama* 'but' or *a* 'and,' as in the following:[11]

(23) a. ǹ   tím   bá   ń   nàwá ˈjááŋ <pause> àmá ǹ   dááˈyá mìŋ
      1SG PAST want 1SG pick thing   but 1SG forgot AFF
      'I intended to get something, but I forgot.'

  b. ʊ̀   gàwá ˈnyʊ́ŋ <pause> àmá ʊ̀   ká   dá   ˈkpááŋ
      3SG went market   but 3SG NEG buy oil
      'S/he went to market, but she didn't buy oil.'

  c. ʊ̀   gàwá kʊ́áŋ[12] <pause> à   kpà   sìŋkpááŋ
      3SG went farm   and harvest groundnuts (peanuts)
      'S/he went to farm and harvested groundnuts.'

Compound sentences generally follow the intonational pattern of monoclausal sentences, with four additional observations. First, as elicited here, they often have a pause before the coordinating conjunction, as indicated in (23). If the sentence was in answer to a question, then the pause in my data is quite reduced or even absent, as in (24).

(24) Q: bíá   ʊ́   gáà   kʊ́áŋ   dúù   yì ?   (duu = di + u)
      what 3SG go farm that.3SG do?
      'What did s/he go to farm to do?'

  A: ʊ̀   gàwá   kʊ́áŋ   á   kpà   sìŋkpááŋ   (no pause)
     3SG went farm and harvest groundnuts
     'He went to farm to harvest groundnuts.'

---

[11] There are three words for 'and' in Kɔnni. *Anaŋ* joins noun phrases. *Ta* joins independent clauses, with the pronoun specified in the second clause:

n naŋ ga **ta** ŋ keŋ   'I will go and come (back)'
1s FUT go **and** 1s come

The form *a* 'and' in this study joins verb phrases. The second clause in (23c), that is not a full clause, since it has no overt subject. However, in all the intonation data available at this point, the *a* conjunction example here behaves in the same way as the coordinating conjunction *ama* 'but.'

[12] The citation forms for 'market' and 'farm' in (23) are *nyʊ̌ŋ* and *kʊ̌áŋ*. The downstepped ˈ*nyʊ́ŋ* in (23) results from the L in *nyʊ̌ŋ* dissociating in the context of HLH, as discussed in Section 2.4.

Second, the first clause of the compound sentences is significantly higher in pitch than the second one. This may be seen in the following data. The frequency measurements of underlined syllables are in Hz, and the pause measurements are in milliseconds, both being the average of three repetitions for Salifu.

(25) a. I intended to bring something but I forgot.

<u>ǹ</u> <u>tím</u> bá <u>nàwá</u> <u>ˈjááŋ</u> <pause> <u>àmá</u> <u>ǹ</u> <u>dáá</u>ˈyá mìŋ
144 213   153/170 133   <361>   133-173 137 165

b. I intended to bring something   c. I forgot.
<u>ǹ</u> <u>tím</u> bá <u>nàwá</u> <u>ˈjááŋ</u>   <u>ǹ</u> <u>dáá</u>ˈyá mìŋ
135 196   141/154 123   135 171

(26) An example of the above, with all three utterances in the same recording session, with the initial L and H of the clauses marked

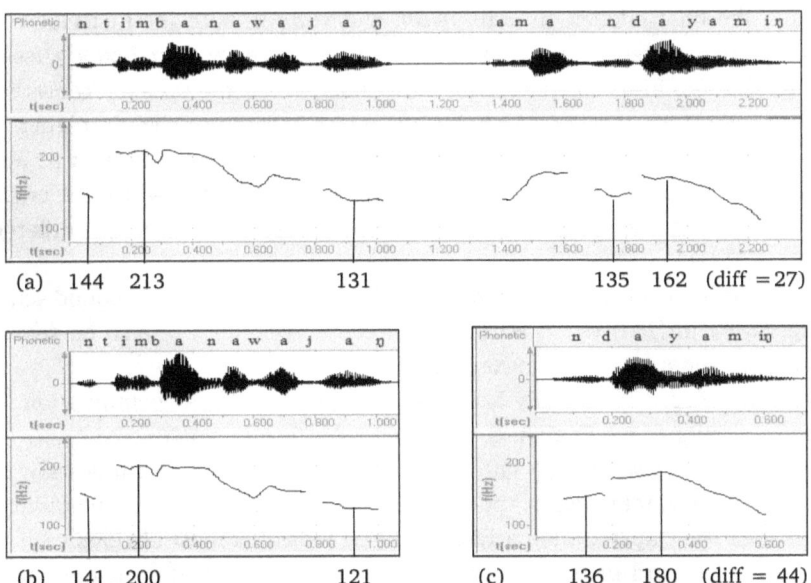

(a) 144 213   131   135 162 (diff = 27)

(b) 141 200   121   (c)   136 180 (diff = 44)

The higher *n* in (a) in the second clause in (25a) and (26a) is attributable to its position between two Highs. Other compound sentences are in (27)–(28), again displaying the averages of three repetitions.

(27) a. He went to market but he didn't buy oil.
 ʊ̀ gàwá ˈnyʋ́ŋ <pause> àmá ʊ̀ ká dá ˈkpááŋ
 147 198 147 <416> 132-167 142 160

 b. He went to market
 ʊ̀ gàwá ˈnyʋ́ŋ
 146 188 143

 c. He didn't buy oil.
 ʊ̀ ká dá ˈkpááŋ
 146 177

(28) a. He went to farm, and harvested groundnuts.
 ʊ̀ gàwá ˈkʋ́áŋ <pause> à̀ kpà sɩ̀ŋkpááŋ
 149 205 185 <586> 135 145

 b. He went to farm.
 ʊ̀ gàwá ˈkʋ́áŋ
 147 183 163

 c. He has harvested groundnuts.
 ʊ̀ kpàwá sɩ̀ŋkpááŋ
 145 193 141

From the final pitches on *jááŋ*, *nyʋ́ŋ*, and *kʋ́áŋ* in both the first clause of the compound sentence and their occurrences in the independent clauses, it is seen that the former is higher than the latter. When the speaker knows there is a second clause coming, he pitches the entire first clause slightly higher.

Third, the range of the second clause is wider when it uttered as an independent sentence. This is seen most dramatically in (27) in which the embedded *ʊ̀ ká* LH difference in (27) is 18 Hz, but the independent *ʊ̀ ká* LH difference in (27) is 31 Hz.

Fourth, the range of the initial LH is larger in the longer compound sentences, e.g. 56 Hz in (28a) vs. 36 Hz in the shorter (28b). This will also be seen in the complex sentences in the next section.

One effect I specifically examined the data for was a "continuation intonation," similar to the English contrast between "I think you're cool." and "I think you're cool..." where the latter invites the expectation of a following clause, probably beginning with "but." This would indicate a H% boundary tone between the clauses. Such a H% would be indicated most obviously by a pitch on the last word of the first clause that is relatively higher in the compound sentence than in that clause as an independent sentence. The key word here is "relatively." While this last word of the first clause is definitely higher than in the independent clause, the whole first clause is higher as well, and the last word merely participates in that general raising, with no additional local raising. There appears to be a slight upflip in *jááŋ* in (26a), but this is only 1–2 Hz, does not appear in all graphs of this sentence, and so is not considered significant.

Another possibility for manifestation of a H% might be that a previous H of the first clause would be raised higher than normal, e.g. in [ǹ tím bá nàwá ˈjááŋ, àmá ǹ dááˈyá mìŋ], the [-wá] would be relatively higher in this compound sentence than in the independent sentence. As above, [-wá] is higher in the compound sentence, but again merely participates in the general raising of the first clause of that sentence. So there is no evidence for a H% boundary tone in compound sentences.

As seen in the measurements, the generalizations discussed here are tendencies, being gradient rather than categorical changes. In (30) are pitch graphs of the compound sentence ʊ̀ gàwá ˈnyʊ́ŋ, àmá ʊ̀ ká dáá ˈkpááŋ, with the pitches of the separate clauses ʊ̀ gàwá ˈnyʊ́ŋ and ʊ̀ ká dáá ˈkpááŋ superimposed on it (by dotted lines).

(29) a. ʊ̀   gàwá   ˈnyʊ́ŋ   <pause> àmá ʊ̀   ká   dá   ˈkpááŋ (solid lines)
      3SG   went   market   but   3SG   NEG   buy   oil

    b. ʊ̀   gàwá   ˈnyʊ́ŋ   (dotted lines, left part of graph)

    c. ʊ̀   ká dá   ˈkpááŋ   (dotted lines, right part of graph)[13]

(30) ʊ̀ gàwá ˈnyʊ́ŋ, àmá ʊ̀ ká dá ˈkpááŋ, as a complex sentence and as separate clauses

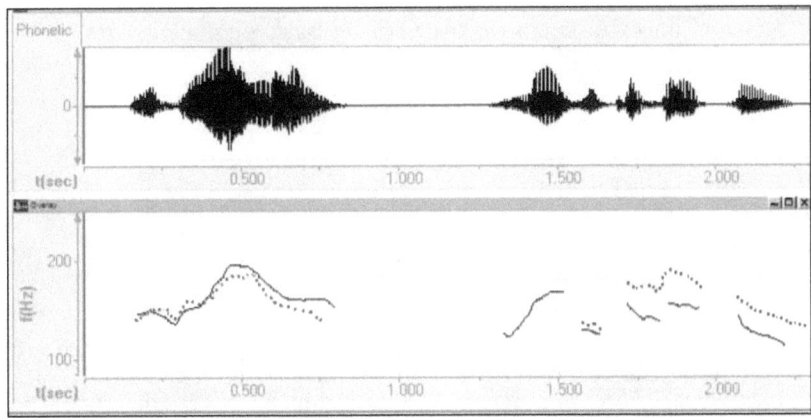

---

[13] In (29), kpááŋ is presumably downstepped due to a Low tone licensed by the verb in this aspect (also see (37b)). This contrasts with the lack of downstep in (31), in which the final tone of the verb is unambiguously High.

It can be clearly seen that ʊ̀ ká dáá ꜜkpááŋ as an independent clause is higher than the second clause in the compound sentence. It can also be seen that the first clause of the compound sentence is somewhat higher than the independent clause ʊ̀ gàwá ꜜnyʊ́ŋ.

3.3 Complex sentences: Direct and indirect quotes

Data at this point is quite limited on complex sentences; only a comparison of direct and indirect quotes is presented here (though (21) is a complex sentence, systematic data was not available for that). The target sentences were:

(31) a. ʊ̀   dàwá   kpááŋ   'S/he bought oil.'
3SG bought oil

b. ʊ̀   bàá?   ʊ̀   dàwá   kpááŋ   'S/he said (that) s/he bought oil.'
3SG said (that) 3s bought oil

c. ʊ̀   bàà   dí?   ʊ̀   dàwá   kpááŋ   'S/he said s/he bought oil.'
3SG said QUOT 3s bought oil

These differ from English; it is the *direct* quote in Kɔnni that has an extra word *dí* in it, rather than the indirect quote (cf. English 'he said *that*...'). The second speaker, Salifu, not only had a higher voice, as seen in the data in (32), but attached an extra suffix on the verb *ba* 'say', producing *bàrí*. There were significant differences in the speakers, and averages are presented separately below (S1 = Solomon, S2 = Salifu).

(32) a.   ʊ̀   dàwá kpááŋ
      S1 145 173   166   ʊ̀...wá LH difference = 28 Hz
      S2 158 187   173   ʊ̀...wá LH difference = 29 Hz

b.1   ʊ̀   bàá? <pause> ʊ̀   dàwá kpááŋ
      S1 138 172 <107>   135 150   147   ʊ̀ bá LH difference = 29 Hz
                                                 ʊ̀...wá LH difference = 16 Hz

b.2   ʊ̀   bàrí? <pause> ʊ̀   dàwá kpááŋ ʊ̀...rí LH difference = 56 Hz
      S2 159 216 <444>   145 159   149   ʊ̀...wá LH difference = 14 Hz

c.1   ʊ̀   bàà dí? <pause> ʊ̀   dàwá kpááŋ
      S1 144 198   <199>   131 146   146   ʊ̀...dí LH difference = 54 Hz
                                                 ʊ̀...wá LH difference = 15 Hz

c.2   ʊ̀   bàrí dí? <pause> ʊ̀   dàwá kpááŋ ʊ̀...dí LH difference = 55 Hz
      S2 155 210   <945>   144 156   151   ʊ̀...wá LH difference = 12 Hz

Sample pitch graphs for these are presented below. One noteworthy difference between speakers is that Solomon (S1) had little or no difference between frequency of the final *kpááŋ* and the preceding High syllable. There is also little if any declination in the *kpááŋ*, which actually shows a slight final rise, as seen in the graphs (33a), (34), and (35) below. Salifu (S2), in contrast, had a slight decrease in frequency of the final *kpááŋ*, and the graph shows a final drop in pitch, as seen in (33b). In terms of possible boundary tones, then, Salifu may possibly have a final L% (or it may be he just has more pronounced declination), but there is no sign of this in Solomon's speech here.

(33) a.   *ʊ̀ dàwá kpááŋ* (32a, S1)

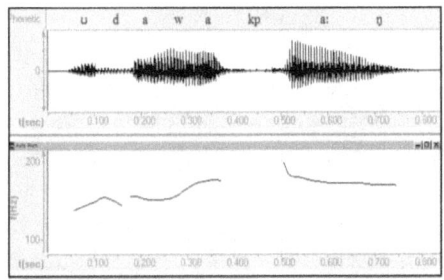

   b.   *ʊ̀ dàwá kpááŋ* (32a, S2)

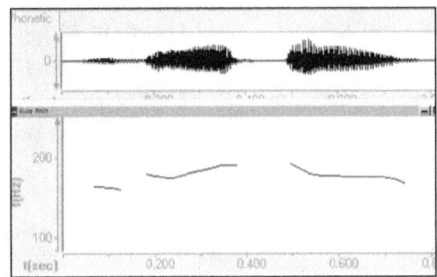

(34)   *ʊ̀ bàá? <pause> ʊ̀ dàwá kpááŋ* (S1)[14]

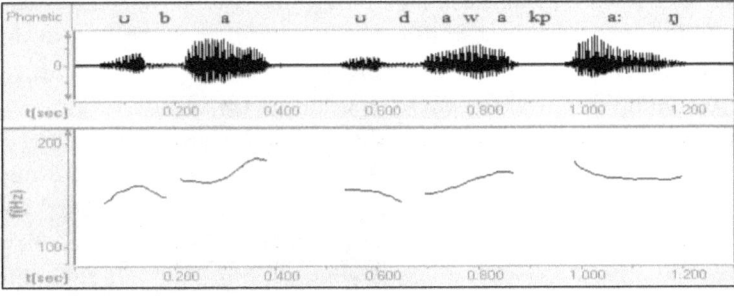

---

14 It is unclear why *bàá* has a rising tone in (34) but not in (35). One possibility is that the verb phrase requires a final High. Another hypothesis is that the clear glottal stop at the end of *bàá* in (34) raises the pitch. Data to decide between these hypotheses is currently unavailable.

(35)   ʊ̀ bàà dí? <pause> ʊ̀ dàwá kpááŋ (S1)

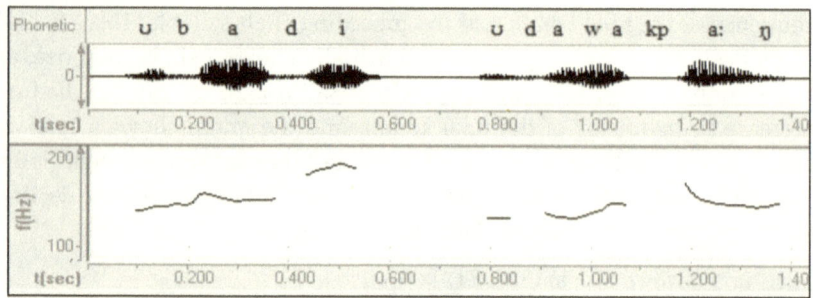

As with compound sentences, there is a pause before the embedded clause, and in the second clause, the embedded 's/he bought oil' has a narrower range than when it is an independent clause. Again as with compound sentences, the embedded clause is usually lower in pitch than when that clause is an independent sentence.

Of particular note is that the sentence-initial LH range in (32a, b.1) is much less (29 Hz) than the LH range when either the suffix -rí or the quotative particle dí contributes the High tone (55 Hz). One would be tempted to say that the -rí/dí contributes an extra-High tone as an intonational pattern for quotations, except that 55 Hz for a LH range appears to be the normal value for longer sentences such as (25)–(27). Thus the lesser LH rise in (32a, b.1) seems more the anomaly in this data. However, this is more in the range of LH differences in other short sentences, such as in the neutral emotional sentence in (51). It is probable that the range of the initial LH is larger in longer sentences, as seen in the compound and complex sentences in the last two sections.

3.4 Fronted elements

Elements, generally noun phrases, may be fronted either for emphasis, as in (36a–b) or as a natural response to a content question, as in (36c–d). In many languages, emphasis is marked by a higher pitch, but for many African languages, including Kɔnni and most of the languages in this volume, morphosyntactic strategies rather than intonation are used to indicate focus. Of the twelve languages in this volume, only Akan, Bemba, Chimiini, and Shingazidja have any prosodic manifestation of focus. Perhaps because temporal elements tend to be one-word expressions, when these temporal elements are mentioned at all, they are almost always fronted. In contrast, it is quite rare to find locative phrases fronted; they are almost always post-verbal (though more investigation of answers to questions in natural discourse may reveal a higher frequency).

(36) a. jìnnɛ́ Ámìnà nàŋ kéŋ
today Amina FUT come
'today Amina will come'

b. Bìyáŋsì-mà wʊ̀-rìáŋ wʊ̀ wàà ká¹lí
Nangurima-LOC 3SG-also 3SG now sit
'at Nangurima he also is now living'

c. bíá? ʊ́ dàà what did he buy?

d. kpáá? ʊ́ dàà oil he bought

The study here focuses on fronted single-word object nouns. There is no phonemic tonal difference in the subject pronoun, verb, or object noun from the basic sentence to the fronted object one (<p> indicates a phonetic pause):

(37) a. ú ¹dígì nyʊ́à¹⁵   nyʊ́à <p> ú ¹dígì   She cooked yams, yams she cooked

b. ʊ́ ¹dáà kpááŋ   kpááŋ <p> ʊ́ ¹dáà   She bought oil, oil she bought

c. ú ¹dígì gílà   gílà <p> ú ¹dígì   She cooked eggs, eggs she cooked

d. ʊ́ ¹chɔ̂ŋ gílà   gílà <p> ʊ́ ¹chɔ̂ŋ   She fried eggs, eggs she fried

e. ú ¹díì sààŋ   sààŋ <p> ú ¹díì   She ate TZ (porridge), TZ she ate

f. ʊ́ ¹chɔ́gìsì bòlíŋ   bòlíŋ <p> ʊ́ ¹chɔ́gìsì She fetched fire, fire she fetched

Intonation patterns specific to a fronted element are minimal. I note first of all that there is usually a pause between the fronted object and the rest of the sentence. The other issue to note is the behavior of the tone across the pause. In general, a pause often marks a new utterance, or at least sentence, and this resets the register of the tone range, raising a High in a new sentence to higher than the last High of the first sentence. Also, in an extended discourse, there is a general downtrend of sentences. This is schematized in (38), where each line represents the pitch track of a sentence (also see discussion in Section 6).

---

15 For Solomon, the corresponding basic form that sparked the fronted object form was a sentence with the perfective suffix on the verb, as in ù dìgì-wó nyʊ́à. The fronted form he produced was the same, however.

(38) Downtrend of sentence pitches within paragraphs

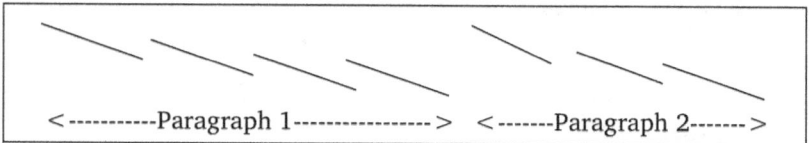

Here, the pause acts as if it were absent, in two ways. First, in a H<p>H sequence in a fronted element sentence, the High after the pause is normally the same level as the High before the pause, unlike the pattern in (38). This is illustrated in (39).

(39) sààŋ <p> ú ꜝdîi 'TZ porridge she ate'[16]

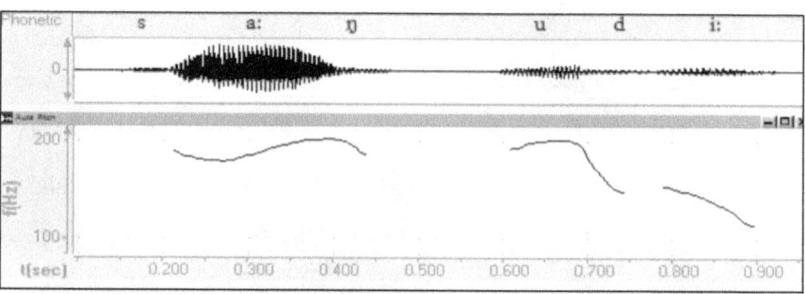

Second, on a more local level, the pause in these does not reset the domain of downdrift; the second High tone in a HL<p>H will be downstepped as if the pause was absent. This local downstep is a different phenomenon, more predictable and quantifiable, than the downtrend between sentences in a discourse.

4 Intonation of questions

4.1 Content questions

Content questions of Kɔnni merely add an interrogative marker in place of the subject noun or noun phrase, with no additional tonal phonology. The following examples have exactly the same pitch pattern:

---

[16] The Low in sààŋ is considerably higher than the initial Low-toned pronouns in (33)–(35). The initial Low tone of the disyllabic bòlíŋ in (37f) is approximately the same as sààŋ, both being around 150 Hz. This is the only place in my data which may possibly indicate a H%, but requires more data and analysis before any conclusions can be solidified.

(40) a. tígíŋ wǔn'ná   'this is a house'   (lit. 'house this.is')[17]

b. bíá wǔn'ná   'what is this?'

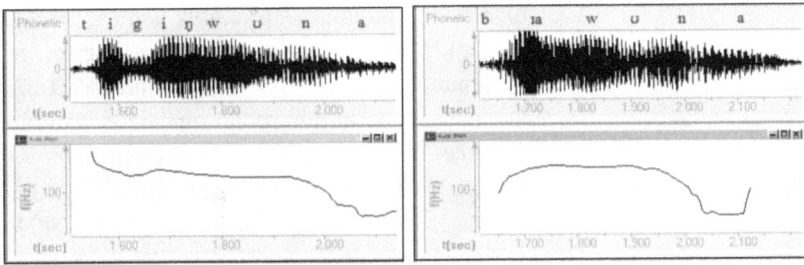

Note the raising effect of the voiceless [t] and lowering effect of the voiced [b] in the onset of the sentences above.

Questions which have a corresponding object in their answer have the same syntax in both question and answer:

(41) a. bíá ʔʋ́ dàà   'what did he buy?'[18]

b. kpáá ʔʋ́ dàà   'oil he bought'

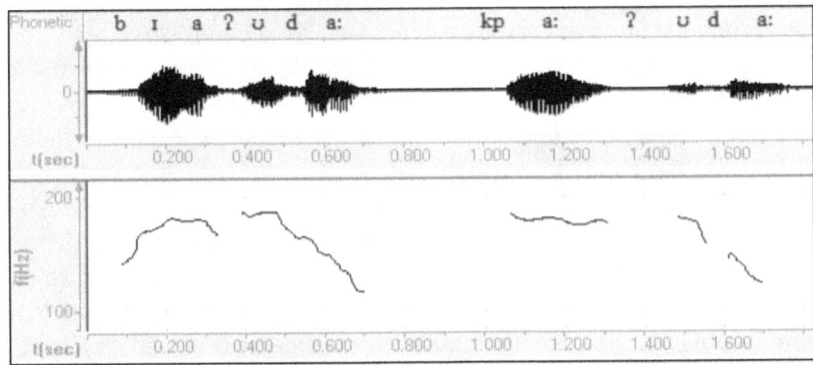

Interestingly, there is a measurable and somewhat variable pause after the fronted noun *kpáá*, but not after the interrogative *bíá*. This may be there to set off the fronted noun for emphasis (as new information), but this is somewhat speculative at this point.

---

[17] Note the lack of pause after the initial noun. This is not a fronted noun, as in the previous section, but a subject noun.

[18] The verb *daa* 'buy' has a long vowel here because of a bimoraic requirement for verbs in final position. If a suffix such as *-wa* perf is added, the underlying /da/ surfaces, as in (50).

4.2 Polar questions

Polar questions in Kɔnni have a number of interesting distinctives, more so than content questions. Polar question intonation has probably been subjected to the most detailed cross-linguistic study of any African intonation pattern, in works by Rialland and Clements (Clements and Rialland 2008, Rialland 2007, 2009). Cross-linguistically, the most common pattern for polar questions is to raise their pitch at the end of the utterance, in languages as diverse as English, French, Italian (Chapallez 1964), Huastec of Mexico (Larsen & Pike 1949), Kunimaipa of Papua New Guinea (Pence 1964), and the tone languages Chrau of Vietnam (Thomas 1966), Thai (Luksaneeyanawin 1998), and Hausa (Miller & Tench 1982, Cowan & Schuh 1976). In light of this, Bolinger (1978: 471) wrote: "Terminals are almost universally low or falling for finality and assertion, and high or rising for the opposite, including yes-no questions..." Ohala (1984: 2) makes a similar generalization. What Rialland and Clements (2008) found, however, was that in the more than 100 African languages for which they obtained data, over half lower their final pitch to indicate a polar question, rather than raise it. Furthermore, there were a number of other qualities that accompanied polar questions besides pure pitch. We will first examine the Kɔnni situation, then compare it to the other characteristics of what Rialland terms "lax question intonation." The information below contains the essential facts from Cahill (2012).

While content questions in Kɔnni have no particular extra tonology or intonation, polar questions, in contrast, lengthen the final vowel or nasal, and have some variety of a falling final pitch. I say "some variety of a falling final pitch," because Kɔnni surprisingly has at least three distinct patterns of how this falling pitch is realized. This differs from other languages attested in the polar question literature, and also from all the other languages in this volume, which attest one single way to manifest falling pitch on the final syllable. (Some of the original sources in the literature are sketchy enough so that there may be more complexity than has thus far been documented; indeed, my own earlier presentation in Cahill 2007 had an overly simplified and incorrect analysis.)

In Kɔnni, polar question intonation is categorial, not paralinguistic. It is analyzed in terms of added phonemic tones, as in (42). This first pattern of Kɔnni polar question intonation adds a downstepped High to the final mora of the lengthened vowel, giving a H!H final contour.

(42) a. ʊ̀ ŋmìá gúúm⌐bú   's/he is rolling the rope'[19]

b. ʊ̀ ŋmìá gúúm⌐bú⌐ú   'is s/he is rolling the rope?'

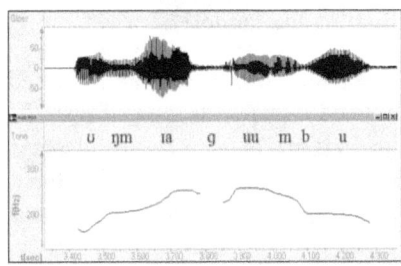 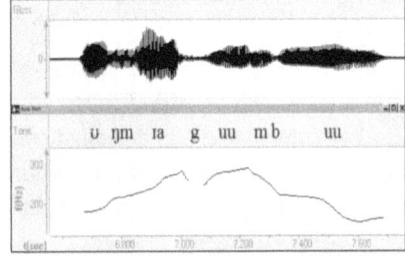

The additional statements and questions below follow the same tonal pattern, adding an additional downstepped High to the final syllable that itself is a High, whether downstepped or not.

(43) a. ʊ̀ yèsʊ̀wá gbíá⌐bíŋ   's/he has carved a door'

b. ʊ̀ yèsʊ̀wá gbíá⌐bí⌐ŋ   'has s/he carved a door?'

(44) a. tì díè sààbʊ́   'we are eating the TZ'   (a porridge)

b. nì díè sààbʊ́⌐ʊ́   'are you (pl) eating the TZ?'

The entire pitch in a polar question is also higher than in the corresponding statement.

The second pattern, exemplified in (45), adds a Low tone to a sentence-final High, creating a HL final contour, distinct from a H⌐H contour.

(45) a. ù sìé gìlìnsìèlé   's/he is dancing gilinsiele dance'

b. ù sìé gìlìnsìèléè   'is s/he dancing gilinsiele dance?'

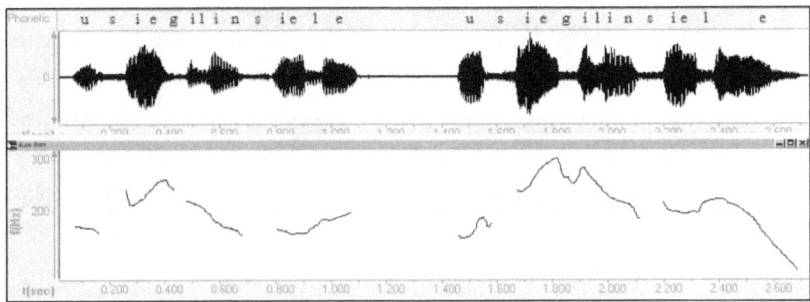

---

19 The sentences in (42)–(48) were recorded from a different Kɔnni speaker, James Amadu, with a higher voice than Salifu's or Solomon's.

An additional example is:

(46) a. ʋ̀ yásíná jɔ́ríkʋ́ 's/he is climbing the ladder'

b. ʋ̀ yásíná jɔ́ríkʋ́ʋ̀ 'is s/he climbing the ladder?'

Phonologically, gúúmˈbú, sààbʋ́, gìlìnsìèlé, and jɔ́ríkʋ́ all end with a H autosegment, but LH is added to the first two and only a L to the last two.

The third pattern is the most complex in terms of autosegments, and appears with statements ending with a noun with final Low tone. In these, the pitch is actually raised before falling, again giving a HˈH final contour.

(47) a. ʋ̀ dàwá níígè 's/he has bought cows'

b. ʋ̀ dàwá níìˈgéˈé 'has s/he bought cows?'

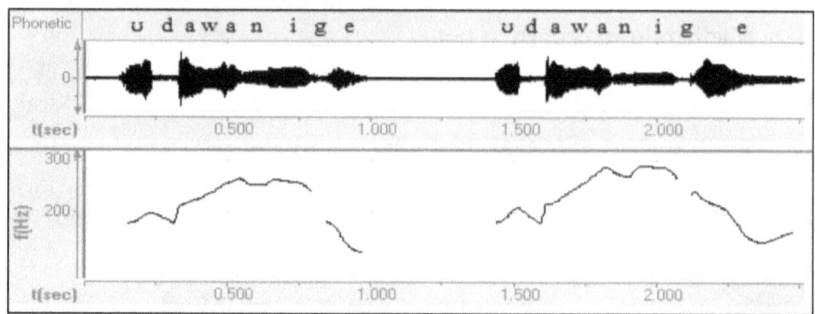

Changing níígè to níìˈgéˈé is a complex tonal change, and is accomplished by adding HLH to the statement.

In these three examples, we see that a falling pitch on the final long syllable is accomplished in autosegmental terms by adding either LH, L, or HLH. Note that these are categorial changes, not gradient. A gradient change, however, can be added to a polar question when the person expresses surprise, even astonishment.

(48) 3 repetitions of nì dìè sààbʋ́ˈʋ́ 'you (pl.) are eating the TZ?' in normal and surprise question intonation (pitches superimposed; surprise is the higher pitch)

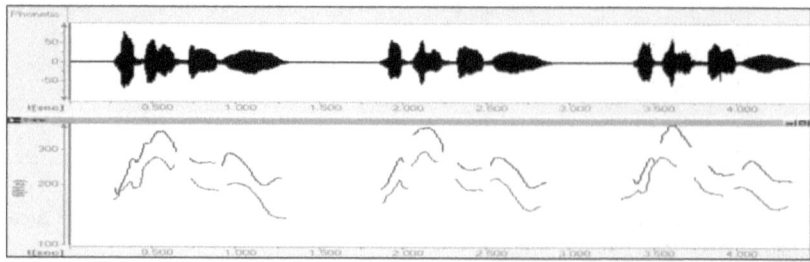

The chapter on Chimiini in this volume also briefly alludes to this pattern. In this case, the F0 of the whole utterance is raised. Other emotional factors and the gradient changes they cause are covered in Section 5.

An "upflip", a very short rise utterance-finally, is a phonetic detail that occurs in most polar questions, as in (42b), (47b), and (48) and is always present in the "surprise question" forms. The upflip was not initially audible to this non-native listener. However, its regularity, occurring in the speech of the two speakers in Cahill (2012), as well as the speaker who gave "surprise" data for this new study (Salifu, Section 5), indicates that it is learned as a normal pattern of a child acquiring Kɔnni question intonation. The fact that it does not rise as far as the phonemic LH rising tone in Kɔnni makes it likely that this upflip is probably more a phonetic than a categorical phonological phenomenon, perhaps an enhancement phenomenon.

The three varieties of realizing a falling polar pitch in Kɔnni are surprising, being quite uneconomical from a language learning or analytical point of view. The complexity of the change of *níígè* to *níí!gé!é*, especially, with added HLH autosegments, is as far as I know unattested in any other language.[20] However, the phonetics is clear, and all attempts to unify the phenomenon using a single autosegmental representation meet insurmountable obstacles. Study of polar questions with a larger number of final lexemes may shed more illumination on this admitted perplexity, but at this point, which polarity pattern applies is assumed to be a lexical matter.[21]

Rialland (2007, 2009) lists characteristics of what she terms "lax question intonation." 36 out of 78 African languages in the database of Rialland (2007), and 66 of 119 languages in the expanded database of Rialland (2009), have some form of this "lax question intonation." Some languages in Africa display most of these; others display a subset. These characteristics include:

(49) Characteristics of "lax question intonation" in Africa (Rialland 2009)
    a. Low or L%
    b. length
    c. breathy termination
    d. [open] vowel

---

[20] Upon request, one other Kɔnni speaker recorded *ʊ̀ dàwá níí!géè*, necessitating adding HL rather than HLH. This is simpler, but still is a separate pattern than the others. I will check this with other speakers as opportunity allows.

[21] Salifu, in data for "surprise" emotion (Section 5), produced polar questions, and all of these had a final downstepped High. The polar questions are shown here, with citation forms of

Of the characteristics in (49), Kɔnni demonstrates one of these partially, and one fully. As has been demonstrated, Kɔnni lowers pitch, but usually manifests downstepped H tone, not Low (with the exception of a few lexical items), so it demonstrates (49a) only partially. It turns out there are other, more complex, ways to lower a pitch besides merely adding a L tone to it. Regarding (49b), increased length of the final vowel or nasal is fully present. For (49c, d), there is no trace of breathiness or any change in vowel quality in polar questions in Kɔnni. So Kɔnni partly exhibits (49a), and fully exhibits (49b), but not the others.²²

Other Ghanaian languages I have examined with this same methodology (Cahill 2015) show varied results. Adele [ade], a Kwa language, always lowers the final pitch, whatever the final underlying tone of the final noun in declarative sentence form. It lengthens the final existing vowel. Safaliba [saf], a Gur language like Kɔnni, is quite variable in the specifics of how it manifests a polar question, but there is always a lowering of the final syllable. It also lengthens the final vowel. Buli [bwu], Kɔnni's closest relative (Gur), does not lengthen the final original vowel, but adds another morpheme /-áà/, which has falling tone over the last syllable. Deg [mzw], a Gur language, also adds /-áà/ to the final noun. Chumburung [ncu] (Kwa) often has a slightly different suffix than Buli and Deg, adding the falling-toned /-áàh/ to form a polar question. This is the only language to exhibit breathiness.

All these except Adele appear to be analyzable in autosegmental terms as Kɔnni was, with added tones that themselves conform to normal tone patterns. Adele phonetically lowers all final tones, even a Low tone, and this can be analyzed as a L% boundary tone.

The four characteristics of "lax question intonation" in (49) all appeared at least partially in these languages. However, the only criteria always present in

---

nouns in parentheses. Unfortunately, he did not record questions ending with nouns that above exhibited other patterns, so it is not known how general a pattern this could be.

ù dìgì-wó nyʊ́ˈáá (nyʊ́à)   HL base, add H → H!H   S/he has cooked yams?
ʊ̀ dàwá kpáˈáŋ (kpááŋ)   H base, add LH → H!H   S/he has bought oil?
ù dìgìwó gíˈláá (gílà)   HL base, add H → H!H   S/he has cooked eggs?
ù dùùwó ˈsáˈáŋ (sààŋ)   LH base, add LH → H!H   S/he has eaten TZ?
ʊ̀ chɔ̀gìsìwó ˈbólíˈŋ (bòlíŋ)   LH base, add LH → H!H   S/he has fetched fire?

22 Rialland (2007, 2009) refers to Kɔnni, using the single example given in Watters (2000). I supplied that information to Watters before the present detailed study, and the present chapter corrects and supersedes the transcription *nì díè sààbʊ̀ʊ̀* in that publication (see (44)). The form actually ends in downstepped High, not Low.

all languages were falling intonation and long final vowels, and even these were not uniform:
- "Falling intonation" does not have to be a L or L% tone. It can be an added ꜜH tone, and it is not always consistent within a single language.
- Long final vowels were sometimes lengthened root vowels, and were sometimes the added /-aa/ vowel.

5 Emotions and intonation patterns

In Kɔnni and many other languages, expressing emotion by intonation[23] is a paralinguistic feature, not a matter of discrete phonological units. In the data gathered for this section, Mr. Kpeebi asked the Kɔnni speakers to first utter a particular sentence, and then asked them to say it as if they were surprised, bored, angry, contemptuous, or "with emphasis." (The way the instructions were given would elicit broad focus, not narrow focus on any particular word or phrases.) I suggested these particular emotions on the basis of some of the literature cited in Ladd (2008). These certainly do not exhaust the list of emotions which may affect intonation patterns. In their paper on emotions and intonation, Murray and Arnott (1993), for example, list anger, joy/happiness, sadness, fear/anxiety, and disgust/contempt as "primary emotions," and grief/sorrow, affection/tenderness, sarcasm, and surprise as "secondary emotions." This part of the research must therefore be considered preliminary and not exhaustive, but it did produce some definite patterns.

For reasons beyond my control, Solomon only produced recordings on emotions for one sentence, so the bulk of this data refers to Salifu's speech.

The sentences in this part of the study are the following, with the bold syllables being the ones measured.

(50) ʋ̀ dìgìwó nyʋ́à   's/he has cooked yams'
      ʋ̀ gàwá ꜜnyʋ́ŋ   's/he has gone to market'
      ʋ̀ dàwá kpááŋ   's/he has bought oil'
      ù dìgìwó gílà   's/he has cooked eggs'
      ù chʋ̀ŋwá gílà   's/he has fried eggs'
      ù dùùwó ꜜsááŋ   's/he has eaten TZ'
      ʋ̀ chɔ̀gìsìwó ꜜbólíŋ   's/he has fetched fire'

---

[23] This section summarizes Cahill (to appear), where more details as well as specific measurements may be found.

All the sentences started with the Low-toned third singular pronoun ʊ̀/ù and had a High-toned perfective verbal suffix -wá/-wó (vowels alternate because of ATR vowel harmony). The representative example in (51) illustrates the methodology for this section.

(51) She has gone to market: ʊ̀ gàwá ˈnyʊ́ŋ (Salifu)

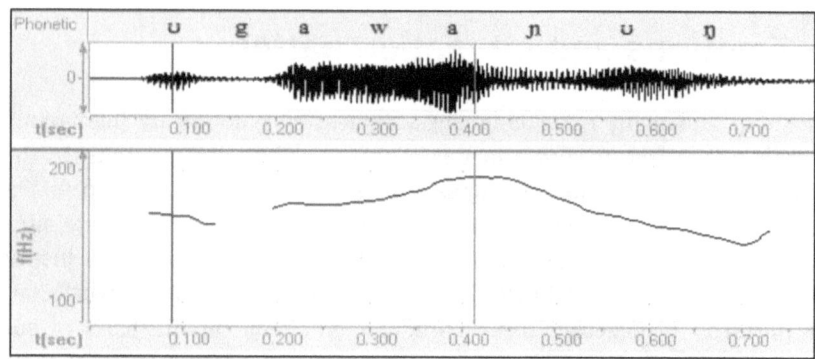

For F0, the goal was to measure both the *level* of the sentence (how high it was) and its *range* (the difference between High and Low tones). To quantify these, the crucial measurements of Low and High were made on the initial pronoun ʊ̀/ù and the first High tone, the suffix -wá/-wó, as shown in the position of the vertical cursors in (51).[24] Data for one sentence with all the emotional variants are given below (EXP = expanded F0 range, CONT = contracted F0 range).

(52) 's/he has gone to market': ʊ̀ gàwá ˈnyʊ́ŋ (Salifu)

	L (Hz)	H (Hz)	range (H-L)	duration	compared to neutral
neutral	157	194	37	678	—
	150	187	37	657	
	144	185	41	617	
	ave 150	ave 189	ave 39	ave 651	
bored	134	172	38	574	lower, CONT, faster
	137	165	28	529	
	135	169	34	554	
	ave 135	ave 169	ave 34	ave 552	

---

24 The measurement is made at the peak of the High tone, which often is later than the midpoint of the vowel. This is considered the articulatory target. As discussed in Section 3.1, measuring the first Low and the first High in the sentence was judged to be adequate for analyzing base level and range.

	L (Hz)	H (Hz)	range (H-L)	duration	compared to neutral
contempt	143	170	27	557	lower, CONT, faster
	126	166	40	531	
	142	161	29	555	
	ave 134	ave 166	ave 32	ave 548	
angry	144	202	58	531	—, EXP, faster
	153	208	55	569	
	152	198	46	575	
	ave 150	ave 203	ave 53	ave 558	
emphatic	160	218	58	752	higher, EXP, slower
	162	214	52	700	
	159	205	51	659	
	ave 159	ave 212	ave 53	ave 704	
surprise (Q)	159	231	71	851	higher, EXP, longer
	163	230	67	817	
	153	216	63	745	
	ave 158	ave 226	ave 67	ave 804	

The measurement of the initial Low is taken to indicate the base level of the sentence. If it is higher, then the whole utterance is higher; if lower, then lower. The difference between the initial Low and the suffixal High indicates the *range* of the utterance. The rightmost column summarizes the difference between the emotion in that row and the neutral utterance.

Thus for this particular sentence, the "emphatic" utterance was a somewhat higher F0 than the neutral utterance, and also had an expanded range, and was uttered more slowly. There is no comment on initial F0 for the "angry" utterance because in this data, the base level was the same level as that of the neutral utterance. The "surprise" utterance was uttered as a polar question, which entailed additional changes. As discussed in Section 4, there is an extra mora added in polar questions, so I note duration as "longer" rather than "slower" or "faster."

I also note in passing the volume of these, though this is not in the table. The "bored" and "contemptuous" versions were quieter, and "emphatic" was louder ("angry," somewhat surprisingly, was approximately the same volume for this speaker).

A summary of all the sentences is displayed below, with the caveat that these high level generalizations conceal detail.

(53) Properties of emotions in Kɔnni compared to "neutral"

	base pitch	range	speech rate	volume
bored	neutral	contracted	faster	quieter
contemptuous	neutral	contracted	varied/faster	quieter
angry	little higher	expanded	faster	same
emphatic	higher	expanded	slower	louder
surprise	higher	expanded	longer	

The "bored" expressions in Salifu's speech were consistently faster than the neutral, and most of the time had a contracted range. No consistent pattern of raising or lowering was found (despite the measure for the single sentence in (52)). The "contemptuous" expressions in Salifu's speech varied in speed, but were generally faster than neutral, and most of the time had a contracted range. Again, no consistent pattern of raising or lowering was found. The "bored" and "contemptuous" patterns thus resembled each other. The "angry" expression was sometimes higher than neutral, mostly faster, but always with an expanded range. The "emphatic" expression was always higher, always with expanded range, and almost always slower. As in the previous section, the "surprise" was always higher, with an expanded range, and longer. I use "longer" rather than "slower" because there is always an extra mora added when the utterance was expressed as a polar question.

The similarity between the "bored" and the "contemptuous" measurements may suggest that these are closely related in Kɔnni speakers' minds. It is easy to imagine that someone who is expressing contempt would act as if he were bored. This brings up the challenge of what emotions are active in the minds of people in different cultures, so the relation between "bored" and "contemptuous" must be somewhat speculative at this point. If we count "bored/contemptuous" as one, there are four distinct patterns of intonation in this data that indicate emotional states. A good follow-up experiment would test if naïve Kɔnni speakers (or speakers of other languages) could reliably distinguish these.

Since this was a controlled and not a natural situation, there may be questions raised as to the acting abilities of the speakers. As Murray and Arnott (1993:1099) note, "Speakers vary markedly in their ability to express emotive meaning vocally in controlled circumstances." This may explain why "anger" in the studies referred to by them, as well as in Bänziger and Scherer (2005), produced a definitely higher raise in pitch than was shown by the relatively modest raise in this study.

Another question is how universal these intonational patterns of emotions are. Some researchers have indeed found cross-linguistic similarities. Gussenhoven (2004: 72) cites Bezooijen (1984: 128) discussing a study in which Taiwanese and Japanese speakers identified (with above chance results) sadness, anger, and surprise by Dutch speakers. However, contempt and shame were not recognized. It is possible that at least some emotions have common, even universal, intonational expressions. A challenge, however, is that the lexical terms which are translated as "anger, sadness, etc." may not represent the exact same mental state from culture to culture.

Still, the changes in pitch shown here for various emotions are consistent with the more controlled study of Bänziger and Scherer (2005), who found the base level and range of F0 (also measured in this study) varied strongly with the specific emotion acted out in the experiments. They are also compatible with patterns found in other languages (Cruttenden 1997), and specifically add to the knowledge of how tone languages are able to express paralinguistic intonation in a systematic way.

6 Concluding remarks

This study has only scratched the surface of intonation in Kɔnni. There are other constructions which could be investigated, phonological phrasing determined, and of course more extensive data on the constructions examined here would further validate the conclusions of this work.

One major area which could fruitfully be investigated is intonation in discourse, to mark off information in larger units than single sentences (Halford 1994), which was briefly mentioned in Section 3.4. The effects of discourse context on intonation have been known for some time. Grimes (1959) notes that in Huichol, a tone language of Mexico, there are paragraph-size pitch patterns involving a downdrift before resetting to a higher pitch, and this pattern also occurs in West African languages. Bolinger (1979) notes several languages with "extra low at paragraph end." Cahill (1995) briefly noted a related pattern in Kɔnni as well. The following is an extract of four sentences from a single paragraph in a dramatic story, "The Spider and the Monkey." Note the general downtrend from one sentence to the next. The following sentence, not shown here, starts a new paragraph, and is pronounced at a higher level. At this point, the data is not conclusive, but is suggestive.

(54) Four sentences from Spider and Monkey story (lines divide sentences)

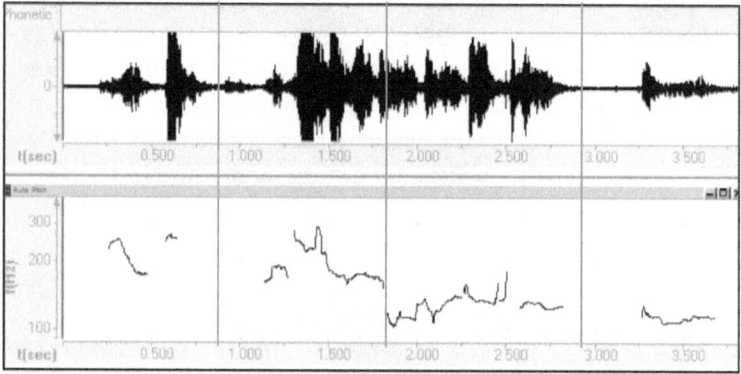

Pearce (2000) also briefly discusses the range of tones increasing as a function of excitement in a story; at the beginning of the story, the range between L and H is 2–4 semitones, whereas at the climax of the story, L stays at the same pitch while H can be an octave higher.

Returning to the bifurcation of intonation types, it is evident that Kɔnni contains both linguistic and paralinguistic types of intonation. The linguistic type is clearly illustrated by polar questions, in which discrete autosegments are added to a statement to make it a question. The paralinguistic type is most clearly indicated in the use of pitch level and range, as well as duration, to indicate various emotional states.

Acknowledgements

I am grateful first of all to Konlan Kpeebi and Kɔnni speakers Mr. Naaza Solomon Dintigi and Mr. Mumuni Salifu Barnabas, who were the source of most of the intonation data in Sections 3–5. I also acknowledge a debt to the editors of this volume and two other referees, who gave valuable input which vastly improved this chapter.

References

Antilla, Arto, and Adams Bodomo. 1996. Stress and tone in Dagaare. http://roa.rutgers.edu/files/169-1296/169-1296-ANTTILA-0-0.PDF.
Banziger, Tanja and Scherer, Klaus R. 2005. The role of intonation in emotional expressions. *Speech Communication* 46: 252–267.

Bezooijen, R.v. 1984. *Characteristics and recognizability of vocal expressions of emotion.* Dordrecht: Foris.
Bolinger, Dwight. 1978. Intonation across Languages. In Greenberg. J. H. (ed.), *Universals of Human Language 2 (Phonology).* Stanford University Press, pp. 471–524.
Cahill, Michael. 1995. Peaking at Zero: Null Anaphora and other Indicators of Peak in Kɔnni. In Akinbiyi, Akinlabi (ed.), *Theoretical Approaches to African Linguistics. Trends in African Linguistics 1.* Trenton, NJ: Africa World Press, Inc. pp. 345–357.
Cahill, Michael. 2000. Tonal Associative Morphemes in Optimality Theory. *Ohio State University Working Papers in Linguistics* 53: 31–70.
Cahill, Michael. 2004. Tonal Polarity in Kɔnni Nouns, *Studies in African Linguistics* 33.1: 1–33.
Cahill, Michael. 2007. *Aspects of the Morphology and Phonology of Konni.* Dallas: SIL International.
Cahill, Michael. 2012. Polar Question Intonation in Kɔnni. In *Selected Proceedings of the 42nd Annual Conference on African Linguistics,* ed. Michael R. Marlo, Nikki B. Adams, Christopher R. Green, Michelle Morrison, and Tristan M. Purvis, 90–98. Somerville, MA: Cascadilla Proceedings Project. http://www.lingref.com/cpp/acal/42/index.html, document #2761.
Cahill, Michael. 2015. Polar Question Intonation in Five Ghanaian Languages. In *Selected Proceedings of the 44th Annual Conference on African Linguistics,* ed. Ruth Kramer, Elizabeth C. Zsiga, and One Tlale Boyer, 28–36. Somerville, MA: Cascadilla Proceedings Project. www.lingref.com, document #3124. http://www.lingref.com/cpp/acal/44/paper3124.pdf.
Cahill, Michael. to appear. Intonation and emotions in Kɔnni. In Payne, Doris L., Sara Pacchiarotti & Mokaya Bosire (eds.). *Contemporary African Linguistics, Selected papers from the 46th Annual Conference on African Linguistics.* Language Science Press.
Carlson, Robert. 1983. Downstep in Supyire. *Studies in African Linguistics* 14: 35–45.
Casali, Roderic F. 1995. An Overview of the Nawuri Verbal System. *Journal of West African Languages* XXV.1: 63–86.
Chapallaz, Marguerite. 1964. Notes on the Intonation of Questions in Italian. In David Abercrombie, D.B. Fry, P.A.D. MacCarthy, N.C. Scott and J.L.M Trim (eds.), *In Honor of Daniel Jones.* Longman, pp. 306–312.
Clements, G.N. 2000. Phonology. In Heine, Bernd, and Derek Nurse (eds.), pp. 123–160.
Clements, G.N. and Annie Rialland. 2008. Africa as a phonological area. In Heine, Bernd, and Derek Nurse (eds.) *A Linguistic Geography of Africa.* Cambridge: Cambridge University Press, pp. 36–85.
Cowan, J. Ronayne, and Russell G. Schuh. 1976. *Spoken Hausa.* Spoken Language Services, Inc., Ithaca, NY. (see esp. pp. 198–199)
Cruttenden. 1997. *Intonation.* Cambridge: Cambridge University Press.
Essien, Okon E. 1990 A Grammar of the Ibibio Language. Ibadan: University Press Ltd.
Grimes, Joseph. 1959. Huichol tone and intonation. *International Journal of American Linguistics* 25: 221–232.
Gussenhoven, Carlos. 2004. *The Phonology of Tone and Intonation.* Cambridge: Cambridge University Press.
Halford, Brigitte, K. 1994. The Discourse Function of Intonation. In Halford and Pilch (eds.), *Intonation,* 69–88. Tübingen: G. Narr Verlag Tübingen.
Heine, Bernd, and Derek Nurse (eds.). 2008. *A Linguistic Geography of Africa.* Cambridge: Cambridge University Press.
Hirst, Daniel, and Albert DeCristo (eds.). 1998. *Intonation Systems: A Survey of Twenty Languages.* New York: Cambridge University Press.

Kenstowicz, Michael, Emmanuel Nikiema, and Meterwa Ourso. 1988. Tonal Polarity in two Gur Languages. *Studies in the Linguistic Sciences* 18:1, 77–103.

Ladd, D. Robert. 2008. *Intonational Phonology*. Second Edition. Cambridge Studies in Linguistics 119. New York: Cambridge University Press.

Ladd, D. Robert, Klaus Scherer, and Kim Silverman. 1986. An integrated approach to studying intonation and attitude. In Johns-Lewis (ed.), *Intonation in Discourse*, 125–138. Breckenham, Kent: Croom Helm.

Larsen, Raymond S., and Eunice V. Pike. 1949. "Huasteco intonation and phonemes." *Language* 25: 268–277.

Lewis, M. Paul, Gary F. Simons, and Charles D. Fennig (eds.). 2016. *Ethnologue: Languages of the World, Nineteenth edition*. Dallas, Texas: SIL International. Online version: http://www.ethnologue.com.

Luksaneeyanawin, Sudaporn. 1998. Intonation in Thai. In Hirst & Di Cristo, pp. 376–394.

Miller, Jennifer, and Paul Tench. 1982. Aspects of Hausa Intonation, 1: Utterances in isolation. *Journal of the International Phonetic Association* 12(2): 45–63.

Murray, Iain R., and Arnott, John L. 1993. Toward the simulation of emotion in synthetic speech: A review of the literature on human vocal emotion. *Journal of the Acoustical Society of America* 93: 1097–1108.

Naden, Tony. 1986. Première note sur le kɔnni. *Journal of West African Languages* XVI.2: 76–112.

Odden, David. 1982. Tonal phenomena in KiShambaa. *Studies in African Linguistics* 13: 177–208.

Odden, David. 1995. Tone: African Languages. In Goldsmith, John (ed.). *The Handbook of Phonological Theory*. Cambridge, MA: Basil Blackwell. Pp. 444–475.

Ohala, John J. 1984. An ethological perspective oncommon cross-language utilization of F0 of voice. *Phonetica* 41: 1–16.

Pearce, Mary. 2013. *The Interaction of Tone with Voicing and Foot Structure: Evidence from Kera Phonetics and Phonology*. Stanford: CSLI Publications.

Pence, Alan R. 1964. Intonation in Kunimaipa (New Guinea). *Linguistic Circle of Canberra Publications* A3: 1–15.

Rialland, Annie. 2007. Question prosody: an African perspective. In Gussenhoven, Carlos, and Tomas Riad (eds.), *Tunes and Tones, Volume 1: Typological Studies in Word and Sentence Prosody*, 35–62. Berlin: Mouton deGruyter.

Rialland, Annie. 2009. The African lax question prosody: Its realisation and geographical distribution. *Lingua* 119.6: 928–949.

Schwarz, Anne. 2009. Tonal focus reflections in Buli and some Gur relatives. *Lingua* 119: 950–972.

Thomas, Dorothy. 1966. Chrau Intonation. *Mon-Khmer Studies* 2: 1–13.

Watters, John. 2000. Syntax. In Heine, Bernd and Derek Nurse (eds.), pp. 194–230.

Yip, Moira. 2002. *Tone*. Cambridge: Cambridge University Press.

Frank Kügler
Tone and intonation in Akan

Abstract: This chapter provides an account of the intonation patterns in Akan (Kwa, Niger-Congo). Tonal processes such as downstep, tonal spreading and tonal replacement influence the surface tone pattern of a sentence. In general, any Akan utterance independent of sentence type shows a characteristic downtrend in pitch. This chapter proposes that Akan employs a simple post-lexical tonal grammar that accounts for the shapes of an intonation contour. The unmarked post-lexical structure is found in simple declaratives. The downward trend of an intonation contour is shaped by local tonal interactions (downstep), and sentence-final tonal neutralization. In polar questions, an ι-phrase-final low boundary tone (L%) accounts for the intensity increase and lengthening of the final vowel compared to a declarative. Complex declaratives and left-dislocations show a partial pitch reset at the left edge of an embedded ι-phrase. Underlying lexical tones are not affected by intonation with the exception of sentence-final H-tones.

Keywords: downstep, low boundary tone, polar question, constituent question, imperative, complex declarative, Akan, pitch register reset, prosodic phrasing, tonal neutralization, avoidance, lax question prosody

1 Introduction

This chapter provides an account of the intonation patterns in the tone language Akan. Akan belongs to the Kwa branch of the Niger-Congo family and the name also refers to the largest ethnic group in Ghana (Nkansa-Kyeremateng 2004); the language is spoken by about 8.3 million people in Ghana and some eastern parts of the Ivory Coast (Christaller 1933; Lewis 2009). Akan consists of several dialects, some of which are more mutually intelligible than others (Schachter & Fromkin 1968). The dialects differ at the level of segments as well as tones (cf. Cahill 1985; Dolphyne 1988; Dolphyne & Kropp Dakubu 1988; Abakah 2000, 2005b; Abakah & Koranteng 2007 among others). Asante Twi is one of the three largest dialects, and "Akan is growing in its influence as a potential national language" of Ghana (Osam 2003: 3). The data discussed in this chapter are based on the Asante Twi dialect, and we will use Akan as a cover term throughout the chapter.[1]

The tone system of Akan is well studied (Stewart 1965; Schachter & Fromkin 1968; Clements 1983; Dolphyne 1988; Abakah 2005a, 2005b, 2010a; Paster 2010). Likewise, the interaction of tone and morpho-syntactic structure (Abakah 2010b; Abakah & Koranteng 2007; Paster 2010; Genzel 2013), the interaction of tone and segmental aspects (Marfo 2004; Manyah 2006, 2014), as well as the interaction of tone and information structure (Genzel & Kügler 2010; Kügler & Genzel 2012; Genzel 2013) have been studied. A number of studies have been concerned with tonal interactions, in particular downstep (Clements 1979; Stewart 1993; Dolphyne 1994; Abakah 2000, 2002; Abakah, Amissah & Ofori 2010; Genzel & Kügler 2011; Genzel 2013).

Genzel (2013) intensively studied the intonation of Akan in her dissertation. We will base our analysis of intonation on Genzel (2013) and extend the proposal to the following simple intonational grammar for Akan. First, a low intonation phrase boundary tone (L%) signals polar questions. In particular, the intonation in polar questions has been reported to exhibit sentence-final low pitch, lengthening of the sentence-final vowel and an intensity increase on the final vowel (Saah 1988; Rialland 2007, 2009; Saah & Dundaa 2012; Genzel 2013; Genzel & Kügler 2016). Second, an intonation phrase is associated with an initial high and final low pitch register tone (h and l, respectively) (Genzel 2013), which together with a phonetic implementation algorithm à la Liberman & Pierrehumbert (1984) account for the general downward trend in pitch in all Akan sentence types. This general downtrend in pitch, which is found in many West African tone languages, led Welmers (1959) to classify languages such as Akan as terraced-level tone languages (cf. also Clements 1979). Third, our data on complex declarative sentences suggest that the cues pitch reset and pause at the boundary of embedded clauses signal complex sentence structure.

---

[1] The acoustic data presented in this chapter (except for Figure 3) come from four native speakers of Asante Twi (two females and two males) who were recorded in Ghana in 2014. The speakers were in their mid-twenties and born and raised in the region where Asante Twi is spoken. All of them are fluent in English. Some parts of the sentence materials were taken from Genzel (2013), Genzel & Kügler (2016) and Kügler & Genzel (2012), and were partly adapted for the purposes of the present study. Data annotation and acoustic F0 analysis were conducted in Praat (Boersma & Weenink 2014). The data were hand-labelled at the levels of the syllable and segments. F0 means of syllabic nuclei were measured; these were either a vowel or a sonorant consonant (cf. Section 2). Stylized F0 contours present time-normalized F0 values averaged across the four speakers. The acoustic raw data in Figure 3 are from Genzel (2013).

This chapter is structured as follows. Section 2 introduces the basic tone patterns of Akan, showing that tone spreading affects surface tonal patterns and that floating tones as grammatical morphemes appear on the surface changing underlying lexical tone patterns. In addition, the well-known phenomenon of pitch downtrend over the course of an utterance, i.e. downstep or downdrift, is shown to have a crucial influence on the intonation in Akan. Section 3 presents the intonational patterns of declaratives, interrogatives and imperatives. All sentence types show a general downtrend in pitch over the utterance. Complex declaratives in contrast to simple declaratives show a pitch reset accompanied by a pause before the embedded clause. Interrogatives appear to end low in pitch, and, in addition, polar questions show a characteristic lengthening and increased intensity of the phrase-final vowel, which is interpreted as a low intonational phrase boundary tone. Finally, similar to declaratives and interrogatives, imperatives show a general downtrend in pitch. Section 4 briefly presents data on the prosodic expression of focus, where speakers employ a strategy of pitch register lowering, and in spontaneous speech, glottal stop insertion. Section 5 concludes the chapter and presents a table listing the individual intonational and prosodic events and their distribution in Akan.

2 Tonal patterns and tonal processes in Akan

Akan can be classified as a [+tone] and [−stress] language according to the classification of word prosodic systems of Hyman (2006).[2] The [+tone] feature characterizes Akan as a language in which "an indication of pitch enters into the lexical realization of at least some morphemes" (Hyman 2001: 1368 based on Welmers 1959: 2). Lexical tones are level tones characterizing Akan as a level tone language (Pike 1948). Unlike many Bantu languages, which are claimed to represent only H-tones underlyingly (cf. Myers 1998; Kisseberth & Odden 2003; see also the chapters in this collection on Bemba, Kula & Hamann this volume, on Chichewa and Tumbuka, Downing this volume, on Chimwiini, Kisseberth this volume, on Shingazidja, Patin, this volume, and on Tswana, Zerbian this volume), Akan distinguishes between lexical L-tones and H-tones, transcribed as [ˋ] and [ˊ],

---

[2] There is no phonetic indication of Akan having word stress (Dolphyne 1988; Purvis 2009; Anderson 2009). Note however that Christaller (1933: XXVIII) characterized stress in Akan as "emphasis put on a syllable", the details of which remain unclear though.

respectively (Dolphyne 1988).³ Tones both distinguish word meanings (1) and carry grammatical function (2) (Dolphyne 1988). Among other things, the grammatical function of tone relates to the expression of verb aspect, tense, and argument structures of the verb. For instance, in (2), the final tone of the verb determines verb aspect: the habitual form (2a) is characterized by a H-tone, and the stative form (2b) by a L-tone. The underlying lexical H-tone is postlexically replaced by a grammatical tone (Paster 2010). The grammatical function of tone in Akan plays a more important role than its lexical function (Dolphyne 1988).

(1)   a.   pápá   'good'

       b.   pàpà   'fan'

       c.   pàpá   'father'   (Dolphyne 1988: 52)

(2)   a.   kòfí   d͡ʑìná   hó
             Kofi   stand.HAB   there
             'Kofi stands there.'

       b.   kòfí   d͡ʑìnà   hó
             Kofi   stand.STAT   there
             'Kofi is standing there.'   (Dolphyne 1988: 67)

According to several scholars, the tone-bearing unit (TBU) in Akan is the syllable since tone sandhi affects the whole syllable and not just a mora (Stewart 1965; Dolphyne 1988: 52; Abakah 2002: 194, 2005a, 2005b). Dolphyne (1988) shows that Akan distinguishes three syllable types as shown in (3), which are either open syllables (CV, V), or a single sonorant (C) functioning as a syllabic nucleus (cf. also Christaller 1933: XXVIII; Stewart 1965; Abakah 2002).⁴ Any vowel constitutes a syllable, and hence, two adjacent vowels constitute two syllables (3e) (Christaller 1933: XVII; Dolphyne 1988).

---

3 All speech data of this chapter appear in standard IPA transcription. Glossing is based on the Leipzig Glossing Rules (Bickel et al. 2008). The following abbreviations are used in the glosses: ASS = associative marker; COMPL = completive; COORD = coordination; DEF = definite; DIM = diminutive; FM = focus marker; FUT = future; GEN = genitive; HAB = habitual; IMP = imperative; N = noun class prefix; NEG = negation; OBJ = object; PFT = perfective; PRS = present; PST = past; PRO = pronoun; PROG = progressive; SBJ = subject; SG = singular; STAT = stative; TOP = topic; QP = question particle.

4 Underlyingly, a syllabic consonant constitutes a syllable onset, and the vowel is dropped word-finally rendering the sonorant as syllabic (cf. Dolphyne 1988: 102ff; Abakah 2002: 195).

(3) a. ɔ́-fá 'he takes it' b. sò-ḿ 'hold it'
    c. ǹ-sú 'water' d. dà-ǹ 'turn it over'
    e. ò-hú-ì 'he saw it' (Dolphyne 1988: 52f)

The distinction of lexical H-tones and L-tones is also reflected at the level of segmental duration. According to Manyah (2006; 2014), vowels that carry a L-tone are significantly, about 80 to 100 ms, shorter than vowels carrying a H-tone. Vowel quality does not differ for different tones.

Relevant tonal processes in Akan discussed below concern downstep, tonal spreading and tonal replacement by grammatical tone insertion. Because both L-tones and H-tones are active in tonal processes, they can be considered to be lexically specified. In addition, toneless syllables exist in Akan, which receive their tonal specification either by tonal spreading, by tone polarization or by default L-tone insertion. According to Abakah (2002; 2005b) toneless elements comprise nominal prefixes, optional nominal suffixes, pronominal clitics, and tense and aspect affixes. Further tonal processes can be found in Schachter & Fromkin (1968: 105ff), Abakah (2002; 2010a), and Paster (2010).

2.1 Downstep

Akan has been classified as a terraced-level tone language, indicating that lexical H-tones are subject to a lowering process after L-tones (Welmers 1959).[5] This downtrend in Akan is triggered by the presence of a lexical L-tone, be it overt (automatic downstep or downdrift) or covert (non-automatic downstep).[6] In any underlying tonal sequence of /H-L-H/, the second H-tone is realized lower than the first H-tone. Automatic downstep arises when the underlying tonal sequence /H-L-H/ is realized as in (4a). The schematized pitch register shows the H-tone and L-tone with a following lower H-tone. Non-automatic downstep arises when the underlying L-tone trigger loses its segmental association and results

---

[5] Clements (1979: 537) lists a number of other languages that show tone terracing, which are not limited to sub-Saharan languages such as Niger-Congo (e.g. Yoruba) or Bantu (e.g. Sotho), but also occur in Nilo-Saharan (e.g. Luo) and Chadic languages (e.g. Ga'anda), as well as in some native North American languages such as Acatlán Mixtec.

[6] For clarification of terminological aspects concerning downtrends, see Connell (2011), as well as the introduction to this collection (Downing & Rialland this volume). Since there is no phonetic difference between different types of downstep in Akan (Genzel & Kügler 2011), we use the term 'downstep' as a cover term.

in a floating L-tone as in (4b); in this case, downstep is indicated by a superscript exclamation mark ('!'). The schematic pitch register shows two downstepped H-tones without an intervening L-tone realized. Tonal stability (Yip 2002: 67) ensures that the L-tone of the noun class prefix ɔ̀ is not deleted when the segment is deleted in (4b). As a result, the floating L-tone triggers downstep on the surface.

(4) a. kòfí + pàpá → kòfí pàpá
       Kofi   father   Kofi.GEN father

   b. kòfí + ɔ̀-dáń → kòfí ꜝdáń
      Kofi   N-house   Kofi.GEN house

Contributing to the debate whether the two types of downtrends (automatic and non-automatic downstep) have different phonetic effects, Genzel & Kügler (2011) investigated the amount of downstep in structures like (4) which were embedded in a tonally identical sentence frame. Contrary to Dolphyne (1994), who claimed that there exist phonetic differences in the amount of downstep, Genzel & Kügler (2011) found that the amount of downstep is identical in the two types of downstep. Hence, the phonetic realization of downstep is independent of whether the L-tone trigger is phonetically realized (4a) or not (4b).

2.2 Tonal spreading

Another phonological process is H-tone spreading, or "L-stepping" in Stewart (1993). Across word boundaries, a word-initial L-tone is deleted and the H-tone of the preceding word spreads onto the L-tone segmental anchor of the following word. In (5), the initial L-tone of the object àtàadíɛ́ is affected by H-tone spread from the verb, gets dissociated and turns up as a floating L-tone that causes downstep on the spread H-tone. Note that Marfo (2005) and Paster (2010) discuss further cases of H-tone spread across words that do not necessarily involve downstep.

(5) ɔ́bɛ́tɔ́   + àtàadíɛ́ → ɔ́bɛ́tɔ́ ꜝátáádíɛ́
    3SG.FUT.buy   garment   'S/he will buy (a) garment.'

(Stewart 1993: 194)

A case of rightward L-tone spread is discussed in Abakah (2005b: 115f). This tonal process can however be conceived of as an association of a floating L-tone (represented as L̥) rather than tonal spreading of an associated tone. The floating L-tone is underlyingly present (e.g. hɔhʊ – H L̥ H in (6)). This floating L-tone associates to the rightward adjacent TBU with the effect of a dissociation of a H-tone that in turn shows up on the next (toneless) TBU. There are three toneless TBUs in (6) (indicated by Ø); the re-associated H-tone shows up on the third one, an obligatory pronoun ɔ in the case of class-II nouns that are possessed that cliticizes to the associative construction (Abakah 2005b: 115). There are other processes taking place in (6): the associative tone is segmentless and constitutes only a floating H-tone (represented as H̥), which is followed by the underlying tone of the possessed noun. In the case of (6), this floating H-tone merges with the first underlying H-tone of the noun hɔhʊ 'guest'. The class 2 noun prefix ɔ is deleted, and the first person singular pronoun mɪ receives its tone from tone polarization with the following noun (Abakah 2005b: 123).

(6) mɪ   + Ø   + ɔ-hɔ́ˈhʊ́ + ɔ   →   mɪ̀hɔ́hʊ̀ɔ́
    1.SG.PRO   ASS   N2-guest   PRO   'my guest'
    /Ø   H̥   Ø H L̥ H   Ø /   [L H L H]

Marfo (2004) argues that H-tone spreading occurs across phonological phrase boundaries, and he takes the occurrence of this spreading process as a diagnostic for the presence of phonological phrases. However, Marfo (2004) also states that the H-tone spreading only occurs in certain circumstances, such as higher speech rate, which may indicate that para-linguistic effects drive the spreading process rather than prosodic phrasing. As for grammatically induced tone spreading, Paster (2010: 83f) discusses H-tone spreading in the case where the H-tone spreads from a subject noun phrase to a verb phrase in the case of the negative habitual. The negation marker, which underlyingly bears a L-tone /ǹ/, appears as a H-tone in the case of a preceding H-toned subject (7).

(7) ésí ń-ˈtɔ́   pèn
    Esi NEG-buy   pen
    'Esi doesn't buy pens.'   (Paster 2010: 83)

The H-tone spreads from the subject to the negative marker, and delinks the underlying L-tone of the negative marker /ǹ/, which results in a floating L-tone that causes downstep on the following H-tone of the verb. The negative marker cliticizes to the verb stem, and thus belongs to the verb phrase. If H-tone spread were sensitive to phonological phrase boundaries, we would not expect a H-tone spread to occur between the subject noun phrase and the verb phrase (cf. section 3.1, and Kügler 2015). However, exactly this process takes place, and

Paster (2010) analyses this process with a rule of Nasal Tone Assimilation that accounts for the association of the preceding tone (be it H or L) of the negative marker. In sum, there seems to be no clear evidence that tonal spreading is sensitive to phonological phrasing such that it might be blocked at a phonological phrase boundary.

2.3 Tonal replacement

A very common tonal process in Akan is referred to as 'tonal replacement' (Abakah 2005b) or 'grammatical tone insertion' (Paster 2010), referring to the grammatical function of tone in Akan. A lexical tone is replaced by a grammatical tone, for example to indicate a particular verb aspect or tense (Dolphyne 1988: 67f; Abakah 2005b; Paster 2010: 101ff). The following illustrates a process involving a floating L-tone, and one involving a floating H-tone. For instance, the verb tense 'PAST' is represented as a grammatical floating L-tone that associates to the edge of a morpheme, in (8b) to the left edge of a verb root. The effect of the association of the floating L-tone is illustrated in (8a). Applying the rule in (8a), the floating L-tone in (8b) associates to the verb /tɔ́/ to the effect that the underlying H-tone of the verb dissociates. Hence, the verb [tɔ̀ɔ̀] appears as L-toned in the past tense in (8b). The general property of (8a) is that the dissociated tone does not re-associate to the next TBU if it is a lexically specified one.

In associative constructions, a similar tonal process occurs, yet with a floating H-tone. As illustrated in (6), the associative marker is a floating H-tone, which is followed by the underlying tone of the possessed noun (Abakah 2010b: 57). The association of this floating tone appears to follow the rule in (8a) although neither Paster nor Abakah formalize the H-tone association in associative constructions in this way. The association of the floating H-tone results in the dissociation of the initial L-tone of the noun *pòmá* in (8c). Since the adjacent TBU is lexically specified with a H-tone, this L-tone becomes floating and causes the following H-tone to be downstepped.

(8) a. Grammatical tone association   (adapted from Paster 2010: 101)

$$[_{root}\ \sigma$$
$$\underset{T}{} \neq$$
$$T \rightarrow \emptyset$$

b. Past tense: floating L-tone   (Paster 2010: 101)
/ésí L tɔ́ pèn/ → [ésí tɔ̀-ɔ̀ pèn]
Esi PST buy pen   'Esi bought a pen.'

c. Associative tone: floating H-tone
/nè H̥ pòmá/ → [nè pó¹má]
PRO ASS walking stick 'her walking stick'
(cf. Cahill 1985: 45; Abakah 2005b: 115, 2010b)

This overview of tonal patterns and tonal processes in Akan has shown that the two tones are lexically specified and active in tonal processes. Local tonal interaction causes a downward trend of pitch in intonation. In addition, the grammatical function of tone in Akan becomes obvious by means of tonal processes like tonal replacement. The interaction of lexical tones and tonal processes accounts for the surface pitch contour of an Akan utterance.

3 Sentence-level intonation in Akan

This section presents the intonation of declarative sentences – both simple and complex, polar and constituent questions, as well as the imperative sentence type. As background, the first subsection briefly introduces some basic facts of Akan syntax, and relates them to prosodic phrasing.

3.1 Basic Akan syntax and corresponding prosodic structure

Akan is an SVO language, which is illustrated in (9a). NPs are right-branching, and post-nominal modifiers follow a strict order, i.e. the adjective is closest to the head noun, followed by numerals, the determiner, and finally by quantifiers (Boadi 2005; Saah 1994); cf. (9a), which illustrates the sequence of an adjective and a quantifier.

(9) a. kòfí dí kɔ́tɔ́ kɔ̀kó: bèbré:
Kofi eat.PRS crab red many
'Kofi eats many red crabs.' (Kügler 2015: 194)

b. [CP [TP [DP kofi] [VP di [DP kɔtɔ kɔko bebre:]]]]

c. ((kofi)φ (di (kɔtɔ kɔko bebre:)φ)φ)ι

Following a general approach to the syntax-phonology interface (Selkirk 2011), the assumption for prosodic phrasing is that any syntactic word, phrase, and clause is matched with a corresponding prosodic word (ω), phonological phrase (φ) and intonation phrase (ι). The assumption for Akan is that phonological phrase structure is isomorphic to syntactic structure (Kügler 2015). The syntactic structure of (9a) is illustrated in (9b) (cf. e.g. Saah 1994). Lexically headed phrases are matched with phonological phrases (φ-phrase), which results in one φ-phrase containing the subject, one containing the verb phrase and one containing the object noun phrase (9c). The object φ-phrase is recursively embedded in the VP φ-phrase. As outlined in section 2.2, tone spreading appears not to be sensitive to, and thus does not indicate prosodic phrasing. Instead, the process of regressive vowel harmony between prosodic words (RVH) motivates the recursive structure (Kügler 2015). RVH occurs in a number of African languages (Casali 2008; Kügler 2015). Kügler (2015) argues that the right edge of a maximal φ-phrase blocks the general process of RVH.

RVH occurs if two adjacent words differ in [ATR] specification, more specifically, if a [−ATR] word precedes a [+ATR] word as in (10a). In some cases, however, this regressive assimilation process is blocked, as is illustrated in (10c). The subject noun and the verb fulfil the requirement of adjacent words differing in [ATR] specification, yet RVH does not affect the subject noun.

(10) a. /àdàm̀fʊ̀ tʊ́   kùbé/   / tʊ́ + kùbé / → [tú kùbé]
        friend   throw   coconut | \/   \/
        'A friend throws a coconut.'   [−ATR] [+ATR]   [+ATR]

    b. [[àdàm̀fʊ̀]φ [tú kùbé]φ]ι

    c. /àdàm̀fʊ̀ dí   kùbé/   / àdàm̀fʊ̀ + dí / → *[àdàm̀fù dí]
        friend   eat   coconut   \/ | \|
        'A friend eats a coconut.'   [−ATR] [+ATR]   [+ATR]

    d. [[àdàm̀fʊ̀]φ [dí kùbé]φ]ι

The proposal advocated in Kügler (2015) bears on recursive phonological phrasing of lower-level, or non-maximal, and higher-level, or maximal, phonological phrases (cf. Selkirk 2011; Itô & Mester 2012). A maximal φ-phrase is defined such that it is not dominated by any further φ-phrase. In (10a), the object noun forms a lower-level, i.e. non-maximal, φ-phrase, and hence RVH can affect the verb, which results in the prosodic structure (10b). In (10c), however, the verb phrase and the subject noun phrase form higher-level, i.e. maximal, φ-phrases. In this context, RVH fails to apply, which results in the prosodic structure (10d). The structural fact is that neither the verb phrase nor the subject noun phrase are headed by lexical projections in the syntax (cf. e.g. Saah 1994), which results in the prosodic structure of maximal φ-phrases. Other structures with maximal φ-phrase edges that block RVH comprise serial verb constructions or time adverbials; for a detailed analysis and data, see Kügler (2015).

Left-dislocated structures represent deviations from simple SVO word order. For instance, a topic constituent is fronted to the sentence-initial position, thus dislocated from its base position. A sentence topic may be marked morphologically with a topic marker *deɛ* (11a), but need not necessarily be (11b) (Boadi 1974; Marfo 2005; Ermisch 2006 among others). If a constituent is topicalized, an obligatory resumptive pronoun is realized in the position of the topicalized constituent in the matrix clause. Syntactically, the topic forms its own phrase, and the matrix clause starts with an embedded TP,[7] as illustrated in (11c) (Marfo 2005).

(11) a. [kòfí déɛ́]_TOP   ɔ́-à-bá   hà.
        Kofi TOP   3SG.SBJ-PFT-come here
        'As for Kofi, he has come here.'

   b. [wɔ̀fà Kòfí]_TOP,   ɔ́-à-bá   hà.
        uncle Kofi   3SG.SBJ-PFT-come here
        'Uncle Kofi, he has come here.'

   c. [_TopP kofi deɛ [_TP ɔ-a-ba ha]]

A focused constituent may also be fronted but need not be (e.g. Boadi 1974; Kügler & Genzel 2012).[8] If fronted, a focus constituent is obligatorily followed by a focus marker *na*, and a resumptive pronoun is realized at the position of the focused constituent in the matrix clause (12a) if it is an animate referent (cf. Boadi 1974; Saah 1988, 1994; Ermisch 2006 among others). Syntactically, the matrix clause starts with an embedded TP (12b) as is the case for topic fronting (11c).

(12) a. àmáǹgò   nà   ànúm̀   tɔ̀-ɔ́   ánɔ̀pá   jí
        mango   FM   Anum   buy-COMPL   morning this
        'It is a mango that Anum bought this morning.'
                                              (Kügler & Genzel 2012: 341)

   b. [_FocP amango na [_TP anum tɔɔ anɔpa ji]]

---

[7] Note that Boadi (2005) and Marfo (2005) use the term IP instead of TP for the syntactic phrase containing tense or inflectional phrasal elements. TP is used here in order to avoid a misinterpretation of the abbreviation IP as 'intonation phrase'.

[8] In the case of subject focus, subjects preferably occur dislocated in sentence-initial position (Pfeil et al. 2015). Non-subjects, in particular objects, show a preference for occurring in their base position (Genzel & Kügler 2010). Thus, Akan shows a case of a so-called subject-object asymmetry in focus marking (Fiedler et al. 2010), although not in a categorical sense, since Pfeil et al. (2015) showed that in the case of non-exhaustive focus interpretation, speakers show a tendency to realize a focused subject in its base position.

The left-dislocated topic and focus constituents form their own syntactic phrase (Marfo 2005), and the matrix clause is embedded in the entire clause (13a). Applying the syntax-phonology match (Selkirk 2011), the entire clause is matched with an intonation phrase (ι-phrase). In addition, the embedded TP is matched with an ι-phrase, which thus results in a recursively embedded ι-phrase (13b). For more elaborated syntactic analyses of Akan, see Saah (1994) and Boadi (2005). Recursive ι-phrases are prosodically expressed by means of pitch register reset before the embedded clause; cf. section 3.2.2 and Kügler (2016).

(13)   a.   [TopP/FocP Topic/Focus [TP matrix clause]]

       b.   (Topic/Focus (matrix clause)ι)ι

3.2 Declarative sentence type

Welmers (1959) introduced the term "terraced-level languages" for describing languages such as Akan where "an effect of terraced descent is heard" (p. 4), and where the phonological tone quality remains identical to previous non-low tones although the phonetic realization is lower, i.e. downstepped to a new terrace level which "becomes the new point of reference" (p. 4). According to Clements (1979: 537), terracing languages display a regular process of register shift which affects the F0 realization of successive tones. The shift of the total pitch register can apply downward (downstep) and/or upward (upstep). An important feature of tone terracing is that there is no limit on the number of register lowering steps in a tone group. External limits can be set by lexical, grammatical, and/or phonological factors. Terracing is thus a process on the level of the pitch register, which defines reference lines (top line, bottom line) relative to which tones are scaled (Huang 1985). The terracing property is illustrated in Figure 1; the example sentence, originally mentioned in Schachter & Fromkin (1968), is given in (14) (cf. also Abakah 2000; Abakah et al. 2010).

(14)   ɔ̀-bé-kɔ́   kùmásé   ánɔ̀pá   jí
       3SG-FUT-go   Kumase   morning   this
       '(S)he will go to Kumase this morning.'
                             (Schachter & Fromkin 1968: 105; glosses added)

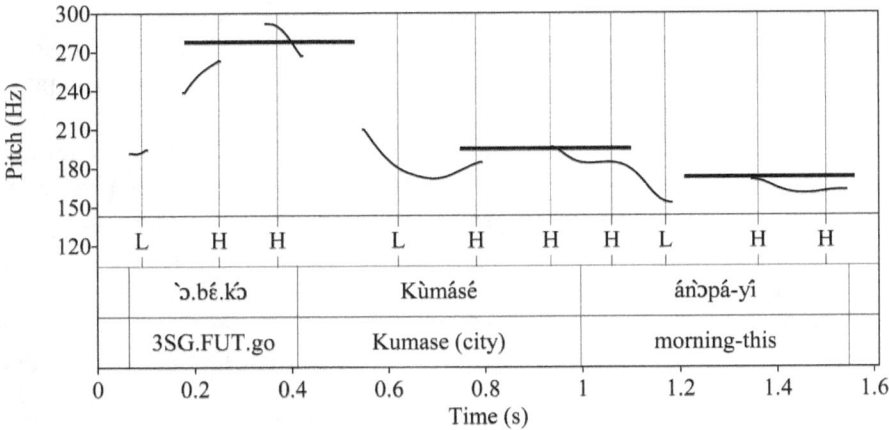

Figure 1: Tonal terracing at three distinct register levels exemplified with sentence (14). L-tones between H-tones lower the pitch register in a staircase fashion illustrated by horizontal lines (Figure from Kügler & Genzel 2012: 334)

3.2.1 Simple declaratives

The terracing property causes the intonation of every sentence to step down until a low end of the phrase, which usually lies in the lower pitch register of a speaker (cf. Figure 1); this downward trend in pitch also applies to sentences which contain like tone sequences, such as only H-tones for instance (cf. Figure 2 below). The downtrend is a result of local tonal interaction (cf. Section 2.1, example (4), and Clements 1983; Dolphyne 1988; Stewart 1993; Abakah 2000; Abakah et al. 2010). As a first approximation, no post-lexical intonational tones seem to mark a simple declarative sentence. Following Genzel (2013), Akan declarative sentences show neither an initial nor a final ɩ-phrase boundary tone. Hence, it appears that in a simple declarative sentence, only lexical tones shape the intonational contour.

Consider the sentences in (15). Both sentences have ten syllables, but they differ in the final lexical tone. (15a) has a sentence-final H-tone, while (15b) has a sentence-final L-tone. As shown in Figure 2 with dashed black and grey lines, the F0 declines over the course of the utterance, and the F0 of the final syllables is identical and hence independent of lexical tone. Paster (2010: 79) mentions a final lowering rule applicable in Akan that turns a sentence-final H-tone into a L-tone. We interpret this final lowering as a case of tonal neutralization at the end of an intonation phrase. In final position, a lexical H-tone neutralizes to low. There are instances where a final lowered H-tone is realized higher than a final low tone; see for instance the polar question with a sentence-final question particle in Figure 8. The realization of the sentence-final H-tone on the question particle could be a case of non-complete neutralization. It appears to happen in such cases where a speaker marks the final H-tone to maintain the tonal distinction. However, the variation in final H-tone realization needs further investigation. Note that in other languages final lowering of tones happens independently of tonal category. For instance, in Yoruba sentence-final L-tones are reported to be lowered (La Velle 1974). As the chapters in this collection show, final lowering indicates some kind of downtrend across languages, and its realization appears to be language specific. While we find tone neutralization in Akan, in Chichewa and Bemba it can be realized as a low register plateau (Downing this volume; Kula & Hamann this volume), as a gradual fall in Embosi (Rialland & Aborobongui, this volume), or as a sharp fall in Bemba (Kula & Hamann this volume).

(15) a. pàpá kòfí má mè-dɔ́ sìká nó.
father Kofi give 1SG-love money DEF
'Father Kofi gives my lover the money.'

b. pàpá kòfí má mè-dɔ́ àbɛ́ tɔ̀.
father Kofi give 1SG-love palm nut buy
'Father Kofi sells a palm nut to my lover.'

Sentences containing only H-tones (16a) show a similar descent of F0 over the whole utterance although no L-tone is present to trigger downstep (cf. solid black line in Figure 2). Similar to sentences with a final H-tone, the sentence-final H-tone in (16a) is neutralized to low. Similarly, sentences with only L-tones (16b) show a gradual descent of F0 terminating in a sentence-final low (cf. solid grey line in Figure 2). The downward descent of H-tones in Akan differs from tone languages such as Mambila (Connell this volume) and Mandarin Chinese where H-tones in a sentence containing only H-tones are realized at an equal F0 level (Xu 1999).[9]

---

[9] In Mandarin, however, declination, a gradual decline of F0 over an utterance, has been observed in a stretch of adjacent H-tones in a sentence frame with initial low or rising tones (Shih 2000). The amount of declination in Mandarin is however much smaller than the general downward trend in Akan.

(16) a. kúkúó-bá pápá nó bɔ́ dáá.[10]
pot-DIM good DEF break everyday
'The good small pot breaks everyday.'

b. wɔ̀fà àdò fìrì àtɕèm̀fò
uncle Ado come.from Akyemfo
'Uncle Ado comes from Akyemfo.' (cf. Genzel 2013: 57)

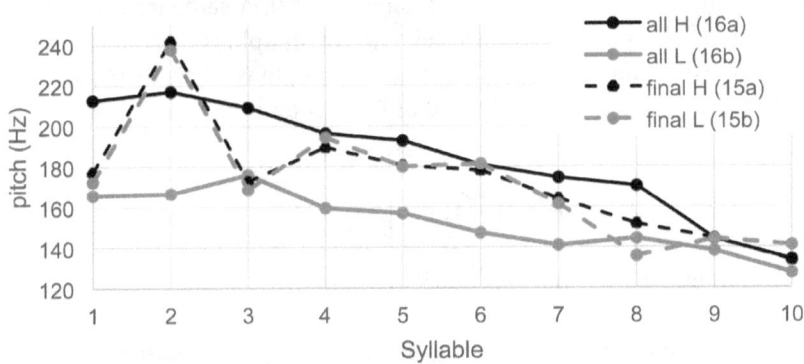

Figure 2: Averaged F0 means of four speakers per declarative sentence; examples (15) represent sentences with alternating tone sequences, and examples (16) represent sentences with like tone sequences. All sentences have ten syllables

There are different analyses available to account for the downtrend in F0. Traditionally, downtrends have been modelled with metrical trees (Ladd 1990) or with register trees (Clements 1990; Snider 1999). Myers (1996) modelled downtrend in Chichewa in terms of a phonetic tone implementation rule à la Liberman & Pierrehumbert (1984). Metrical trees treat the global downtrend in terms of local downstep which is triggered in a particular phonological context. For instance, in the Bantu language Llogoori, adjacent H-tones are subject to downstep (Clements 1990). In Akan, a L-tone is the downstep trigger (cf. section 2.1). However, sentences that contain only like tones show a similar downward trend in F0 to sentences that contain both H-tones and L-tones (cf. Figure 2). Neither

---

10 Note that the word *daa* 'everyday' consists of a long vowel which appears to be affected by tonal neutralization as a whole, not just in its second part. This becomes visible in Figures 2 and 3.

metrical trees nor register trees can easily account for this similarity. Therefore, Genzel (2013) concluded that in Akan downstep is phonologized declination, and the downward trend in F0 is accounted for by a phonetic implementation rule (cf. Liberman & Pierrehumbert 1984 for English and Myers 1996 for Chichewa). In particular, Genzel (2013) proposed that there is a phonetic implementation rule for both H-tones and L-tones independently. As a phonological trigger for the implementation rule, Genzel (2013) proposed an initial high register tone (h) and a final low register tone (l) for the domain of the downward trend. We will adopt this analysis here. The tonal representation of the declarative sentence (16) together with its prosodic phrasing is shown in (17). A sentence-initial high pitch register tone is associated with the left edge of an ɩ-phrase, and a sentence-final low pitch register tone with the right edge of an ɩ-phrase. This representation has the effect of a global downward trend of F0 over an utterance.

(17)   h   l
        | H   H   H   H   H |
        | /|\\   /\ | | |\ |
        [kúkúó-bá pápá   nó bɔ́ dáá   ]ɩ

Genzel's (2013) conclusion that downstep in Akan is phonologized declination makes the prediction that the tonal realization should show effects of preplanning (cf. Connell 2011). This is indeed the case. The initial pitch height for each sentence depends on the length of the sentence itself. Longer sentences start higher, which reflects a general preplanning effect (Genzel 2013). We illustrate the effect of preplanning on the tonal realization with data and recordings from Genzel (2013: 138ff). The examples compare short and long sentences with five or six, and ten syllables, respectively (18). In general, H-tone sentences start higher (solid lines in Figure 3) than L-tone sentences (dashed lines in Figure 3), both short and long ones. If sentences are longer (black lines in Figure 3), speakers start higher. On average, speakers started 20 Hz higher in the longer utterances, which is shown in Figure 3.

(18) a. kúkúó-bá   nó.
          pot-DIM   DEF
          'The small pot.'

      b. kúkúó-bá   pápá   nó   bɔ́   dáá.
          pot-DIM   good   DEF break everyday
          'The good small pot breaks everyday.'

c. jàw̃ fì àtɕèm̀fò.
   Yaw originate.HAB Akyemfo
   'Yaw comes from Akyemfo.'

d. wɔ̀fà àsàrè fì àtɕèm̀fò.
   uncle Asare originate.HAB Akyemfo
   'Uncle Asare comes from Akyemfo.' (Genzel 2013: 138ff)

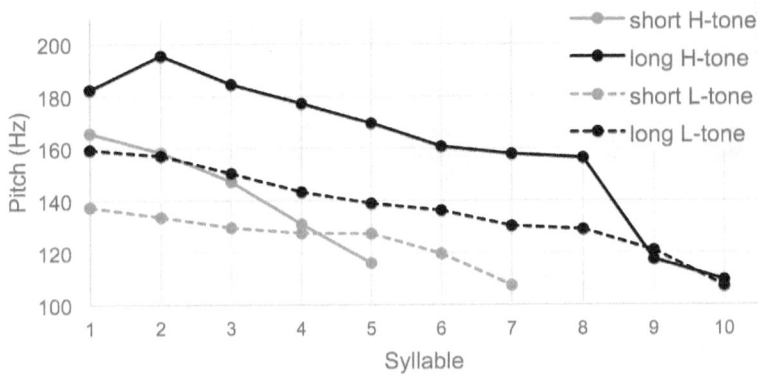

Figure 3: Averaged F0 means of six speakers (1 female, 5 male) per sentence split by short and long sentences with only H-tones (18a/b) or L-tones (18c/d); speech materials and acoustic raw data from Genzel (2013: 138ff), data plot is our own

3.2.2 Complex declaratives

This section deals with complex declaratives, comparing a complementizer sentence and a coordination structure. Embedded sentence structures with a complementizer show a pitch reset at the left edge of the embedded clause; note that the complementizer is phrased with the matrix clause (Kügler 2016). The matrix clause ends on a low pitch at the level of the neutralized ι-phrase-final tone. The prosodic realization also includes pauses (cf. also Genzel 2013: 150); the pause is realized after the complementizer, but before the conjunction in the coordination.

The first structure contains the complementizer sɛ as shown in (19), which prosodically belongs to the matrix clause. As illustrated in Figure 4, speakers usually realize a pause after the complementizer. The embedded clause then starts at a higher F0 level as if it were integrated in the downward trend of an SVO sentence, yet not as high as a completely new sentence. The pitch reset is indicated by the "%reset" transcription in the prosodic phrasing in (19c) and in Figure 4. This transcription convention is borrowed from Peng et al. (2005). The complementizer sɛ is usually realized with a falling tone (Dolphyne 1988: 65; Genzel 2013: 151), and the vowel is lengthened. The syntactic structure is given in (19b) following Boadi (2005). As introduced in section 3.1, a clause, be it CP or TP, is matched with an ι-phrase. The embedded TP (19b) thus is matched with an embedded ι-phrase (19c).

(19) a. nàná kà-à ènórà sè kúkúó-bá bɔ́.
Nana say-COMPL yesterday that pot-DIM break
'Nana said yesterday that the small pot breaks.' (Genzel 2013: 59)

b. [CP nana ka-a ɛnora sɛ [TP kukuo-ba bɔ]] (cf. Boadi 2005)

c. (nana ka-a ɛnora sɛ %reset(kukuo-ba bɔ)ι)ι

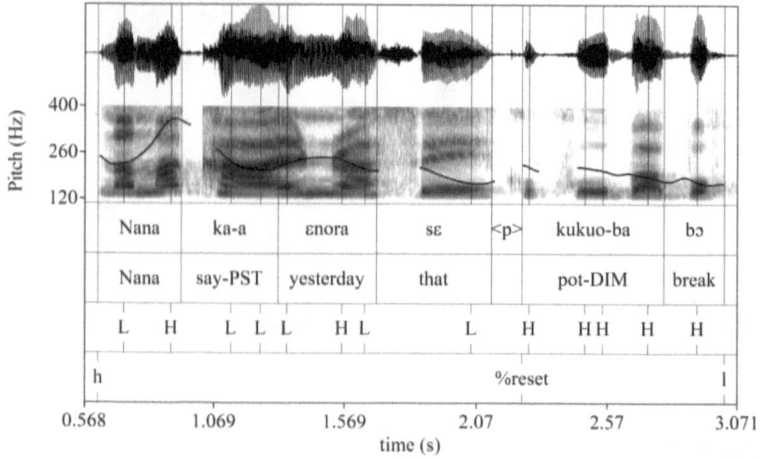

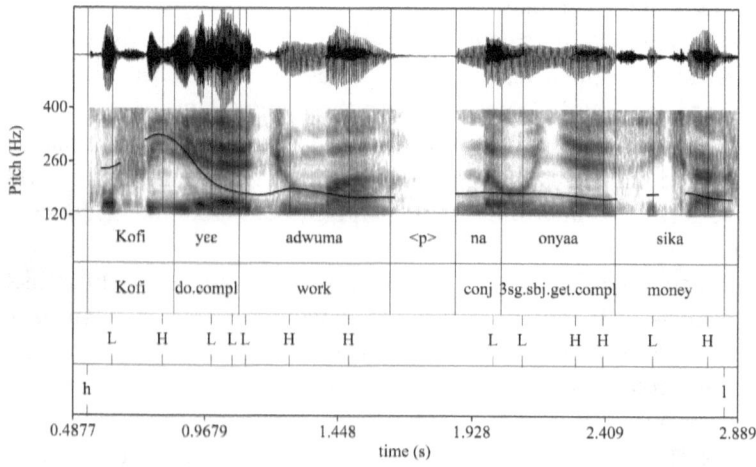

Figure 4: Waveform, spectrogram, and F0 contour of embedded declarative sentence (19) showing pitch reset (upper panel) and coordinated declarative sentence (20) with no pitch reset (lower panel)

An example with the coordination conjunction *nà* is given in (20). Speakers realize a pause before the conjunction (see Figure 4). The prosodic structure is given in (20c) and illustrates that both conjuncts of the coordination prosodically belong to one ι-phrase. We assume a flat syntactic structure in (20b) in which each of the conjuncts functions as a head of the coordinated structure. Note that the exact syntactic phrasing of the coordination is subject to speculation here and needs further investigation.

(20) a. kòfí   yὲὲ   ǽdɥúmá   nà   òɲǽǽ   sìká
         kofi   do.COMPL work   COORD   3SG.SBJ.get.COMPL money
         'Kofi worked and he got money.'

   b. [cp kofi yɛɛ ædɥuma & oɲææ sika]

   c. (kofi yɛɛ ædɥuma na oɲææ sika)ι

The averaged pitch contours of these complex structures are compared in Figure 5. The point of comparison is syllable 10. The solid black line represents a declarative sentence containing only H-tones (cf. 16a) with ten syllables and shows the downtrend pattern with ι-phrase-final low pitch. The dotted black line represents the embedded sentence with the complementizer *sɛ* (19). The matrix clause contains seven syllables up to *sɛ*, which is divided into three parts to represent measures of the falling tone realized on the complementizer. The end of the matrix clause plus *sɛ* is thus reached at syllable 10, and it shows that the final pitch of the matrix clause ends at the identical pitch height of a simple declarative. After the pause (cf. Figure 4) there is a pitch reset at the beginning of the embedded clause, which starts with a phrase-initial lexical H-tone. The phrase-initial H-tone of the embedded clause is realized lower than an initial H-tone of a matrix clause and lower than an initial H-tone of a simple declarative (solid black line). The conclusion is thus that the pitch register reset signals embedding.

The solid grey line in Figure 5 illustrates the coordinated structure (20). The first conjunct ends at syllable 10, and the conjunction *nà* appears at syllable 11. The comparison with the embedded structure reveals that the L-tone on the conjunction (syllable 11) is realized higher than both the sentence-final low of the matrix clause of the embedded sentence, and the final low of the simple declarative (syllable 10). In addition, the first conjunct ends in a lexical H-tone (syllable 10) which is not neutralized as is the case for the ι-phrase-final H-tone of the simple declarative (solid black line, syllable 10). Thus, the first conjunct of the coordination does not constitute a case of a sentence-final low pitch register but shows that both coordinated constituents are integrated into the downward trend in F0 of an ɩ-phrase. If the second conjunct constituted a separate phrase which was recursively embedded, the expectations would be, first, that the L-tone of the conjunction *na* would be higher indicating a pitch reset, and, second, that the final H-tone of the first conjunct would be neutralized to low. The conclusion is thus that a coordinated structure is phrased within one ɩ-phrase.

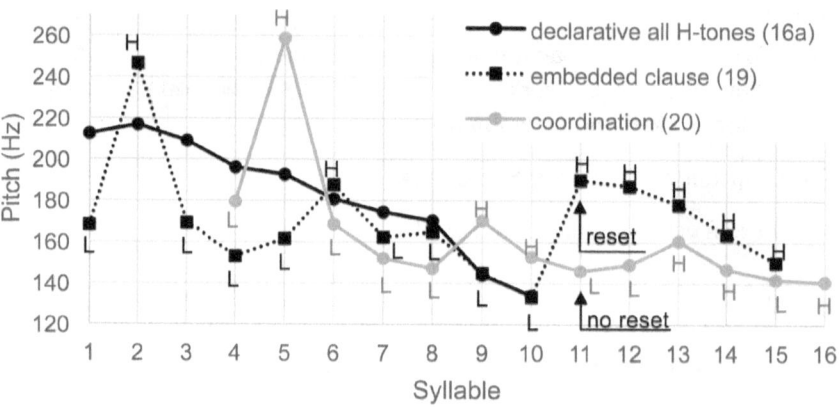

Figure 5: Averaged F0 means of four speakers per complex sentence; solid black line: declarative all H-tone sentence (16a) as reference; dotted black line: embedded *sɛ* clause (19); solid grey line: coordinated structure (20)

3.2.3 Left-dislocation

In Akan, a topic is syntactically expressed by means of constituent fronting; cf. (11) above. The topicalized constituent is dislocated to the left periphery of the sentence, and is resumed by a co-referential pronoun in its base position (Boadi 1974; Saah 1994; Marfo 2005; Ermisch 2006). Of particular interest here is the prosodic realization of topicalized constituents since a fronted topic may be accompanied by the morphological topic marker *deɛ* (21a), but need not be; cf. (21b) and (21c). This allows for an investigation of different tone patterns in the left-dislocated element. The dislocated structures in (21a–c) are compared with a simple declarative with an identical number of syllables (21d). Prosodically, speakers tend to realize a pause after the topicalized constituent; there is usually no pause within a simple declarative (cf. Figure 6). According to Marfo (2005), a topic and the matrix clause are phrased separately, each as an ɩ-phrase; see section 3.1 for the syntax-phonology match, which accounts for this prosodic phrasing.

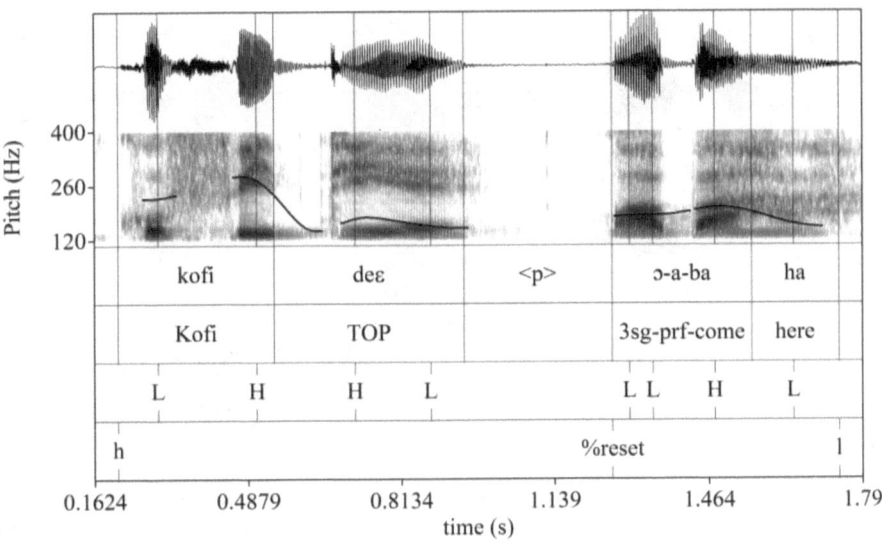

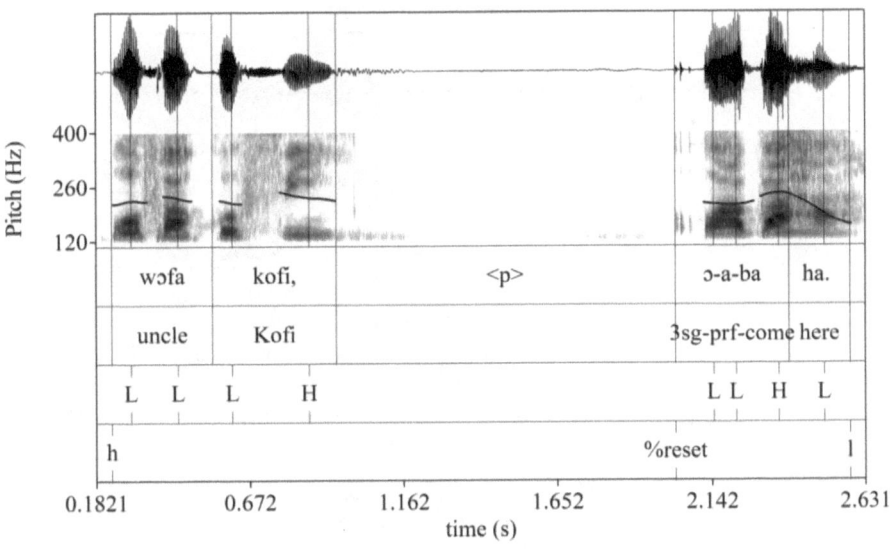

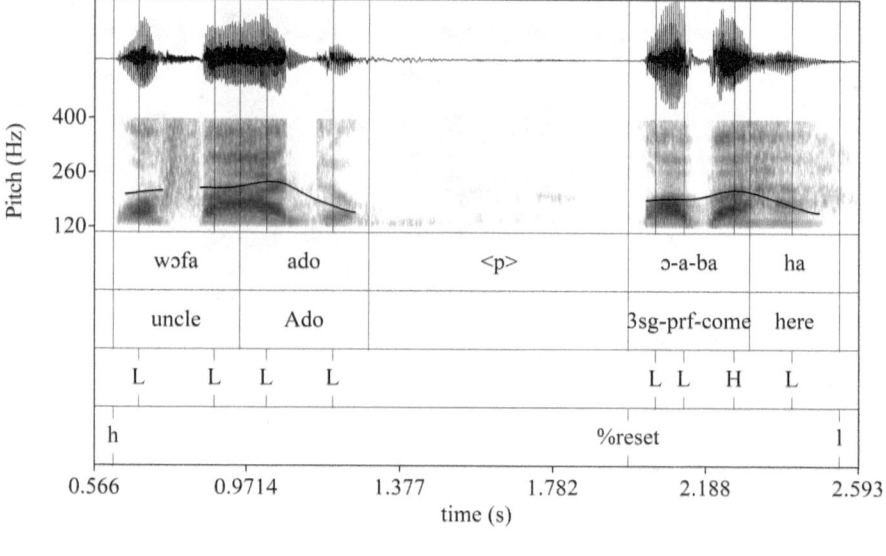

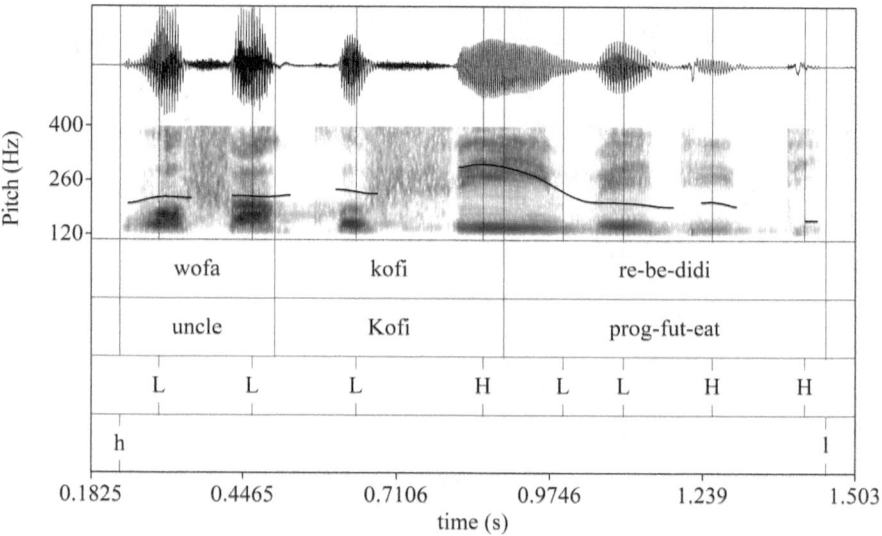

Figure 6: Waveform, spectrogram, and F0 contour of left-dislocated sentences (21a) (upper panel, p. 109), (21b) (lower panel, p. 109), (21c) (upper panel, p. 110), and simple declarative with identical number of syllables (21d) (lower panel, p. 110)

(21) a. kòfí déɛ̀, ɔ́-à-bá   hà.
       Kofi TOP   3SG.SBJ-PFT-come here
       'As for Kofi, he has come here.'

   b. wɔ̀fà kòfí, ɔ́-à-bá   hà.
      uncle Kofi   3SG.SBJ-PFT-come here
      'Uncle Kofi, he has come here.'

   c. wɔ̀fà àdò, ɔ́-à-bá   hà.
      uncle Ado   3SG.SBJ-PFT-come here
      'Uncle Ado, he has come here.'

   d. wɔ̀fà kòfí rè-bè-dídí.
      uncle Kofi PROG-FUT-eat
      'Uncle Kofi is about to eat.'

The mean F0 contours averaged over four speakers of sentences containing a topic in (21a–c) are illustrated in Figure 7 and are compared to a simple declarative sentence (21d) (solid black line). All sentences have an identical number of syllables. The topic phrases end at syllable 4. The dashed black line in Figure 7 illustrates that the topic phrase with the topic marker *deɛ* (21a) ends at a low pitch register (syllable 4) comparable to the left-dislocated topic phrase with a final L-tone (solid grey line, (21c)). The left-dislocated topic phrase with a final H-tone (dotted grey line, (21b)) ends higher.[11] This indicates that at this point no intonation-phrase-final tonal neutralization has taken place. After the topic phrase, all matrix clauses in (21a–c) start with phrase-initial lexical L-tones (syllable 5). The L-tones are realized higher than the topic-phrase-final L-tones (syllable 4), which indicates pitch reset. In line with the analysis of prosodic phrasing of Marfo (2005), the proposed prosodic structure of (21) is given in (22). The pitch reset is equivalent to the pitch reset of embedded clauses found in complex declaratives (cf. section 3.2.2). Thus, a pitch reset indicates the left edge of a recursively embedded ι-phrase (cf. Kügler 2016).

(22) Prosodic structure of a sentence containing a left-dislocated topic phrase (cf. (13) in section 3.1)

(kòfí déɛ̀ %reset(ɔ́-à-bá hà)ι)ι

---

11 Note that the topic-phrase-final H-tone is realized lower than the equivalent H-tone in the declarative (syllable 4). It appears that speakers anticipate the pitch reset of the upcoming embedded structure in (21b), while in the case of a declarative, the first H-tone needs to set the pitch register frame for the whole sentence.

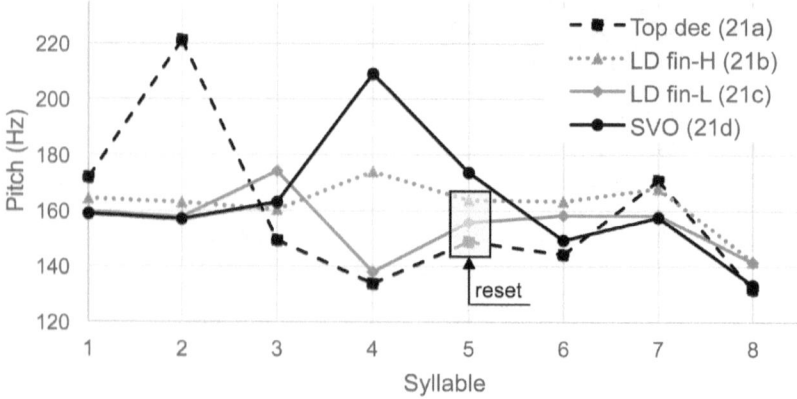

Figure 7: Averaged F0 means of four speakers for left-dislocated structures and corresponding simple declarative (solid black line); dashed black line represents left-dislocated phrase with a morphological topic marker *deɛ* (21a); dotted grey line represents a left-dislocated phrase that ends in a H-tone (21b); solid grey line represents a left-dislocated phrase that ends in a L-tone (21c)

3.3 Interrogative sentence type

Interrogativity in Akan is expressed by means of syntax, morphology or prosody. Polar questions and constituent questions differ in their linguistic means. While polar questions are marked either prosodically or morphologically, constituent questions are marked morphologically by a wh-word, which syntactically may appear in-situ, or ex-situ in sentence-initial position. We start our overview with the intonation of polar questions.

3.3.1 Polar questions

Polar questions are either marked prosodically (Dolphyne 1988; Genzel 2013; Genzel & Kügler 2016) or by means of a question particle (Boadi 1990, 2005), which appears in sentence-final position. Polar questions without a question particle are syntactically identical to declaratives and the only difference arises through prosody (Dolphyne 1988: 55; Boadi 2005; Genzel 2013; Genzel & Kügler 2016). In particular, polar questions are prosodically characterized by a raised pitch register and a sentence-final downward glide of F0 (Dolphyne 1988; Boadi

1990; Genzel 2013: chap 6). The final low pitch is accompanied by a lengthening of the sentence-final vowel (cf. Figure 8 and Table 1), higher intensity as well as breathy termination (Boadi 1990; Rialland 2009; Genzel 2013). In her seminal overview of the question prosody of a large number of African languages, Rialland (2007: 45, 2009: 936) classified Akan as a language with lax question prosody, which characteristically involves sentence-final low pitch, vowel lengthening and breathy termination. In a quantitative evaluation of question intonation in Akan, breathy termination was however not obligatorily present (Genzel 2013).

The data set in (23) compares a polar question that contains the question particle *ànáá* (23a) with a corresponding polar question without a question particle (23b) and a declarative (23c). All three sentences contain eight syllables and have an identical tone pattern. The question particle appears sentence-finally. Figure 8 illustrates the time-normalized averaged intonation contours. Both polar question contours show the characteristics of a raised pitch register compared to the declarative. In sentence-final position, characteristic differences appear between the polar questions with and without a question particle. The contour of the polar question containing the question particle shows higher F0 in sentence-final position compared to the polar question without a question particle. It appears that the raised pitch register compared to the declarative is maintained throughout the whole phrase, or that the sentence-final neutralization of H-tones is incomplete in the case of the polar question with a question particle. In the case of a polar question without a question particle, the sentence-final F0 is identical to that of the declarative. In this position, there is no raised pitch register and tonal neutralization takes place.

(23) a. àtó wɔ̀ hítà ànáá?
Ato possess.PRS heater QP
'Is it the case that Ato possesses a heater, or not?'

b. àtó wɔ̀ hítà bèbréé?
Ato possess.PRS heater many
'Does Ato possess many heaters?'

c. àtó wɔ̀ hítà bèbréé.
Ato possess.PRS heater many
'Ato possesses many heaters.' (cf. Genzel & Kügler 2016)

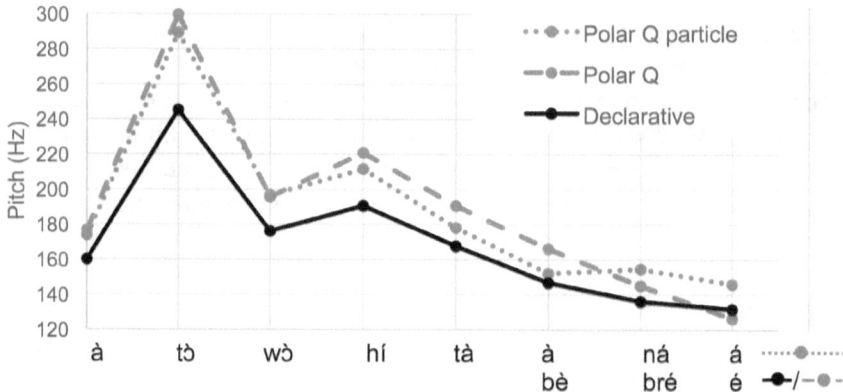

Figure 8: Averaged F0 means of four speakers; comparison between polar questions with and without question particle and corresponding declarative with identical tone patterns, sentences (23)

All four speakers recorded for this study also showed the characteristic sentence-final vowel lengthening in polar questions without a question particle. In Table 1, the individual duration of the sentence-final vowels of the declaratives ((23c) and (24c)) and the corresponding polar questions ((23b) and (24b)) are presented. On average, the sentence-final vowel of the polar question (23b) is 57 ms longer than the corresponding vowel of the declarative, and the sentence-final vowel of the polar question (24b) is 23 ms longer than the corresponding vowel of the declarative. In both polar questions, the sentence-final vowel is on average 29% longer than that of the corresponding declarative. The lengthening reported in Genzel (2013) and in Genzel & Kügler (2016) was about 20% on average. In addition to the lengthening, the vowels of the polar question show a higher intensity on average, and thus are perceptually louder than their corresponding declarative counterparts.

Table 1: Duration of sentence-final vowel in milliseconds (ms) – Comparison of declarative (D) and polar question (Q) and their difference (diff.) for sentences (23) and (24)

Speaker	D (23c)	Q (23b)	diff.	D (24c)	Q (24b)	diff.
1	105	157	52	109	138	29
2	135	150	15	111	117	6
3	148	181	33	48	65	17
4	134	191	57	44	82	38
mean	131	170	39	78	101	23

In order to evaluate whether global register raising or the local cues sentence-final F0 lowering, vowel lengthening and higher intensity are the most salient perceptual cues of polar questions, Genzel & Kügler (2016) ran a forced choice identification perception test where listeners were asked to rate each stimulus as a question or a declarative. Stimuli were either original polar questions and declaratives, or cross-spliced stimuli, which were cut at the last syllable and combined with either a question or declarative beginning. Overall, listeners identified original stimuli correctly most of the time (questions 98%, declaratives 89%). For cross-spliced stimuli listeners based their decision on the last syllable of the sentence: stimuli containing a final declarative syllable with the preceding raised register of a polar question were rated 80% as declaratives; stimuli containing a final question syllable with the preceding pitch register of a declarative were rated 94% as questions. This result suggests that listeners unambiguously decide on the identity of a question or declarative at the end of the sentence, where the sentence-final cues duration, intensity and F0 differentiate between polar questions and declaratives. The global cue of raised pitch register appears to be a universal phonetic side-effect of interrogativity (cf. Gussenhoven 2004).

From the acoustic analysis and the perceptual results, we can conclude that in Akan, local prosodic cues are used to identify polar questions. These local cues should thus be phonologically represented. Therefore, the proposal for Akan is that a polar question is phonologically marked by a low ι-phrase boundary tone (L%). The effect of this low boundary tone is an enhancement of the prosodic cues of duration and intensity of the sentence-final vowel, while sentence-final F0 is identical to declarative sentences. Note that the downward trend in F0 of an utterance is characteristic for all Akan sentence types. The L% boundary tone is a language-specific expression of polar questions and has only local scope over the sentence-final syllable. Similar findings of language-specific local cues of questions are found in the Bantu languages Xhosa (Jones et al. 1998) and Sesotho (Mixdorff et al. 2011), and in Cantonese (Ma et al. 2011). In all these languages including Akan, global register raising is also present in questions. At least in Xhosa, a globally raised register at the beginning of a sentence is already functionally interpreted as a question (Jones et al. 1998). For Akan, it is a matter of future research to determine what role the cue of global register raising plays in the disambiguation of sentence types.

3.3.2 Constituent questions

Constituent questions in Akan are characterized by a wh-word, or by an interrogative pronoun (Saah 1988). According to Saah (1988), the wh-word may remain in-situ or may be fronted to the sentence-initial position. A fronted wh-word is obligatorily followed by a focus marker *na* (cf. focus fronting in (12)), and this construction expresses greater emphasis on the wh-word.

The data in (24) show a comparison between a constituent question with an in-situ wh-word (24a), a polar question (24b), and a declarative (24c), which are illustrated in Figure 9. All three sentences contain five syllables with an identical tonal sequence. In Figure 9, the characteristic lengthening of the sentence-final vowel in a polar question compared to a declarative is visible (157 ms vs 105 ms).

The comparison of the time-normalized averaged intonation contours in Figure 10 reveals a similar overall pattern for all three sentences. Similar to polar questions, globally raised pitch register is also found in constituent questions. Perceptually, however, the sentence-final wh-word is not as salient as the final syllable in polar questions. Nor is there a particular lengthening of the vowel or of the syllabic nasal of the wh-word *dɛn* 'what' in (24a). The phonetic cues which seem to be correlates of a low ι-phrase boundary tone in polar questions are not found in constituent questions. Hence, we propose that constituent questions are not marked by an ι-phrase boundary tone.

(24) a. ésí jí dɛ́ṅ?
Esi take_away.PRS what
'What does Esi take away?'

b. ésí jí lɛ́tà?
Esi take_away.PRS letter
'Esi takes away the letter?'

c. ésí jí lɛ́tà.
Esi take_away.PRS letter
'Esi takes away the letter.' (cf. Genzel & Kügler 2016)

From the data shown so far, we can propose the following phonological analysis. Akan exhibits a low intonational phrase boundary tone, which signals polar questions (cf. Genzel 2013; Genzel & Kügler 2016) but not constituent questions. A phonological representation of (24) is given in (25). The sentences are divided into two phonological phrases: one phonological phrase contains the subject noun phrase, the other one contains the verb phrase including the object noun phrase (cf. section 3.1, and Kügler 2015). Both phonological phrases are dominated by the intonation phrase, which is associated with a sentence-initial high register tone and a sentence-final low register tone. In all sentence types, the domain for the downward intonation contour is between the two register tones, and downstep is accounted for by phonetic implementation rules for L- and H-tones (cf. Genzel 2013). In the case of a polar question, a low ι-phrase boundary tone is associated sentence-finally (25b) causing lengthening and higher intensity of the final syllable.

Tone and intonation in Akan — 117

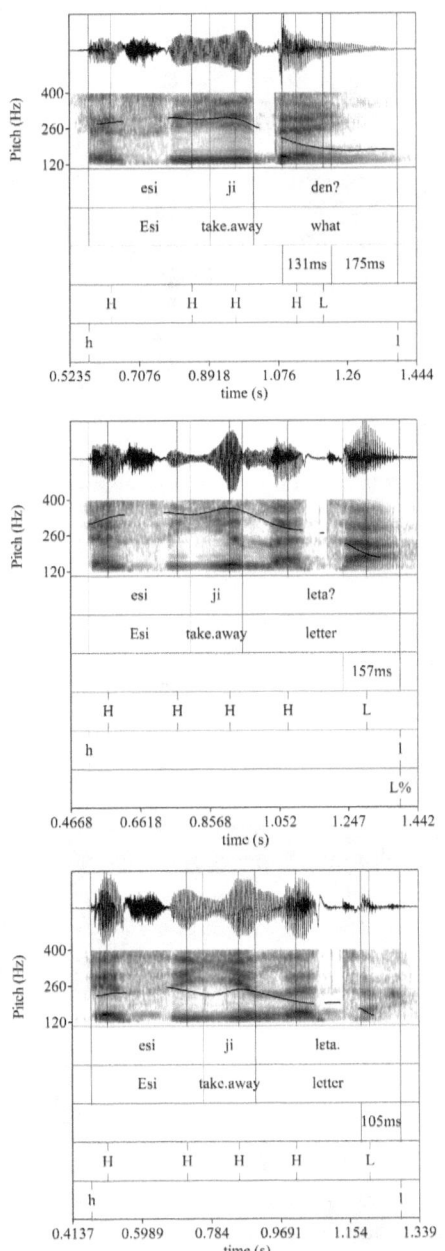

Figure 9: Waveform, spectrogram, and F0 contour of interrogatives: constituent question (24a) (upper panel), polar question (24b) (mid panel), and corresponding declarative of identical sentence length (24c) (lower panel)

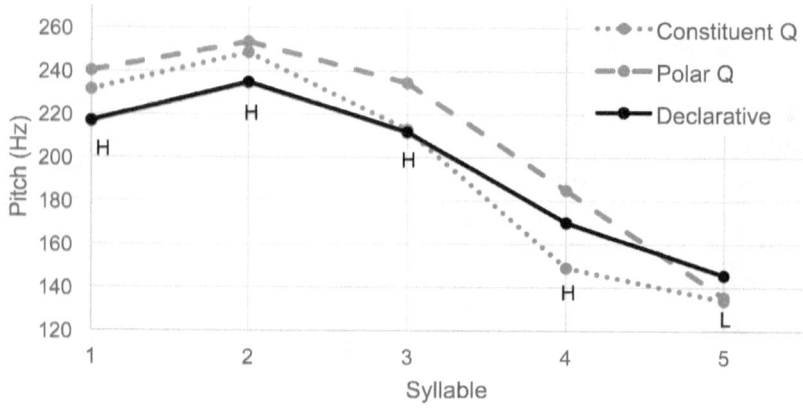

Figure 10: Averaged F0 means of four speakers; comparison between a constituent question (24a), a polar question (24b) and a declarative (24c) with identical tone patterns and sentence length

(25) a. h   l
         | H   H H L |
         | /\ | | | |
         [[esi]φ [ji dɛn]φ]ι   constituent question

   b. h   l
         | H   H H L | L%
         | /\ | | | | /
         [[esi]φ [ji leta]φ]ι   polar question

   c. h   l
         | H   H H L |
         | /\ | | | |
         [[esi]φ [ji leta]φ]ι   declarative

3.4 Imperative sentence type

The imperative sentence type is characterized by lexical tonal changes on the verb (Dolphyne 1988; Paster 2010). In (26a/b) for instance, the underlying form of the verb 'to ask' is bìsá, which changes to bísà in the imperative. Apart from this grammatical tonal replacement (cf. section 2.3), the intonation pattern of imperatives seems to deviate slightly from that of simple declarative sentences. An imperative sentence lacks sentence-final tonal neutralization. The intonation contour in general is the result of local tonal interaction as in other sentence types.

Consider the imperatives with a sentence-final H-tone (26a) and a sentence-final L-tone (26b). In Figure 11, these two examples are compared with the simple declarative sentence (18a), which is repeated as (26c) here.[12] The tonal structure of the two imperatives is identical up to the sentence-final word. In Figure 11 (26a) is represented by the solid black line, and (26b) by the dashed black line. The sentence-final H-tone of (26a) is realized higher than the sentence-final L-tone of (26b), and higher than the sentence-final H-tone of the declarative sentence. This difference in tonal scaling seems to point to the fact that the sentence-final tone neutralization does not happen in the imperative sentence type. However, as noted before, the conditions of sentence-final H-tone lowering require further research. Hence, our findings that sentence-final H-tones are incompletely neutralized should be taken as tentative results.

(26) a. kɔ̀-bísà   nò   sìká.
       go-ask.IMP 3SG.OBJ money
       'Go ask him for money!'

   b. kɔ̀-bísà   nò   pájà.
       go-ask.IMP 3SG.OBJ papaya
       'Go ask him for papaya!'

   c. kúkúó-bá   nó.
       pot-DIM   DEF
       'The small pot.'

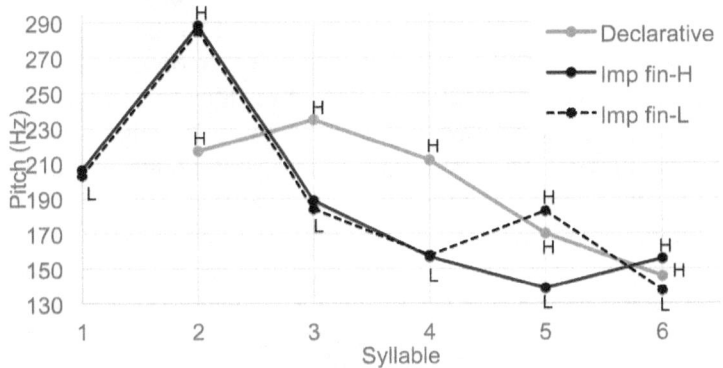

Figure 11: Averaged F0 means of four speakers; comparison between imperatives with a final H-tone (solid black line) and with a final L-tone (dashed black line), and a declarative (solid grey line); data from (26)

---

[12] Note that the average F0 of the declarative (26c) in Figure 11 differs from that of (18a) in Figure 3. This is because in Figure 3, the data are based on the six speakers who were recorded and analysed in Genzel (2013). All other figures including Figure 11 represent the average F0 data of the four speakers recorded for this study.

4 Prosodic realization of focus

Focus is known to affect the intonation, more specifically the pitch register, of utterances in many languages, among them intonation languages like German (Féry & Kügler 2008) or tone languages like Mandarin (Xu 1999). In Mandarin, for instance, register expansion leads to higher scaling of H-tones (tone 1), lower scaling of L-tones (tone 3) and higher and/or lower scaling of rising (tone 2) and falling tones (tone 4) (Xu 1999). In an overview of prosodically marked focus in selected African languages Zerbian et al. (2010) argued that, independent of the language family, neither prosodic marking of focus in general nor expansion of pitch range under focus or deaccentuation can be considered language universals. Indeed, the majority of languages in this volume do not show prosodic effects of focus. As an exception, both Akan (see below) and Bemba (Kula & Hamann this volume) show pitch register lowering under focus. The difference between the two languages is in the domain of register lowering. In Akan, the pitch register is lowered on the focused constituent whereas in Bemba, the post-focal domain is lowered.

Instead of changes of the pitch register, many languages, including African tone languages, show an effect of focus on the phrasing pattern such that a prosodic phrase break occurs left and/or right of the focused constituent (cf. e.g. Ewe: Fiedler & Jannedy 2013; Shingazidja: Patin this volume; Chichewa: Kanerva 1990; however, see Downing & Pompino-Marschall 2013, who argue against an influence of focus on prosodic phrasing in Chichewa). The tendency for languages to rephrase their prosodic structure under focus has been analysed as a tendency for focus to align with an edge of a prosodic phrase (Féry 2013).

Akan shows prosodic marking of focus in terms of pitch register effects and phrasing. The pitch register effect shows up as pitch register lowering both for H-tones and L-tones and both for in-situ and ex-situ focus (Kügler & Genzel 2012), contrary to the well-known register expansion or higher scaling of tones (cf. Gussenhoven 2004). Note however that Boadi (1974) reported tonal raising of both H- and L-tones on ex-situ focused words on impressionistic grounds. The pitch register lowering effect is illustrated in Figure 12, where the solid black line represents the course of F0 on the target word àmáǹgò 'mango' in the neutral, i.e. baseline, condition. In the case of contrastive focus (dashed black line), speakers lowered their pitch register significantly by about 1 to 1.5 semitones on average (Kügler & Genzel 2012: 345). The experimental data were elicited with question-answer pairs. Speakers listened to a pre-recorded question (27Q) and were asked to answer the question by reading out a provided answer (27A). The prosodic expression of correction resulted in a pitch register lowering, all other tones being equal in the target sentence.

(27) Q: ànúm̀ tɔ̀-ɔ́ kòbí ánɔ̀pá jí?
Anum buy-PST salty fish morning this
'Did Anum buy salty fish this morning?'

A: ànúm̀ tɔ̀-ɔ́ àmáǹgò ánɔ̀pá jí
Anum buy-PST mango morning this
'Anum bought a mango this morning.' (cf. Genzel & Kügler 2010: 83)

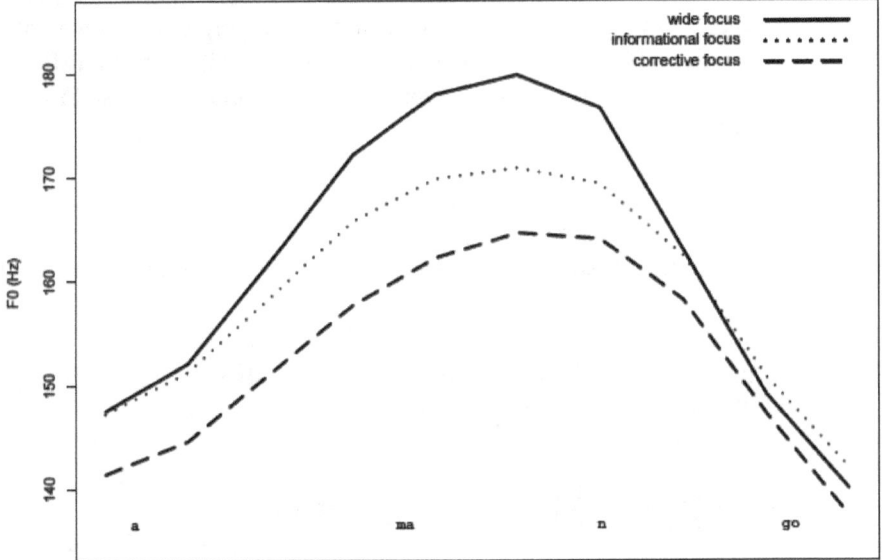

Figure 12: Illustration of pitch register lowering of a H-tone in corrective focus (dashed black line) compared to wide focus (solid black line) or narrow information focus (dotted grey line), from Kügler & Genzel (2012: 344)

As for phrasing, Genzel (2013: 195ff) shows data where a glottal stop is inserted before and/or after the focused constituent; cf. Figure 13.[13] The observation of inserted glottal stops was made on the basis of semi-spontaneous data. Glottal stop insertion was not found in the experimentally controlled data set of Kügler & Genzel (2012). The occurrence of a glottal stop may be interpreted as a prosodic boundary delimiting the focused constituent. Such a boundary would be in line with a so-called emphasis boundary observed in Kwa-languages other than Akan (Leben & Ahoua 2006). The example in Figure 13 comes from

---

[13] A reviewer notes that glottal stop insertion in example (28) may be due to a strategy to prevent coarticulation of vowels in a focused position. We have no example with nasals to show a general glottal stop insertion.

a situation-description task in which speakers were asked to spontaneously answer questions based on a picture that depicts a particular situation (Genzel & Kügler 2010). In the case cited here, two persons were visible in the picture, one in a boat and one in the water. The one in the boat is helping the other person to climb into the boat. Both persons were labelled with proper names. One of the context questions was a constituent question asking for a narrow informational object focus (28), and the answer of one of the speakers is illustrated in Figure 13 showing the focused object flanked by glottal stops. Since these are impressionistic observations, we cannot draw any quantitative conclusions about the effect of focus and phrasing. However, it seems that focus may be marked by means of a prosodic break, at least to some extent and under certain circumstances.

(28) a. ɕɥáǹ   nà   ad͡ʑɪ̀màǹ   bóà-à   ánɔ̀pá   jí
         who   FM   Agyeman   help-COMPL morning   this
         'Whom did Agyeman help this morning?'   (Genzel & Kügler 2010: 83)

    b. àd͡ʑɪ̀màǹ   bóà-à   ʔ àdò ʔ   ánɔ̀pá   jí
        Agyeman   help-COMPL Ado   morning   this
        'Agyeman helped Ado this morning.'

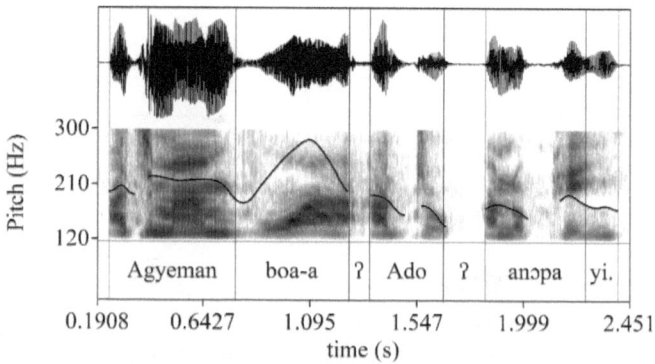

Figure 13: Glottal stop insertion before and after a focused constituent (Ado), analysis from Genzel (2013: 197), data from Genzel & Kügler (2010)

5 Conclusion

This chapter presented an analysis of the intonation in the tone language Akan. Akan employs a simple post-lexical tonal grammar that accounts for the shapes of an intonation contour. Table 2 lists the prosodic events discussed in this chapter. The unmarked post-lexical structure is found in simple declaratives. The downward trend of an intonation contour is shaped by local tonal interactions (downstep), and sentence-final tonal neutralization. The downward trend is modelled phonologically by means of a high and low pitch register tone, and the actual F0 curve is achieved by means of phonetic implementation rules à la Liberman & Pierrehumbert (1984). In the case of polar questions, an ι-phrase-final low boundary tone (L%) accounts for the intensity increase and lengthening of the final vowel compared to a declarative. Complex declaratives and left-dislocations show a partial pitch reset at the left edge of an embedded ι-phrase. The pitch reset occurs independent of the type of clause (matrix or complementizer clause). The examples discussed in this chapter contained a subordinate complementizer clause and left-dislocated structures, which both are marked by a pitch reset at the left edge of the embedded clause (cf. Kügler 2016).

The very prominent downward trend in pitch in Akan utterances was acknowledged as a terracing property occurring in many West African tone languages (Welmers 1959; Clements 1983; Abakah et al. 2010). The detailed phonetic study of downtrends in Akan of Genzel (2013) revealed the interesting insight that the downtrend is identical in utterances with differing tone qualities and in utterances which contain only like tone sequences (either only H-tones or only L-tones). Downstep as a phonological phenomenon and declination as a gradient phonetic pitch lowering (cf. Gussenhoven 2004: 98; Connell 2011) appear to be identical in surface intonation. Genzel's conclusion, which we adopt here, was that declination has been phonologized in Akan with the result that downstep is a fundamental concept in sentence-level intonation in Akan. Phonetic implementation rules predict the amount of downstep within an utterance.

Sentence-final tone neutralization as proposed in this chapter may enhance the requirement of downstepping. This tonal neutralization is clearly marked since elsewhere in the sentence tonal distinctions are maintained. Sentence-final lowering of H-tones is fairly common, as the collection of chapters in this volume shows. However, not all languages show sentence-final tone lowering. For Tswana for instance, Zerbian (this volume) presented evidence that lexical H-tones are clearly distinguished from surface L-tones in sentence-final position; in some contexts such as lists the tonal distinction may even be enhanced as an effect of intonation, i.e. Tswana sentence-final H-tones are realized higher in pitch than a surface L-tone.

Table 2: Prosodic events in Akan and their distribution

Prosodic event	Distribution
L%	right edge of the ɩ-phrase in polar questions
h, l	high and low pitch register tone associated with the left and right edge of an ɩ-phrase, respectively
%reset	left edge of an embedded ɩ-phrase
tone neutralization	declaratives, interrogatives sentence-final H-tone drops to a low pitch level
downstep	downtrend in all sentence types, local tonal interactions

Regarding the interaction of lexical tone and intonation, this chapter has demonstrated that underlying lexical tones are not affected with the exception of sentence-final H-tones. The presence of a low ɩ-phrase boundary tone enhances the phonetic cues intensity and duration phrase-finally. In terms of the possible tonal interactions with intonation proposed by Hyman & Monaka (2008), Akan shows the strategy of *avoidance*. That is, intonational events are clearly separated from lexical tones. The presence of sentence-final tone neutralization could however speak in favour of Akan constituting a case of tonal *accommodation* (Hyman & Monaka 2008), i.e. a minimal interaction between intonation and lexical tone. Regarding the interaction of pitch reset and lexical tones, it is clearly a strategy of *avoidance* in Akan because the phonological distinction of lexical tones after a pitch reset is maintained, i.e. the reset is higher when a H-tone follows than when a L-tone follows.

To conclude, the interaction of tone and intonation is minimal in Akan. Intonational events consist of a low boundary tone, register tones and pitch register manipulations in terms of pitch reset. A tone language like Akan thus clearly shows intonation, corroborating the view that every language has intonation (Bolinger 1962; 1978); see however the absence of intonational cues in Mambila (Connell this volume). The inventories of intonational events that the tonal grammars of languages employ, however, necessarily differ between languages, partly also depending on the prosodic typological profiles of the languages.

Acknowledgements

Financial support for this research came from a German Research Foundation (DFG) grant, SFB 632 "Information Structure," project D5. Special thanks to Susanne Genzel, Reginald Duah, Kofi Dorflo, Rike Schlüter, and Lisa Baudisch. Thanks to two anonymous reviewers and the editors of this volume, Laura Downing and Annie Rialland, whose comments allowed me to improve the quality of this chapter.

References

Abakah, Emmanuel N. 2000. A closer look at downstep in Akan. *Afrika und Übersee* 83. 1–23.
Abakah, Emmanuel N. 2002. The low tone in Akan. In Theda Schumann, Mechthild Reh, Roland Kießling & Ludwig Gerhardt (eds.), *Aktuelle Forschungen zu afrikanischen Sprachen: Sprachwissenschaftliche Beiträge zum 14. Afrikanistentag, Hamburg, 11.–14. Oktober 2000*, 193–210. Köln: Köppe.
Abakah, Emmanuel N. 2005a. Tone in Akan nominals. In Mary E. Kropp Dakubu & Emmanuel K. Osam (eds.), *Studies in the Languages of the Volta Basin 3*, 193–218. Legon: Linguistics Department, University of Ghana.
Abakah, Emmanuel N. 2005b. Tone rules in Akan. *Journal of West African Languages* 32(1–2). 109–134.
Abakah, Emmanuel N. 2010a. The tonomorphology of reduplication in Akan, Dangme and Gurene. In Mary E. Kropp Dakubu, Nana A. Amfo, E. Kweku Osam, Kofi K. Saah & G. Akanlig-Pare (eds.), *Studies in the Languages of the Volta Basin 6*, 121–140. Legon: Linguistics Department, University of Ghana.
Abakah, Emmanuel N. 2010b. Tone and the Associative Construction in Akan. *Journal of West African Languages* 37(2). 57–79.
Abakah, Emmanuel N., Comfort Amissah & Kwaku Ofori. 2010. Tone Terracing in Akan. *Journal of African Cultures and Languages* 1(1). 1–20.
Abakah, Emmanuel N. & Louisa Koranteng. 2007. The Interaction of Tone, Syntax and Semantics in Akan. In Mary E. Kropp Dakubu, G. Akanlig-Pare, E. Kweku Osam, Kofi K. Saah & (eds.), *Studies in the Languages of the Volta Basin 4*, 63–86. Legon: Linguistics Department, University of Ghana.
Anderson, Jonathan C. 2009. Preliminary to Preliminary: Speech Rhythm in Akan (Twi). In Jonathan C. Anderson, Christopher R. Green & Samuel G. Obeng (eds.), *African Linguistics across the Discipline*, 133–143. Bloomington: IULC Publications.
Bickel, Balthasar, Bernard Comrie & Martin Haspelmath. 2008. The Leipzig Glossing Rules. Available (December 2015) at http://www.eva.mpg.de/lingua/resources/glossing-rules.php.
Boadi, Lawrence A. 1974. Focus-marking in Akan. *Linguistics* 140. 5–57.
Boadi, Lawrence A. 1990. Questions in Akan. *Frankfurter Afrikanistische Blätter* 2. 70–92.
Boadi, Lawrence A. 2005. *Three major syntactic structures in Akan: Interrogatives, complementation, and relativisation*. Accra: Black Mask Ltd.
Boersma, Paul & David Weenink. 2014. Praat: Doing phonetics by computer [Computer program]. Available (December 2015) at http://www.praat.org.
Bolinger, Dwight L. 1962. Intonation as a universal. In *Proceedings of the International Congress of Linguistics*, 833–848: Oslo.
Bolinger, Dwight L. 1978. Intonation across languages. In J. Greenberg (ed.), *Universals of Human Language*, 471–524. Palo Alto: Stanford University Press.
Cahill, Michael. 1985. *An autosegmental analysis of Akan nasality and tone*. Arlington: University of Texas, MA Thesis.
Casali, Roderic F. 2008. ATR Harmony in African Languages. *Language and Linguistics Compass* 2(3). 496–549.
Christaller, Johan G. 1933. *Dictionary of the Asante and Fante language called Tshi (Twi)*. Basel: Evangelical Missionary Society.

Clements, George N. 1979. The description of terraced-level tone languages. *Language* 55(3). 536–558.

Clements, George N. 1983. The Hierarchical Representation of Tone Features. In Ivan R. Dihoff (ed.), *Current approaches to African linguistics vol. 1* (Publications in African languages and linguistics 1), 145–176. Dordrecht: Foris.

Clements, George N. 1990. The status of register in intonation theory: Comments on the papers by Ladd and by Inkelas and Leben. In John Kingston & Mary E. Beckman (eds.), *Papers in Laboratory Phonology I*, 58–71. Cambridge: Cambridge University Press.

Connell, Bruce. 2011. Downstep. In Marc Oostendorp, Colin J. Ewen, Elizabeth Hume & Keren Rice (eds.), *The Blackwell Companion to Phonology*, 824–847. Malden, MA: Wiley-Blackwell.

Dolphyne, Florence A. 1988. *The Akan (Twi-Fante) language: Its sound systems and tonal structure*. Accra: Ghana Universities Press.

Dolphyne, Florence A. 1994. *A phonetic and phonological study of downdrift and downstep in Akan* (Paper, 25th Annual Conference on African Linguistics, Rutgers University). Rutgers University.

Dolphyne, Florence A. & Mary E. Kropp Dakubu. 1988. The Volta-Comoe Languages. In Mary E. Kropp Dakubu (ed.), *The Languages of Ghana*, 50–90. London: Kegan Paul.

Downing, Laura J. & Bernd Pompino-Marschall. 2013. The focus prosody of Chichewa and the Stress-Focus constraint: A response to Samek-Lodovici (2005). *Natural Language & Linguistic Theory* 31(3). 647–681.

Ermisch, Sonja. 2006. Focus and topic Akan constructions in Akan. In Sonja Ermisch (ed.), *Frankfurter Afrikanistische Blätter* (18), 51–68. Köln: Köppe.

Féry, Caroline. 2013. *Focus as prosodic alignment*. Natural Language & Linguistic Theory 31(3). 683–734.

Féry, Caroline & Frank Kügler. 2008. Pitch accent scaling on given, new and focused constituents in German. *Journal of Phonetics* 36(4). 680–703.

Fiedler, Ines, Katharina Hartmann, Brigitte Reineke, Anne Schwarz & Malte Zimmermann. 2010. Subject Focus in West African Languages. In Malte Zimmermann & Caroline Féry (eds.), *Information structure: Theoretical, typological, and experimental perspectives* (Oxford linguistics), 234–257. Oxford: Oxford University Press.

Fiedler, Ines & Stefanie Jannedy. 2013. Prosody of focus marking in Ewe. *Journal of African Languages and Linguistics* 34(1). 1–46.

Genzel, Susanne. 2013. *Lexical and post-lexical tones in Akan*. Potsdam: Universität Potsdam, Humanwissenschaftliche Fakultät, PhD Thesis. Available (December 2015) at https://publishup.uni-potsdam.de/opus4-ubp/frontdoor/index/index/docId/7796.

Genzel, Susanne & Frank Kügler. 2010. How to elicit semi-spontaneous focus realizations with specific tonal patterns. In Mira Grubic, Susanne Genzel & Frank Kügler (eds.), *Linguistic Fieldnotes I: Information Structure in different African Languages* (Interdisciplinary Studies on Information Structure (ISIS), vol. 13), 77–102. Potsdam: Universitätsverlag Potsdam.

Genzel, Susanne & Frank Kügler. 2011. Phonetic Realization of Automatic (Downdrift) and Non-automatic Downstep in Akan. In Eric Zee & Wai-Sum Lee (eds.), *Proceedings of the 17th International Congress of Phonetic Sciences (ICPhS XVII), Hong Kong*, 735–738.

Genzel, Susanne & Frank Kügler. 2016. *Prosodic question marking in Akan – what do listeners hear?* MS, University of Potsdam.

Gussenhoven, Carlos. 2004. *The Phonology of Tone and Intonation*. Cambridge: Cambridge University Press.

Huang, Cheng-Teh J. 1985. The autosegmental and metrical nature of tone terracing. In Didier L. Goyvaerts (ed.), *African Linguistics: Essays in Memory of M. W. K Semikenke*, 209–238. Amsterdam: John Benjamins.

Hyman, Larry M. 2001. Tone systems. In M. Haspelmath, E. König, H. E. Wiegand & H. Steger (eds.), *Language typology and language universals: An international handbook*, 1367–1380: Berlin: Mouton de Gruyter.

Hyman, Larry M. 2006. Word-Prosodic Typology. *Phonology* 23(2). 225–257.

Hyman, Larry M. & Kemmonye C. Monaka. 2008. Tonal and Non-Tonal Intonation in Shekgalagari. In *UC Berkeley Phonology Lab Annual Report*, 269–288. Berkeley.

Itô, Junko & Armin Mester. 2012. Recursive prosodic phrasing in Japanese. In Toni Borowsky, Shigeto Kawahara, Takahito Shinya & Mariko Sugahara (eds.), *Prosody Matters: Essays in Honor of Elisabeth Selkirk*, 280–303. London: Equinox Press.

Jones, J., J. A. Louw & J. C. Roux. 1998. Perceptual experiments on Queclaratives in Xhosa. *South African Journal of Linguistics* 16, Supplement 36. 19–31.

Kanerva, Jonni. 1990. Focusing on phonological phrases in Chichewa. In Sharon Inkelas & Draga Zec (eds.), *The Phonology-Syntax Connection*, 145–161. Chicago: University of Chicago Press.

Kisseberth, Charles W. & David Odden. 2003. Tone. In Derek Nurse & Gérard Philippson (eds.), *The Bantu Languages*, 59–70. London: Routledge.

Kügler, Frank. 2015. Phonological phrasing and ATR vowel harmony in Akan. *Phonology* 32(1). 177–204.

Kügler, Frank. 2016. Embedded clauses and recursive prosodic phrasing in Akan. In *Proceedings of the Fifth International Symposium on Tonal Aspects of Languages (TAL 2016)*.

Kügler, Frank & Susanne Genzel. 2012. On the Prosodic Expression of Pragmatic Prominence: The Case of Pitch Register Lowering in Akan. *Language and Speech* 55(3). 331–359.

Ladd, D. R. 1990. Metrical representation of pitch register. In John Kingston & Mary E. Beckman (eds.), *Papers in Laboratory Phonology I*, 35–57. Cambridge: Cambridge University Press.

La Velle, C. R. 1974. An experimental study of Yoruba tone. *Studies in African Linguistics*, (Suppl. 5), 185–194.

Leben, William R. & Firmin Ahoua. 2006. Phonological Reflexes of Emphasis in Kwa Languages of Cote d'Ivoire. In Paul Newman & Larry M. Hyman (eds.), *Studies in African Linguistics*, 145–158. Columbus, Ohio: The Department of Linguistics and the Center for African Studies, Ohio State University.

Lewis, M. P. 2009. *Ethnologue: Languages of the world*, 16th ed. Dallas, TX: SIL International.

Liberman, Mark & Janet B. Pierrehumbert. 1984. Intonational invariance under changes in pitch range and length. In Mark Aronoff & Richard T. Oehrle (eds.), *Language Sound Structure: Studies in Phonology presented to Morris Halle*, 157–233. Cambridge: MIT Press.

Ma, Joan K.-Y., Valter Ciocca & Tara L. Whitehill. 2011. The perception of intonation questions and statements in Cantonese. *Journal of the Acoustical Society of America* 129(2). 1012–1023.

Manyah, Kofi A. 2006. Relation between Tone and Vowel Quality in Twi. In *Proceedings of the Second International Symposium on Tonal Aspects of Languages*, 37–40. La Rochelle.

Manyah, Kofi A. 2014. Relationship between Lexical Tone Contrasts and Vowel Quality. *European Scientific Journal* 10(17). 418–428.

Marfo, Charles O. 2004. On tone and segmental processes in Akan phrasal words: A prosodic account. *Linguistik online* 18(1/04). 93–110.

Marfo, Charles O. 2005. Akan Focus and Topic Constructions and the Prosody-Syntax Interface. *Journal of West African Languages* 32(1). 45–59.

Mixdorff, Hansjörg, Lehlohonolo Mohasi, Malillo Machobane & Thomas Niesler. 2011. A Study on the Perception of Tone and Intonation in Sesotho. *Proceedings of the 12th Interspeech*. 3188–3191.

Myers, Scott. 1996. Boundary tones and the phonetic implementation of tone in Chichewa. *Studies in African Linguistics* 25(1). 29–60.

Myers, Scott. 1998. Surface underspecification of tone in Chichewa. *Phonology* 15(3). 367–391.

Nkansa-Kyeremateng, K. 2004. *The Akans of Ghana: Their customs, history and institutions*. Accra: Sebewie Publishers.

Osam, Emmanuel K. A. 2003. An Introduction to the Verbal and Multiverbal System of Akan. In Dorothee Beermann & Lars Hellan (eds.), *Proceedings of the workshop on multi-verb constructions* (Trondheim Summer School 2003). Available (December 2015) at http://www.ling.hf.ntnu.no/tross/osam.pdf.

Paster, Mary. 2010. The verbal morphology and phonology of Asante Twi. *Studies in African Linguistics* 39(1). 77–120.

Peng, Shu-hui, Marjorie K. M. Chan, Chiu-yu Tseng, Tsan Huang, Ok Joo Lee & Mary E. Beckman. 2005. Towards a Pan-Mandarin System for Prosodic Transcription. In Sun-Ah Jun (ed.), *Prosodic Typology: The Phonology of Intonation and Phrasing*, 230–270. Oxford: Oxford University Press.

Pfeil, Simone, Susanne Genzel & Frank Kügler. 2015. Empirical investigation of focus and exhaustivity in Akan. In Mira Grubic & Felix Bildhauer (eds.), *Mood, Exhaustivity & Focus Marking in Non-European Languages* (Interdisciplinary Studies on Information Structure (ISIS), vol. 19), 87–109. Potsdam: Universitätsverlag Potsdam.

Pike, Kenneth L. 1948. *Tone languages*. Ann Arbor: University of Michigan Press.

Purvis, T. M. 2009. Speech rhythm in Akan oral praise poetry. *Text & Talk – An Interdisciplinary Journal of Language, Discourse & Communication Studies* 29(2). 201–218.

Rialland, Annie. 2007. Question prosody: An African perspective. In Tomas Riad & Carlos Gussenhoven (eds.), *Tones and Tunes: Volume 1. Typological Studies in Word and Sentence Prosody* (Phonology and phonetics 12, 1), 35–62. Berlin: De Gruyter.

Rialland, Annie. 2009. The African lax question prosody: Its realisation and geographical distribution. *Lingua* 119(6). 928–949.

Saah, Kofi K. 1988. Wh-questions in Akan. *Journal of West African Languages* 18(1). 17–28.

Saah, Kofi K. 1994. *Studies in Akan Syntax, Acquisition, and Sentence Processing*. Ottawa: University of Ottawa, PhD Thesis.

Saah, Kofi K. & Mark Dundaa. 2012. *Interrogative sentences in Akan and Kaakyi: A comparative study* (Paper at the 5th Linguistics Association of Ghana conference). University of Education, Winneba.

Schachter, Paul & Victoria Fromkin. 1968. Phonology of Akan. In *Working Papers in Phonetics* 9, 1–268. Department of Linguistics, UCLA.

Selkirk, Elisabeth O. 2011. The Syntax-Phonology Interface. In John A. Goldsmith, Jason Riggle & Alan C. L. Yu (eds.), *The Handbook of Phonological Theory*, 2nd ed. (Blackwell handbooks in linguistics), 435–484. Chichester: Wiley-Blackwell.

Shih, Chilin. 2000. A declination model of Mandarin Chinese. In Antonis Botinis (ed.), *Intonation: Analysis, Modelling and Technology*, 243–268. Dordrecht: Kluwer.

Snider, Keith L. 1999. *The geometry and features of tone*. Arlington: SIL International and the University of Texas.

Stewart, John M. 1965. The typology of the Twi tone system. In *Bulletin of the Institute of African Studies*, 1–27: Institute of African Studies, University of Ghana, Legon.
Stewart, John M. 1993. Dschang and Ebrié as Akan-type total downstep languages. In Harry van der Hulst & Keith L. Snider (eds.), *The phonology of tone: The representation of tonal register*, 185–244. Berlin: De Gruyter.
Welmers, William E. 1959. Tonemics, morphotonemics, and tonal morphemes. *General Linguistics* 4. 1–9.
Xu, Yi. 1999. Effects of tone and focus on the formation and alignment of f0 contours. *Journal of Phonetics* 27(1). 55–105.
Yip, Moira J. 2002. *Tone*. Cambridge: Cambridge University Press.
Zerbian, Sabine, Susanne Genzel & Frank Kügler. 2010. Experimental work on prosodically-marked information structure in selected African languages (Afroasiatic and Niger-Congo). In *Workshop on Experimental Approaches to Focus, Chicago, Speech Prosody 2010*. Chicago. Available (December 2015) at http://speechprosody2010.illinois.edu/abstracts/100976.htm.

Bruce Connell
Tone and Intonation in Mambila

Abstract: Mambila is a Bantoid language spoken in the Nigeria-Cameroon borderland. It is a language with four level lexical tones and two grammatical tones. Previous work by the author (see references) indicates that pitch realization in Mambila is rather tightly constrained with respect to downtrends, the intrinsic F0 of vowels, and the overall scaling of tones. The present chapter combines this earlier work with newly reported research to present an overview of tone and intonation in Mambila. The major question addressed is whether Mambila, with its complex and crowded tone space, uses F0 differences to signal differences in sentence type: declaratives, polar questions, and content questions. The results of a series of experimental investigations reveal no consistent contribution of F0 in distinguishing sentence type: Mambila is a language which does not have intonation, as this concept is usually understood. The implications of these findings for intonation theory are discussed in the closing paragraphs of the chapter.

Keywords: downtrend, declination, downdrift, final lowering, polar question, content question, F0 scaling, question

1 Background

1.1 Tone and intonation in tone languages

There are a number of important and interesting issues with respect to the realization of intonation in tone languages. Since both tone and intonation have as their principal phonetic correlate controlled variation of F0, the potential for interaction between the two leading to ambiguity or miscommunication exists; so, it is of interest to know what strategies are employed with tone languages to resolve or avoid possible conflicts. It is reasonable to suggest that there would not be one 'blanket' strategy, but that the nature of the tone system in question would to a large extent be the determining factor. That is, and simply put, tone

---

Bruce Connell, York University

DOI 10.1515/9783110503524-005

in a language with a small tone inventory, or one in which tone carries a relatively small functional load, would be less susceptible to misinterpretation than otherwise.

The aim of this chapter is to provide an account of the role of pitch and other phenomena related to intonation in Mambila. The variety of Mambila examined here features four level lexical tones and two grammatical tones, the latter realizing several tonal morphemes. Together, these tones may combine to form a number of contour tones. As tone in Mambila is, like in most African languages, realized primarily through F0, it is of interest to learn how tone-based F0 variations interact with possible intonation-based F0 variations. Alternatively, one might ask to what extent intonation functions in Mambila are realized through F0 variations or by other conceivable means. A number of studies of pitch realization in Mambila have been undertaken, including Connell (1999a, b, 2002a, b, 2003, 2004, 2005). There are two studies on phonological aspects of Mambila tone, Perrin (1974, 1991), both of which are difficult of access, as is Perrin & Hill (1969), which provides a sketch of the phonology of Mambila. The present chapter draws on this work as well as the results of further as yet unreported work en route to an admittedly still partial characterization of intonation in Mambila. The remainder of this section looks at certain terminological issues and gives background on Mambila. Section 2 examines the status of tone in Mambila; §3 reports a series of instrumental studies into downtrends in Mambila, looking at the extent to which declarative utterances are marked intonationally. Section 4 looks at F0 scaling relative to sentence length; §5 presents results of experimental work investigating polar questions compared to the associated declarative utterances, and §6 at the pitch characteristics of content questions compared to similar statements. Section 7 gives discussion pertaining to the possible phonological representation of intonation in Mambila and §8 provides a summary and concluding statement.

1.2 Terminological concerns

The terminology used in describing pitch phenomena – both tone and intonation – has been used somewhat inconsistently in the Africanist literature, or differently than in other traditions. In the present chapter, and following the rationale given in Connell (2011), I use the relevant terminology defined in the following manner.

Declination: a gradual lowering of the phonetic backdrop of F0 over the course of an utterance. It is often said, or assumed to be, phonologized to mark declarative intonation.

Downstep: the lowering of a High tone following another High tone with the effect that a new ceiling is established for subsequent High tones within a specifiable domain. Downstep is *automatic* when a surface Low tone triggers the lowering, and *non-automatic* when there is no surface trigger; in such cases it is often attributable to a floating L tone. The new ceiling set for Hs leads to a terracing effect, hence the description of many languages as *terrace-level* languages.

Final lowering: a relatively abrupt lowering of F0 restricted to the ends of utterances. Liberman & Pierrehumbert (1984) and Pierrehumbert & Beckman (1988) report final lowering in English and Japanese respectively, and suggest it is restricted to (or extends over) approximately the last 250 ms or so of an utterance, i.e. approximately the last syllable. It is often said to fall to the bottom of a speaker's normal pitch range. It is often attributed to an utterance final boundary or edge tone. For African languages, Welmers (1973) notes that final (pre-pausal) L tones are typically falling. Two experimental studies investigating final lowering in African languages are Herman (1996) for Kipare, and Myers (1996) for Chichewa, both Bantu languages. Final lowering is often assumed to have a demarcative function relative to utterance boundaries in the form of a low boundary tone (L%).

Downdrift: Downdrift is most often used in the literature synonymously (and confusingly) with either automatic downstep and declination; here, and following the practice adopted in Connell (2002a, 2011) downdrift refers to a lowering of F0 that is the result of successive cumulative local lowerings through tone coarticulation; i.e., as shown in Connell 2002a, a H tone is lowered by a preceding L tone. However, in sequences involving a string of H tones, e.g. HLHHH, within two to three syllables the H has achieved its earlier, initial, height. In sequences of alternating High(er) and Lowe(er) tones, e.g. HLHLHL, H does not have the possibility to achieve its initial height, but rather, the lowering effect of the intervening Ls is cumulative. So while in certain contexts this effect may be indistinguishable from automatic downstep, unlike downstep, it does not impose a new, lower, ceiling on succeeding Hs, as is a characteristic of downstep. In this, downstep (either automatic or non-automatic) can be seen as phonologically based while downdrift, as described here, is phonetic in nature.

Register: Clements (1990: 59) defines register as the "frequency band internal to the speaker's range which determines the highest and lowest frequency within which tones can be realized at any given point in an utterance", to distinguish it from an individual's normal pitch *range*. The register can be raised or lowered, expanded or narrowed.

1.3 Mambila

Mambila is a Bantoid language spoken on both sides of the Nigeria-Cameroon border, in Taraba State in Nigeria and Adamawa Region in Cameroon. With approximately 100,000 speakers[1], it is the largest language of the Mambiloid group. It comprises two dialect clusters, East and West Mambila, most of whose lects are mutually unintelligible, within as well as across clusters. Mambila speakers of whichever variety who claim to understand other lects are able to do so largely through exposure; exceptions would be in certain cases of neighbouring lects, i.e. a restricted dialect chain. The division into two clusters has been established on the basis of a number of phonological and morphological characteristics (Connell 2000a); one of these characteristics appears to be that languages of the eastern set have three lexical tones, while those of the western grouping operate a system of four lexical tones. In making this claim it should be noted that the presence of four tones in West Mambila vs three in East Mambila has not been confirmed for all varieties of the two clusters, though it does appear to be true of all that have been examined thus far; the circumstances of the development from three in the east to four in the west are relatively transparent. The only Mambila lect that has been the subject of detailed phonetic investigation is Ba Mambila; Ba is spoken principally in three villages on the Tikar Plain in Adamawa Province, Cameroon: Atta, Sonkolong and Somié, together with smaller villages and hamlets in the orbit of these three. There are some relatively minor subdialectal differences across the Ba speaking area; to the extent that these bear on the present work, they are mentioned below where relevant. Perrin & Hill (1969) is a sketch of the phonology of Ba as spoken at Atta, and Mouh & Perrin (1995) is a lexicon based on Ba as spoken at Sonkolong. Perrin (1974) is a sketch of the tone system of Tungba Mambila spoken in Gembu and environs, to some extent in comparison with that of Atta. (Tungba is a

---

1 There are no reliable census figures, particularly for Nigeria, since questions pertaining to ethnic affiliation (including language) are not used in the national census.

distinct, and in fact the largest, variety of West Mambila; Gembu is the seat of local government in the Mambila region in Nigeria.) Finally, while Perrin (1991) is presented as an update ('Some further comments...') on tone in Mambila, comments therein are in fact based on Ba spoken at Sonkolong. Other than these, a number of studies by the present writer which, as mentioned above, inform this chapter, have been carried out at Somié, the third and smallest of the three main Ba speaking villages. In the remainder of the chapter I refer to simply to 'Mambila', though my remarks should be understood as being specific to Ba as spoken at Somié unless otherwise mentioned.

2 The status of tone in Mambila

Tone can be said to function on three different levels in Mambila: lexically, grammatically and deictically. Perrin (1974, 1991) identifies three units she says are required to describe tone in Mambila: the syllable, the phonological word, and a larger, grammatically determined, unit referred to by Perrin as the span. There are four level lexical tones; for ease of reference, these are numbered from 1 to 4 (High to Low). The positing of four underlying level tones is defended in Perrin (1991), who considers and rejects an analysis that tone 3 be analyzed as underlyingly 42, and need not be explored in detail here. Motivation for the identity of underlying tones is based in the fact that most tone patterns on verbs occur in what Perrin (1991) refers to as the narrative tense and these correspond to patterns on verbs given in citation form. Every syllable bears at least one of the four level tones. Contour tones, which can be analyzed as combinations of level tones borne on a single syllable, are not uncommon. This analysis is straightforward and to some extent will be seen as justified in the discussion below, though detailed discussion is outside the scope of the present work.

2.1 Lexical tone in Mambila

There is sufficient lexical contrast based solely on tone that it is not problematic to find minimal pairs or triplets; minimal quadruplets are less common but do exist, as shown in (1).

(1) Examples of lexical tonal contrasts, level tones[2].

Word	Tone	Gloss
baŋ	1	defensive trench around village
	2	type of wild cat (genet sp.)
	3	begin
	4	wound (n.)
go	1	guardian
	2	habit, custom
	3	sell
	4	journey (n.)
ker	1	sparrowhawk
	2	new field
	3	cut (v.), dig
	4	cup used for palm wine
jere	1	dirtiness
	2	pity
	3	go up (e.g. smoke)
	4	type of flea

Figure 1 illustrates pitch differences for the four tones spoken in collocation with the 1SG-POSS marker mò (tone 4). Since baŋ T3 is a verb (as are the other T3 words in the above examples) it is not possible to place it in the comparable tone environment, so two minimal sets are used, baŋ (tones 1, 2, 4 and ba (tones 2, 3, 4); ba T1 is a grammatical form and so it too cannot fit into the environment used.)

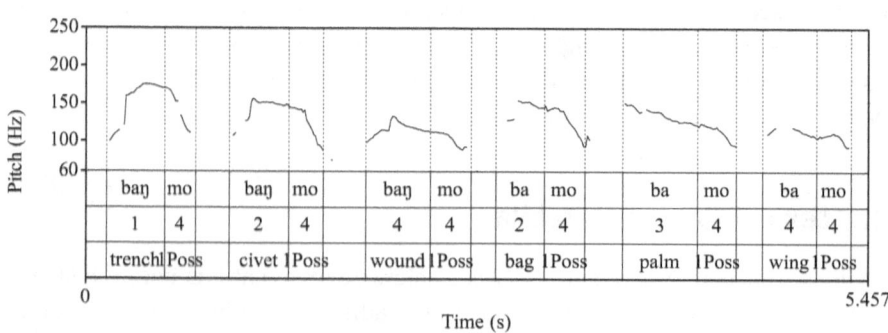

Figure 1: Pitch tracks for the four tones of Mambila, illustrated using two minimal sets, baŋ (tones 1, 2, 4 and ba (tones 2, 3, 4); speaker CD

---

[2] Examples throughout are given in the accepted Mambila orthography, with the exception of tone marking. The orthography provides for marking only T1 (H = ´) and T4 (L = `); in this chapter I use one of two conventions, according to which is best suited for a given example: either numbers (1 to 4, High to Low) or diacritics with T2 being marked with a macron (= ¯) and T3 left unmarked. When using tone numbers the syllable boundary is indicated (.) where necessary.

Possible tonal combinations or sequences of tones within the syllable are limited to 2-1, 3-1, 4-1, 1-4, 2-4, 3-4, 2-1-4. These patterns appear to define the phonological word, along with others introduced through the addition or influence of grammatical tones, whether a word is of one, two, or three syllables. Two tritonal contours, which occur only rarely, have been identified in monosyllabic or disyllabic nouns: 214 and 314. In disyllabic words bearing these tone sequences the contour is always on the second syllable (i.e. 2.14, 3.14). The majority of words in Ba Mambila are monosyllabic, while three syllable words are uncommon. It is worth noting, though tangential to the concerns of this study, that the four way lexical contrast is found only on the initial syllable of nouns. The functioning of grammatical tone gives a four way contrast on the second (final) syllable of verbs.

Contour tones on one syllable are normally restricted to monosyllabic words. On disyllabic words they occur only rarely (except as a result of grammatical conditioning, discussed below) and when they do, the contour is invariably on the second syllable. The presence of contour tones on monosyllables gives evidence the syllable is the relevant tone bearing unit in Mambila. Examples of contours, in contrast with level tones are given in (2).

(2) Examples of lexical tonal contrasts involving compound contour tones.

Word	Tone	Gloss	Word	Tone	Gloss
man	14	thus	lam	1	row
man	24	small	lam	4	type of tree
man	31	learn	lam	21	lose consistency
beh	1	we	lan	3	today
beh	3	aspect marker	lan	4	society
beh	4	arm, handle	lan	31	invite to work
beh	14	me and …	bam	3	traditional 10 week
beh	21	to spoil, ruin	bam	34	day in the 10 day week
beh	31	braid (v.)			
beh	24	our			

Level tones and contours combined give 11 surface tone contrasts; these are augmented by other contours found on grammatical morphemes, e.g. na 212, a tense marker.

2.2 Grammatical tone in Mambila

Tonal morphemes exist in Mambila which serve a number of grammatical functions; with disyllabic words, these result in a contour on the final syllable of the word. Grammatical modifications of inherent tones can also level a pre-existing contour. Modifications occur in both noun phrases and verb phrases.

2.2.1 The noun phrase

In dependent constructions (associative, attributive, genitive, possessive), a tone 4 is suffixed: i.e. final T1 > T14; T2 > T24; T3 > T34, T21 > T214; T31 > 314. Perrin describes this as a floating tone morpheme in Atta/Sonkolong which still has a segmental counterpart in Gembu. The segmental morpheme is also said to be still in use by older speakers in Atta, though only with CVC nouns. My own work confirms the existence of this segmental counterpart in a small number of forms in Gembu as well as all varieties of East Mambila examined to date, and I am aware of at least one instance in Ba as spoken at Somié which appears to be a fossilization of the segmental marker. An example of the productive tonal morpheme is given in (3), with tones indicated by number.

(3) T4 as a marker of dependent (genitive) constructions
 feh 1 'head'
 wo   sie   jule   feh
 4   31   2.1   1-4
 2SG comb hair   head-GEN
 'You comb (your) hair of head.'

2.2.2 The verb phrase

There are several grammatical functions of tone at the level of the verb phrase, unlike the situation of the noun phrase, just described. That is, inherent tone patterns are changed, and in some cases contrasts neutralized, through the addition of grammatical tones. It is not within the scope of this chapter to give a complete description of the grammatical role tone plays in Mambila, though the following paragraphs attempt to illustrate at least some of them. Imperative and negative formation involve changes to the inherent tonal pattern of verbs in which existing contours are leveled rather than new contours created: T2, T21 > T1; T3, T31, T34 > T4. Negative formation also sees a permutation of the basic SVO word order to SOV. These are illustrated in (4).

(4) Imperative and negative formation
    a. T2 > T1: yila 2.2 'enter'

car	yila	lɔ
2	2.2	2
monkey	enter	village

'The monkey enters (into) the village.'

yila	lɔ
1.1	2
enter.IMP	village

'Enter the village.'

car	lɔ	yila	ŋgweh
2	2	1.1	1
monkey	village	enter	NEG

'The monkey doesn't enter (into) the village.'

    b. T21 > T1: yila 21 'call'

car	yila	mi
2	2.1	4
monkey	call	1SG.OBJ

'The monkey calls me.'

yila	mi
1.1	4
call.IMP	1SG.OBJ

'Call me.'

car	mi	yila	ŋgweh
2	4	1.1	1
monkey	1SG.OBJ	call	NEG

'The monkey doesn't call me.'

In past tense formation, verbs with inherent level tone (i.e. either tone 2 or 3) form a contour with the addition of a polar tone: i.e. 2 > 24, 3 > 31. This is illustrated in (5), which may be compared with (4a).

(5) Past tense
    T2 > T24: yila 2.2 'enter'

car	le	yila	na	lɔ
2	1	2.4	212	2
monkey	PST	enter	COP	village

'The monkey entered (into) the village.'

In discontinuous verb phrases (Perrin 1991) the verb comes at the end of the clause, with a tone 1 morpheme being suffixed to the verb. This neutralizes the 2–21 distinction, though tone 3 remains unchanged. Verbs may be repeated clause finally for emphasis; in these cases, the inherent tone of the verb is replaced with a 24 contour. Finally, in verb nominalization or infinitive formation, a tone 4 is suffixed to the existing tone of the verb (together with a reduplicative prefix), which may already be a contour as a result of being clause final; hence 2, 21 > 214; 3, 31 > 314. Examples are given in (6):

(6) Infinitive formation
    luo (2) 'push'   bə (31) 'plait'
    lu-luo-INF   bə-bə-INF
    2-2-4   4-31-4
    'to push'   'to plait'

2.3 Tone as a deictic marker

Finally, tone serves what may be termed a deictic function in Mambila: e.g. motion toward can be indicated by replacing the inherent tone with tone 4 (7a, b), and nouns with a 21 contour bear tone 2 when indicating location (7d–f). As the examples in (7) show, these sometimes involve segmental changes as well as tone alternations. As 7c indicates, use of tone to mark deixis is not restricted to nouns.

(7) Tonal deixis
    a. nde (2) 'go'   nde (2-4) 'come'
    b. Ndeba (3) Somié   Ndeba (4) 'comes from Somié'
        (the village name in Ba)
    c. nji (21) 'verb indicating a certain nji (24) 'action/movement towards
        direction'   the speaker'
    d. lɔ (21) 'village'   lɔ (2) 'in(to) the village'
    e. ton (21) 'market'   tan (2) 'to the market'
    f. cibi (2.1) 'night'   cibi (2) 'in the night'

2.4 The span

Little mention is made by Perrin of pitch or tonal behaviour with respect to what she terms 'the span', though she does say it corresponds to the grammatical clause, which I assume is equivalent to the intonational phrase. If this is the case, many of the phenomena under examination in this chapter can be seen as properties of, or corresponding to, the span. These are the subject of the following sections of the chapter, which look at downtrends generally, to arrive at a characterization of the intonation of unmarked affirmative declarative utterances, at possible intonation differences between declaratives and interrogatives in polar questions, and at differences between questions and answers in content-word questions.

3 The use of pitch in declarative sentences in Mambila

Cross linguistically different sentence types are typically characterized by different intonations, with declarative utterances being marked by a fall in pitch across the utterance and interrogatives by a suspension of the fall or heightened pitch being the default expectations (Gussenhoven (2004) offers a possible biological basis to these tendencies). While this seems generally as true of tone languages as it is of non-tone languages, Rialland (2007; see also Clements & Rialland 2008) provides numerous counterexamples to this with respect to question intonation. The complex tonal structure of Mambila as presented above suggests that even slight downtrends could introduce a potential for ambiguity and so it is of interest to investigate and ascertain to what extent the use of a downward course in F0 serves intonation purposes in the language. Research investigating downtrends in Mambila was first published in Connell (1999a, b, c) and summarized in Connell (2003). It was known already from early phonological work on Mambila (Perrin 1974, 1991; Perrin & Hill 1969) that non-automatic downstep, as is found in such classic terracing languages as Akan, Efik, and Igbo, is not present in Mambila. However, it was not known to what extent different types of downtrend existed in the language and might therefore be associated with different sentence types. Thus the aim of this work was to establish whether, or to what extent, any of the various downtrends attested generally in tone languages, as defined above in §1.2, exist in Mambila.

The essence of the method in these experimental investigations was to test for pitch effects using sentences comprised of words bearing the same phonemic tone ('like-tone sentences'); in this way any observed downtrend would be attributable to phrase or utterance level effects rather than to phonemic tone. Inclusion of sentences with sequences of different tones ('mixed-tone sentences') allowed for testing of local effects, and use of sentences of different lengths permitted testing for pitch effects that might be tied to utterance length, such as heightened pitch initially for longer sentences. Standard experimental procedures were used for all the investigations described here;[3] details are available in the different published reports. The investigations typically involved between four and six speakers, both male and female (the first, published as Connell 1999a was conceived as a pilot study and used just two speakers, both male). Since they were conducted in the field over a period of approximately a decade, the pool of participants inevitably varied; despite this there is a core set of speakers who participated in each study. All participants were adult native speakers of Ba Mambila, were born and had grown up in Somié. All were also fluent in French and Fulfulde (both non-tone languages) and many had varying degrees of competence in various other local languages.

3.1 Experiment 1

The preliminary investigation of the occurrence of pitch downtrends in Mambila is reported in Connell (1999a). This study used both like-tone sentences and mixed tone sequences, where for the latter, for the most part all but one tone were the same. The odd tone was placed in some cases early in the sentence, and other cases late in the sentence. Sentences ranged in length from two to nine syllables (the same range was not possible for all four tones). In all, 30 sentences were used. The corpus was recorded by two male speakers, both native speakers of Mambila in their early twenties. The results of this study suggested that downtrends are minimal in Mambila pitch realization. The clearest example of an effect on F0 of was the lowering of tone 1 when following a tone 4, considered to be tone coarticulation (as discussed above in the section on terminology). This is a local effect, with the lowered tone typically regaining its target value within one or two syllables; in, for example, 4111 sequences, the first in the tone 1 sequence did not reach the height of an earlier tone 1, though typically the second did so. Mid tones (2 and 3) in similar circumstances appeared to be only slightly affected, if at all. Evidence for utterance-level effects, e.g. declination, was somewhat ambiguous, particularly for the mid tones, where it was not clear whether observed slight downtrends were evidence of declination or final lowering. Tone 1 however, showed no tendency to declination for these two speakers, while tone 4 seemed subject to final lowering. There was no evidence of downstep (the lowering attributed to tone coarticulation did

---

[3] All recordings were done during fieldwork in Cameroon, and so were not done in a recording studio. High quality digital recording equipment was used and multiple (usually five) randomized repetitions of test items recorded.

not set a new, lowered, ceiling for the H tone), while evidence for final lowering was clearest for tone 4 and nonexistent for tone 1. This near absence of downtrends was accounted for by postulating that the relatively crowded tonal space, phonologically, left little room for flexibility with respect to the phonetic realization of tone.

3.2 Experiment 2

3.2.1 Declination and final lowering

A follow up investigation (Connell 1999b) using a modified set of sentences and an expanded subject pool attempted to test the results of the pilot study and to explore in greater depth two questions which arose from the earlier study: whether the mid tones, tone 2 and tone 3, are subject to declination or final lowering, and whether the local lowering of tones observed earlier is cumulative, e.g. in a 414141 sequence, therefore resulting an apparent downdrift effect. The test materials comprised 16 declarative sentences, including like-tone sequences for all four tones and mixed tone sequences alternating tone 1 and tone 4, tone 4 and tone 1, and tone 2 and tone 3. Short and long sentences of each of these patterns were included. F0 measurements were taken of each syllable at a point judged to be the tonal target;[4] these were analyzed using linear regression, first to determine whether a significant F0 downtrend occurred in a particular sentence type, and then to separate a potential effect of final lowering from that of declination.[5] Inspection of the data suggested that in potential cases of final lowering, a relatively steep drop in F0 occurred over the last 1–2 syllables of an utterance; these were therefore examined separately in the regression analysis. In previous attempts to separate declination from final lowering, somewhat different statistical techniques were used: Laniran (1992) used a regression analysis, but rather than looking at the F0 slope of the final syllable(s), she examined the decline in F0 when successive final syllables were removed. If the slope became less steep, she concluded that final lowering had contributed to the overall downtrend. Herman (1996) used an ANOVA rather than regression, and examined whether the F0 value of a target syllable was more greatly affected by its distance from

---

[4] An effort to help establish standard procedures for determining tonal targets is presented in Connell & Ladd 1990; Connell (2002) elaborates these for Mambila.

[5] I am grateful to Mario Cortina Borja, Statistics Consultant at Oxford University for his help with this aspect of the research.

the beginning of the utterance, or its proximity to the end of the utterance; the former case she took to be evidence for declination and the latter to be evidence of final lowering. While both of these techniques provide some insight into F0 downtrends, neither of them asks directly whether the F0 decline over the last syllable or two is significantly different (steeper) from that of the preceding part of the sentence. The technique adopted here specifically addresses this question. Figure 2 illustrates the output of the regression analysis. The black dots represent raw F0 values; in the left panel, the dotted trace represents the F0 curve, an average of the raw measurements represented by the dots, and the solid trace is the regression line. In the right panel, the regression line for the main part of the utterance is compared to the regression line for the final two syllables. The table at (8) gives the regression summary for the left panel, and shows a significant downtrend over the entire utterance (p = 0.0000). The regression summaries at (9) and (10) examine the main part of the utterance (9) and the final two syllables (10); these show that slope of the first part is not significant (p = 0.1228) while that for the final two syllables is significant (p = 0.0019).

(8) Regression summary for all the data (Figure 2, top panel):
Coefficients:

	Value	Std. Error	t value	Pr(>|t|)
(Intercept)	237.9867	3.6410	65.3624	0.0000
NSO	5.1486	0.9349	−5.5069	**0.0000**

(9) Regression summary for first part of the data (Figure 2, bottom panel):
Coefficients:

	Value	Std. Error	t value	Pr(>|t|)
(Intercept)	231.5000	3.9574	58.4980	0.0000
NSO	−2.3400	1.4450	−1.6193	**0.1228**

(10) Regression summary for last two syllables (Figure 2, bottom panel):
Coefficients:

	Value	Std. Error	t value	Pr(>|t|)
(Intercept)	320.8000	24.8827	12.8925	0.0000
NSO	−20.4000	4.5056	−4.5277	**0.0019**

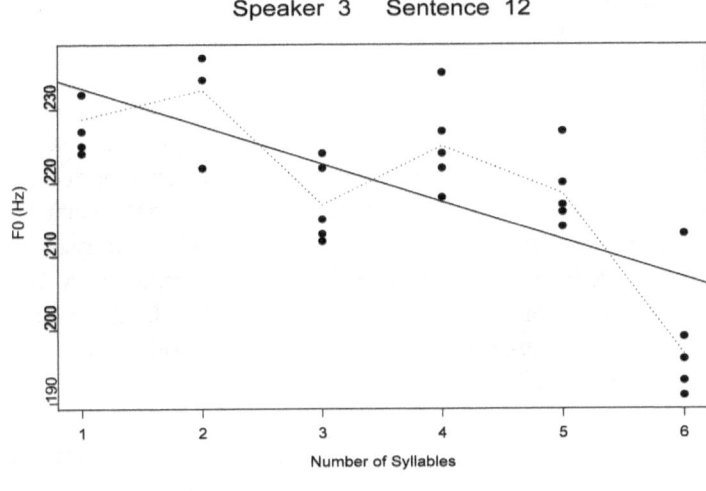

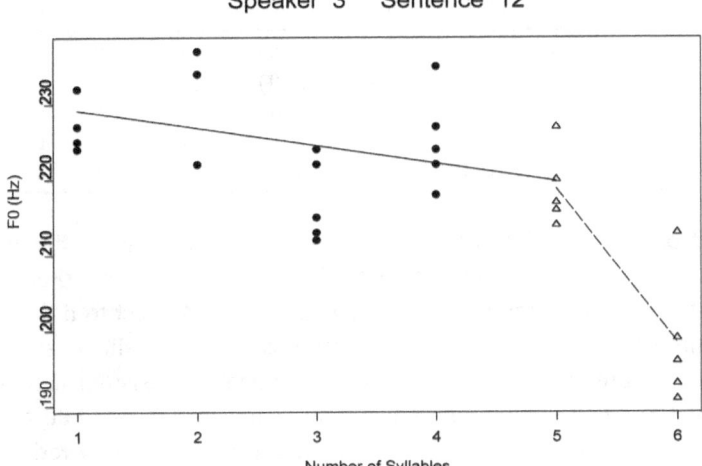

Figure 2: Regression line superimposed on averaged pitch trace for a short (six syllables) T2 utterance (top), and for the main part of the utterance compared to that for last two syllables (bottom). (Speaker 3, VM, female)

Finally, the results of T-tests comparing the two slopes (11) and the mean F0 of the two portions of the sentences (12) are both significant:

(11) Difference of slopes = 18.06 StdError = 4.7316
      T-value = 3.8169, p-value = **0.0001**

(12) Standard Two-Sample t-Test
      t = 4.6377, df = 28, p-value = **0.0001**

With the difference between the two slopes being significant and with a significant drop in F0 between the first and last parts of the utterance, we can say final lowering is present.

A regression analysis of this sort was applied to results from data for all the like-tone sentences. Conclusions based on the results of the regression analysis are summarized in Table 1. 'D' or 'F' in a cell indicates the presence of declination or final lowering, respectively. (F) indicates final lowering was present but accompanied by a slight rise in F0 on the penultimate syllable. This rise was slight, typically on the order of 2–4 Hz relative to the antepenultimate. A dash in a cell indicates an absence of either or both of declination or final lowering. S, M or L denote the length of the sentence, short, medium or long. For tone 4, three sentence lengths were used.

Table 1: Summary of results for like tone sentences across five speakers

Speaker	Tone 1 S	Tone 1 L	Tone 2 S	Tone 2 L	Tone 3 S	Tone 3 L	Tone 4 S	Tone 4 M	Tone 4 L
1 (M)	-, -	-, -	-, -	-, -	-, -	D, (F)	-, F	D, F	D, -
2 (M)	D, -	-, -	D, -	D, -	-, -	D, (F)	-, F	D, -	D, F
3 (F)	-, -	-, -	-, (F)	-, (F)	D, -	-, (F)	-, F	D, F	D, -
4 (F)	-, -	D, -	D, -	D, -	-, (F)	D, -	-, F	D, F	D, (F)
5 (M)	-, -	D, -	D, -	D, (F)	-, (F)	D, (F)	-, F	D, F	D, (F)

A striking aspect of these results is the different treatment accorded different tones; in particular, the lower the tone, the more likely it is subject to either or both of declination or final lowering. Tone 1, the high tone, is subject to little in the way of downtrends, while tone 4, the low tone, consistently shows some form of downtrend. Moreover, the effects seen are relatively consistent across speakers: e.g. for tone 4, the short utterance shows final lowering, while the two longer sentences offer evidence of both declination and final lowering. However it may be noted that, given the length of the short utterance – four syllables – it may not be possible to conclusively distinguish between declination and final lowering. The two mid tones, however, are less regular in exhibiting either declination or final lowering. While a downtrend of some sort appears for these two tones more often than not, one is not always present and, when there is, there is no consistency as to whether declination or final lowering is used, either across the two tones or across speakers. What does appear to be consistent is that when final lowering does occur with these tones it is facilitated by a slight rise in F0, of approximately 2–4 Hz, on the penultimate syllable relative to the antepenultimate. The more consistent appearance of a downtrend with tone 4 is presumably possible because there is no lower tone whose space it would be violating. Or, from the opposite perspective, tones 1–3 do not show downtrends consistently because they would risk impinging on the space of the lower tone(s).

3.2.2 Downdrift vs. tone coarticulation

The pilot study indicated that lowering of tone 1 following tone 4 in 4111 sequences was a local effect, lasting only one or two syllables. In addition to looking at final lowering and declination, the follow up study also addressed the question whether this lowering effect in mixed tone sentences is cumulative; i.e. in sequences alternating tones 4 and 1, does tone 1 still reach its normal value, or does it show a downdrifting effect. Figures 3 and 4 show T1–T4 alternations for three utterances of difference lengths for two speakers, male and female respectively, representing an average of five repetitions. Utterances were four, six, and eight syllables in length; note that in Figure 3 the trajectory of the medium and long utterances are virtually identical (one superimposed upon the other) and so are difficult to distinguish.

For speaker CD (male, Figure 3), the difference between the initial tone 1 and the final tone 1 (syllables one and seven) is not large, but it is significant ($p = 0.032$); similarly the difference between initial and final tone 4 (syllables two and eight) is significant ($p = 0.000$). Tone 1 showed no declination for this speaker in the earlier experiments (i.e. in like-tone sentences), so it may be assumed here that the consistent drop in values across the sentence for tone 1 is a result of the local interaction with tone 4 observed in the pilot study, and that this effect is cumulative. A syllable by syllable analysis of the lowering of tone 4 values for all three utterances shows that the difference between the last

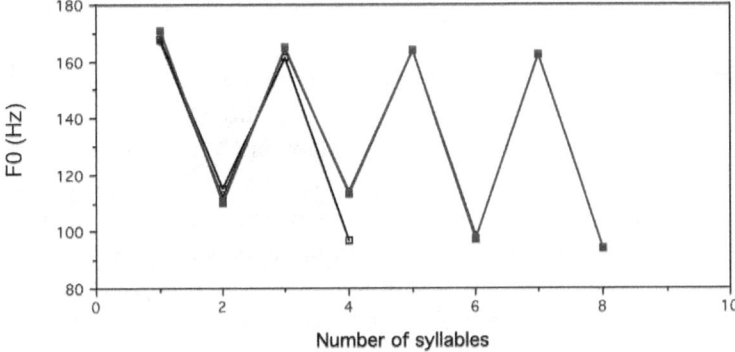

Figure 3: Averaged pitch traces for alternating tone 1–tone 4 sequences of three different lengths. (Speaker CD, male)

two syllables is significant for the two shorter phrases ($p = 0.005; p = 0.006$), though not for the longer phrase. This appears consistent with the behaviour observed above for this speaker with tone 4.

For the second speaker (VM, female), there were no significant differences between initial and final tone 1, or initial and final tone 4, for any of the three utterances. This suggests that the local lowering effect observed in the preliminary study may not exist for all speakers. We note that this speaker showed what appeared to be declination with T1 in the like tone sequences reported above, though the evidence was ambiguous; in the absence of declination or downdrifting effects here, it is tempting to suggest the possible declination effect noted above maybe due to other, as yet undetermined, causes. This reanalysis would then be in line with observations for other speakers, where T1 shows no declination. The absence of a downtrend for T4 here, where one was reported above for this speaker in the like tone sequences, may be due to the interrupting effect of T1.

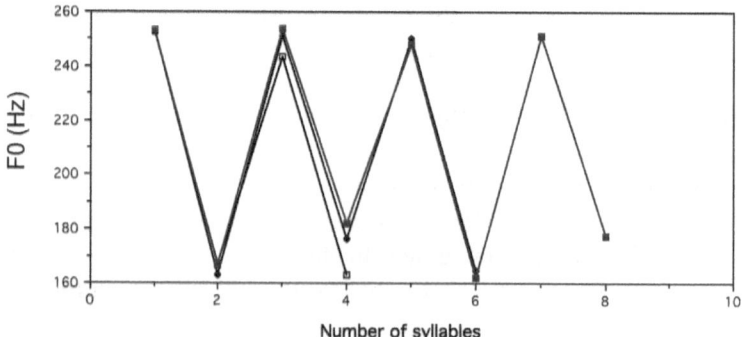

Figure 4: Averaged pitch traces for alternating tone 1–tone 4 sequences of three different lengths. (Speaker VM, female)

The pilot study also found little interaction between tone 2 and tone 3 or between these two tones and the others, but the possibility of such effects was not systematically investigated. Figures 5 and 6 show pitch traces (averages of five repetitions) for sequences of alternating tone 2 and tone 3 which shed some light on possible interactions between these two tones. Note that in the longer utterance syllables five and six represent a bisyllabic tone 2 word.

For speaker CD, the short utterance shows a noticeable lowering of tone 2 following tone 3, though the difference between initial and final tone 2 is not significant; in the longer utterance, however, the difference between initial and final tone 2 is significant ($p = 0.006$). It may be concluded that the slight lowering effect found in the shorter utterance is cumulative, i.e. downdrifting does occur in tone 2–tone 3 sequences for this speaker. A slight lowering of tone 3 is also observable in the longer utterance, though this is not statistically significant.

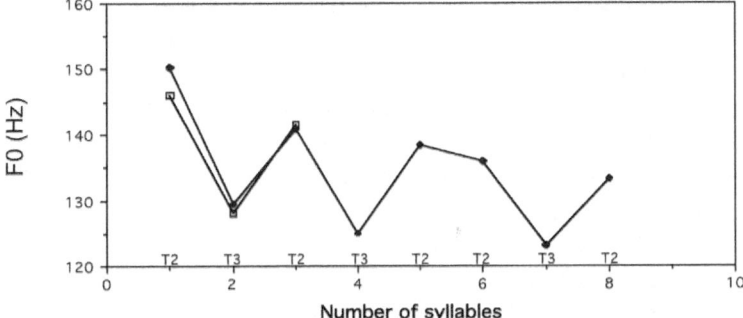

Figure 5: Averaged pitch traces (5 repetitions) for T2–T3 alternating tone sequences of two different lengths. (Speaker CD, male)

For the second speaker, a similar trend exists, confirming the existence of downdrift as a cumulative local effect. In her case, though, the difference between initial and final tone 2 in the shorter utterance is significant ($p = 0.028$), as well as that in the longer utterance ($p = 0.005$). Final tone 2 also appears to show final lowering here, though the downtrend is not statistically significant. This speaker also agrees with the other in showing no significant downtrend for tone 3.

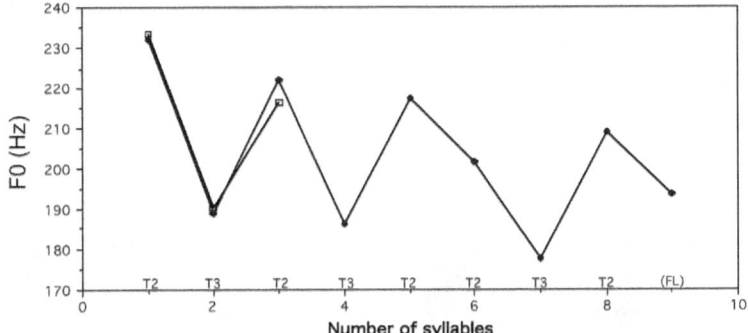

Figure 6: Averaged pitch traces for T2–T3 alternating tone sequences of two different lengths. (Speaker VM, female)

3.3 Experiment 3

Another issue of relevance to the possibility of pitch contributing to identifying declaratives is the scaling of F0. A basic hypothesis in this is that, assuming a constant rate of declination, utterance length will be a determining factor of initial and/or final pitch height. Longer utterances will involve either a higher initial F0 and/or a lower final F0 than is found in shorter utterances. The first of these two possibilities, higher initial F0, suggests a preplanning mechanism by which utterance initial F0 is raised proportionate to utterance length. An alternative is that adjustment is made 'on-the-fly', and given that F0 range is finite, its bottom may be reached before utterance end. Preplanning is most often taken as a means of phonetically accommodating utterance length; alternatively, it could be taken as evidence that declination has been phonologized, in the sense that it has gone beyond simply being phonetic and serves specifically to signal (declarative) utterance type. Research on preplanning has been conducted primarily on non-tone languages (see, e.g. Cooper & Sorenson 1981, 't Hart 1979, Ladd & Johnson 1986). The general finding is that initial pitch height does increase with sentence length, though Ladd & Johnson (investigating English) hold the opposite view, that utterance length has no effect on F0 scaling.[6] Lindau (1986, for Hausa), and Snider (1998, for Chumburung) are two studies conducted on tone languages. Lindau's results appear to support the general finding, but Snider reports this to be true of H but not L tone. In Mambila, the use of F0 scaling is an open question; first, as reported above, declination appears not to be used for intonation purposes as it only really appears in L tone utterances. However, if F0 is scaled upwards utterance initially for longer sentences in low tone contexts in Mambila, it could be interpreted as lending support to a claim that Mambila has phonologized the use of declination, at least to this limited extent.

A third experiment investigated the possibility of F0 scaling in Mambila, details of which were originally reported in Connell (2004). The procedures summarized above were also employed for this study. The focus was on tone 4 utterances since it most reliably showed declination in the earlier work; tone 1 utterances were also investigated since, even though previous experiments did not show declination for this tone, in theory it could rise without endangering tonal contrasts since it is the highest tone. (And note, it was with H that Snider found scaling in Chumburung.) Our findings indicate that for Mambila speakers

---

[6] This conclusion was supported by only one of two speakers who participated in Ladd & Johnson's study; they suggest metrical factors are responsible for the raising or non-raising of utterance initial pitch.

utterance length does not play a role in determining either the beginning or the end point F0 of either High or Low tone utterances. We show this first for tone 4 and then for tone 1.

Figure 7 presents results for one speaker (MD, female) for tone 4, to illustrate the nature of the Mambila data. The findings for this speaker are typical of those of the other speakers in several respects: first, although there is variation as to which utterance length had the highest initial F0, for none of the speakers did the longest sentence have the highest; second, for all speakers, the final F0 of each utterance, regardless of utterance length, was approximately the same; and third, all speakers showed the shortest sentence to have the steepest slope.

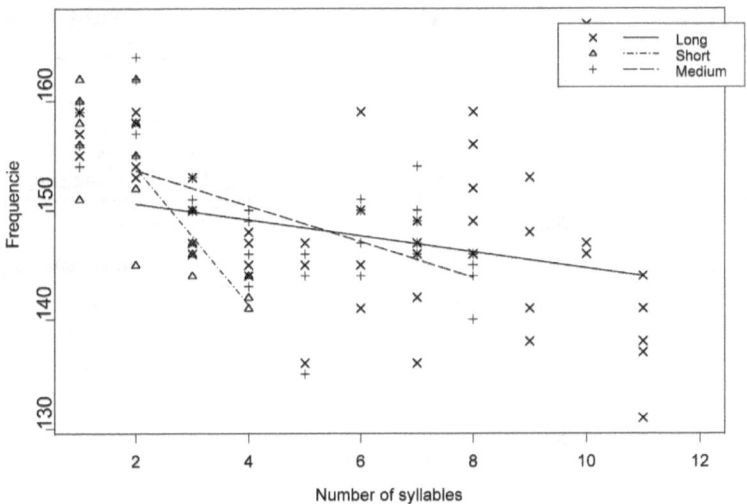

Figure 7: Regression trends for short, medium and long utterances of L tone sentences. (Speaker MD, female)

Table 2 presents the statistics for all speakers (three male, two female), male and female speakers are treated separately. To test for differences in initial F0, an analysis of variance was run, comparing measurements for the three different sentence lengths. Values for the first two syllables were tested. Table 2 gives means and standard deviations for F0 of these syllables, and the significance levels. Neither group, male or female, showed a significant difference in initial F0 for the three sentence lengths.

Table 2: Means, standard deviations and statistical results of F0 for the first two syllables of Mambila Low-toned utterances for three different sentence lengths, Short, Medium and Long

Mean	Male		Female	
	F01 (SD)	F02 (SD)	F01 (SD)	F02 (SD)
S	105.7 (10.3)	108.7 (11.6)	167.4 (13.5)	173.6 (21.6)
M	112.3 (11.3)	113.6 (11.4)	166.5 (12.5)	173.9 (20.0)
L	107.1 (10.2)	111.8 (10.7)	168.8 (14.4)	173.9 (20.6)
Stats	$F(2, 49) = 1.887$; $p = 0.162$, ns	$F(2, 49) = 0.863$; $p = 0.428$, ns	$F(2, 28) = 0.08$; $p = 0.923$, ns	$F(2, 28) = 0.001$; $p = 0.999$, ns

Differences in utterance final F0 for each of the three sentence lengths were tested for significance in a similar fashion (Table 3); again no significant differences were found for either group of speakers.

Table 3: Means, standard deviations and statistical results of F0 for the final syllable of Mambila Low-toned utterances for three different sentence lengths, Short, Medium and Long

Mean	Male	Female
	F0-final (SD)	F0-final (SD)
S	92.47 (7.3)	152.6 (13.8)
M	91.4 (6.7)	153.7 (11.4)
L	96.75 (11.3)	151.1 (14.3)
statistic	$F(2, 49) = 1.838$; $p = 0.170$, ns	$F(2, 28) = 0.105$; $p = 0.901$, ns

Figure 8 illustrates the results for one speaker (SM, male) for tone 1. Four of the five speakers showed very similar tendencies. First, the longer utterance did begin slightly higher than the shorter one, their end points were approximately the same, and the slopes of the regression line for each ran nearly parallel.

Statistical analyses of beginning and endpoints were done as above, presented in Tables 4 and 5. Despite the tendencies just noted for individual speakers, e.g. that longer utterances start with a slightly higher F0 for High tone, none of the differences observed is statistically significant.

The absence of significant differences in either initial or final pitch height concurs with Snider's (1998) results for Low tone in Chumburung, a typical two tone language, but not his findings for High, in which higher initial F0 correlated with longer utterance length. There are a number of possible explanations for this. First, one might argue that for L to increase in F0 would risk overlap with the tone above, thereby creating a situation of potential ambiguity. A constraint to inhibit this potential overlap need not apply to initial High, which

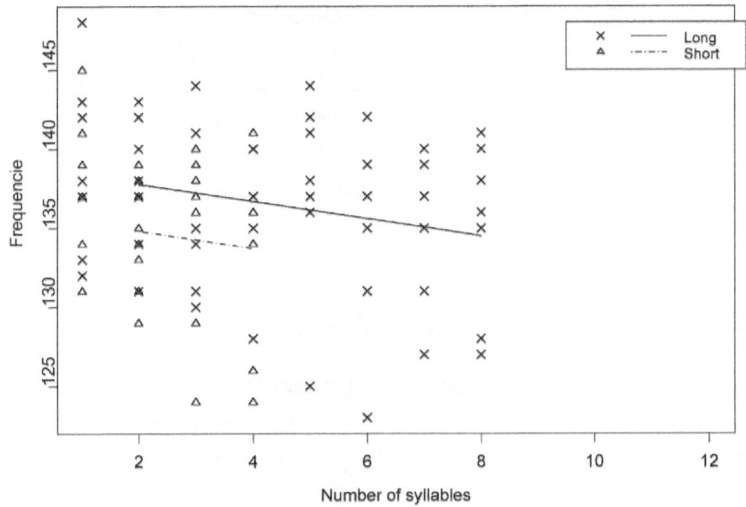

Figure 8: Regression trends for short and long utterances of H tone sentences. (Speaker SM, male)

Table 4: Means, standard deviations and statistical results of F0 for the first two syllables of Mambila High-toned utterances for two different sentence lengths, Short and Long

	Male		Female	
	F01 (SD)	F02 (SD)	F01 (SD)	F02 (SD)
S	141.2 (17.9)	142.2 (21.2)	224.1 (26.0)	226.5 (26.6)
L	140.6 (17.8)	141.2 (18.5)	228.3 (28.6)	231.1 (31.3)
Stats	$F(1, 31) = 0.009$; $p = 0.924$ (ns)	$F(1, 30) = 0.02$; $p = 0.888$ (ns)	$F(1, 19) = 0.125$; $p = 0.728$ (ns)	$F(1, 19) = 0.130$; $p = 0.722$ (ns)

Table 5: Means, standard deviations and statistical results of F0 for the final syllable of Mambila High-toned utterances for two different sentence lengths, Short and Long

	Male	Female
Mean	F0-final (SD)	F0-final (SD)
S	139.1 (20.0)	221.5 (24.2)
L	140.4 (19.5)	222.6 (24.2)
Statistic	$F(1, 31) = 0.038$; $p = 0.846$ (ns)	$F(1, 19) = 0.10$; $p = 0.922$ (ns)

would be free to rise in order to accommodate declination in a longer utterance where the end point is specified. While this may be the case for H in Chumburung, in Mambila, since neither tone 4 nor tone 1 is scaled, an alternative suggestion is that both start and end points are specified; this corresponds to Snider's proposal for Chumburung L, that is, rather than the rate of declination being constant or predetermined in Mambila and Chumburung, it may be seen as a byproduct of tone specifications.

4 Experiment 4, Polar Questions in Mambila

Polar (Yes/No) questions in Mambila take the same word order as corresponding declarative statements, and there is no alternative order as is permitted in some languages. They are obligatorily marked by the addition of a sentence final particle, wā; if the question is emphatic, the marker is wò. Of course, the presence of a question particle does not preclude the possibility of pitch signalling questions: register raising or expansion, or a rise in pitch over the terminal part of the sentence are all possible manipulations of pitch that, except perhaps for the latter, would not necessarily threaten tone contrasts. More generally, one might argue that contextual and pragmatic concerns would lessen the possibility of intonation based pitch manipulations having a detrimental effect on tone contrasts. The question thus arises whether Mambila, despite the general absence of pitch marking for declaratives, marks interrogatives through pitch differences.

The possibility of differences in intonation between declarative utterances and associated polar questions was again investigated using like-tone sentences, one declarative, one the associated polar question (originally reported in Connell 2005). The sentence pair on tone 1, is given as an example at (13).

(13) bɔ́   bú   kúkúm   témá   ké   ŋgwéh   (wā)
     3PSBJ 3SOBJ cassava   send   PRP   NEG   (Q)
     They didn't send the cassava to him. (?)

Figure 9 shows pitch tracks for this sentence pair, with the declarative form in the top panel and the question form, with the Q-marker wā (tone 2), in the bottom.[7]

---

[7] All pitch tracks were produced using Praat 5.4 (Boersma & Wineenk 2015).

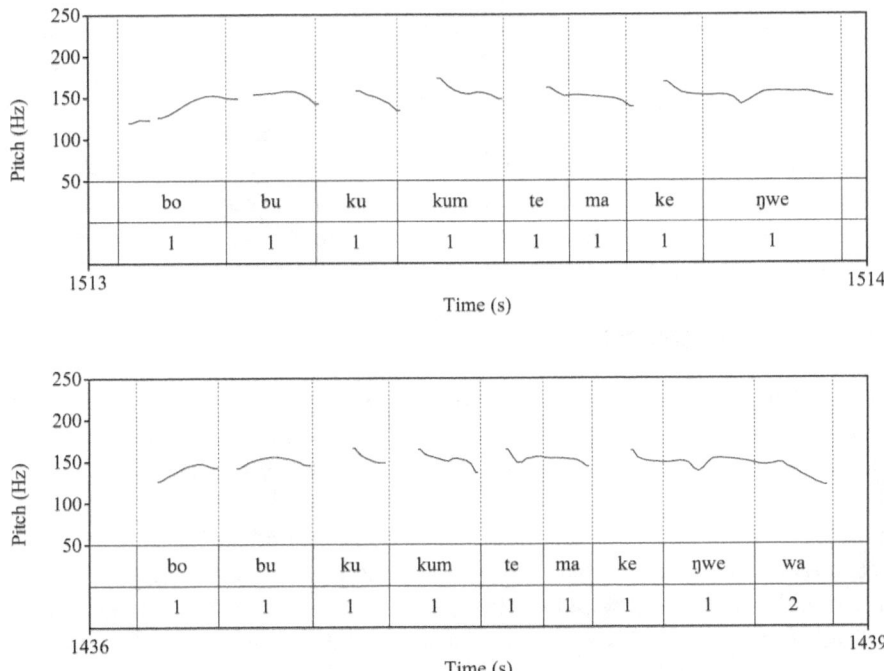

Figure 9: Pitch traces for the sentence pair bɔ́ bú kúkúm témá ké ŋgwéh (top) and bɔ́ bú kúkúm témá ké ŋgwéh wā (bottom). (Speaker BP, male)

Measurements of F0 were taken for each syllable and an analysis of variance was run on the data to compare, syllable by syllable, the F0 of statements vs questions. Six hundred pairs of syllables (4 speakers × 5 repetitions × 30 syllables) were compared in total. Overall, no statistically significant differences were found for the pairs of sentences of like-tone sequences. There were occasional individual pairs of syllables which did show a significant difference, but these were not systematic and cannot taken as indicative of a difference in pitch realization between statements and questions. Given the results of earlier work, these sentences were not tested for declination; however based on the results obtained, any downtrend that does exist must be present in both questions and statements.

A fifth sentence pair allowed comparison of mixed tone utterances, where the sentence wē ŋgie cār bē (wā), i.e. 2-3-2-2(-2) was used.[8] With three of the

---

[8] Literally, 'Fire burn monkey hand (Q)'. The collocation 'cār bē' bears comment; in order to maintain the desired tone sequence the intended reading was 'monkey hand' rather than 'monkey's hand' as the latter would have involved an added tone 4 (see §2.2.1 above). At least one speaker consistently used the latter reading; to accommodate this measurements were taken earlier in the syllable to recognize the tone 2 target.

four speakers, again there were no significant differences in F0 between corresponding syllables of the statement and question. For one speaker (SM), however, the step between tones 2 and 3 was smaller in questions, i.e. a narrowing of the register. This result is remarkable on two counts: first, a narrower register for questions, though not unheard of, is not expected; and second, this particular speaker already operates with a relatively narrow range. These points aside, since only one speaker showed this narrowing, it is difficult to see this as a strategy to differentiate polar questions and statements in Mambila.

4.1 Question particle wā

A few remarks as to the realization of the question marker wā are of interest. This is described as bearing an inherent tone 2 by Mouh & Perrin (1995; Mouh per. comm.) It is sometimes realized in the data here with a slight fall, typically from tone 2 to the range of tone 3; this occurs only infrequently. It might be possible to suggest this to be the influence of a L boundary tone, however this leaves two problems, first that it does not fall to the level one might expect of a L% (i.e. the bottom of the pitch range), and second is its infrequency. However, wā itself, could arguably be seen as a segmental manifestation of intonation. This possibility is taken up in the concluding section, below.

4.2 Summary

The results presented here indicate declarative sentences and the associated polar questions are not differentiated in Ba Mambila by pitch. A functional explanation may be offered for this, that greater flexibility in the realization of tone, given the dense nature of the tonal space in Mambila, would potentially endanger the stability of tone contrasts. It is worth noting however that pitch manipulations such as overall register shift or expansion could potentially be used without endangering tone contrasts, yet these variations are absent. A structural, as opposed to functional, account is discussed in §7.

5 Content questions

Content questions are coded in Mambila through use of specific question markers. These include: nī 'who'; kī 'what'; hī 'where'; hêh 'when'; nân 'how'; mèn 'how many'; mé ŋgī 'why' (or dé kì; the former is more polite, the latter more demanding in its pragmatics). Perrin (ms) reports question markers occur clause finally, and wā is not used, as in the following example (and using her transcription conventions):

(14) lé   haá   naâ   wò   nēì?
     PST   give PST   2SG Q
     Who gave (it) to you?

Perrin does not specify where these data were collected, but as mentioned earlier, her work was on Tungba, spoken at Gembu, and Ba as spoken at Sonkolong.

In Somié (also recognized as Ba Mambila), Q-words for content questions are found in-situ, i.e. in the grammatical slot being questioned, and the Q-marker wā still appears finally; e.g.

(15) nī   lé   hǎ   nā   wò   wā?
     Q   PST   give PST   2SG Q
     Who gave (it) to you?

Perrin does, though, present her examples as having neutral focus; similarly, when investigating interrogatives in Somié, our language assistants were asked to supply 'basic' or 'default' structures, so we presume the differences in structure are (sub-)dialectal and not due to pragmatic factors.

The possible role of F0 in the realization of Mambila question intonation was investigated using a basic set of sentences comprised of like-tone sequences, as in previous work and, also as in previous work, one sentence which alternated tone 1 and tone 4 was included, to give a total of five base sentences. These were then adapted to form questions which asked for the subject or the object, using the question markers ní 'who', kī 'what', and hī 'where' from the above possibilities. These introduced tone-induced pitch variations into the like-tone sentences, such that the pairs of sentences (question and answer) were neither segmentally nor tonally identical (i.e. as was the case for the polar questions described above); paired sentences however did contain a portion of shared material.

The sentences were arranged to form mini-dialogues which were played out in two groups of three people each, such that Speaker A said the question to Speaker B, who answered and then asked the question of Speaker C; Speaker C answered and the repeated the question to Speaker A, who in turn answered.[9] This process was repeated for each of the five sentence sets, for both subject

---

[9] This method is adopted from Myers (1996).

and object questions. The alternating tone sentence formed the basis of three questions, asking for the subject, for the object, and for the object of a preposition. Sentence sets were arranged in a randomized list, and five repetitions were recorded. An example of the procedure, using the tone 3 sentences and questioning the subject is given in (16). Only the first portion is morphologically glossed. For analysis purposes, as discussed below, the tonally identical shared portion in this pair is 'bele tele yaga tele'.

(16) Example sentence (tone 3), Subject questioned:

Speaker A: Q   nī   mé   bele   tele   yaga   tele   wā
               Q   REL   shave   father wash   father Q
               'Who washed and shaved the father?'

Speaker B: A   kwer   bele   tele   yaga   tele
               slave shave   father wash   father
               'The slave washed and shaved the father.'

Speaker B: Q   nī mé bele tele yaga tele wā?
               'Who washed and shaved the father?'

Speaker C: A   kwer bele tele yaga tele.
               'The slave washed and shaved the father.'

Speaker C: Q   nī mé bele tele yaga tele wā?
               'Who washed and shaved the father?'

Speaker A: A   kwer bele tele yaga tele.
               'The slave washed and shaved the father.'

Recording and analysis followed standard procedures, as with the previously reported work, including use of high quality digital recording equipment.[10] The pitch tracks in Figure 10 represent the question and answer for the pair of sentences in (16), as produced by speaker MD (female).

The results reported here are based on one of the two groups, comprised of two female speakers (VM and MD) and one male (CD), each of whom had participated in some or all of the studies reported above. Several measurements were taken (e.g. F0 at various points within the sentence, final vowel duration); of relevance here is mean F0 of the shared portions of the sentence pairs. An analysis of variance was run to test for differences between the mean F0 of

---

[10] A report of this work was presented at WOCAL8, Kyoto, as Connell & Im (2015). I am grateful to Hannah Im for her input to the present chapter.

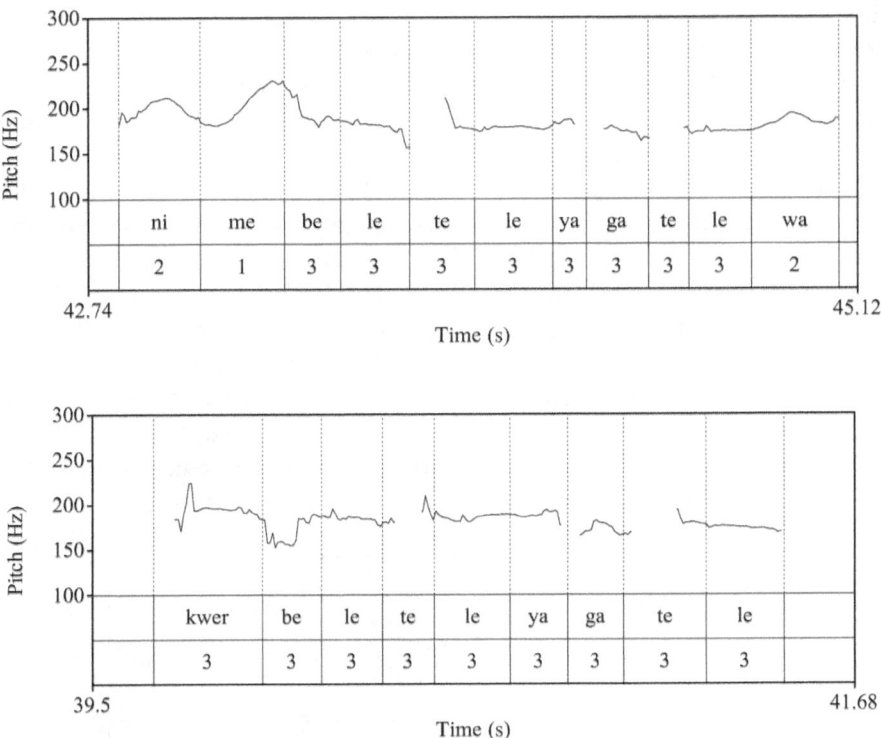

Figure 10: The sentence pair nī mé bele tele yaga tele wā? Who washed and shaved the father? (top) and kwer bele tele yaga tele. 'The slave washed and shaved the father.' (bottom) (Speaker MD, female)

question vs statement of the shared portions of the utterances. A significant difference between the two would indicate F0 is used to signal content-Qs, through raising (or lowering) the pitch range. The results are given in Table 6.

Table 6: Mean F0 of Questions and Answers for tones 3 and 4 compared, with significance levels

	Mean F0 (SE) of Q	Mean F0 (SE) of A	Significance Level
CD 3	150.00 (1.770)	141.93 (1.375)	$p = 0.002$
CD 4	135.91 (2.698)	131.56 (2.001)	$p = 0.212$
VM 3	200.46 (2.152)	194.32 (2.351)	$p = 0.070$
VM 4	180.84 (2.781)	174.72 (1.284)	$p = 0.061$
MD 3	184.24 (1.520)	183.62 (1.797)	$p = 0.794$
MD 4	167.07 (2.187)	161.30 (1.907)	$p = 0.062$

The results of the comparison of the shared portions of the utterance pairs for tones 3 and 4, shown in Table 6 showed in only one of the six comparisons is significance achieved (speaker CD, for tone 3; p = 0.002).[11] In short, like polar questions, content questions in Mambila appear not to be differentiated from corresponding statements by pitch.

Yet further confirmation of this is reflected in the pitch curves of the tone 4 sentence pair shown in Figure 11. The question form of this pair, ní bɔ̀ bùnɔ̀ mò gwàn bèh wā? Who don't my enemies like?', begins with ní 'who' and ends with wā (Q); the intervening content, bɔ̀ bùnɔ̀ mò mì gwàn bèh 'My enemies don't like me.' is entirely on tone 4 and also constitutes the statement, or reply. It is noticeable that the shared tone 4 portion of the two sentences is spoken on approximately the same pitch (the mean F0s are 131 Hz for the question and 133 Hz for the statement), and both show a slight downtrend; for the statement this lowering continues across the last two syllables of the sentence, but in the presence of final wā, is not present in the question form.

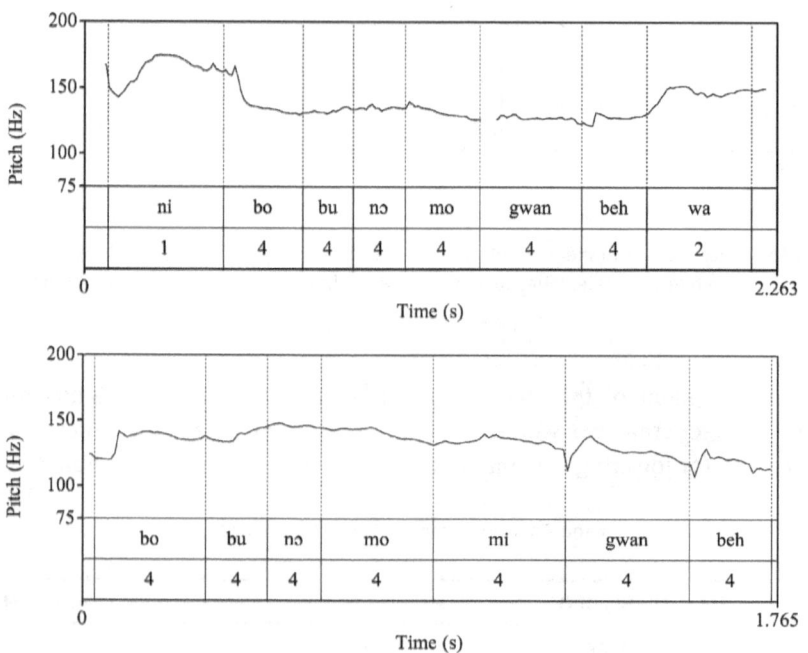

Figure 11: The sentence pair ní bɔ̀ bùnɔ̀ mò gwàn bèh wā? 'Who don't my enemies like? (top) and bɔ̀ bùnɔ̀ mò mì gwàn bèh 'My enemies don't like me.' (bottom). (Speaker CD, male)

---

[11] Comparison of the mean F0 of the entire utterance did show differences, but given the results of the shared portions these can be safely attributed to the contribution of the tone 1 and tone 2 question words to the overall F0. In confirmation of this, comparison of the tone 2 sentences showed no significant difference between questions and statements for any of the speakers.

6 Tone and intonation in Mambila

The results of the experiments contributing to this chapter show that pitch variations play a minor role at best in marking Mambila sentence types. Declination and/or final lowering appear to be present in lower tone contexts (tones 3 and 4, and more consistently in tone 4) in declarative sentences, but declination is present in questions in these tone contexts as well. Polar questions showed no significant difference in pitch relative to corresponding statements; the same is true of content questions where the words and tonal structures are comparable. In this respect Mambila is similar to Yoruba (Connell & Ladd 1991). Where content questions and statements differ in Mambila is in the absence of a steeper fall over the last two syllables (final lowering) in the lower tone contexts in questions. Mambila differs in this respect from Yoruba, where questions too show a final fall in L tone contexts. In Yoruba however the Q-marker (sẹ́ or ńjẹ́) occurs sentence initially whereas, as seen, in Mambila the Q-marker wā is final, removing the environment for a final fall. This is evident in Figure 11, where bèh shows a slight fall when final (Fig 11, right panel) but maintains a level trajectory when followed by wā (left panel).

The question then arises as to whether the final lowering is the implementation of a L boundary tone (L%); if so its presence must be dependent on the specification of the final lexical tone: it may mark the intonational phrase in the two lower tone contexts (or at least tone 4), but not the higher tones. This raises the question as to whether the two upper tones are marked by a H%. If so, it would offer an interesting, albeit limited, symmetry with the tone alternations induced by grammatical tones reported in §2 with imperative and negative formation, in which upper level tones alternate to tone one (H) and lower level tones to tone 4 (L). There is, though, little positive evidence to support this; e.g. tones 1 and 2 do not differ markedly in their realization when occurring finally or prepausally compared to when they are not, and in particular tone 2 does not rise to the level of tone 1. Similarly, tone 3 does not fall as low as tone 4 in the presence of an ostensible L%. (In addition at least some speakers occasionally showed what appeared to be final lowering – a relatively steep fall over the last syllable or two – in tone 2 sentences.) Apart from these concerns, the degree of inconsistency across speakers within tone contexts must be noted. This may not be particularly unusual; Connell & Ladd (1991) note this in their discussion of Yoruba, as does Myers (1996) for Chichewa. This suggests that if present, boundary tones may be optional. Gussenhoven (2004), citing data from Venlo Dutch, along with data from a number of other languages, advocates this possibility, contrary to the more accepted view that they are obligatory. It is not clear however that Gussenhoven would use their optionality as an explanation for variation of the sort seen in Mambila; rather, an interesting alternative also suggested by Gussenhoven (2004) may be considered: just as some people are better swimmers or better writers than others, some speakers may have better control over the phonetic implementation of their phonological representations. For Chichewa, Myers suggests that boundary tones are associated to a higher node than lexical tones, and this presumably accounts for their transparency with respect to interactions between adjacent tones within an intonational phrase, as well as influences on the entire phrase such as register raising or expansion. The same is possibly true of Mambila since one of the effects of L% might be seen as inducing declination in tone 4.

The prevailing view of intonational phonology (see Ladd 2008 for an overview), divides the phonological effects that determine the pitch contour of an utterance into core tones and edge tones, the former essentially being lexical, and the latter being postlexical and governing phrase level phenomena. There is no insistence that both types of tone appear in a given language; indeed Ladd (2008) speculates that Yoruba may not have edge tones, and that this is reflected in the absence of intonational differences between questions and statements. A similar conclusion may drawn regarding Mambila. The relative absence of pitch phenomena attributable to phonological elements beyond those that may be specified in the lexicon, or predictable from those specified in the lexicon, points strongly in this direction.

It is possible to equate the division of labour between core and edge tones in intonation phonology, at least loosely, with the distinction between lexical and register tones, current in some approaches to tonal phonology, e.g., register tier theory. That is, tones specified on the register tier are in some sense equivalent to edge tones, in that they function postlexically and modulate the realization of tones on the lexical tier (cf. Leben et al 1989). The representation of Mambila tone in such a framework, however, requires use of the tones on both tiers to specify its four lexical tones, presumably leaving register tones unavailable for such postlexical functions as distinguishing questions and statements. While other versions of register tier theory may vary in their handling of the lexical – postlexical divide (see, e.g. several of the contributions to van der Hulst & Snider 1993; Snider 1999), a reasonable expectation would be that the more tones a language has functioning lexically, the more restricted would be the use of register (or edge) tones for marking intonation and other phrase level phenomena.

Finally, to address the question, 'Does Mambila have intonation'? The answer, not surprisingly, depends at least in part on how one defines intonation. Ladd's (2008: 4) definition, "... the use of *suprasegmental* phonetic features to convey "postlexical" or *sentence-level* pragmatic meanings in a *linguistically structured* way" (emphasis in the original) can be taken as standard; by this, and based on the present evidence, we are obliged to conclude that while Mambila does indeed make sentence level distinctions, it does not do so through use of pitch. Ongoing research in Mambila may reveal whether suprasegmental features other than pitch play a role, as e.g. Rialland's (2007) Lax Prosody question marking or Hyman & Monaka's (2011) treatment of intonational phenomena in Shekgalagari, and while it is still premature to draw conclusions, indications thus far seem to show features such as duration and intensity are not used in marking such contrasts in Mambila. A more restrictive definition of intonation such as that at least implicit in the various contributions to Jun (2005) or in Beckman & Venditti (2011), and which forms the basis of the ToBI transcription system, is apparently exclusive even of suprasegmental features other than pitch. But, in Mambila the difference between question types and declaratives is only marked segmentally, with a final Q-marker, wā. This may fit in the constellation of features identified by Rialland (where a final low vowel is found to mark interrogatives in some languages), but it is excluded in Ladd's insistence on suprasegmental rather than segmental marking of intonation, and the ToBI reliance only on pitch. So in order to say Mambila 'has intonation', it would be necessary to adopt a broader definition, one that permits segmental marking of discourse functions and as such would be based in function, not in structure.

7 Summary

In this chapter I have looked at a possible intonational role or roles for pitch in distinguishing different sentence types. Simple declaratives, F0 scaling with respect to sentence length, polar questions vs corresponding declaratives, and content questions compared to associated statements have all been examined, using as a basis, sentences constructed of words bearing the same tone. With the tones within a sentence being phonologically lexically equivalent, pitch differences found will be due to post-lexical effects. Unlike the other languages discussed in this volume, few have been found. The possibility of attributing the final fall found over the last two syllables of low tone sequences to final lowering, reflecting a L%, was considered but seen as unlikely; arguments for a H% governing phrase boundaries for the upper tones are even less convincing. Still the work presented here, while covering those areas where exploitation of pitch differences might be most expected, represents only a beginning. Other areas, such as a role for pitch in signalling the clause structure of complex sentence structures, or indeed the detailed examination of other suprasegmental features such as duration and intensity are waiting to be examined.

Acknowledgements

The research contributing to this paper was conducted over a period of approximately two decades; as a result there are more than the usual number of people and agencies whose contribution to the ongoing investigation deserve mention. Inevitably some may be omitted. Funding has come from different sources at different times. Much of the research was done while conducting fieldwork associated with ESRC grant R000237450 (1997–2000) to the author and AHRC grant 112306 (2006–2009) to David Zeitlyn, both of which projects were aimed at the situation of language endangerment in the Mambiloid region, but permitted other work to be done during 'down time'. Despite the extended period, the Mambila speakers I have worked with have remained mostly the same: not for the first time (nor the last) I express my gratitude to Begimi Jean, Ciebeh Daniel, Lelo Lilianne, Mbiti Donique, Sondue Michel and Veyo Marguerite for their continued interest and assistance; to the people of Somié for their welcoming nature; and to David Zeitlyn for continued collaboration working on Mambila and Mambiloid. Thanks are also due to Hannah Im for timely help with statistical and other matters, and to an anonymous reviewer whose comments and suggestions, though not adopted in their entirety, resulted in making this a better paper. Last, though by no means least, I'm grateful to Annie Rialland and Laura Downing for the invitation to contribute to this volume, for their patience and suggestions along the way, and their work in putting this much needed volume together.

References

Beckman, Mary E. & Jennifer J. Venditti. 2011. Intonation. In John Goldsmith, Jason Riggle & Alan C. L. Yu (eds.), *The Handbook of Phonological Theory*, 2nd edition. Oxford: Blackwell. Pp. 485–532.

Boersma, Paul & David Wineenk. 2015. Praat: Doing phonetics by computer [Computer program]. Version 5.4.17, retrieved 20 August 2015. http:// www.praat.org/

Clements, George N. 1990. The status of register in intonation theory: comments on the papers by Ladd and by Inkelas and Leben. In M. Beckman and J. Kingston (Ed.), *Papers in Laboratory Phonology I: Between the grammar and physics of speech*. Cambridge: C.U.P. Pp. 58–71.

Clements, George N. & Annie Rialland. 2008. Africa as a phonological area. In Bernd Heine & Derek Nurse (Eds.) *A Linguistic Geography of Africa*. Cambridge: Cambridge University Press. Pp. 36–85.

Connell, Bruce. 1999a. Four tones and downtrend: a preliminary report on pitch realization in Mambila. In P. F. A. Kotey (Ed.), *New Dimensions in African Linguistics and Languages. Trends in African Linguistics, Vol. 3*. Trenton, N.J.: Africa World Press. Pp. 75–88.

Connell, Bruce. 1999b. Mid tone downtrends in Mambila. Paper presented to the 7th Manchester Phonology Meeting, May 1999.

Connell, Bruce. 1999c. Downdrift, declination and final lowering in Mambila. Poster presentation, 6th Conference on Laboratory Phonology, York University, York, U.K, July 1999.

Connell, Bruce. 2002a. Downdrift, downstep and declination. In U. Gut, & D. Gibbon (Eds.), *Typology of African Prosodic Systems*. Bielefeld: University of Bielefeld. www.spectrum.uni-bielefeld.de/BEST/Research/TAPS/proceedings.html.

Connell, Bruce. 2002b. Tone languages and the universality of intrinsic F0: Evidence from Africa. *Journal of Phonetics, 30:* 101–129.

Connell, Bruce. 2003. Pitch realization and the four tones of Mambila. In S. Kaji (ed.) *Cross-Linguistic Studies of Tonal Phenomena: Historical development, phonetics of tone, and descriptive studies*. Tokyo: Research Institute for the Language and Cultures of Asia and Africa. Pp. 181–197.

Connell, Bruce. 2004. Tone, utterance length and F0 Scaling. In B. Bel & I. Marlien (eds.) *International Symposium on Tonal Aspects of Languages: Emphasis on tone languages. Proceedings*. Beijing: Institute of Linguistics, Chinese Academy of Social Sciences. Pp. 41–43.

Connell, Bruce. 2011. Downstep. In M. van Oorstendorp et al (eds.). *Companion to Phonology*. Oxford: Blackwell Publishing. Pp. 824–847.

Connell, Bruce & Hannah Im. 2015. Question prosody in Mambila. Paper presented at the 8th World Congress of African Linguistics, Kyoto, Japan, 20–24 August 2015.

Cooper, William E. & John M. Sorenson. 1981. *Fundamental Frequency in Sentence Production*. Heidelberg: Springer.

Gussenhoven, Carlos. 2004. *The Phonology of Tone and Intonation*. Cambridge: Cambridge University Press.

't Hart, Johan. 1979. Explorations in automatic stylization of F0 curves. *IPO Annual Progress Report, 14:* 61–65.

Herman, Rebecca. 1996. Final lowering in Kipare. *Phonology 13:* 171–196.

Hulst, Harry v. d. & Keith Snider (eds.). 1993. *The Phonology of Tone. The representation of tonal register*. Berlin: Mouton de Gruyter.

Hyman, Larry M. & Kemmonye C. Monaka. 2011. Tonal and non-tonal intonation in Shekgalagari. In Sónia Frota, Gorka Elordieta & Pilar Prieto (eds.), *Prosodic categories: Production, perception and comprehension*, 267–290. Dordrecht: Springer.

Inkelas, Sharon, & Leben, William R. 1990. Where phonology and phonetics intersect: the case of Hausa intonation. In Mary E. Beckman, & John Kingston (Ed.), *Papers in Laboratory Phonology I: Between the grammar and physics of speech* (pp. 17–34). Cambridge: C.U.P.

Jun, Sun-Ah (ed.) *Prosodic Typology: The Phonology of Intonation and Phrasing*. Oxford: Oxford University Press.

Ladd, D. Robert. 2008. *Intonational Phonology (2nd Edition)*. Cambridge: Cambridge University Press.

Ladd, D. Robert & Catherine Johnson. 1987. 'Metrical' factors in the scaling of sentence-initial accent peaks. *Phonetica, 44:* 238–245.

Laniran, Yetunde. 1992. Intonation in a tone language: the phonetic implementation of tone in Yoruba. Ph.D., Cornell.

Leben, William R., Sharon Inkelas & Mark Cobler. 1989. Phrases and phrase tones in Hausa. In Newman, P. & R. Botne (eds.) *Current Approaches to African Linguistics (vol. 5)*. Dordrecht: Foris, 45–61.

Liberman, Mark & Janet Pierrehumbert. 1984. Intonational invariance under changes in pitch range and length. In Aronoff, M. & R. Oehrle (eds.) *Language and Sound Structure*. Cambridge MA: MIT. Pp. 157–233.

Lindau, Mona. 1986. Testing a model of intonation in a tone language. *Journal of the Acoustical Society of America, 80:* 757–764.

Mouh, Marc & Mona Perrin. 1995. *Lexique mambila–français*. Yaoundé: SIL.

Myers, Scott. 1996. Boundary tones and the phonetic implementation of tone in Chichewa. *Studies in African Linguistics 25*: 29–60.

Perrin, Mona. 1974. Mambila. In J. Bendor-Samuel (Ed.), *Ten Nigerian Tone Systems*. Jos: Summer Institute of Linguistics. Pp. 93–108.

Perrin, Mona. 1991. The tone system in Mambila: some further comments. Yaoundé: SIL.

Perrin, Mona (ms) Morphemes, Words and Phrases in Mambila. Preliminary draft.

Perrin, Mona & Margaret Hill. 1969. *Mambila (Parler d'Atta): Description phonologique*. Yaoundé: Université Fédérale du Cameroun.

Pierrehumbert, Janet & Mary Beckman. 1988. *Japanese Tone Structure*. Cambridge MA: MIT Press.

Rialland, Annie. 2007. Question prosody: An African perspective. In Tomas Riad & Carlos Gussenhoven (Eds.). *Tones and Tunes Volume 1: Typological studies in sentence prosody*. Berlin: Mouton de Gruyter. Pp. 35–62.

Snider, Keith. 1998. Tone and utterance length in Chumburung: An instrumental study. Paper presented at the 28th Colloquium on African Languages and Linguistics. Leiden.

Snider, Keith. 1999. *The Geometry and Features of Tone*. Dallas: Summer Institute of Linguistics.

Welmers, William. 1973. *African Language Structures*. Berkeley: University of California Press.

Emmanuel-Moselly Makasso, Fatima Hamlaoui, and Seunghun J. Lee
Aspects of the intonational phonology of Bàsàá

Abstract: Two major aspects of the intonational phonology of Bàsàá, a Northwest Bantu language spoken in Southern Cameroon with an underlying opposition between high, low and toneless tone bearing units, are presented in this chapter. First, two tonal processes, high tone spreading (HTS) and falling tone simplification (FTS), show sensitivities to prosodic domains: the phonological phrase and the intonational phrase, respectively. Second, tones do not seem to be affected by sentence modalities or information structure. Declarative sentences and *yes-no* questions show nearly identical intonation patterns, and varying the location of focus in a sentence does not significantly affect sentence prosody either. So far, Bàsàá is a language that shows little interaction between tone and intonation.

Keywords: Bàsàá, Tone and tone rules, Intonation, Prosodic structure, Absence of focus marking

1 Introduction

This chapter presents tonal and intonational aspects of Bàsàá, a narrow Bantu language (A43 in Guthrie's classification), spoken by approximatively 300,000 people (SIL 2005, Lewis et al. (2015)) in southern Cameroon. Most of the Bàsàá speakers are found in the Littoral Region – within the Sanaga Maritime, the Wourri and the Nkam divisions – and in the Center Region of Cameroon – within the Nyong and Kelle Divisions. Bàsàá is also used as a language of trade with neighboring and related ethnic groups, like the Bakoko and the Bati. In this chapter we concentrate on Bàsàá as it is spoken in Nyong and Kelle. A number of studies on Bàsàá report and analyze tonal and segmental processes (Bot ba Njock, 1970; Lemb and De Gastines, 1973; Dimmendaal, 1988; Bitjaa Kody, 1993; Hyman, 2003; Makasso, 2008; Hamlaoui et al., 2014; Hamlaoui and Szendrői, 2015). An overview of the sound system appears in Makasso and Lee (2015).

Emmanuel-Moselly Makasso and **Fatima Hamlaoui**, Centre for General Linguistics (ZAS) Berlin
Seunghun J. Lee, International Christian University, Tokyo University of Venda, Thohoyandou

DOI 10.1515/9783110503524-006

First, we will present the basic features of the Bàsàá tonal system and tonal processes. After discussing new findings from data on intonation with respect to sentence modality, the (in-)sensitivity of intonation to information structure will be presented.

2 Tone

2.1 Tonal inventory

Bàsàá is a tonal language. The pitch of a word can thus determine its core-meaning (Yip, 2007). The studies that have addressed the tonal aspects of this Northwest Bantu language generally agree on the fact that Bàsàá underlyingly distinguishes high-toned (H) and low-toned (L) tone bearing units (TBUs). Additionally, certain tense affixes, verbal extensions and noun-class prefixes have no underlying tone of their own, suggesting that Bàsàá displays an underlying ternary opposition between H, L and Ø. For example, the Past 1 tense marker (-n-) is an underlyingly toneless TBU (Bitjaa Kody, 1993), which acquires its tone from an immediately preceding TBU. This tense marker thus surfaces with a H tone if it is preceded by a H-toned subject marker, as in (1)a. After a L-toned subject marker as in (1)b, the Past 1 marker surfaces with a L tone that is inserted by default.[1]

(1)   a.   ɓ-ɔ̀r   ɓá-ń-téhé   ɓ-ɔ́ɔ́ŋgé
           2-people   2.AGR-PST1-see   2-children
           'The people saw the children.'

       b.   sóɣól   à-ǹ-téhé   ɓ-ɔ́ɔ́ŋgé
           1.grandfather   1.AGR-PST1-see   2-children
           'The grandfather saw the children.'

As a result of a number of tonal processes, on the surface Bàsàá shows a 5-way tonal opposition: H, L, ↓H (called "downstepped" H), LH, HL. Minimal tonal contrasts are given in Fig. 1.

---

[1] Abbreviations: AGR: agreement, AUG: augment, CONN: connective, DEM: demonstrative, FTS: falling tone simplification, HTS: High tone spread, LOC: locative, PRES: present, PRO: pronoun, PST: past

H tone		L tone		HL tone		LH tone	
jáχ	'to annoy'	jàχ	'also'				
ɓáŋ	'to tolerate'	ɓàŋ	'to make'				
ɓó:	'to move out'	ɓò:	'(smell) bad'			ɓŏ:	'nine'
		tù:	'to be unable to cut'	tû:	'shoulder (CL7)'		
		ɲɔ̀:	'to copulate'			ɲɔ̌:	'snake (CL9)'
				ɓáŋgà	'drug (CL7)'	ɓàŋgá	'great'

Figure 1: Tonal Minimal Pairs in Bàsàá (Makasso and Lee, 2015)

Register lowering of a H tone (↓H) often emerges under the influence of a preceding delinked or unaffiliated (floating) L tone, as in (2).

(2) ɓ-ɔ̀ɔŋέ ɓá-ḿ-↓ɓárá m-áŋgòlò má ɓ-á↓sáŋ.
    ɓ-ɔɔŋέ ɓa-ḿ`-ɓárá   m-áŋgòlò   má   ɓ-àsáŋ
    2-children 2.AGR-PRES-take 6-mangoes 6.CONN 2-fathers
    'The children take the mangoes of the fathers.'

The first downstep in *ɓá-ḿ-↓ɓárá* '2.AGR-PRES-take' is created by a floating L tone introduced by the tense marker, while the second downstep in *ɓá↓sáŋ* '2-fathers' is the result of an extension of the H from the preceding connective marker, onto the first TBU of /ɓàsáŋ/. This spreading process delinks the underlying L tone, which in turn lowers the following H. In contrast, in (1)a, the fact that no downstep is observed on the TBU following the toneless *-n-* further indicates that no underlying L tone is carried by this tense marker.

As the word-pairs in (3) illustrate, Bàsàá also has contrastive vowel length.

(3) a. lɔ́ 'to come' ~ lɔ́ɔ́ 'to surpass'

    b. lá 'to taste' ~ láá 'how'

    c. kúr 'blow' ~ kúúr 'maritime tortoise'

    d. kàr 'to chase away' ~ kààr 'book'

In contrast with many of its relatives, Bàsàá does not have a general restriction on tone contours; both falling (HL) and rising (LH) contours are allowed. Tonal contours are however restricted to bimoraic syllables, suggesting that the mora (and not the syllable) is the TBU, and that each mora can be represented with a level tone. According to Bitjaa Kody (1993), HL tones are derived either synchronically through the "doubling" of an underlying H or L or diachronically, through the loss of a syllable nucleus. The former process is illustrated in (4), where the H of the first syllable of the verb 'to help' spreads onto the second syllable – underlyingly specified as L – which, as a result, surfaces with a falling tone. The latter process is illustrated in (5), where the historical loss of a syllable resulted in the delinking of a L tone which reassociates to the left, and creates a falling tone on the remaining syllable of the noun stem 'udder'.

(4)   -hól + -à → hólâ 'to help' (High Tone Spreading)

(5)   Proto Bantu *-bédè → Bàsàá -bê 'udder'

As for LH tones, they result from the loss of a final vowel (6) or a medial vowel (7) (Bitjaa Kody, 1993).

(6)   nàɲí (Western dialect) → nǎŋ (Eastern dialect) 'bed'

(7)   lì- + -áy → jǎy 'flyswatter'

Bisyllabic word stems exhibit the four surface tonal patterns illustrated in (8) to (11) respectively: HH, LH, LL, and H-HL (Hyman, 2003). The H-HL pattern in (11) results from an extension of the initial H to the right (High Tone Spreading).

(8)   a.   /kwémbé/ → [kwémbé] 'box'

      b.   /sókól/ → [sóɣól] 'grandfather'

(9)   a.   /hi-nùní/ → [rìnùní] 'bird'

      b.   /nùká/ → [nùɣá] 'animal'

(10) a.   /lɔ̀lɔ̀/ → [lɔ̀lɔ̀] 'duck'

      b.   /ma-kàlà/ → [màkàlà] 'doughnuts'

(11) a.   /kɛ́mbɛ̀/ → [kɛ́mbɛ̂] 'goat'

      b.   /li-pɛ́hɛ̀l/ → [lìpɛ́hɛ̂l] 'comb'

No automatic prominence on the penultimate or final vowel is observed in Bàsàá. If anything, segmental contrasts suggest that the initial syllable of a stem has a priviledged prosodic status as the word's head (Hyman, 2003). No prosodic correlates of this status as a word head has however been identified so far.[2]

Now that we have laid out some basic facts concerning the tonal system of Bàsàá, let us turn to two major tonal processes, which are the main source of contour tones and downstepped H tones: High Tone Spreading (Dimmendaal, 1988; Hyman, 2003; Hamlaoui et al., 2014) and Falling Tone Simplification (Bitjaa Kody, 1993; Hamlaoui and Szendrői, 2015).

2.2 Tonal rules and prosodic structure

According to Hyman (2003), High Tone Spreading (HTS) is the "major tone rule in present-day Bàsàá". HTS consists in an underlying H tone associating to one or more L/Ø toned TBUs to its right. This tonal rule applies both at the word and phrasal level. At the word level, HTS applies both within the root, as shown in (11), and from a root to one or more derivational suffixes, as shown with the causative extension in (12) (Dimmendaal, 1988; Hyman, 2003).[3]

(12)   a.   hól + V̀s → húlûs – 'to make sharpen'

   b.   lék + V̀s → lígîs – 'to make warm up'

In Hamlaoui et al. (2014), we argue that HTS, and in particular its bounded nature, provides a window into the prosodic structuring of clauses into separate phonological phrases (noted ϕ), the level of the prosodic hierarchy corresponding to (lexical) syntactic phrases (Selkirk, 1995; Truckenbrodt, 1999). More precisely, we propose that it allows us to detect the right edge of ϕs.

Typically, HTS applies between a verb and a phrase that immediately follows it, suggesting that they form a single phonological phrase.[4] When the post-verbal

---

[2] As pointed out to us by an anonymous reviewer, it is unclear whether segmental contrasts indicate the strong/head status of the initial syllable of a stem. Bantu languages that display penultimate lengthening, such as Chichewa, also display more segmental contrasts in initial position.

[3] Examples in (12) show vowel raising in Bàsàá. For further details, see Makasso and Lee (2015) and references therein.

[4] There are a few exeptions to this generalization. We refer the interested reader to Hyman and Lionnet (2012) on Abo (Bantu, A42), a close relative of Bàsàá, as well as to Makasso (2012). A number of cases are discussed in which the verb fails to assign a H to the word that follows it. We also refer the reader to Hamlaoui et al. (2014) for a detailed discussion of the application of HTS within various types of phrases.

phrase has an underlying LH tonal pattern, as "animal" in (13), the L tone is delinked and creates a downstep on the following H.

(13) (sóɣól)_φ (à-ǹ-téhé nú⁺ɣá)_φ.
 sóɣól   à-nˊ-téhé   nùɣá
 1.grandfather   1.AGR-PST1-see   7.animal
 'The grandfather saw the animal.'

When the post-verbal phrase is monosyllabic and carries a L tone, as "today" in (14), HTS creates a HL tone on that syllable.

(14) (m-ùr)_φ (à-ń-sèβél lên)_φ.
 m-ùr   à-ń-sèβél   lɛ̀n
 1-man   1.AGR-PRS-call   today
 'The man calls today.'

Note that as briefly illustrated by examples (13) and (14), the syntactic nature of the phrase that follows the verb (i.e. argument or adjunct) does not affect the application of HTS (see Hamlaoui et al., 2014, for more detail on this point).

At the clausal level, there are three syntactic contexts in which HTS does not apply. First, HTS never applies between subject and verb, whether the subject is pronominal or not, suggesting that, as expected, separate phonological phrases are formed. This is illustrated in (15) and (16).

(15) (sóɣól)_φ (à-ń-sèβèl)_φ.
 sóɣól   à-ń-sèβèl
 1-grandfather   1.AGR-PRS-call
 'Grandfather calls.'

(16) (n-dʒé)_φ (à-ń-sèβèl)_φ
 n-dʒé   à-ń-sèβèl
 1-who   1.AGR-PRS-call
 'Who calls?'

Second, HTS also fails to apply between post-verbal complements whether they are pronominal or not.[5] In (17), the first post-verbal complement is a noun, while it is a pronoun in (18).

---

[5] See however Hamlaoui et al. (2014) regarding the participation of non-subject *wh*-pronouns to HTS, pointing to their clitic status.

(17) (sóɣól)_φ (à-ǹ-tí ɓɔ́ɔ́ŋgɛ́)_φ (mà-kàlà)_φ.
    sóɣól   à-n´-tí   ɓɔɔŋgɛ́   ma-kàlà
    1.grandfather 1.AGR-PST1-give 2-children 6-doughnuts
    'The grandfather gave the children doughnuts.'

(18) (sóɣól)_φ (à-ǹ-tí ɓɔ́)_φ (mà-kàlà)_φ.
    sóɣól   à-n´-tí   ɓɔ́   ma-kàlà
    1.grandfather 1.AGR-PST1-give 2.PRO 6-doughnuts
    'The grandfather gave them doughnuts.'

Finally, HTS also fails to apply between a complement and a modifier of the verb, as in (19), and between modifiers, as in (20).

(19) (mùr)_φ (à-ń-sèβél m-ááŋgɛ́)_φ (lɛ̀n)_φ.
    mùr   à-ń`-sèβél   m-aaŋgɛ́   lɛ̀n
    1-man 1.AGR-PRS-call   1-child   today
    'The man calls the child today.'

(20) (mùr)_φ (à-ǹ-sé↓βél βí↓sú)_φ (βí ndáp)_φ (lɛ̀n)_φ.
    mùr   à-n´-sèβél   βìsú   βí   ndáp   lɛ̀n
    1.man 1.AGR-PST1-call 8.front 8.CONN 9.house today
    'The man called in front of the house today.'

The domain of application of HTS is both distinct from and smaller than the domain of application of the next tonal process: falling tone simplification (FTS). FTS turns a HL-H sequence into H-↓H. Let us illustrate this process by examining the behavior of the phrase *all the children*, which in isolation or sentence final position (as in (21)) displays a final HL tone.[6]

(21) (, sóɣól à-ǹ-téhɛ́ ɓ-ɔ́ɔ́ŋgɛ́ ɓɔ́-ɓá-sô).
    sóɣól   à-n´-téhɛ́   ɓ-ɔɔŋgɛ́   ɓɔ́-ɓá-só`
    1.grandfather 1.AGR-PST1-see 2-children 2.PRO-2.CONN-all
    'The grandfather saw all the children.'

---

6 The form *sô* "all" derives from the form *sónà* (Lemb and De Gastines, 1973). The loss of the final syllable for certain speakers and in certain contexts creates a floating L tone that either reassociates to the left or to the right, depending on the context.

When the phrase *all the children* is in the subject position and followed by the H-toned subject marker ɓá-, as in (22), the final HL tone simplifies into a H tone and creates downstep on the following H.

(22) (ᵢ ɓ-ɔ̀ɔ̀ŋgɛ́ ɓɔ́-ɓá-só ↓ɓá-ḿ-ɓárá máŋgòlò).
  ɓ-ɔɔŋgɛ́ ɓɔ́-ɓá-só` ɓá-ḿ-ɓárá m-áŋgòlò
  2-children 2.PRO-2.CONN-all 2.AGR-PST1-pick.up 6-mangoes
  'All the chilren picked up the mangoes.'

FTS applies between a verb and the phrase that immediately follows it (23), as well as between any postverbal phrases (24), (25) (when the required tonal configuration is met).

(23) (ᵢ mùr à-ǹ-lɔ́ ↓ hálà).
  mùr à-n´-lɔ́   hálà
  1.man 1.AGR-PST1-arrive like.this
  'The man arrived in this fashion.'

(24) (ᵢ sóɣól à-ǹ-tí ɓ-ɔ́ɔ́ŋgɛ́ ɓɔ́-ɓá-só ↓ ndáp).
  sóɣól à-n´-tí ɓ-ɔɔŋgɛ́ ɓɔ́-ɓá-só` ndáp
  1.grandfather 1.AGR-PST1-buy 2-children 2.PRO-2.CONN-all 9.house
  'The grandfather bought all the children a house.'

(25) (ᵢ Lìŋgòm à-ǹ-ʤɛ́ má-kàlà mɔ́-má-só ↓ kɛ́kɛ̀là).
  Lìŋgòm à-n´-ʤɛ́ ma-kàlà mɔ́-má-só` kɛ́kɛ̀là
  Lingom 1.AGR-PST1-eat 6-doughnuts 6.PRO-6.CONN-all morning
  'Lingom ate all the doughnuts in the morning.' (adapted from Bitjaa Kody)

The data we have examined so far suggests that the domain of application of FTS is the intonational phrase (ι), the level of the prosodic hierarchy that relates to syntactic clauses (Truckenbrodt, 2007; Selkirk, 2011).

 The application of FTS thus reveals what type of clauses form their own ι. In this respect, Bàsàá displays the type of root vs non-root clause asymmetry displayed in well-studied languages like English (a.o Downing, 1970; Selkirk, 2011) and observed in a number of other languages (e.g. Xhosa (Jokweni, 1995), Durban Zulu (Cheng and Downing, 2007)). Complement clauses, introduced by lɛ́ ('that'), do not block the application of FTS, indicating that they do not introduce an ι edge at their left edge. This is illustrated in (26).

(26) (ⁱ mè ń-sòmból jí lɔ́ŋgɛ́ ↓ lɛ́ mbómbó à-ń-lɔ̀)
    mè ń`-sòmból jí   lɔ́ŋgɛ̀ lɛ́   mbómbó   à-n´-lɔ̀
    I   want   to.know   well   that 1.grandmother   1.AGR-PST1-arrive
    'I really want to know that the grandmother came.'
    (Hamlaoui and Szendrői, in press)

Temporal and purpose clauses in post-verbal position also show the application of FTS. In the examples (27) with a temporal clause and (28) with a purpose clause, a surface HL tone on the final mora of the verb is expected. This HL tone would be created when a floating H that accompanies the recent past (PST1) associates with an underlying L on the last mora of these verbs (Makasso, 2012, 2014). However, FTS applies and the final mora of the verbs *arrive* and *leave* has a H tone on the surface, indicating that these clauses do not introduce an ɩ boundary of their own.

(27) (ⁱ sóɣól à-ń-kɛ̀ ↓í ↓ŋgɛ́ŋ Lìngòm à-ń-lɔ̀)
    sóɣól   à-n´-kɛ̀   í`   ŋgɛ́ŋ   Lingom   à-n´-lɔ̀
    1.grandfather 1.AGR-PST1-leave   at   hour   Lingom   1.AGR-PST1-arrive
    'The grand-father left when Lingom arrived.'

(28) (ⁱ Lìngòm à-ń-lɔ̀ ↓ lɛ́ á-tí ɲɛ́ βìdʒék)
    Lingom   à-n´-lɔ̀   lɛ́   bá-tí   ɲɛ́   βidʒék
    Lingom   1.AGRPST1-arrive   that 2AGR-SUBJ.give 1.PRO   8.food
    'Lingom came so that they give him food.'

Crucially, FTS also applies between a root clause and a right extraposed subject clause, as in (29). This suggests that FTS is not sensitive to the right-edge of root clauses.

(29) (ⁱ (ⁱ hálà à-jè lɔ́ŋgɛ́) ↓lɛ́ sóɣól à-ń-dʒɛ́ jɔ̂)
    hálà à-jè   lɔ́ŋgɛ̀ lɛ́   sóɣól   à-n´-dʒɛ́   jɔ̂
    so   1.AGR-be.PRES well   that 1.grandfather 1.AGR-PST1-eat   9.pro
    'This is good that the grandfather ate it.' (Hamlaoui and Szendrői, in press)

Rather, what is observed in sentences displaying a clause-initial temporal clause (as in (30)) or a fronted object (31), where FTS fails to apply, suggests that FTS is sensitive to the left-edge of intonational phrases. The fact that these clause-initial constituents fail to integrate to the ɩ formed by the remainder of the sentence is expected – due to the presence of a root-clause left-edge – and independent of the prosodic status of the clause-initial constituent, that is, whether it is itself a ϕ or an ɩ (Hamlaoui and Szendrői, 2015, Subm).

(30) (ᵢ í ↓ŋgéŋ Lìngòm à-ǹ-kɛ̂ (ᵢ sóɣól à-ǹ-lɔ̂))
 î̀   ŋgéŋ   Lingom   à-ŋ́-kɛ̀   sóɣól   à-ń-lɔ̂
 at   hour   Lingom   1.AGR-PST1-leave   1.grandfather   1.AGR-PST1-arrive
'When Lingom left, the grandfather arrived.'
(Hamlaoui and Szendrői, Subm)

(31) (ᵢ ɓɔ̀ɔ̀ŋgɛ́ ɓɔ́-ɓá-sô (ᵢ sóɣól à-ǹ-tɛ́hɛ́ ɓɔ́))
 ɓɔ̀ɔ̀ŋgɛ́   ɓɔ́-ɓá-só̀   sóɣól   à-ń-tɛ́hɛ́   ɓɔ́
 2-children   2.PRO-2.CONN-all   1.grandfather   1.AGR-PST1-see   2.PRO
'All the children were seen by the grandfather'
(Hamlaoui and Szendrői, 2015)

Note that, together with other simplification processes, FTS generally limits the distribution of falling tones in Bàsàá. The occurrence of clause-medial HL-H sequences, as for instance in (32) to (34), however further shows that falling tones are not limited to ι right edges and thus do not constitute a diagnostic for right ι edges (Hamlaoui and Szendrői, 2015, Subm).[7]

(32) màlêr   à-ǹ-ʤɛ́   lí-kɔ̀ndɔ̀.
 1.teacher   1.AGR-PST1-eat   6-plantain
'The teacher ate plantains.'

(33) à-ǹ-tí   ndáp   jêm   ʤɔ̀ŷɔp
 1.AGR-PST1-give   9.house   9.my   5.bath
'He/she gave away my bathroom.'

(34) à-ŋ́-↓gwês   nì   ɓèn.
 1.AGR-PRES-like   and/with   hate
'He/she likes and hates' (Hamlaoui et al., 2014)

In sum, what we have seen so far is that tonal processes, and in particular HTS and FTS, show how word sequences are phrased in Bàsàá. So far, they provide evidence for two levels of phrasing, the phonological phrase and the intonational phrase (like in most Bantu languages in this volume, except for Embosi and Chichewa). Let us now turn to sentence-level prosody and the (lack of) involvement of tone in expressing certain semantic/pragmatic contrasts.

---

7 The simplification of HL-L sequences into H-L is also possible but seems to be dependent on factors like speech rate. Note also that certain falling tones never simplify, no matter the tonal context or syntactic position. Both issues require further research.

3 Tone and intonation

As pitch differences are used to convey meaningful, phonemic contrasts, a recurring question concerning tonal languages is whether pitch is also used to express postlexical meanings. Wong et al. (2005) have shown that in the Standard Hong Kong dialect of Cantonese, melodic events at phrase edges correlate with different sentence modalities. In this variety of Cantonese, a boundary H tone (H%) at the end of an uttrance indicates an incredulous echo question modality, while a HL% expresses the speaker's sense of sudden realization ("Oh I get it!"). Cantonese is but one example of tonal languages that utilize pitch to express postlexical contrasts. Embosi (Bantu C25), a two-tone language similar to Bàsàá, exhibits intonational phrase final L% and HL% boundary tones that mark assertions and *yes-no* questions respectively. These boundary tones are superimposed on the lexical tones and modify their pitch characteristics by either lowering or raising their realization (Embanga Aborobongui et al., 2011; Downing and Rialland, 2012; Embanga Aborobongui et al., 2012) (see also Rialland and Embanga Aborobongui, this volume). In this respect, Embosi displays a crosslinguistically common behaviour, as *yes-no* questions are often marked with a rising intonation (Ultan, 1978; Cruttenden, 1997; Gussenhoven, 2004). Nevertheless, Rialland (2009) has shown that in a number of African languages that are spoken around the equator, just like Bàsàá, *yes-no* questions are characterized by a "lax" question intonation, that is, a final low tone, a low or falling pitch contour or a breathy termination. In this section, we show that sentence modality has little effect on Bàsàá tonal specifications. In Bàsàá *yes-no* questions are primarily marked by morpho-syntactic devices.

3.1 Declarative Sentences

While the effects of postlexical meanings on the realization of tone, if there are any, are expected to occur regardless of the tonal make-up of particular sentences, they are certainly most visible in sentences in which all tones have the same phonological value (Connell, 2001). As briefly illustrated in Fig. 2, sentences which displays a mixed tone sequence present so-called 'automatic downstep', that is, each H subsequent to a L is realized on a lower register than previous H tones. In this type of sentences, it is thus not an easy task to determine which effect is responsible for observed lowerings.

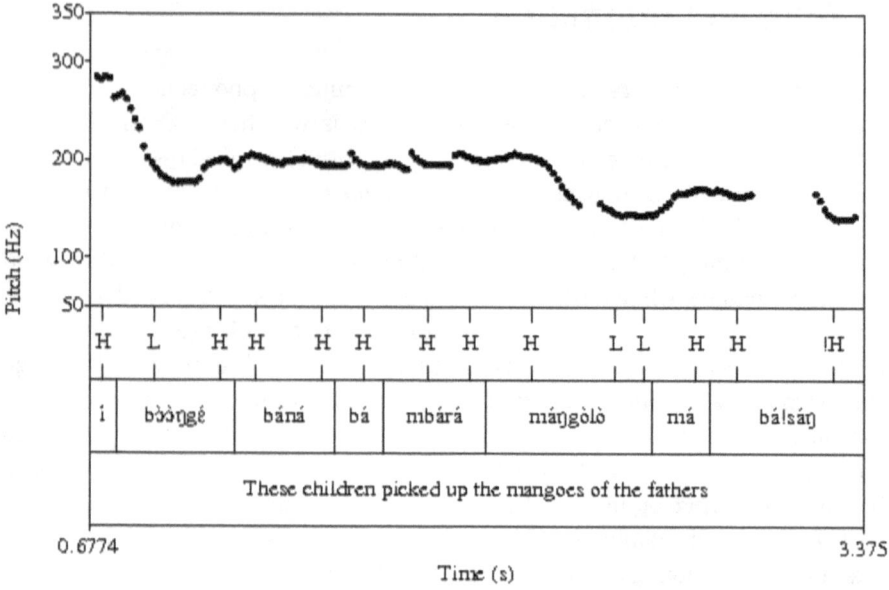

Figure 2: Bàsàá sentence with a mixed tone sequence (see Item 4 in Appendix)

This section thus reports results from a preliminary investigation of the effect of sentence modality on the realization of Bàsàá tones. A set of sentences, with only H tones or only L tones, is recorded in a neutral context. Both types of sentences were produced by a female and a male adult speaker and each sentence was repeated three times. Two illustrative sentences are provided in (35) and in (36).

(35) híndá   í   kóp   í-ń-lámá   jéŋ   ŋwér.
     7.black   7.CONN   hen   7.AGR-PST1-may   search   1.owner
     'The black hen may look for its owner.'   all H tone

(36) tòlò   à-jè   ŋgì   dʒàm.
     1.mouse 1.AGR-be.PRES   no   problem
     'The mouse has no problem.'   all L tone

In Fig. 3a and 4a, pitch tracks of declarative sentences with only H tones are illustrated.

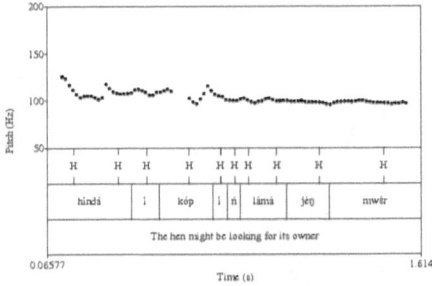
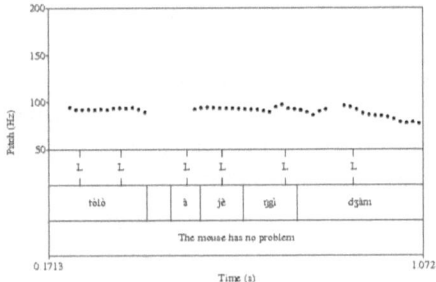

(a) Declarative sentence – High tones only   (b) Declarative sentence – Low tones only

Figure 3: Declarative sentences – Male speaker

There is a slight f_0 declination throughout the sentence and H tones form a plateau until the end of the utterance. The absence of a steeper final lowering toward the end of the sentence suggests that there is no L boundary tone at the end of declarative sentences in Bàsàá.

Declarative sentences with words that only have low tones in Fig. 3b and 4b present similar f_0 patterns as sentences with only high tones. The lowering of f_0 at the end of these sentences is a natural declination, rather than an effect of a low boundary tone.

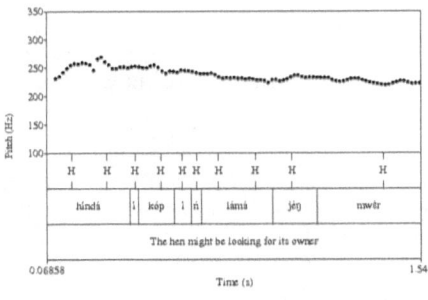
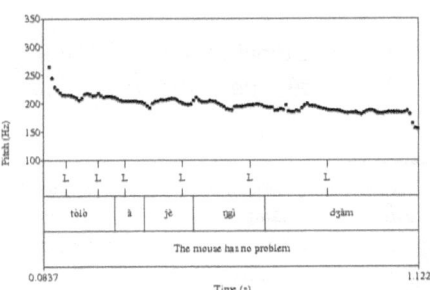

(a) Declarative sentence – High tones only   (b) Declarative sentence – Low tones only

Figure 4: Declarative sentences – Female speaker

In all sentences we recorded, no particular pitch movement seems to correlate with prosodic phrase edges, indicating that pitch does not serve as an indicator for prosodic phrasing in all H tone or all L tone contexts.[8]

---

[8] See however Hamlaoui & Makasso, forth, for evidence that certain successive H tones are distinguished at specific syntactic edges and might be indicators of recursive phonological phrasing.

3.2 Yes-No Questions

In Bàsàá, *yes-no* questions are formed by adding a clause-final question marker {-ɛ} (glossed as Q) to a corresponding declarative sentence.[9] There is no change in word order. Two statement-question pairs (a and b, respectively) are presented in (37) and (38).

(37) a. màlêr   à-ń-↓ʤé.
        1.teacher   1.AGR-PRES-eat
        'The teacher is eating.'

   b. màlêr   à-ń-↓ʤé-ɛ̀.
        1.teacher   1.AGR-PRES-eat-Q
        'Is the teacher eating?'

(38) a. mùràá   à-ɓí-gwâl.
        1.woman   1.AGR-PST2-give.birth.
        'The woman gave birth.'

   b. mùràá   à-ɓí-gwàl-ɛ̀.
        1.woman   1.AGR-PST2-give.birth-Q
        'Did the woman give birth?'

The surface tonal specification of the question marker depends on the structure and the final tone of the word it attaches to. Whenever the preceding word ends

---

9 Note that the question marker sometimes seems to harmonize with the immediately preceding vowel, as in examples (i) and (ii). An account of this phenomenon extends the scope of the present chapter, so we leave this issue open for future research.

(i) a. Paul à-nìɲí.
       Paul 1.AGR-lie.down
       'Paul is lying down.'

   b. Paul à-nìɲí-ì.
       Paul 1.AGR-lie.down-Q
       'Is Paul lying down?'

(ii) a. màànge̋   à-ɓíí   ŋwáá.
        1.child   1.AGR-FUT2.take   1.wife
        'The boy will take a wife.'

   b. màànge̋   à-ɓíí   ŋwáá-à.
        1.child   1.AGR-FUT2.take   1.wife-Q
        'Will the boy take a wife?'

with a coda consonant and carries a final H tone, as in (39) and (40), the question marker realizes a H tone. This contrasts with what is seen in (37) and (38), where it seems to us that the question marker simply realizes a default L tone.[10] Note that no full-fledged analysis of questions has been offered yet.

(39) a. Paul à-gwèé támb.
Paul 1.AGR-PRES.have 7.shoe
'Paul has a shoe.'

b. Paul à-gwèé támb-ɛ́.
Paul 1.AGR-PRES.have 7.shoe-Q
'Does Paul have a shoe?'

(40) a. Paul à-ɓèèyá màlép.
Paul 1.AGR-carry.DUR water
'Paul is carrying water.'

b. Paul à-ɓèèyá màléβ-ɛ́.
Paul 1.AGR-carry.DUR water-Q
'Is Paul carrying water?'

The interrogative counterpart of sentences (35) and (36) are shown in (41) and (42).

(41) híndá í kóp í-ńlámá jéŋ ŋwɛ́r-ɛ́.
7.black 7.CONN hen 7.AGR-PST1-may search owner-Q
'May the black hen look for its owner?' all H tones

(42) tòlò à-jè ŋgì dʒàm-ɛ̀.
1.mouse 1.AGR-be.PRES no problem-Q
'Does the mouse have no problem?' all L tones

The pitch tracks of sentences (41) and (42) are shown in Fig. 5 and 6. In *yes-no* questions, there is a small difference between the male speaker and the female speaker. The male speaker has a f_0 plateau, similar to declarative sentences, both in H tone and L tone contexts, as in Fig. 5a and 5b. The female speaker, however, begins with a raised f_0 and shows gradual f_0 declination as in Fig. 6a and 6b.

---

[10] A reviewer wondered whether the underlying tone of the Q morpheme could be a L tone. Such an analysis predicts that the surface tone of the Q morpheme should be a falling tone in (39)b to (41), which is not the case.

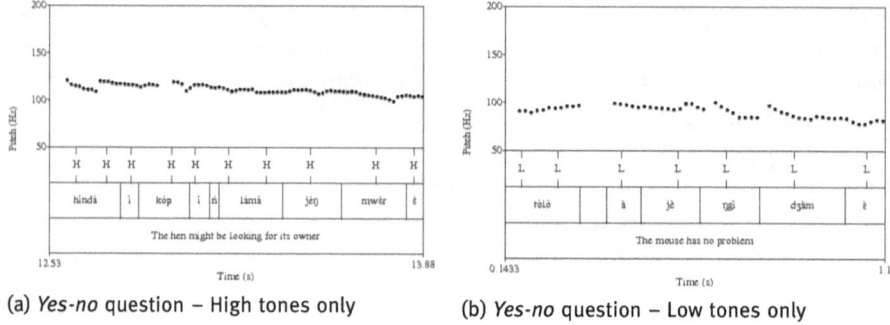

(a) *Yes-no* question – High tones only (b) *Yes-no* question – Low tones only

Figure 5: *Yes-no* question – Male speaker

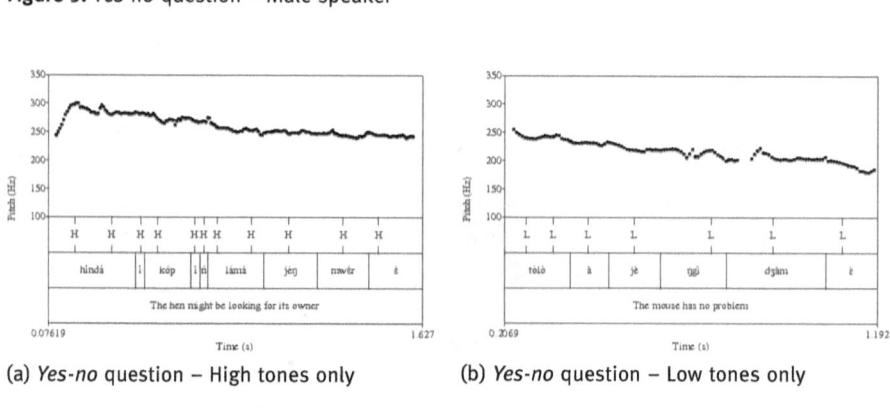

(a) *Yes-no* question – High tones only (b) *Yes-no* question – Low tones only

Figure 6: *Yes-no* question – Female speaker

What we can conclude so far is that tonal specifications are not affected by sentence modality and that there is no systematic initial or final tonal rising or lowering that would be indicative of the presence of modality-related boundary tones. A more systematic study is however needed to confirm this observation and to determine whether there are more subtle but nonetheless systematic prosodic differences between declaratives and their corresponding *yes-no* questions (e.g. expansion of the overall pitch range or downdrift manipulations). As suggested by Makasso (2012), creaky termination (low f_0, aperiodic glottal pulses and lower amplitude) might ultimately be found and lead to the classification of Bàsàá into the languages described by Rialland (2009) as displaying a lax question prosody.

Let us now turn to the final section of this chapter, which examines the influence of focus and discourse-givenness on Bàsàá tones.

4 Tone and discourse context

In intonation languages such as Germanic or Romance languages, information-structural notions such as focus and discourse-givenness have been shown to affect prosodic prominence. Despite a number of differences between these languages families, focused information tends to present a prominence boost, while discourse-given information is prosodically reduced (a.o. Cruttenden, 1993; Swerts et al., 2002; Ladd, 2008; Breen et al., 2010). Although it is commonly assumed that tonal languages do not exploit prosody as much as intonation languages do in expressing information-structural categories, a growing number of (sometimes complex) tonal languages have been shown to utilize prosodic cues to encode focus. Xu (1999) and Jannedy (2007) have shown that in Mandarin Chinese and Northern Vietnamese, respectively, focus and post-focal givenness have an effect on pitch range. In African tonal languages too, prosody has been shown to correlate with information structural status, even if in some cases prosodic focus marking is only optional and rather secondary (a.o. Fiedler and Jannedy (2013) on Ewe, or Kügler, this volume, on Akan). In Bantu languages such as Chichewa (Kanerva, 1990) and Xhosa (Zerbian, 2004), it has been argued that focus triggers the insertion of additional prosodic boundaries, which correlate for instance with the presence of penultimate vowel lengthening of the focused phrase (see for instance Patin, this volume, on Shingazidja). Recently, the systematic influence of focus on the prosody of Bantu languages has however been questioned, as no or only optional prosodic cues could be found in languages such as Northern Sotho (Zerbian, 2006) and Chichewa (Downing and Pompino-Marschall (2013), Downing, this volume).

In Bàsàá, the tone-sandhi rules discussed in Section 2.2 remain unaffected by information structure, suggesting that focus is not encoded by means of changes in the prosodic structure (i.e. by insertion or deletion of phrasal boundaries). The question we address in this section is whether Bàsàá nonetheless prosodically encodes information-status. The results of our production study suggest that f_0, duration and intensity are not reliable indicators of information-structural status.

4.1 Methodology

Focus is expressed either in situ or by means of inverted pseudo-clefts (Hamlaoui and Makasso, 2015) in Bàsàá. To determine whether focus affects prosodic prominence, we elicited 10 simple transitive sentences in which word order was kept constant. For each sentence, a context was set by means of a *wh*-question, so as to elicit focus either on the entire sentence (baseline condition), on the object constituent, on the subject constituent or on a locative or temporal adjunct. A sample paradigm is given in (43) to (46).

(43) All-new
    A: kí   í-ŋ-↓únɓáhá   ńlóm?
       7.what 7.AGR-PRES-upset.CAUS 1.husband
       'What upsets the husband?'

    B: ɲàŋgó à-ɓí-nùŋúl móó í ɓòm.
       1.wife 1.AGR-PST2-sell 6.oil LOC 7.market
       '[The wife sold the oil at the market]$_{Focus}$'

(44) Object focus
    A: ɲàŋgó à-ɓí-nùŋúl kí í ɓòm?
       1.wife 1.AGR-PST2-sell 7.what LOC 7.market
       'What did the wife sell at the market?'

    B: ɲàŋgó à-ɓí-nùŋúl móó í ɓòm.
       1.wife 1.AGR-PST2-sell 6.oil LOC 7.market
       'The wife sold [the oil]$_{Focus}$ at the market'

(45) Subject focus
    A: ndʒé à-ɓí-nùŋúl móó í ɓòm?
       1.who 1.AGR-PST2-sell 6.oil LOC 7.market
       'Who sold the oil at the market?'

    B: ɲàŋgó à-ɓí-nùŋúl móó í ɓòm.
       1.wife 1.AGR-PST2-sell 6.oil LOC 7.market
       '[The wife]$_{Focus}$ sold the oil at the market'

(46) Adjunct focus
    A: ɲàŋgó à-ɓí-nùŋúl hé móó?
       1.wife 1.AGR-PST2-sell where 6.oil
       'Where did the wife sell the oil?'

    B: ɲàŋgó à-ɓí-nùŋúl móó í ɓòm.
       1.wife 1.AGR-PST2-sell 6.oil LOC 7.market
       'The wife sold the oil [at the market]$_{Focus}$'

The tonal make-up of the sentences was as varied as possible, as we did not expect focus to affect only some tones. We also varied the length of the words and the constituents, for more naturalness (see Appendix for a full set of sentences).

Three participants (1 male and 2 female) took part in this production study. Each pair of a context question and a target response was presented on a computer screen in a randomized manner in a quiet room. Context questions were pre-recorded. Participants were instructed to first push a key to hear the context question, read the target sentence silently and then pronounce it as naturally as possible. Each sentence was repeated three times, yielding a total of 360 utterances (3 speakers * 10 items * 4 contexts * 3 repetitions).

A segment-by-segment and phrase-by-phrase alignment of the data was created using the Prosodylab Aligner (Gorman et al., 2011), trained on our own experimental data. We here report two types of measures. We first report phrasal measurements, for which we looked at the entire phrase (including both vocalic and consonantic segments). Additionally, we also examined particular vowels, which in Bàsàá can be considered to be part of the prosodic head of a word, as they belong to the first syllable of the prosodic stem (root + suffixes) (Hyman, 2003). Whenever a subject, an object or an adjunct was phrasal, the examined vowel is the one pertaining to the syntactic head of this phrase (see underlined vowels in the Appendix). Measures of maximum f_0, maximum intensity and duration were obtained for each head vowel and each phrase using PRAAT scripts (Boersma and Weenink, 2014).[11] All statistical analyses were conducted in the R environment software (R Core Team (2015), version 3.2.2). Linear mixed effects models were used to analyze the data, with random intercepts and slopes for items and participants.

4.2 Results

4.2.1 Fundamental frequency

Stylized f_0 contours for each item are given in Fig. 7 and 8. For both vowels and phrases, absolute and relative pitch (using difference in semitones between Subject and Verb, Verb and Object and Object and Adjunct, respectively) were examined. None of the comparisons turned out to be significant, indicating that focus does not affect pitch in Bàsàá.

---

[11] Many thanks go to Michael Wagner and the McGill ProsodyLab for sharing with us their tools for data analysis, and to Jonas Engelmann for assistance in the processing and the statistical analysis of the data.

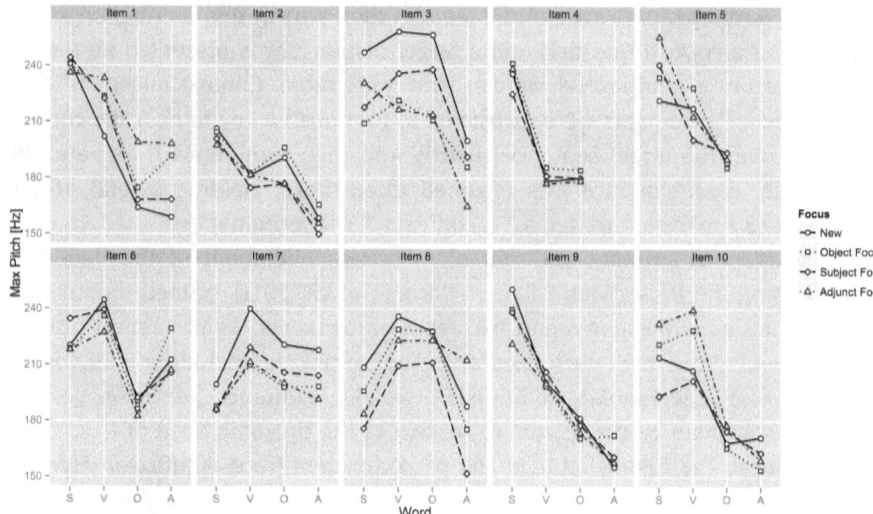

Figure 7: Focus: mean maximum f_0 in phrases (3 speakers * 3 repetitions)

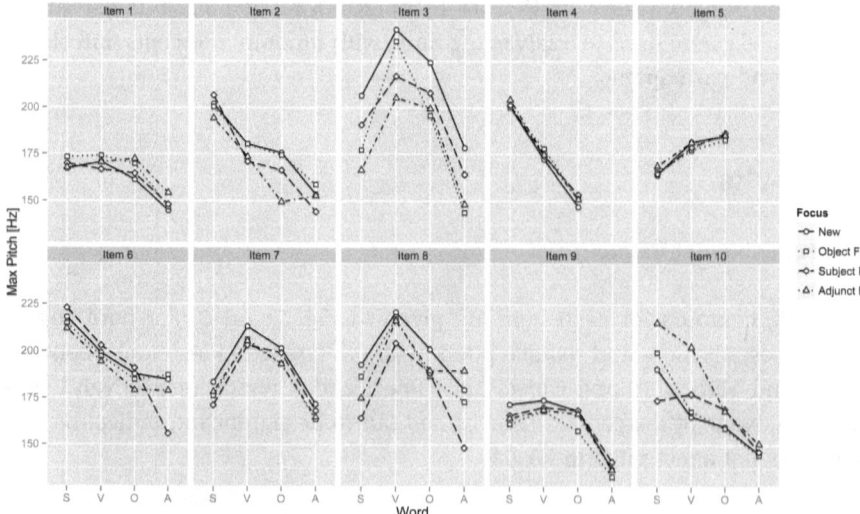

Figure 8: Focus: mean maximum f_0 for head vowels (3 speakers * 3 repetitions)

Bàsàá thus does not pertain to tone languages in which focus participates in determining the fundamental frequency of tones.

4.2.2 Duration

Measures of duration for the target phrases and their head vowels are given in Fig. 9 and 10, respectively. We examined absolute and relative duration (using difference in log duration between Subject and Verb, Verb and Object and Object and Adjunct, respectively).

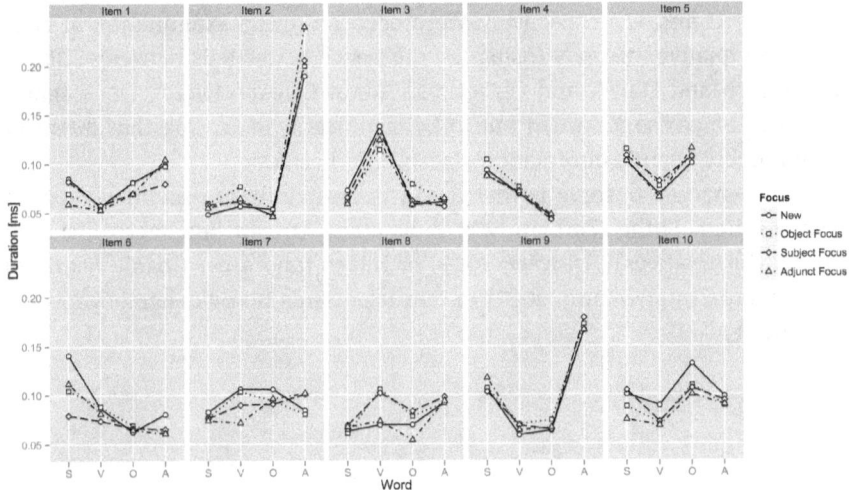

Figure 9: Focus: mean duration for phrases (3 speakers * 3 repetitions)

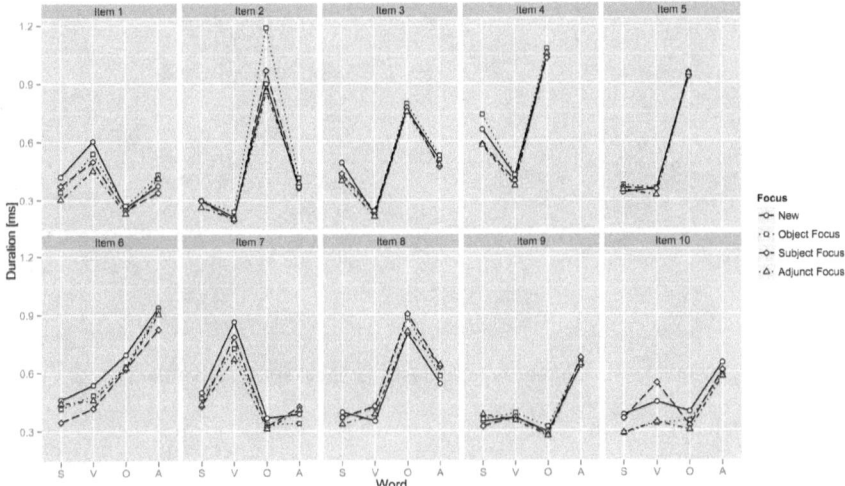

Figure 10: Focus: mean duration for head vowels (3 speakers * 3 repetitions)

Neither the duration of the entire phrase, nor the duration of the head vowel was found to distinguish focused constituents from the non-focused ones. Duration is thus not a reliable cue to distiguish between focused and non-focused constituents in Bàsàá.

4.2.3 Intensity

Finally, measures of intensity for focused phrases and their head vowels are shown in Fig. 11 and 12, respectively. We proceeded to the examination of both absolute and relative intensity (using the difference in decibels between Subject and Verb, Verb and Object and Object and Adjunct, respectively). Once again, none of the comparisons turned out to be significant, indicating that intensity does not reliably encode information structure in Bàsàá.

In sum, what we observe is that Bàsàá is comparable to Bantu languages such as Northern Sotho (Zerbian, 2007), or other African languages like Buli (and other Gur relatives) (Schwarz, 2009) or Hausa (and other Chadic relatives) (Hartmann and Zimmermann, 2007) in that it presents no evidence of prosodic focus marking.

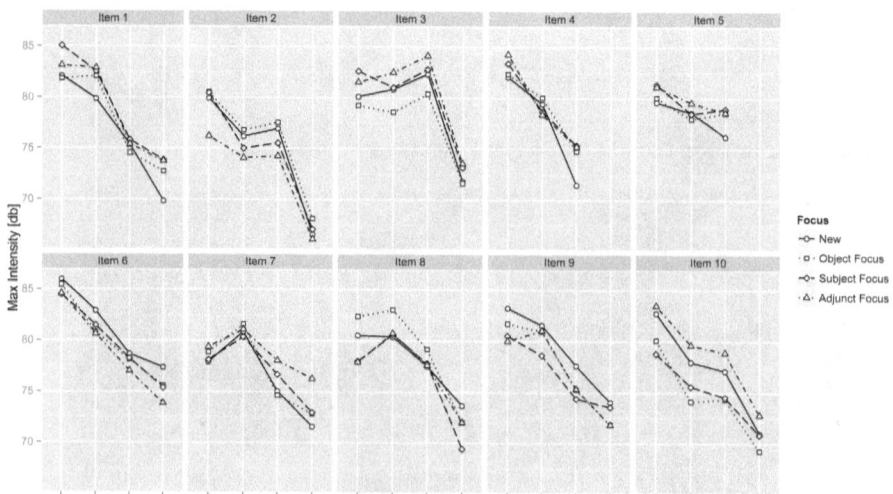

Figure 11: Focus: mean maximum intensity for phrases (3 speakers * 3 repetitions)

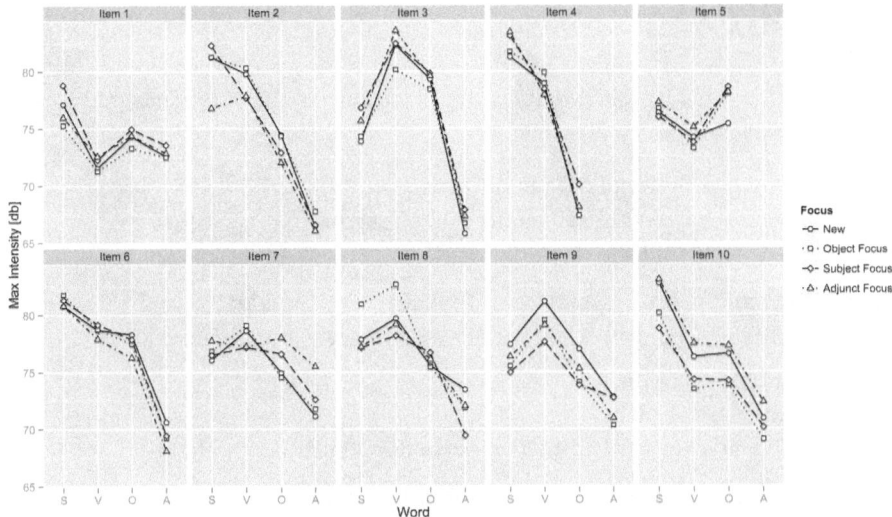

Figure 12: Focus: mean maximum intensity for head vowels (3 speakers * 3 repetitions)

5 Conclusion

Two major aspects of the intonational phonology of Bàsàá, a Bantu language with an underlying opposition between high, low and toneless TBUs, have been reported in this chapter. First, Bàsàá has two major tone rules (high tone spreading and falling tone simplification) that show sensitivities to prosodic domains. HTS applies within a phonological phrase, but not across right phonological phrase boundaries. FTS, on the other hand, applies within an intonational phrase and fails to apply across left intonational phrase boundaries. The other intonational aspect of Bàsàá is that tones do not seem to be affected by sentence modalities or information structure. Declaratives and *yes-no* questions show nearly identical intonation patterns. Finally, varying the location of focus in a sentence does not affect sentence prosody in any significant way either. Other structures will have to be studied to determine whether there is intonational structure to speak of in the grammar of Bàsàá.

Acknowledgement

We would like to thank the editors as well as two anonymous reviewers for their comments on previous versions of this chapter, and Sergio Quiroz for proofreading it. All remaining errors are our own.

Appendix

Underlined vowels in the examples are head vowels that are measured in the analysis in section 4.

Item 1 ɲàŋgó à-βí-nùŋúl m-óó í ɓòm.
1.wife 1.AGR-PST2-sell 6.oil LOC 7.market
'The wife sold the oil at the market.'

Item 2 lì-wándá lí málêr lí-ŋ-wáŋ má-kàlà má
5.friend 5.CONN 1.teacher 5.AGR-PST1-fry 6.doughnut 6.CONN

ḿ-ɓòŋ ʤ-ùú.
3.cassava 5.night
'The teacher's friend fried cassava doughnuts last night.'

Item 3 rì-nùní rí-ŋ-ɔ̀ŋ m-ú↓mbúl mà-láám í pùmá.
13-birds 13.AGR-PST1-build 6.nests 6.beautiful LOC 1.orange.tree
'The birds built beautiful nests on the orange tree.'

Item 4 í-ɓ-ɔ̀ɔ̀ŋgé ɓáná ɓá-ḿ-ɓárá m-áŋgòlò má ɓ-á↓sáŋ.
AUG-2-children 2-DEM 2.AGR-PST1-pick.up 6-mangoes CONN 2.fathers
'These children have picked up the mangoes of the fathers.'

Item 5 m-àáŋgé à-ǹ-níp ŋ́-hóólàk lí-kɔ̀ndɔ̀.
1-child 1.AGR-PST1-steal 3.ripe 3.CONN.5.plantain
'The child stole the ripe plantain.'

Item 6 lì-húá lí-βí-↓nɔ́l ŋgándàk á-òr í ŋwǐi ú-β-í↓táγɓè.
5.alcool 5.AGR-PST2-kill many 2-people 3.DEM 3.year 3.AGR-PST2-pass.
'Alcohol killed a lot of people last year.'

Item 7 hì-ŋgɔ̀ndà hí-ŋ-hójá sɔ́mb ŋ́lámb í ɓòm.
19.girl 19.AGR-PST1-forget buy 3.meat LOC 7.market
'The girl forgot to buy the meat at the market.'

Item 8 βì-lɔ̀lɔ̀ βí-ŋ́-ʤé hí-ònde̋ hɔ́-só↓ná βì-kékèlà.
8-ducks 8.AGR-PST1-eat 19-peanut 19.PRO-all 8-morning
'The ducks ate all the peanuts this morning.'

Item 9 m-àáŋgé à-ɓárá lɔ̀lɔ̀ ɓèèhéé.
1-child 1.AGR-PST3.pick.up 7.duck a.long.time.ago
'The child picked up the duck a long time ago.'

Item 10 ɓɔ́lí í-ŋ́-nɔ̀ŋ m-ááŋgé βì-kékèlà.
7.wasp 7.AGR-PST1-chase 1.child 8-morning
'The wasp chased the child this morning.'

References

Bitjaa Kody, Zachée Denis. 1993. Le système tonal du basaa. *Journal of West African Languages* 23(1). 65–72.
Boersma, Paul, and Weenink, David. 2014. *Praat: doing phonetics by computer*. Computer program. http://www.praat.org/.
Bot ba Njock, H. M. 1970. *Nexus et nominaux en bàsàa*. Ph.D. thesis, Université Paris 3 Sorbonne Nouvelle.
Breen, Mara, Fedorenko, Evelina, Wagner, Michael, and Gibson, Edward. 2010. Acoustic correlates of information structure. *Language and Cognitive Processes* 25(7). 1044–1098.
Cheng, Lisa Lai-Shen, and Downing, Laura Jo. 2007. The Prosody and Syntax of Zulu Relative Clauses. *SOAS Working Papers in Linguistics* 15. 51–63.
Connell, Bruce. 2001. *Downdrift, downstep and declination*. In: *Proceedings of the Typology of African Prosodic Systems Workshop*. University of Bielefeld.
Cruttenden, Alan. 1993. *The de-accenting and re-accenting of repeated lexical items*. In: *Proceedings of the ESCA workshop on Prosody* 16–19, Lund.
Cruttenden, Alan. 1997. *Intonation*. Cambridge: Cambridge University Press.
Dimmendaal, Gerrit 1988. *Aspects du basaa*. Peeters/SELAF. [translated by Luc Bouquiaux].
Downing, Bruce T. 1970. *Syntactic structure and phonological phrasing in English*. Ph.D. thesis, University of Texas at Austin.
Downing, Laura Jo, and Pompino-Marschall, Berndt. 2013. The focus prosody of Chichewa and the stress-focus constraint: a response to Samek-Lodovici (2005). *Natural Language and Linguistic Theory* 31(3). 647–681.
Downing, Laura Jo, and Rialland, Annie. 2012. *Superimposed boundary tones in selected Bantu languages*. Paper presented at WOCAL 7, Buea, Cameroon.
Embanga Aborobongui, Martial, Beltzung, Jean-Marc, Hamlaoui, Fatima, and Rialland, Annie. 2011. Questions partielles en ɛmbɔ́sí (C25). In: Downing, Laura Jo (ed.), *Questions in Bantu Languages: Prosodies and Positions*. ZAS Papers in Linguistics, 7–21. ZAS.
Embanga Aborobongui, Martial, Rialland, Annie, and Beltzung, Jean-Marc. 2012. *Tones and intonation in Boundji ɛmbɔ́sí (C25)*. In: *Proceedings of the 6th World Congress of African Linguistics*, 237–244, Köln. Köppe Verlag.
Fiedler, Ines, and Jannedy, Stefanie. 2013. Prosody of focus marking in Ewe. *Journal of African Languages and Linguistics* 34(1). 1–46.
Gorman, Kyle, Howell, Jonathan, and Wagner, Michael. 2011. Prosodylab-aligner: a tool for forced alignment of laboratory speech. *Canadian Acoustics* 39(3). 192–193.
Gussenhoven, Carlos. 2004. *The phonology of tone and intonation*. Cambridge: Cambridge University Press.
Hamlaoui, Fatima, Gjersøe, Siri, and Makasso, Emmanuel-Mosely. 2014. *High Tone Spreading and Phonological Phrases in Bàsàá*. In: *Proceedings of the 4th International Symposium on Tonal Aspects of Languages*. ISCA Archive.
Hamlaoui, Fatima, and Makasso, Emmanuel-Mosely. 2015. Focus marking and the unavailability of inversion structures in the Bantu language Bàsàá. *Lingua* 154. 35–64.
Hamlaoui, Fatima, and Makasso, Emmanuel-Mosely. forth. *Downstep in Bàsàá*. In: *Proceedings of the 47th Annual Conference on African Linguistics*.
Hamlaoui, Fatima, and Szendrői, Kriszta. 2015. A flexible approach to the mapping of intonational phrases. *Phonology* 32(1). 79–110.

Hamlaoui, Fatima, and Szendrői, Kriszta S.ubm. The syntax-phonology mapping of intonational phrases in complex sentences: a flexible approach.

Hartmann, Katharina, and Zimmermann, Malte. 2007. In place – out of place: Focus in Hausa. In: Schwabe, Kerstin, and Winkler, Susanne (eds.), *On information structure: Meaning and form*, 365–403. Amsterdam: John Benjamins.

Hyman, Larry. 2003. *The Bantu languages*, chap. Bàsàa (A43), 257–282. Routledge.

Hyman, Larry, and Lionnet, Florian. 2012. *Metatony in Abo*. In: Marlo, Michael, Adams, Nikki, Green, Christopher, Morrison, Michelle, and Purvis, Tristan (eds.), *Selected Proceedings of the 42nd Annual Conference on African Linguistics: African Languages in Context*. 1–14. Cascadilla.

Jannedy, Stefanie. 2007. Prosodic focus in Vietnamese. In: Ishihara, Shin, Jannedy, Stefanie, and Schwarz, Anne (eds.), *Interdisciplinary Studies on Information Structure*, Vol. 08, 209–230. University of Potsdam.

Jokweni, Mbulelo. 1995. *Aspects of IsiXhosa phrasal phonology*. Ph.D. thesis, University of Illinois at Urbana Champagne.

Kanerva, Jonni. 1990. *The phonology-syntax connection*, chap. Focusing on phonological phrases in Chichewa. The University of Chicago Press.

Ladd, Robert D. 2008. *Intonational Phonology*. Cambridge: Cambridge University Press.

Lemb, Pierre, and De Gastines, François. 1973. *Dictionnaire basaá-français*. Collège Libermann.

Lewis, Paul M., Simons, Gary F., and Fennig, Charles D. (eds.). 2015. *Ethnologue: Languages of the world*. Dallas, Texas: SIL International, eighteenth edition.

Makasso, Emmanuel-Moselly. 2008. Melisms and subjectivity in Bàsàa oral spontaneous discourse. *Journal of West African Languages* 35, 33–44.

Makasso, Emmanuel-Moselly. 2012. *Metatony in Basaa*. In: Marlo, Michael (ed.), *Selected Proceedings of the 42nd Annual Conference on African Linguistics*, 15–22, Somerville. Cascadilla Proceedings Project.

Makasso, Emmanuel-Moselly. 2014. The melodic tone pattern in Basaa. *Africana Linguistica* 20. 225–241.

Makasso, Emmanuel-Moselly, and Lee, Seunghun Julio. 2015. Basaá. *Journal of the International Phonetic Association* 45(1). 71–79.

R Core Team. 2015. *R: A Language and Environment for Statistical Computing*. R Foundation for Statistical Computing, Vienna, Austria.

Rialland, Annie. 2009. The African lax question prosody: its realisation and geographical distribution. *Lingua* 119(6). 928–949.

Schwarz, Anne. 2009. Tonal focus reflections in Buli and some Gur relatives. *Lingua*, 1196, 950–972.

Selkirk, Elisabeth. 1995. Sentence prosody: Intonation, stress and phrasing. In: Goldsmith, J. A. (ed.), *The Handbook of phonological theory*. 550–569. London: Blackwell.

Selkirk, Elisabeth. 2011. The syntax-phonology interface. In: Goldsmith, John, Riggle, Jason, and Yu, Alan (eds.), *The Handbook of Phonological Theory*, 485–532. Oxford: Blackwell Publishing.

Swerts, Marc, Krahmer, Emiel, and Avesani, Cinzia. 2002. Prosodic marking of information status in Dutch and Italian: a comparative analysis. *Journal of Phonetics* 30. 629–654.

Truckenbrodt, Hubert. 1999. On the relation between syntactic phrases and phonological phrases. *Linguistic Inquiry* 30(2). 219–282.

Truckenbrodt, Hubert. 2007. The syntax-phonology interface. In: de Lacy, Paul (ed.), *The Cambridge Handbook of Phonology*, 435–456. Cambridge: Cambridge University Press.

Ultan, Russell. 1978. Some general characteristics of interrogative systems. In: Greenberg, Joseph Harold (ed.), *Universals of human language*, Vol. IV, 211–248. Stanford: Stanford University Press.
Wong, Wai-Yi Peggy, Chan, K.-M. Marjorie, and Beckman, Mary E. 2005. An autosegmental-metrical analysis and prosodic annotation conventions for Cantonese. In: Jun, Sun-Ah (ed.), *Prosodic typology: The phonology of intonation and phrasing*, 271–300. Oxford: Oxford University Press.
Xu, Yi. 1999. Effects of tone and focus on the formation and alignment of f_0 contours. *Journal of Phonetics* 27(1). 55–105.
Yip, Moira. 2007. Tone. In: *The Cambridge Handbook of Phonology*. Cambridge University Press.
Zerbian, Sabine. 2004. Phonological phrases in Xhosa (Southern Bantu). In: *ZASPiL* 37. 71–99. ZAS.
Zerbian, Sabine. 2006. *Expression of Information Structure in the Bantu Language Northern Sotho*. Ph.D. thesis, Humbolt-Universität zu Berlin. ZASPiL 45.
Zerbian, Sabine. 2007. Subject/object-asymmetry in Northern Sotho. In: Schwabe, Kerstin, and Winkler, Susanne (eds.), *Information Structure and the Architecture of Grammar: A Typological Perspective*, 323–346. Amsterdam: John Benjamins.

Annie Rialland and Martial Embanga Aborobongui
How intonations interact with tones in Embosi (Bantu C25), a two-tone language without downdrift

Abstract: This chapter presents a study of the intonational system of Embosi, a two-tone Bantu language without downstep (or downdrift) in which boundary tones are superimposed on tones and not inserted on the same line. To account for the interaction between lexical tones and boundary tones, a model with a dual register organization is proposed. It involves a basic register for the tone realizations and enlargements above and below this basic register, due to extra-high or extra-low boundary tones. Expansions were found in yes-no questions and in the expression of emphasis. Boundary tones are involved in the marking of assertions (L%), polar questions (HL%), wh-questions (L%), among others. Focus is not indicated by prosodic means. Embosi has a prosodic hierarchy with Phonological Words and Intonational Phrases but lacks Phonological Phrases.

Keywords: Boundary tone, Downdrift, Final lowering, Focus, Emphasis, Phonological phrase, Polar question, Register expansion, Superimposition, Wh-question

1 Introduction

Downdrift (or "automatic downstep") is one of the best studied prosodic phenomena. It is fascinating as it is not a simple, linear and automatic declination but it results from interval calculations, which could be modeled in mathematical terms (see Lieberman & Pierrehumbert 1984, Pierrehumbert & Beckman 1988, Prieto & al. 1996, Laniran & Clements 2003 and Laniran 1992, for example). Studies on downdrift were performed on many tonal and non-tonal languages from various continents and families. In Africa, they concern Igbo (Liberman 1993), Yoruba (Laniran 1992, Clements & Laniran 2003), Chichewa (Myers 1996), Kono (1996), Dagara (Rialland & Some, 2011), among others.

Annie Rialland, Laboratory of Phonetics and Phonology, (CNRS) Paris
Martial Embanga Aborobongui, Marien Ngouabi University

DOI 10.1515/9783110503524-007

However, as far as we know, there is no research on a two-tone African language without downdrift. The present chapter will fill this gap, investigating tone realizations and intonations in Embosi, a two-tone language without downdrift. Embosi is a Bantu language (C25) spoken in Congo-Brazzaville. The number of Embosi speakers in the 'Cuvette region' can be roughly estimated at 150000, based on the 2009 census of the region's inhabitants and the knowledge of the main languages spoken in the villages and towns. There is also an unknown number of Embosi speakers in Brazzaville and in the diaspora. Knowledge of the Embosi language is rapidly increasing, with a number of recent articles and PhD dissertations. The current main references on Embosi are: Fontaney (1988, 1989), Amboulou (1998), Embanga Aborobongui (2013). However, so far, there exist no studies on its intonational system.

This chapter will first present the basic features of Embosi tonology and some relevant features of its segmental phonology, which are necessary to understand the overall architecture of the prosodic system. Next, we examine tonal realizations in assertive utterances, showing that there is no downdrift. Simple and complex assertive sentences will be considered, as well as yes-no questions and wh-questions. Based on these different types of intonation, we will argue that the observed realizations result from a superimposition of intonational tones (H%, L% or HL%) on tonal realizations, which trigger extra-high or extra-low realizations. A dual-register model will be introduced to account for this superimposition. Focus, as an answer to a *wh*-question and as distinct from emphasis, will also be studied. The final section will be devoted to prosodic subdivisions of complex sentences.

2 Basic features of Embosi tonology

Embosi is a two-tone language whose tone-bearing unit is the mora. There is no word or root level tonal patterns like the ones found in neighboring languages such as Kukuya, which provided well-known examples in phonology books (Paulian 1975, Hyman 1997, van Oostendorp & al. 2011, Archangeli & Pulleyblank 1994). Thus, any type of tone combination can be found on mono, bi or tri-moraic nominal roots, as shown by Embanga Aborobongui (2013). The following examples illustrate this broad range of possibilities. Note that only H tones are transcribed in the examples, for simplicity and clarity reasons.

(1) a. Monomoraic roots:
   H   a-kɔ́   "cl9. forest"
       ɔ-tá   "cl3. gun"
   L   o-mbo   "cl3. now"
       ɔ-dzɛ   "cl3. mockery"

b. Bimoraic roots (with a long vowel)
   HH   i-báá   "cl5. knife"
   LL   i-baa   "cl5. man"
   HL   i-báa   "cl5. marriage"
   LH   i-baá   "cl8. walls"

c. Bimoraic roots (with two syllables)
   HH   ɔ-mbɔ́ndɔ́   "cl3. leg"
   LL   i-mbamba   "cl5. frog"
   HL   o-lómi   "cl1. husband"
   LH   o-kondó   "cl3. tail"

d. Trimoraic roots
   HHH   e-bóndílí   "cl7. understanding"
         nzúbhúlɛ́   "cl9. smoke"
   LLL   a-jɛngili   "cl6. flattery"
         o-baɲaa   "cl3. type of eatable caterpillar"
   HLL   ngóloma   "cl9. palm wine esp."
         i-βímbisi   "cl7. hide and seek"
   LHH   mbaβílí   "cl9. heat of the sand"
         tsalálá   "cl9. scattered, disorganized"
   HHL   ngólómi   "cl9. uncle"
         támáre   "cl1a. aunt"
   LLH   ɛ-juɔmí   "cl7. shade, rest spot"
         ɛ-waamí   "cl7. joke"
   LHL   ɛ-kaláa   "cl7. afternoon"
         i-kaáɣa   "cl5. coal"
   HLH   le-kúulú   "cl11. darkness"
         ɔ-ngɔ́ngɔmbí   "cl3. collarbone"

Embosi does not have any tonal shift rules like the ones occurring in Eastern Bantu languages, such as Chichewa (Mtenje 1987) or Shingazidja (Casimjee & Kisseberth 1998, Patin 2007) among others. Its tonal rules are local and mainly triggered by vowel elision and glide formation. They conspire in order to provide adequate solutions after the loss of a mora, given that Embosi does not allow tonal contours on a single mora or downstep. These rules occur very frequently in Embosi speech, as semi-vocalization and elision are common processes. Thus, at any word junction within a sentence, when two vowels come into contact, a hiatus is avoided by the deletion of the first vowel in contact or the coalescence of the two vowels in contact. This vowel deletion or coalescence can be combined with a compensatory lengthening due to the loss of a prefix initial consonant (see Embanga Aborobongui 2013, Rialland & al. 2012, 2015). When a vowel is deleted and there is no compensatory lengthening, a tone is left without any tone bearing unit and has to be anchored, or eventually deleted. Contour avoidance rules and OCP rules then apply, as shown by the following examples:

(2) a.   morábve < moro ábve "somebody fell"
    b.   morakɔ́si < moro ákɔ́si "somebody hurts himself"

In 2a, the final vowel *o* of *moro* is elided. It leaves behind a L tone, which is itself deleted, and the H tone stands alone on the vowel *á* of *ábve*. Generally, when a L tone and a H tone compete for a single mora, the H tone wins but this is not always the case, as exemplified in 2b. In this example, the H tone of the vowel *á* of *ákɔ́si* undergoes deletion, which is due to an OCP process triggered by the H tone of the root *kɔ́si*. Before a lexical H tone, the potential LH contour on the remaining vowel *–a* is simplified to L. The fact that the L tone is active in the tonal process indicates that the contrast between H and L tones in Embosi is a binary one and not a privative one. A detailed study of these tonal processes in various contexts can be found in Embanga Aborobongui (2013).

Embosi also has "metatony", that is the alternation between a L and a H tone at the end of some verb categories. 'Metatony' is a relatively common process in Bantu languages and it is known to vary depending upon syntactic factors, verb tenses and categories involved (Schadeberg 1995; Hyman and Lionnet, 2011). In Embosi, several tenses undergo metatony. Thus, in present and future, verbs exhibit a final H tone when they are followed by a complement, or a L tone when they are not followed by a complement. Metatony occurs also in some other tenses and in infinitives but varies depending upon the fact that a stem is monosyllabic or not (Embanga Aborobongui, 2013). This metatony helps indicating whether a verb is clause final and, consequently provides a cue for the ending of a clause (see ex. 18). Metatony-like alternations target also two pronouns with L tones (3sgPRO *wa* and 2sgPRO *nɔ*) but do not have any form of demarcative role.

To summarize, Embosi has very productive local tonal rules triggered by vowel elision, and no rule of tonal spreading, doubling or retraction. We signaled metatony for its demarcative role, though it is morphosyntactically determined.

3 Some relevant features of segmental phonology

Various segmental processes occur at two levels of the prosodic hierarchy: the Phonological Word and the Intonational Phrase.

Some major processes occurring within the Phonological Word are vowel harmony, glide formation, and consonant dissimilation. Among these processes, the total dissimilation of the class prefix consonant is typologically remarkable and deserves a short excursus. It consists in the elision of the initial consonant of the prefix when the root begins with a consonant, as illustrated in the following alternations of class prefixes:

(3) Alternations of the class 1 prefix: mo-
    a. mo-ási → mw-ási "spouse"
        mo-ána → mw-ána "child"

    b. mo-kondzi → o-kondzi "chief"
        mo-lómi → o-lómi "husband"

Alternations of the class 2 prefix: ba-
    a. ba-ási → b-ási "spouses"
        ba-ána → b-ána "children"

    b. ba-kondzi → a-kondzi "chiefs"
        ba-lómi → a-lómi "husbands"

Beltzung & al (2011) analyzed these alternations, which are found in most of the other C20 Group languages and in some languages of other groups spoken in the region, as resulting from a total dissimilation rule. It was also shown that their elision leaves a C slot which is revealed by compensatory lengthening (Embanga Aborobongui 2013, Rialland & al. 2012, 2015). As class-prefixes occur not only in nouns but also in verbs, as subject markers, and in relative and connective constructions, this process is an important mechanism in the formation of the Phonological Word.

Embosi does not have any segmental rules whose domain could be the Phonological Phrase. There are no phrasal rules as the ones which are found in Eastern Bantu languages such as Chichewa, Kimatuumbi (see Downing 2012, for an overview). Conversely, it has processes whose domain is the Intonational Phrase. Within an Intonational Phrase in Embosi, hiatus is avoided at every word junction: the final vowel of the first word in contact is elided when the following word begins with a vowel. Vowel elision can be accompanied by vowel coalescence when the vowels in contact are $a + i$. Compensatory lengthening occurs when vowel elision is combined with the loss of a prefix consonant (Embanga, 2013). Elisions of word-final vowels are very frequent and can be seen in almost any Embosi sentence, as all words end with a vowel and that 40% begin with a vowel (Rialland & al. 2012, 2015). Many examples of these elisions will be shown and analyzed in the remainder of this chapter, at least one in every utterance. Let's first consider more closely one utterance, which will be studied later on from an intonational point of view (Figure 1).

(4) [ekoojɔ́ɔtɔɔmbílédibémbélé]
    e-koo   já   (m)ɔ-tɔɔmbílí   é-di   bémbélé
    cl7-foot   cl7.CON   cl8-automobile   cl7-be.PRES   cl10.inflated
    "The tire of the automobile is inflated."

In connected speech, the vowel *á* in *já* is elided in front of the vowel *ɔ* in the word *ɔtɔɔmbílí*. The *(m)* of the class prefix of *(m)ɔtɔɔmbílí*, which has been deleted, is responsible for the formation of the long vowel *ɔɔ*.

To summarize, we found segmental rules whose domains are either the Phonological Word or the Intonational Phrase, but we did not find any processes related to in-between prosodic constituents. Thus, we arrive at the following conclusion: in Embosi, the Phonological Phrase is not associated with any tonal or segmental rule. Let's now examine tone realizations and intonations in various types of utterances.

4 Tone and intonation in assertive utterances: a two-tone language without downdrift

Considering tonal realization and intonation in assertive utterances, that is in utterances where downdrift could be expected, we provide evidence that Embosi is a language without downdrift. The fact that there is no downdrift does not imply that tone is realized only on two pitch levels from the beginning to the end of an utterance but rather that observed pitch decay is due to other processes. In order to determine which processes are involved in the realization of assertive utterances, we will perform an intonational analysis of some assertive utterances and then consider quantitative data. These analyses will allow us to identify the reference lines that structure the tonal and intonational system and introduce a dual register model. Juxtaposed assertive sentences will also be considered.

4.1 Analyzing some assertive utterances

To introduce our study on tone realizations and intonations, our starting point will be the analysis of three assertive utterances. These utterances are extracted from a corpus which includes 350 sentences, as well as isolated words (not considered in this study). This corpus was read by two male speakers (MEA and GNK[1]). For each example included in this chapter, a phonetic notation is given, followed by a morphological gloss and a translation. The comparison between the two lines illustrates the segmental rules involved in the formation of the utterances, particularly the elision of word-final vowels at word junction, mentioned previously.

(4) (repeated)
     [ekoojɔ́ɔtɔɔbílédibémbélé]
     ekoo   já   (m)ɔtɔɔmbílí   édi   bémbélé
     "The tire of   the automobile   is   inflated."

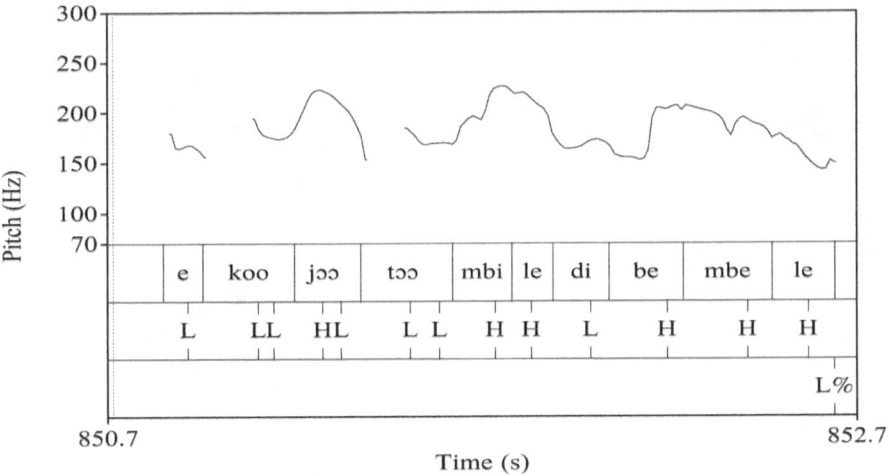

Figure 1: F0 curve of [ekoojɔ́ɔtɔɔmbílédibémbélé] "The tire of the car is inflated." (Speaker MEA)

In this sentence, H and L tones in the sequence *ekoojɔ́ɔtɔɔmbílédi* are realized on two levels (around 220Hz for the H tones and 165Hz for the L tones) separated by roughly two musical tones. There is no downdrift. In the remaining part, that

---

1 Speaker MEA is the second author of this chapter. Currently, he is Assistant Professor at Marien-Ngouabi University in Brazzaville. Speaker GNK holds a post-doctorate position in Paris. Both speaks the Boundji variety of Embosi.

is on *bémbélé*, H tones are lowered, the very last tone being realized much lower, indeed even lower than the L tones of the sentence. We can explain this gradual lowering as being due to the L%. The L% boundary tone pulls down the final H tones, its lowering being strongest at the very end of the sentence. We can recognize here the effects of a final lowering, which is a well-known process found in many languages (see 3.4. for a more detailed study of final lowering). To summarize, the first part of this assertive sentence (*ekoojɔ́ɔtɔɔmbílédi*) displays undisturbed tonal realizations while the last part is affected by a lowering intonation.

This is the typical intonational pattern found in an Embosi assertive utterances (without any focus or emphasis), which is also illustrated in (5):

(5) [wáβaaɲibeabóowée]
wa á.βaaɲi bea bá (m)o-we
3g.PRO 3sg.take away.REC cl8.property cl8.GEN[2] cl1-deceased
'He took away the properties of the deceased.'

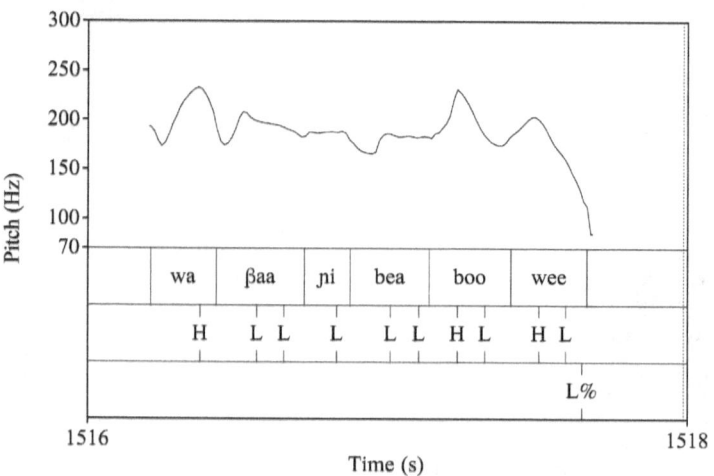

Figure 2: F0 curve of [wáβaaɲibeabóowée] "He took away the properties of the deceased." (Speaker MEA)

Figure 2 exemplifies the absence of downdrift between two H tones, even if they are separated by a rather long stretch of L tones. Note that the stretch of L tones is realized as a plateau.

---

2 GEN = genitive

The following example displays the realization of sequences of identical H tones, which are realized as plateaus.

(6) [ikɔ́ɔ́bíílámbíɲéeβíílaapóimisɔ́ɔ́βámina]
 (b)i-kɔ́ɔ́   bíílámbí   ɲéeβíí   la   (m)a-póa   (b)í-misáá
 cl8-manioc cl8.REL.cook.REC Gneebii at cl6-yesterday cl8-already.is
 ɔ-βámina
 cl15-toughen
 'The manioc that cooked Gneebii yesterday is already toughened.'

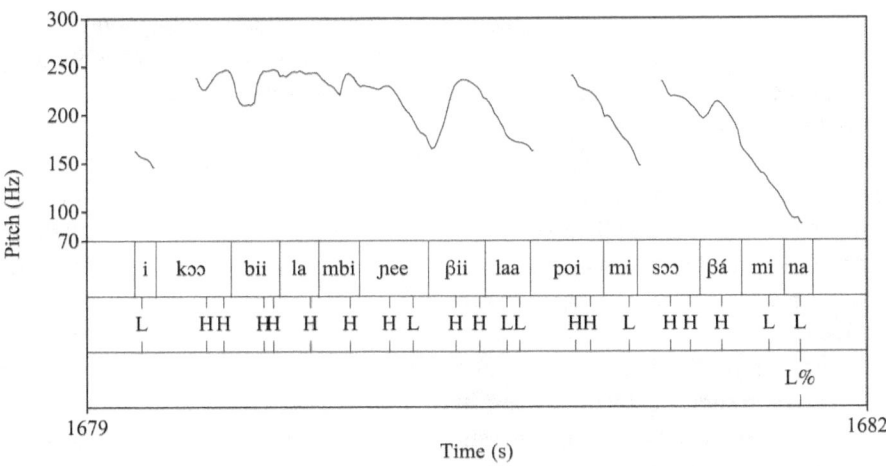

Figure 3: F0 curve of [ikɔ́ɔ́bíílámbíɲéeβíílaapóimisɔ́ɔ́βámina] "The manioc that Gneebii cooked yesterday is already toughened" (Speaker MEA)

These three utterances could seem ideal. However, such a precision in the implementation of the two tones on two levels is not uncommon, particularly in read utterances. There are also irregularities in the rendition of the two tones within an utterance. Some H tones are realized higher than expected while other ones are realized lower. These irregularities might occur on any word, and they are not related to the beginning or the end of a constituent. However, we observe that a local lowering of H tones tends to occur on grammatical words, which could be interpreted as a reduction, being related to the weakness of these words.

In the following section, we provide a quantative analysis of the relationships between successive H tones (separated by L tones) in assertive utterances.

4.2 Absence of downdrift in assertive utterances: a quantitative analysis

The corpus includes 100 assertives utterances that were read by speaker MEA and 78 assertive utterances that were read by speaker GNK[3]. At first glance, it seems that there is no regular decay in the section of assertive sentences not affected by final lowering, but only local raisings or lowerings of H tones. If there were downdrift in this section, it would affect successive H tones separated by L tones, and we would expect to find an exponential decay toward an asymptote. Despite differences between languages, exponential decay toward an asymptote is a signature of downdrift (Liberman & Pierrehumbert 1984, Myers 1996, Laniran 1992, Clements & Laniran 2003, Prieto 1996, Liberman & al. 1993, Bird 1994, among others). Due to its exponential nature, downdrift decay is particularly important at the beginning of a sentence.

To determine the presence (or absence) of downdrift, we measured the F0 peak values of H tones in sections of the utterances, which were not affected by final lowering. These undisturbed sections start at the beginning of an utterance and do not include the final part of utterances, which undergoes final lowering. 146 measurements from 100 utterances were performed for speaker A, and 108 measurements from 78 utterances for speaker B were performed. Measurements where taken on the peak of an H tone's realization.

Hn represents a given H tone and H (n+1) the following H tone, being separated from Hn by a L tone or a string of L tones. Most of the time, Hn corresponds to the first H tone (H1) and H(n+1) to the second tone (H2) of an utterance. We compared the F0 values of Hn with the F0 value of H(n+1).

The following graphs present the values of Hn on the x-axis plotted against the values of H(n+1) on the y-axis for Speaker MEA (Figure 4a) and Speaker GNK (Figure 4b).

We can observe that for both speakers, the regression line is close to the diagonal, which means that the values of Hn and H(n+1) tend to be similar. In both figures, the regression line crosses the diagonal, which is due to the fact that the difference between H and H(n+1) can be positive or negative: H(n+1) can be either lower or higher than Hn.

---

[3] Sound examples with text-grids in PRAAT format for both speakers (MEA and GNK) are provided with this chapter.

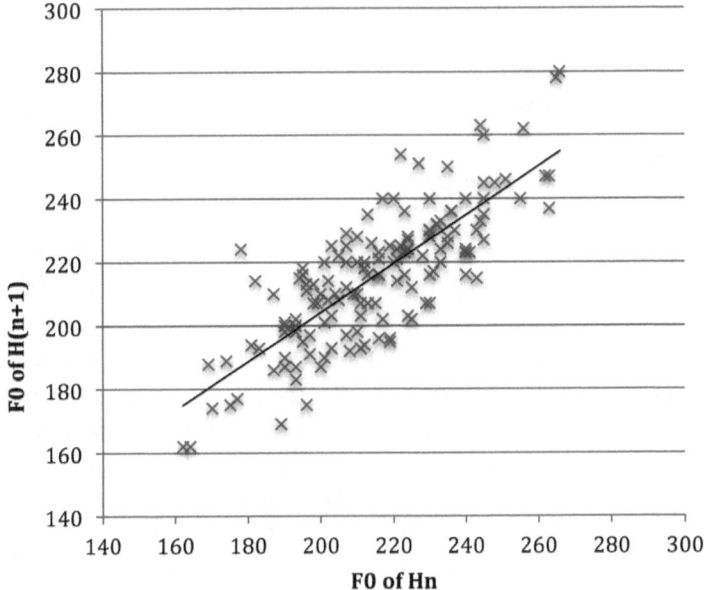

Figure 4a: F0 value of a H tone (Hn) plotted against F0 value of the following H tone (H (n+1)), separated by L tone(s) in sections of utterances unaffected by Final lowering (Speaker MEA)

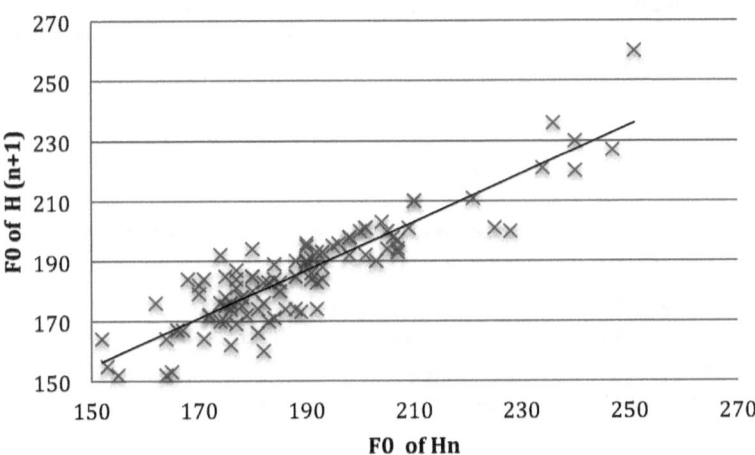

Figure 4b: F0 value of a H tone (Hn) plotted against F0 value of the following H tone (H (n+1)), separated by L tone(s) in sections of utterances unaffected by Final lowering (Speaker GNK)

The mean values with standard deviations of Hn and H(n+1) values for both speakers are presented in Table 1:

Table 1: Mean values with standard deviations of Hn and H(n+1) values for Speaker MEA and Speaker GNK

Speaker MEA:	mean of Hn = 215Hz	σ = 18Hz
	mean of H(n+1) = 216hz	σ = 7hz
Speaker GNK:	mean of Hn = 189Hz	σ = 4Hz
	mean of H(n+1) = 185Hz	σ = 7hz

For both speakers, despite the dispersion of the pitch realisation, which is mainly due to variations in register spans (see 3.3.), the mean values of Hn and H(n+1) are very close. For speaker GNK, there is a slight decaying tendency (around 4 Hz). But this slight decay is very small compared to the steps of a downdrift. For example, in Yoruba, a language with downdrift, the difference between a first H and a second H separated by a L tone is roughly 30Hz for speakers with similar pitch range (Laniran 1992). Based on this data, we can conclude that there is no downdrift in these utterances.

We can also remark that the standard deviation is more important for Hn, which is often the first H in a sentence than it is for H(n+1) with speaker MEA. This can be explained by the fact that the first H tone tends to be carried by a grammatical word and that grammatical words tend to display more variation than verbs or nouns, as they are occasionally reduced.

We next consider an important source of variation in tone realization: variations in the register span.

4.3 Variations of the register span

The register of tonal realization varies within the speech of a single speaker as well as across speakers. In our corpus, variations mainly involve the span of the register, which can be expanded or reduced. Expansion or reduction correlates mainly with the level of the ceiling of the register, which can be raised or lowered. The following example is a sentence read by the same speaker as the preceding examples, showing how he can expand his register of tonal realizations.

(7) [ɔkɔnímóobénálalekú]
ɔkɔní   móobémá   la   lekú
cl1.patient   cl1.wail.PRES   with   cl.11.agony
"The patient wails in agony"

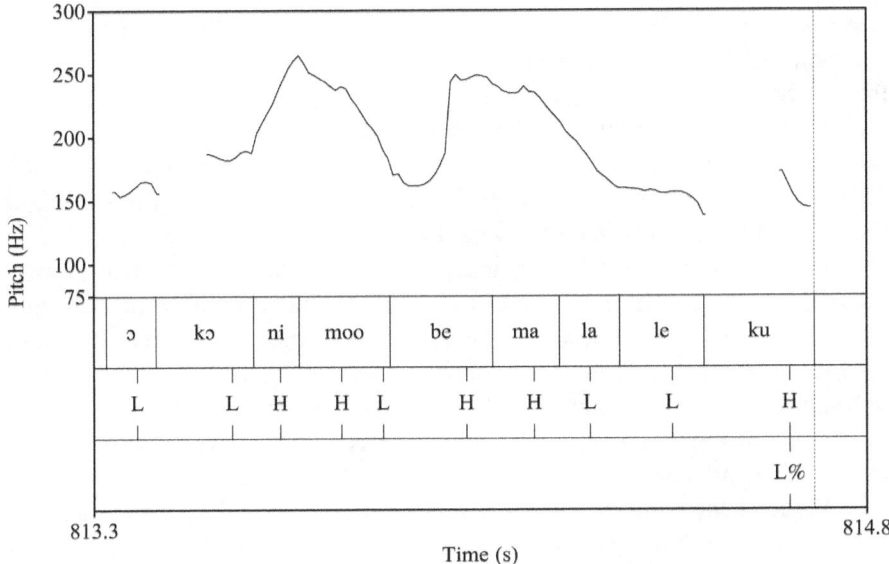

Figure 5: F0 curve of the utterance: [ɔkɔnímóobémálalekú] "The patient wails in agony." (Speaker MEA)

In Figure 5, the register span of the tone realizations in the section, which is not affected by the final lowering, ranges from 158Hz to 264 Hz, which can be compared with the 165Hz–220Hz span of the similar section in Figure 1. The register span in Figure 5 covers 9 semitones while the register span in Figure 1 covered only 5 semitones. Aside from this difference in the register spans both examples are similar, with a L% realized lower than any tone and pulling down the preceding H tones. Let's consider final lowering more closely.

4.4 Final lowering

Final lowering, as distinct from declination or downdrift, has been studied in many languages: in Japanese by Poser (1984) and Pierrehumbert & Beckman (1988); in English by Pierrehumbert & Liberman (1984) and by Arvaniti (2007), in Spanish by Prieto & al (1996), in Yoruba by Connell & Ladd (1990) and Laniran (1992), and in Kipare (Herman 1996), among others. In all these languages, final lowering had to be separated from other decaying processes, particularly downdrift. In Embosi, final lowering appears in its purest state, without being intricated with downdrift phenomena.

As in most languages in which final lowering has been documented, final lowering in Embosi is triggered by a L%. Cross-linguistically, this L% is very common, particularly at the end of assertions. The phonetic implementation of this L% has been studied in many languages. It has been found that it is not a L tone but an extra-low tone, going down to the bottom of the speaker's pitch range (see Maeda 1976 for a pioneering study on English, Rialland and Robert 2001 on Wolof, among others). In Embosi, the L% also reaches the bottom of the pitch range and it is often associated with devoicing.

This L% boundary tone is 'superimposed' on the realization of tones, lowering both final L and H tones. Figures 1, 5 and 8 exemplify the strong lowering of a final H tone, pulled down by the L%. An utterance-final string of H tones displays a progressive lowering, as shown in Figure 1. The final lowering does not only lower the last tone or string of tones but it is gradual: it affects also preceding tones but at a lesser degree. It triggers a progressive lowering toward the end of the utterance (Figure 2, 3, 5).

This final lowering recalls the Kipare lowering, after the other sources of decay were factored out (Herman 1996). The points in common are a strong lowering at the end of the utterance and an anticipation of this final strong decay on some syllables before the end.

4.5 Identifying reference lines in the realizations of tone and intonation in assertive utterances

One of the important results of the numerous previous studies on downdrift and downstep is that they were able to identify reference lines guiding the realization of tones. Asymptotes recognized by downdrift studies are examples of these reference lines. In performing downdrift, speakers tend to reach these asymptotes. Other reference lines were also identified such as the L, M and H tone reference lines in Yoruba, the H reference line being also the downdrift asymptote in this language (Laniran 1992, Laniran & Clements 2003). In their study of downstep in Dagara, Rialland and Somé (2010) posited a reference line for the last downstep in sequences of downsteps and even a second reference line in longer sentences when the number of downsteps exceeds five steps. There is also a reference line which seems common to many languages (if not all languages): the bottom of the pitch range, which is reached by the L%. Let us consider the Embosi data and begin to determine which reference lines can be posited for it.

The melodic organization of these Embosi assertive utterances is quite simple and results from the interaction of the following elements: H and L tones, and a

L%. In a given utterance, H and L tones stay essentially at the same level. Two references lines can be posited: one for the H tones and another for the L tones. The L% tone is realized lower, toward the bottom of the speaker's pitch range. This organization can be schematized as follows in Table 2:

Table 2: Pitch references lines in assertive utterances

H reference line	H_____H_____H_____
L reference line	_____L_____L_____L__
L% bottom of the pitch range	_____ L%

As we examine juxtaposed assertive sentences (in section 4.6) and yes-no questions (in section 5), we will show that there are also extra-high intonational tones, which will provide a type of symmetry to the whole system, with the span of the tonal realization in the middle.

4.6 Sequences of juxtaposed assertive sentences: introducing the H%

Juxtaposed assertive sentences are very frequent in Embosi narratives. Each of them forms an intonational phrase, ending either with a L% or a H%. Starting with examples extracted from the beginning of an interview conducted by the second author, we introduce the H% and show some of its properties. At the end of a sentence, H% plays a similar role as the continuation rise in languages such as English and can be found in a similar context. In Embosi, its specificity is to be attracted by the last H of the intonational phrase. Consequently, it is realized on the last mora, which bears a H tone in example 8 and in Figure 6. The result is an extra-high tone at the end of the sentence and a rising contour that sounds like a continuation rise. In example 9 and in Figure 7, it is realized as an extra-high tone on the penultimate syllable, which bears the last H tone. Thus, the final contour is falling.

(8) [ngáβámwánájookoβapɔ́ɔjéédijé]
 ngá βá mwána ájɛɛ okoβa pɔ́ɔ
 1sgPRO here cl1.child cl1.come.PAST cl15.take.Hm. cl.9.stories
 jéé di jé
 cl9.REL. be.PRES cl9.DEM.
 (litt.) "To me, here, the child came to collect stories which are these (ones)..."
 'To me, here, the child came to collect stories from here.'

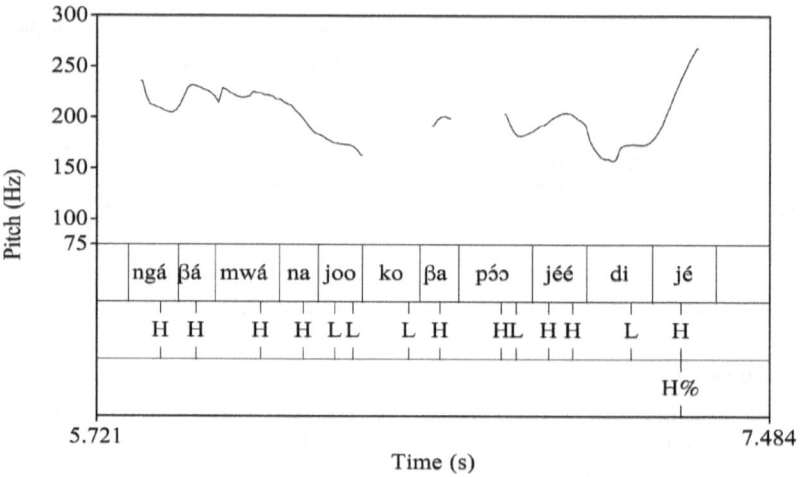

Figure 6: F0 curve of [ngáβámwánajookoβapɔ́ɔjéédijé] "To me, here, the child came to collect stories from here..." (Speaker: Catherine S., interview)

(9) [ádzaábísímóondzési]
ádzaá bísí mó (m)ondzési
"it was us during childhood" = "It was during our childhood..."

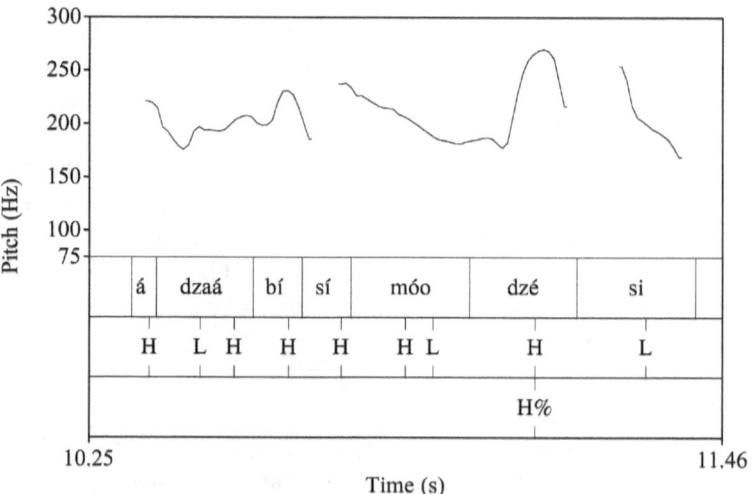

Figure 7: F0 curve of [ádzaábísímóondzési] "It was during our childhood..." (speaker: Catherine S., interview)

This H% is not only present in sequences of assertives sentences, but it is also involved in yes-no intonation marking, as we shall see in the next section.

5 Intonations of yes-no questions: a HL% contour boundary tone

A HL melody is one of the intonational markers of yes-no questions found in Bantu languages (Clements & Rialland 2008, Downing, this volume). For Embosi yes-no questions, an HL melody is also present, and we propose that this melody results from a combination of two boundary tones: a H% and a L%, forming together a HL% boundary contour. Similar to the L% in assertive utterances (see 2), the L% of this HL% contour has a strong lowering effect, particularly on final H tones. It is associated with the end of an utterance. Similar to the H% in juxtaposed assertive utterances (see 3), the H% of this HL% triggers extra-high realizations and is attracted by H tones. The alignment of this HL% contour with the tone tier of the utterance is as follows: the L% is found at the end of the utterance while the H% occurs on the last H tone if the final tone is a L tone. Otherwise, the H% of the HL% is pushed forward towards a preceding H tone, extending the contour on a larger domain. Besides these intonational HL%, the yes-no questions are also characterized by a general register expansion. Consider the realization of the following assertive and interrogative pairs:

(10) [bánabáadzáa] (assertion/question)
 b(a)-ána   báadzáa
 cl2-enfant cl2.eat.PRES
 "The children eat" / "Do the chidren eat?"

(11) [oβémbóódzɔɔbvɛ́] (assertion/question)
 (m)o-βémbá   (m)ódze   (m)ɔ-bvɛ́
 cl3-journey cl.3.be.REC cl3-good
 "The journey was good." / "Was the journey good?"

In these assertive/interrogative pairs (Figures 8 and 9), the interrogative counterpart is realized on a higher and expanded register. This effect is exaggerated in these examples, due to the fact that these interrogative utterances were read in pairs with their assertive counterparts. In the assertive forms (Fig. 8a and 9a), final lowering due to the L% can be observed. In questions (Fig. 8b and 9b), this final lowering is still present, pulling strongly down realizations of a final H tone

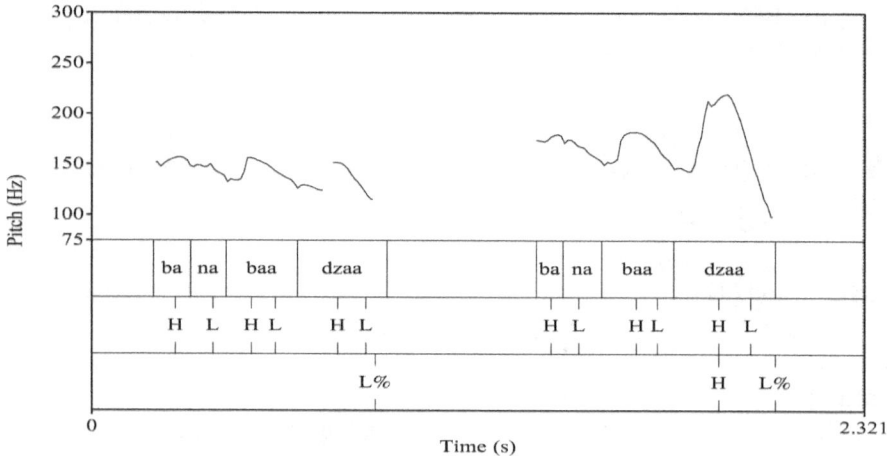

Figure 8: F0 curve of [bánabáadzáa], a) "The children eat." / b) "Do the children eat?" (Speaker MEA).

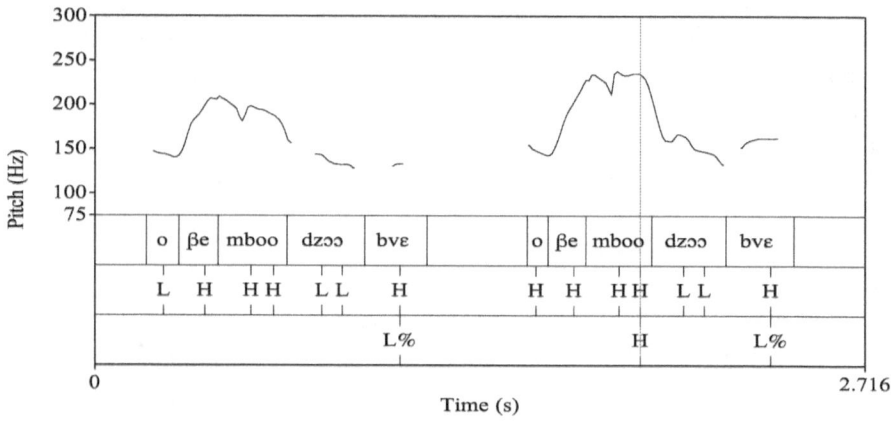

Figure 9: F0 curves of [oβémbóódzɔɔbvɛ́], a) "The journey was good." / b) "Was the journey good?" (Speaker MEA)

like in *bvɛ́* (Fig. 8b). The H% of the HL% contour is found on the last H tone when the sentence ends with a L tone. Then, this last high tone becomes extra-high (see Figure 8b). If there is a H tone at the end of the utterance, this final H tone is lowered by the L% boundary tone, and the H% of the HL% contour is found on the preceding H, raising it to an extra-high (Figure 9b). This analysis is confirmed by the other 15 assertions/yes-no question pairs recorded by speaker

A, the same corpus recorded by speaker B, and yes-no questions occurring in the 3 interviews conducted by the second author.

The existence of this H% tone has an interesting consequence for our overall model: this H% provides a higher-level reference line above the reference lines of the tone realizations (Table 3).

Table 3: Pitch references lines of H and L tones and L% and H% boundary tones

H%	_____H%_____
H reference line	H_____H_____H_____
L reference line	____L_____L_____L__
L% bottom of the pitch range	_____ L%

6 Intonation of *wh*-questions

Wh-questions in Embosi have been investigated by various theses and publications (Amboulou 1998) but the most detailed study is found in Embanga Aborobongui & al. (2011). Embosi has two sets of interrogatives pronouns: 1) *nda/nde* with *nda* referring to humans, among others (ex. 13) and *nde* referring to inanimate objects and some animals (ex. 12, 14 & 15); and 2) interrogatives words, agreeing in class with the noun that they modify or replace. Embosi also possesses interrogative adverbs. Two types of constructions are possible for questions on the subject, on the direct and indirect objects: constructions with relatives (ex. 12 & 13) and in situ constructions (ex. 14). Only in-situ constructions are permitted for questions on place, manner or cause. Here are some examples (partly from Embanga Aborongui & al. 2011):

(12) [ɲamajeébomíingobasákɔ́édzende]
 ɲama   jeébomí   ingoba   sá   kɔ́   édze   nde
 cl1.animal cl1a.REL.kill.REC Ingoba   in   forest cl.7.be.REC which
 'Which animal did Ingoba kill in the forest?'

(13) [morojɛɛpɛníitswétswelélawádzenda]
 moro   jɛɛpɛ   nɔ́   itswétswelé la   wa
 cl1.person cl1.REL.give.REC 2sgPRO.Hm   cl4.oranges to   3sgPRO
 ádze   nda
 3sg.be.REC who
 'To whom did you give oranges?'

(14) [nódziindɔɔféti]
    nɔ   ódzii   nde   (m)ɔ   féti
    2sgPRO 2sg.find.REC. what   during   festivities
    'What did you find during the festivities?'

(15) [nópfeβándéngénde]
    nɔ   ópfe   βá   ndéngé   nde
    2sgPRO 2sg.arrive.REC   here cl9.manner   which
    'How did you arrive here?'

Whatever their construction (with relatives or in-situ), *wh*-questions in Embosi do not have any specific intonations. They display the same intonations as assertive utterances, as illustrated by the following F0 curve of a realization of example 12 (Figure 10):

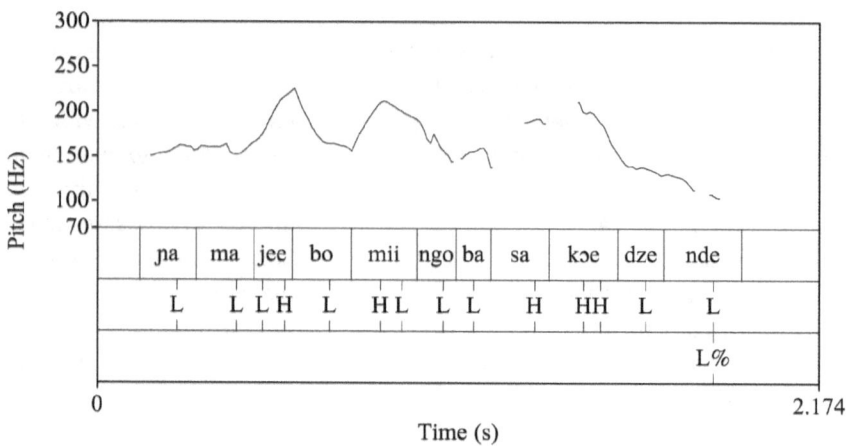

Figure 10: F0 realization of the utterance [ɲamajeébomíingobasákɔ́édzende] "Which animal did Ingoba kill in the forest?" (Speaker MEA)

The similarity of intonation between assertive utterances and wh-questions, observed in Embosi, is shared by all the languages of this volume, except Moro (Rose & Piccinini, this volume) and is common cross-linguistically (Cruttenden 1997, Frota and Prieto 2015 in Romance languages, for example).

7 Absence of specific intonation of focus

In Embosi, an answer to a *wh*-question could typically be a single word, a word with a copula or a sentence with a relative clause. Thus, the answers given by MEA to the question in (12), repeated below for convenience are as follows:

(12) repeated
[ɲamajeébomíingobasákɔ́édzende]
ɲama   jeébomí   ingoba   sá   kɔ́   édze   nde
cl1.animal cl1a.REL.kill.REC. Ingoba in forest cl.7.be.REC which
(translation word by word: the animal that Ingoba killed was which?"
'Which animal did Ingoba kill in the forest?'

(16) answers
a. one word answer
   ngombá   "a porcupine"

b. answer with a copula
   édze   ngombá
   cl7.be.REC. porcupine
   'It was a porcupine.'

c. answer with a relative clause
   [ɲamajeébomíingobasákɔ́édzengombá]
   ɲama   jeébomí   ingoba   sá   kɔ́   édze   ngombá
   cl1.animal cl1a.kill.REC. Ingoba in forest cl7.be.REC porcupine
   'The animal that Ingoba killed in the forest was a porcupine.'

In these various answers, *ngombá* is the focus. These utterances display the typical assertive pattern with the final part being lowered by the L%. As a result of this final lowering, the final H of *ngombá* is strongly lowered and there is no prosodic indication of its focus role: no increase of the pitch range, no lengthening. Possible answers to five *wh*-questions by speakers A and B were recorded and none of them showed any form of prominence or prosodic subdivision or lengthening.

Embosi can be added to the growing list of languages without any prosodic focus marking. It includes Bantu languages (Northern Sotho, Zerbian 2006; Tumbuka, Downing 2012, this volume; Chichewa, Downing, this volume; Basaa, Makasso and al., this volume), non Bantu African languages (Wolof, Rialland & Robert 2001; Buli and related Gur Languages, Schwartz 2009; Hausa, Hartmann & Zimmermann 2007; selected African languages, Zerbian & al. 2010, Moro,

Rose and Piccinini, this volume; Mambila, Connell, this volume; Kɔnni, Cahill, this volume) as well as languages spoken outside of Africa (Yucatec Mayan, Gussenhoven & Teeuw 2008, Kügler & al. 2007; Thompson River Salish, Koch 2008). Embosi provides also an additional counterexample to the view that focus is necessarily associated with some type of prominence. (See Downing & Pompino-Marschall 2013, for a discussion of this issue.)

8 Intonation of emphasis: local register expansion

Emphasis is a local highlighting of a word or an expression and is signaled by a register expansion. It is often found in association with expressions of quantity or deictic expressions as illustrated in the following example:

(17) [beabíbíidzwambváangala / bíbíidzwambváapéndzi]
    bea bí   biídzwa   mbváa Ngala / bí
    food cl.8.DEMPROX cl.8.go.FUT to   Ngala / cl.8.DEMPROX
    biídzwa   mbváa Pendzi
    cl.8.go.FUT to   Pendzi
    'This food will go to Ngala, this one will go to Pendzi.'

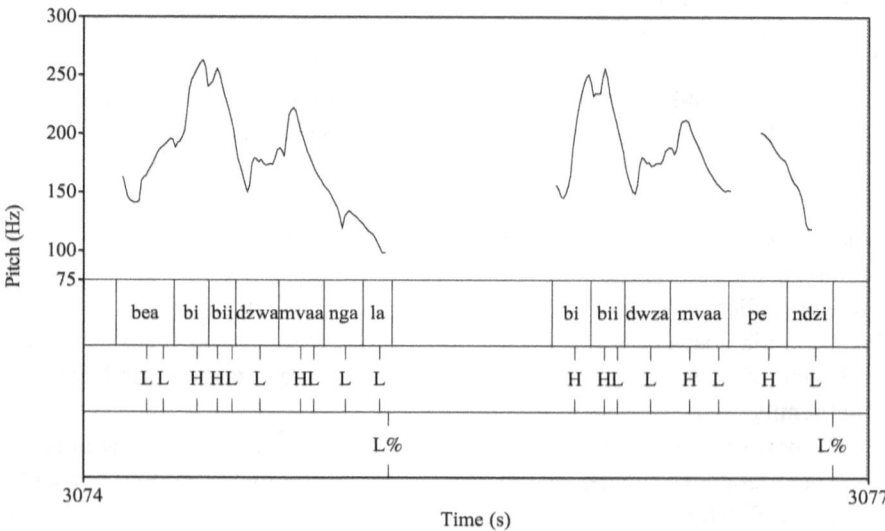

Figure 11: F0 realization of the utterance [beabíbíidzwambváangala/bíbíidzwambváapéndzi] "This food will go to Ngala's home, this one will go to Pendzi's home." (Speaker MEA)

In (17), two sets of food are pointed at, one intended for Ngala and the other one for Pendzi. The proximal demonstratives (*bí* "this") are realized with an expanded register (Figure 11). In association with a deictic expression or an expression of quantity, this local register expansion has an iconic value, enhancing the importance of the designated item. In all of its usages, it has a local highlighting function. It is clearly not related with focus as an answer to a wh-question as seen previously in 7, it is often involved in contrastive expression but it is also present when there is no contrast to insist on a given word or as a metaphoric expression of bigness. In our view, the main difference between this emphasis and focus is that it is a gradient phenomenon: a term or an expression could be more or less emphasized, depending upon the importance of the register expansion. This local register expansion has also a mirror image which is local register compression, indicating that a given term or expression is less important or backgrounded within the discourse. In this chapter, we are keeping "emphasis" separate from focus which is marked syntactically, without any involvement of intonation as seen in 7. Focus divides an utterance into two parts: a new or contrastive part and given or presupposed part while we assume that emphasis (or backgrounding) modulates locally the informative weight.

9 Subdivisions of complex sentences

In our corpus of isolated words and sentences, which include 45 complex sentences, there were no pauses or any other prosodic events between subordinate clauses and main clauses. Like in simple assertive sentences, vowel deletion processes can occur at any word junction, without any disruption. One process is sensitive to clause boundary: metatony, as mentioned previously. Thus, a verb, which undergoes metatony, will end with a L when it is clause final as in the following example (from Embanga Aborobongui 2013):

(18) [ojúluláalámbatsínadílandzaa]
(m)o-júlu   láalámba   tsína   adí   la   N-jaa
cl1-woman   cl1.PRES-cook because   cl1.PRES-be.Hm with cl9-hunger
'The woman cooks because she is hungry.'

In (18), the verb *alámba* which undergoes metatony, displays a final L tone because it is clause final, while it would have had a final H tone if it were followed by a complement. Conversely, the verb *di*, which is also sensitive to metatony, is realized with a final H because it is followed by a complement.

In a study on relative clauses in Embosi (Beltzung & al. 2011) based on a different corpus recorded by Speaker A, it was also found that utterances including relative clauses are overwhelmingly realized without any intonative subdivision. In more careful speech (perhaps sometimes too careful), pauses might occur between the antecedent and the relative clause and between the relative clause and the matrix clauses. We also found few occurrences of boundary tones, which indicate Intonational Phrase boundaries, in the same positions.

We also studied dislocations in Embosi, from syntactic and prosodic points of view. The study was based on a separate corpus recorded by speaker EMA (Embanga Aborobongui & al. 2014). An asymmetry was found between right and left dislocations. In right dislocations, the main clause ends with a L% boundary as well as the dislocated part. Cross-linguistically, this pattern is very common, found in African languages (Hyman 1999, Downing 2011) but also in non-African languages such as French (Clech-Darbon & al. 1999), among others. Here is one example:

(19) [[ojúluláaβelɔ́pɛ́wamúa L%/ɔkwáí L%] (Embanga Aborobongui & al. 2014)
(m)o-júlu   láaβelá   ɔ-pé   wa   mú-a   (m)ɔ-kwáí.
1-woman   1.PRES.can.Hm cl15-give 1a.PRO   3sg.PRO   3-machete
'The woman can give him it, the machete.'

In left dislocations, no boundary tones are realized. In our corpus, generally a pause was observed between the dislocated element and the main clause but there were few cases of continuity between them, with the final vowel of the dislocated part being deleted. Interestingly, if a pause is generally present between the dislocated element and the main clause, there is often no pause between two dislocated elements: they are often combined into a single unit, without any pause or discontinuity in the process of vowel elision at word junction. The following example illustrates this configuration:

(20) [básópoo /báabáaβelótonánɔ]
básí   ó poo   / báa   báaβelá   o-toná   nɔ.
cl2.woman at cl7.village cl2.PRO   cl2.can.PRES.Hm   cl15-refuse.Hm 2sgPRO
'The women, at the village, they can refuse you.'

In (20), there is a pause between the two dislocated elements (*básí* and *ó poo*), and the main clause, and the two dislocated elements are grouped together, as shown by the elision of the vowel *-i* of *básí* 'women' at the junction with the word *ópoo*. To account for this phrasing, we do not introduce a notion of Intermediate Intonational Phrase, but rather we propose a recursive structure of IPs as follows:

(21) [Dislocated element [core clause]]IP

This representation formally accounts for the fact that there is no boundary tone at the end of the dislocated part and that the beginning of the main clause is similar to the beginning of an Intonational Phrase.

In the eight folktales extracted from Obenga (1984) that were read by speaker MEA, we observed no dislocation, and complex sentences were rarely prosodically divided. In the three interviews that were conducted by the second author in Brazzaville, dislocations were rare and intonational breaks mainly occurred onlly between the sentences, even if the sentences were complex.

10 Conclusion

Embosi (Bantu C25) is a two-tone language without downdrift. To account for the superimposition of intonational tones on tone realizations, a dual-register model is proposed. It involves a basic register for lexical tone realization and enlargements above and below this basic register due to extra-high or extra-low boundary tones. The basic register of tone realizations can be compressed or expanded. Expansions were found in yes-no questions and in the expression of emphasis.

The prosodic hierarchy of Embosi includes Phonological Words and Intonational Phrases, which are both associated with phonological processes. No correlate, either segmental or tonal, was found for a potential Phonological Phrase. Absence of a Phonological Phrase seems typologically rare (Jun 2014). However, it is probably more common than usually assumed, as the prosodies of many languages, and among them many Bantu languages, are still undocumented. (See Downing, this volume, for another case.)

The prosody of Embosi is distinguished by its economical features: an intonational structure without downdrift and a prosodic hierarchy skipping the level of the Phonological Phrase (or at least with an invisible Phonological Phrase).

Acknowledgements

We would like to express our gratitude to our Embosi speaking consultants in France and in Brazzaville, particularly to Guy-Noël Kouarata and Angélique Otsanaa. This chapter has benefited from comments from Laura Downing, Caroline Féry and Sonia Frota, whose suggestions for improvements were very useful.

References

Amboulou Célestin. 1998. *Le Mbochi : langue bantoue du Congo Brazzaville (zone C, groupe C20)*. Thèse de Doctorat, INALCO, Paris.

Archangeli Diana & Douglas Pulleyblank. 1994. *Grounded Phonology*. Cambridge (MA, USA): MIT Press.

Arvaniti Amalia. 2007. On the presence of final lowering in British and American English. In Carlos Gussenhoven & Tomas Riad (eds.), *Tones and tunes, vol. 2: Experimental studies in word and sentence prosody*, 317–347. Berlin & New York: Mouton De Gruyter.

Beltzung Jean-Marc, Annie Rialland & Martial Embanga Aborobongui. 2010. Les relatives possessives en ɛmbɔ́sí (C25). In Downing, Laura, Annie Rialland, Jean-Marc Beltzung, Sophie Manus, Cédric Patin & Kristina Riedel (eds.), *Papers from the Workshop on Bantu Relative Clauses* (ZAS Papers in Linguistics 53), 7–37. Berlin.

Casimjee, Farida & Kisseberth Charles. 1998. Optimal domains theory and Bantu tonology: a case study from Isixhosa and Shingazidja. In Larry M. Hyman & Charles W. Kisseberth (eds.), *Theoretical aspects of Bantu tone*, 33–133. Stanford: CSLI.

Clech-Darbon Anne, Georges Rebuschi & Annie Rialland. 1999. Are there cleft sentences in French? In G. Rebuschi & L. Tuller (eds.), *The Grammar of Focus*, 83–118. Amsterdam: Benjamins.

Clements George N. & Annie Rialland. 2008. Africa as a phonological area. In Bernd Heine & Derek Nurse (eds.), *A Linguistic Geograohy of Africa*, 36–85. Cambridge: Cambridge University Press.

Cruttenden Alan. 1997. *Intonation (2nd ed.)*. Cambridge: Cambridge University Press.

Downing, Laura J. & Bernd Pompino-Marschall. 2013. The focus prosody of Chichewa and the Stress-focus constraint: a Response to Samek-Lodovici (2005). *Natural Languages and Linguistic Theory* 31. 647–681.

Downing, Laura J. 2012. On the (Non)-congruence of focus and prominence in Tumbuka. In Michael R. Marlo, Nikki B. Adams, Christopher R. Green, Michelle Morrison, and Tristan M. Purvis (eds.), *Selected Proceedings of the 42nd Annual Conference on African Linguistics: African Languages in Context*, 122–133. Somerville (USA): Cascadilla Press.

Downing, Laura J. 2012. Issues in the Phonology-Syntax Interface in African Languages. In Ọlanikẹ Ọla Orie and Karen W. Sanders (eds.), *Selected Proceedings of the 43rd Annual Conference on African Linguistics: Linguistic Interfaces in African Languages*, 26–38. Somerville (USA): Cascadilla Press.

Downing, Laura J. 2011. The prosody of 'dislocation' in selected Bantu languages. In Leston Buell, Kristina Riedel & Jenneke van der Wal (eds.), *Movement and Word Order in Bantu, Lingua* (Special Issue) 121(5). 772–786.

Embanga Aborobongui Martial, Fatima Hamlaoui & Annie Rialland. 2014. Syntactic and Phonological Aspects of Left and Right Dislocation in Embɔsi. In Fatima Hamlaoui (ed.), *Proceedings of the Workshop BantuSynPhonIS : Preverbal Domain(s)* (ZAS Papers in Linguistics 57), 26–48. Berlin: ZAS.

Embanga Aborobongui Martial, Jean-Marc Beltzung, Fatima Hamlaoui, Annie Rialland. 2011. Questions partielles en ɛmbɔ́si (C25). In Laura Downing (ed.), *Questions in Bantu Languages: Prosodies and Positions* (ZAS Papers in Linguistics 55), 7–32. Berlin: ZAS.

Embanga Aborobongui Martial. 2013. *Les processus segmentaux et tonals en mbondzi (variété de la langue ɛmbɔ́sí. C25)*. PhD dissertation, Université Sorbonne-Nouvelle, Paris.

Fontaney Louise. 1988. Mboshi: Steps toward a Grammar: Part I. *Pholia 3*. 87–169.
Fontaney Louise. 1989. Mboshi: Steps toward a Grammar: Part II. *Pholia 4*. 71–131.
Frota, Sonia & Prieto Pilar. 2015. *Intonation in Romance*. Oxford: Oxford University Press.
Gussenhoven, Carlos & Teeuw, Renske. 2008. A moraic and a syllabic H-tone in Yucatec Maya. In Esther Herrera Zendejas & Pedro Martín Butrageño (eds.), *Fonología instrumental: Patrones fónicos y variación*, 49–71. Mexico City: El Colegio de México.
Hartmann, Katharina & Malte Zimmermann. 2007. In place – out of place? Focus strategies in Hausa. In Kerstin Schwabe & Susanne Winkler (eds.), *On Information Structure, Meaning & Form: Generalizations Across Languages*, 365–403. Amsterdam: John Benjamins.
Herman, Rebecca. 1996. Final lowering in Kipare. *Phonology* 13.2. 171–193.
van Heuven, Vincent J. 2004. Planning in speech melody: production and perception of downstep in Dutch. In H. Quené and V. J. van Heuven (eds.), *On speech and language: Studies for Sieb G. Nooteboom* (LOT Occasional Series), 83–93. Utrecht: Utrecht University.
Hogan John T. & Morie Manyeh. 1996. Study of Kono Tone Spacing. *Phonetica* 53. 221–229.
Hyman, Larry. M. 1997. Prosodic domain in Kukuya. *Natural Language and Linguistic Theory* 5.3. 311–333.
Hyman, Larry. M. & Lionnet, Florian. 2012. Metatony in Abo (Bankon), A2. In Michael R. Marlo, Nikki B. Adams, Christopher R. Green, Michelle Morrison, and Tristan M. Purvis (eds.) *Selected Proceedings of the 42nd Annual Conference on African Linguistics: African Languages in Context*, 1–14. Somerville (USA): Cascadilla Press.
Hyman Larry. 1999. The interaction between focus and tone in Bantu. In G. Rebuschi & L. Tuller (eds.), *The Grammar of Focus*, 151–171. Amsterdam: Benjamins.
Jun, Sun-ah. 2014. *Prosodic Typology II: the Phonology of Intonation and phrasing*. Oxford: Oxford University Press.
Koch, Karsten. 2008. *Intonation and Focus in Nɬeʔkepmxcin (Thompson River Salish)*. Ph.D. dissertation, University of British Columbia, Vancouver.
Kügler, Frank, Stavros Skopeteas & Elisabeth Verhoeven. 2007. Encoding information structure in Yucatec Maya: on the interplay of prosody and syntax. *Interdisciplinary Studies on Information Structure* 8. 187–208.
Laniran, Yetunde. O. 1992. *Intonation in tone languages: the phonetic implementation of tones in Yoruba*. Ph.D. dissertation, Cornell University, Ithaca (NY).
Laniran, Yetunde O. & George N. Clements. 2003. Downstep and high raising: interacting factors in Yoruba tone production. *Journal of Phonetics* 31. 203–250.
Liberman, Mark, J. Michael Shultz, Soonhyun Hong & Vincent Okeke. 1993. The phonetic interpretation of tone in Igbo. *Phonetica* 50. 147–160.
Liberman Mark & Janet Pierrehumbert. 1984. Intonational invariance under changes in pitch range and length. In M. Aronoff, & R. T. Oehrle (eds.), *Language and sound structure*, 157–233. Cambridge (MA, USA): MIT Press.
Maeda Shinji. 1976. *A characterization of American English*. Doctoral Dissertation, MIT, Cambridge (MA, USA).
Myers Scott. 1996. Boundary tones and the phonetic implementation of tone in Chichewa. *Studies in African Linguistics* 25, 29–60.
Obenga, T. 1984. *Littérature traditionnelle des mbochi: etsee leyamba*. Paris : Présence Africaine.
Van Oostendorp Marc, Colin J. Ewen, Elizabeth Hume & Karen Rice. 2111. *The Blackwell Companion to Phonology: Suprasegmental phonology*. vol 2, Chichester: Blackwell.
Patin Cédric. 2007. *La tonologie du shingazidja, langue bantu (G44a) de la Grande Comore : nature, formalisation, interfaces*. Thèse de doctorat, Université Sorbonne-Nouvelle, Paris.

Paulian Christiane. 1975. *Le Kukuya, langue teke du Congo: phonologie, classes nominales.* B49–50. Paris: SELAF.

Pierrehumbert Janet B. & Mary E. Beckman. 1988. *Japanese Tone Structure*. Linguistic Inquiry Monographs 15. Cambridge (MA, USA): The MIT Press.

Prieto Pilar, Chilin Shih & Holly Nibert. 1996. Pitch downtrend in Spanish. *Journal of Phonetics* 24. 445–473.

Rialland Annie, Martial Embanga Aborobongui, Martine Adda-Decker & Lori Lamel. 2012. Réanalyse de processus phonologiques et exploration automatisée de corpus en Embosi (Bantu C25). In Chantal Enguehard, Mathieu Mangeot & Gilles Seraset (eds.), *Traitement Automatique des Langues Africaines (TALAf 2012: African Language Processing)*, http://aclweb.org/anthology/W12-1301.

Rialland Annie, Martial Embanga Aborobongui, Martine Adda-Decker & Lori Lamel, 2015, Dropping of the Class-Prefix Consonant, Vowel Elision and Automatic Phonological Mining in Embosi (Bantu C 25) In Ruth Kramer, Elizabeth C. Zsiga, and One Tlale Boyer (eds.), *Selected Proceedings of the 44th Annual Conference on African Linguistics: African Languages in Context*, 221–230. Somerville (USA): Cascadilla Press.

Rialland Annie & Penou-Achille Some. 2011. Downstep and linguistic scaling in Dagara-Wulé. In John Goldsmith, Elizabeth Hume & Leo Wetzels (eds.), *Tones and Features: Phonetic and Phonological Perspectives*, 108–134. Berlin & New York: Mouton De Gruyter.

Rialland Annie & Stéphane Robert. 2001. The intonational system of Wolof. *Linguistics* 39. 5. 893–939.

Schadeberg, Thilo C. 1995. Object diagnostics in Bantu. In E. Nolue Emenanjo & Ozomekuri Ndimele (eds), *Issues in African languages and linguistics*, 173–180. Aba: National Institute for Nigerian Languages.

Schwarz, Anne. 2007. Tonal focus reflections in Buli and some Gur relatives. *Lingua* 119. 950–972.

Zerbian, Sabine, Susanne Genzel & Frank Kügler. 2010. Experimental work on prosodically-marked information structure in selected African languages (Afroasiatic and Niger-Congo). *Proceedings of Speech Prosody 2010*, Chicago 100976, 1–4.

III Eastern Africa

Charles W. Kisseberth
Chimiini Intonation

Abstract: This chapter investigates tonal accent and intonation at the word and phrase level in Chimiini, a Bantu language formerly spoken in Somalia and heavily influenced by Somali. The study shows that a distinction between penult and final accent is morphosyntactically contrastive. However, accent is realized at the (recursive) Phonological Phrase level and can be conditioned by non-syntactic factors, like focus. Focus and emphasis also have an effect on pitch register. Phonological Phrases in Chimiini are mainly conditioned by the right edges of XP. The prosody and prosodic phrasing of constructions such as relative clauses and pseudo-relatives, dislocations, time adverbials, negatives, IAV focus, preverbal focus and questions are examined in detail.

Keywords: Final accent, penultimate accent, downstep, IAV focus, preverbal focus, left dislocation, Match theory, pseudo-relative, cleft, right dislocation, yes/no question, constituent question, Phonological Phrase, Accent Phrase

1 Introduction

Chimiini, a Bantu language closely related to the northern Kiswahili dialects (e.g. Ki̠tikuu/Bajuni and Kiamu), has been spoken for centuries in the town of Brava (=Miini) in southern Somalia. The civil war in Somalia in the 1990's, however, drove much of the population into a diaspora stretching from Mombasa in Kenya to London and Manchester in the United Kingdom to Atlanta and Columbus in the United States (to mention only the largest concentrations of speakers).

The connection between Chimiini and Kiswahili is strong; indeed, at times Chimiini has been viewed as a dialect of Kiswahili, but the major differences in phonology, morphology, and lexicon invalidate this classification. This chapter focuses on the Chimiini prosodic system, which differs strikingly from Kiswahili. At the word level, there are two principal differences. In Chimiini, accent (realized as High pitch) is contrastive, falling on the final syllable in certain mostly morphosyntactically-determined evironments, and on the penult otherwise. Swahili lacks such contrasts. In addition, Chimiini has contrastive vowel length (due to

---

Charles W. Kisseberth, Tel Aviv University and University of Illinois

retaining long vowels from Proto-Bantu and borrowing many words with long vowels from Arabic and Somali), whereas Swahili lacks such a contrast, instead predictably lengthening penult vowels by rule. Long vowels in Chimiini may be underlying, or they may arise as aconsequence of morphophonemic rules; however, whatever their origin, the long vowel may actually be realized only in either the penult or the antepenult position in the word (but not in both positions at the same time). In any other position, a long vowel must shorten.

What makes Chimiini of most interest, however, is that the principles of accent placement and vowel length distribution do not operate at the word level, but in terms of larger prosodic units. We have discussed in various places the formation of these prosodic constituents (cf. Kisseberth 2005, 2010a,b, 2011 and Kisseberth and Abasheikh 1974, 2004, 2011). The present chapter begins the task of looking closely at the issue of the realization of the pitch on the accented syllables of a sentence, i.e. the intonation of the sentence.

The data in this chapter are drawn from the speech of Mohammad Imam Abasheikh (=MI) and Gelani Mohamed Diini (=GM). The MI data were gathered in the 1970's and 1980's, while the GM data were gathered from 2009 until the present. There are two principal phonological differences between these two speakers: (a) the *mw* sequence in MI's speech is simplified to *m* in GM's speech, as well as the other speakers we have observed; (b) the sequence *ml* is replaced by *mn*. One striking phonetic difference is that in the sound we write *ndr*, the rhotic element is not present in MI's speech, while it is very noticable in the present-day speakers we have observed.

The Chimiini prosodic data are extremely complex, and presenting complex data patterns from an unfamiliar language is challenging even without the severe limitations of space that a chapter like this faces. Perhaps it will be useful to summarize at the outset the contents of each section, and the progression of ideas from one section to the next. By the term "prosody" we mean specifically (a) vowel quantity, (b) accent, and (c) intonation (by which we mean the way in which the pitch realization of the accented syllables are modulated across sentences). There is no aspect of Chimiini prosody that can be understood except by recognizing that every Chimiini sentence is exhaustively parsed into a sequence of prosodic constituents. Section 2 provides an introduction to the nature of the evidence for prosodic constituents in Chimiini and discusses the fundamental principle that guides the formation of these constituents. The evidence for prosodic constituents is provided by the distribution of vowel length and accent in sentences as opposed to the word level. The formation of prosodic constituents is shown to depend on the notion "maximal projection": the right edge of a maximal projection (roughly NP, VP, AdjP, AdvP) is always at the end of a prosodic constituent. This principle is referred to as R/XP.

In section 3 we begin our examination of Chimiini intonation. Specifically, we claim that sentences with "canonical word order" are phrased in accordance with R/XP and have a specific intonational pattern (as long as there is no focus associated with an element inside the verb phrase). We call this intonational pattern "downstep intonation", since each successive accented syllable in the sentence is downstepped. In this section we detail two critical aspects of canonical sentences: specifically, how final accent is assigned in such sentences, and how yes-no questions are formed when they have a canonical sentence as their input.

There are a variety of non-canonical sentences which have specific phrasing and intonational aspects associated with them. Sentences are mostly rendered non-canonocal by virtue either of the presence of focus or the reordering of phrases. Section 4 discusses focusing strategies. Since one of these strategies involves putting the verb into the shape of a relative clause, there is also some discussion of relativization proper in this section. Section 5 begins the examination of the reordering of phrases, discussing two quite distinct patterns where a subject is repositioned after the verb. Section 6 looks at the left dislocation of complements that are not focused, while section 7 looks at sentences where there is repositioning of both subjects and complements. Time adverbials show a different behavior from other types of complements to the verb and are examined in section 8. Section 9, the final substantive section, takes a quick look at sentential complements. Section 10 gives some brief concluding remarks.

2 Chimiini prosodic constituent structure

In the papers referred to above we have argued that an accent (High pitch) is assigned to the last word of a prosodic phrase. This accent is on the final syllable if the phrase contains a final-accent "trigger." (This statement is an oversimplification, as we shall demonstrate later.) The triggering element may be a morphosyntactic feature complex (e.g. a first/second person affirmative verb in the present or past tense, a relative verb), but in other cases may be a function word. (See the appendix for a list of final accent-triggers.) In the absence of a final-accent trigger, accent falls on the penult syllable of the word. If the final word in the phrase is monosyllabic, then that syllable bears the default accent, effectively masking the contrast between final and default accent.

Accent is never heard earlier than the last word of the phrase. An example is given in (1). (We indicate the right edge of a prosodic constituent by the symbol ")$_\varphi$". Accent is indicated by an acute accent over the vocalic nucleus of the syllable. If the nucleus has a long vowel, we write the vowel symbol twice. The acute accent mark is placed over the first vowel symbol.)

(1) **Halíima)$_\varphi$ ∅-m-pashile mw-áana)$_\varphi$ dáwa)$_\varphi$**
'Haliima rubbed medicine on the child'
(cf. isolation forms: **Halíima**, personal name; **∅-m-pashíle**
'(s)he rubbed him/her', **mw-áana** 'child', **dáwa** 'medicine')

There are no final-accent triggers in this example, hence default penult accent appears on the last word of each prosodic constituent. This example illustrates the basic principle that the right edge of a (lexical) maximal projection matches up with the right edge of a prosodic constituent in Chimiini. In (1), the verb **∅-m-pashile** is not a lexical maximal projection and thus it is not at the right edge of a prosodic constituent. One significant fact about Chimiini verbal morphology needs to be noted: there is an obligatory subject marker (SM) in finite verbs, but in certain cases this subject marker is phonologically null, as in (1). Both second person singular and third person singular human subjects require the null prefix in various affirmative tenses like the past tense shown here. In the past tense, the second person form triggers final accent, whereas the third person form does not. An object marker (OM) may appear on the verb; when the object is human, as in (1), the OM is generally used. It appears as *m* in front of a consonant and as *mw* in front of a vowel.

The example in (2) also has no final-accent triggers, thus penult default accent is predicted for the final word in each phrase. However, the final phrase consists of a monosyllabic word, thus the default accent must fall on it, since there is no penult syllable available.

(2) **Abunawáasi)$_\varphi$ ∅-ch-ala m-sál̠a)$_\varphi$ n-t̠ʰí)$_\varphi$**
'Abunawaasi spread the mat on the floor'[1]
(cf. isolation forms: **Abunawáasi**, name of a character in stories; **∅-ch-áala**
'(s)he spread s.t. out', **m-sál̠a** 'mat', **n-t̠ʰí** 'floor'

---

[1] Most examples in this chapter use the past tense form that employs the perfect extension, but this example uses the past tense form based on the tense-aspect-mood element *chi*, which coalesces with the verb stem *–ala* as *–ch-aala*)

An example with a final-accent trigger is shown in (3).

(3) a. **mw-a̱limu Ø-bozelo chi-buukú)**_φ_ **ni Huséeni)**_φ_
'the teacher who stole the book is Huseeni'
(cf. **mw-aalímu** 'teacher', **Ø-boozeló** 'who stole', **chi-búuku** 'book',
Huséeni 'personal name')

b. **mw-aalímu)**_φ_ **Ø-bozele chi-búuku)**_φ_ 'the teacher stole the book'
(cf. **Ø-boozéle** '(s)he stole')

(3a) has a subject which consists of a head noun and a relative clause modifier. In subject relativization, there is no relative particle between the head and the relative verb. Observe that the head is phrased together with the relative verb. This indicates that the head is not a lexical maximal projection. Relative verbs in Chimiini are marked in many cases by the use of a final vowel *o* at the end of the verb, rather than the *a* and *e* final vowels that occur in main clauses. The *o*, however, does not occur in the case of relative passives and relative negative verbs. All relative verbs, however, trigger final accent. Thus we find final accent in **mw-a̱limu Ø-bozelo chi-buukú)**_φ_. The predicate, on the other hand, displays default penult accent: **ni Huséeni)**_φ_. In (3b), the subject **mw-aalímu)**_φ_ is a lexical maximal projection and thus is at the end of a prosodic constituent. The verb in (3b) is not a final-accent trigger, thus we have default penult accent in **Ø-bozele chi-búuku)**_φ_.

The two examples in (3) provide a useful introduction to the second phonological phenomenon that leads to the need to recognize a critical role for prosodic constituent structure in Chimiini. In (3b), the subject noun **mw-aalímu)**_φ_ has a long vowel in its initial syllable, but the head noun in **mw-a̱limu Ø-bozelo chi-buukú)**_φ_ instead has a short vowel. Kisseberth & Abasheikh (1974) observed that at the word level, long vowels may be underlying or derived by phonological or morphological processes, but regardless of origin, the long vowel may surface only in either the penult or the antepenult position in the word. Moreover, setting aside loan words, long vowels do not occur in both the penult and the antepenult at the same time. Kisseberth & Abasheikh went on to demonstrate, however, that it is penult or antepenult position in the phonological phrase that is critical. Thus **mw-aalímu)**_φ_ is permitted to have a long vowel because that vowel is antepenult in the phrase, but the head noun in **mw-a̱limu Ø-bozelo chi-buukú)**_φ_ cannot have a long vowel since it is far removed from the end of the prosodic constituent.

Selkirk (1986) provides an insightful analysis of Chimiini vowel length. Her analysis goes as follows: Chimiini has an abstract stress system that follows the principles of the Latin Stress Rule. Stress is assigned to the penult syllable if long, otherwise to the antepenult (regardless of length). If there are only two syllables, then stress is on the penult regardless of length. If there is a single syllable, it is stressed. What is crucial is that metrical structure in Chimiini is constructed at the right edge of a prosodic constituent and not the right edge of a word. Given this assignment of stress, the rule accounting for vowel shortening in Chimiini is simple: unstressed vowels must be short.

The examples in (4) illustrate the alternations in vowel length due to the Chimiini stress system. (In (4) we indicate the stressed syllable by underlining; nowhere else in the chapter do we mark the abstract stress. Note that a sequence of vowels across word-boundary does not contract to a single syllable in Chimiini.)

(4) a. ∅-so<u>mée</u>le)_φ 'he read'
    b. ∅-somele chi-<u>búu</u>ku)_φ 'he read a book'
    c. ∅-somele chi-bu<u>ku</u> íchi) 'he read this book'

In (4a), the verb root **soom** is followed by the bimoraic perfect extension **ee**. Stress falls on the penult syllable since that syllable has a long vowel. The root vowel is shortened since it is not stressed. In (4b), stress is assigned to the long penult vowel of **chi-búuku**. Thus neither the root **soom** nor the perfect extension **ee** are stressed and thus their long vowels must shorten. In (4c), the long vowel in the initial root syllable of the noun does not receive stress since it is a pre-antepenult syllable. Thus the long vowels in the verb and also the noun must shorten since they are unstressed. It is important to emphasize that stress is assigned in terms of the right edge of a prosodic phrase, but it is not necessarily located on the last word of that phrase (in contrast to accent).

The stress system in Chimiini is an abstract system in the sense that there is no physical correlate connected to the presence of stress. The absence of stress correlates with the absence of vowel length. The presence of stress allows a vowel to be long, but does not require it to be long. We will not indicate the location of abstract stress in Chimiini sentences since it plays no role in the intonational pattern; the only thing that is important for the present chapter is the observation that the Latin Stress Rule in Chimiini searches for the very same right constituent edges as accent assignment. We are dealing with a system of prosodic constituents that determines two entirely distinct phonological phenomena: the location of abstract stress and the presence of accent.

There are two competing theories of how prosodic constituents are formed: the "align/wrap" version of Selkirk's (1986) edge-based, indirect reference to syntactic structures theory, and Selkirk's more recent "match" theory. (For the align/wrap approach, see Selkirk (1986, 1996, 2000) and Truckenbrodt (1999); for the Match approach, see Selkirk (2009, 2011).) We shall not discuss the differences between these two theories since both are consistent with the idea that it is the right edge of a prosodic constituent which is critical for the analysis of vowel length and accent. For discussion of the "align/wrap" analysis of Chimiini prosodic constituents, see Selkirk (1986), Kisseberth (2010a,b, 2011) and Kisseberth and Abasheikh (2011); for some discussion of the "match" analysis, see Selkirk (2011).

Given that the φ-phrase determines both the assignment of accent to the final word of the phrase and also the assignment of a foot at the right edge of the phrase, the critical question is: how is a φ-phrase structure assigned to the sentence. Selkirk (1986) was the first to identify the basic generalization: the right edge of a φ-phrase corresponds to the right edge of a (lexical) maximal projection (e.g. NP). We will refer to this as the R/XP Principle, without committing ourselves to how a particular theory expresses the principle. In any case, it soon becomes apparent that there must be more to the story of the assignment of prosodic constituency. Most significantly, as we discuss in detail in section 4, below, a focused word must be final in a φ-phrase even if it is not a lexical maximal projection.

3 Canonical sentences and their intonation

We use the term "canonical sentence" to refer to a sentence where the word order follows what we take to be the preferred sequencing and there is no internal focus in the sentence. Such sentences exhibit a prosodic constituent structure that reflects R/XP: prosodic constituents end at the right edge of an XP and do not end anywhere else.

(5) a. subject precedes verb:
   mu-ke óyo)$_φ$ **Ø-pishíle)**$_φ$ 'that woman cooked'
   (cf. **mú-ke** 'woman', **óyo** 'that', **Ø-pishíle** 'she cooked')

   b. verb precedes complement
   mu-ke óyo)$_φ$ **Ø-pishilee zíjo)**$_φ$ 'that woman cooked **zijo**'

   c. indirect object precedes direct object:
   Núuru)$_φ$ **Ø-pakize gáari)**$_φ$ **ma-jíwe)**$_φ$
   'Nuuru loaded stones onto the truck'
   (cf. **Núuru**, a personal name; **Ø-pakíize** 'he loaded', **gáari** 'truck', **ma-jíwe** 'stones')

k-onyesha wáa-nt^hu)ᵩ ú-so)ᵩ
'lit.to show people the face – i.e. to make a brief appearance'
(cf. **k-oonyésha** 'to show', **wáa-nt^hu** 'people', **ú-so** 'face')

mw-aalímu)ᵩ Ø-mw-andiki̱li̱le mw-áana)ᵩ kháti̱)ᵩ
'the teacher wrote a letter to/for the child'
(cf. **Ø-mw-andiki̱líile** 'he wrote to/for', **kháti̱** 'letter')

wó)ᵩ wa-m-bozele mw-aalímu)ᵩ chi-buku ch-a hisaáabu)ᵩ
'they stole the arithmetic book from the teacher'
(cf. **wó** 'they', **wa-m-boozéle** 'they stole', **ch-a hisáabu** 'of mathematics')

d. "causee" precedes direct object:
Núuru)ᵩ Ø-m-kamulishize mw-áana)ᵩ n-gúwo)ᵩ
'Nuuru caused the child to wring out the clothes'
(cf. **Ø-m-kamulishíize** 'he caused him to wring out', **n-gúwo** 'clothes')

e. direct/ indirect object precedes prepositional or locative phrase
Háaji)ᵩ Ø-t̲unzile i-bohóli)ᵩ ka i-yéembe)ᵩ 'Haaji dug a hole with a hoe'
(cf. **Háaji**, a personal name, **Ø-t̲uunzíle** 'he dug', **i-bohóli** 'hole',
ka i-yéembe 'with a hoe')

Ø-mw-osheze mw-áana)ᵩ ú-so)ᵩ ka saabúni)ᵩ
'she washed the child's face with soap'
(cf. **Ø-mw-oshéeze** 'she washed', **ka saabúni** 'with soap')

A canonical sentence is characterized by what we call "downstep intonation": the first accented syllable in the sentence represents the pitch peak and each accented syllable following is lowered in pitch. In a simple *subject-verb* sentence the pitch drop between the subject and the verb is rather substantial (e.g. 40 kHz or so). If the verb phrase has multiple phrases, the drop between phrases is less radical than between the subject and the verb. (Cf. figure 1.)

Although canonical sentences can be argued to represent the preferred word order, other word orders are possible without altering the downstep intonation (and without representing a case where the reordered element is focused). The sentences in (6) illustrate the reordering of elements in the verb phrase with no effect on intonation.

(6) **Múusa)ᵩ Ø-m-pele mw-áana)ᵩ chi-búuku)ᵩ**
'Muusa gave the child a book'

Or: **Múusa)ᵩ Ø-m-pele chi-búuku)ᵩ mw-áana)ᵩ**
'Muusa gave a book to the child'
(cf. **Múusa**, a personal name, **Ø-m-péele** '(s)he gave him')

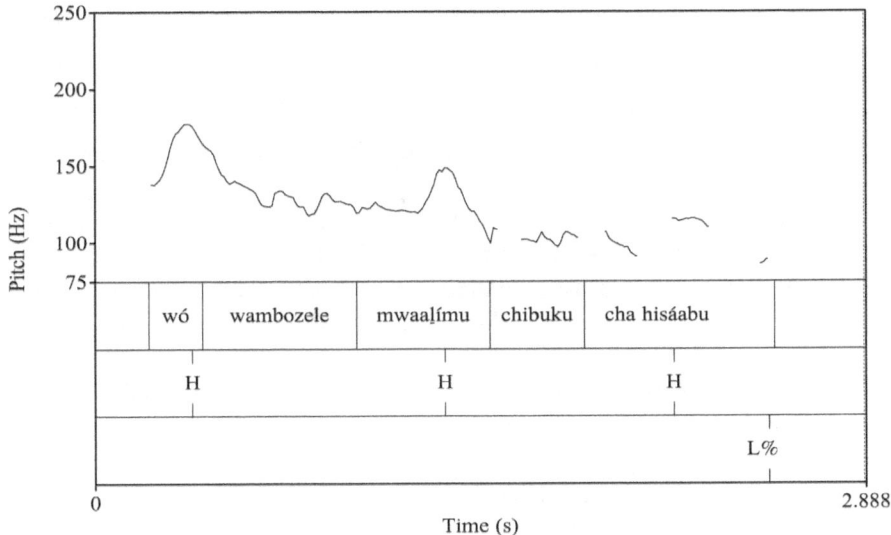

Figure 1: F0 curve of *wó wambozele mwaalímu chibuku cha hisáabu* 'They stole the arithmetic book from the teacher.'

Before we can turn our attention to non-canonical sentences and their intonational properties, there are two topics that must be addressed with respect to canonical sentences. The first topic is the problem of the realization of final accent in canonical sentences. The second topic is the formation of yes-no questions based on canonical sentences.

3.1 Final accent in canonical sentences

There is a significant puzzle that any full account of Chimiini prosody must tackle. This puzzle revolves around the fact that certain morphosyntactic word forms "trigger" the assignment of final accent and the requirement that accent appears on the last word of the φ-phrase. If the final-accent trigger were always at the end of a φ-phrase, then the issue of where this accent appears would be moot. The accent would appear on the triggering word itself.

(7) **n-jiilé)**φ 'I have eaten'

The fact is, however, the trigger is not always at the end of a φ-phrase. The first guess that one would make in that case is that the final accent will appear at the end of the φ-phrase containing the trigger. Such an analysis would account for examples like those in (8).

(8) **n-jilee n̠amá)**_φ 'I have eaten meat'
(cf. the isolation forms: **n-jiilé** 'I have eaten' and **ná̠ma** 'meat')

It is at this point that we run into some surprising data (surprising in the sense that we have not encountered any parallel data involving accent/tone or indeed any other phonological material). Specifically, look at what happens when there is more than one complement in the verb phrase.

(9) a. **n-uzize maandrá)**_φ **sukhuu=ní)**_φ 'I sold bread in the market'
or with word order variation:
n-uzize sukhuu=ní)_φ **maandrá)**_φ 'I sold in the market bread'
(cf. isolation forms: **n-uziizé** 'I sold', **máandra** 'bread', **sukhúu=ni** 'in the market')

b. **sî)**_φ **chi-m-bozele mw-aa̠limú)**_φ **chi-buku ch-a hisaabú)**_φ
'we stole the arithmetic book from the teacher'

c. **ni-m-ul̠ile mw-aaná)**_φ **gaarí)**_φ **ka do̠tooré)**_φ
'I bought for the child a car from the doctor'
(cf. isolation forms: **ni-m-ul̠iilé** 'I bought for', **gáari** 'car', **ka do̠tóore** 'from doctor')

The descriptive generalization seems to be this: when the final-accent trigger is a verb, the final accent appears at the end of each φ-phrase in the verb phrase. Consequently, in the last example there is a final accent not only on **mw-aaná**, but also on **gaarí** and **ka do̠tooré** (i.e. all three phrases are realized with final accent rather than their default penult accent).

Assuming that the realization of final accent is not a matter that must make reference to syntax directly, it seems likely that resort to some sort of recursive prosodic constituency will be necessary to account for these data. In Kisseberth and Abasheikh (2011), we suggested that the appropriate phonological principle may be: realize a final H tone on every prosodic phrase that contains the triggering verb. This analysis was based on the "align/wrap" theory of prosodic constituency and is dependent on recursive φ-phrases and the *absence* of the left edge of φ-phrases. Specifically, it assumed a prosodic structure such as **(ni-m-ul̠ile mw-aaná)**_φ **gaarí)**_φ **ka do̠tooré)**_φ where the verb is an element in three different phrases: **(ni-m-ul̠ile mw-aaná)**_φ, **(ni-m-ul̠ile mw-aaná)**_φ **gaarí)**_φ and **(ni-m-ul̠ile mw-aaná)**_φ **gaarí)**_φ **ka do̠tooré)**_φ. Given this recursive prosodic structure, the generalization holds that final accent occurs in every phrase containing the trigger.

"Match" theory (Selkirk 2011) would not allow for this solution (since when a syntactic XP is matched to a φ-phrase, both the left and the right edge are matched). Match theory would perhaps seek a solution where final accent is realized on each φ-phrase that the triggering verb c-commands. It is beyond the scope of this chapter to examine the theoretical issues. We will continue with transcriptions of sentences where just the "lowest" prosodic constituency is shown (moreover, one that ignores the possible presence of left edges of these constituents). We shall show, however, that focus, the phenomenon that we consider in some detail below, has a striking effect on the realization of final accent.

Regardless of the theoretical account of these multiple final H tones, in canonical sentences they exhibit the same downstep intonation as penult accents. (Cf. figure 2.)

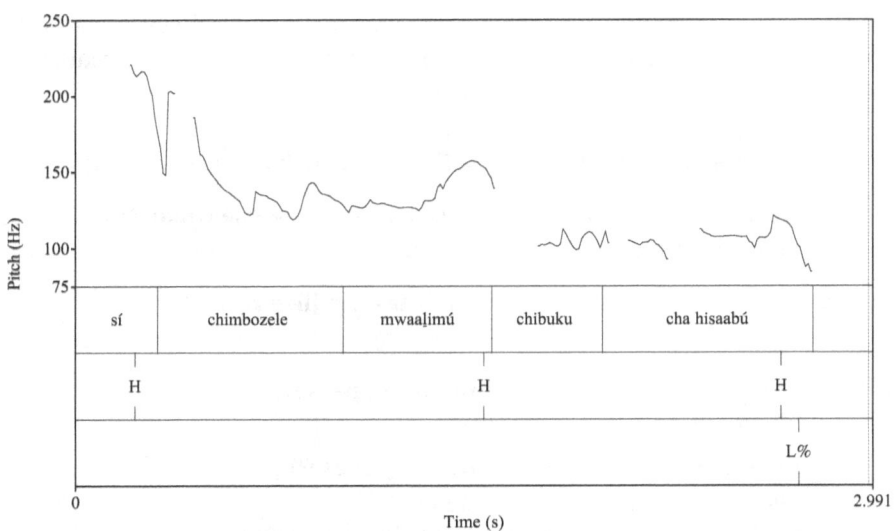

Figure 2: F0 curve of *sí chimbozele mwaaḷimú chibuku cha hisaabú* 'We stole the arithmetic book from the teacher.'

3.2 Yes-no questions based on canonical sentences

Before proceeding in section 4 to examine Chimiini sentences containing focused elements, it will be useful to briefly review the formation of yes-no questions based on canonical sentences. There are two types of yes-no questions in Chimiini: simple yes-no questions and exclamatory yes-no questions. The former is a straight-forward attempt to confirm whether something is or is not the case. The exclamatory question on the other hand seems to express disbelief/amazement that something is or is not the case. It was not possible to research the issue of usage with Mohammad Imam, who provided data on these questions via a tape recording that could not be analyzed until more than twenty years after our collaboration essentially ended. Our discussion here is restricted to the prosodic form of these questions rather than their precise use.

In a canonical sentence (including word order variants that do not involve focus), the simple yes-no question undergoes a phenomenon we refer to as Q-Raising, but no other phonological alteration occurs. The principal characteristic of Q-Raising is that the pitches of the accented syllables in the sentence are not downstepped. Although not downstepped, they do tend to show some declination in pitch height across the sentence. In MI's speech, the last accented syllable is raised to the pitch peak. This extra raising of the last accented syllable is absent from GM's speech. It should be stressed that the location of the accent in a phrase remains unaltered when one compares canonical statements with their corresponding questions. Q-Raising is indicated by the question mark that we put at the end of a simple yes-no question.

(10) a. ∅-**fakéete**)$_\varphi$ '(s)he ran away' > ∅-**fakéete?**)$_\varphi$ 'did (s)he run away?'

b. ∅-**m-wene Omári**)$_\varphi$ '(s)he saw Omari' > ∅-**m-wene Omári?**)$_\varphi$ 'did (s)he see Omari?'

c. **mí**)$_\varphi$ **n-jilee namá**)$_\varphi$ 'I ate meat' > **mí**)$_\varphi$ **n-jilee namá?**)$_\varphi$ 'have I eaten meat?'

d. **mw-aalímu**)$_\varphi$ ∅-**m-pasize Túuuma**)$_\varphi$ **péesa**)$_\varphi$
'the teacher lent Tuuma money' >

mw-aalímu)$_\varphi$ ∅-**m-pasize Túuma**)$_\varphi$ **péesa?**)$_\varphi$
'did the teacher lend Tuuma money?'
(cf. isolation forms: ∅-**m-pasíize** '(s)he lent'; **Túuma**, personal name; **péesa** 'money')

e. **mw-aalímu**)$_\varphi$ ∅-**m-pasize péesa**)$_\varphi$ **Túuma**)$_\varphi$
'the teacher lent money to Tuuma' >

mw-aalímu)$_\varphi$ ∅-**m-pasize péesa**)$_\varphi$ **Túuma?**)$_\varphi$
'did the teacher lend money to Tuuma?'

f. **wó**)$_\varphi$ **wa-m-bozele mw-aalímu**)$_\varphi$ **chi-buku ch-a hisáabu?**)$_\varphi$
'did they steal the arithmetic book from the teacher?'
(Cf. figure 3 for an example of Q-Raising from MI and figure 4 for GM.)

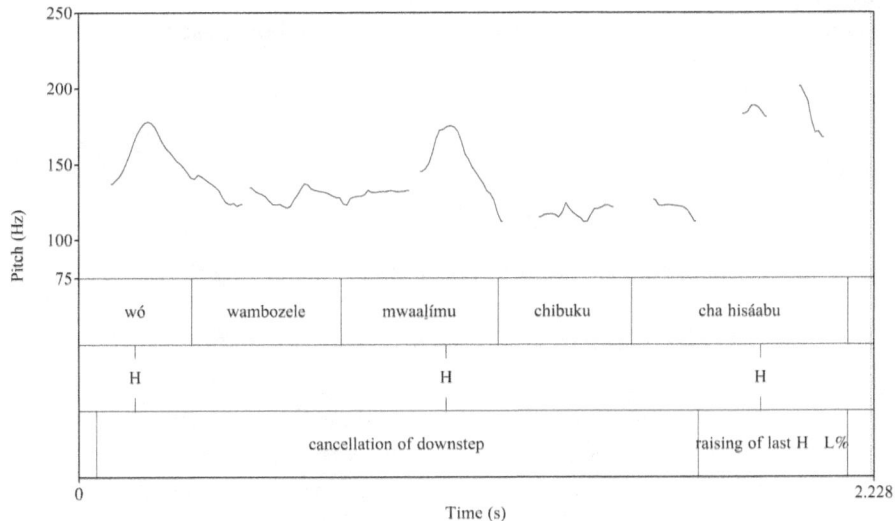

Figure 3: F0 curve of *wó wambozele mwaalímu chibuku cha hisaáabu* 'Did they steal the arithmetic book from the teacher' (speaker MI)

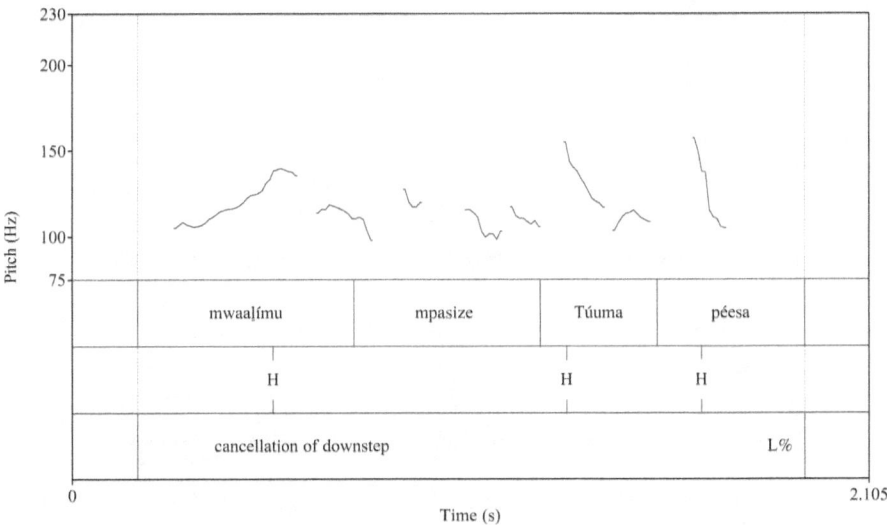

Figure 4: F0 curve of *mwaalímu mpasize péesa T̲úuma?* 'Did the teacher lend money to Tuuma?' (speaker GM)

Exclamatory yes-no questions differ from simple yes-no questions in important ways. First of all, exclamatory questions exhibit downstep intonation (not just in canonical sentences but also in non-canonical sentences, as we shall see later). Furthermore, in the speech of MI, the pitch register of the exclamatory question is also clearly lowered in comparison to the corresponding statement. Secondly, the location of accent shifts to the final syllable of each prosodic constituent in the VP. Third, the sentence-final accented syllable has a lengthened vowel and falling pitch in the pronunciation of GM, though this is not prominent in the speech of MI. We do not directly mark the phonetics of the sentence-final vowel, but instead use the symbol "!?" to indicate the various attributes of emphatic yes-no questions.

(11) **wó) wa-m-bozele mw-aalimú) chi-buku ch-a hisaabú!?)**
'did they really steal the arithmetic book from the teacher?'
cf. the case of a final-accent trigger verb, where the shift of accent in the verb phrase is is vacuous:

sí)$_\varphi$ chi-m-bozele mw-aalimú)$_\varphi$ chi-buku ch-a hisaabú!?)$_\varphi$
'did we really steal the arithmetic book from the teacher?'
(Cf. figure 5 for an example of an exclamatory yes-no question.)

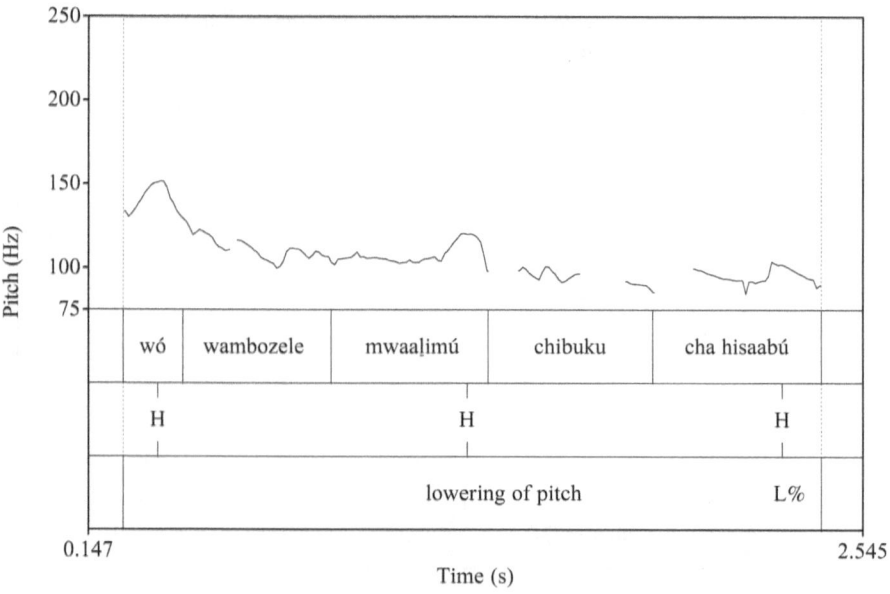

Figure 5: F0 curve of *wó wambozele mwaalimú chibuku cha hisaabú!?* 'Did they really steal the arithmetic book from the teacher?' (Exclamatory yes/no question)

4 Focus

Sentences containing focused elements do not in every case display the constituent structure predicted by the R/XP principle, nor do they display the downstep intonation pattern associated with canonical sentences. Furthermore, yes-no questions based on sentences containing focused elements have properties not present in yes-no questions based on canonical sentences.

There are a variety of instances of focus that need to be examined in terms of their effect on prosodic constituent structure, on the distribution of final accents, on intonation, and even in some cases on the morphological structure. We will discuss these various cases of focus in turn. For the most part, the presence of focus can be identified in terms of an examination of *wh*-questions (where the *wh*-word or particle identifies the locus of focus) and their possible answers. It is important to note that there are also cases of what we refer to as *emphasis*, which have some (but not all) of the prosodic effects of focus. A particularly prominent case of this is what we refer to as verb emphasis.

4.1 Focus in IAV position

The position immediately after the verb (=IAV) is a preferred position for focusing a complement of the verb in Chimiini as well as other Bantu languages. The examples in (12) illustrate.

(12) **Múusa)$_\varphi$ ∅-m-pele ᶠmw-áana)$_{f\text{-}\varphi}$ chi-búuku)$_\varphi$**
'Muusa gave the *child* a book'

Or with indirect object immediately after the verb:
Múusa)$_\varphi$ ∅-m-pele ᶠchi-búuku)$_{f\text{-}\varphi}$ mw-áana)$_\varphi$
'Muusa gave a *book* to the child'

wó)$_\varphi$ wa-m-bozele ᶠmw-aalímu)$_{f\text{-}\varphi}$ chi-buku ch-a hisáabu)$_\varphi$
'they stole from the *teacher* the arithmetic book'

In (12), R/XP predicts that the complement in IAV position is at the end of a prosodic constituent, so in that respect focus on this complement does not alter the phonological phrasing. But the presence of focus does have a clear effect on the intonation. We have placed the symbol ᶠ in front of the word bearing the accent in the focused phrase. The immediate phonetic manifestation of the focus is that the accented syllable is not subject to downstep intonation. It is raised in pitch, though not necessarily above or even to the precise same level as the initial accented syllable in the sentence. The accented syllable of a complement that follows the focused element, on the other hand, is clearly downstepped. It is, of course, not immediately obvious whether the focused phrase should be considered just another φ-phrase, or whether the notion of a "focus phrase" has a special status in prosodic constituent structure. For convenience, we show the focused element to be at the end of a f-φ-phrase, but do not pursue theoretical issues. (Cf. figure 6.)

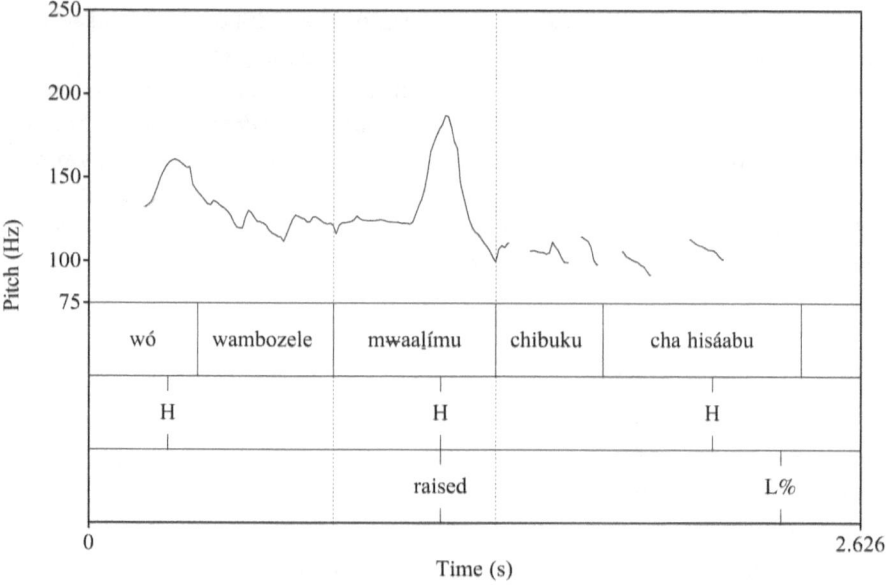

Figure 6: F0 curve of *wó wambozele ⁽ᶠmwaalímu⁾f chibuku cha hisáabu* 'They stole from the *teacher* the arithmetic book' (focus on ⁽ᶠmwaalímu⁾f)

There is another phonetic manifestation of focus on an IAV complement. In order to see this evidence, we must shift to the case where the verb is a final-accent trigger.

(13) *canonical sentence and reordered variant*:
    a. **ni-m-pele mw-aaná)φ chi-buukú)φ** 'I gave the child a book'
       (cf. **ni-m-peelé** 'I gave him/her')

    b. **ni-m-pele chi-buukú)φ mw-aaná)φ** 'I gave a book to the child'

focus on IAV complement:
    c. **ni-m-pele ᶠmw-aaná)f-φ chi-búuku)φ** 'I gave the *child* a book'

    d. **ni-m-pele ᶠchi-buukú)f-φ mw-áana)φ** 'I gave a *book* to the child'

What we see from (c–d) in comparison to (a–b) is that realization of the final accent is confined to the f-φ-phrase when there is focus, while in the canonical sentences the final accent is realized on both prosodic constituents in the verb phrase. The phrase to the right of the f-φ-phrase does not realize the final accent, even though syntactically speaking it is a complement of the triggering verb. Kisseberth and Abasheikh (2011) explained such data by claiming that the verb could not be recursively wrapped into a phrase with the second complement due to a requirement that a focused element must be final in any prosodic phrase containing it. A match theory analysis might propose that the verb that triggers final accent c-commands only the first complement, since the second complement is outside the f-φ-phrase. In the rest of this chapter, we will refer to this phenomen as the Accentual Law of Focus (=ALF); it simply says that the effect of a final accent cannot extend past a focused element.

The assumption that there is a contrast between the presence and absence of focus on the IAV complement is supported by evidence from discourse. For example, if someone asks the question: ∅-m-pele náani)$_{f-φ}$ chi-búuku)$_φ$ 'you gave whom a book?', the only appropriate answer from among the sentences in (13) would be: **ni-m-pele ᶠmw-aaná)$_{f-φ}$ chi-búuku)$_φ$**; but if the question were ᶠ∅-m-peele=ní)$_{f-φ}$ mw-áana)$_φ$ 'what did you give the child?', the only appropriate response would be **ni-m-pele ᶠchi-buukú)$_{f-φ}$ mw-áana)$_φ$**. Neither (a) nor (b) would be a felicitous answer to either of these questions.

The formation of a simple yes-no question based on a sentence with IAV focus is rather surprising. Recall that the Q-Raising found in a simple yes-no question has the effect of raising the pitch of an accented syllable (nullifying downstep). It is not clear whether there is any difference in this raising when operating on a f-φ-phrase, as opposed to an ordinary φ-phrase. A careful phonetic study of this matter is needed. What is clear, however, is that the phrases subsequent to the f-φ-phrase are pronounced differently in the question than in the statement: specifically, accent in these phrases is shifted to the final syllable. Thus an out-of-focus noun like **péesa** has default accent in the statement, but final accent in the question: **peesá**. Only the "out-of-focus" phrases following the f-φ-phrase exhibit this accent shift. The f-φ-phrase itself does not show a shift, nor does a preceding subject.

(14) a. **mw-aalímu)$_φ$ ∅-m-pasize ᶠTúuuma)$_{f-φ}$ péesa)$_φ$**
'the teacher lent *Tuuma* money' >

mw-aalímu)$_φ$ ∅-m-pasize ᶠTúuma)$_{f-φ}$ peesá?)$_φ$
'did the teacher lend *Tuuma* money?'

mw-aalímu)_φ ∅-m-pasize ᶠpéesa)_{f-φ} Ṯúuma)_φ
'the teacher lent *money* to Tuuma' >

mw-aalímu)_φ ∅-m-pasize ᶠpéesa)_{f-φ} Ṯuumá?)_φ
'did the teacher lend *money* to Tuuma?'

b. wó)_φ wa-m-bozele ᶠmw-aalímu)_{f-φ} chi-buku ch-a hisáabu)_φ
'they stole from the *teacher* the arithmetic book'

> wó)_φ wa-m-bozele ᶠmw-aalímu)_{f-φ} chi-buku ch-a hisaabú?)_φ
cf. the exclamatory question: wó)_φ wa-m-bozele mw-aalimú)_{f-φ} chi-buku ch-a hisaabú)_φ

wó)_φ wa-m-bozele chi-buku ch-a ᶠhisáabu)_{f-φ} mw-aalímu)_φ
'they stole the *arithmetic book* from the teacher'

> wó)_φ wa-m-bozele chi-buku ch-a ᶠhisáabu)_{f-φ} mw-aalimú?)_φ

> wó)_φ wa-m-bozele chi-buku ch-a hisaabú)_φ mw-aalimú!?)_φ

sí)_φ chi-m-bozele ᶠmw-aalimú)_{f-φ} chi-buku ch-a hisáabu)_φ
'we stole from the *teacher* the arithmetic book'

> sí) chi-m-bozele ᶠmw-aalimú)_{f-φ} chi-buku ch-a hisaabú?)_φ

Our consultant GM does not ordinarily form exclamatory questions based on sentences containing a focused element. MI, however, provided examples of such questions. An exclamatory question like sí)_φ chi-m-bozele mw-aalimú)_φ chi-buku ch-a hisaabú!?)_φ 'did we really steal an arithmetic book from the teacher!?' exhibits downstep (and register lowering) across the sentence. There is no reflection of the f-φ phrase found in the corresponding statement. In addition to this downstep intonation, there is also accent shift throughout the verb phrase. Accent shift in exclamatory questions does not differentiate phrases "in focus" from phrases "out of focus", thus they provide no evidence bearing on matters of focus.

There is one point that we need to stress here. Our hypothesis here is that there is a kind of phonological phrase (the f-φ phrase) that is a barrier to the projection of final accent into subsequent phrases in the syntactic verb phrase. Our assumption is that, in the absence of an f-φ phrase, final accent triggered by the verb will extend to the end of the verb phrase. We will suggest later in this chapter that there are elements that seem to stand outside the verb phrase proper (specifically, time adverbials and right-dislocated subjects) and thus are outside the scope of the verb's final accent. We do not resort to the notion of a f-φ to explain these cases.

4.2 Emphasis on the verb

IAV focus does not yield prosodic constituents that are inconsistent with R/XP. There is, however, a very common phenomenon of *verb emphasis* which does yield prosodic constituents which we do not expect on the basis of R/XP. The phonological consequences of verb emphasis are several. First of all, the verb is raised in pitch and not downstepped in comparison to the initial accent in the sentence (although there are significant restrictions on this observation: for example, relative verbs do not exhibit downstep). Second, the verb is necessarily at the end of a prosodic constituent. While the verb is not downstepped, the following complement is. Third, if the verb is a final accent-trigger, then the final accent is realized at the end of the verb and does not extend throughout the verb phrase (due to the Accentual Law of Focus discussed in 4.1). Fourth, in a simple yes-no question based on a sentence with verb focus, all of the complements to the verb undergo accent shift to the final vowel of the prosodic constituent (just like the phrases following an IAV-focused phrase).

Due to the parallelism between the effects of IAV-focus and verb emphasis, we will continue to use the terms "focus" and "f-φ" in our description even for verb emphasis. But it is important to note that the use of verb emphasis in Chimiini is extremely flexible and does not correlate with any notions of predicate-centered focus. Texts and elicitation sessions are alike in being rife with examples of verb emphasis where the question of focus as ordinarily construed seems irrelevant. Some vague concept of stylistic "high-lighting" is appropriate for many cases of verb emphasis, although it is undoubtedly true that the device can be adapted intonationally to contrast one verb with another. We do not examine this particular use of verb emphasis. The first three points are illustrated by the examples in (15):

(15) **wáawe)$_φ$ ^{f}Ø-m-bishíle)$_{f-φ}$ mu-nt^{h}u úyu)$_φ$** 'my father *beat* this man'
cf. the canonical sentence: **wáawe)$_φ$ Ø-m-bishile mu-nt^{h}u úyu)$_φ$**
'my father beat this man'
(cf. isolation forms: **Ø-m-bishíle** '(s)he hit him/her'; **múu-nt^{h}u**
'person, man'; **úyu** 'this one')

mí)$_φ$ ^{f}n-t^{h}iinzilé)$_{f-φ}$ náma)$_φ$ kaa chí-su)$_φ$ 'I *cut* the meat with a knife'
cf. the canonical sentence: **mí)$_φ$ n-t^{h}inzilee namá)$_φ$ kaa chi-sú)$_φ$**
(cf. **n-t^{h}iinzilé** 'I cut'; **náma** 'meat'; **chí-su** 'knife')

wó)$_φ$ ^{f}wa-m-boozéle)$_{f-φ}$ chi-buku ch-a hisáabu)$_φ$ mw-aalímu)$_φ$
'they stole the math book from the teacher'

In the first example, the verb is a third person past tense form and does not trigger final accent. The focused verb stands at the end of a prosodic constituent and bears a penult accent that is not downstepped relative to the first accented syllable in the sentence. The complement, however, is downstepped. (Cf. figure 7.)

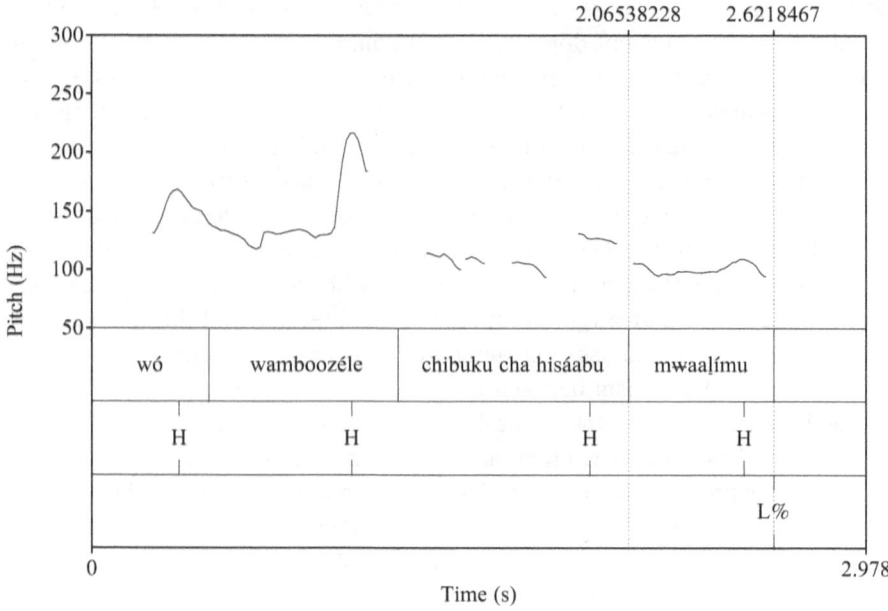

Figure 7: F0 curve of *wó ꜝwamboozéle$_f$ chibuku cha hisáabu mwaalímu* 'they *stole* the math book from the teacher' (focus on ꜝ*wamboozéle$_f$*)

In the second sentence in (15), the first person past tense verb is a final-accent trigger, but because this verb is at the end of a f-φ, the final accent appears on this verb and not on the following complement.

The formation of yes-no questions is shown in (16).

(16) **mí)$_φ$ ꜝn-t^{h}iinzilé)$_{f-φ}$ náma)$_φ$ kaa chí-su)$_φ$** 'I *cut* the meat with a knife'
> mí)$_φ$ ꜝn-t^{h}iinzilé)$_{f-φ}$ namá)$_φ$ kaa chi-sú?)$_φ$

yé)$_φ$ ꜝØ-tiinzíle)$_{f-φ}$ náma)$_φ$ kaa chí-su)$_φ$ 'he *cut* the meat with a knife'
> yé)$_φ$ ꜝØ-tiinzíle)$_{f-φ}$ namá)$_φ$ kaa chi-sú?)$_φ$

wó)$_φ$ wa-m-bozele chi-buku ch-a ꜝhisáabu)$_{f-φ}$ mw-aalímu)$_φ$
'they stole the *arithmetic book* from the teacher'
> wó)$_φ$ ꜝwa-m-boozéle)$_{f-φ}$ chi-buku ch-a hisaabú)$_φ$ mw-aalimú?)$_φ$

In these examples, Q-Raising eliminates the downstepping of the complements, but both complements undergo accent shift to their final syllable.

The exclamatory question provided by MI is quite different, as it exhibits downstep (and register lowering), eliminating any reflection of the f-φ phrase found in the statement. Accent shift, as always in the exclamatory question, affects all the phrases in the syntactic verb phrase.

(17) wó)_φ wa-m-boozelé)_φ chi-buku ch-a hisaabú)_φ mwaalimú!?)_φ
'did they really steal the arithmetic book from the teacher!?'

4.3 Pre-verbal focus

There are various pre-verbal elements: subjects, adverbials, preposed verbal complements. Sentences may have more than one preverbal prosodic constituent. R/XP predicts correctly that there will be a phrase break after each pre-verbal XP. In the absence of focus, the intonation of the sentence is straightforward. There is always a major downstep between the phrase immediately before the verb and the following phrase. Subsequent phrases in the VP are also downstepped. If there are multiple pre-verbal phrases, the pitch peak is on the first phrase and there is a declination of pitch on subsequent pre-verbal phrases. This declination is not as radical, however, as the downstep affecting the phonological phrases in the VP.

For the most part, pre-verbal constituents are not necessarily focused, but they *may* be. Since the initial phrase in a sentence is the pitch peak, pitch alone is not a clear indication that an initial element is focused. The presence of focus on a pre-verbal element, however, is clearly marked by the fact that the verb must be put into what we call a "pseudo-relative" form. In order to explain what we mean by "pseudo-relative" form, we must briefly sketch the prosody of relative clauses.

4.3.1 True relative clauses

The morphology of a relative verb parallels closely the morphology of the corresponding main clause verb in that it follows the same basic structure: (neg)-SM-(TAM)(OM)-verb stem-FV (where "neg" refers to a possible negative element; "SM" refers to the obligatory subject marker, which may be phonologically null in some cases; "TAM" refers to the possible presence of a tense-aspect-mood marker; "OM" refers to a possible object marker; the verb stem consists of a verb root plus various possible extensions, including the past tense and passive extensions, which have considerable complexities; "FV" refers to the final vowel that is obligatory in every verb form. The relative verb is distinct from the non-relative verb in some, but not all, cases due to its use of the final vowel *o* in affirmative tenses (except for those involving a passive verb). A second difference between relative verbs and non-relative verbs is that the former triggers final accent in all tenses regardless of the nature of the subject.

The contrast between main clause verbs and relative verbs is shown in (18):

(18) a. **mu-ke Ø-pishiló)**$_\varphi$ 'the woman who cooked' or: **mú-ke)**$_\varphi$ **Ø-pishiló)**$_\varphi$
(cf. isolation forms: **mú-ke** 'woman', **Ø-pishiló** 'who cooked')

cf.

b. **mú-ke)**$_\varphi$ **Ø-pishíle)**$_\varphi$ 'the woman cooked'

There is variation between whether the head in subject relativization is phrasally separated from the relative verb or not; both options are illustrated in (18a). No such option exists when the verb is a main clause verb. A preceding NP is always in a separate phonological phrase from the verb, as in (17b). In affirmative, active tenses, the relative verb ends in a final vowel *o*, as in (18a). The final vowel of the past tense main clause verb is *e*, as in (17b). The relative verb in (18a) triggers a final accent; a third person main clause past tense verb triggers default penult accent, as in (18b).

In (19a), we see that a passive verb retains its final vowel in the relative clause, but does trigger final accent (cf. the corresponding main verb in (19b).

(19) a. **mu-nt^{h}u Ø-na-ku-meroowá)**$_\varphi$ **ni úyu)**$_\varphi$
'the person who is being looked for is this one'
(cf. isolation form: **Ø-na-ku-meroowá** 'who is being looked for')

cf.

b. **múu-nt^{h}u)**$_\varphi$ **Ø-na-ku-meróowa)**$_\varphi$ 'the man is being looked for'

In (20a), we see that the final accent triggered by the relative verb is realized on its infinitival complement; in (20b), the main verb triggers default accent, which is also realized on the infinitival complement.

(20) a. **mu-nt^{h}u Ø-ofeto kh-fakatá)**$_\varphi$ **Ø-na-kh-pumúla)**$_\varphi$
'the man who is tired from running is resting now'
(cf. isolation forms: **Ø-ofeetó** 'who is tired', **kh-fakáta** 'to run',
Ø-na-kh-pumúla '(s)he is resting')

cf.

b. **múu-nt^{h}u)**$_\varphi$ **Ø-ofete kh-fakáta)**$_\varphi$ 'the man is tired from running'

Given that in subject relativization, the relative clause is a modifier of the head, one would expect that the head is not a maximal projection and thus would not be at the edge of a phonological phrase by virtue of R/XP. Thus the forms where the head phrases with the verb are expected. But as we mentioned above, it is also quite possible for the head to be phrasally separated from the relative verb, as in (21).

(21) **ni-m-wene mw-aa̱limú)**$_\varphi$ **∅-bozelo chi-buku ch-a mw-aaná)**$_\varphi$
'I saw the teacher who stole the child's book'
(cf. **ni-m-weené** 'I saw him', **mw-aa̱límu** 'teacher', **∅-boozeló** 'who stole', **chi-búuku** 'book', **ch-a hisáabu** 'of mathematics')

n-t^hále)$_\varphi$ **i-la̱ziló)**$_\varphi$ ^{f}**ha-y-rúudi)**$_{f\text{-}\varphi}$ **chi-núme)**
'an arrow that has left does not come back' (a proverb)
(cf. **n-t^h ále** 'arrow'; **i-la̱ziló** 'which has left'; **ha-y-rúudi** 'it does not return'; **chi-núme** 'back')

It is beyond the scope of this chapter to explore whether there are stylistic, discourse, or even structural factors that play a role in whether the head in these sentences phrases with the verb or not.

When there is (a) a head of a relative clause that is co-referential to a complement of the verb, and (b) when there is an overt subject of the relative clause, the head is obligatorily followed by what we will refer to as the relative particle ***AGR-a***. The agreement on this particle is with the head.

(22) **ni-m-wene mw-aaná)**$_\varphi$ **w-aa mí)**$_\varphi$ **ni-m-bozelo chi-buukú)**$_\varphi$
'I saw the child whom I stole a book from'
(cf. **ni-m-weené** 'I saw him', **mw-áana** 'child', **w-a** relative particle, **mí** 'I', **ni-m-boozeló** 'whom I stole from', **chi-búuku** 'book')

n-uzize chi-buukú)$_\varphi$ **ch-a Núuru)**$_\varphi$ **∅-m-bozelo mw-aaná)**$_\varphi$
'I sold the book that Nuuru stole from the child'
(cf. **n-uziizé** 'I sold', **chi-búuku** 'book', **ch-a** relative particle, **Núuru** personal name, **∅-m-boozeló** 'that he stole from him', **mw-áana** 'child')

Notice that in these examples the head noun of the relative clause is in a separate prosodic constituent from the relative particle. This is by no means an invariable phrasing pattern, as shown in (23), where the head and the relative particle plus subject are phrased together.

(23) **chi-su ch-aa mí) n-uuziló)** 'the knife that I bought'
or: **chi-su ch-aa mí) ni-ch-uuziló** 'the knife that I bought (it)'

n-uzize chi-buku ch-aa mí) ni-m-bozelo mw-aaná)
'I sold the book that I stole from the child'

n-uzize chi-buku ch-a Nuurú)_φ ∅-m-bozelo mw-aaná)_φ
'I sold the book that Nuuru stole from the child'

n-uziizé)_f-φ Núuru)_φ ∅-m-bozelo mw-aaná)_φ
'I sold/the book that Nuuru/stole from the child'

In these examples, the head of the relative is phrased together with the relative verb. Again, this is what we might expect if the head is a noun that is modified by the structure consisting of the relative particle and the relative clause. The problem, of course, is that (just as in subject relativization) the head in object relativization may be at the end of a prosodic constituent. This variation is beyond the scope of this chapter.

The ***AGR-a*** relative particle is absent if the head of the relative clause is not the subject, but the subject is postposed after the relative verb. Look at the variations in the relative clause shown below in (24).

(24) **fat̲úura)_φ y-a Núuru)_φ ∅-t̲a-k-uuló)_φ** 'the car that Nuuru will buy'

fat̲ura y-a Núuru)_φ ∅-t̲a-k-uuló)_φ 'the car that Nuuru will buy'

fat̲úura)_φ ∅-t̲a-k-ulo Nuurú)_φ 'the car (that) he will buy, Nuuru'

fat̲ura ∅-t̲a-k-ulo Nuurú)_φ 'the car (that) he will buy, Nuuru'

gáari)_φ ∅-pakizo Nuurú)_φ ma-jiwé)_φ
'the truck that was loaded (i.e. by) Nuuru with stones'

gáari)_φ ∅-uzilo Haají)_φ s-páandri)_φ 'the truck that bought Haaji I will not ride (in it)'

Núuru)_φ ∅-inenzeze gáari)_φ ∅-uzilo Haají)_φ
'Nuuru drove the truck (that) bought Haaji'

We should note that the postposed subjects in these examples *are* the subjects of the relative verb, as indicated by the fact that they control the subject marker on the relative verb. The head nouns do not control the subject marking.

With that much background on true relative clauses, let us turn our attention to pre-verbal focus and the pseudo-relativization that it triggers on the verb.

4.3.2 Pre-verbal focus and pseudo-relativization

Whenever there is focus on a pre-verbal element, the verb *looks* like a relative verb (i.e. ends in the final vowel *o* in many tenses and triggers final accent in all tenses with all subject markers), hence the use of the term "pseudo-relative" to describe the morphological effect of pre-verbal focus on the verb. There is no doubt that the immediate reaction to the data might be to say that we are dealing with a so-called "cleft" sentence (i.e. a biclausal construction consisting of the focused element, a copula verb in the main clause, and a subordinate relative clause). While such an analysis may be possible, there are some factors that render the issue a bit complex. First of all, while the copular verb **ni** may precede the focused element in many cases, it is much more common for the **ni** to be absent. Second, there are various cases where **ni** is not permitted to precede the focused element. Third, there are verb tenses that cannot be used in true relative clauses, but can be used in what we refer to as pseudo-relative clauses. Fourth, the accentual facts are not the same in pseudo-relative clauses as in true relative clauses. All of the preceding points will be seen in the discussion below. One instance of pre-verbal focus involves the subject.

(25) no internal focus:
 Abú)$_φ$ Ø-ṯumbile ḻ-kúta)$_φ$
 'Abu made a hole in the wall'

 verb focus:
 Abú)$_φ$ ^{f}Ø-ṯumbíile)$_{f-φ}$ ḻ-kúta)$_φ$
 'Abu *made a hole* in the wall'

 subject focus:
 ^{f}Abú)$_{f-φ}$ Ø-ṯumbilo ḻ-kutá)$_φ$
 '*Abu* made a hole in the wall'

 subject focus:
 ni ^{f}Abú)$_{f-φ}$ Ø-ṯumbilo ḻ-kutá)$_φ$
 'it is *Abu* who made a hole in the wall'

 (cf. **Abú**, a person name, **Ø-ṯumbíile** 'he made a hole', **Ø-ṯumbiiló** 'who made a hole', **ḻ-kúta** 'wall')

In preceding sections, we have seen that failure to undergo downstep is one piece of evidence that a constitutent is focused. In (25), the subject is in initial position and regardless of focus is the pitch peak in the sentence. That the subject is focused in the third example is indicated by the shift of the verb to pseudo-relative form. The fourth example illustrates that a copular verb *ni* may precede the focused subject. Additional examples are provided below:

(26) ^f**máandra)**_{f-φ} **i-jiilá)**_φ '*bread was eaten*'
(cf. **máandra)**_φ **i-jiila)**_φ 'bread was eaten')

^f**Omári)**_{f-φ} **Ø-m-ulilo mw-aana=w-é)**_φ **fatuurá)**_φ
'Omari (is the one who) bought a car for his son'
(cf. isolation forms: **Omári**, personal name; **Ø-m-uliiló** '(s)he bought for him/her'; **mw-aaná=w-e** 'his/her son'; **fatúura** 'car')

^f**Huséeni)**_{f-φ} **khámri)**_φ **hu-nó)**_φ '*Huseeni beer drinks*'
(cf. isolation forms: **Huséeni**, personal name; **khámri** 'liquor, beer'; **hu-nó** 'who drinks')

fatúura)_φ ^f**Túuma)**_φ **Ø-uziló)**_φ 'a car *Tuuma* bought'
(cf. isolation forms: **Túuma**, personal name; **Ø-uziló** 'who bought')

The particle **tú** 'only' (a phrasal isolate that never phrases with a preceding or following element) induces a pseudo-relative verb when it is located after a pre-verbal NP. Its pitch is raised in this environment and we consider it to be a focus-phrase. When attached to a post-verbal NP, **tú** does not induce pseudo-relativization. This is a consistent fact about the language: post-verbal focus leaves the form unaltered with respect to its morphological form, but pre-verbal focus requires pseudo-relativization.

(27) **Múusa)**_φ ^f**tú)**_{f-φ} **Ø-somelo zi-buukú)**_φ **z-ont^hé)**_φ 'only Muusa read all the books'
(cf. isolation forms: **Múusa**, personal name; **Ø-someeló** 'who read'; **z-ónt^he** 'all')

Omári)_φ **tú)**_{f-φ} **Ø-lumila naa noká)**_φ 'only Omari was bitten by a snake'
(cf. isolation forms: **Ø-lumiilá** 'who was bitten'; **nóka** 'snake')

cf. when **tú** attaches to a post-verbal NP:
Báana)_φ **hu-wa-barsha w-áana)**_φ ^f**tú)**_{f-φ} **adábu)**_φ 'Baana punishes only children'
(cf. isolation forms: **Báana**, personal name; **hu-wa-bársha** 'x teaches them'; **adábu** 'manners')

A preposed complement may also be focused, in which case the verb is again put in pseudo-relative form.

(28) ᶠmáayi)_{f-φ} Múusa)_φ Ø-leeseló)_φ 'water Muusa brought'
(cf. isolation forms: máayi 'water'; Ø-leeseló 'who brought')

ᶠw-áana)_{f-φ} Múusa)_φ Ø-wa-pelo maandrá)_φ 'children Muusa gave them bread'

chi-buku ch-a ᶠMúusa)_{f-φ} m-pʰeetó)_φ 'Muusa's book, I found'
(cf. isolation form: m-pʰeetó 'which I got/found')

ᶠMúusa)_{f-φ} chi-buukú=ch-e)_φ m-pʰeetó)_φ 'Muusa his book I found'

ᶠpéesa)_{f-φ} n-t̠ʰulubilo kaakó)_φ 'money, I demanded from you'
(cf. isolation forms: n-t̠ʰulubiiló 'which I demanded'; káako 'yours')

ᶠkáako)_{f-φ} n-t̠ʰulubilo peesá)_φ 'from you I demanded money'

w-áana)_φ ᶠtú)_{f-φ} Halíima)_φ Ø-wa-'ul̠ilo zi-buukú)_φ
'only the children, Haliima bought books for'

zi-búuku)_φ ᶠtú)_{f-φ} Halíima)_φ Ø-wa-'ul̠ilo waaná)_φ
'only books, Haliima bought for the children'

Preverbal adverbials and locative phrases may also be focused and trigger pseudo-relativization:

(29) kharibu y-a ᶠnúumba)_{f-φ} Ø-kaleent̠ʰó)_φ 'near the *house* he sat'
(cf. the isolation forms: kharíibu 'near'; y-a núumba 'of house'; Ø-kaleent̠ʰó 'who sat')

muda y-a ᶠmw-éezi)_{f-φ} Ø-liinziló)_φ 'for a period of a *month* he waited'
(cf. the isolation forms: múda 'period'; y-a mw-éezi 'of month', Ø-liinziló 'who waited')

Núuru)_φ ᶠnumbáa=ni)_{f-φ} u-kó)_φ 'Nuuru *at home* is'
(cf. the isolation forms: numbáa=ni 'at home'; u-kó 'who is')

When there are two pre-verbal elements, the focused one may be initial, but it also may be in second position. When in second position, its pitch is realized a bit higher than the accented syllable of the first phrase.

(30) a. ᶠpéesa)_{f-φ} káako)_φ n-t̠ʰulubiiló)_φ '*money* from you I demanded'
   or:
   káako)_φ ᶠpéesa)_{f-φ} n-t̠ʰulubiiló)_φ 'from you *money* I demanded'
   (cf. péesa 'money', káako 'from you', n-t̠ʰulubiiló 'that I demanded')

b. ᶠkhamri)_f-φ Huseeni)_φ hu-nó)_φ '*liquor* Huseeni drinks'
Huseeni)_φ ᶠkhamri)_f-φ hu-nó)_φ 'Huseeni *liquor* drinks'
(cf. khámri 'liquor', Huséeni, personal name, hu-nó 'that drinks')

c. zi-búuku)_φ ᶠtú)_f-φ Halíima)_φ Ø-uziló)_φ '*only books*, Haliima bought'
Halíima)_φ zi-búuku)_φ ᶠtú)_f-φ Ø-uziló)_φ 'Halima *only books* bought'
(cf. zi-búuku 'books', tú 'only', Halíima, personal name, Ø-uziló 'that bought')

If there is both a pre-verbal subject and a pre-verbal complement, the order of the two is variable and the location of focus is variable. (31) illustrates the possibilities:

(31) ᶠTúuma)_f-φ fatúura)_φ Ø-uliilá)_φ '(for) *Tuuma* a car she was bought'
ᶠfatúura)_f-φ Túuma)_φ Ø-uliilá)_φ '(for) Tuuma a *car* was bought'
Túuma)_φ ᶠfatúura)_f-φ Ø-uliilá)_φ '(for) Tuuma a *car* was bought'
Fatúura)_φ ᶠTúuma)_f-φ Ø-uliilá)_φ 'a car (for) *Tuuma* was bought'
(cf. fatúura 'car', Túuma personal name, Ø-uliilá 'that was bought')

4.3.3 Pseudo-relativization versus true relativization

We have seen that pre-verbal focus triggers the appearance of a verb that is the same as a relative verb in terms of the choice of the final vowel and in terms of being a final-accent trigger. Why do we label these "pseudo-relatives" rather than simply relative verbs? There are two considerations that lead us to adopt this terminological distinction. First of all, not all pseudo-relative verbs could actually occur as relative verbs. Second, pseudo-relative verbs show a greater likelihood of respecting the Accentual Law of Focus in comparison to true relatives.

Consider first the existence of pseudo-relative verbs that do not occur as true relatives. There are verb tenses that are not used in true relative clause constructions; specifically, the imperative and the subjunctive verb do not occur in relative constructions. But these verb forms do have the potential to appear in pseudo-relative form. (Note that third person subjunctive verbs in Chimiini have a formative *na* located between the subject marker and the verb stem.)

(32) absence of focus:
fanya gaarí=y-a)$_\varphi$ 'fix my truck!'

verb focus:
^{f}**fáanya)**$_{f\text{-}\varphi}$ **gaarí=y-a)**$_\varphi$ '*fix* my truck!'

focus on preposed complement:
^{f}**gaarí=y-a)**$_{f\text{-}\varphi}$ **faanyá)**$_\varphi$ '*my truck*, fix it!'

no relative clause version:
*****gari yaa wé)**$_\varphi$ **faanyá)**$_\varphi$ **ni nd-aaká)**$_\varphi$ 'the car that you fix it is mine'

(33) absence of focus:
Múusa)$_\varphi$ **Ø-na-'olóke)**$_\varphi$ 'let Muusa go'

subject focus:
Múusa)$_{f\text{-}\varphi}$ **Ø-na-'oloké)**$_\varphi$ 'let *Muusa* go
Múusa)$_\varphi$ **tú)**$_{f\text{-}\varphi}$ **Ø-na-'oloké)**$_\varphi$ 'let only *Muusa* go'

no relative clause version:
*****múu-nt^{h}u) Ø-na-'oloké)**$_\varphi$ **ni Múusa** 'man who should go is Muusa'

absence of focus:
Núuru)$_\varphi$ **Ø-na-'ule gari íyi)**$_\varphi$ 'Nuuru should buy this car'

preposed NP focus:
gari íyi)$_{f\text{-}\varphi}$ **Múusa)**$_\varphi$ **Ø-na-'ulé)**$_\varphi$ '*this car* Muusa should buy it'

no relative clause version:
*****gari y-a Núuru)**$_\varphi$ **Ø-na'ulé)**$_\varphi$ **ni nd-aaká)**$_\varphi$ 'the car that Nuuru should buy is mine'

Both the affirmative imperative and the affirmative subjunctive verb seen in (32) and (33) respectively are not final-accent triggers and consequently exhibit default penult accent in case there is no pre-verbal focus. But when there is a pre-verbal focus, the verb is put in the pseudo-relative form and has final accent. Neither verb, however, can be a true relative verb. It is perhaps worth noting that while focused pre-verbal constituents often may be preceded by the copular *ni* (though the variant without *ni* seems more common), no copular may occur in cases such as these where the verb is not in fact a possible true relative: *****ni Múusa)**$_{f\text{-}\varphi}$ **Ø-na-'oloké)**$_\varphi$ and *****ni gari íyi)**$_{f\text{-}\varphi}$ **Múusa)**$_\varphi$ **Ø-na-'ulé)**$_\varphi$.

A second way in which pseudo-relative verb forms differ from true relatives is with respect to the interaction of the focus phrase and the projection of final accent. Recall that we have shown that in non-relative clauses, if a focus phrase contains a final-accent trigger, the final accent appears only on the focus phrase and not on subsequent phrases (in the verb phrase). We refer to this as the

Accentual Law of Focus (=ALF). A natural question to ask is whether we see the effects of ALF in relative clauses. In our data from true relative clauses, we *generally* have not observed cases where the presence of a focus phrase prevents the final accent from appearing in all the phrases contained in the relative verb phrase. Some examples involving verb focus are given in (34):

(34) a. **mw-áana)_φ ^fØ-uziizó)_{f-φ} chi-buukú)_φ** 'the child who sold a/the book'
(cf. **mw-áana** 'child', **Ø-uziizó** 'who sold', **chi-búuku** 'book')

b. **múu-nt^hu)_φ ^fØ-m-weenó)_{f-φ} mw-iizí)_φ** 'the man who saw the thief'
(cf. **múu-nt^hu** 'person', **Ø-m-weenó** 'who saw him', **mw-íizi** 'thief')

c. **mw-áana)_φ ^fØ-naa=ch-ó)_{f-φ} chi-buukú)_φ** 'the child who has a/the book'
(cf. **mw-áana** 'child', **Ø-naa=ch-ó** 'who has it', **chi-búuku** 'book')

d. **mw-anáamke)_φ úyu)_φ ^fwa-náa=cho)_{f-φ} chi-gúwo)_φ ^fØ-peelá)_{f-φ} na waawa=y-é)_φ**
'this girl had a piece of cloth that she had been given by her father'
(cf. **mw-anáamke** 'girl', **úyu** 'this', **wa-náa=cho** 'she had it', **chi-gúwo** 'piece of cloth', **Ø-peelá** 'she had been given', **na** 'by', **waawá=y-e** 'her father')

The examples in (34) are cases where the verb is prosodically separated from its complement. There is a somewhat different range of cases where the verb is separated from a postposed subject. We consider this another case where the verb is at the end of a focus-phrase, but once again the final accent is not confined to this focus phrase.

(35) **n-guwo ^fØ-fuziló)_{f-φ} Faa_timá)_φ nz-aaká)_φ**
'the clothes which she washed, Faatima, are mine'
cf. the ungrammatical: **fuziló)_φ Faa_tíma)_φ nz-aaká)_φ**

cf. without subject postposing:
n-guwo z-a Faa_tíma)_φ Ø-fuziló)_φ nz-aaká)_φ
'the clothes that Faatima washed are mine'
(cf. the isolation forms: **n-gúwo** 'clothes'; **Faa_tíma**, personal name; **Ø-fuziló** 'who washed'; **nz-aaká** 'are mine')

fatúura)_φ ^fØ-inenzeezó)_{f-φ} Nuurú)_φ ki_la muu-nt^hí)_φ nd-aaká)_φ
'the car that he drove, Nuuru, each day is mine'
(cf. the isolation forms: **Ø-inenzeezó** 'that he drove'; **kí_la** 'each'; **múu-nt^hi** 'day'; **nd-aaká** 'is mine')

ALF-effects are overwhelmingly absent in both our textual and our elicited data on true relative clauses. However, it would be incorrect to say we have never encountered a case where ALF appeared to come into play. Recently we collected the following data set, where the second example violates ALF:

(36) a. **Ø-na-mw-iiwá)**_f-φ_ **mw-áana)**_φ_ **Ø-bozelo chi-buku ch-a Hamadí)**_φ_
'I *know* the boy who stole Hamadi's book'
(cf. **Ø-na-mw-iiwá** 'I know', **mw-áana** 'child/boy', **Ø-boozeló** 'who stole', **ch-búuku** 'book', **ch-a** associative particle, **Hamádi**, personal name)
(there is no focus internal to the relative clause in this example)

b. **Ø-na-mw-iiwá)**_f-φ_ **mw-áana)**_φ_ **ᶠØ-boozeló)**_f-φ_ **chi-buku ch-a Hamadí)**_φ_
'I *know* the boy who *stole* Hamadi's book'
(the relative verb is focused, but ALF does not block projection of final accent to the next phrase)

c. **Ø-na-mw-iiwá)**_f-φ_ **mw-áana)**_φ_ **ᶠØ-boozeló)**_f-φ_ **chi-buku ch-a Hamádi)**_φ_
'I *know* the boy who *stole* Hamadi's book'
(the relative verb is focused, but ALF blocks the projection of final accent to the next phrase)

d. **Ø-na-mw-iiwá)**_f-φ_ **mw-áana)**_φ_ **Ø-bozelo ᶠchi-buukú)**_f-φ_ **ch-a Hamadi)**_φ_
'I *know* the boy who stole the *book* of Hamadi's'

When we turn to pseudo-relative clauses, on the other hand, we find that there is much evidence that ALF *usually* controls the appearance of final accent (though it would be incorrect to claim that ALF holds invariably). Some examples:

(37) a. no internal focus in the verb phrase:
ᶠmw-aaná=w-a)_f-φ_ **ni-m-ul̪ilo fatuurá)**_φ_
'*my son* I bought a car for him'
(cf. **mw-aaná=w-a** 'my child', **ni-m-ul̪iiló** 'that I bought for him', **fat̪úura** 'car')

vs.

verb focus:
ᶠmw-aaná=w-a)_f-φ_ **ᶠni-m-ul̪iiló)**_f-φ_ **fat̪úura)**_φ_
'*my son I bought for him* a car' (ALF effect)

b. no internal focus in the verb phrase:
mw-ana w-a ᶠOmári)$_{f-\varphi}$ **Ø-bozelo chi-buukú)**$_\varphi$
'*Omari's son* stole a/the book'

vs.

verb focus:
mw-ana w-a ᶠOmari)$_{f-\varphi}$ **ᶠØ-boozeló)**$_{f-\varphi}$ **chi-búuku)**$_\varphi$
'*Omari's son stole* a book' (with ALF effect[2])
(cf. **mw-áana** 'child', **w-a**, associative particle, **Omári**, personal name, **Ø-boozeló** 'that stole', **chi-búuku** 'book')

c. no internal focus in the verb phrase:
ᶠFardóosa)$_{f-\varphi}$ **Ø-pela peesá)**$_\varphi$
'*Fardoosa* was given money'

vs.

verb focus:
ᶠFardóosa)$_{f-\varphi}$ **ᶠØ-peelá)**$_{f-\varphi}$ **péesa)**$_\varphi$
'*Fardoosa was given* money'
(with ALF effect)
(cf. **Fardóosa**, personal name, **Ø-peelá** 'that was given', **péesa** 'money')

Although it cannot be maintained that true relatives *never* show the effect of ALF while pseudo-relatives *always* do, nevertheless in our research the preponderance of the evidence so far does suggests ALF effects are very likely with pseudo-relative clauses and very unlikely with true relative clauses. This difference in behavior suggests that there is a significant contrast between true relatives and pseudo-relatives.

4.4 Focus and wh-questions

So-called ***wh***-questions in Chimiini are formed either through the use of a question word (e.g. **náani** 'who(m)', **líini** 'when', **gáni** 'which') or an interrogative enclitic (e.g., **=ni** 'what?', **=yi** 'how?', **=pi** 'where?'). The ***wh***-question word or the word marked with the interrogative enclitic bears focus. When the question word/particle precedes the verb, it is phrase-final like any other focused element

---

[2] But our consultant also suggested that it is possible to say: **mw-ana w-a ᶠOmari)**$_{f-\varphi}$ **ᶠØ-boozeló)**$_{f-\varphi}$ **chi-buukú)**$_\varphi$, where ALF does not block the projection of the H tone from the verb; he suggested that in this latter pronunciation, it is a specific book that is being referred to; this issue needs to be explored.

and it triggers pseudo-relative clause structure for the verb (just like other pre-verbal focused elements). There are no intonational properties associated uniquely with **wh**-questions.

We will illustrate the prosody of **wh**-questions using one question word (**náani** 'who/m?') and one enclitic (=**ni** 'what?'). Look first at examples of **náani** in pre-verbal position.

(38) ᶠ**náani**)_f-φ **Ø-pishiló**)_φ 'who cooked?'
  (cf. **Ø-pishíle** 'he cooked')

  ᶠ**náani**)_f-φ **Ø-somelo chi-buukú**)_φ 'who read the book?'
  (cf. **Ø-soméele** 'he read'; **chi-búuku** 'book')

  ᶠ**náani**)_φ **Ø-na-m-ulilo Nuurá**)_φ **chi-buukú**)_φ 'who is buying a book for Nuura?'
  (cf. **Ø-na-m-uulíla** 'he is buying for her, **Núura**, personal name, **chi-búuku** 'book')

  ᶠ**náani**)_f-φ **Ø-latilo i-ji-wé**)_φ **ch-olokoo=ní**)_φ 'who threw a stone at the window?'
  (cf. **Ø-latíile** 's/he threw', **i-jí-we** 'stone', **ch-olokóo=ni** 'at the window')

  with ALF effects due to focus in the pseudo-relative clause:
  ᶠ**náani**)_f-φ ᶠ**Ø-someeló**)_f-φ **chi-búuku**)_φ '*who read* the book?'

  ᶠ**náani**)_f-φ **Ø-na-m-ulilo** ᶠ**Nuurá**)_f-φ **chi-búuku**)_φ '*who* is buying for *Nuura* a book?'

The morphological shift of the verb to a relative clause structure (final vowel **o**, final accent) is obvious in these data, as well as the application of the Accentual Law of Focus when there is focus internal to the verb phrase.

When **naani** is post-verbal and not a subject, the verb is not in the pseudo-relative form:

(39) a. **Halíima**)_φ **Ø-m-wene** ᶠ**náani**)_f-φ
    'Haliima saw whom?'
    (cf. **Halíima**, personal name, **Ø-m-wéene** 'she saw him')
    (but cf. ᶠ**náani**)_f-φ **Halíima**)_φ **Ø-m-weenó**)_φ 'whom did Haliima see?')

  b. **chi-buku íchi**)_φ **n-chʰ-a** ᶠ**náani**)_f-φ
    'this book is whose?'
    (cf. **chi-búuku** 'book', **íchi** 'this', **n-chʰ-a** 'is of')

c. **Múusa)_φ Ø-m-bozele ^fnáani)_{f-φ} chi-búuku)_φ**
'Muusa stole from whom a/the book?'
(cf. **Múusa**, personal name, **Ø-m-boozéle** 'he stole from him',
chi-búuku 'book')

d. **Jáama)_φ Ø-m-tindilile ^fnáani)_{f-φ} náma)_φ**
'for whom did Jaama cut meat?'
(cf. **Jáama**, personal name, **Ø-m-tindilíile** 'he cut for him', **náma** 'meat')

e. **wé)_φ Ø-m-ulile ^fnaaní)_{f-φ} chi-búuku)_φ**
'you bought for whom a/the book?'
(a possible answer: **mí)_φ ni-m-ulile ^fHuseení)_{f-φ} chi-búuku)_φ**
'I bought for *Huseeni* a/the book')
(cf. **wé** 'you', **Ø-m-ulíile** 'you bought for', **chi-búuku** 'book')

These data provide clear evidence that post-verbal **naani**, even though it does not trigger pseudo-relativization like pre-verbal **naani**, nevertheless is focused. When the verb is a final-accent trigger, the final accent cannot project past **naani**. This is an effect of the Accentual Law of Focus.

Further evidence that **naani** is focused is provided by what constitutes an appropriate answer to the question like Ø-**pasize ^fnaaní)_{f-φ} péesa)_φ** 'whom did you lend money?' Only the first possibility below is an acceptable answer; the symbol # indicates that the sentence is grammatical, but not acceptable as an answer to the question:

(40) **ni-m-pasize ^fTuuma)_{f-φ} péesa)_φ** 'I lent Tuuma money'

#**ni-m-pasize Tuumá)_φ peesá)_φ** 'I lent Tuuma money'

#**ni-m-pasize ^fpeesá)_{f-φ} Túuma)_φ** 'I lent *money* to Tuuma'

#**ni-m-pasize peesá)_φ Tuumá)_φ** 'I lent money to Tuuma'

In the appropriate answer cited, there is focus on **Tuuma**, as is clear from the fact that the final accent triggered by the first person verb appears on **Tuuma** but not on the following complement. The other sentences are inappropriate because either they do not put any focus on **Tuuma** or they put focus on **peesa**. What appears to be going on is this: **naani** in the question is focused, and an appropriate answer is one where the noun phrase supplying the answer to **naani** is also focused.

Let us turn our attention to the case of the enclitic =**ni** 'what?' In (41), we illustrate the case where =**ni** is encliticized to a verb.

(41) Ø-jíile)_φ '(s)he ate', but: ᶠØ-jiilé=ni)_f-φ 'what did (s)he eat?'
Huséeni)_φ ᶠhu-ná=ni)_f-φ 'what does Huseeni drink?'
(a possible answer: Huséeni)_φ hu-na ch-áayi)_φ 'Huseeni drinks tea')
(cf. Huséeni, personal name, hú-na 'x drinks', ch-áayi 'tea')

ᶠØ-m-pasiize=ní)_f-φ T̲úuma)_φ 'what did you lend to Tuuma?'
(a possible answer: ni-m-pasize ᶠpeesá)_f-φ T̲úuma)_φ 'I lent money to Tuuma')
(cf. Ø-m-pasiizé 'you lent him/her', T̲úuma, personal name, péesa 'money')

ᶠØ-m-peele=ní)_f-φ Núuru)_φ 'what did you give Nuuru?'
(cf. Ø-m-peelé 'you gave him/her', Núuru, personal name)

Núuru)_φ ᶠØ-m-boozelé=ni)_f-φ mw-áana)_φ 'what did Nuuru steal from the child?'
(cf. Núuru, personal name, Ø-m-boozelé 'you stole from him/her', mw-áana 'child')

wé)_φ ᶠØ-m-ul̲iile=ní)_f-φ Núura)_φ 'you bought what for Nuura?'
(a possible answer: mí)_φ ni-m-ul̲ile ᶠchi-buukú)_f-φ Núura)_φ 'I bought a book for Nuura')
(cf. wé 'you', Ø-m-ul̲iilé 'you bought for him/her', Núura, personal name, mí 'I', ni-m-ul̲iilé 'I bought for you', chi-búuku 'book')

The =*ni* is not necessarily encliticized to a verb. In the following example it is encliticized to the associative marker:

(42) nt̲ʰini ᶠy-a=ni)_f-φ weshelo zi-buukú)_φ
'under what did you put the books?'

Here we see a couple of crucial points. First of all, the enclitic does not behave like a monosyllabic word (e.g. a pronoun). If it did, the vowel in the associative particle *y-a* would be lengthened. Second, being in pre-verbal position, the following verb is put into the pseudo-relative form.

The =*ni* may be cliticized to the preposition *ka* to ask the question 'with/by what?' and to *ka khisa* 'because' to form the question 'why? for what reason?' When these expressions are in pre-verbal position, the verb is in the pseudo-relative form.

(43) a. **Alí)**_φ **ᶠká=ni)**_{f-φ} ∅-**oloshelo Mkhodiishó)**_φ
'by what means did Ali go to Mogadisho?'
(cf. **Alí**, personal name, **ka** 'with', ∅-**oloshelό** 'that went', **Mkhodíisho** 'Mogadishu')

b. **ᶠká=ni)**_{f-φ} ∅-**tinziloo namá)**_φ
'*what* did you cut the meat with?'
(cf. **ka** 'with', ∅-**tiinziló** 'that you cut', **náma** 'meat')

c. **ᶠka khisá=ni)**_{f-φ} **Súufi)** ∅-**latilo i-ji-wé)**_φ **ch-olokoo=ní)**_φ
'*why* did Suufi throw a stone at the window?'
(cf. **ka khísa** 'reason', **Súufi**, personal name, ∅-**latiiló** 'that he threw', **i-jí-we** 'stone', **ch-olokóo=ni** 'at window')

In post-verbal position, however, there is no pseudo-relativization:

(44) ∅-**tinzile ᶠka=ní)**_{f-φ} **náma)**_φ '*what* did you cut the meat with?'
or:

náma)_φ ∅-**tinzile ᶠka=ní)**_{f-φ}
(cf. **ka** 'with', ∅-**tiinzilé** 'you cut', **náma** 'meat')

Núuru)_φ **nt**ʰ-**a-ku-ya ka ᶠkhisá=ni)**_{f-φ} '*why* didn't Nuuru come?'
(cf. **Núuru**, personal name, **nt**ʰ-**aa-kú-ya** 'he did not come', **ka khísa** 'reason')

4.5 The non-canonical nature of morphologically negative verbs

Up until this point we have discussed cases of focus (IAV focus, verb focus, and pre-verbal focus of subjects, complements, locatives, adverbials) where focus is a marked option, contrasting with corresponding sentences lacking the focus. We have also discussed pre-verbal question words/enclitics that are necessarily focused and do not have alternative versions lacking focus. We turn now to the case of morphologically negative verbs, which are not *necessarily* focused, but in the default case behave exactly like focused verbs. Specifically, in the default case the negative verb is separated prosodically from a complement and is raised in pitch (not subject to downstepping). We consider negative verbs to be inherently focused. They *can* appear without focus (and thus not be final in a phrase), but just in case there is focus elsewhere in the sentence.

We provide some examples in (45) of the usual pronunciation of negative verbs. (The only negative verb tense that is a final accent-trigger is the negative imperative. See the appendix for a list of the final accent-triggers.)

(45) a. T̲úuma)_φ ᶠntʰ-a-kh-píka)_f-φ zíjo)_φ 'Tuuma did not cook **zijo**'
 (cf. T̲úuma, personal name, **ntʰ-a-kh-píka** 'he did not cook', **zíjo** 'food from cooked cereals')

 b. T̲úuma)_φ ᶠhaa-fúli)_f-φ n-gúwo)_φ 'Tuuma does not wash clothes'
 (cf. T̲úuma, personal name, **haa-fúli** 'she does not wash', **n-gúwo** 'clothes')

 c. ᶠs-kú-m-pa)_f-φ Omári)_φ zi-láatu)_φ 'I did not give Omari shoes'
 (cf. **s-kú-m-pa** 'I did not give him', **Omári**, personal name, **zi-láatu** 'shoes')

 d. **Huséeni)**_φ ᶠntʰ-aa-kú-na)_f-φ khámri)_φ m-gahawáa=ni)_φ
 'Huseeni did not drink beer at the restaurant'
 (cf. **Huséeni**, personal name, **ntʰ-aa-kú-na** 'he did not drink', **khámri** 'beer', **gahawáa=ni** 'at the restaurant')

 e. ᶠsi-m-vuundé)_f-φ mw-eenzí=w-o)_φ 'don't contradict, belie your friend (e.g. if your friend has put on airs, made false claims, etc.)!'
 (cf. **si-m-vuundé** 'don't break!', **mw-eenzí=w-o** 'your friend')

 f. mí)_φ ᶠs-k-oolóka)_f-φ madrasáa=ni)_φ 'I did not go to *madrasa*'
 (cf. **mí** 'I', **s-k-oolóka** 'I did not go', **madrasáa=ni** 'to school')
 > mí)_φ ᶠs-k-oolóka)_f-φ madrasaa=ní?)_φ
 > mí)_φ s-k-ooloká)_φ madrasaa=ní!?)_φ

The raised pitch on the negative verb and its phrase-final position is clear evidence of the parallelism between negative verbs and focus. Negative verbs are for the most part not final-accent triggers, thus the applicability of ALF is usually not relevant. However, the negative imperative verb is a final-accent trigger, and we see from the example ᶠsi-m-vuundé)_f-φ mw-eenzí=w-o)_φ that the final accent does not project to the complement in the default case. This, of course, is a reflection of ALF. A further parallelism between the negative verb and focus comes from yes-no question formation, illustrated by the last data set in (45). What we see is that the complement to the negative verb undergoes accent shift in the simple yes-no question, just like other complements that are out-of-focus. In the case of an emphatic yes-no question, the accent of the negative verb as well as the complements is shifted to the end. Recall, accent shift in the emphatic question is not connected to an out-of-focus status.

Focus on negative verbs is absent in various situations: (a) relative verb clauses, where it appears that narrow focus is dispreferred; (b) interrogatives, where focus is on the questioned constituent rather than the verb; (c) cases where there is a non-verb focus. Look at the data in (46).

(46) a. **ha-fundrowi na maama=y-é)ᵩ hu-m-fundro l-mweengú)ᵩ**
'the one who is not taught by his mother is the one whom the world teaches'
(cf. **ha-fundróowi** 'he is not taught', **na** 'by', **maamá=y-e** 'his/her mother', **hu-m-fuundró** 'who teaches her/him', **l-mwéengu** 'the world')

b. **mu-ntʰu ha-ṯa-kh-fanya kaazí)ᵩ** 'the man who won't work'
(cf. ᶠ**ha-ṯa-kh-fáanya)f-ᵩ káazi)ᵩ** 'he won't work')
(cf. **múu-ntʰu** 'person', **ha-ṯa-kh-fáanya** 'he won't do'/ **ha-ṯa-kh-faanyó** 'who won't do', **káazi** 'work')

c. **yé)ᵩ ha-ṯa-kh-fanya káazi)ᵩ ᶠlíini)f-ᵩ** 'he won't work when?'
(cf. ᶠ**ha-ṯa-kh-fáanya)f-ᵩ káazi)ᵩ** 'he won't work')
(cf. **yé** '(s)he', **ha-ṯa-kh-fáanya** 'he won't do', **káazi** 'work', **líini** 'when?')

d. **ntʰ-a-ku-leta chi-buku ᶠgáni)f-ᵩ** 'which book did he not bring?'
(cf. ᶠ**ntʰ-a-ku-=léeta)f-ᵩ chi-buku chi-hába)ᵩ** 'he didn't bring the small book')
(cf. **ntʰ-a-ku-léeta** 'he did not bring', **chi-búuku** 'book', **gáni** 'which?')

e. **ntʰ-a-k-endra ᶠnumbáa=ni)f-ᵩ** 'he did not go *home*
(i.e. he went somewhere else, not home)'
(cf. ᶠ**ntʰ-a-k-éendra)f-ᵩ numbáa=ni)ᵩ** 'he did not go home')
(cf. **ntʰ-a-k-éendra** 'he did not go', **numbáa=ni** 'to home')

f. **yé)ᵩ ntʰ-a-m-letela ᶠNúuru)f-ᵩ chi-búuku)ᵩ Ø-m-letelele Múusa)ᵩ**
'he did not bring Nuuru, a book, he brought Muusa (one)'
(cf. **yé** 'he', **ntʰ-a-m-leetéla** 'he did not bring to him', **Núuru**, personal name, **chi-búuku** 'book', **Múusa**, personal name)

g. **yé) ntʰ-a-m-letela ᶠchi-búuku)f-ᵩ Núuru) Ø-m-letelele khalámu)ᵩ**
'he did not bring a book to Nuuru, he brought him a pen'
(cf. **yé** 'he'; **ntʰ-a-m-leetéla** 'he did not bring to him', **Núuru**, personal name, **chi-búuku** 'book', **Ø-m-leteléele** 'he brought to him', **khalámu** 'pen')

The negative verb in (46a–c) is not phrase-final and therefore does not bear the high pitch associated with a focused element. But in each case, there is a focused element elsewhere in the sentence. If there is no other focus, the negative verb must be itself be focused.

Before leaving the topic of negative verbs, we should point out that the focus on the negative verb is present only in the case where the negative verb is followed by a complement. In the absence of a complement, there is no focus (as evidence by the absence of pitch raising). Consider the following examples.

(47) **mí)**_φ **s-ku-téza)**_φ 'I did not play' (cf. **mí** 'I', **s-ku-téza** 'I did not play')
    madrasáa=ni)_φ **yé)**_φ **nt^h-a-k-oolóka)**_φ 'to school he did not go'
    (cf. **madrasáa=ni** 'to school', **yé** 'he', **nt^h-a-k-oolóka** 'he did not go')
    yé)_φ **madrasáa=ni)**_φ **nt^h-a-k-oolóka)**_φ 'he to school did not go'

In the first example, the verb is intransitive and thus there is no complement. The pronominal subject is the pitch peak and the negative verb is downstepped. In the next two examples, the complement to the verb has been preposed, putting the negative verb in sentence-final position. Once again, it undergoes downstep. This behavior of the negative verb is parallel to the behavior of an affirmative verb in sentence-final position, where the contrast between an emphasized and an unemphasized verb is not present.

5 Post-verbal subjects

The postposing of subjects is a topic of some interest in terms of phrasing and intonation. There are different sub-cases, which we examine in turn.

5.1 Right-dislocation

A subject may be dislocated to the end of the verb phrase, in which case it is separated phrasally from whatever precedes and radically lowered in pitch (this lowering is indicated by the raised exclamation symbol). We refer to this as right-dislocation. We have the impression that this downstepping is more extreme than the ordinary downstep inside the VP, but this needs to be verified by detailed phonetic study.

(48) a. **Múusa)**_φ **Ø-fíile)**_φ 'Muusa died'
       Ø-fíile)_φ **!Múusa)**_φ 'died Muusa' (but not *Ø-file Múusa)_φ)

   b. **Omári)**_φ **Ø-tezéeze)**_φ 'Omari played'
       Ø-tezéeze)_φ **!Omári)**_φ 'he played, Omari' (but not *Ø-tezeze Omári)_φ)

   c. **n-jiilé)**_φ **!mí)**_φ 'ate I' (but not *n-jilee mí)_φ)

d. **wá-ke)**ᵩ **ka-wa-pikaa zijó)**ᵩ ... 'if the women had cooked **zíjo**...'
(cf. **wá-ke** 'women', **ka-wa-piká** 'if they had cooked', **zíjo** 'cooked cereals')

ka-wa-pikaa zijó)ᵩ ¹**wá-ke)**ᵩ ... 'if they had cooked, the women...'
(not *ka-wa-pikaa zijó) wa-ké)...)

The final example in (48) shows clearly that the right-dislocated subject is outside the verb phrase proper since the final accent that is required by all subject forms of the *ka*-conditional tense projects to the end of the verb phrase, but cannot project to the right-dislocated subject. (See the appendix for a list of final accent-triggers.)

One might view this radical lowering of the right-dislocated subject as following from the prosodic constituent structure. One possible analysis would be that what we have shown throughout this chapter as φ-phrases are more precisely **minimal** φ-phrases, and that there are also **maximal** φ-phrases that correspond to larger syntactic phrases such as the "verb phrase". In this sort of account, we would have a prosodic constituent structure like **Ø-fíile)**ᵩ^{max} **Múusa)**ᵩ – i.e. the postposed subject is a phrase that is not part of the maximal phrase that precedes it. Such a configuration might be claimed to trigger radical downstepping. An alternative analysis would be to assume that the postposed subject is an embedded intonational phrase. Such sentence-final embedded intonational phrases could be claimed to undergo radical downstepping. (See Selkirk 2005 for some discussion of the intonational phrase.) We lack evidence to choose between these two kinds of analysis and will refrain from indicating prosodic constituents other than φ-phrases, relying on the symbol ¹ to indicate the radical downstepping and leave open the issue of the precise structure that triggers it.

Right dislocated subjects undergo Accent Shift in simple yes-no questions:

(49) **Omári)**ᵩ **Ø-tulubile péesa)**ᵩ 'Omari demanded money'
> **Omári)**ᵩ **Ø-tulubile péesa?)**ᵩ 'did Omari demand money?'
(cf. **Omári**, personal name, **Ø-tulubíile** 'he demanded', **péesa** 'money')

but with right dislocation:

Ø-tulubile péesa)ᵩ ¹**Omári)**ᵩ 'he demanded money, Omari'
> **Ø-tulubile péesa)**ᵩ, **Omarí?)**ᵩ 'did he demand money, Omari'

Accent shift in simple yes-no question affects any post-verbal phrase that is not focused.

Right-dislocation of the subject can be observed in =*ni* 'what?' questions:

(50) a. ᶠØ-fuzilé=ni)_{f-φ} ˈFaatíma)_φ 'what did Faatima wash?'
(possible answer: Ø-fuzilee ᶠn-gúwo)_{f-φ} ˈFaatíma)_φ 'she washed *clothes*, Faatima') (cf. Ø-**fuzíle** 'she washed', **Faatíma**, personal name, **n-gúwo** 'clothes')

b. ᶠØ-bozelé=ni)_{f-φ} ˈmaskíini)_φ 'what did he steal, the poor man?
(possible answer: Ø-bozele ᶠpéesa)_{f-φ} ˈmaskíini)_φ 'he stole *money*, the poor man')
(cf. Ø-**boozéle** 'he stole', **maskíini** 'poor person', **péesa** 'money')

c. ᶠØ-vunzilé=ni)_{f-φ} ˈmw-íizi)_φ 'what did he break, the thief?'
(possible answer: Ø-vunzile ᶠm-náango)_{f-φ} ˈmw-íizi)_φ 'he broke the *door*, the thief') (cf. Ø-**vuunzíle** 'he broke', **mw-íizi** 'thief', **m-náango** 'door')

d. ᶠwa-talishiizá=ni)_{f-φ} ˈw-aana)_φ 'what were they made to take, the children?'
(cf. **wa-talishíiza** 'they were made to take', **w-áana** 'children')

e. ᶠØ-hadiilé=ni)_{f-φ} ˈsul_táani)_φ 'what did he say, the sultan?'
(cf. Ø-**hadíile** 'he said', **sul_táani** 'sultan')

The right-dislocated subjects in these examples are radically lowered in pitch and separated phrasally from the preceding verb (though this separation would be required anyhow by virtue of the =*ni* enclitic, which focuses the verb).

We might also add that GM volunteered the existence of a kind of question that seeks confirmation as to what the answer to the question was:

(51) ᶠØ-pishile=ní)_{f-φ} ↑mu-ké)_φ 'what did (you say) the woman cooked?'
(cf. Ø-**pishíle** 'she cooked', **mú-ke** 'woman')

ᶠØ-bozele=ní)_{f-φ} ↑maskíini)_φ 'what did (you say) the poor man stole?'
(cf. Ø-**boozéle** 'he stole', **maskíini** 'poor man')

ᶠØ-fuzile=ní)_{f-φ} ↑Faatimá)_φ 'what did (you say) Faatima washed?'
(cf. Ø-**fuzíle** 'she washed', **Faatíma**, personal name)

ᶠØ-vunzile=ní)_{f-φ} ↑mw-iizí)_φ 'what did (you say) the thief broke?'
(cf. Ø-**vuunzíle** 'he broke', **mw-íizi** 'thief')

This intonation shares with emphatic yes-no questions the accent shift in the verb and the postposed subject. However, it is quite different in that there is no downstepping, indeed the postposed subject is radically raised in pitch (indicated by the upward-pointing arrow).

There is data that suggests that right-dislocation has the effect of eliminating the default focus on negative verbs:

(52) **nt^h-a-k-oloka madrasáa=ni)$_\varphi$!yé)$_\varphi$** 'he did not go to school, him'
(cf. **nt^h-a-k-oolóka** '(s)he did not go';

madrasáani 'to school'; **yé** '(s)he') > **nt^h-a-k-oloka madrasáa=ni)$_\varphi$ yé?)$_\varphi$**
> **nt^h-a-k-oloka madrasaa=ní)$_\varphi$ yé!?)$_\varphi$**

It is not clear to us why right-dislocation requires the complement to be part of the focus (eliminating narrow focus on the verb). We leave the matter to further research.

It is possible for a right-dislocated subject to appear internal to the verb phrase, as illustrated in the following example. Once again the subject is radically lowered in pitch.

(53) **s-k-oolóka)$_\varphi$!mí)$_\varphi$ madrasáa=ni)$_\varphi$** 'I did not go, I, to school'
(cf. **s-k-oolóka** 'I did not go', **mí** 'I',

madrasáa=ni 'to school') > **s-k-oolóka)$_\varphi$ mí)$_\varphi$ madrasaa=ní?)$_\varphi$**
> **s-k-ooloká)$_\varphi$ mí)$_\varphi$ madrasaa=ní!?)$_\varphi$**

In the simple yes-no question, Q-Raising counteracts the radical lowering associated with a right-dislocated subject; in the speech of MI, where this example comes from, the pitch peak is at the end of the sentence. In the emphatic question, the right-dislocated subject displays normal downstep, and not the radical lowering characteristic of the statement.

5.2 Postposed subjects in IAV position

So far we have looked at cases where a subject is postposed, but not phrasally grouped with the preceding constituent. There are cases, however, where a postposed subject is not separated from the preceding element by the right edge of a prosodic constituent. This situation is commonly encountered in sentences containing a passive verb. Look first at the example in (54), where the passive subject is pre-verbal.

(54) **Fardóosa)**_φ_ ∅-**pe̱la péesa)**_φ_ 'Fardoosa was given money'
(cf. **Fardóosa**, personal name, ∅-**pée̱la** 'she was given', **péesa** 'money')

This example exhibits the canonical form for a passive sentence: subject-passive verb-complement(s). The subject is the indirect object of the corresponding active sentence and not the direct object; thus in (54), the subject marker on the passive verb is phonologically null, since the subject is the [cl.1] noun **Fardóosa** and not **péesa**. The intonation in (54) is canonical downstep intonation.

There are, of course, variants of (54) where **Fardoosa** is focused.

(55) ᶠ**Fardóosa)**_f-φ_ ∅-**pe̱la peesá)**_φ_ '*Fardoosa* was given money'
ᶠ**Fardóosa)**_f-φ_ ᶠ∅-**pee̱lá)**_f-φ_ **péesa)**_φ_ '*Fardoosa was given* money.'

or with **peesa** preposed:

ᶠ**Fardóosa)**_f-φ_ **péesa)**_φ_ ∅-**pee̱lá)**_φ_ '*Fardoosa* money (she) was given'

Although the passive subject precedes the passive verb in what we consider the canonical form of the passive, there is another perhaps somewhat surprising version of the passive where the subject is postposed after the verb, forming a phrase with that verb, while the complement is preposed.

(56) **péesa)**_φ_ ∅-**pe̱la Fardóosa)**_φ_ 'money was given to Fardoosa'

The null SM on the verb establishes clearly that **Fardóosa** is the subject and not **péesa**. If **péesa** were the subject, the verb would have to agree with it: ***s-pe̱la Fardóosa)**_φ_.

The sentence in (56) could be a response to the question: **péesa)**_φ_ ∅-**pe̱la náani)**_f-φ_ 'money was given to whom?' But notice that the verb ∅-**pe̱la** is not phrase-final; if it were, it would be pronounced ∅-**pée̱la**, since accent would fall on the penult syllable and the long vowel in the penult syllable would be allowed to surface due to the presence of abstract stress on this syllable. The simple yes-no question version of (56) is **péesa)**_φ_ ∅-**pe̱la Fardóosa?)**_φ_ 'money, was Fardoosa given it?' Notice that **Fardóosa** does not undergo Accent Shift in the question, indicating that it is not an out-of-focus element.

(56) displays downstep intonation. This is due to the fact that although **náani** is certainly focused, in clause-final position it does not show pitch-raising (cf. a similar observation made above with regard to negative verbs in clause-final position).

There are variants of the (56) where **peesa** is focused:

(57) ᶠ**péesa)**ᵩ ∅-**pela Fardoosá)**ᵩ '*money* Fardoosa was given (lit. she was given Fardoosa)'

ᶠ**péesa)**ᵩ ∅-**peelá)**ᵩ **Fardóosa)**ᵩ '(it was) money (that) Fardoosa was *given*'

Although **Fardoosa** is not a right-dislocated subject in the preceding sentences, it is possible for a passive verb to exhibit a right-dislocated subject:

(58) ∅-**pela péesa)**ᵩ, ᶦ**Fardóosa)**ᵩ 'she was given money, Fardoosa'

The contrast with the earlier examples is obvious. Here the subject is phrasally separated from what precedes and shows a radical pitch drop.

6 Left dislocation of non-focused elements

Earlier we discussed focused pre-verbal elements. It is important, however, to recognize that left-dislocation is not necessarily associated with focus. (59) illustrates left-dislocated elements that are not focused and consequently do not trigger pseudo-relativization of the verb.

(59) a. **akhíli)**ᵩ **múu-ntʰu)**ᵩ **hu-zalilóowa)**ᵩ 'intelligence, a person is born with it'
(cf. **akhíli** 'intelligence', **múu-ntʰu** 'person', **hu-zalilóowa** 'x is born with')

b. **ka tartíibu)**ᵩ **kilaa chíi-ntʰu)**ᵩ **hu-patikána)**ᵩ 'slowly everything can be achieved'
(cf. **ka tartíibu** 'slowly', **kíla** 'each', **chíi-ntʰu** 'thing', **hu-patikána** 'x is achieved, gotten')

c. **mw-íizi)**ᵩ **ni-m-bishilé)**ᵩ 'the thief, I beat him'
(cf. **mw-íizi** 'thief', **ni-m-bishilé** 'I beat him')

d. **mw-áana)**ᵩ **ni-m-bigilile chi-lutí)**ᵩ 'the boy, I hit him with a stick'
(cf. **mw-áana** 'child'; **ni-m-bigiliilé** 'I hit him'; **chi-lúti** 'stick')

e. **chi-búuku)**ᵩ **mw-áana)**ᵩ **Ø-boozéle)**ᵩ 'a book, the child stole'
(cf. **chi-búuku** 'book'; **mw-áana** 'child'; **Ø-boozéle** '(s)he stole')
cf. **mw-áana)**ᵩ **chi-búuku)**ᵩ **Ø-boozéle)**ᵩ 'the child, a book, stole'

Sentences of this type show downstep intonation as long as they do not have a focused element elsewhere in the sentence.

In (60) we show the way yes-no questions are formed when there is a left-dislocated element present.

(60) a. **madrasáa=ni)**$_\varphi$ **yé)**$_\varphi$ **Ø-oloshéle)**$_\varphi$ 'to school he went'
(cf. **madrasáa=ni** 'to school'; **yé** '(s)he' **Ø-oloshéle** '(s)he went')
> **madrasáa=ni)**$_\varphi$ **yé)**$_\varphi$ **Ø-oloshéle?)**$_\varphi$
> **madrasaa=ní)**$_\varphi$ **yé)**$_\varphi$ **Ø-oloshelé!?)**$_\varphi$

b. **Halíima)**$_\varphi$ **búni)**$_\varphi$ **Ø-poonzéle)**$_\varphi$ 'Haliima, coffee beans, she pounded'
(cf. **Halíima**, personal name, **búni** 'coffee beans', **Ø-poonzéle** 'she pounded')
> **Halíima)**$_\varphi$ **buní)**$_\varphi$ **Ø-poonzéle?)**$_\varphi$
> **Halíima)**$_\varphi$ **buní)**$_\varphi$ **Ø-poonzelé!?)**$_\varphi$

c. **sí)**$_\varphi$ **chi-buku ch-a hisáabu)**$_\varphi$ **chi-m-bozele mw-aalimú)**$_\varphi$
'we, the arithmetic book, stole from the teacher'
(cf. **sí** 'we', **chi-búuku** 'book', **ch-a**, associative particle, **hisáabu** 'arithmetic';
mw-aalímu 'teacher')
> **sí)**$_\varphi$ **chi-buku ch-a hisáabu)**$_\varphi$ **chi-m-bozele mw-aalimú?)**$_\varphi$
> **sí)**$_\varphi$ **chi-buku ch-a hisaabú)**$_\varphi$ **chi-m-bozele mw-aalimú!?)**$_\varphi$

d. **wó)**$_\varphi$ **chi-buku ch-a hisáabu)**$_\varphi$ ^{f}**nt^{h}a-wa-m-bóola)**$_{f-\varphi}$ **mw-aalímu)**$_\varphi$
'they, the math book, did not steal from the teacher'
(cf. **wó** 'they', **chi-búuku** 'book', **ch-a**, associative particle, **hisáabu** 'arithmetic', **nt^{h}a-wa-m-bóola** 'they did not steal from him/her', **mw-aalímu** 'teacher')
> **wó)**$_\varphi$ **chi-buku ch-a hisáabu)**$_\varphi$ ^{f}**nt^{h}a-wa-m-bóola)**$_{f-\varphi}$ **mw-aalimú?)**$_\varphi$
> **wó)**$_\varphi$ **chi-buku ch-a hisaabú)**$_\varphi$ **nt^{h}a-wa-m-boolá)**$_\varphi$ **mw-aalimú!?)**$_\varphi$

e. **chi-buku ch-a hisáabu)**$_\varphi$ **wó)**$_\varphi$ ^{f}**wa-m-boozéle)**$_{f-\varphi}$ **mw-aalímu)**$_\varphi$
'math book, they stole from teacher'
> **chi-buku ch-a hisáabu)**$_\varphi$ **wó)**$_\varphi$ ^{f}**wa-m-boozéle)**$_{f-\varphi}$ **mw-aalimú?)**$_\varphi$
> **chi-buku ch-a hisaabú)**$_\varphi$ **wó)**$_\varphi$ **wa-m-boozelé)**$_\varphi$ **mw-aalimú!?)**$_\varphi$

Notice that in the simple yes-no question, the left-dislocated phrase does not undergo accent-shift. This is important because post-verbal elements that are out-of-focus *do* undergo accent shift in the simple question (cf. **mw-aalimu** in the last two data sets, where the verb is focused. Thus it seems that out-of-focus elements in the verb phrase have a different discourse status from the left-dislocated elements that lack focus. The emphatic yes-no question, on the other hand, shifts accent in all phrases regardless of the issue of focus, affecting left-dislocated phrases as well as prosodic constituents in the verb, regardless of whether they are focused or not.

There is some evidence that accent shift in emphatic yes-no questions may be affected by pauses. The data in (61) is an example from MI where he paused after the left-dislocated phrase and failed to shift the accent to the final syllable.

(61) **mw-aalímu...) wó) nt ha-wa-m-bóola) chi-buku ch-a hisáabu)**
'teacher, they stole math book from'
> **mw-aalímu...) wó) nt ha-wa-m-bóola) chi-buku ch-a hisaabú?)**
> **mw-aalímu...) wó) nt ha-wa-m-boolá) chi-buku ch-a hisaabú!?)**

Our data on this point from MI is restricted. Our more robust data from GM, while not focusing on the issue of pauses, does suggest considerable variability with respect to whether accent shift affects an initial (non-verbal) phrase in emphatic questions. We suspect that this variation is connection to the nature of the "juncture" between the initial phrase and the following phrase, where pause represents one end of the spectrum. More research is required.

7 Left- and right-dislocation in the same sentence

It is possible to combine left dislocation and right dislocation in the same sentence.

(62) a. **chi-búuku)$_\varphi$ Ø-boozéle)$_\varphi$!mw-áana)$_\varphi$** 'a book, he stole it, the child'

b. **zi-nóolo)$_\varphi$ wa-naa-kú-ja)$_\varphi$!w-áana)$_\varphi$** '*zinoolo*, they are eating, the children'
(cf. **zi-nóolo** 'banana bread', **wa-naa-kú-ja** 'they are eating', **w-áana** 'children')

c. **chi-buku ícho)$_\varphi$ Ø-na-ki-chi-sóoma)$_\varphi$!mw-áana)$_\varphi$** 'that book, he is reading it, the boy'
(cf. **chi-búuku** 'book', **ícho** 'that', **Ø-na-ki-chi-sóoma** 'he is reading it', **mw-áana** 'child, boy')

d. háanzu)_φ Ø-ulíila)_φ ꜜFáatma)_φ '(yes,) a dress, she was bought for, Faatma'
(cf. háanzu 'dress', Ø-ulíila 's/he was bought for', Fáatma, personal name)

e. zíjo)_φ Ø-pishíle)_φ ꜜHalíima)_φ 'zijo she cooked, Haliima'
(cf. zíjo 'food from cooked cereals', Ø-pishíle 'she cooked', Halíima, personal name)

The right-dislocated subject is separated prosodically from the verb and the corresponding yes-no question establishes the out-of-focus nature of this element. The left-dislocated verbal complement, on the other hand, is unaffected by any accent-shift in the simple yes-no question. Accent is shifted only in post-verbal out-of-focus phrases.

(63) a. chi-buku ícho)_φ Ø-na-ki-sóoma)_φ mw-aaná?)_φ 'this book, is he reading it, the child?'

b. chi-búuku)_φ Ø-boozéle)_φ mw-aaná?)_φ 'did book, steal, the child?'

c. háanzu)_φ Ø-ulíila)_φ Faatmá?)_φ 'dress, was she bought one for, Faatma?'

d. zíjo)_φ Ø-pishíle)_φ Haliimá?)_φ 'zijo did she cook, Haliima?'

e. chi-buku ch-a hisáabu)_φ chi-m-bozele mw-aalimú)_φ ꜜsí)_φ
'the math book, we stole from the teacher, we'
> chi-buku ch-a hisáabu)_φ chi-m-bozele mw-aalimú)_φ sí?)_φ
> chi-buku ch-a hisaabú)_φ chi-m-bozele mw-aalimú)_φ sí!?)_φ

It is critical to distinguish between a postposed subject and a predicate noun. Look at the following sentence.

(64) búni)_φ Ø-poonzeló)_φ Halíima)_φ 'coffee beans, the one who pounded them is Haliima'
> búni) Ø-poonzeló) Halíima?)
(cf. búni 'coffee beans', Ø-poonzeló 'the one who pounded', Halíima, personal name)

In (64), there is no radical lowering of **Halíima** since it is not a right-dislocated subject, but rather a predicate noun. In the simple yes-no question, accent remains on the penult of **Halíima** since it is included in the focus and not out-of-focus.

8 Time adverbials

Some discussion of the intonation of time adverbials is merited, as they are quite distinct from other adverbials when located in the verb phrase. Let us focus initially on the time adverbial in sentence-final position.

(65) a. **Omári)**$_\varphi$ **Ø-oloshele numbáa=ni)**$_\varphi$ **yána)**$_\varphi$ 'Omari went home yesterday'
(cf. **Omári**, personal name, **Ø-oloshéle** 'he went', **numbáa=ni** 'to home', **yána** 'yesterday')

b. **n-andishilee khatí)**$_\varphi$ **yána)**$_\varphi$ 'I wrote a letter yesterday'
(cf. **n-andishilé** 'I wrote', **kháti̱** 'letter', **yána** 'yesterday')

c. **Omári)**$_\varphi$ **Ø-m-pele Nuréeni)**$_\varphi$ **péesa)**$_\varphi$ **yána)**$_\varphi$ 'Omari gave Nureeni money yesterday'
(cf. **Omári**, personal name, **Ø-m-péele** 'he gave him', **Nuréeni**, personal name, **péesa** 'money', **yána** 'yesterday')

Adverbial phrases, like any other lexical maximal projections, are expected to be phrasally separate from a preceding lexical maximal projection. Thus the data in (65) do not immediately appear to exhibit any special prosodic properties with respect to phrasing. However, the data in (66) are surprising:

(66) a. **Omári)**$_\varphi$ **Ø-oloshéle)**$_\varphi$ **yána)**$_\varphi$ 'Omari went yesterday'
(cf. **Omári**, personal name, **Ø-oloshéle** 'he went', **yána** 'yesterday')

b. **múu-nt^{h}u)**$_\varphi$ **oo Ø-fakee̱tó)**$_\varphi$ **Ø-shiishíla)**$_\varphi$ **yána)**$_\varphi$
'the man who ran away was caught yesterday'
(cf. **múu-nt^{h}u** 'person', **óo** 'that one', **Ø-fakee̱tó** 'who ran away', **Ø-shiishí̱la** 'he was caught', **yána** 'yesterday')

The sentences in (66) represent the default pronunciation for an intransitive verb followed by a time adverbial: the verb is in phrase-final position, but is not raised in pitch, unlike a verb bearing focus/emphasis. The adverb is in a separate phrase from the verb. This indicates that the time adverbial stands outside the VP.

In the examples in (65) and (66), the time adverbial is lower in pitch than the preceding phrase. We have sometimes had the impression that the downstepping of the time adverbial may be greater than that found in ordinary downstep intonation, but this is not at all certain. There is, however, substantial evidence that the relationship of the time adverbial with respect to the preceding phrase is different from the relationship observed in canonical sentences with downstep intonation. Specifically, in the preceding examples where the verb is a final-accent trigger, the final accent does not project into the time adverbial: **n-andishilee khatí)**φ **yána)**φ 'I wrote a letter yesterday.'

Simple yes-no questions based on sentences with time adverbials present clear evidence that the time adverbial should be regarded as "out-of-focus", since just like complements following a focused phrase and like right-dislocated subjects, the time adverbial undergoes accent shift. Of course, in exclamatory questions, the time adverbial also undergoes accent shift, but in these questions *all* verb phrase elements undergo obligatory accent shift (thus accent shift is not a means to distinguish between phrases in and out of focus).

(67) **yê)**φ **Ø-enzele sukhúu=ni)**φ **na mapéema)**φ **yána)**φ
'he went early to the market yesterday'
(cf. **yé** 'he', **Ø-enzéle** 'he went', **sukhúu=ni** 'to the market', **na mapéema** 'early', **yána** 'yesterday')
> **yê)**φ **Ø-enzele sukhúu=ni)**φ **na mapéema**φ **yaná?)**φ
> **yê)**φ **Ø-enzele sukhuu=ní)**φ **na mapeemá)**φ **yaná!?)**φ

mí)φ **sukhúu=ni)**φ **n-enzele na mapeemá)**φ **yána)**φ
'I went early to the market yesterday'
(cf. **mí** 'I', **sukhúu=ni** 'to the market', **n-eenzelé** 'I went', **na mapéema** 'early', **yána** 'yesterday')
> **mí)**φ **sukhúu=ni)**φ **n-enzele na mapeemá)**φ **yaná?)**φ
> **mí)**φ **sukhuu=ní)**φ **n-enzele na mapeemá)**φ **yaná!?)**φ

A time adverbial may be located in IAV position and bear focus.

(68) **n-andishilee ᶠyaná)**f-φ **kháṯi)**φ 'I wrote yesterday a letter'
(cf. **n-andishilé** 'I wrote', **yána** 'yesterday', **kháṯi** 'letter')
(This sentence would be used in response to a question:
Ø-andishile ᶠliiní)f-φ **kháṯi)**φ 'when did you write a letter?')

yê)φ **Ø-enzelee ᶠyána)**f-φ **na mapéema)**φ **sukhúu=ni)**φ
'he went *yesterday* early to the market'
(cf. **yé** 'he', **Ø-enzéle** 'he went', **yána** 'yesterday', **na mapéema** 'early', **sukhúu=ni** 'to the market')
> **yê)**φ **Ø-enzelee ᶠyána)**f-φ **na mapeemá)**φ **sukhuu=ní?)**φ
> **yê) Ø-enzelee yaná)**φ **na mapeemá)**φ **sukhuu=ní!?)**φ

A time adverbial may also be focused *in situ*.

(69) **n-andishilee khatí)**_φ_ **ᶠyaná)**_f-φ_ 'it was yesterday that I wrote a letter'

This *in situ* focus is accompanied by pitch raising. Notice that the verb is a final accent-trigger and its final accent project to the focused phrase. *In situ* focusing of sentence-final elements doubtless exists for other sentence-final phonological phrases as well, but it is not attested in our texts and quite sparse in our elicitation sessions. IAV-focusing or pre-verbal focusing are preferred strategies in comparison with *in situ* focusing.

9 Embedded complement clauses

We do not examine in this chapter the intonation of subordinate clauses (e.g. adverbial clauses, conditional clauses, conjoined clauses), but in this final section we will look briefly at sentential complements functioning as objects of a main verb. The three most important clause types are (a) finite clauses introduced by the complementizer **kuwa** (which may be elided), (b) infinitival clauses which may or may not have an overt subject, (c) subjunctive clauses. The examples below mostly illustrate **kuwa**-complements.

If there is no internal focus/emphasis within the verb + sentential complement structure, then the phrasing follows from the R/XP principle and exhibits downstep intonation.

(70) a. **Omári)**_φ_ **Ø-hadile kuwaa n-vúla)**_φ_ **i-taa-kú-nya)**_φ_
'Omari said that rain will rain'
(cf. **Ø-hadíile** 'he said', **n-vúla** 'rain', **i-taa-kú-nya** 'it will rain')

b. **Hamádi)**_φ_ **Ø-tanabahile kuwa zi-wóvu)**_φ_ **ha-zi-dúumi)**_φ_
'Hamadi reawakened to the fact that evil never lasts'
(cf. **Ø-tanabahíile** 'he reawakened to', **zi-wóvu** 'evil', **ha-zi-dúumi** '[cl.10] does not last')

c. **Ø-na-kh-tosha kuwa mw-áana)**_φ_ **Ø-ta-kh-pita imtiháani)**_φ_
'he thinks that the child will pass the exam'
(cf. **Ø-na-kh-tósha** 'he thinks', **mw-áana** 'child', **Ø-ta-kh-píta** 'he will pass', **imtiháani** 'exam')

d. **mw-áana)**_φ **Ø-sh-fikíra)**_φ **Ø-chi-wona kuwa ni khéeri)**_φ **yé)**_φ **ku-wa-ráasha)**_φ
'the boy thought and realized that it was better for him to follow them [the soldiers]'
(cf. **mw-áana** 'child', **Ø-sh-fikíra** 'he thought', **Ø-chi-wóna** 'he saw/realized', **ni** 'x is', **khéeri** 'better', **yé** 'he', **ku-wa-ráasha** 'to follow them')

e. **Múusa)**_φ **Ø-na-kh-su̱la mw-áana)**_φ **kú-ja)**_φ 'Muusa wants the child to eat'

In such cases, if the main verb is a final-accent trigger, final accent occurs at the end of each phonological phrase following the main verb, even if the phrase in question would otherwise exhibit default penultimate accent.

(71) a. **n-faramile Jaamá)**_φ **∅-na-'oloké)**_φ 'I advised Jaama that he should go.'
(cf. **n-faramiilé** 'I advised', **Jáama**, personal name, **∅-na-'olóke** 'that he should go')

b. **Ø-na-kh-fila̱ta Fariidá)**_φ **kh-pita imti̱haaní)**_φ 'I expect Farida to pass the examination'
(cf. **Ø-na-kh-filatá** 'I expect', **Faríida**, personal name, **kh-píta** 'to pass'; **imti̱háani** 'exam')

c. **n̄-na-'iwa kuwa Nureení)**_φ **∅-ta-kh-faka̱tá)**_φ 'I know that Nureeni will run away'
(cf. **n̄-na-'iwa** 'I know', **Nuréeni**, personal name, **∅-ta-kh-faká̱ta** 'he will go')

d. **n-ink^hiri̱le kuwaa yé)**_φ **∅-bozele peesá)**_φ 'I denied that he stole (the) money'
(cf. **n-ink^hiriilé** 'I denied', **yé** 'he', **∅-boozéle** 'he stole', **péesa** 'money')

e. **Ø-na-kh-su̱la Omarí)**_φ **ku-m-pa Nuurú)**_φ **peesá)**_φ
'I want Omari to give Nuuru money'
(cf. **Ø-na-kh-suu̱lá** 'I want', **Omári**, personal name, **kú-m-pa** 'to give him', **Núuru**, personal name, **péesa** 'money')

In each one of these examples, the complement clause would be expected to have default accent, but has final accent due to the fact that the main verb triggers final accent throughout its verb phrase.

It is not uncommon for the main verb to be located at the end of a phonological phrase and thus separated prosodically from the sentential complement.

In this case, if the main verb is a final-accent trigger, the Accentual Law of Focus predicts that the final accent does not project out of the verb. The complement clause thus will have default accent (as long as it does not itself have a verb that triggers final accent).

(72) a. ᶠØ-na-kh-tósha)_{f-φ} kuwa mw-áana)_φ Ø-ta-kh-pita imṯiháani)_φ
'he *thinks* the child will pass the exam'
(cf. Ø-na-kh-tósha 'he thinks', mw-áana 'child', Ø-ṯa-kh-píta 'he will pass', imṯiháani 'exam')

b. Omári)_φ ᶠØ-hadíile)_{f-φ} kuwaa n-vúla)_φ i-ṯaa-kú-nya)_φ
'Omari *said* that rain will rain'
(cf. Omári, personal name, Ø-hadíile 'he said', n-vúla 'rain', i-ṯaa-kú-nya 'it will rain')

c. yé) ᶠØ-iwíile)_{f-φ} kuwa Hasáni)_φ Ø-tila habáasa)_φ
'he *knew* that Hasani had been put in prison'
(cf. yé 'he', Ø-iwíile 'he knew', Hasáni, personal name, Ø-ṯíila 'he was put', habáasa 'prison')

d. ᶠØ-na-kh-suuḻá)_{f-φ} Omári)_φ ku-m-pa Núuru)_φ péesa)_φ
'I *want* Omari to give Nuuru money'
(cf. Ø-na-kh-suuḻá 'I want', Omári, personal name, kú-m-pa 'to give him', Núuru, personal name, péesa 'money')

e. ᶠØ-na-kh-filaṯilá)_{f-φ} Farίida)_φ kh-pita imṯiháani)_φ
'I *expect* Fariida to pass the examination'
(cf. Ø-na-kh-filaṯilá 'I expect', Farίida, personal name, kh-píta 'to pass', imṯiháani 'examination')

It is possible for focus to be located in positions other than after the main verb. The subject of the complement sentence may be focused, in which case it triggers pseudo-relativization of the complement verb. However, it is also possible to emphasize the subject (thus barring the projection of a final accent past the subject) but not cause pseudo-relativization of the complement verb. This contrast between focus and emphasis (and the lack of either) is illustrated in (73).

(73) a. ɲ-na-'iwa kuwa Nureení)_φ Ø-ṯa-kh-fakaṯá)_φ
'I know that Nureeni will run away'
(cf. ɲ-na-'iwá 'I know', Nuréeni, personal name, Ø-ṯa-kh-fakáṯa 'he will run away')

vs.

b. n-na-'iwa kuwa ᶠNureení)_{f-φ} Ø-ta-kh-fakáta)_φ
'I know that *Nureeni* will run away'

vs.

c. n-na-'iwa kuwa ᶠNureení)_{f-φ} Ø-ta-kh-fakató)_φ
'I know that *Nureeni* will run away'

The data in (73) provide evidence for a three-way contrast. In (a), the subject **Nuréeni** is simply a φ. As such, it allows the final accent from the main verb to project past it and appear on the complement verb. In (b) and (c), there is pitch raising on **Nuréeni**, giving support to the idea that this word has some special status in these cases. In (b), if we claim that **Nuréeni** is focused, this will explain why the final accent triggered by the higher verb does not extend to the lower verb (an ALF effect). The problem is this: we have argued that focus on a pre-verbal word triggers pseudo-relativization of the verb. But there is no pseudo-relativization in (b). The sentence in (c) shows thata focus on **Nuréeni** can indeed induce pseudo-relativization of the complement verb. Thus (c) constitutes an example where **Nuréeni** shows both properties that a focused element is expected to show. If (c) is an example of focus, what then is (b)?

We suggest that it may be useful to postulate two types of phrases, an emphasis phrase (e-φ) as well as a focus phrase (f-φ). Both would trigger the Accentual Law of Focus, but only the latter would trigger pseudo-relativization. What we have called verb emphasis would, under such an analysis, create an e-φ rather than a f-φ. We have not implemented this proposal in the present chapter, in large part due to the fact that so far we have found a three-way contrast to be present only in a context like (73), i.e. the element is pre-verbal but located in a complement sentence.

The object of the complement clause may be focused. In (74), this focus explains why **Nuurú** exhibits final accent but **péesa** does not: the focus on **Nuurú** prevents final accent from projecting past it (an ALF effect).

(74) Ø-na-kh-sula Omarí)_φ ku-m-pa ᶠNuurú)_{f-φ} péesa)_φ
'I want Omari to give *Nuuru* money'
(cf. **Ø-na-kh-suulá** 'I want', **Omári**, personal name, **kú-m-pa** 'to give', **Núuru**, personal name, **péesa** 'money')

The verb in the sentential complement may be emphasized, as we can see from the following examples. There are, however, some issues that require exploration.

(75) a. ᶠØ-na-kh-toshá)_{f-φ} kuwa Núuru)_φ ᶠØ-boozéle)_{f-φ} gáari)_φ
'I *think* that Nuuri *stole* a car'
(cf. Ø-na-kh-toshá 'I think', **Núuru**, personal name, Ø-boozéle 'he stole', **gáari** 'car')

b. Ø-na-kh-tosha kuwa Nuurú) ᶠØ-boozéle)_{f-φ} gáari)_φ
cf.

c. Ø-na-kh-tosha kuwa Nuurú) Ø-bozele gaarí)_φ

d. Ø-na-kh-tosha kuwa ᶠNuurú)_{f-φ} Ø-bozelo gaarí)_φ
cf.

e. Ø-na-kh-tosha kuwa ᶠNuurú)_{f-φ} Ø-boozeló) gáari)_φ

In (75a), the main verb is emphasized, thus the final accent that it triggers cannot project past the verb itself. The elements in the sentential complement all exhibit default accent. We can see that the verb in the complement is emphasized, since it stands in phrase-final position, separated phrasally from its object. In (75b), the main verb is not emphasized, so the final accent can appear on the subject of the complement sentence. What is surprising, however, is that the final accent does not extend to the emphasized complement verb. This could be explained, given the discussion above, by claiming that **Núuru** is emphasized (but not focused). However, that analysis would imply a sentence should exist where **Núuru** is not emphasized, resulting in a pronunciation like **Ø-na-kh-tosha kuwa Nuurú)_φ ᶠØ-boozélé)_{f-φ} gáari)_φ**. Such a form was not given when the data in (75) were collected, raising the possibility that it is not a valid pronunciation. More research on this matter is required.

Notice that in (75c) the complement verb is not emphasized and final accent does project to the end of the sentence. In (75d), the final accent in the complement verb phrase is not the consequence of the main verb but rather is due to the focus on the subject **Núuru** requiring the complement verb to be put in pseudo-relative form. The verb and its object are phrased together and thus the final accent triggered by the pseudo-relative verb appears on the object. In (75e), the complement verb is emphasized and the final accent does not project out of the verb, as predicted by the Accentual Law of Focus.

In (76), we find some evidence that an emphasized complement verb may be in the scope of final accent from the main verb. In this example the emphasized verb is an infinitive.

(76) Ø-na-kh-sula Omarí)_φ ᶠku-m-pá)_f-φ Núuru)_φ péesa)_φ
'I want Omari to *give* Nuuru money'
(cf. **Ø-na-kh-suulá** 'I want', **Omári**, personal name, **kú-m-pa** 'to give him', **Núuru**, personal name, **péesa** 'money')

We see that the emphasis on the complement verb prevents the main verb's final accent from projecting past the infinitive verb onto the complements **Núuru** and **péesa**. (76) suggests either that the missing example from (75), **Ø-na-kh-tosha kuwa Nuurú)_φ ᶠØ-boozelé)_f-φ gáari)_φ**, is in fact a valid sentence, or there is a difference in behavior between infinitive and finite complement verbs.

We have seen now that focus or emphasis may be placed on the subject, the object, and the verb of the complement sentence. These focused elements exhibit the raised pitch associated with focus and also, due to the Accentual Law of Focus, bar a projection of the main verb's final accent from crossing past the focused element. There are, of course, other ways in which complement clauses may be manipulated (left dislocation and right dislocation inside the complement clause, left dislocation of elements of the complement sentence to a position before the main verb, preposing of the entire complement clause). But all this richness of options is beyond the scope of the present chapter.

10 Conclusion

Our understanding of Chimiini prosody has made substantial strides over the past several years. We have a very good idea of what the possible phrasings of a Chimiini sentence are. We also have a very good idea of whether a phrase will display final accent or default penult accent; however, there are certainly areas (e.g. the applicability of the Accentual Law of Focus) where some variation is possible. Departures from downstep intonation due to the pitch raising associated with focus are quite widespread and well-understood; it is less clear how to separate focus on pre-verbal elements that triggers pseudo-relativization from focus that does not. The radical lowering of right dislocated subjects represents a modification of canonical downstep intonation. Further research will doubtless establish that there are other modifications to downstep intonation associated with specific constructions and phrasings.

In this chapter we have also examined two intonational patterns associated with yes-no questions. One pattern involves pitch raising that subverts the canonical downstepping that occurs in the corresponding statement. The second pattern imposes systematic downstepping even when the corresponding statement departs from the canonical downstepping pattern. The yes-no questions strikingly may also show the shift of accent from a penult to a final syllable in some phrases, although the conditions under which this shift takes place are different in simple yes-no questions from emphatic yes-no questions.

Chimiini exhibits an extremely complex prosodic pattern. We have worked in great detail on this pattern for many years, but there is no question that much remains to be done. Given that Chimiini is an endangered language, greatly at risk, it can only be hoped that chapters such as this will stimulate additional research. The availability of speakers in Kenya, the United Kingdom, and the United States does make accessibility to speakers greater than it would be if Brava were still the exclusive home to the **want^{h}u wa Miini**.

Acknowledgements

I wish to thank the editors and reviewers for helpful feedback on an earlier version. I am particularly grateful to Annie Rialland for her help with producing and annotating the pitch tracks.

References

Kisseberth, C. W. 2005. Accent and phrasing in Chimwiini. In: S. Kaji (ed.), *Proceedings of the Symposium: Cross-linguistic Studies of Tonal Phenomena*. Research Institute for Languages and Cultures of Asia and Africa (ILCAA), Tokyo University of Foreign Studies: Tokyo, 129–145.

Kisseberth, C. W. 2010a. Optimality Theory and the theory of phonological phrasing: The Chimwiini evidence. In: N. Erteschik-Shir and L. Rochman (eds.), *The Sound Patterns of Syntax*. Oxford University Press: Oxford and New York, 217–246.

Kisseberth, C. W. 2010b. Phrasing and relative clauses in Chimwiini. In: Downing, L., Rialland, A., Beltzung, J-M., Manus, S., Patin, C., Riedel, K. (eds.), *ZAS Papers in Linguistics* 53: 109–144.

Kisseberth, C. W. 2011. Phonological phrasing and questions in Chimwiini. In: Downing, L. (ed.), *ZAS Papers in Linguistics* 55: 83–116.

Kisseberth, C. W. & M. I. Abasheikh. 1974. Vowel length in Chi-Mwi:ni – a case study of the role of grammar in phonology. In: A. Bruck, A. Fox & M.W. La Galy (eds.), *Papers from the Parasession on Natural Phonology*. Chicago: Chicago Linguistic Society, 193–209.

Kisseberth, C. W.& M. I. Abasheikh. 2004. *The Chimwiini Lexicon Exemplified*. Asian and African Lexicon no. 45: Research Institute for Languages and Cultures of Asia and Africa (ILCAA), Tokyo University of Foreign Studies. Tokyo.

Kisseberth, C. W. & M. I. Abasheikh. 2011. Chimwiini phonological phrasing revisited. *Lingua* 121: 1987–2013.
Selkirk, E. 1986. On derived domains in sentence phonology. *Phonology Yearbook* 3, 371–405.
Selkirk, E. 1996. The prosodic structure of function words. In: J. L. Morgan and K. Demuth (eds.), *Signal to syntax: Prosodic bootstrapping from speech to grammar in early acquisition*, 187–214. Mahwah, NJ: Lawrence Erlbaum.
Selkirk, E. 2000. The interaction of constraints on prosodic phrasing. In: M. Horne (ed.), *Prosody: theory and experiments*, 231–262. Dordrecht: Kluwer.
Selkirk, Elisabeth. 2005. Comments on intonational phrasing. In Sonia Frota, Marina Vigario, Maria Joao Freitas, eds. 2005. *Prosodies*. Mouton de Gruyter, Berlin.
Selkirk, E. 2009. On clause and intonational phrase in Japanese: The syntactic grounding of prosodic constituent structure. *Gengo Kenkyu* 136: 35–73.
Selkirk, E. 2011. The syntax-phonology interface. In: Goldsmith,J., Riggle, J., Yu, A.C.L. (eds.), *The handbook of phonological theory*, Second Edition, 435–484. Oxford: Blackwell.
Truckenbrodt, H. 1999. On the relationship between syntactic phrases and phonological phrases. *Linguistic Inquiry* 30:2, 219–255.

Appendix: Final Accent-Triggers

The default accent for a phonological phrase in Chimiini is penult. There are, however, a variety of what we term "final accent-triggers". These triggers require that the phrase have final accent. Final accent-triggers are primarily of three types. There are several very important *morphosyntactic* triggers. There are a variety of *lexical* triggers, mostly particles and kinship terms. Finally, there seem to be *intonational* triggers of final accent. This third type will not be discussed here (due to the fact that we have not established fully the range of data involved), but examples drawn from yes-no questions are discussed in some detail in the main text.

1 Morphosyntactic triggers

The morphosyntactic final accent-triggers in Chimiini are listed below. As explained in the main text, the final accent is not necessarily heard on the trigger, but rather at the end of a phrase containing the trigger.

- first and second person, singular and plural, subject forms in the affirmative past tense

    n-vuunzilé)$_\varphi$ 'I broke', **∅-vuunzilé)**$_\varphi$ 'you broke', **chi-vuunzilé)**$_\varphi$ 'we broke', **n-vuunzilé)**$_\varphi$ 'you (pl.) broke'
    (cf. **∅-vuunzíle)**$_\varphi$ 'he broke', **wa-vuunzíle)**$_\varphi$ 'they broke')

ni-m-uzize Hamadí)ᵩ **k-ooloká)**ᵩ 'I asked Hamadi to go'
(cf. ∅**-m-uzize Hamádi)**ᵩ **k-oolóka)**ᵩ 'he asked Hamadi to go')

- first and second person, singular and plural, subject forms in the affirmative present tense

  n-naa-ku-já)ᵩ 'I am eating', ∅**-naa-ku-já)**ᵩ 'you are eating', **chi-naa-ku-já)**ᵩ 'we are eating', **n-naa-ku-já)**ᵩ 'you pl. are eating' (cf. third person forms: ∅**-naa-kú-ja)**ᵩ 'he is eating', **wa-naa-kú-ja)**ᵩ 'they are eating')

  n-na-ku-jaa zijó)ᵩ 'I am eating zíjo', ∅**-na-ku-jaa zijó)**ᵩ 'you are eating zíjo', **chi-na-ku-jaa zijó)**ᵩ 'we are eating; zíjo', **n-na-ku-jaa zijó)**ᵩ 'you (pl.) are eating zíjo'

  (cf. third person forms ∅**-na-ku-jaa zíjo)**ᵩ 'he is eating zíjo' and **wa-na-ku-jaa zíjo)**ᵩ 'they are eating zíjo')

- all subjects, *ka*-conditional

  kaa-ni-já)ᵩ 'if you (pl.) had eaten', **n-kʰa-liindrá)**ᵩ 'if I had waited', **wê)**ᵩ ∅**-ka-soomá)**ᵩ 'if you had read', **Múusa)**ᵩ ∅**-ka-baashá)**ᵩ 'if Muusa had lost (it)', **ka-waa-bigá)**ᵩ 'if they had hit', **ka-chi-limá)**ᵩ 'if we had cultivated'

  Hamádi)ᵩ ∅**-ka-bola gaarí)**ᵩ 'if Hamadi had stolen a car'
  (cf. **Hamádi**, personal name, ∅**-ka-boolá** 'if he had stolen', **gáari** 'car')

  n-kʰa-'ula garii m-pʰiyá)ᵩ 'if I had bought a new car'
  (cf. **n-kʰa-'ulá** 'if I had bought', **gáari** 'car', **m-pʰíya** 'new')

  Núuru)ᵩ ∅**-ka-teza na Saalimú)**ᵩ **sukhuuní)**ᵩ 'if Nuuru had played in the market with Saalimu'
  (cf. **Núuru** personal name, ∅**-kaa-tezá** 'if he had played', **na** 'with', **Saalímu** personal name, **sukhúu=ni** 'in the market')

- negative imperative, singular and plural subject forms

  s-piké)ᵩ 'don't cook! (cf. **píka**ᵩ 'cook!') **s-pikee=ní)**ᵩ '(pl.) don't cook!'
  (cf. **pikáa=ni)**ᵩ)

  si-mizé)ᵩ 'don't swallow!' (cf. **míza)**ᵩ 'swallow!')

  si-mizee=ní)ᵩ '(pl.) don't swallow!' (cf. **mizáa=ni)**ᵩ)

  si-soomeshé)ᵩ 'don't teach!' (cf. **soomésha)**ᵩ 'teach!')

  si-someshee=ní)ᵩ 'pl. don't teach!' (cf. **somesháa=ni)**ᵩ)

  s-uulé)ᵩ 'don't buy!', ᶠ**s-uulé)**f-ᵩ **fatura íyo)**ᵩ 'don't buy that car', but (with focus removed from verb):

  s-ule fa̱tura iyó)ᵩ **tú)**f-ᵩ 'just don't buy that car!'

- all subjects, relative clause form of any tense

   múu-nthu)ᵩ Ø-fanyiizó)ᵩ 'the man who has done s.t.'; **hu-m-waajibó)ᵩ** '(the things) that are required of him'; **ha-zi-m-waajibí)ᵩ** '(the things) that are not required of him'; **chi-búuku)ᵩ ch-uziizá)ᵩ** 'the book that was sold'

   chi-búuku)ᵩ sh-teta ka mw-aalimú)ᵩ na mw-anafuunzí)ᵩ 'the book that was taken from the teacher by the student'
   (cf. **chi-búuku** 'book', **sh-teetá** 'which was taken', **mw-aalímu** 'teacher', **na** 'by', **mw-anafúunzi** 'student')

- *na*-conjunction

   naa m-pʰaná)ᵩ 'and a rat', **na Jaamá)ᵩ** 'and Jaama', **na khasaará)ᵩ** 'and misfortune', **na i-jambiya=y-é)ᵩ** 'and his dagger' (cf. **m-pʰána, Jáama, khasáara, i-jambiyá=y-e**)

   na chi-ti ichó)ᵩ 'and that chair' (cf. **chí-ti** 'chair', **ícho** 'that')

   na m-tanaa=ní)ᵩ k-aaké)ᵩ 'and in his room' (cf. **m-tanáa=ni** 'in the room', **káake** 'at his')

2 Lexical triggers

- *amó* 'or'

   mí)ᵩ n-tʰaa-kú-fa)ᵩ amó)ᵩ n-tʰa-m-úbla)ᵩ dugháaghi)ᵩ amó)ᵩ n-tʰa-ki-'i-rudila

   k-íitu)ᵩ ka wáawe)ᵩ na maamé)ᵩ
   'I will die or I will kill the beast or I will return home to my father and mother'

- *hatá* 'until'

   Omári)ᵩ Ø-na-k-iiníka)ᵩ m-belee m-béle)ᵩ hatá)ᵩ Ø-tuushíle)ᵩ
   'Omari was tilting forward until he fell'

- *naankʰó* 'again'

   naankʰó)ᵩ Ø-chi-mw-aambíla)ᵩ ᶠsi-n-soongé)f-ᵩ lawa ka mu-yi úyu)ᵩ
   'again he said to him: don't come near to me, get out of this town'

- *n-tʰaasá* 'not yet, before'

   m-géeni)ᵩ ntʰaasá)ᵩ k-anzaa kú-ja)ᵩ 'the guest has not yet begun to eat'

- *ntʰangú* 'since'

   ntʰangú)ᵩ fijíri)ᵩ hatá)ᵩ laakúja)ᵩ ni-m-niinziló)ᵩ
   'from/since morning until dusk I waited for him'

- **kinship terms**

  amiyá 'my paternal uncle', **amiyó** 'your paternal uncle', **amiyé** 'his/her paternal uncle'

  baayá 'my older sister', **baayó** 'your older sister', **baayé** 'her older sister'

  daadá 'my grandmother', **daadó** 'your grandmother'

  khaajá 'my maternal uncle', **khaajó** 'your maternal uncle', **khaajé** 'his/her maternal uncle'

  m-bujá 'my sister (of a boy)', **m-bujó** 'your sister', **m-bujé** 'his sister'

  mku̱lá 'my older brother (of a male)', **mku̱ló** 'your older brother (of a male)', **mku̱lé** 'his older brother'

  mu̱ná 'my younger sibling of same sex', **mu̱nó** 'your younger sibling of same sex', **mu̱né** 'his/her younger sibling'

  waankʰu̱lá 'my grandfather', **waankʰu̱ló** 'your grandfather', **waankʰu̱lé** 'his grandfather'

  yaayá 'my aunt', **yaayó** 'your aunt', **yaayé** 'his/her aunt'

Cédric Patin
Tone and Intonation in Shingazidja

Abstract: This chapter investigates the intonation system of Shingazidja, a Bantu (G44a) language of Comoros, and the way it interacts with lexical tones. The intonation of various sentence types, from complex declaratives to wh-questions, is investigated, and several prosodic features of the language are discussed, such as downstep. Special attention is paid to the way tone-intonation interaction varies in Shingazidja, depending on the dialect. I show that intonation tends to override the lexical High tones in some contexts. This is, for instance, the case for the L% and H% boundary tones that are associated with the end of Intonation Phrases. However, I also demonstrate that, on the contrary, tones dominate intonation in many contexts. For instance, the superhigh tone that signals polar questions is displaced when the final syllable of a sentence is high-toned.

Keywords: prosody, downstep, boundary tones, prosodic phrasing, focus, polar questions, Wh-questions, tone shift, Bantu, Comorian, alternative questions, biased questions

1 Introduction

This chapter describes the intonation of Shingazidja in the framework of the Autosegmental-Metrical model of intonation (Pierrehumbert 1980, Beckman & Pierrehumbert 1986, Ladd 1996). Shingazidja is a Bantu language, referenced as G44a in Guthrie's classification of the Bantu languages (Guthrie 1967–1971), which is spoken in Ngazidja (or Grande Comore), the largest island of Comoros. It is one of the four Comorian languages, along with Shindzuani (G44b, spoken in Ndzuwani – or Anjouan), Shimwali (G44c, spoken in Mwali – or Mohéli) and Shimaore (G44d, spoken in Maore – or Mayotte).[1]

The tonal system of Shingazidja has been described in great detail by various scholars (Tucker & Bryan 1970; Philippson 1988, 2005; Cassimjee & Kisseberth 1989, 1992, 1998; Jouannet 1989; Rey 1990; Patin 2007). Its intonation

---

[1] Full (2006) adds Shikombani, a language also spoken in Mayotte, to this group.

Cédric Patin, University of Lille

DOI 10.1515/9783110503524-009

system, however, has never been addressed extensively, though certain aspects were briefly discussed in Cassimjee & Kisseberth (1989) and Patin (2007), for example. A notable exception is O'Connor & Patin (2015), which discusses the intonation of Intonation Phrases. While part of the analysis in the present chapter is based on early work from the author, most of the sections thus introduce new material.

Data for this chapter have been gathered from different speakers starting in 2006. These speakers use different varieties of Shinagzidja; the variety will be indicated in the examples and figures: Moroni refers to the capital of the country, Washili to an area in the center of the island, Mbeni to a city in the North of the island and Fumbuni to the South.

The structure of this chapter is as follows. Section 2 provides an overview of the tone system of the language, focusing on how the shift of high tones signals Phonological Phrase boundaries. Section 3 discusses various parameters that can be observed in a simple sentence, from downstep (Section 3.1) to the intonation of Phonological Phrases (Section 3.3), including a discussion of the H* accent that is inserted in Phonological Phrases lacking a lexical high tone (Section 3.2). Section 4 is devoted to the intonation of non-final Intonation Phrases. Section 5 discusses the intonation of yes-no questions (Section 5.1), biased questions (Section 5.2) and content questions (Section 5.3). Section 6 provides a brief conclusion.

As we shall see, tones and intonation interact in very various ways in Shingazidja. While intonation may prevail over lexical tones in many situations, there are numerous cases where the lexical tones have an influence on intonation.

2 Tone patterns

In this section, I provide a short description of tone rules of Shingazidja and discuss their importance for phrasing. Given space restrictions, I will not mention optional tone rules, such as tone spreading; some of these rules, however, will be briefly addressed in Section 2.

2.1 Tone rules

The major characteristics of the Shingazidja tone system are well known. The system has been extensively discussed in Tucker & Bryan (1970), Cassimjee & Kisseberth (1989, 1992, 1993, 1998), Philippson (1988, 2005) and Patin (2007, 2008, 2010).

Shingazidja has a 'privative' tone system in the sense of Hyman (2001), where /H/ contrasts with Ø (there is no phonemic low tone in Shingazidja). In this language, a high tone shifts to its right, unless an underlying tone blocks it (in this study, an underlying tone is underlined). In (1b), for instance, the tone of the noun *maβáha* 'cats'[2] shifts to the penult of the adjective *mailí* 'two'.

(1) a. i. -ilí 'two'
    ii. ma-βáha 'cats (6)'

    b. ma-βaha ma-ílí
       6[3]-*cat* 6-*two*
       'two cats'

The shift of the tone leads to the deletion of every even-numbered underlying tone (e.g. the second tone, the fourth, the sixth, etc.), following the Obligatory Contour Principle. In (1b) for instance, the tone of the noun *maβáha* 'cats' shifts to the penult of the adjective *mailí* 'two', and the (even-numbered underlying) tone of the adjective is thus deleted. In (2), however, the odd-numbered tone of the adjective is free to appear, because the even-numbered tone of the noun has been deleted by the tone of the verb *tsiwóno* 'I saw' that has shifted from the penult of the verb to the first syllable of *maβáha* 'cats' (further rightward shift is blocked by the underlying tone of the noun).

(2) tsi-(w)ono má-βaha ma-i!lí
    1SG.PER-*see* 6-*cat* 6-*two*
    'I saw two cats.'

Note that the tone of the adjective is downstepped with respect to the first surface tone (see Section 2.1 for details on downstep).

A consequence of these rules is the surface neutralization of several underlying tonal oppositions. While the two words in (3) differ in their underlying tone patterns, both will surface with a single high tone on their penult.

(3) a. H Ø /ndrúme/ ndrúme 'messenger'

    b. H H /ndróví/ ndróvi 'banana'

---

[2] Words mentioned in the text are in their citation form, i.e. as they appear in isolation.
[3] In this chapter, numbers refer to noun classes. Other abbreviations are AG = augment, APP = applicative, FOC = focalizer, HAB = habitual, IMP = imperfective, OM = object marker, P = pronoun, PAS = passive, PAST = past, PER = perfective, REL = relative, SG = singular, Q = question marker.

For reasons that will be made explicit in Section 2.2, however, the surface realizations will differ slightly, with the rise of the F_0 associated with (3a) being sharper than the one associated with (3b) (see also Cassimjee & Kisseberth 1989).

2.2 Tone and phrasing

As in many other Eastern Bantu languages (Philippson 1991; Kisseberth & Odden 2003), the tone is not bounded in Shingazidja by the limits of the prosodic word. In (1b) and (2), for instance, the tones of the nouns and/or verbs are free to move to the following word(s). More precisely, in Shingazidja the tone shifts as far as possible toward the end of a 'maximal syntactic phrase' in the sense of Truckenbrodt (1999), i.e. 'the maximal projection of a lexical head' (Truckenbrodt 1999:233).

In (4), for example, the high tone of the verb shifts onto the first syllable of the direct object *mapésa* 'money' through the beneficiary *wándu* 'persons', which is underlyingly low[4] (/wandu/).

(4) [(tsi-nika   wa-ndu   má-pe!sá)_φ]_I
    1SG.PER-*give* 2-*person* 6-*money*
    'I gave money to people.'   [Mbeni]

However, a tone cannot cross the boundaries of phonological phrases. In (5a) – the symbol ')_φ' signals the end of a phonological phrase, the symbol ']_I' signals the end of an Intonation phrase – the tone of the subject NP stops on the last syllable of the noun even though the first syllable of the verb *haréme* 'he beat' is not a tone-bearing unit and is thus a possible target (5b).

(5) a. [(m-limadjí)_φ   (ha-re!mé   paha)_φ]_I
         1-*farmer*   1.PER-*beat* 5.*cat*
         'A farmer beat a cat.'

    b. *(mlimadji háreme !páha)_φ   [Moroni]

The shift of the tone is thus a reliable indicator of phonological phrase boundaries in Shingazidja. Following Selkirk's (1986) End-Base Theory, I will assume that the right boundary of a Phonological Phrase is aligned with the right boundary of a

---

[4] The tone that appears on its penult in its citation form will be explained in Section 3.3.1.

maximal syntactic phrase in Shingazidja. A Phonological Phrase boundary also separates, for instance, a dislocated element from its host, or two coordinated NPs. Both the subject NP and the VP, however, belong to a single Intonation Phrase, as illustrated in (5); evidence for this fact, which is valid for all varieties, will be provided in Section 3.

It is important to note that a phonological phrase boundary is also associated with the so-called 'augment' (whose behavior is similar to that of the definite article in Romance languages). In (6b), as opposed to (6a), the tone of the verb cannot shift onto the object because the noun is preceded by an augment.[5] The boundary precedes the augment when it cliticises to a following noun (6b) in formal speech, and follows the augment when it cliticises to a preceding element (6c) in casual speech.

(6) a. [(ha-ni̱ka   ɲ-úŋgu̱   n-dziɾo)_ɸ]_I
       1.PER-*give* 9-*pot*   9-*heavy*
       'He gave a heavy cooking pot.'

    b. [(ha-ni̱ká)_ɸ (ye=ɲ-uŋgu   n-ˈdzíɾo)_ɸ]_I
       1.PER-*give*   AG_9=9-*pot* 9-*heavy*
       'He gave the heavy cooking pot *(formal speech)*.'

    c. [(ha-ni̱k'=é)_ɸ   (ɲ-uŋgu   n-ˈdzíɾo)_ɸ]_I
       1.PER-*give*=AG_9   9-*pot*   9-*heavy*
       'He gave the heavy cooking pot *(casual speech)*.'   [Fumbuni]

Phrasing is also conditioned by focus in Shingazidja (Patin 2007, 2008), as it is in other African languages, such as Akan (Kügler, this volume). In (7b), for instance, a Phonological Phrase boundary follows the focused verb, while there is no such boundary in the all-focus sentence in (7a).

(7) a. [(ŋgam-a̱ndzo   tʃáy̱)_ɸ]_I   < /tʃaí/
       1.IMP-*like*   9.*tea*
       'I like tea.'

    b. [(ŋgam-a̱ndzó)_ɸ (tʃaˈi̱)_ɸ]_I
       'I LIKE tea.'   [Moroni]

In (8a), the underlying tone stays on the penultimate syllable of the sentence. The tone does not shift, as might be expected, to the final syllable (8b). Moreover, the shift of a tone also stops on the penult – see (6b, 6c).

---

5 The boundary is optional in the present tense.

(8) a. [(ze=m-ɓudá   pia   za-vuˈndzíha)_φ]_I
       AG₁₀=10-*stick*   *all*   10.REL.PER-*break*
       'All the sticks that broke.'

b. *ze=mɓudá pia zavundzihá

This non-finality effect, i.e. the fact that a tone cannot shift to the final syllable of a sentence, has been said to be the clue for Intonational Phrases in Patin (2007, 2008, 2010), following Cassimjee & Kisseberth (1998). We will see in Section 4, building upon intonational evidence, that this analysis is debatable.

To conclude this section, I will briefly discuss stress in Shingazidja, since stress will be of notable importance for some aspects of this study (see Section 3.3.1). As in several closely related languages such as Swahili (Ashton (1944), among many others), stress falls regularly on the penult of words. However, stress also relates to the Phonological Phrase in the sense that it seems to be strengthened on the penult of prosodic phrases: in (7a), for instance, the penult of *tʃaí* 'tea' is longer and more intense than the penultimate syllable of the preceding verb.

To my knowledge, only one phonetic study has been conducted on stress in Shingazidja: Rey (1990). However, as interesting as it is, in particular the discussion of length as a phonetic correlate of stress (Rey 1990: 153, 165), Rey's analysis suffers from several issues, such as the fact that it is based on only one speaker, that make it difficult to exploit for the present research.

Thus, a detailed study of stress in Shingazidja still remains to be done. Such a study would have to determine the precise nature of the interactions between stress and tones. Indeed, numerous examples in my corpus indicate that stress and tones may or may not align according to parameters that still need to be identified

3 Intonation of simple declarative sentence

In this section, I focus on the intonation of simple sentences. In Section 3.1, I show that downstep operates in Shingazidja, though it may be suspended. Section 3.2 is dedicated to the L% boundary tone that signals the end of a declarative in Shingazidja. In Section 3.3, I discuss the intonation of Phonological Phrases: Section 3.3.1 introduces the H* accent that is inserted in Phonological Phrases that lack any lexical high tone; Section 3.3.2 briefly shows that there is no other intonation pattern that is associated with Phonological Phrases.

3.1 Downstep(s)

In a simple declarative sentence (but also in wh-questions – see Section 5.3), all high tones are downstepped with respect to the preceding high tone(s) – see for instance (9), illustrated in Figure 1, where each high tone appears at the end of a Phonological Phrase.

(9)   [(ye=m-limadjí)_Φ   (ha-ni¹ká)_Φ   (e=m-le¹ví)_Φ   (e=ɲ-u¹mɓá)_Φ]_ι
      AG₁=1-*farmer*   1.PER-*give*   AG₁=1-*drunkard*   AG₉=9-*house*
      'The farmer gave the house to the drunkard.'   [Moroni]

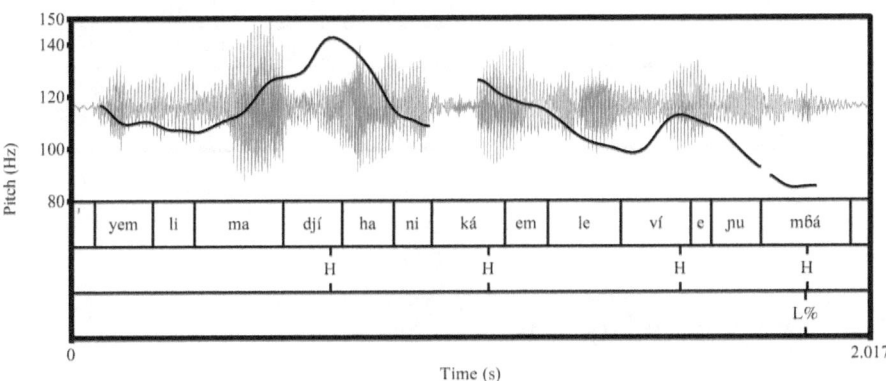

Figure 1: cf. (9) – [Moroni]

As can be observed in (9) and in Figure 1, the tone of the verb *haníka* 'he gave', which surfaces on the final syllable, is downstepped with respect to the tone of the subject. In addition, the tone of the beneficiary *mleví* 'drunkard' is downstepped with respect to the tone of the verb (the tone of the final word is also downstepped, but the phenomenon is obscured by the presence of a L% tone – see Section 3.2).

However, in a (long) phonological phrase that contains several tones, especially in non-final positions, downstep may optionally be suspended – there is no evidence that the final tone is raised. Compare the two realizations of (10) that are provided in Figure 2.

(10)   [(ze=m-ɓuɗá   n-djeu   m-ɓi⁽¹⁾lí)_Φ   (¹zí-wu)_Φ]_ι
       AG₁₀=10-*stick*   10-*white*   10-*two*   10.PER-*fall*
       'Two white sticks fell.'   [Moroni]

In the first iteration, the final tone of the first Phonological Phrase is downstepped with respect to the first high tone of the utterance. In the second version of the sentence, however, the final tone of the first Phonological Phrase is realized at the same level as the first tone of the sentence, leading to the formation of a plateau.

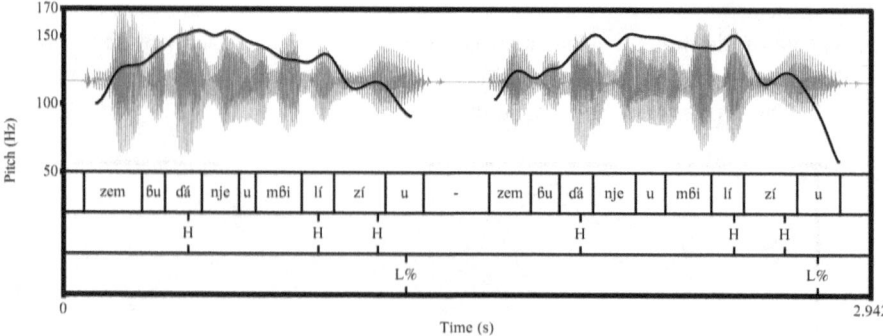

Figure 2: cf. (10) – [Moroni]

3.2 The L% boundary tone

In Figure 2, the F_0 falls dramatically at the end of the sentence, especially in the second realization. This final lowering, which is generally associated with a partial or complete devoicing of the final syllable, indicates that the end of a (simple) sentence is associated with an L% boundary tone. The presence of an L% tone at the end of a sentence is attested in other Bantu languages (e.g. Chimiini – Kisseberth *this volume* – or Tumbuka – Downing *this volume*), and widely observed among the languages of the world (Jun 2005, 2014). However, the way the L% boundary tone interacts with the lexical high tones in Shingazidja, as we shall now see, is uncommon.

As seen in Figure 1, the association of a lexical high tone and the L% boundary tone leads to a flat shape of the F_0. Such a realization is unsurprising. More interestingly, the L% tone extends its influence to a high tone that appears on the penultimate syllable,[6] as shown in (11a), illustrated in Figure 3. What is unusual here is the fact that the L% does not interact with a high tone on the penultimate syllable if the final syllable of the sentence is underlyingly high, as in (11b). In Figure 3, the tone that appears on the word *mleví* 'drunkard' is

---

[6] F. Cassimjee and C. Kisseberth noted this difference in the realization of the tones on the penult in their seminal paper on Shingazidja tonology (Cassimjee & Kisseberth 1989: 46).

realized with a sharp rise of the F_0, in contrast with the tone that is associated with the word *ndóvu* 'elephant'.

(11) a. [(ha-wono n-ᶦdóvu)_φ]_I
          1.PER-*see* 9-*elephant*
          'He saw an elephant.'

     b. [(ha-wono m-lévi)_φ]_I
          1.PER-*see* 1-*drunkard*
          'He saw a drunkard.'   [Moroni]

Furthermore, there are some interesting dialectal differences in the relationship that links the high tones to the L%. In the variety of Fumbuni, in contrast with Moroni, the L% does not extend its influence to a tone that appears on the penult, even if there is no underlying tone associated with the final syllable. Compare the realizations of the sentences in (12) in Figure 4 with the realizations of (11) in Figure 3: in Fumbuni, the presence or absence of an underlying tone on the final syllable has no effect on the shape of the F_0.

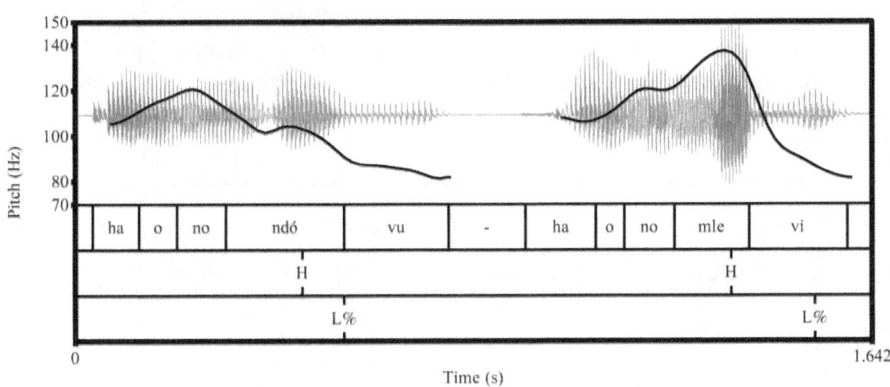

Figure 3: cf. (11) – [Moroni]

(12) a. [(ha-piha ɲ-áma)_φ]_I
          1.PER-*cook* 9-*meat*
          'He cooked some meat.'

     b. [(ha-piha djándze)_φ]_I
          1.PER-*see* 5.*crab*
          'He cooked some/a crab.'   [Fumbuni]

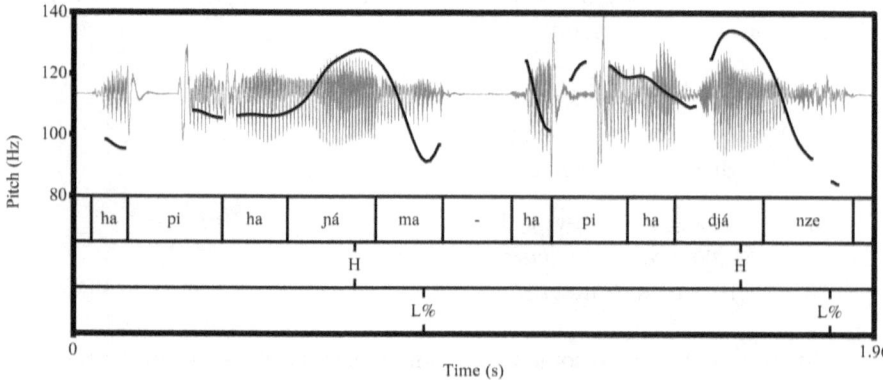

Figure 4: cf. (12) – [Fumbuni]

The peripheral dialects also differ from the dialects of the center of the island regarding the interaction of the L% boundary tone with lexical high tones. As previously mentioned, the association of L% with lexical high tones results in a flat shape of the F_0 in Moroni, which is also the case in Washili. In the peripheral varieties, i.e. in Mbeni or Fumbuni, there is no L% boundary tone on a syllable where a lexical high tone surfaces. See for instance Figure 5, which corresponds to (4): the final high tone, while downstepped, is realized as a sharp rise of the F_0.

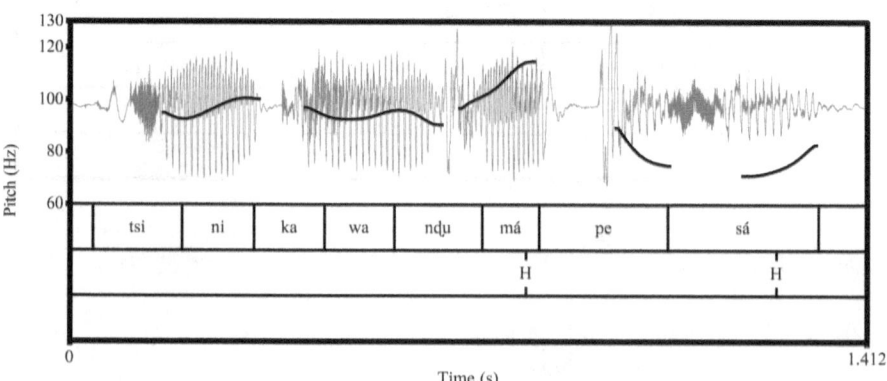

Figure 5: cf. (4) – [Mbeni]

At this point in my research, it is not clear if the L% boundary tone signals the end of a final Intonation Phrase or the end of a prosodic phrase at a higher level, e.g. a hypothetical Utterance Phrase level. Besides this boundary tone, other prosodic clues for the end of a simple clause include non-finality (see Section 2), the lengthening of high-toned penultimate syllables in Mbeni, and an intensity peak on the penult in all varieties. As may be observed in the signal that is provided in several figures in this chapter, this intensity peak on the penult is not consistent in my data; understanding why is left for future research.

3.3 The intonation of phonological phrases

This section is dedicated to the Intonation of non-final Phonological Phrases. In 3.3.1, I discuss the H* accent that is inserted in Phonological Phrases that lack a lexical high tone. In 3.3.2, I show that no other intoneme characterizes Phonological Phrases.

3.3.1 H* insertion

Examples (11a) and (12a) in Section 2.2 involve nouns that have no underlying tone. As noted by other researchers (Cassimjee & Kisseberth 1989, Philippson 2005), these nouns emerge with a default high tone on their penult when they are realized in isolation (13).

(13) a. /N-ama/   →   [ɲámạ]   'meat (9)'

 b. /N-dovu/ →   [ndóvụ]   'elephant (9)'

Philippson (2005:204) claims: "[...] it must be assumed that no unaccented utterance is allowed in Shingazidja. If no element of the P[honological] P[hrase] can lexically supply an accent,[7] a default accent will appear on the penult of the phrase." As mentioned in Section 2.2, the penult of a phrase is the stressed syllable in a phrase.

It is not clear, however, if the tones in examples such as (13) should be considered H* accents that are inserted at the Intonation level, or if the usually toneless words have high-toned allomorphs that are selected when the word is realized in isolation. There is independent evidence in favor of the existence of high-toned allomorphs of usually toneless words (see also Cassimjee & Kisseberth (1989)). In (14), for instance, the word 'elephant', which usually lacks

---

[7] Philippson uses the term 'accent' for what is here referred to as 'tone'.

a lexical high tone – see (11a), (13b), etc. – is associated with a lexical high tone that surfaces on its final syllable.

(14) [(ze=n-dovú   nfu¹káre)_Φ]_I
         AG₁₀-10-*elephant*   *seven*
         'Seven elephants.'

The tone on the last syllable of *ndóvu* 'elephant' has to be underlyingly associated with the noun: not only does it appear on the final syllable of the word (contrary to the claim from Philippson that the default high tone appears on the penultimate syllable of the phrase – see also (13)), but it also triggers the deletion of the first underlying tone of *nfúkare* 'seven'.

However, I will claim here that the default tone in (13) and similar examples is an intoneme. A first argument in favor of the insertion of H* comes from the comparison of sentences such as (15a), which involves a usually toneless (subject) noun, and (15b), which involves a usually toned (subject) noun. In the first case, the tone generally appears on the penult of the Phonological Phrase, whereas the tone surfaces at the end of the Phonological Phrase in the second (Figure 6).

(15) a. [(ze=n-dovu   n-dzíro)_Φ (¹zí-dja)_Φ]_I
             AG₁₀-10-*elephant*   10-*heavy*   10.PER-*come*
             'The heavy elephants came.'

      b. [(ze=m-ɓuɗa   n-dziró)_Φ (¹zí-wu)_Φ]_I
             AG₁₀-10-*stick*   10-*heavy*   10.PER-*fall*
             'The heavy sticks fell.'   [Moroni]

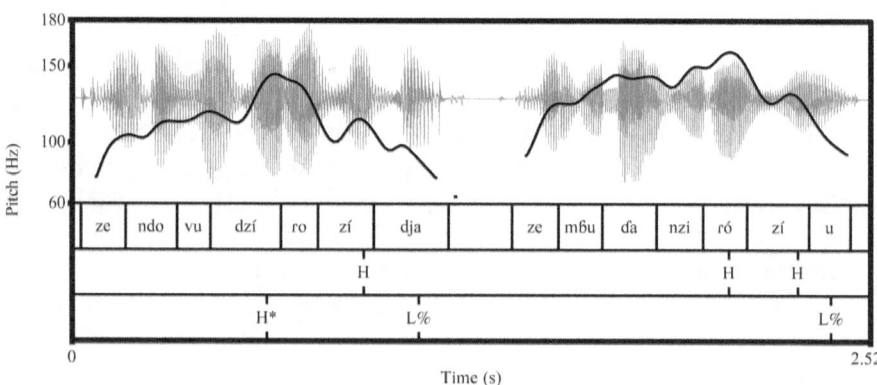

Figure 6: cf. (15) – [Moroni]

I consider the fact that the high tone does not shift to the final syllable of the first Phonological Phrase in (15a), in contrast to (15b), to be evidence that this tone is not a lexical high tone, but rather an H* accent.

Additional evidence comes from phrases such as (16) that contain three usually toneless words. In such a situation, a high appears on both the adjectives in the dialect of Moroni (16a). In Mbeni (16b), however, only one high tone emerges on the penult of the sentence. (In (16), the brackets, indicating the *phonetic* – rather than phonological – notation, do not refer to syntactic or prosodic structures.)

(16) /ze=n-dovu   n-djema   n-dziro/   >
      AG$_{10}$-10-*elephant* 10-*nice*   10-*heavy*

   a. [ze=ndovu ndjéma ndzíro]   [Moroni]

   b. [ze=ndovu ndjema ndzíro]   [Mbeni]
      'The nice heavy elephants.'

The association of a H* with both adjectives in (16a) may indicate that a prosodic level below the Phonological Phrase, defined as aligning a prosodic phrase with the syntactic phrase (instead of the maximal syntactic phrase, as defined in Section 2.2, as it is the case for Phonological Phrases), is relevant in the dialect of Moroni. I leave this point for further research, but see O'Connor & Patin (2015) for a brief discussion.

Rephrasing due to eurythmic constraints leads to another pattern in longer sentences. As shown in (17), a default tone is only inserted on the second adjective in Moroni, and no default tone is inserted in Mbeni, indicating that the insertion of a default high tone is a rule that operates at the Intonation Phrase level in this dialect.

(17) /ze=n-dovu   n-djema   n-dziro   zí-djá/ >
      AG$_{10}$-10-*elephant* 10-*nice*   10-*heavy*   10.PER-*come*

   a. [ze=ndovu ndjema ndzíro | zídja]   [Moroni]

   b. [ze=ndovu ndjema ndziro | zídja]   [Mbeni]
      'The nice heavy elephants came.'

This latter fact confirms that the default high tone is an intoneme, here represented as an H*. Surprisingly, this intoneme, as a lexical tone, triggers the downstep of a following lexical high tone (see Figure 6).

A final argument in favor of the existence of an H* is the comparison of (4-Mbeni), illustrated in Figure 5, with a similar example from the dialect of Moroni (18), illustrated in Figure 7.

(18) [(tsi-ni̱ka   m̩-ndu̱   má-pe̱ˈsá̱)_ϕ]_I
     1SG.PER-*give* 1-*person* 6-*money*
     'I gave money to somebody.'   [Moroni]

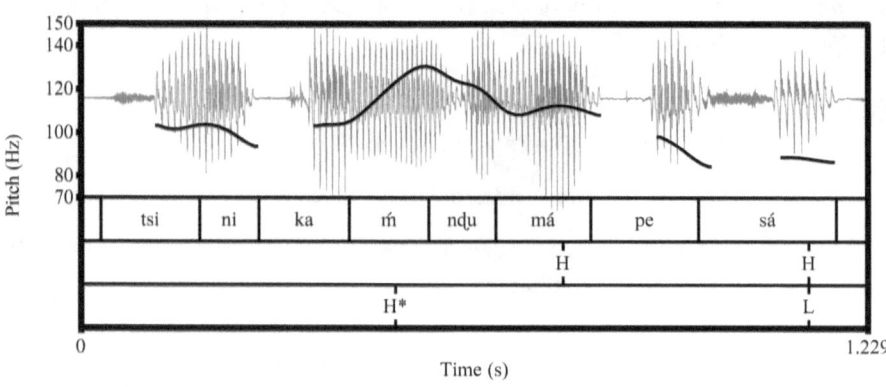

Figure 7: cf. (18) – [Moroni]

In Figure 5, which corresponds to the production of a speaker from Mbeni, no rising of the F₀ is observable on the beneficiary *wándu̱* 'persons'. In Figure 7, on the other hand, a sharp rise of the F₀ can be observed on the penult of *m̩ndu̱* 'person'. This rise cannot be attributed to the lexical tone of the verb, since this tone shifts in (18) onto the first syllable of *mape̱sa̱* 'money', as it did in (4). As a consequence, it must be explained by the presence of the H* that emerges on the penult of phrases in the dialect of Moroni.

3.3.2 The right edge of the Phonological Phrase

When there is a lexical high tone in a Phonological Phrase, no H* is inserted on the penult, even if the final two syllables of the Phrase lack any surface tone. Moreover, no intoneme appears on the final syllable of a non-final Phonological Phrase. See for instance (19), where the word *ndóvu* 'elephant' lacks any tone, either underlyingly or on the surface.

(19) [(e=mw-i̱dz[i]   yá-i̱ɓa   n-dovu)_ϕ   (ha-tˈá̱wa)_ϕ]_I
     AG₁=1-*thief* 1.REL.PER-*steal* 9-*elephant* 1.PER-*run away*
     'The thief who stole an elephant ran away.'

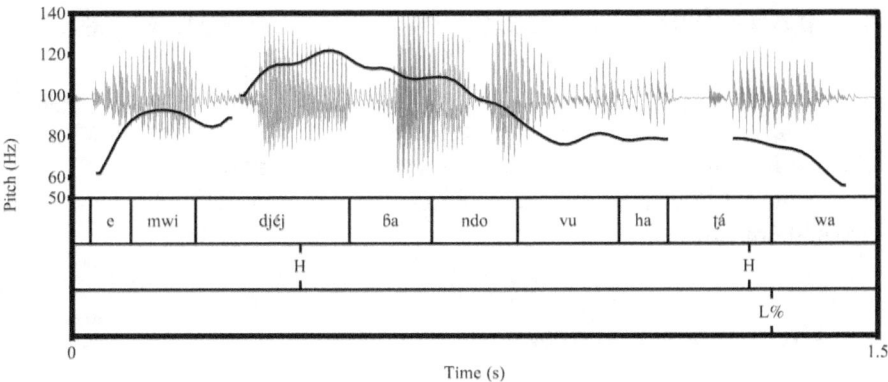

Figure 8: cf. (19) – [Moroni]

However, examples where no tone appears on the final syllables of a Phonological Phrase, such as (19), are extremely rare in my data. Since the shift of a tone stops on the final syllable of a Phonological Phrase, most of Phonological Phrases end with a high tone (see for instance (9)). Moreover, several rules seem to conspire to increase the number of H-final Phonological Phrases. For example, one of the underlying tones of the verb, either the tone of the object marker or the tone of the root, is deleted in (20b),[8] leading to a surface realization where a high tone emerges at the end of the Phonological Phrase, whereas the form *hazínika* would have been expected.

(20) a. [(ha-niká)_φ   (ze=ˈsír[i])_φ]_I
         1.PER-*give*   AG$_{10}$=10.*pants*
         'He gave the pants.'

    b. [(ha-zi-niká)_φ   (ze=ˈsír[i])_φ]_I
         1.PER-OM$_{10}$-*give*   AG$_{10}$=10.*pants*
         'He gave them, the pants.'   [Washili]

The realization in (20b) is representative of a general tendency in the language to avoid Phonological Phrases where no tone appears on the final two syllables of the prosodic group. I consider this an indication that the language is evolving towards a pitch-accent system; due to space restrictions, I cannot explore this analysis here.

---

8 Note that the phrase boundary that prosodically separates the verb from the object in (20a) is due to the presence of the augment (see the end of Section 2 for a discussion).

4 Intonation of complex declarative sentences

This section focuses on the intonation of non-final Intonational Phrases. In Section 4.1, I present data supporting the existence of an H% boundary tone, which is here considered to be the main cue for (non-final) Intonation Phrases. In Section 4.2, I discuss a LH*!H contour that is associated with contrastive topics in Shingazidja.

4.1 The H% boundary tone

In Shingazidja, a sharp rise of the F_0, here referred to as an H% boundary tone and frequently accompanied by a short pause, is associated with the end of a non-final clause. In O'Connor & Patin (2015), just such an H% was observed at the end of non-restrictive appositives, at the end of non-restrictive relatives (building upon Patin (2010)), and at the end of the first part of two coordinated clauses. In (21), illustrated in Figure 9, an H% is also observable at the end of the first clause, on the final syllable of the word *mizíkí* 'music'.

(21) [(ha-ka-u-ʃília   mizikí)_φ]_I [(βo   na-ka-u-fanyá   hazi)_φ]_I
      1.PER-PAST-15-*listen* 9.*music*   *while* 1SG.PER-PAST-15-*do* 9.*job*
      'He was listening music while I was working.'   [Washili]

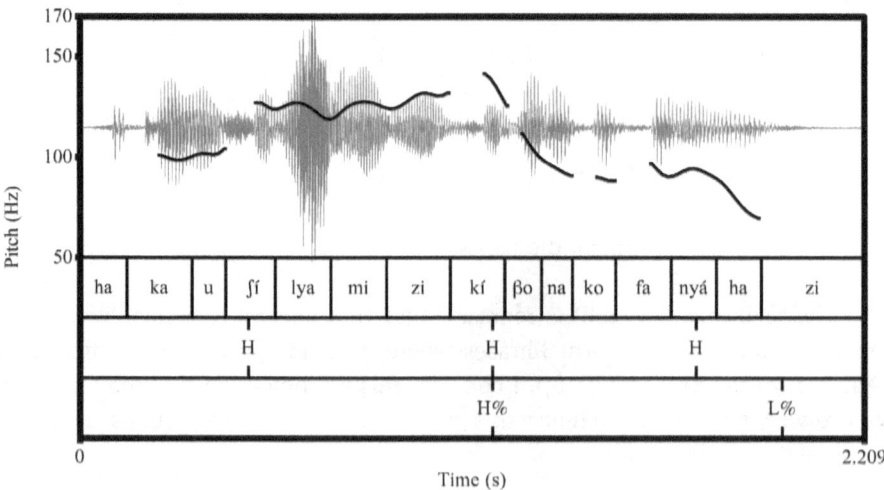

Figure 9: cf. (21) – [Washili]

Note that the rising of the F_0 in Figure 9 cannot be attributed to the lexical tone. As was shown in O'Connor & Patin (2015), the rise is observable even when no surface tone emerges on the final syllables of the Intonation phrase – (22), illustrated in Figure 10.

(22) [(ye=m-limadjí)_Φ   ([h]a-[h]ulu   ɲ-úŋ[g]u   n-jeu)_Φ]_I
      AG₁=1-*farmer*   1.PER-*buy*   9-*cooking pot* 9-*white*

      [(ʃ[a]=ye=fúndî)_Φ   (ŋ[g]w-[y]i-wonó   ā̊lį)_Φ]_I
      but=AG₁=1.*teacher*   1.PER-OM₉-*see*   *expensive*
      'The farmer bought a white cooking pot, but the teacher thinks it is expensive.'   [Washili]

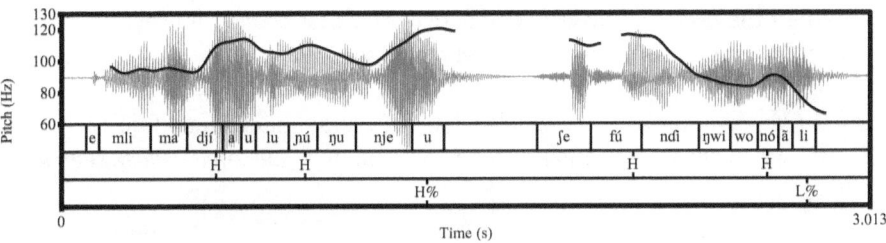

Figure 10: cf. (22) – [Washili]

When several clauses are stacked, an H% appears at the end of all non-final clauses (the final clause being associated with a L%). In Figure 11, illustrating (23), all the tones are downstepped with respect to the preceding tones, except the tones at the end of the clauses, which are significantly raised.

(23) [(yek[a]=[y]é)_Φ   (ma-siʹhú)_Φ   (ya-ˈdjá)_Φ]_I   [(yeʹká)_Φ   (m-ndru)_Φ
      if=AG₄   4-*night*   4.PER-*come*   *if*   1-*person*

      (ha-woʹnó)_Φ   (ze=ɲ-ora   z-a=mw-andó)_Φ]_I   [(ze=m-ˈɓé)_Φ
      1.PER-*see*   10-*star*   10-*of*=3-*first*   AG₁₀=10-*cow*

      (zo-u-ndji[h]=ˈhó)_Φ   (paʹʃé=ni)_Φ]_I
      10.HAB-15-*enter*=AG₁₇   9.*kraal*=*in*
      'When the night comes, when one sees the first stars, the cows come back to the kraal.'   [Washili]

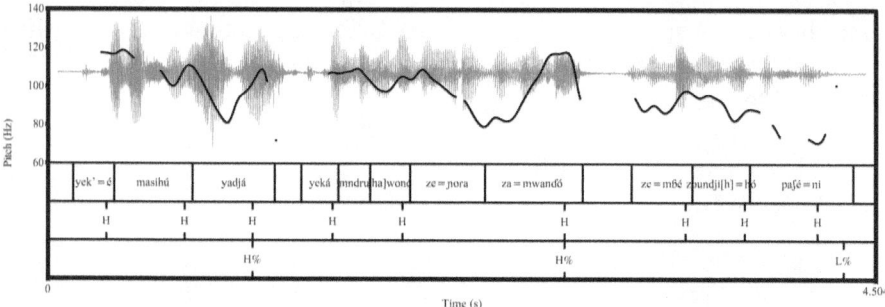

Figure 11: cf. (23) – [Washili]

When the second clause is embedded in a first clause, however, as is the case in (24), no H% is in general observable (see Figure 12).[9]

(24) [(ye=mw-aná)_Φ (ha-leme̩ˈwá)_Φ   (ha[ta] ha-siuʃi[a]=ˈ[h]ó)_Φ
     AG₁=1-*child*   1.PER-*being tired*   *until* 1.PER-*fell asleep*.APP=AG₁₇

  (ga̩ˈrí=ni)_Φ]_I
  9.*car=in*

'The child was so tired that he fell asleep in the car.' [Washili]

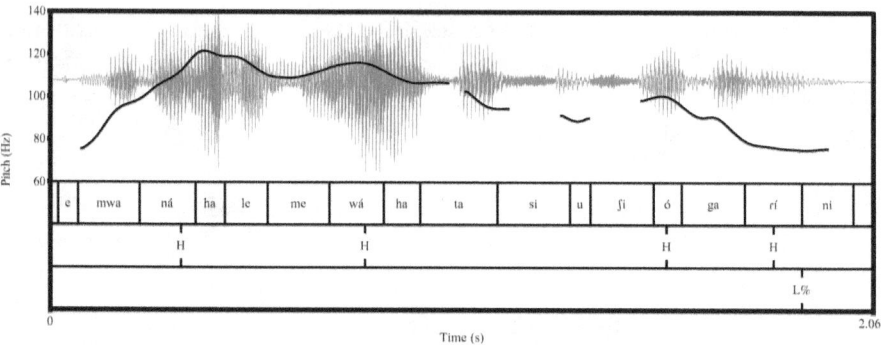

Figure 12: cf. (24) – [Washili]

However, the H% may also emerge in these situations, depending on parameters such as speech rate or idiolectal variation. More generally, an H% can appear at the end of – or before – any non-final clause. In (25), for instance, an H% associated with a short pause follows the relative.

---

9 I have no evidence here that an Intonation Phrase is embedded in another, as could be expected.

(25) [[(wa-dj<u>e</u>ni wa-wá-n<u>i</u>ka ma-ɓamɓú)_Φ]_I (w<u>a</u>-ˈdjíβiwa)_Φ]_I
      2-*visitors* 2.REL.PER-OM₂-*give* 6-*present*   2.PER-*please*.PAS
      'The visitors to whom they gave gifts are pleased.'   [Moroni]

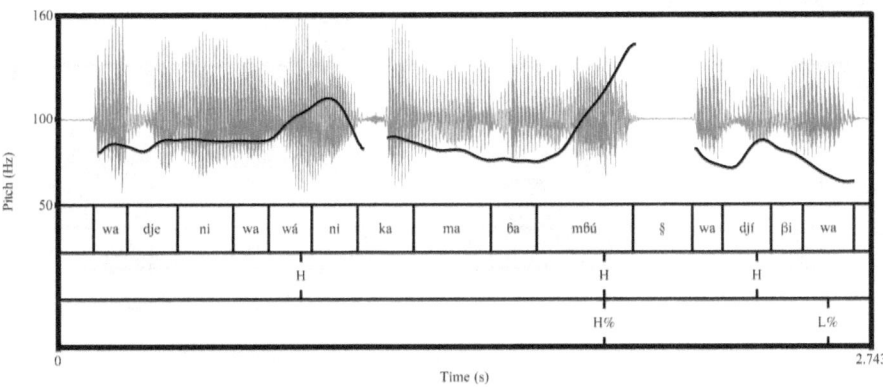

Figure 13: cf. (25) – [Moroni]

Note that the insertion of an Intonation Phrase boundary in (25), signaled by an H%, must be linked to the length of the sentence and idiolectal variation, since it has previously been shown that not all relatives are followed by an H% (cf. (19) in Section 3.3.2, and Patin (2010)).

4.2 The LH*!H% contour

As demonstrated in (26a) and Figure 14, the H% boundary tone can appear in contexts other than the end of (or before) a clause. In (26a), the fronted dislocated object is followed by an Intonation Phrase boundary; evidence for this boundary comes from the pause that separates the dislocated NP from the matrix.

(26) a. [[(ʃe=i-t<u>a</u>nďá)_Φ]_I (tsi-ʃi-ˈrénge)_Φ]_I
        AG₇=7-*bed*   1SG.PER-OM₇-*take*
        'The bed, I took it.'

    b. [[(ʃe=it<u>á</u>nďā)_Φ]_I (tsiʃiˈrénge)_Φ]_I
        'THE BED (= not the chair), I took it.'   [Moroni]

Interestingly, a contrastive topic is associated with a specific contour composed of a LH* bitonal tone associated with the penult of the dislocated element and a downstepped H% boundary tone, which is, as expected, associated with the final syllable of the Intonation Phrase: compare (26a) with (26b), which exhibits this contour, in Figure 14. As we shall see later (see Section 5.2), this contour is also associated with specific types of questions that involve emphasis: surprise and echo questions.

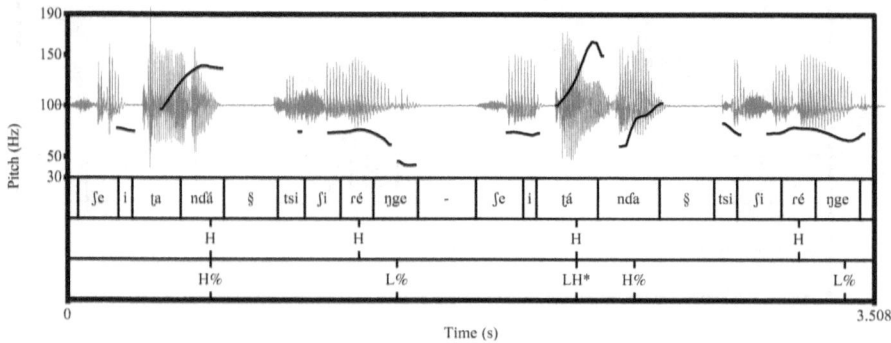

Figure 14: cf. (26) – [Moroni]

If the lexical high tone at the end of the contrastive topic is underlyingly associated with the final syllable, this syllable is lengthened in order for the contour to emerge – see (27), illustrated in Figure 15.

(27) [[(leo̱ō̄)_φ]_I (ha-li¹mí̱)_φ]_I   < /leó/
       today   1.PER-*cultivate*
       'TODAY (= not yesterday), I have cultivated.'

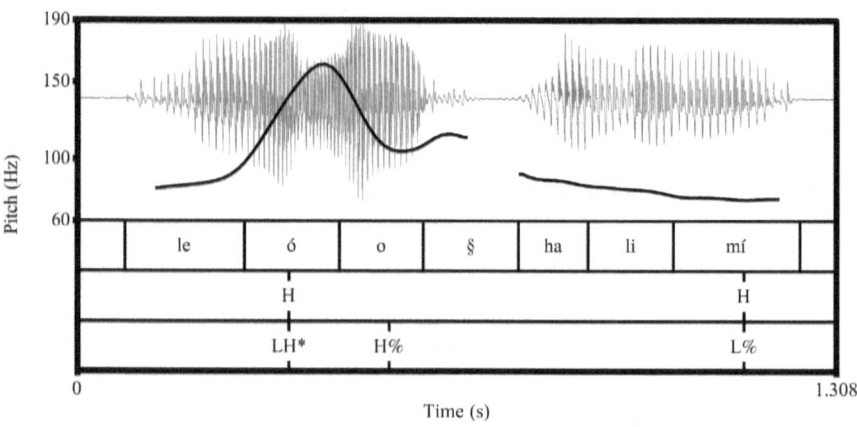

Figure 15: cf. (27) – [Moroni]

5 Question intonation

This section is dedicated to the prosody of questions in Shingazidja. In Section 5.1, I discuss yes-no questions extensively, especially the interesting tone-intonation relationship exemplified by these questions. In Section 5.2, I briefly introduce biased questions. Finally, Section 5.3 is dedicated to content questions.

5.1 Yes-no questions

In this section, I will discuss the prosody of yes-no questions in Shingazidja in detail. The results come from the analysis of an experiment where 100 questions were produced by four different speakers from various dialectal backgrounds. All the examples and F_0 curves in this section correspond to the realizations of the speaker from Moroni.

5.1.1 The superhigh tone

In Shingazidja, as in many other Bantu languages, polar questions do not differ from their declarative counterparts in their morphology or word order. Rather, polar questions are marked by prosody, and optionally by the question particle *yé*. As noted in Cassimjee & Kisseberth (*in prep.*), the distinctive feature of polar questions is a 'superhigh tone' that appears on the penultimate syllable of the utterance, i.e. the last stressed syllable. In (28), for instance, the polar question differs from its declarative counterpart by the presence of a superhigh tone on its penultimate syllable (28b), as opposed to a downstepped high tone (28a).

(28) a. [(ha-wonó)_φ (le=ꞌpáha)_φ]_I
        1.PER-*see*   AG₅=5.*cat*
        'He saw the cat.'

    b. [(hawonó)_φ (lé=páha)_φ]_I
        'Did he see the cat?'   [Moroni]

The insertion of a (super)high tone or a rising intonation pattern is a widely observed strategy in yes-no questions in Bantu languages, though the pattern is more frequently associated with the last syllable of the utterance (e.g. Ekoti – Schadeberg & Mucanheia 2000; Herero – Möhlig et al. 2002; Kinyarwanda – Kimenyi 1980) than with the penult (but see for instance Chichewa, Chitumbuka – Downing 2004, Downing *this volume* –, Chimiini – Kisseberth *this volume*).

Recordings of the utterances in (28)[10] show that there is no clear observable difference in the average fundamental frequency of the word *hawóno* 'he saw' when it occurs in the declarative or the polar question. On the other hand, the F_0 of the penultimate syllables of theses utterances – i.e. the first syllable of the word *páha* 'cat' in both cases – differs radically depending on the status of the clause. This difference is illustrated in Figure 16. Generally, the superhigh tone is realized as a sharp F_0 rise, though it is also regularly realized as a rising-falling F_0 movement. In Figure 16 and subsequent figures, the superhigh tone is represented as a bitonal pitch accent LH* linked to the stressed syllable of the utterance. This bitonal accent forms a contour with the boundary L% tone that is also attested in yes-no questions.

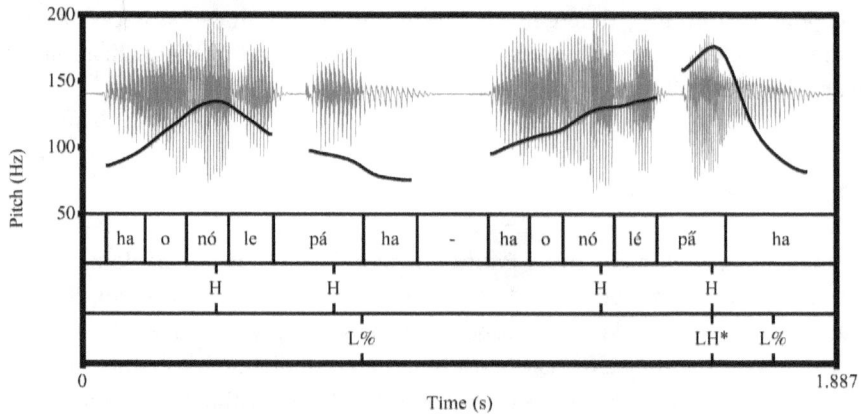

Figure 16: cf. (28) – [Moroni]

When more than two high tones surface in the utterance, the yes-no question differs from the declarative in that the downstep is suspended: in (29b), for example, the tone of the word *uká(ya)* 'that'[11] is not downstepped with respect to the tone of *ŋgudjúo* 'he knows', while it is downstepped in the statement in (29a).

(29) a. [(ŋgu-dju-ó)ᵩ (uˈká)ᵩ (ŋge-ˈɲá-o)ᵩ]ᵢ
        1.IMP-*know*-IMP   *that*   9.IMP-*rain*-IMP
        'He knows that it (= the rain) is raining.'

    b. [(ŋgudjuó)ᵩ (uká)ᵩ (ŋgéɲá-o)ᵩ]ᵢ
        'Does he know that it (the rain) is raining?'   [Moroni]

---

10 Six to ten repetitions of each sentence were recorded.
11 *uká(ya)* 'that' comes from the verb *ukáya* 'to be, live, stay'.

In (28b) and (29b), the syllables that immediately precede the superhigh tone are high, whereas they are low in the corresponding declaratives (28a, 29a). Generally, the syllables that separate the superhigh tone from the preceding high tone in the declarative are raised, independently of the number of syllables that separates the former from the latter. In (30) for instance, the three syllables that precede the superhigh tone are realized at the same level as the tone of the last syllable of the verb.

(30) a. [(ha-niká)_ɸ (e=ɲ-uŋgu   n-ˈdzíro)_ɸ]_I
        1.PER-*give*   AG_9=9-*pot*   9-*heavy*
        'He gave the heavy cooking-pot.'

    b. [(haniká)_ɸ (é=ɲúŋgú   ndzíro)_ɸ]_I
        'Did he give the heavy cooking-pot?'   [Moroni]

The high plateau (or tone bridge) that links the superhigh tone from a preceding high tone is illustrated in Figure 17, which corresponds to (30). This figure also illustrates the fact that there is no systematic peak of intensity on the penult of yes-no questions.

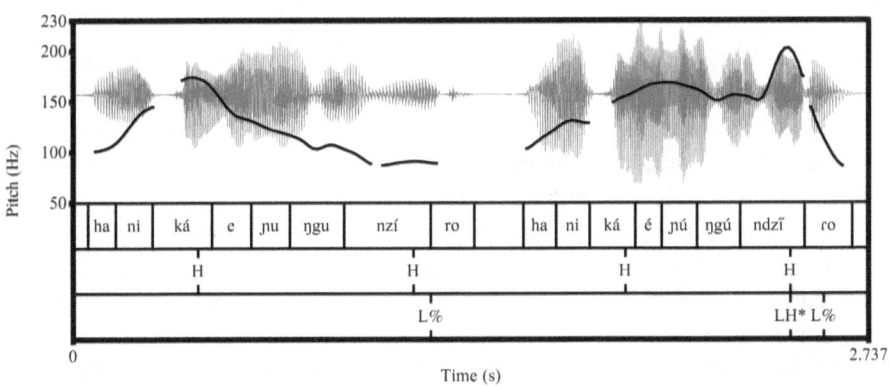

Figure 17: cf. (30) – [Moroni]

It is important to note that the Phonological Phrase boundaries are maintained in yes-no questions, at least in the dialect of Moroni (the situation is less clear in northern and southern varieties). In (30b), for instance, the plateau starts on the last syllable of the verb, whereas one might expect the beginning of the bridge to occur on the first syllable of the noun if there were no prosodic break before the augment. Thus, we can conclude that the tone bridge rule occurs at the Intonation Phrase level.

Since the superhigh tone that marks polar questions overlaps a high tone in (28)–(30), one may wonder if the marker of polar questions is a superhigh tone or a rising of the last tone of a sentence, a strategy that has been identified in some Bantu languages (e.g. Ganda, Dzamba – see Rialland 2007; Chimiini – Kisseberth *this volume*). As pointed out in Cassimjee & Kisseberth (*in prep.*), the latter hypothesis is ruled out by examples such as (31b). In this example, a superhigh tone appears on the penultimate syllable of the sentence, while there is no tone on the penultimate syllable of the corresponding declarative (31a).

(31) a. [(ha-nika ɲ-úŋgu n-dziro)_Φ]_I
   1.PER-*give* 9-*pot* 9-*heavy*
   'He gave a heavy cooking-pot.'

 b. [(hanika ɲúŋgú ndzíro)_Φ]_I
   'Did he give a heavy cooking-pot?'   [Moroni]

5.1.2 A case of tone-intonation interaction: superhigh tone retraction

Hyman & Monaka (2008) distinguish three main tone-intonation strategies: (a) 'Accommodation ('peaceful coexistence'), whereby the terrain is divided up somehow such that the lexical and intonational tones minimally interact'; (b) 'Submission ('surrender'), whereby the intonational tones invade and override the lexical tones'; (c) Avoidance ('blockade') [...]: intonation is minimized'. While Shingazidja mostly belongs to the second type (Submission), there are situations in which the lexical tones influence intonation – e.g. the L% tone that cannot be associated with high tones in peripheral dialects. Such a situation arises in yes-no questions.

Indeed, there is a set of polar questions that does not follow the pattern that has been sketched up to this point: the superhigh tone is not associated with the penultimate syllable of yes-no questions that correspond to declaratives with a high tone on their last syllable. In such cases, the superhigh tone appears instead on the *ante*penultimate syllable. In (32b), for instance, illustrated in Figure 18, the superhigh tone appears on the augment,[12] while it might have been expected on the penult (32c).

---

[12] In such a sentence, the presence of the superhigh tone on the vowel [e] of the augment or on the (nasal) prefix of the noun (then syllabic: [m̩]) varies depending on speech rate. In any case, it cannot appear on the penult.

(32) a. [(ha-wonó)_φ   (ye=m-le¹ví)_φ]_I
          1.PER-*see*   AG₁=1-*drunkard*
          'He saw the cat.'

    b. [(hawonó)_φ   (yĕ=mle¹ví)_φ]_I
        'Did he see the cat?'

    c. *[(hawonó)_φ   (yé=mlĕ¹ví)_φ]_I   [Moroni]

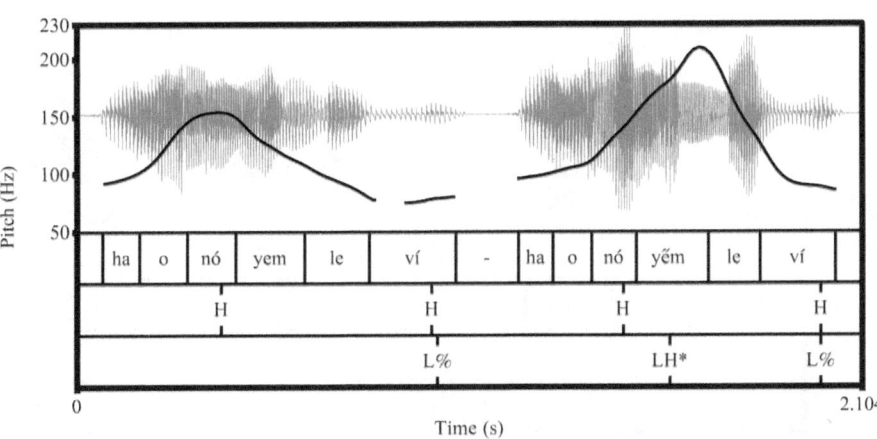

Figure 18: cf. (32) – [Moroni]

It must be noted that this category of polar questions also constitutes an exception in Cassimjee & Kisseberth (*in prep.*). However, their data do not correspond to mine on this point. According to F. Cassimjee and C. Kisseberth, the superhigh tone does not appear in this situation, either on the penult or the antepenult, and the final high tone is deleted. The deletion of the final tone, while infrequent, is also observable in my data; the presence of the superhigh tone, however, is mandatory.

Importantly, no displacement of the superhigh tone occurs when the lexical tone appears on the antepenult, as in (33). It is only when a lexical high emerges on the final syllable that the superhigh tone is retracted.

(33) a. [(ha-wonó   paha)_φ]_I
          1.PER-*see* 5.*cat*
          'He saw a cat.'

    b. [(ha-wonó   pǎha)_φ]_I
        'Did he see a cat?'   [Moroni]

When both the antepenult and the final syllable are associated with a high tone, the superhigh still appears on the antepenult, which is then raised – (34).

(34) a. [(ha-wonó   m-pi¹rá)_ɸ]_I
       1.PER-see   3-ball
       'He saw a ball.'

   b. [(ha-wonő   mpi¹rá)_ɸ]_I
       'Did he see a ball?'   [Moroni]

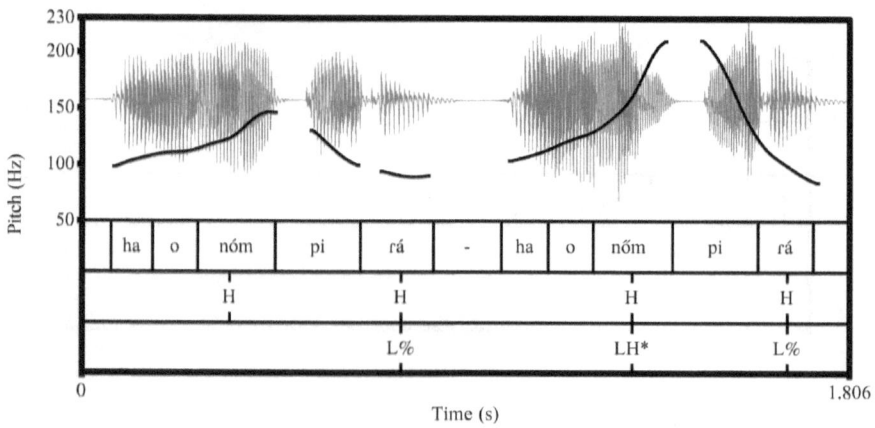

Figure 19: cf. (34) – [Moroni]

5.1.3 Alternative questions

Alternative questions in Shingazidja share many features with polar questions. Like the latter, they do not differ syntactically from their declarative counterparts – i.e. the alternative statements – and they are not associated with an obligatory morpheme (like other types of questions in Shingazidja, however, they may be associated with the question particle *yé*).

A superhigh tone is also associated with alternative questions, where it appears on the penultimate syllable of the first conjunct. The superhigh tone cannot appear only on the second part of the alternative. While some speakers claim that the raising of both the first and the second elements of the alternative is possible, such a realization has not been observed for any speaker, whether the expected answer is 'A(/B)' or 'yes(/no)' (e.g. 'coffee(/tea)' or 'yes(/no)' when the question is 'Do you want tea or coffee?'). This pattern supports the idea that, prosodically speaking, a polar question in Shingazidja corresponds to the first part of an alternative question.[13]

(35b) illustrates the placement of the superhigh tone on the penultimate syllable of the first element of the alternative, i.e. the NP *le=páha* 'the cat'. Note that while there is a high tone on the last syllable of the first element in the declarative (due to the shift of the tone – (35a)), the superhigh tone is still associated with the penult (in other words, there is no tone retraction) in the alternative question. This indicates (i) that the high tone that triggers the retraction of the superhigh has to be underlyingly associated with the final syllable of the first segment; and (ii) that the alternative question is composed of two distinct Intonational Phrases, as opposed to its declarative counterpart. As for the second point, it is important to note that the end of the first part of the alternative is not associated with an H%, but with an L%.

(35) a. [(ha-wonó)_φ (le=pa!há)_φ (ha!wú)_φ (ye=m-!ɓwá)_φ]_I
      1.PER-*see*   AG₅=5.*cat*   or   AG₉=9-*dog*
      'He saw the cat or the dog.'

   b. [(ha-wonó)_φ (lé=páha)_φ]_I [(ha!wú)_φ (ye=m-!ɓwá)_φ]_I
      'Did he see the cat or the dog?'   [Moroni]

The 'tone bridge' phenomenon that characterizes polar questions also arises in alternative questions, including alternative questions corresponding to declaratives that have a 'lexical' high tone on the last syllable (i.e. a tone that does not come from shifting) of the first member of the alternative. In (36), the antepenult – not the penult – of the first element of the alternation bears the superhigh tone.

(36) [(ha-wono má-ꞵáhá má-i!lí)_φ]_I [(ha!wú)_φ (m-ɓwa m-!ɓíli)_φ]_I
     1.PER-*see* 6-*cat* 6-*two*   or   9-*dog* 9-*two*
     'Did he see two cats or two dogs?'   [Moroni]

Example (36) is illustrated in Figure 20. Alongside the position of the superhigh tone, special attention must be paid to the register of the second conjunct of the alternative, which is considerably reduced with respect to the register of the first part.

---

[13] Whether a polar question should or should not be considered an alternative question with an ellipsis has been extensively discussed in the literature – cf. for instance the seminal work of Bolinger (1978).

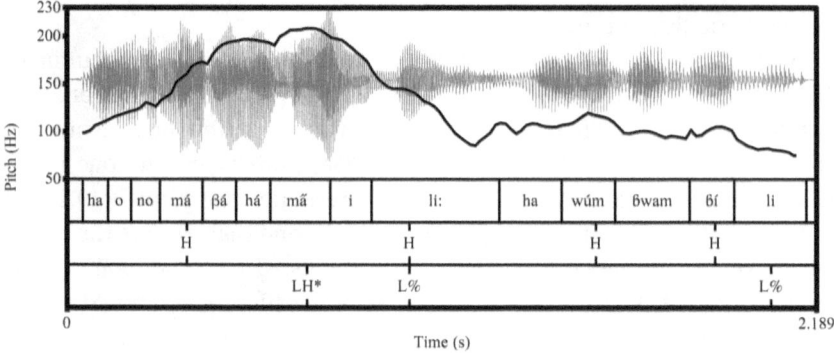

Figure 20: cf. (36) – [Moroni]

5.2 Biased questions

Biased questions in Bantu languages have received very little attention so far (but see for instance Schadeberg & Mucanheia (2000: 27): 'a surprised question is marked by a downstepped Hi on the final syllable'). In this section, I shall briefly discuss some features of biased questions in Shingazidja, building upon readings of sentences by a speaker from Washili. Due to the lack of corpora of natural speech, and since only one speaker has been tested for biased questions, this analysis should be considered tentative and will have to be confirmed by further research.

Rhetorical questions share some prosodic properties with yes-no questions, including the presence of a superhigh tone on the penult. However, they differ from polar questions in terms of pitch range: the superhigh tone is much higher in rhetorical questions than in yes-no questions. The difference between yes-no questions and rhetorical questions is illustrated in Figure 21, which corresponds to (37).

(37) a. [(ŋga-we   na=naf<u>a</u>sí)$_\phi$[14]   (m<u>á</u>űɗu)$_\phi$]$_I$
            1.IMP-P2SG   with=9.space   tomorrow
            'Are you free tomorrow?'

     b. [(ŋga-mi   na=naf<u>a</u>sí)$_\phi$ (m<u>á</u>↑űɗu)$_\phi$]$_I$
            1.IMP-P1SG   with=9.space   tomorrow
            'Am I free tomorrow??'   [Washili]

---

14 Several adverbs, such as *m<u>á</u>uɗu* 'tomorrow', are preceded by Phonological Phrase boundaries.

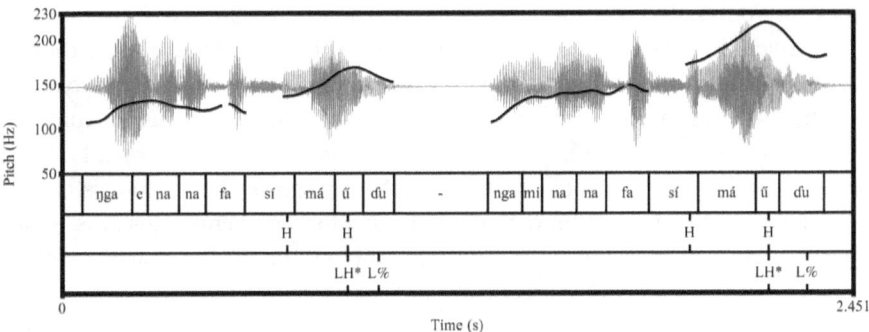

Figure 21: cf. (37) – [Washili]

The overall expansion of the pitch range of the sentence, along with a relative reduction in the intensity of the syllables that precede the penult or an increase of the delivery, has also been observed, but none of these cues seem to be obligatory.

Echo questions have the same segmental and syntactic properties as partial questions (see Section 5.3), but they differ from the latter in terms of prosody. Echo questions are minimally signaled by a LH*!H% contour on a lengthened final syllable, a pattern that recalls contrastive topics (Section 4.2). The second 'mora' of this lengthened syllable is regularly devoiced. Compare in Figure 22 the F_0 shape and the length of the final syllable of a simple wh-question (38a) with the same parameters in the corresponding echo question (38b).

(38) a. [(ha-wọno)_φ   (ndó̱)_φ]_I
        1.PER-*see*   *who*
        'Who did he see?'

   b. [(ha-wọno)_φ   (ndó̱̊ó̱)_φ]_I
        'WHO did he see? [Echo]'   [Washili]

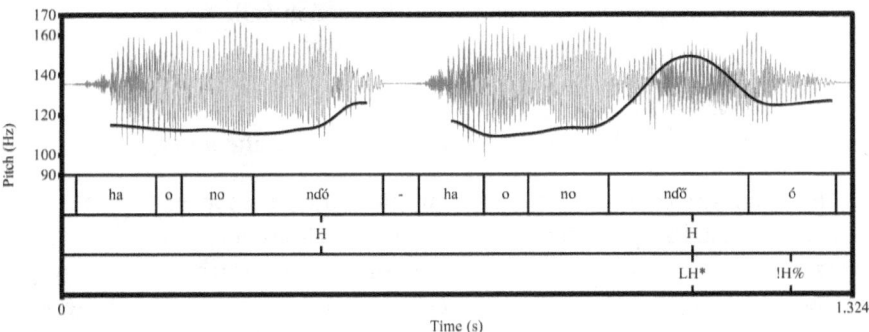

Figure 22: cf. (38) – [Washili]

A plateau optionally links the final LH*!H% 'contour' to the preceding tone(s), and the overall register of the echo question is regularly louder or raised, though Figure 22 demonstrates that this expansion of the register is not obligatory.

Surprise questions, insofar as prosody is concerned, have much in common with echo questions. Indeed, surprise questions are also signaled by a LH*!H% contour on a lengthened final syllable, but the register of the contour is clearly and systematically higher than that of the contour in Echo questions – see Figure 23, corresponding to (39). The remnant portion of the question is de-accented and the tones are frequently delinked.

(39)   [(hu-re↑ndḛ́ːḛ́)_φ]_I
         2SG.PER-*do s.t.*
         'You did [what]?? [Surprise – after, e.g., 'I won the lottery']'   [Washili]

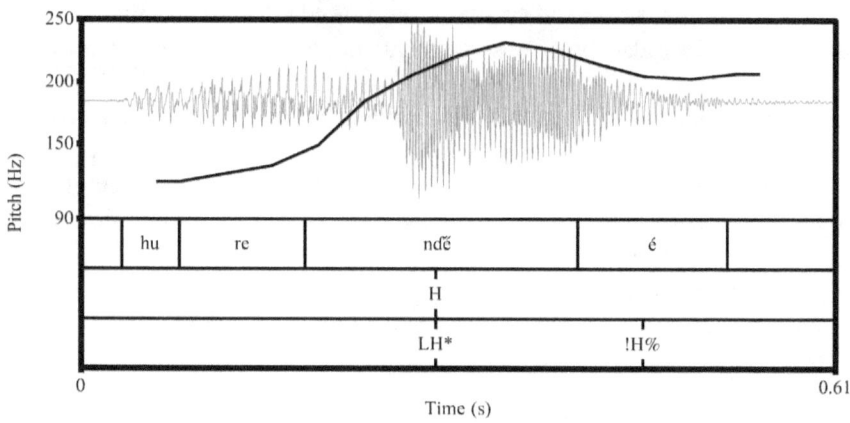

Figure 23: cf. (39) – [Washili]

Importantly, the LH*!H% contour is also observable when the last lexical high tone is on the penult (40), rather than on the final syllable – as compared to what has been observed for contrastive topics (Section 4.3).

(40)   [(hu-fáɲ↑áːá)_φ]_I
         2SG.PER-*do s.t.*
         'You did [what]?? [Surprise – after, e.g., 'I won the lottery']'   [Washili]

The properties of polar and biased questions are summarized in Table 1. All types of questions are associated with the superhigh LH* tone that also characterizes yes-no questions, but the expansion of the register (rhetorical, surprise) and the LH*!H% contour on a lengthened syllable (echo, surprise) are each associated with two types of questions, which raises the possibility that they form natural classes.

Table 1: Biased questions features

	Superhigh tone (LH*)	Register expansion	Lengthening + !H%
POLAR	✓		
RHETORICAL	✓	✓	
SURPRISE	✓	✓	✓
ECHO	✓		✓

5.3 Content questions (and answers)

A content question, or Wh-question, in Shingazidja is primarily identified by an interrogative phrase or pronoun. No intoneme or superhigh tone is associated with the wh-word or the whole clause and, at first glance, the prosody of a wh-question does not seem to differ from that of a statement. In (41), illustrated in Figure 24, for instance, the tone of the wh-word is downsptepped with respect to the preceding tone(s),[15] and there is no expansion of the register of the utterance.

(41) a. [([y]é)_Φ   (ya-re̱¹má)_Φ   (nɗo=¹βí)_Φ]_I
         Q   1.REL.PER-*hit*   who=FOC
       'Which one did hit?'

    b. [(ya̱remá)_Φ   (nɗo=β¹í)_Φ]_I
       'Which one did hit?'   [Moroni]

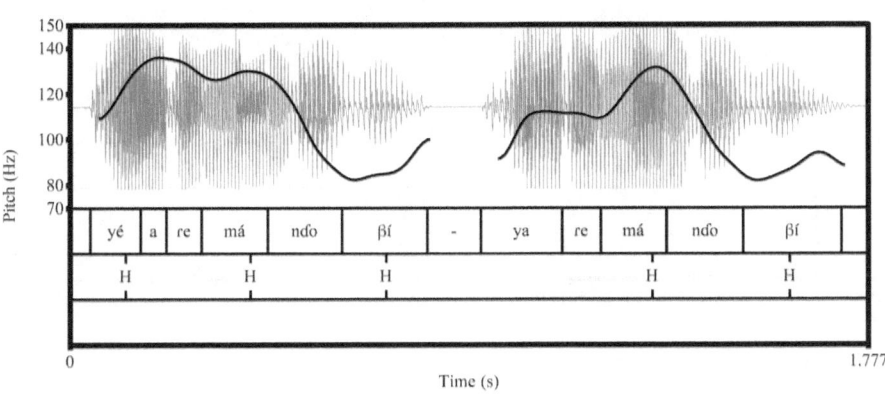

Figure 24: cf. (41) – [Moroni]

---

[15] The verb appears in the relative form when the subject is questioned, as in many other Bantu languages – e.g. in Nguni languages, where questioning the subject leads to Cleft formation (Sabel & Zeller 2006, Zerbian 2006).

The lexical tone of a wh-word can even be deleted due to the OCP, as in (42), though it is regularly maintained.

(42) [([y]ḗ)_Φ (ya-re̱ˈmá)_Φ   (ndo̱)_Φ]_I
     Q   1.REL.PER-*hit* who
     'Who did hit?'   [Moroni]

However, a content question differs from a statement in that it does not exhibit the L% boundary tone that characterizes the latter. In Figure 24, for instance, the final high tones of the questions are realized as a shallow rise of the F_0, while the final tone of the statement has a flat shape (see Section 2).

The absence of L% is even clearer in the dialect of Washili,[16] which also exhibits a L% in statements. While the tone of the wh-word is downstepped in (43) with respect to the preceding tones of the utterance, it is associated with a significant, sharp rise of the F_0 (see Figure 25).

(43) [([y]e̱)_Φ (n-ts[ih]u̱ [y]-á[17] [y]i̱di)_Φ (Djuˈmwá̱)_Φ
     Q   9-*day*   9-*of*   Eid   Juma

     ([h]a-[h]undu̱)_Φ   ([h]iˈndi̱)_Φ]_I
     1.PER-*obtain*   what

     'What did Juma get for Eid?' (lit. = [for] Eid Juma get what?)   [Washili]

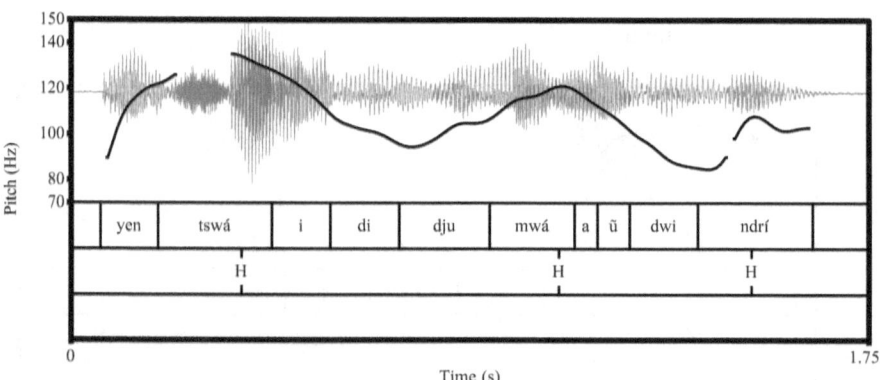

Figure 25: cf. (43) – [Washili]

---

16 Unfortunately, I do not have data on wh-questions from northern and southern speakers.
17 The tone that appears on this vowel comes from the initial question marker *yé* due to a rule that shifts an utterance initial high tone (a high tone cannot be aligned with the left edge of an utterance in the dialect of Washili). The rule also applies in (45).

Interestingly, the L% boundary tone emerges when the wh-word is dislocated. In (44), illustrated in Figure 26, the last syllables of the question are associated with a L%, indicating that the fronted wh-word is followed by an IP boundary.

(44)　[[¹⁸ (hiˈndí̱)_φ]_I　(ha-ˈré̱me)_φ]_I
　　　　what　　　　　1.PER-*hit*
　　　'What did he hit?'　　　　　　　　　　　　　　　　　　　　　[Moroni]

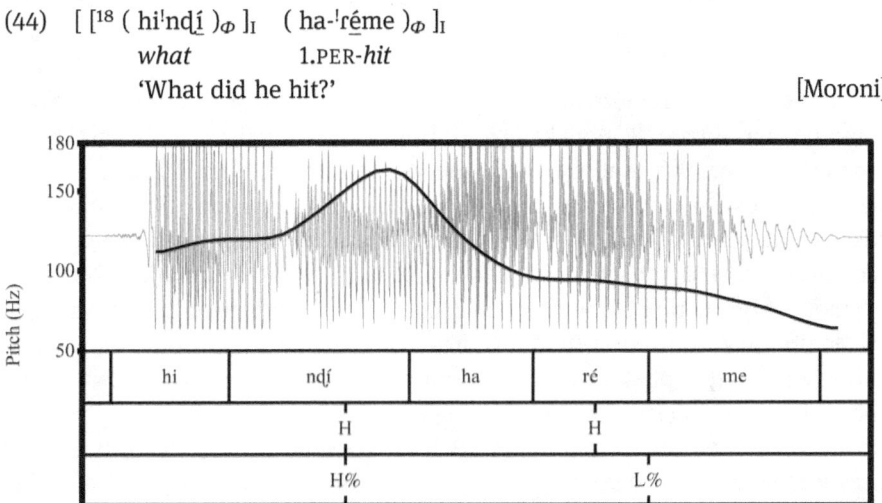

Figure 26: cf. (44) – [Moroni]

No prosodic difference has been observed between statements and answers of content questions. In (45), no intoneme is linked to the focalized subject *Alí*, and a L% boundary tone is associated with the final syllables of the answer.

(45)　a.　[([y]e̱)_φ　(yá-wo̱na　　ˈDjúmwa̱)_φ　(ˈndó̱)_φ]_I
　　　　　　Q　　　　1.REL.PER-*see*　Juma　　　　who
　　　　　'Who saw Juma?'

　　　b.　[(Alí̱)_φ　(ha-m-ˈm¹⁹ó̱no)_φ]_I
　　　　　　Ali　　　　1.PER-OM₁-*see*
　　　　　'Ali saw him.'　　　　　　　　　　　　　　　　　　　　　　[Washili]

---

18 It is not clear at this point in my research if the IP that corresponds to the fronted wh-word is embedded in another IP (the hypothesis I adopt in this example), or if the two IPs are distinct.

19 /w/ assimilates to [m] after another [m].

6 Conclusion

In this chapter, I have presented an analysis of intonation in Shingazidja, a Bantu language of Comoros, focusing on the interaction of intonation with lexical high tones. As is the case for the H% boundary tone that signals the end of non-final Intonation Phrases, intonation tends to override the lexical high tones in several situations, indicating that Shingazidja may be assumed to belong to the 'submission' type in the typology of tone-intonation interface introduced in Hyman & Monaka (2008). However, I also discussed several cases where tones, on the contrary, dominate intonation. The position of the super-high tone of yes-no questions on the penult or the antepenult of utterances, for instance, depends on the presence or absence of a high tone on the last syllable. Moreover, the L% tone that signals the end of a final Intonation Phrase is excluded from content questions that end with a high tone in the varieties of Moroni or Washili, and from any sentence that has a high tone on its final syllable in the peripheral dialects (Mbeni, Fumbuni). This mixed system in the tone-intonation interface reflects the prosody of the language, which exhibits characteristics of both a tone language (e.g. the shift of the tone) and a pitch-accent language (e.g. the insertion of a default tone on a toneless phrase, discussed in Section 3.3.1).

While progress has been made these last years in the understanding of the non-tonal prosody of Shingazidja, there are still many unresolved issues and challenges for future research. Indeed, several structures or features discussed in this chapter deserve a closer look. This is for example the case for H* insertion in the variety of Moroni, whose conditions of emergence are not properly defined, or biased questions, which need to be studied in context, using a dedicated corpus of natural speech. In particular, it would be highly interesting to compare the results sketched in this chapter with a closer examination of the parameters that do not involve F_0. These parameters include segment reduction (which is considerable in Shingazidja), and most importantly intensity and vowel length, which are related to stress.

Acknowledgements

I would like to thank Laura J. Downing and Annie Rialland for the invitation to participate in this volume. I would also like to thank Kathleen M. O'Connor, as well as an anonymous reviewer and the editors of the volume, for their comments, which allowed me to make significant improvements to the chapter.

References

Ashton, E. O. 1944. *Swahili grammar, including intonation*. Longmans, Green.
Beckman, M. & J. Pierrehumbert. 1986. Intonational Structure in Japanese and English. *Phonology Yearbook* 3. 255–309.
Bolinger, D. 1978. Yes-No Questions Are Not Alternative Questions. In H. Hiz (ed.), *Questions*. Dordrecht (Neth): Reidel. 87–105.
Cassimjee, F. & C. Kisseberth. *In preparation*. The Shingazidja Lexicon Exemplified.
Cassimjee, F. & C. Kisseberth. 1998. Optimal Domains Theory and Bantu Tonology: a Case Study from Isixhosa and Shingazidja. In L. Hyman & C. Kisseberth (eds.), *Theoretical Aspects of Bantu Tone*. Stanford: CSLI. 33–132.
Cassimjee, F. & C. Kisseberth. 1993. The phrasal tonology of Shingazidja. 24th Annual Conference on African Linguistics. Ohio State University, July 23–25 1993.
Cassimjee, F. & C. Kisseberth. 1992. Metrical Structure in Shingazidja. *CLS* 28. 72–93.
Cassimjee, F. & C. Kisseberth. 1989. Shingazidja Nominal Accent. *Studies in the Linguistic Sciences* 19.1. 33–61.
Downing, L. 2004. The prosody of focus in Bantu languages and the primacy of phrasing. TIE conference, Santorini, september 2004.
Full, W. 2006. *Dialektologie des Komorischen*. Köln: Rüdiger Köppe Verlag.
Guthrie, M. 1967–71. *Comparative Bantu: an introduction to the comparative linguistics and prehistory of the Bantu languages*. 4 vols. Farnborough: Gregg Press.
Hyman, Larry. 2001. Privative tone in Bantu. In Shigeki Kaji (ed.), *Cross-linguistic studies of tonal phenomena*. Tokyo: Institute for the Study of Languages and Cultures. 237–257.
Hyman, L. & K. Monaka. 2008. Tonal and Non-Tonal Intonation in Shekgalagari. *UC Berkeley Phonology Lab Annual Report* (2008). 269–288.
Jouannet, Francis. 1989. *Des tons à l'accent. Essai sur l'accentuation du comorien*. Université de Provence Aix-Marseille.
Jun, S.-A. (ed.). 2014. *Prosodic Typology II: The Phonology of Intonation and Phrasing*. Oxford: Oxford University Press.
Jun, S.-A. (ed.). 2005. *Prosodic Typology: The Phonology of Intonation and Phrasing*, Oxford: Oxford University Press.
Kanerva, J. 1990. *Focus and Phrasing in Chichewa Phonology*. New York: Garland.
Kimenyi, A. 1980. *A relational Grammar of Kinyarwanda*. Berkeley: University of California publications.
Kisseberth, C. & D. Odden. 2003. Tone. In D. Nurse & G. Philippson (eds), *The Bantu Languages*. Routledge. 59–70.
Ladd, D. R. 1996. *Intonational Phonology*. Cambridge: Cambridge University Press.
Möhlig, W., L. Marten & J. Kavari. 2002. *A grammatical sketch of Herero (Otjiherero)*. Köln: Köppe.
O'Connor, K. & C. Patin. 2015. The Syntax and Prosody of Apposition in Shingazidja. *Phonology* 32.1, Special issue 'Constituent structure in sentence phonology', edited by S. Lee & E. Selkirk. 111–145.
Patin, C. 2010. The prosody of Shingazidja Relatives. In L. Downing, A. Rialland, J.-M. Beltzung, S. Manus, C. Patin & K. Riedel (eds.), *ZAS papers in Linguistics* 53. 187–210.
Patin, C. 2008. Focus and Phrasing in Shingazidja. In M. Zygis & S. Fuchs (eds.), *Papers in Phonetics and Phonology. ZAS papers in Linguistics* 49. 167–189.

Patin, C. 2007. *La tonologie du shingazidja, langue bantu (G44a) de la Grande Comore: nature, formalisation, interfaces.* Thèse de doctorat, Université Paris 3.

Philippson, G. 2005. Pitch accent in Comorian and Proto-Sabaki tones. In K. Bostoen & J. Maniacky (eds.), *Studies in African Comparative Linguistics with special focus on Bantu and Mande: Essays in Honour of Yvonne Bastin & Claire Grégoire.* Tervuren, Musée Royal de l'Afrique Centrale. 199–220.

Philippson, G. 1991. *Tons et accent dans les langues bantu d'Afrique orientale: étude typologique et diachronique.* Thèse d'Etat, Université Paris V René Descartes, Paris.

Philippson, G. 1988. L'accentuation du comorien: essai d'analyse métrique. *Etudes Océan Indien (Paris)* 9. 35–79.

Pierrehumbert, J. 1980. *The Phonology and Phonetics of English Intonation.* Ph.D. dissertation. Massachusetts Institute of Technology.

Rey, Véronique. 1990. *Approche phonologique et expérimentale des faits d'accent d'une langue africaine, le shingazidja (parler de la Grande Comore).* Thèse de doctorat, Université Aix-Marseille 1.

Rialland, A. 2007. Question prosody: an African perspective. In C. Gussenhoven & Thomas Riad (eds.), *Tones and tunes: studies in word and sentence prosody* vol. 2. Berlin: Mouton de Gruyter. 35–62.

Sabel, J. & J. Zeller. 2006. Wh-Question Formation in Nguni. In J. Mugane (ed.), *Selected Proceedings of the 35th Annual Conference on African Linguistics.* Somerville, MA: Cascadilla Proceedings Project. 271–283.

Schadeberg, T. & F. Mucanheia. 2000. *Ekoti: the Maka or Swahili language of Angoche.* Köln: Köppe.

Selkirk, E. 1986. On derived domains in sentence phonology. *Phonology Yearbook* 3. 371–405.

Truckenbrodt, H. 1999. On the relationship between syntactic phrases and phonological phrases. *Linguistic Inquiry* 30.2. 219–255.

Tucker, A. & M. Bryan. 1970. Tonal classification of nouns in Ngazija. *African Language Studies* 11. 351–383.

Zerbian, S. 2006. Questions in Northern Sotho. *ZAS Papers in Linguistics* 43. 257–280.

Nancy C. Kula and Silke Hamann
Intonation in Bemba

Abstract: This chapter identifies a number of key features in the intonation of Bemba. Final lowering is a robust feature found in all sentence types but which is implemented in two different ways. At the end of clauses a boundary L% affects the last few syllables of a clause-final word but at the end of minimal intonational phrases, like fronted topics, the boundary L% affects only the final syllable. Polar questions show pitch range expansion with a final L%. Such global effects are seen to result in suspension of downstep. Constituent questions and focus constructions show a suppression of downdrift with pitch range expansion occurring before the focus, leaving the focused constituent prosodically unmarked. Right dislocated clauses which are outside the matrix clause show pitch range compression. We treat global effects of pitch range expansion and compression as the result of left edge intonational tones (-H or -L) and local effects of pitch lowering as resulting from right edge boundary tones which then interact with lexical tones.

Keywords: tone-intonation, final lowering, pitch range compression (PRC), pitch range expansion (PRE), downstep, focus, Phonological Phrase, minimal i-Phrase, maximal i-Phrase, contrastive topic, that-clause, relative clause, dislocation, preverbal topic, polar question, constituent question, multiple question, OCP

1 Introduction

This chapter presents an initial investigation of Bemba intonation. Bemba is a Niger-Congo language of the Central Narrow Bantu branch that is classified as part of Zone M in Guthrie's (1948, 1967–71) classification. It is spoken in Zambia (mainly in the Northern, Luapula and Copperbelt provinces) and in the Southern Democratic Republic of Congo by approximately 3.3 million speakers (Lewis, Simons & Fening 2013). Bemba has several dialects, though there are no systematic studies on the exact number and the differences between possible dialects (but see Bickmore & Kula 2013 for a discussion of tonal differences between

---

Nancy C. Kula, University of Essex
Silke Hamann, University of Amsterdam

two dialects). Some information on the possible number of dialects can be found in Ohannessian & Kashoki (1978), Kashoki (1978), Chanda (1996) and Kula (2006). This work is based on the Copperbelt dialect.[1] Like the majority of languages in this volume, Bemba is a tone language that does not have stress or any kind of accent marking.

The present chapter discusses the following robust intonational patterns in Bemba that correlate to different kinds of declarative sentences and questions: final lowering, pitch range expansion and compression, pitch register raising and pitch reset, which will be demonstrated and defined in ensuing discussion. For the notation of intonation we follow basic assumptions within autosegmental-metrical theory as reviewed in Ladd (2008). We employ a number of intonational tones to account for the intonational structure of Bemba. L% and H% are used as the boundary markers of local register effects at the right edges of intonational phrases. It is demonstrated that intonational phrases are the main domain marked in Bemba intonation. We further propose to indicate global effects of pitch range expansion and compression as the anchoring of -H and -L at the left edges of intonational phrases for the specific sentence types in which they occur (polar and constituent questions and right dislocations). Multiple questions and focus constructions also use -H to indicate pitch raising in a more restricted domain within an intonational phrase. A final necessary intonational tone is !H for a downstepped High indicated at the beginning of the domain of downstep. Thus the intonational grammar we will utilize and motivate in the remainder of the chapter consists of the set { L% H% -L -H !H }.

The chapter is organised as follows: Section 2 presents the general tone patterns and tonal processes of Bemba that are relevant to the current chapter; section 3 discusses the intonational structure of declaratives with particular focus on subordinate clauses, dislocations and topics. Section 4 looks at questions considering polar and constituent questions, multiple questions and the interaction between questions and focus. In section 5 we evaluate how these intonational patterns interact with prosodic phrasing in particular with phonological and intonational phrases; and in section 6 we offer some concluding remarks.

---

[1] Copperbelt Bemba as used here is not intended to refer to what has been labeled *Town Bemba* which is widely used on the Copperbelt and which evolved as a lingua franca on the mines of the Copperbelt province involving a mixture of languages (see Kashoki 1972, Kabinga 2010). Rather indigenous Bemba speaking peoples migrating from the Northern Province from around the 1920s is what is intended. Needless to say there is inevitable interaction between this Copperbelt Bemba and Town Bemba that we abstract away from here.

2 Tone patterns and tonal processes of Bemba

This section introduces the main tone patterns and tonal processes in Bemba[2] which will be important for understanding surface tone patterns of data discussed in following sections. For example, our pitch track notations (section 3 onwards) are only going to signal lexical H tone on the lexical tone tier with the actual surface forms of words understood as following from the tonal interactions discussed in this section.

Bemba contrasts two level tones, high and low, which are generally phonologically treated as H vs. Ø following basic Bantu language assumptions (Kisseberth & Odden 2003). This means that phonologically low tones are not active and surface low-toned forms are considered to be lexically toneless but surface as low-toned if they are not affected by High tone spreading rules. In the remainder of the chapter High tone is marked with an acute accent and low tone with a grave accent. Vowels in Bemba can be short or long with the mora as the tone-bearing unit.[3] The attested syllables are Cv̀, Cv̀v̀, Cv́, Cv́v́ and Cv́v̀, therefore a rising sequence is ungrammatical (*Cv̀v́). Verbs are lexically specified as either high or toneless. Nouns are also lexically specified for particular tone patterns. Bemba tone descriptions and analyses can be found in Bickmore and Kula (2013), Guthrie (1945), Kula & Bickmore (2015), Mann (1977), Sharman (1956) and Sharman & Meeussen (1955).

Within verbs, tones are of two types; (a) lexical tone on roots and various affixes (e.g. /lúk-/ 'vomit' vs. /lùk-/ 'weave'); and (b) melodic or grammatical tone which is morpho-syntactically assigned by various Tense-Aspect-Mood markers. The following sub-sections illustrate the main tonal processes involved based on Bickmore & Kula (2013) and Kula & Bickmore (2015). These works should be consulted for more detailed analyses and additional examples, with the focus here being mainly on those processes relevant to the current chapter.

---

[2] The following abbreviations are used in the remainder of the chapter: H = high tone; TBU = tone bearing unit; TAM = tense aspect mood; CB = Copperbelt Bemba; IP = intonational phrase; PP = phonological phrase; PRC = pitch range compression; PRE = pitch range expansion; OCP = obligatory contour principle; MH = melodic high tone; FV = final vowel; V2 = verb stem second vowel; SM = subject marker; OM = object marker; PL = plural; SG = singular; Q = question particle; HAB = habitual; COMPL = complementizer; IMP = imperative; PROG = progressive; SUBJ = subjunctive; IAV = immediate after verb; FUT = future; FUT1/2/3 refer to different futures; P1/2/3/4 refer to different pasts; and numbers on nominals indicate noun class markers.

[3] A description of the phonetic properties, realizations and phonotactic restrictions of the vowel and consonantal system of Bemba is given in Hamann & Kula (2015).

2.1 High tone spreading

There are two main H tone spreading processes central to the tonology of Bemba; unbounded spreading and bounded spreading. Unbounded spreading spreads a H rightwards up to the end of the verb form, targeting all following toneless moras in a phrase-final word. The examples in (1) show unbounded spreading in a verb form where the initial mora of the subject marker is lexically H-toned (1a) and the following TAM marker and verb are toneless. (Lexical Highs are underscored throughout). This contrasts with (1b) where the subject marker is toneless and the verb form therefore surfaces as all low.

(1) a. bá̱-ká-lóóndólól-á
2SM-FUT3-explain-FV
'They will explain'

b. tù-kà-lòòndòlòl-à
2PLSM-FUT3-explain-FV
'We will explain'

Unbounded spreading contrasts with bounded spreading which does not spread a H to the end of the verb form. There are two contexts where bounded spreading applies; (i) when the verb is followed by another constituent, such as the adverb in (2a) or (ii) when there is another H following within the verb form as shown in (2b). The final H in (2b) is a grammatical tone that marks the imperative. In Copperbelt Bemba (CB) bounded spreading is ternary. Thus the verb form in (2a) differs from (1a) only in having bounded rather than unbounded spreading when there is a following constituent. In this case the H does not continue to spread even though there are potential target toneless moras. (2b) further shows bounded spreading of the initial H because there is another H following within the verb form. In this case as well, there are possible target toneless moras to which the H does not spread, illustrating that it is ternary.

(2) a. bá̱-ká-lóòndòlòl-à   bwììnò
2SM-FUT3-explain-FV   well
'They will explain well'

b. bá̱-ká-lóòndòlòl-é̱
2SM-FUT3-explain-SUBJ
'They should explain'

Thus in terms of High tone spreading a H spreads unboundedly until the last TBU if there is no other H tone following within the word (1a). If there is another H tone following within the word, then H tone spreading is bounded and is specifically ternary in Copperbelt Bemba (2b) i.e. it spreads twice after the source creating a ternary domain including the source of H tone spread (HHH..). Bounded spreading also occurs in a word that is not phrase final i.e. if another constituent follows as seen in (2a).

2.2 OCP and Downstep

The preceding example in (2b) illustrates bounded spreading where a H follows within the same word. Consider now a similar case (3a–b) where another H tone follows but where there are fewer intervening moras such that the application of ternary spread would result in adjacent lexical Hs. We assume a standard autosegmental representation where lexical tones are represented on a suprasegmental/tonal tier. In this case ternary spreading is ungrammatical (3b). If the initial lexical H underwent ternary spreading, associating to the following two moras, then the lexical H would be adjacent to the following lexical H on the suprasegmental/tonal tier and therefore consist of an OCP violation. This is avoided by spreading once, rather than not at all, as seen in (3a).

(3) a. béléèng-á
     read-FV.IMP
     'Read!'

   b. *bélééng-á

This partial spreading in a ternary spreading context led Bickmore & Kula (2013) to conclude that ternary spreading is achieved by two independent rules namely High Doubling (binary spread) and Secondary High Doubling (SHD). High Doubling spreads a H one mora to the right and SHD spreads it one mora further which then achieves the surface ternary pattern. There are a number of arguments that Bickmore & Kula present in favour of this analysis, which we do not replicate in full here, but one of the central motivations is the application of the OCP. Whereas SHD is subject to the OCP, as the example in (3a) shows, High Doubling is not, so that a H still spreads even though it will create a sequence of lexical Hs. This dispreferred sequence is adjusted by producing the second lexical H at a lower register than the first i.e. downstep (indicated by superscript !). In many languages the trigger of downstep is usually a low tone or a floating low tone preceding a H (see, for example, Clements 1990, Connell 2001, Connell

& Ladd 1990, Ladd 1990, Lindau 1986, Steward 1965, among others).[4] In Bemba there is no evidence of a low tone as the trigger of downstep and we must conclude that in this case downstep is a reflex to remedy an OCP violation. The same also applies in Moro (Rose & Piccinini, this volume) and Tswana (Zerbian, this volume). Interestingly, there is no downstep between underlyingly adjacent Hs in Bemba, with downstep only occurring in derived environments. The disparity between violation of the OCP and concomitant downstep in High Doubling, versus OCP violation avoidance in SHD is further illustrated in (4a) vs. (4b).

(4) a. bá-ká-!tú-lúk-á
    2SM-FUT3-1PLOM-plait-FV
    'They will plait us (our hair)'

  b. bá-ká-mù-lás-á
    2SM-FUT3-1OM-hit-FV
    'They will hit him/her'

In (4a) the subject marker *bá-* and the object marker *-tú-* are lexically H-toned. The H of the subject marker is subject to bounded spreading because of the following lexical H but can only spread once (High Doubling) and does so resulting in downstep of the following lexical H of the object marker. This H itself undergoes unbounded spreading to the end of the verb form. Pitch tracks of downstep examples can be seen in figures 6 and 9 below. By contrast the subject marker H in (4b) spreads once but does not spread further – no Secondary High Doubling – to complete its ternary span, thereby avoiding an OCP violation. There is therefore also no downstep in this case.

2.3 Melodic high tones

Like other Bantu languages Bemba also has the so-called Melodic Highs (MH; see Odden & Bickmore 2014) which are particular tones/tone patterns associated to specific TAMs. MHs have 3 docking sites in Bemba (Bickmore & Kula 2013): (i) on the final vowel (FV) as in examples (2b, 3a); (ii) on the second vowel of

---

[4] Connell (2001, this volume) recognizes two types of downstep from the literature. Automatic downstep in cases where Hs are separated by a low tone (HHLHH) and non-automatic downstep where there is no low tone (HH!HH). The latter case is generally assumed to involve a floating low tone. Downstep is not usually seen to affect low tones but see Hyman (1985) for a case in Dschang. The idea of downstep as involving a change in register, where register is understood as a phonetic frame of reference for tone, owes to the work of Clements (1979), Clements and Ford (1979).

the stem (V2); or (iii) on the domain from V2 to the FV. See Kula & Bickmore for a full list of TAMs showing these patterns. The motivation for treating these Hs as MHs is because they cannot be readily explained by the tone spreading rules discussed above, with their occurrence determined by the TAM. They are in this sense grammatical tones. Consider the example in (5) illustrating the V2-FV MH.

(5) bá-mú-lùk-íílé
     2SM-1OM-plait-PERF
     'They have woven for him'

As (5) illustrates, the final three Hs in the verb form cannot be explained by a spreading process from the initial lexical H but are associated with perfective verbs. Note that the application of ternary spread remains the same – only High Doubling applies in this case because there is a following H of the MH V2-FV pattern. MHs will be pointed out where they occur in the following discussion and will also be underscored like lexical Hs as in (5).

2.4 Phrasal tone and prosodic phrasing

At the phrasal level Kula & Bickmore (2015) show that H tone spreading is used as a cue for phonological phrasing with unbounded spreading indicating an immediately following *phonological phrase* (p-phrase) boundary while bounded spreading indicates the absence of such a boundary. Recall from earlier discussion that one of the contexts of bounded spreading was the presence of a following constituent (2a). The more precise description of this condition is that bounded spreading applies in word$_1$ if a following word$_2$ is in the same p-phrase as word$_1$. If the two words are in different p-phrases, then unbounded spreading applies in word$_1$. If the following word or sequence of following words are all toneless, and are each in independent p-phrases, then the H of word$_1$ (indirectly) spreads through each of the following words. The examples in (6a–d) illustrate H spreading at the p-phrase level. (6a) indicates a p-phrase boundary between an object-marked verb and its complement, while (6b) shows no such boundary when the object marker is absent. (6c) indicates long-distance H spreading over four words but this spreading is arrested when the verb and first complement phrase together (6d). In this case we see bounded (ternary) H spreading on the verb form.[5]

---

[5] There is information structure involved in the interpretation of the complement in (6a–b) with the complement in (6b) being focused. See Kula (to appear) for discussion.

(6) a. (bá̠-ká-mú-lóóndólól-á)_PP (Bùùpé)_PP
2SM-FUT3-1OM-explain-FV Bupe
'They will introduce him, Bupe'

b. (bá̠-ká-lóòndòlòl-à Bùùpé)_PP
2SM-FUT3-explain-FV Bupe
'They will introduce Bupe'

c. (bá̠-ká-mú-shíík-íl-á)_PP (Chítúúndú)_PP (cáángá)_PP (bwíínó)_PP
2SM-FUT3-1OM-bury-APPL-FV Chitundu 1a.bushbaby well
'They will bury the bushbaby for Chitundu well'

d. (bá̠-ká-shíìk-ìl-à Chìtùùndù)_PP (càànga̠)_PP (bwììnò)_PP
2SM-FUT3-bury-APPL-FV Chitundu 1a.bushbaby well
'They will bury the bushbaby for Chitundu well'

It cannot be assumed in an example such as (6c) that the initial H just spreads unboundedly to the final word. There are a number of data that do not support such an analysis. For example, if a second word (w_2) contains a high tone, a final H in the preceding first word (w_1) still spreads into w_2 but it does not spread any further. This is illustrated in example (7).

(7) tù-kà-lás̠-á   Kápèèmbwá̠
1PL-FUT3-hit-FV Kapembwa
'We will hit Kapembwa'

In (7) the H on the verb spreads to the final mora in unbounded fashion and then spreads into w_2 which only has the final H as lexical. However the H on the initial syllable of w_2 does not spread further, even in bounded fashion, although there are available targets. This is used to conclude that there is an independent process of inter-word H doubling that doubles a final high tone from w_1 to w_2.[6] Such doubling also applies even if it results in an OCP violation in w_2. This means that in order to achieve the long distance H spreading effects, spreading between words must be interspersed with inter-word H doubling. This process is formalized as following from the constraint *INTER-WORD HL which militates against a HL sequence between two words and therefore forces a final

---

[6] There are additional examples illustrating that the spread from w_1 to the initial of w_2 is not creating a ternary domain. Namely in cases of w_1 with a final lexical H, the spread is still only to the initial of w_2, if there is a H in w_2, despite following possible targets. The reader is advised to consult Kula & Bickmore (2015) for further details and exemplification.

H of w₁ to spread into w₂ (see Kula & Bickomore 2015 for details). The crucial point about this constraint is that it only affects a sequence of TBUs which are in the same *intonational phrase* (i-phrase). If two TBUs are part of words/p-phrases that belong to different i-phrases then inter-word H doubling does not apply. This process is therefore a good diagnostic for p-phrases and i-phrases. Consider the examples illustrating the difference below.

(8) a. ùmú-límí)_PP _PP(tú-ká-pát-á
       1-farmer   1PL-FUT3-hate-FV
       'the farmer we will hate, (the teacher we will like)' (contrastive focus)

    b. ùmú-límí)_IP _IP(tù-kà-pàt-à
       1-farmer   1PL-FUT3-hate-FV
       'as for the farmer, we will hate (him)' (left dislocated object topic)

In (8a) the fronted object is a contrastive focus. In this case the initial H of w₁ undergoes unbounded spreading, showing that a p-phrase boundary follows. The final H in w₁ then spreads into w₂ indicating that the two words are part of the same i-phrase. The doubled inter-word H then undergoes unbounded spreading to the end of w₂. By contrast, in (8b) where the object is a fronted topic we see no spreading between w₁ and w₂ and must conclude that the two identical words in this instance belong to two separate i-phrases. Without inter-word H doubling, w₂ in this case surfaces as all low. We thus see tonal evidence for a distinction between p-phrases and i-phrases in the prosodic phonology of Bemba. This evidence will be used to evaluate whether p-phrases and/or i-phrases are marked in Bemba intonation. We take up this discussion later in section 5.

2.5 Vowel coalescence and tone shift

Vowel coalescence is important in the discussion of the general Bemba tone patterns because it affects surface tones. In Bemba vowel hiatus at morpheme boundaries is resolved in many verbal forms by vowel fusion, where a low vowel (/a/) followed by a high one (/i/ or /u/) results in a long mid vowel (/ee/ or /oo/). If a high vowel precedes the low vowel then the high vowel turns into a glide and the following vowel is compensatorily lengthened (see Kula 2002 for discussion). As the TBU is the mora, there is no tone coalescence for the two moras of a long vowel with a sequence of a low tone followed by a H tone, for example, since rising tone patterns are not permitted. Potential rising sequences are resolved either as level low tone or level H. This depends on the possibility of shifting the H into the next syllable i.e. whether the tone can dissociate from its sponsor and attach to the next mora on the right (see tone shift discussion below) or not.

The numbered examples in this article are given without coalescence to more accurately represent the underlying forms, whereas the transcriptions in the figures indicate all instances of vowel coalescence mirroring the actual realizations.

The class one subject marker -á- which is lexically high toned shows tone shift to a following mora but only if there is no lexical high tone on the target. In (9a) we see vowel fusion between the class one subject marker and the initial vowel of the verb. The resulting long vowel surfaces as all H in this case because shifting from the first to the second mora would result in a rising tone sequence on a long vowel and shifting to the next syllable is not possible since that has a MH. As a result, the MH is downstepped.

Apart from cases involving vowel coalescence, tone shift in Bemba is also seen in other instances. In infinitives, for example, the VCV shaped noun class prefix (class 15) also has the property of shifting its initial H to the following vowel. The infinitive examples in (9b–c) show different realisations of the shifting initial H depending on whether a toneless verb (9b) or a high-toned verb (9c) is involved.

(9)   a.   á̠-ìb-íĺé   léélò → ééb-ˈíĺé léélò
            1SM-steal-perf   today
            'He has stolen today'

     b.   ù̠-kú-sóónték-á
            AUG-CL15-light-FV
            'to light'

     c.   ú-kú-ˈl̠éét-á
            AUG-CL15-bring-FV
            'to bring'

In (9b) the initial H of the augment shifts to the following syllable and is then subject to unbounded spreading in this phrase-final verb form which contains no other Hs. In (9c), on the other hand, where the verb is lexically high-toned, tone shift is blocked, and the H surfaces on the augment, from where it spreads rightwards once, resulting in downstep on the following lexical H of the verb. Our annotation of tone shift in the ensuing discussion will follow the representations in (9) where the source of a H tone that undergoes tone shift is underscored to indicate the source of the lexical H tone even though in fact the relevant vowel may surface low (as in 9b).

In summary, the main tonal processes we see in Bemba are rightward H spreading which may be bounded (binary/ternary) or unbounded; downstep and OCP violation avoidance in different environments; variable application of tone shift; the presence of MHs which are subject to the regular tone processes; and long distance spreading at the phrasal level indicating prosodic phrasing. As rising tones are disallowed, there are also a number of processes resolving such sequences depending on the context. These processes are going to be crucial to the interpretation of the tone patterns in the data to be discussed in the following sections, which we now turn to.

3 Declarative sentences

Word order in Bantu is SVO (see e.g. Bearth 2003) and declarative sentences provide either old or all new information as in the examples in (10).[7] The subject in declarative sentences shows a consistent right edge boundary L%. It remains to be investigated whether this boundary tone replaces the lexical tone or simply causes the final H of the subject noun to be realized at a lower register.[8] An optional pause after the subject is possible.

(10) a. àbááná̱   bá̱-ká-bíl-à   ifyákùfwáálá
        2child   2SM-FUT3-sew-FV   8clothes
        'The children will sew clothes'

    b. bànàmáàyó̱ bá̱-ká-bílà   ifyákùfwáálá
        2woman   2SM-FUT3-sew-FV   8clothes
        'The women will sew clothes'

---

[7] All data are generated by the first named author, a native speaker of CB, for the purpose of this research and are therefore not naturally occurring data, although an effort was made to depict everyday scenarios so that the sentences used are not particularly marked. At least three examples (with at least three repetitions each) were analysed for each of the sentence types investigated and reported here. Pitch tracks for each of the examples were compared to arrive at the final analysis with only select figures shown for illustrative purposes. Pitch tracks and annotations were conducted in Praat (Boersma & Weenink 2014).

[8] We thank Carlos Gussenhoven for raising this point. At least subjects with final low tone will have to be investigated to ascertain the effect of the intonational tone. If the boundary L% alters the register of lexical tone then we expect a final low-tone to be produced at a lower register. We leave a full investigation to future work but preliminary results did not show a lowered register for a final low tone suggesting in this case that the lexical tone succumbs to the boundary tone. Note, however, that a final high tone that can trigger inter-word high doubling does so even when it is superposed by a boundary L%, in this case suggesting the lexical H does not get overridden. See Hyman and Monaka (2008) for some hypotheses on the interaction of lexical and intonational tone.

The other intonational characteristic of significance in declaratives is that (at least) the final three syllables are all lowered. We will treat this as *final lowering* and follow Connell & Ladd (1990) in defining this as a more abrupt lowering effect confined to phrase ends and which affects all tones (high or low) causing them to be lowered. This contrasts with declination, which is more of a phonetic effect. Final lowering can be seen for high-toned words at the right edges of figures 1 and 2. It will be seen in later discussion (e.g. figure 4) that final lowering also affects low-toned words. We cannot precisely define the domain of final lowering, as the target number of syllables varies. In figure 1 at least the last five syllables are affected, in figure 2 about the last three syllables are affected, and in figure 4 at least the final 4 syllables are affected. We treat final lowering as involving a right edge boundary L% following work such as Myers (1996) who argues for possible differences in the phonetic implementation of boundary tones as affecting either only the final TBU or a range of TBUs. In the present case, a single constituent like a subject shows more abrupt L% effects, with only the final syllable affected, while in clause final position (where declination probably also has an effect) a range of TBUs may be affected.

There are 5 tiers in each figure showing; (i) the sentence broken up into syllables with surface tones indicated; (ii) lexical Hs; (iii) intonational tones; (iv) significant intonational effects if present; and (v) the gloss. Note that the lexical tones in tier (ii) are aligned with the phonetic signal (and thus the pitch curve), and therefore might not be fully aligned with the corresponding surface tones transcribed on the syllabic tier (i). Furthermore, it should be kept in mind that lexical H tones in tier (ii) may correspond to surface low tones in tier (i) in cases where they have shifted as discussed in section 2.

Figures 1 and 2 below illustrate examples (10a) & (10b), respectively.

In both cases the subject is finally lexically H-toned but shows a boundary L% and in addition, a boundary L% results in final lowering at the end of the declarative. These findings for declaratives are comparable to Downing and Rialland (2015) for Chichewa and Embosi where they show a local register effect of the final L% on the final and preceding tones. See also Rialland & Aborobongui (this volume) for discussion of final lowering and the superposition of boundary H% on lexical high tone. Patin (this volume) also offers discussion on similar lexical tone-intonation interactions in Shingazija.

A boundary L% after subjects resonates well with the pro-drop status of Bantu and the assumption that subjects are topics at least in most analyses (see Givón 1976, Bresnan & Mchombo 1987, for example). If this hypothesis is correct then we expect the same boundary L% in other topicalised constituents. Similarly, if final lowering marks the end of a major constituent (such as an i-phrase) then we may expect to find it between a matrix and subordinate clause

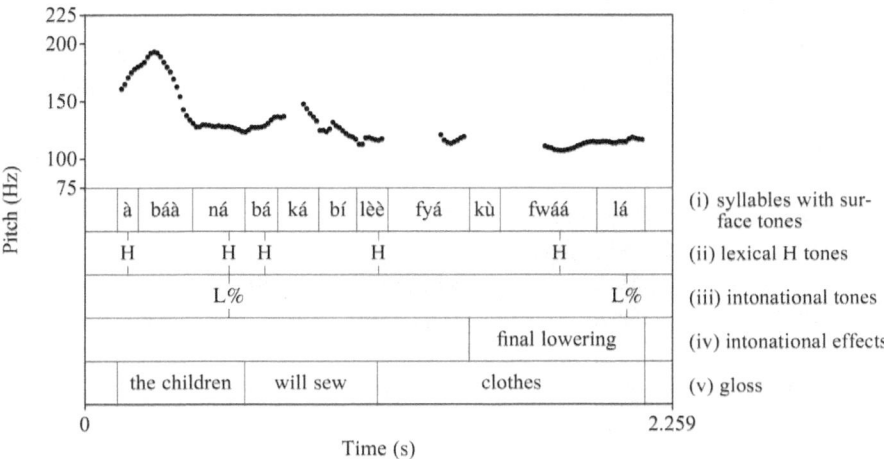

Figure 1: Boundary L% for subject and final lowering in a declarative (10a)

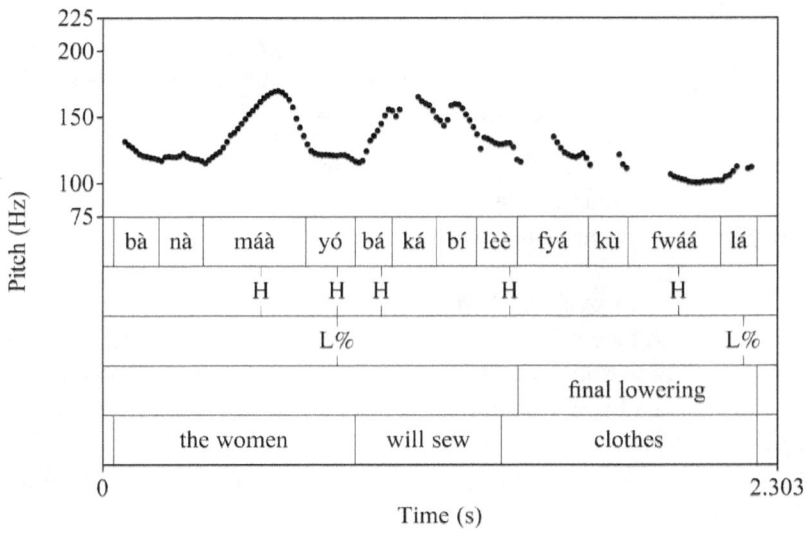

Figure 2: Boundary L% for subject and final lowering in a declarative (10b)

in cases where the two form independent i-phrases. We investigate these structures presently.

Finally, although there is no penultimate lengthening in Bemba, there appears to be some lengthening of the final syllable in both the initial subject and the final constituent in the declarative sentence. We have not carried out systematic durational comparisons but notice it here and in figures discussed below. This may be an issue to investigate in more detail in future work.

3.1 Subordinate clauses

We looked at two kinds of subordinate clauses: those introduced by the complementizer àtì 'that' (11a–b), and relative clauses (11c). (11a) shows the complementizer sentence in its more canonical position after the verb. The intonation of (11a) shows significantly lowered pitch with a fall to the already low-toned complementizer with no pitch reset followed by final lowering after the verb. Thus in order to investigate any right edge effects we use the inverted structure in (11b).[9] This is shown in figure 3.

(11) a. a̱bááná̱ bá̱-lé̱é-súúbìl-à   àtì   bànàmáàyó̱ bá-ká-bíl-á   máíló
       2child 2SM-PROG-expect-FV that 2woman   2SM-FUT3-sew-FV tomorrow
       'The children are expecting that the women will sew tomorrow'

   b. àtì   Chìsàángà a̱líí-sáámbílíl-á máíló,   càà-lí̱-m-pápúsh-á
      COMP Chisanga P3-learn-FV   tomorrow COP-AUX-1SGSM-surprise-FV
      'That Chisanga went to learn/study yesterday surprised me'

   c. a̱báàná̱káshì à-bá-bíl-à   bwììnò bá-lé̱é-ˈángálà   kùmùmànà
      2girl   2AUG.REL-2SM-sew-FV well   2SM-PROG-play-FV 16river
      'The girls who sew well are playing at the river'

The fronted complementizer clause in figure 3 shows a final boundary L% on the final syllable followed by a pause with the following main clause showing pitch reset and final lowering. Note that pitch reset for the main clause that starts with low tone starts at a level very similar to the sentence initial syllable, after which final lowering begins to apply.

Relative clauses, illustrated in figure 4, show a boundary H% signalling continuation on the final syllable of the relative which is itself low-toned. This is followed by a pause before the rest of the main clause. The remainder of the

---

9 We are somewhat unsure of the legitimacy of this move as this makes the complementizer clause look more like a topic, in fact a subject topic since the verb has no subject in (11b). In section 3.2 where we discuss dislocation we use a similar example but with a subject present after the topic to ascertain its topic-hood: [Topic [Subject-Verb]]. But given discussion in Cheng & Downing (2009), (11b) may well be a CP-internal topic.

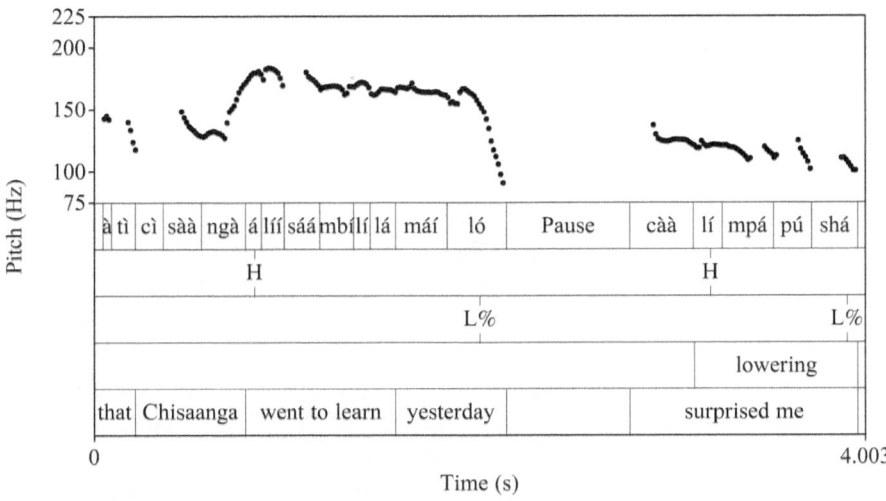

Figure 3: Fronted complementizer clause with boundary L% and main clause with lowering (11b)

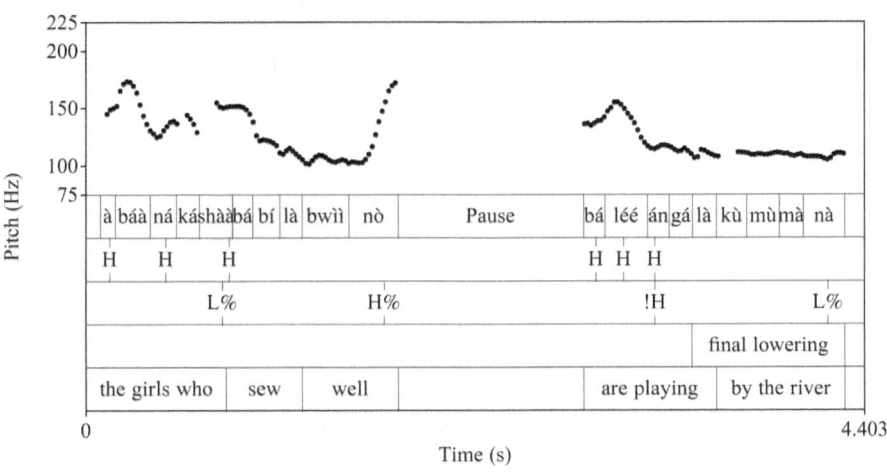

Figure 4: Relative clause with continuation rise and main clause with lowering (11c)

main clause shows pitch reset after the pause and shows expected downstep followed by final lowering indicating the end of the utterance. We again observe lengthening of the final syllable of the relative clause and of the main clause.

A boundary H% (indicating continuation) is also seen to mark the right edges of restrictive relative clauses as well as other subordinate clauses in Embosi and Chichewa (Downing & Rialland, 2015). In Bemba we see that H%

only occurs at the right edge of restrictive relatives but is not seen following other subordinates as in figure 3 (11b).[10]

3.2 Dislocations

We now consider right dislocation of both subjects and objects. Subjects are easily dislocated in Bantu owing to the presence of subject-verb agreement. See Cheng & Downing (2014) for some discussion on contrasting evidence for treating pre-verbal NPs as subjects or topics in Bantu. Similar to subjects, objects can be argued to be right dislocated most clearly in cases where the object is object marked on the verb (Cheng & Downing 2009, Downing 2011, Marten & Kula 2012, Zeller 2015). We assume that the dislocation examples in (12) below show dislocation outside the main clause. The object dislocation example uses a 'disjoint' form in the so-called *conjoint-disjoint* alternation attested in particular tenses in various Bantu languages (Hyman & van der Wal, to appear). In Bemba conjoint forms indicate that a following constituent is phonologically phrased together with the verb, while disjoint forms generally show phrasing that separates the verb and a following constituent. This distribution supports the clause-external status of the final constituents in (12). The conjoint-disjoint alternation also has correlations with information structure on which see Kula (to appear). In both subject (12a) and object (12b) dislocation the right dislocated constituent shows *pitch range compression* (PRC), see figures 5 and 6.[11]

(12) a. bá-láá-bíl-à   kàpùtúlà   lèèló   bànàmáàyó
         2SM-FUT1-sew-FV   1a.trousers   today   2woman
         'They will sew the shorts today, the women'

   b. bá-lá-ˈbélééng-á   bwíínó   ìcítábó
         2SM-HAB-DJ-read-FV   well   7book
         'They read well, the book/they read the book well'

---

[10] Kula & Cheng (2007) investigate the phrasing of a head noun with a following relative clause contrasting restrictive and non-restrictive relatives but do not look at the right edges of RCs.

[11] We take pitch range compression to involve a severe reduction in the f0 range in which tones occur. PRC has been used in contrast to *pitch range expansion* (PRE), which in some languages accompanies focused constituents.

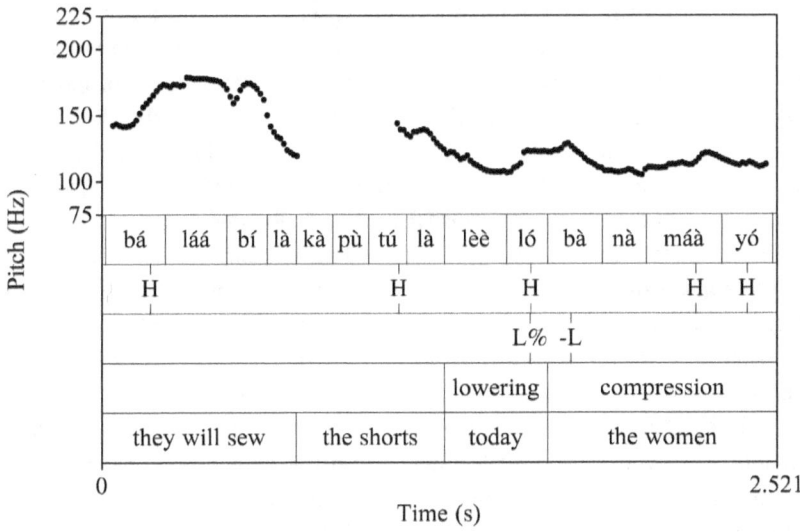

Figure 5: Pitch range compression after lowering on right dislocated subject (12a)

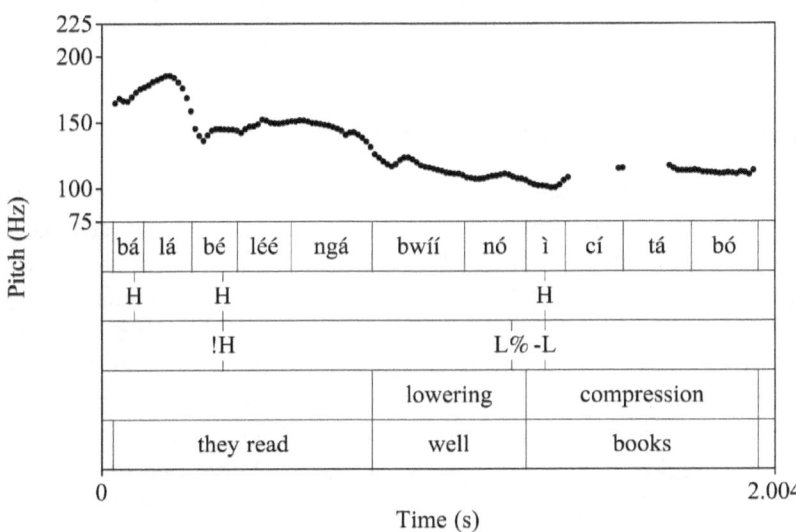

Figure 6: Pitch range compression on right dislocated object after lowering following downstep (12b)

In figure 5 we see lowering on the adverb *lèèló* caused by the boundary tone L% at the end of the clause, and PRC on the right dislocated subject *bànàmáàyó*. PRC is seen to be a global effect affecting the whole constituent. We propose to mark this with the left edge tone -L which then has scope over the dislocated constituent. The PRC analysis is further supported by the fact that the same subject in subject position, cf. figure 2, does not show this effect. Note also that both in this figure and in figure 6 below the right dislocated constituent has a number of high tones for which we see only moderate raising under PRC.

As in the subject dislocation case, object right dislocation in figure 6 shows a boundary L% before the dislocated constituent on which PRC applies, signaled by -L on the left edge of the object. Here we can see that the object despite being High toned on the final three syllables has lower pitch than the initial H on the first two syllables of the sentence as well as the downstepped H. The downstep in this case affects everything that follows within the clause. PRC as triggered by -L in figures 5 and 6 differs from the medial L% in figure 3, for example, because in contrast to figure 3 we see no pitch reset after L% at the beginning of the constituent that undergoes PRC. In figure 3, despite the constituent following the medial L% being low toned, we see pitch reset after the pause matching the low tone level of the initial syllables. This provides justification for distinguishing L% from -L.

3.3 Preverbal topics and contrastive topics

For preverbal topics we consider both clausal objects and single constituent objects in order to compare whether the size of the fronted constituent has a different effect on the intonation. We also look at fronted topics in contrastive contexts. As work by Zerbian (2006) and Downing (2011) shows, languages vary in being either symmetric or asymmetric with respect to the prosodic phrasing of right and left dislocated topics. Bemba is symmetrical in having both kinds of topics phrased separately from the main clause (Kula & Bickmore 2015). The question is whether this translates into identical behaviour of the two topic types at the intonational level. Examples of preverbal clausal and non-clausal topics are given in (13a) and (13b) below with their respective pitch tracks in figures 7 and 8. If fronted topics pattern with initial subjects, which are considered to be topics, then as with subjects (figures 1–2) we expect fronted topics to have a boundary L%. This is the case for clausal topics but not for single constituent fronted object topics but there is possible good motivation for the difference in intonational structure, which we discuss presently.

(13) a. àtì   Chìsàangà   á-álíí-sáámbílíl-á,   nà-àlíí-páp-á
        COMP   Chisanga   3SGSM-P3-learn-FV   1SGSM-P3-surprise-FV
        'That Chisanga went to learn/study surprised me'

   b. kàpùtúlà,   bá-léé-bíl-à lèèló
      1a.trousers   2SM-PROG-sew-FV   today
      'Shorts, they will sew today'

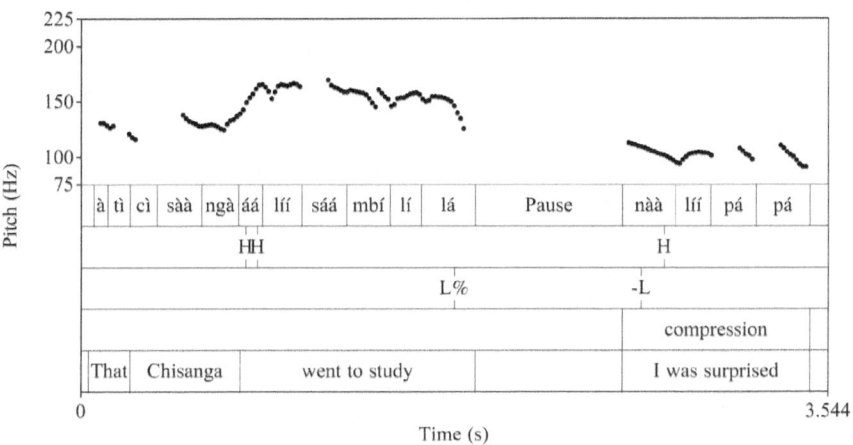

Figure 7: Fronted clausal topic marked with a boundary L% (13a)

The fronted clausal topic in figure 7 shows a boundary L% on the final syllable followed by a pause with the following main clause showing PRC with no pitch reset after the pause. The fronted clausal topic thus patterns with the subject in figures 1–2, but differs in terms of PRC of the following main clause.

A fronted non-clausal object, on the other hand, shows a continuation boundary H%, see figure 8. In this case, as with the H% we saw at the end of a relative clause in figure 4, the continuation boundary H% is superimposed onto the low tone of the final syllable of the fronted object. An optional pause follows the fronted object but notice that in this case there is no PRC of the following clause and there is pitch reset. One possible explanation for the different marking of clausal vs. non-clausal fronted object topics could be the need to more clearly disambiguate the non-clausal object topic from a subject so as to signal the following non-agreeing verb.[12] Interestingly, a fronted headless relative clause shows a similar pattern as a fronted object, with a boundary H% marking its right edge. In this case, too, the main information is still to follow.

---

[12] Perhaps the same could be said of a clausal topic but with a clausal topic it seems that the main information has already been given in contrast to the non-causal one where it is to follow. We leave the formalization of this idea to a future occasion. A more detailed investigation of the context of use of this sentence would also shed more light on the intonation particularly if the discourse function of the fronted topic here turns out to be contrastive, as is possible, but we leave this discussion to future research.

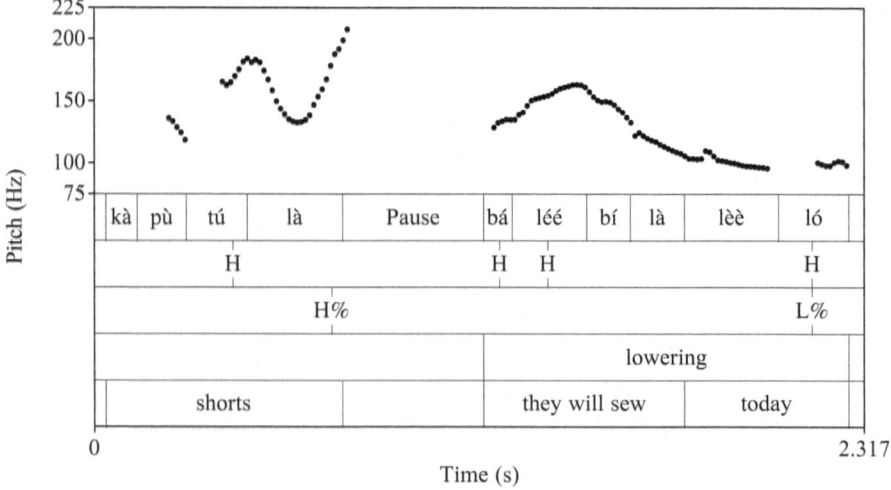

Figure 8: Fronted non-clausal object topic marked with a boundary H% (13b)

The final fronted constituents we look at are contrastive topics occurring as part of two contrastive clauses, as given in the examples in (14).[13]

(14) a. ínyáànyé ná̱á̱-ˈbá̱-shít-à kàlé̱, amá̱tábá, bá̱-ká-shít-á máíló
    10maize ANT-2SM-buy-FV already 6maize 2SM-FUT3-buy-FV tomorrow
    'Maize they have bought already, corn they will buy tomorrow'

b. kàpùtú̱là bá̱-ká-bíl-á máíló, icísóté bá̱-ká-bíl-à pàcìbé̱lú̱shì
   1a.trousers 2SM-FUT3-sew-FV tomorrow 7hat 2SM-FUT3-FV saturday
   'Trousers, they will sew tomorrow, the hat, they will sew on Saturday'

The initial topic in the first clause shows *pitch register raising*, understood as the raising of the pitch contour in the f0 space (Gussenhoven 2004: 76f.), affecting the whole topic, and which we attribute to the presence of a left edge -H. We will show in section 5 below that the domain of -L and -H is (almost always) an i-phrase, which the topic here is. The initial contrastive topic in figure 9 is followed by a right edge boundary L% and in this case followed by a down-

---

[13] (14a) is semantically odd as it contrasts the same object *maize*. Our choice of the synonymous words for *maize* is to ensure a higher number of sonorants for a better pitch track. The sentence is otherwise entirely grammatical.

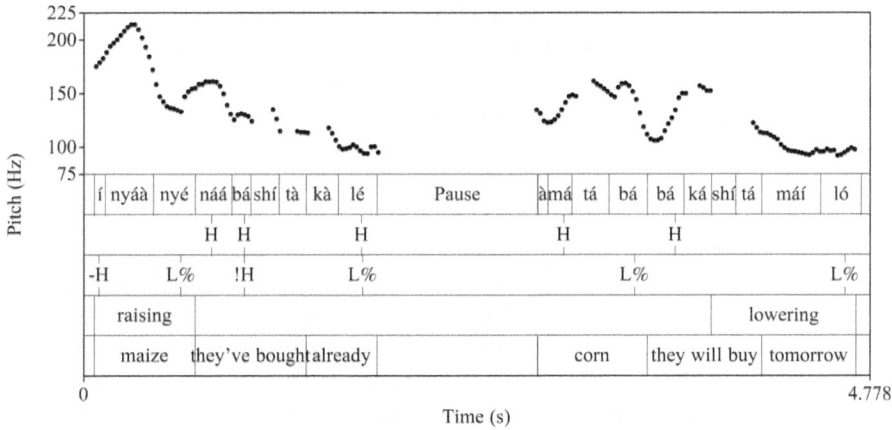

Figure 9: Contrastive topics: 1st topic (inyanye) with pitch raising followed by downstep and 2nd topic (amataba) without raising (14a)

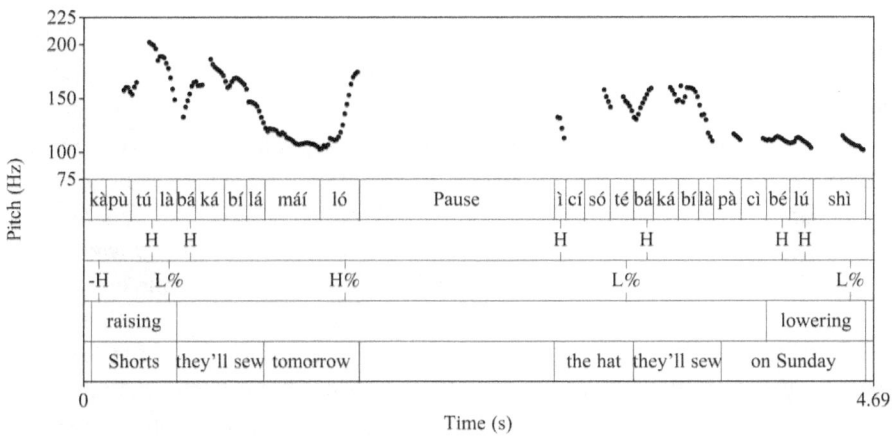

Figure 10: Contrastive topics: 1st topic (kaputula) with pitch raising and clause final H% (14b)

stepped High that affects the rest of the initial clause, showing declination into the pause.[14] We see pitch reset after the pause. The second contrastive topic does not show pitch register raising as the first topic, but has a right edge L%. The final part of the second clause shows normal pitch lowering triggered by the right edge L%.

---

14 Declination refers to the automatic gradual, phonetic lowering or tailing off effect of a series of tones towards the end of utterances or major phrases (see Connell 2001).

The first clause of figure 10 ends with a continuation H% in contrast to figure 9, making us speculate whether this may also have been the case in figure 9 with the effects of the expected boundary H% overridden in this case by the global !H affecting the entire following i-phrase.

4 Questions

In this section, we investigate the two main question types; polar questions and constituent questions. We also look at multiple questions in double object constructions and evaluate any correlation between questions and focus. One of the most robust cross-linguistic characteristics associated with questions is raised intonation (see e.g. Bolinger 1978, Cruttenden 1997, among others). This provides us with an initial testable hypothesis. We begin by first considering polar questions, which in Bemba can optionally occur with the question particle *bùshé*.

4.1 Polar questions

The seminal work of Rialland (2007, 2009) on yes-no questions in a large-scale study of African languages identifies what she terms a *lax* question prosody. Contrary to expectation, the lax question prosody is characterised by a falling pitch contour occurring in isolation or in combination with other phonetic characteristics. These characteristics may involve a sentence final low vowel, vowel lengthening and/or breathy voice utterance termination. Although the lax prosody has mainly been found in the Sudanic belt it is worth investing whether any of its features occur in Bemba.[15] We consider the examples in (15) that illustrate polar questions without (15a) and with (15b) the question particle. In both cases, as figures 11–12 show, we see pitch range expansion (PRE) involving increase in the f0 range of tone (indicated by -H on the left edge) throughout the clause. A final boundary L% occurs but in this case only targets the final syllable. Notice that both in figure 11 and 12, the subject boundary L% is produced at a higher pitch than seen earlier in declaratives. Furthermore, in figure 11 the downstep on both the verb and the final two syllables is suspended as a result of PRE. By comparison in Kano Hausa (Lindau 1986) and Dschang (Hyman 1985) we see

---

[15] A final falling contour can also be found in some Eastern European languages such as Hungarian, Greek, Serbo-Croatian and some varieties of Romanian, as surveyed by Grice et al. (2000). In these languages question intonation involves a low nuclear accent (L*) followed by a high phrase final accent (H-) and a low boundary tone (L%).

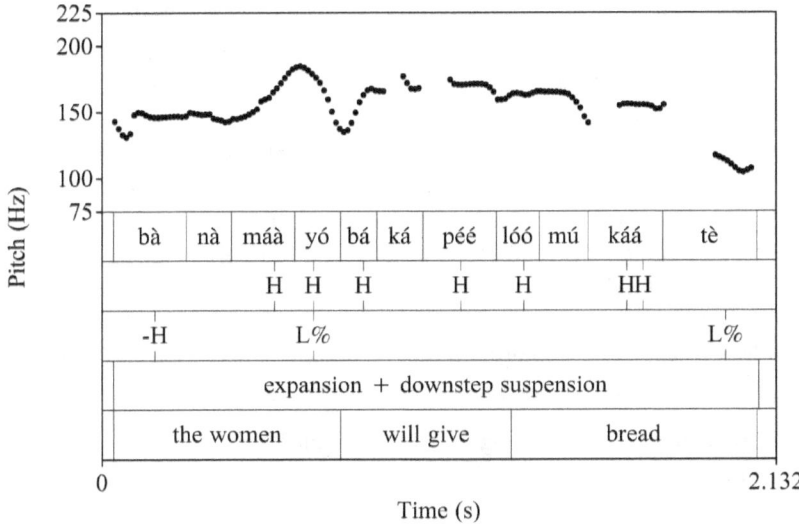

Figure 11: Pitch range expansion in polar question without Q particle with downstep suspension (15a)

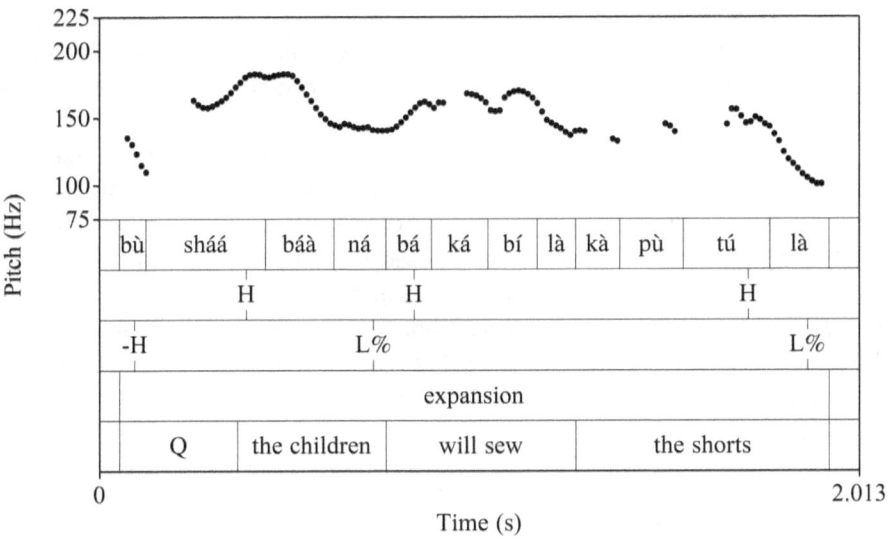

Figure 12: Pitch range expansion in polar question with Q particle (15b)

suspension of declination rather than PRE in questions. In Dschang, in particular, there is then no downstep suspension in questions. In Yoruba, Connell & Ladd (1990) show that there is no consistent effect of pitch raising in questions. These languages show that PRE in questions must be treated as a language specific effect rather than a universal assumption. In the current volume we see cases of downdrift suspension in questions in Chichewa (Downing, this volume) and in Shingazija (Patin, this volume).

As has been discussed, despite Bemba showing PRE in polar questions it nevertheless shows a final fall in pitch, contrary to cross-linguistic expectations, although this occurs fairly late in the utterance. Cahill (2012, 2014 and this volume) shows a more gradual fall in polar questions in Kɔnni (Gur) also providing evidence for a final falling pitch in polar questions. See also Kügler's description of Akan (this volume). The final fall in pitch in Bemba is not associated with low vowels, vowel lengthening, nor breathy voice utterance termination and therefore does not show the lax question prosody.

(15) a. bànàmáàyó   bá-ká-ˈpéél-à   úmúˈkáátè?
         2woman   2SM-FUT3-give-FV   3bread
         'The women will give the bread?'

   b. bùshé   ábáàná   bá-ká-bíl-à   kàpùtúlà?
      Q   2child   2SM-FUT3-sew-FV 1a.shorts
      'Q the children will sew the shorts?'

In figure 12, with the question particle, we see similar PRE of the whole clause with a late final fall on the last syllable. The final word unfortunately has three voiceless stops disrupting the pitch track but PRE can still be discerned before the final fall.

A comparison between a declarative and a polar question for the example in (15a) above shows the difference in pitch we argue indicates pitch range expansion in polar questions. Figure 13 shows the declarative and the polar question of (15a) recapped here as (16) superimposed on the polar question. The polar question shows sustained pitch range expansion before final lowering, while the declarative shows two downsteps and declination before final lowering. This contrasts with the findings of Lindau (1986) on questions in Hausa, which show no pitch range expansion but only suspension of declination (referred to as 'downward slope' in Lindau's work).

(16)   bànàmáàyó   bá-ká-ˈpéèl-à   úmuˈkááte
       2woman   2SM-FUT3-give-FV   3bread
       'The women will give the bread?'

As noted earlier downstep is suspended in the polar question where we see that the final fall comes very late in contrast to the declarative.

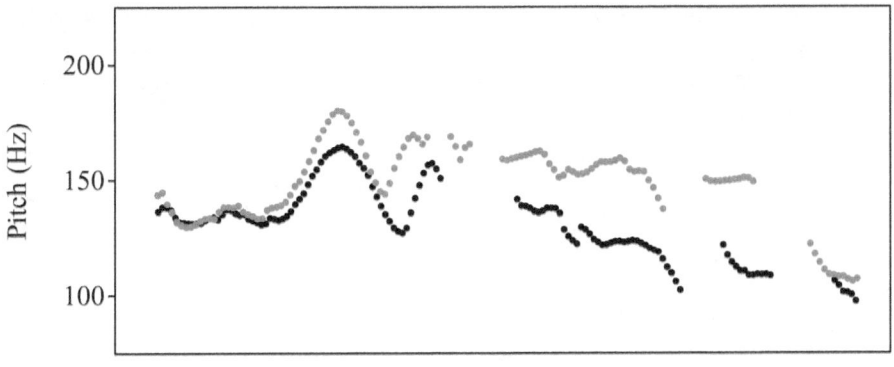

Figure 13: Pitch tracks of a declarative sentence (black) and the corresponding polar question (grey) (16)

4.2 Constituent questions

For constituent questions in Bemba, objects are questioned in-situ, although clefts can also be used, and are identifiable through their relative clause morphology. Constituent questions can also optionally take the question particle *bùshé*, as in polar questions, showing that the particle is not a specific marker of polar questions. Like in a number of Bantu languages (see Sabel and Zeller 2006), subjects are never questioned in-situ in Bemba with clefts as the only available strategy. *Why* uses the same question word as *what*. However, *why* is used with applicatives and literally means 'for what reason'. *Which* either uses the same word as *what* or another independent form. Both forms immediately follow the questioned argument in subject or object position. We will consider *what* and *who* in object questions in the following discussion, using the examples in (17). We consider only simple sentences excluding questions in embedded clauses but see Kandybowicz & Torrence (2015) for a study on the latter in Tano languages of Ghana.

(17) a. bàkàfúndíshá bá-ø-sáámbílìsh-à ínshì lèèló
       2teacher   2SM-HAB.CJ-teach-fv what   today
       'What does the teacher (usually) teach today?'

   b. abáàná bá-!mwééné bààní kúsúkùlù
      2child 2SM-see.PRF who   16school
      'Who did the children see at the school?'

In figures 14–15 illustrating (17a–b) respectively, constituent questions, like polar questions, show pitch range expansion but the question word does not show specific significant pitch raising. When the question word occurs in clause-final position it is subject to final lowering. In contrast to polar questions, final lowering in constituent questions starts earlier: all syllables of the final word usually show lowering triggered by the final boundary L%. In figure 15 downstep applies contrary to expectation when there is pitch range expansion that affects all following constituents.

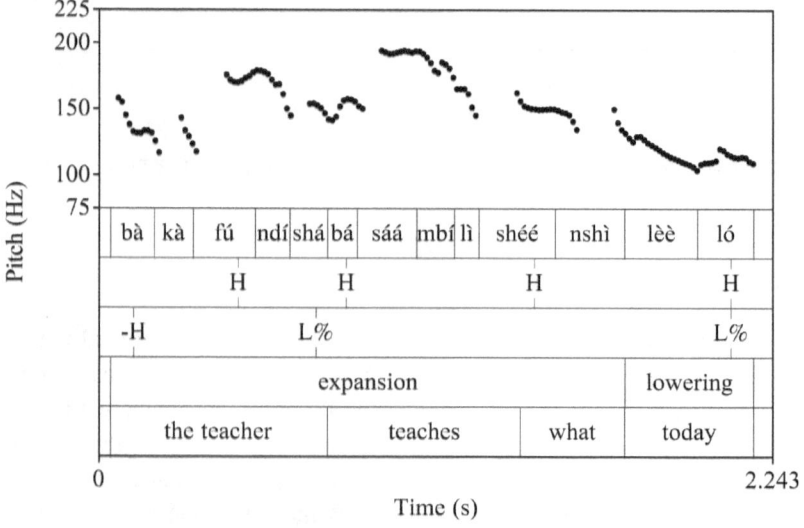

Figure 14: Pitch range expansion in constituent question with question word part of declination (17a)

The average pitch differences between declaratives, polar questions and constituent questions we find in the cases discussed mirrors the findings in Kula (2011). Table 1 below shows average f0 on a verb and following complement which we distinguished in order to assess whether question words showed pitch expansion. The same verb and complement were used for all scenarios with results averaged over three repetitions. As can be seen, the question word itself shows much less expansion than a complement in a polar question. There is some increase in pitch when the question word is non-final, but notice that this is still lower than a final polar question complement relative to the preceding verb.

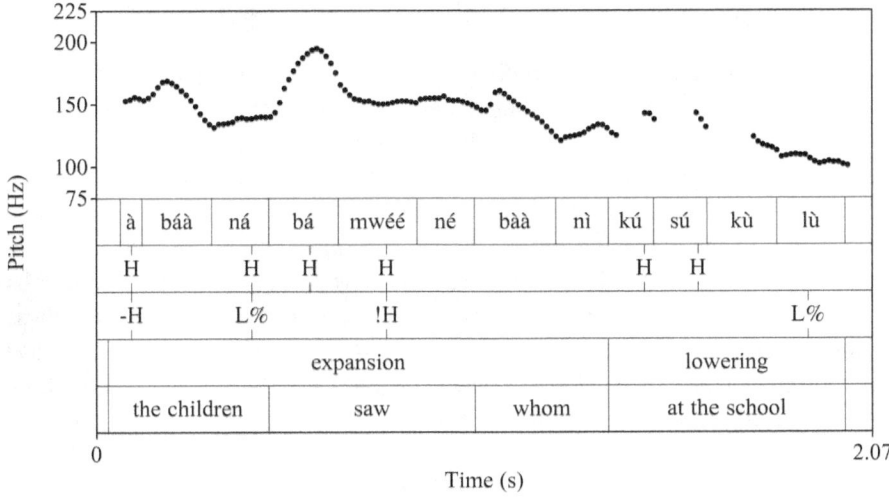

Figure 15: Pitch range expansion in constituent question with question word affected by downstep (17b)

Table 1: Average f0 values on the verb and complement/question word in declaratives vs. questions

Question type	Verb	Complement/ question word
Declarative	149.5 Hz	116 Hz
Polar question	182.5 Hz	150 Hz
Constituent question (question word final)	181.2 Hz	132 Hz
Constituent question (question word non-final)	189 Hz	146 Hz
Constituent question (combined)	183 Hz	136 Hz

Thus in both polar and constituent questions we see an effect of a left edge -H resulting in pitch range expansion. PRE is, however, seen to undergo declination in constituent questions so that they show more drop in pitch towards the final L% than polar questions. Functionally, this difference in phonetic implementation can be regarded as resulting from the functional load of the question word. This fosters the correct interpretation of the utterance as a question in contrast to polar questions where there is more reliance on pragmatic inference carried by pitch expansion. This supports a longer sustained pitch range expansion in polar question contexts. We leave more detailed exploration of the possible interaction between pragmatic inference and phonetic implementation to future research.

4.3 Multiple questions in double object constructions

Bemba is an asymmetric double object language with the requirement that the benefactive object precedes the theme object (Marten et al. 2007). Double objects generally retain their in-situ order when they are questioned although there is some unexpected flexibility in this, perhaps related to focus as discussed below. Riedel & Patin (2011) also show that in some dialects of Fipa (Milanzi and Kwa) a direct object may precede an indirect object in questions in contrast to a non-questioned direct object. It is also possible to have multiple questions in Bemba although these occur infrequently in natural speech. We will consider these using the examples in (18) below where (18a) is an example of a double object construction, (18b) shows a questioned benefactive object, (18c–d) show both objects questioned in alternating order.[16]

(18) a. a̱báàná̱   bá̱-péélé   bà-kàfúndíshà   i̱fítábó
       2child   2SM-give.P4 2teacher   8book
       'The children gave the teacher the book'

   b. bàkàfúndíshà   bá̱-ácí-péél-à   bààní   icítábó
      2teacher   2SM-P2-give-FV 2who   7book
      'The teacher gave who the book?'

   c. a̱báàná̱   bá-péélé   bààní   ínshì   pàlícísàànó
      2child   2SM-give.P4 2who   9what   16.fiday
      'Who did the children give what on Friday?'

   d. a̱báàná̱   bá-péélé   ínshì   bààní   pàlícísàànó
      2child   2SM-give.P4 what   2who   16.fiday
      'What did the children give whom on Friday?'

The expectation is that a single questioned object in a double object construction as well as multiple questions will show pitch range expansion as already seen in the questions discussed above. This, however, does not seem to be the case. Instead, pitch raising of only the verb occurs. This can be seen in figures 16–18 illustrating (18b–c), respectively. In figure 16, for example, there is no pitch difference between the question word and the following non-questioned object with both being fairly low in contrast to the preceding verb. Given the observed pitch raising on the verb, which in figures 17 and 18 can be seen to be

---

16 The verb stem -péélé in (18a, c–d) contains a V2-FV MH. It seems that this MH is applied to the second mora of the verb stem, as we see no downstep within this form. The underlying lexical Hs are fused on the surface.

Intonation in Bemba — 349

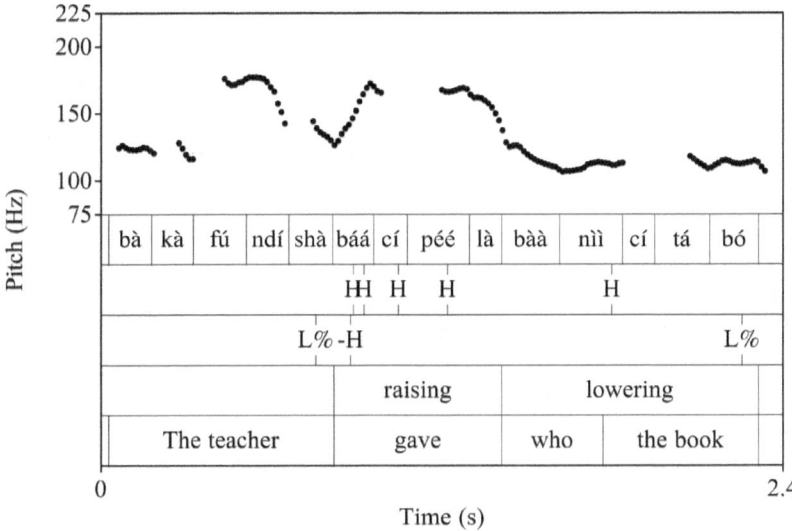

Figure 16: No raising on question word with following complement (theme object) (18b)

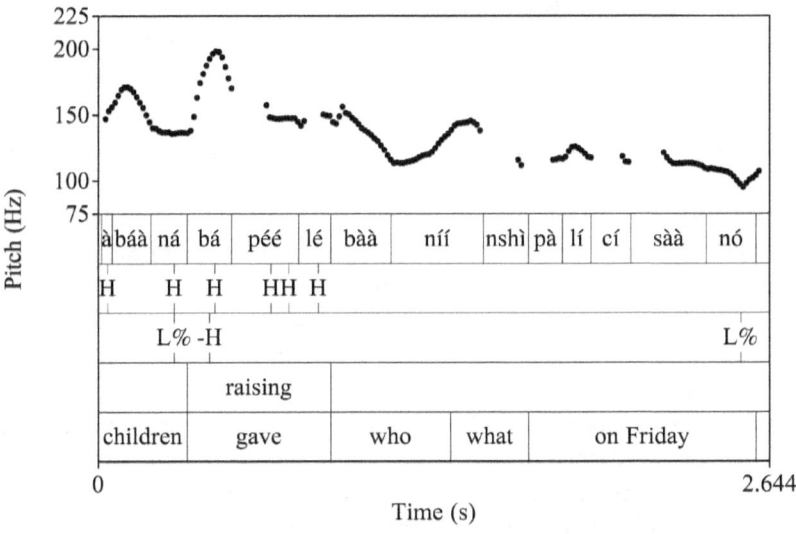

Figure 17: Pitch raising on the verb in a multiple question (18c)

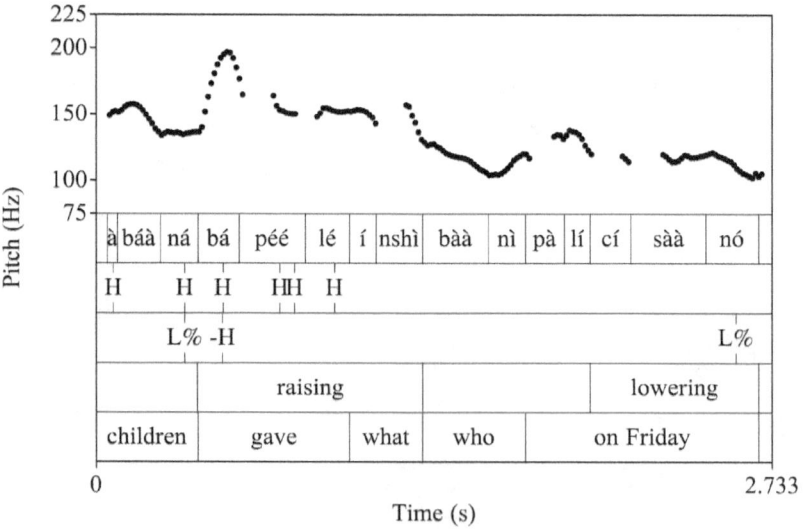

Figure 18: Pitch raising on the verb in a multiple question (18d)

higher than the initial otherwise H toned subject, we are committed to assuming a -H on the left edge of the verb which only targets the verb. In terms of phonological phrasing (Kula & Bickmore 2015) the first object in double object constructions phrases with the verb, while the second object phrases separately. We will discuss the implications of this left edge -H for prosodic domains in section 5.

There are three alternative analyses of these data, which we consider briefly. One would be to assume that the -H is present on the left edge of the verb and has the same pitch range expansion effects as seen in the other questions already discussed. But in this case declination and eventual final lowering, triggered by the final L%, sets in much earlier, as early as the first verbal complement. This, then, instantiates a different phonetic implementation of the final L%. We find this explanation highly improbable as we would expect to see this in at least some declaratives, but we do not.[17] The second possibility would be to have no -H and simply argue that there is no special phrase accent associated to questions in double object constructions. We also do not favour this characterisation because it implies that questions in double object constructions should

---

[17] Needless to say we will have to explore structures with multiple complements to see if final lowering begins much earlier in those cases to rule out the possibility that the final L% is the trigger of the effect.

look like declaratives but they do not, precisely because of the raised pitch on the verb in the question. In addition, this second analysis would fail to capture any similarity with constituent questions with one object, which are treated as involving pitch expansion. The third option would be to have a -L on the left edge of the two objects marking pitch range compression/deaccenting which then has the effect of making the verb appear to be raised in pitch. Although the figures in 16–17 show less consistent PRC than we have seen in right dislocations, there may be some mileage in this argument if we compare this to Turkish (Ipek 2011) which shows post-focus compression. We momentarily treat the restricted expansion as pitch raising on the verb. This leaves us with the question of what prosodic domain is the target of the postulated left edge -H. We offer a possible solution in section 5.

The final issue related to questions that we consider is focus constituents that occur in similar contexts as question words. Since question words have shown no specific prominence we evaluate whether this also holds for other focus bearing constituents.

4.4 Focus and questions

Since question words are considered to be inherently focused, there is an established correlation between focus and questions. A number of languages show identical prosody for focused constituents and question words (see, for example, Deguchi and Kitagawa, 2002, for Japanese). There are different kinds of focus that can be considered (see van der Wal 2009 for some discussion) but for simplicity we will only consider new information focus. Like the restriction we saw in questions, subjects cannot be focused in subject position in Bemba and must obligatorily involve a cleft. Costa & Kula (2008) show that focused constituents occur in post-verbal position in Bemba, in the so-called *Immediate After Verb* (IAV) position (see Buell 2009, van der Wal 2006, among others, on IAV in Bantu). The examples in (19b-c) below illustrate this for locative and adverbial focus from the base sentence (19a).

(19) a. tù-kà-byáál-à ínyànjé mwííbala màìlò (broad focus)
1PLSM-FUT3-plant-FV 9maize 16garden tomorrow
'We will plant maize in the garden tomorrow'

b. tùkàbyáálà mwííbàlà ínyànjé màìlò (locative focus)
'We will plant maize *in the garden* tomorrow'

c. tùkàbyáálà màìlò ínyànjé mwííbàlà (adverbial focus)
'We will plant maize in the garden *tomorrow*'

If IAV is the canonical position for focused constituents in Bemba then we expect questions to occur in this position and this is the case in the constituent questions discussed in section 4.2. The question for double object constructions is whether the requirement for IAV focus will force a violation of the requirement of asymmetric double object structures. The variation seen in the possible positions of question words in double object constructions suggest this might be the case in some instances although it is not categorical. We leave the exploration of this issue to future research and here focus on the intonational structure of focus in relation to questions. Previous work (Costa & Kula 2008, Kula & Bickmore 2015, Kula to appear) argues that focused constituents occur at the right edge of a p-phrase determined by either unbounded H spreading (verb focus) or bounded H spreading (IAV focus). The question is whether these boundaries are signaled in intonation and whether both focused constituents and questions get the same marking. Let us consider this using the question-answer pairs in (20) whose answers we can then compare in terms of intonational structure to that of questions already discussed above. In both answers in (20a–b) the IAV constituent is focused. The answer in (20b) uses a conjoint verb form further confirming the focused status of the complement. Figures 19 and 20 respectively illustrate the answers of (20a–b).

(20) a. *question-answer pair (i)*
    Q: bàkàfúndíshà   bá-léé-ípík-à   ínshì   lèèló
        2teacher   2SM-PROG-cook-FV   what   today
        'What is the teacher cooking today?'

    A: bá-léé-ípíkà   ùbwáálí   lèèló
        2SM-PROG-cook-FV   14ubwaali   today
        'He is cooking *ubwaali* today.'

b. *question-answer pair (ii)*
    Q: bùshé   Chìsàángà   bá-mú-sáàmbìlìsh-à   bùshíkù   nshì?
        Q   Chisanga   2SM-1OM-teach-FV   day   what
        'What day is Chisanga instructed?'

    A: bá-ø-mú-sáàmbìlìsh-à   pàcìbélúshì   (Chisanga)
        2SM-CJ-1OM-teach.CAUS-FV   16saturday   Chisanga
        'They teach him *on Saturday*.'

There is no intonational prominence of the focused constituent in both figures 19 and 20 despite the lexical high tones in these forms. In fact, the sentences here only differ from declaratives (figures 1 and 2) in having a verb with raised pitch.

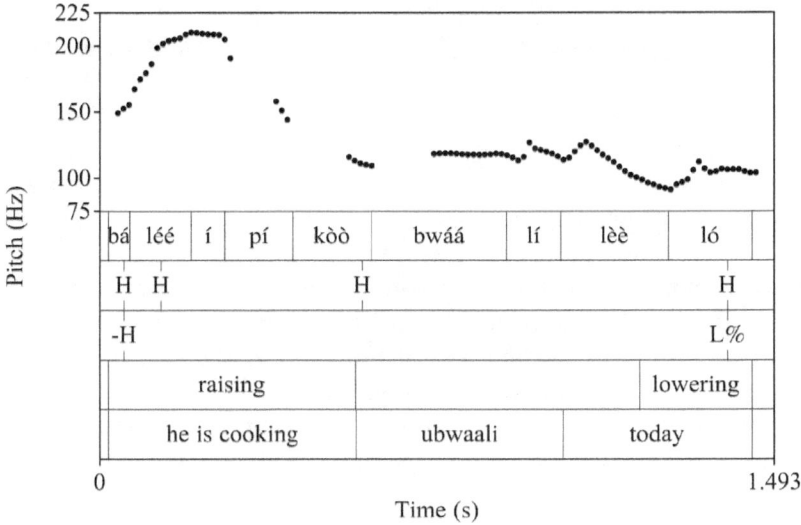

Figure 19: Pre-focus raising in new information focus after the verb (20a answer)

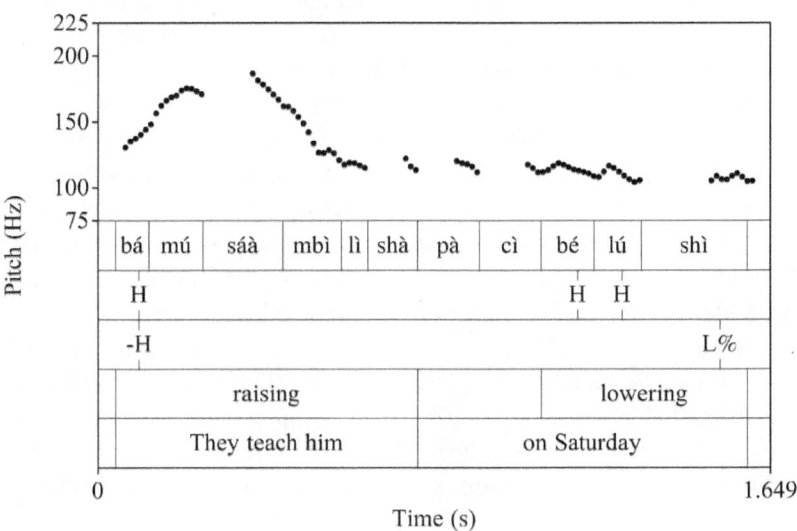

Figure 20: Pre-focus raising with a conjoint verb form (20b answer)

We thus see a complementarity in the intonational structures of focused constituents, whether they are question words or not, particularly when these figures are compared to those of multiple questions (figures 16–18).[18] Kügler (this volume) also shows similar lack of prominence/pitch lowering on focused constituents in Akan.

In summary we can identify the presence of a left edge -H in questions (polar or constituent) that has the effect of pitch raising. Such pitch raising is manifested as pitch range expansion which is sustained throughout a polar question but is more restricted in constituent questions, particularly in double object constructions. The latter effect implies that despite the focus status of question words they show no intonational prominence. The same is seen in focus structures, which after the verb, differ only minimally from declaratives.

We briefly discuss in the following section how the preceding intonational structures in both declaratives and questions correspond to prosodic phrasing.

5 Prosodic phrasing and intonation

We follow standard assumptions in syntax-phonology mapping as in Nespor & Vogel 1986, Selkirk 1986, Truckenbrodt (1999, 2005), which assume prosodic constituents as the domain of interface relations between phonology and syntax. In Align XP-theory, for example, XPs map to p-phrases and CPs to i-phrases. Our approach is to elaborate on what prosodic cues reference which prosodic constituents and then correlate these prosodic constituents to syntactic edges. The assumed syntactic edges are given in table 2. Table 2 provides a summary of the attested boundary/intonational marking and the contexts in which they occur. The motivation for the assumed target prosodic domains is provided in the following discussion.

The most significant marker of the right edge of an intonational phrase is the boundary tone L%. In all cases where L% appears, an i-phrase is signaled. Recall, however, that in most utterances we had more than one L%, e.g. in declaratives, where the subject is followed by L% and the end of the utterance is also followed by L%. The question is whether this implies nested/recursive

---

18 We leave to future investigation the idea mooted in Kula (2011) that this intonational structure as well as the one in questions, which both show significant pitch expansion on the verb (in comparison to declaratives), may indicate an intended intonational structure signaling focus anticipation, comparable to focus delay as discussed for Nagoya Japanese in Tanaka (2010). This contrasts with Turkish, where Ipek (2011) shows that – like in Bemba – focused words show no pitch range expansion but are followed by PRC in the post-focus domain.

Table 2: Summary of intonation marking in Bemba

Structures	Intonational effects	Syntactic edge	Prosodic domain	Examples
Declaratives	L% after subject (optional pause)	RIGHT XP	minimal i-phrase	Figs. 1, 2
	L% (final lowering)	RIGHT CP	maximal i-phrase	Figs. 1, 2
Subordinates				
a) that-clause (complementizer)	L%	RIGHT CP	maximal i-phrase	Fig. 3
b) Relative Clause	H% (continuation) pause	RIGHT CP	minimal i-phrase	Fig. 4
c) Dislocations				
– RD subject	-L (pitch range compression)	LEFT XP	maximal i-phrase	Fig. 5
– RD object	-L (pitch range compression)	LEFT XP	maximal i-phrase	Fig. 6
d) Preverbal topics				
– clausal topic	L%	RIGHT CP	maximal i-phrase	Fig. 7
– non-clausal topic	H% (continuation)	RIGHT XP	minimal i-phrase	Fig. 8
– contrastive topics	1st topic -H; L%	LEFT XP; RIGHT XP	minimal i-phrase	Figs. 9, 10
	2nd topic L%	RIGHT XP	minimal i-phrase	Figs. 9, 10
Questions				
a) polar questions	-H; L% (pitch range expansion)	LEFT CP; RIGHT CP	maximal i-phrase	Figs. 11, 12, 13
b) constituent questions	-H; L% (*partial* pitch expansion)	LEFT CP; RIGHT CP	maximal i-phrase	Figs. 14, 15
c) multiple questions	-H; L% (pitch raising)	LEFT XP; RIGHT CP	minimal i-phrase?; maximal i-phrase	Figs. 16, 17, 18
d) focus	-H; L% (pitch raising)	LEFT XP; RIGHT CP	minimal i-phrase?; maximal i-phrase	Figs. 19, 20

structures and whether the two i-phrases are of the same status and same level. Recursive intonational phrases, as well as phonological phrases, have already been established in the literature (see e.g. Ladd 1986, Gussenhoven 2005, Itô & Mester 2012). We therefore assume recursive i-phrases in Bemba but distinguish minimal and maximal i-phrases where at least three different relations are assumed. (i) Minimal i-phrases can occur recursively to project a maximal i-phrase. (ii) Minimal i-phrases may adjoin to maximal i-phrases to project a maximal i-phrase. (iii) Maximal i-phrases may occur recursively to project an utterance.[19] As can be seen from table 2, minimal i-phrases generally coincide with XPs while maximal i-phrases coincide with CPs. The assumed structures are given in (21) for illustration.

(21) Recursive i-phrases
 a. ((min i-phrase) (min i-phrase))$_{\text{Max i-phrase}}$
 b. ((min i-phrase) (max i-phrase))$_{\text{Max i-phrase}}$
 c. ((max i-phrase) (max i-phrase))$_{\text{Utterance}}$

The crucial indicator of a following minimal i-phrase after a boundary L% is pitch reset. In fact this also extends to a boundary H% so that all boundary tones followed by pitch reset indicate nested structure involving a following minimal i-phrase. This holds for declaratives, complementizer clauses, relative clauses and some topics. Complementizer clauses which are themselves CPs are minimal i-phrases marked by L% and followed by pitch reset of the following minimal i-phrase. Complementizer clauses therefore have the structure in (21a). Relative clauses are the same but end with a H% that is followed by pitch reset into the following minimal i-phrase. Restrictive relatives where the head noun phrases with the relative clause would then have two recursive minimal i-phrases, while non-restrictives, where the head noun phrases separately from the relative, would have three recursive minimal i-phrases. Preverbal topics (in particular objects) and contrastive topics all show a following boundary tone (L% or H%) followed by pitch reset and are thus treated as minimal i-phrases. Downing & Rialland (2015) also treat topics in Chichewa and Embosi as consisting of minimal i-phrases. In Bemba contrastive topics are in addition marked with pitch raising (-H), targeting the initial minimal i-phrase. If there is a following contrastive topic within the same utterance this does not receive pitch raising. Consider the illustration of this below using example (14a) illustrated in figure 9.

(22) Overt multiple contrastive topics
((ínyáànyé)$_{\text{min-ip}}$ (náá-!bá-shít-à kale)$_{\text{min-ip}}$)$_{\text{max-ip}}$
-H L% + pitch reset... L% + pause

((amátábá)$_{\text{min-ip}}$ (bá-ká-shít-á mailo)$_{\text{min-ip}}$))$_{\text{max-ip}}$
pitch reset L% + pitch reset... L%

10maize ANT-2SM-buy-FV already 6maize 2SM-FUT3-buy-FV tomorrow
'Maize they have bought already, corn they will buy tomorrow'

---

[19] We leave open the possibility of structures like (max i-phrase (min i-phrase))$_{\text{Max i-phrase}}$ and other such permutations but leave detailed discussion of a more fully developed analysis to future work perhaps via constraint interaction in Optimality Theory.

In this case in (22) the pause is significant in indicating the right edge of a maximal i-phrase (in each case a CP) composed of multiple minimal i-phrases. We treat the different intonational marking of (different) topics as probably following from their different discourse status and syntactic positions, details of which in Bemba we leave to future work.[20]

Structures where a boundary L% does not show following pitch reset usually have a following left edge phrasal accent that indicates a following maximal i-phrase. Most significantly this is marked by -L after clausal topics and preceding right dislocation. The phonetic effect of a left edge -L is pitch range compression. These structures (figures 5, 6, 7) thus involve the nesting of maximal i-phrases as in (21c). Note that when -L is present on the left edge, and pitch range compression applies, there is no final L% or at best its effects are subsumed by the -L effect. Although it is generally assumed that languages activate a single prosodic edge, either Left or Right, we show that both edges may be referenced in different constructions. There is, however, a difference in effects at the two edges in that on the right edge phrase accents target boundaries (with variable phonetic implementation) while on the left edge phrase accents are global and target the whole following minimal or maximal i-phrase.

Questions and focus constructions are the other cases that involve left edge phrase accents (-H) with global effects in different domains. Polar questions have a -H on the left edge of a maximal i-phrase that results in pitch range expansion of the whole i-phrase terminating in abrupt L%. In constituent questions we see partial PRE targeting a minimal i-phrase and in this case, because expansion does not affect the whole maximal i-phrase, downstep is not suspended and can apply. Note also that final lowering affects a larger domain than just the final syllable in contrast to what is seen in polar questions.

The unexpected finding is the marking observed in multiple questions and in focus constructions where the verb is targeted for pitch raising. The problem as noted earlier is establishing what prosodic domain this coincides with or in what sense this may be deemed a minimal i-phrase as depicted in table 2. The most comparable case, where the right edge of a verb is prosodically referenced is the case of verb focus where a p-phrase boundary (indicated by unbounded H spreading) follows the verb. Such contexts coincide with disjoint forms in Bemba. However, as Givón (1975) and Kula (to appear) show, disjoint forms can

---

[20] Frascarelli & Hinterhölzl (2007), for example, adopting a cartographic approach, argue that different topic constituents are located in specific positions according to their discourse properties. They identify at least three different topics that are also associated with different intonation marking: Aboutness-Shift Topics, Contrastive Topics and Familiar Topics. Similarly, Cheng and Downing (2009) identify CP internal and external Topics.

also occur with a following complement that is part of the focus. This demonstrates that, rather than indicate that only the verb is in focus, disjoint forms instead show that the verb is always *part* of the focus. In such cases the verb shows unbounded H spreading and must be treated as signaling a following p-phrase boundary. In this case we have a mismatch between syntactic structure and prosodic phrasing as depicted in (23) drawn from Kula (to appear).

(23) a. Disjoint pattern (i) (Verb focus, following constituent not part of focus)
 [bá-ka-luk-il-a]$_{VP}$ [Kabwe]$_{ADJT}$ Syntactic Structure
 (bá-ka-luk-il-a)$_\varphi$ (Kabwe)$_\varphi$ Prosodic Structure
 (bá-ká-lúk-íl-á)$_\varphi$ (Kabwe)$_\varphi$ Unbounded Spreading
 (bá-ká-lúk-íl-á)$_\varphi$ (Kábwé)$_\varphi$ Inter-word Doubling & Unbounded Spreading
 'They will weave for Kabwe'

b. Disjoint pattern (ii) (VP focus, following constituent part of focus)
 [bá-ka-luk-il-a Kabwe]$_{VP}$ Syntactic Structure
 (bá-ka-luk-il-a)$_\varphi$ (Kabwe)$_\varphi$ Prosodic Structure
 (bá-ká-lúk-íl-á)$_\varphi$ (Kabwe)$_\varphi$ Unbounded Spreading
 (bá-ká-lúk-íl-á)$_\varphi$ (Kábwé)$_\varphi$ Inter-word Doubling & Unbounded Spreading
 'They will weave for Kabwe'

We could thus argue that multiple questions and focus structures pattern with the distribution in (23b) and therefore that the prosodic domain marked by -H is a p-phrase. This, however, has the problem of being the only structure where a p-phrase would be targeted by a phrase accent. The alternative is to treat this p-phrase as coinciding with a minimal i-phrase. In declaratives, the initial minimal i-phrase consisting of the subject also coincides with a p-phrase so this is already attested. Although we have not indicated this in the pitch tracks there may be evidence of a boundary L% after the verb in these instances which would support a minimal i-phrase analysis. This would support an analysis of the facts as involving pre-focus raising, as was discussed earlier.[21] Another possibility would be to have a -L after the verb to mark the focus as compressed. Intuitively, pre-focus raising resulting in a perception of the focus as compressed is more preferable. More arguments in favour of this analysis will have to be investigated.

---

[21] The structure involved in this case could be (min i-phrase (max i-phrase))$_{Max\ i\text{-phrase}}$. Another alternative is to not reassign the p-phrase if there is no consistent prosodic evidence and rather derive the phrasing through constraint interaction in Optimality Theory. In this case the structure would simply emerge as the most optimal in a system that otherwise aims to match i-phrases with CPs, for example.

We thus see robust prosodic cues in the form of boundary L% and H% followed by pitch reset as indicating the right edge of an i-phrase and a following one, respectively. Final lowering and a continuation H% are both seen to be local effects that can either be abrupt, affecting only one syllable, or wider and affecting the last few syllables. These intonational tones are contrasted with left edge phrase accents that mark i-phrases at different levels, minimal or maximal. Left edge phrase accents generally tend to be global in nature. Our analysis of the phrasal patterns has assumed nesting of i-phrases reflecting recursive structures.

6 Conclusion

This chapter has provided an initial investigation of intonation in particular structures in Bemba. The data show final lowering in *all* sentence types, marked by a boundary L%. Thus, the rightmost CP edge, which coincides with the right edge of an i-phrase, is always marked by a L%. Subordinate clauses show a contrast between a fronted complementizer clause and a relative clause, which are respectively marked by L% and H% at the right edge of the i-phrase. Preverbal topics, including subjects, also show a following boundary tone whose phonetic implementation differs depending on the discourse function of the topic. Topics are treated as minimal i-phrases, which then form a maximal i-phrase with the following minimal i-phrase of the matrix clause. Right dislocations show pitch range compression marked by a left edge -L and form an independent maximal i-phrase. Questions and focus constructions show register raising marked by a left edge -H with pitch expansion affecting the whole maximal i-phrase in polar questions but affecting only a restricted domain (suggested to be a minimal i-phrase) in constituent questions and focus structures.

Future work will have to provide a formal analysis of these findings and in particular explore more complex structures and with more speakers in order to evaluate how robust the current findings are. The chapter draws attention to a number of issues for future research. As in a number of languages the data impressionistically show lengthening of the final syllable that requires some systematic study. The discussion of topics and fronted constituents require a more fine-grained investigation of the left periphery to better understand possible different topics as well as contrastive focus in such positions. Related to this, multiple questions in double object constructions also reveal that multiple complement structures need to be further investigated as well as questions in embedded clauses. Finally, a fuller understanding of the constraints on downstep suspension and sentential downstep would also be beneficial. We take the findings in this work as well as the issues for further exploration as revealing the fertile ground that African languages more generally, and tone languages more specifically, provide for the study of intonation.

Acknowledgements

We would like to thank Bob Ladd for comments on an earlier draft of this chapter and for discussion Carlos Gussenhoven, Louisa Sadler and audiences at the Linguistic Society of Southern Africa (LSSA) 2015 and the Linguistic Society of Great Britain (LAGB) 2015. We also thank two anonymous reviewers and the editors of this volume whose valuable comments have improved the clarity of the arguments made. We take full responsibility for all the ideas expressed.

References

Bearth, Thomas. 2003. Syntax. In Derek Nurse and Gerard Philippson (eds.) *The Bantu Languages*. London and New York: Routledge, 121–142.

Bickmore, Lee & Nancy C. Kula. 2013. Ternary Spreading and the OCP in Copperbelt Bemba. *Studies in African Linguistics* 42(2): 101–132.

Boersma, Paul & David Weenink. 2014. Praat: Doing phonetics by computer. Version 5.4, retrieved 6 November 2014 from http://www.praat.org/.

Bolinger, Dwight. 1978. Intonation across Languages. In Greenberg. J. H. (ed.) *Universals of Human Language 2 (Phonology)*. Stanford: Stanford University Press, pp. 471– 524.

Bresnan, Joan & Sam Mchombo. 1987. Topic, Pronoun, and Agreement in Chichêwa. *Language* 63: 741–782.

Buell, Leston C. 2009. Evaluating the immediate postverbal position as a focus position in Zulu. *Selected Proceedings of ACAL* 38: 166–172. Somerville, MA: Cascadilla Press.

Cahill, Michael. 2012. Polar question intonation in Kɔnni. *Selected Proceedings of ACAL* 42: 90–98. Somerville, MA: Cascadilla Press.

Cahill, Michael. 2014. Polar question intonation in 5 Ghanaian languages. *Selected Proceedings of ACAL* 44: 28–36. Somerville, MA: Cascadilla Press.

Chanda, Vincent M. 1996. Les langues en Zambie. In J-P. Daloz and J.D. Chileshe (eds.) *La Zambie Contemporaine*. Paris: Karthala, Nairobi: IFRA, 301–316.

Cheng, Lisa & Laura J. Downing. 2009. Where's the Topic in Zulu? *Linguistic Review* 26: 207–238.

Cheng, Lisa & Laura J. Downing. 2014. Indefinite Subjects in Durban Zulu. *ZAS Papers in Linguistics* 57: 5–25.

Clements, George N. 1979. The description of terraced-level tone languages. *Language* 55: 536–558.

Clements, George N. & Kevin C. Ford. 1979. Downstep in Kikuyu. *Linguistic Inquiry* 10: 179–210.

Clements, George, N. 1990. The status of register in intonation: comments on the paper by Ladd and by Inkelas and Leben. In Kingston, J. & M.E. Beckman (eds.) 1990. *Papers in Laboratory Phonology I: Between the grammar and physics of speech*, 58–71.
Connell, Bruce. 2001. Downdrift, Downstep, and Declination. *Typology of African Prosodic Systems Proceedings.*
Connell, Bruce & D. Robert Ladd. 1990. Aspects of pitch realisation in Yoruba. *Phonology* 7: 1–29.
Costa, Joao & Nancy C. Kula. 2008. Focus at the interface: Evidence from Romance and Bantu. In Cecile de Cat & Katherine Demuth, eds. *The Bantu-Romance Connection: A comparative investigation of verbal agreement, DPs, and information structure.* Amsterdam: John Benjamins, 293–322.
Cruttenden, Alan. 1997. *Intonation.* (2nd edition). Cambridge: Cambridge University Press.
Deguchi, Masanori and Yoshihisa Kitagawa. 2002. Prosody and Wh-questions. In Masako Hirotani (ed.) *Proceedings of the Thirty-second Annual Meeting of the North Eastern Linguistic Society,* 73–92.
Downing, Laura J. 2011. The prosody of 'dislocation' in selected Bantu languages. In Leston Buell, Kristina Riedel & Jenneke van der Wal (eds.) Special issue on Movement and Word Order in Bantu. *Lingua* 121: 772–786.
Downing, Laura & Annie Rialland. 2015. On the Representation of Intonation and Intonation Phrases: A case study of two Bantu tone languages. Ms., Göteborgs Universitet & Université Sorbonne Nouvelle, Paris 3.
Frascarelli, Mara & Roland Hinterhölzl. 2007. Types of Topics in German and Italian. In Susanne Winkler and Kerstin Schwabe (eds.) *On Information Structure, Meaning and Form,* 87–116. Amsterdam and Philadelphia: John Benjamins.
Givón, Talmy. 1976. Topic, pronoun and grammatical agreement. In C. Li (ed.) *Subject and Topic.* London/New York: Academic Press, 149–88.
Givón, Talmy. 1972. Studies in chiBemba and Bantu grammar. *Studies in African Linguistics.* Supplement 3.
Givón, Talmy. 1975. Focus and the scope of assertion: Some Bantu evidence. *Studies in African Linguistics* 6.2: 185–205.
Gussenhoven, Carlos. 2004. *The Phonology of Tone and Intonation.* Cambridge: Cambridge University Press.
Gussenhoven, Carlos. 2005. Procliticized phonological phrases in English: Evidence from rhythm. *Studia Linguistica* 59: 174–193.
Guthrie, Malcolm. 1945. *The tonal structure of Bemba.* Unpublished PhD thesis, SOAS, University of London.
Guthrie, Malcolm. 1948. *The Classification of Bantu languages.* London: Oxford University Press.
Guthrie, Malcolm. 1967–71. *Comparative Bantu.* 4 vols. Farnborough: Gregg.
Hamann, Silke & Nancy C. Kula. 2015. Bemba. *Journal of the International Phonetic Association* 45.1: 61–69.
Hyman, Larry, M. 1985. Word domains and downstep in Bamileke-Dschang. *Phonology Yearbook* 2: 47–83.
Hyman, Larry, M. & Kemmonye C. Monaka. 2008. Tonal and Non-Tonal Intonation in Shekgalagari. *UC Berkeley Phonology Lab Annual Report (2008),* 269–288.
Hyman, Larry M. & Jenneke van der Wal. to appear. (eds.) *The conjoint-disjoint alternation in Bantu.* Berlin/NY: Mouton de Gruyter.
Itô, Junko & Armin Mester. 2012. Recursive prosodic phrasing in Japanese. In T. Borowsky, S. Kawahara, M. Sugahara & T. Shinya (eds.) *Prosody Matters: Essays in Honour of Elisabeth Selkirk.* Oxford: Elsevier, 280–303.

Ipek, Canan. 2011. Phonetic realization of focus with no on-focus pitch range expansion in Turkish. *ICPhS XVII*: 140–143.
Kabinga, Moonde. 2010. A Comparative study of the Morphosyntax and Phonetics of Town Bemba and Standard Bemba of the Copperbelt, Zambia. MA thesis, University of Cape Town.
Kandybowicz, Jason & Harold Torrence. 2015. The Prosodic Licensing of *Wh-* In-situ: Evidence from Krachi and Wasa. *Selected Proceedings of ACAL* 44: 146–157. Somerville, MA: Cascadilla Press.
Kashoki, Mubanga E. 1972. Town Bemba: A sketch of its main characteristics. *In African Social Research* No. 13. Manchester: Manchester University Press for Institute of African Studies.
Kashoki, Mubanga E. 1978. The Language Situation in Zambia. In S. Ohannessian & M.E. Kashoki (eds.) *Language in Zambia*. London: International African Institute, 9–46.
Kisseberth, Charles W. & David Odden. 2003. Tone. In Derek Nurse and Gerard Philippson (eds.) *The Bantu Languages*. London and New York: Routledge, 59–70.
Kula, Nancy C. 2002. *The phonology of verbal derivation in Bemba*. Ph.D. dissertation University Leiden. Utrecht: LOT.
Kula, Nancy C. 2006. Zambia language situation. In K. Brown (ed.) *Encyclopaedia of Language and Linguistics*. Oxford: Elsevier, Vol 13: 744–745.
Kula, Nancy C. 2011. Constituent questions in Bemba. Presentation at the Bantu Psyn Workshop on WH questions, Lyon.
Kula, Nancy C. to appear. The conjoint-disjoint alternation and phonological phrasing in Bemba. In Hyman, Larry M. & Jenneke van der Wal (eds.) *The conjoint-disjoint alternation in Bantu*. Berlin/NY: Mouton de Gruyter.
Kula, Nancy C. & Lee Bickmore. 2015. Phrasal Phonology in Copperbelt Bemba. *Phonology* 32.1: 147–176.
Kula, Nancy C. & Lisa Cheng. 2007. Phonological and Syntactic phrasing in Bemba relatives. *Journal of African Languages and Linguistics* 28: 123–148.
Ladd, D.R. 1986. Intonational phrasing: The case for recursive prosodic structure. *Phonology* 3: 311–340.
Ladd, D.R. 1990. Metrical representation of pitch register. In Kingston & Beckman (eds.) 1990. *Papers in Laboratory Phonology I: Between the grammar and physics of speech*, 35–57.
Ladd, D.R. 2008. *Intonational Phonology*. 2nd edition. Cambridge: Cambridge University Press.
Lewis, M. Paul, Gary F. Simons & Charles D. Fening (eds.). 2013. *Ethnologue: Languages of the World, Seventeenth edition*. Dallas, Texas: SIL International. Online version: http://www.ethonologue.com.
Lindau, Mona. 1986. Testing a model of intonation in a tone language. *Journal of the Acoustical Society of America* 80: 757–764.
Mann, Michael. 1977. An outline of IciBemba Grammar. In M.E. Kashoki (ed.) *Language in Zambia: Grammatical Sketches*. Lusaka: Institute for African Studies. Reprinted 1999, Lusaka: Bookworld Publishers.
Marten, Lutz & Nancy C. Kula. 2012. Object marking and morphosyntactic variation in Bantu. *Studies in African Linguistics and Applied Language Studies* 30.2: 237–253.
Marten, Lutz, Nancy C. Kula & Nhlanhla Thwala. 2007. Parameters of morpho-syntactic variation in Bantu. *Transactions of the Philological Society* 105: 253–338.
Myers, Scott. 1996. Boundary tones and the phonetic implementation of tone in Chichewa. *Studies in African Linguistics* 25: 29–60.
Nespor, Marina & Irene Vogel. 1986. *Prosodic phonology*. Dordrecht: Foris Publications.

Odden, David & Lee Bickmore. 2014. Melodic tone in Bantu: Overview. *Africana Linguistica* 20: 3–13.
Ohannessian, Sirarpi & Mubanga E. Kashoki. 1978. (eds.) *Language in Zambia*. London: International African Institute.
Patin, Cedric. 2007. La tonologie du shingazidja, langue bantu (G44a) de la Grande Comore: nature, formalization, interfaces. PhD dissertation, Université Paris 3.
Philippson, Gerrard. 1998. *HH and *HL tone patterns in Bemba and the Bemba tone system. In J-M., Hombert, and L.M. Hyman (eds.) *Bantu Historical Linguistics*. Stanford: CSLI Publications, 395–411.
Pierrehumbert, Janet & Mary E. Beckman. 1988. *Japanese Tone Structure*. Cambridge, MA: The MIT Press.
Rialland, Annie. 2007. Question prosody: an African perspective. In Gussenhoven, C. and T. Riad (eds.) *Tunes and Tones, Volume 1: Typological Studies in Word and Sentence Prosody*. Berlin: Mouton deGruyter, 35–62.
Rialland, Annie. 2009. The African lax question prosody: Its realisation and geographical distribution. *Lingua* 119.6: 928–949.
Riedel, Kristina & Cedric Patin. 2011. Question structure and intonation in Fipa. *ZAS Papers in Linguistics* 55: 141–160.
Sabel, Joachim & Jochen Zeller. 2006. wh-Question formation in Nguni. In *Selected Proceedings of ACAL* 35: 271–283.
Schadeberg, Thilo C. 1973. Kinga: a restricted tone system. *Studies in African Linguistics* 4 (1): 23–47.
Selkirk, Elisabeth. 1986. On derived domains in sentence phonology. *Phonology* 3: 371–405.
Sharman, John, C. & Achille E. Meeussen. 1955. The representation of structural tones, with special reference to the tonal behavior of the verb in Bemba, Northern Rhodesia. *Africa: Journal of the international African Institute* 25(4): 393–404.
Sharman, John, C. 1956. The tabulation of tenses in a Bantu language (Bemba: Northern Rhodesia). *Africa: Journal of the international African Institute* 26: 29–46.
Stewart, John M. 1965. The typology of the Twi tone system. *Bulletin of the Institute of African Studies* 1: 1–27.
Tanaka, Yu. 2010. On Wh-Questions and prosodic focus delay in Nagoya Japanese. *Sophia University Working Papers in Phonetics 2010*, 71–93.
Truckenbrodt, Hubert. 1999. On the relation between syntactic phrases and phonological phrases. *Linguistic Inquiry* 30: 219–255.
Truckenbrodt, Hubert. 2005. A Short Report on Intonation Phrase Boundaries in German. *Linguistische Berichte* 203: 273–296.
van der Wal, Jenneke. 2006. The disjoint verb form and an empty Immediate After Verb position in Makhuwa. *ZAS Papers in Linguistics* 43: 233–256.
van der Wal, Jenneke. 2009. *Word order and information structure in Mahuwa-Enahara*. PhD dissertation, University of Leiden. Utrecht: LOT Publications.
Zerbian, Sabine. 2006. Expression of Information Structure in the Bantu Language Northern Sotho. *ZAS Papers in Linguistics* 45.

Laura J. Downing
Tone and Intonation in Chichewa and Tumbuka

Abstract: This study compares the tone and intonation systems of two closely related Bantu languages spoken in Malawi, Chichewa and Tumbuka. The lexical tone systems of the two languages are quite different from each other. Chichewa uses tone contrastively and grammatically. In Tumbuka, tone is predictable except in the ideophonic system. Only Tumbuka provides evidence for both a Phonological Phrase and an Intonation Phrase level. It is surprising, then, that the intonation systems of the two languages turn out to be quite similar. Both have penult lengthening and similar intonation patterns for statements and questions. Both use continuation rises following preverbal topics, and have final lowering at the end of declarative utterances. These similarities raise the question of whether intonation might be an areal phenomenon.

Keywords: penult lengthening, penult High tone, pivot tone languages, phonological phrase, intonational phrase, boundary tone, final lowering, topic, focus, emphasis, questions, superposition, register raising

1 Introduction

Chichewa[1] and Tumbuka are both Bantu languages (N31 and N21, respectively) spoken in Malawi. As we shall see in this chapter, the two languages have quite distinct prosodic systems. Chichewa has contrastive tone, while Tumbuka has predictable tone; Chichewa has only one level of phrasing (Intonational Phrase), while Tumbuka provides evidence for two levels of phrasing (Phonological Phrase and Intonational Phrase). However, the two languages share many aspects of their intonation, notably penult lengthening and the repertoire of boundary tones used, for example, to distinguish declaratives from different question types.

---

[1] Chichewa is often spelled 'Chicheŵa'. The sound represented by 'ŵ' – a voiced bilabial fricative – is not found in standard varieties of Chichewa. This is why I have not chosen to use this spelling variant. Chichewa is known as Nyanja outside of Malawi.

Laura Downing, University of Gothenburg

Pairing a discussion of the two languages in a single chapter provides a striking demonstration that intonation patterns do not necessarily correlate with other aspects of the prosodic system.

2 Lexical tone

2.1 Chichewa: lexical tone with phrasally-conditioned tone realization

Chichewa is a major language of Malawi, and it has contrastive tone, like most Bantu languages (Kisseberth & Odden 2003). The tonal system of Chichewa is quite well studied, and only the main points are summarized here.[2] As demonstrated in some detail in Kanerva (1990) and Bresnan & Kanerva (1989), lexical (and grammatical) High tone realization is conditioned by phonological processes which take the prosodic phrase as their domain. (In section 3.2, below, I argue that the relevant level of phrasing is the Intonational Phrase.) Syntax is the main factor defining prosodic phrasing. In the analyses of Bresnan & Mchombo (1987) and Kanerva (1990), sentences have three main subconstituents – an optional subject noun phrase (NP), an obligatory verb phrase (VP), and an optional topic NP – which can be freely ordered. The VP consists of the verb and all its complements, as shown in (1a, d). According to these authors, each of the three constituents, when they co-occur, is parsed into its own prosodic phrase. As shown in (1b) and (1c), topicalized NPs are in a distinct syntactic and prosodic phrase, and can occur in either order with respect to the VP. Prosodic phrases are indicated with parentheses in the data which follows:[3]

(1) a. (Subj) (VP) – Kanerva (1990: 103, fig (114b))
  (mwaána) (a-na-pézá galú kú-dáambo)
  1.child 1SBJ-TAM-find 1.dog LOC-swamp
  'The child found the dog at the swamp.'

---

[2] See work like Bresnan & Kanerva (1989), Bresnan & Mchombo (1987), Hyman & Mtenje (1999), Kanerva (1990), Moto (1989), Mtenje (1986, 1987), Myers (1996, 1998, 1999a, b), Myers & Carleton (1996) for detailed analyses of tone in Chichewa, including some discussion of the dialectal variation in tone realization mentioned in this section.

[3] The following abbreviations are used in the morpheme glosses: numbers indicate noun agreement class; OBJ = object marker; SBJ = subject marker; TAM = tense-aspect marker; PERF = perfective; LOC = locative; REL = relative; COP = copula; INF = infinitive. Acute accents indicate High tone, and parentheses indicate prosodic phrasing.

b. (Subj) (VP) (Top) – (Kanerva 1990: 107, fig (123b))
 (mwaána) (a-na-ḿ-pézá kú-dáambo) (gaálu)
 1.child 1SBJ-TAM-1OBJ-find LOC-swamp 1.dog
 'The child found it at the swamp, the dog.'

c. (Top) (VP) (Subj) – (Kanerva 1990: 102, fig (110c))
 (a-leenje) (zi-ná-wá-luuma) (njúuchi)
 2.hunter 10SBJ-SIMPLE.PAST-2OBJ-bite 10.bee
 'The hunters, they bit them, the bees [did].'

d. (VP) – (Kanerva, 1990: 98, fig. (101))
 (a-na-mény-á   nyumbá ndí mwáála)
 1SBJ-RECENT.PAST-hit 9.house with 3.rock
 'S/he hit the house with a rock.'

However, Downing & Mtenje (2011a,b) find that the subject NP is only variably followed by a prosodic phrase boundary. This variation in the phrasing of subjects is illustrated in the data below, where we see that the subject is not phrased separately in (2a), but it is in (2b):

(2) a. (Ma-kóló a-na-pátsíra mwaná ndalámá zá mú-longo wáake)
 6-parent 6SBJ-RECENT.PAST-give 1.child 10.money 10.of 1-sister 1.her
 'The parents gave the child money for her sister.'

b. (M-fúumu) (i-na-pátsá mwaná zóóváala)
 9-chief 9SBJ-RECENT.PAST-give 1.child 10.clothes
 'The chief gave the child clothes.'

As Downing & Mtenje (2011a,b) and Cheng & Downing (2009) argue, a prosodic phrase boundary following the subject correlates with topicalization.

Kanerva (1990) and Bresnan & Kanerva (1989) demonstrate that four phonological processes motivate the prosodic phrasing indicated in (1) and (2). First, the phrase penult vowel is lengthened. Chichewa does not have contrastive vowel length, and penult lengthening is the only common vowel lengthening process in the language. While sequences of identical vowels arise across certain morpheme boundaries, all penult long vowels in the data are due to phrasal lengthening. Second, a High tone on a phrase-final vowel is retracted towards the penultimate mora. In the Nkhotakota variety (Kanerva 1990), a High tone on a phrase-final vowel is completely retracted, as shown by the phrase-final tone pattern of the word for /galú/ 'dog' in (1b). In the Ntcheu variety (Downing

& Mtenje 2011a,b), a phrase-final High tone is realized on both the penultimate and final moras: e.g., [gaálú] 'dog'. Third, within a prosodic phrase High tones double to the following syllable. However, the disyllabic window at the end of a prosodic phrase is a barrier to tone doubling. To see this, compare the tone pattern of /kálata/ 'letter' in phrase-medial (3b) vs. phrase-final (3a) position (more on the phrasing of relative clauses in section 3.2, below):

(3) Tone doubling blocked phrase finally (Downing & Mtenje 2011a)
    a. ((m-phunzitsi *a-méné* á-ná-kwiyá   kwámbíiri) a-ná-wélengera
        1-teacher   1-REL   1SBJ-TAM-be.angry very   1SBJ-TAM-read.to
        aná   á súkúlú   kálaata)
        2.child 2.of school 5.letter
        'The teacher who was very angry read the students a letter.'

    b. ((Káláta *i-méné* m-phunzitsi á-ná-weléenga) í-ma-néná   m-fúumu)
        5.letter 5-REL 1-teacher   1SBJ-TAM-read   5SBJ-TAM-criticize 9-chief
        'The letter which the teacher read criticizes the chief.'

There is one principled set of exceptions to the generalization that High tones do not double into the disyllabic phrase-final window, namely a process of High tone plateauing. A High tone can double into the phrase-final disyllabic window if it is followed by another High tone. This is illustrated by the phrase *[ndí mwáála]* 'with a stone' in (1d), where the High tone of the preposition *ndí* doubles onto the phrase-penult vowel, forming a High tone plateau with the (retracted) final High tone of /mwalá/ 'rock'. As Kisseberth & Odden (2003) show, High tone plateauing, tone doubling and avoidance of High tones on final vowels are, in fact, common tonal processes cross-Bantu.

2.2 Tumbuka: phrasal tone or stress?

In contrast to Chichewa, there are no lexical or grammatical tonal contrasts in Tumbuka, except with some ideophones (Vail 1972).[4] Rather, the penult of every word in isolation is lengthened, and the first mora of the lengthened penult is

---

[4] Compared to Chichewa, Tumbuka prosody is relatively understudied. This section summarizes work developed in Downing (2006, 2008, 2010b, 2011a,b, 2012). Note that 'ŵ' in Tumbuka orthography indicates a voiced bilabial fricative [β], which contrasts with both [w] and [b].

associated with a High tone. This is shown in the following representative data (Downing 2012):

(4) No tonal contrasts in nouns

Singular	Gloss	Plural
múu-nthu	'person'	ŵáa-nthu
m-líimi	'farmer'	ŵa-líimi
m-zíinga	'bee hive'	mi-zíinga
m-síika	'market'	mi-síika
khúuni	'tree'	ma-kúuni
báanja	'family'	ma-báanja
ci-páaso	'fruit'	vi-páaso
ci-ndíindi	'secret'	vi-ndíindi
nyáama	'meat, animal'	nyáama
mbúuzi	'goat'	mbúuzi

(5) No tonal contrasts in verbs or verb paradigms
   a. ku-líima   'to farm'   líima!   'farm!'
       ti-ku-líima   'we farm'   ti-ku-líma yáaye   'we do not farm'
       ti-ka-líima   'we farmed'   ti-ka-líma yáaye   'we did not farm'
       t-angu-líima   'we recently farmed'
       n-a-ŵa-limíira   'I have farmed for them'
       ŵ-a-líima   'they have farmed'
       wa-zamu-líima   's/he will farm'   wa-zamu-limilíira   's/he will weed'

   b. ku-zéenga   'to build'   zéenga! 'build!'
       ti-ku-zéenga   'we build'
       nyúumba yi-ku-zengéeka   'the house is being built'
       ŵa-ka-zéenga   'they built'
       ŵa-ka-ku-zengéera   'they built for you sg.'
       ŵa-ka-mu-zengeráa-ni   'they built for you pl.'
       n-a-zéenga   'I have built'
       wa-zamu-zéenga   's/he will build'
       ŵa-zamu-zengeráana   'they will build for each other'

Tumbuka words have the isolation pronunciation in (4) and (5), though, only when they are final in the prosodic phrase (indicated with parentheses in (6) and subsequent examples). As shown in (6), penult lengthening and a penult High tone are not found on every word. Rather, they are found, roughly, on the word at the right edge of each lexical XP (typically, a noun phrase), unless the verb phrase is very short, as in (6c):[5]

(6) Tumbuka prosodic phrasing (Downing 2008)
    a. (ti-ku-phika síima)
       we-TAM-cook porridge
       'We are cooking porridge.' (VP)

    b. (ŵ-áana) (ŵa-ku-ŵa-vwira   ŵa-bwéezi)
       2-child   2SBJ-TAM-2OBJ-help 2-friend
       'The children are helping the friends.' (Subj) (V NP)

    c. (ti-ka-wona mu-nkhúungu) (ku-msíika)
       we-TAM-see 1-thief   LOC-market
       'We saw a thief at the market.' (V NP) (PP)

    d. (ŵ-anakáazi) (ŵa-ka-sona   vy-akuvwara vya mu-kwáati)
       2-woman   2SBJ-TAM-sew 8-clothes   8.of 1-bride
       'The women sewed clothes of the bride.' (Subj) (V NP)

    e. (m-nyamáata) (wa-ka-timba nyúumba) (na   líibwe)
       1-boy   1SBJ-TAM-hit 9.house   with 5.rock
       'The boy hit the house with a rock.' (Subj) (V NP) (PP)

To put these Tumbuka prosodic patterns into perspective, penult lengthening (especially of phrase-penult vowels), interpreted as stress, is very common cross-Bantu. (See, e.g., Doke 1954; Downing 2010a; Hyman & Monaka 2011; Philippson 1998; Zerbian, this volume.) Recall from the preceding section that penult lengthening is a cue to prosodic phrasing in Chichewa. It is also very common cross-Bantu for the High tone of a word to be attracted to the penult (see, e.g., Kisseberth & Odden 2003; Philippson 1998). And other languages of the region (roughly, northern Lake Malawi; it is not clear how widespread this is) have what have been called restricted or predictable tone systems: all words must have a High tone. (See Odden 1988, 1999; Schadeberg 1973 for discussion.) Tumbuka prosody illustrates these regional patterns.

---

[5] High tones are occasionally found on non-lengthened penults, as we see on the verb in example below:

ŵa-líimi) ŵa-lúta ku-múunda)
2-farmer 2-go   LOC-fields
'The farmers have gone to the fields.'

High tones occur so irregularly on non-lengthened penults that it is hard to make a generalization predicting their occurrence. We leave this as a topic for future research.

Because the phrase-penult vowel predictably bears a High tone on its first mora and is lengthened, Tumbuka is sometimes classified as a stress language, rather than a restricted tone language. (See e.g. Kisseberth & Odden 2003.) Pitch change on a lengthened vowel is a cross-linguistically common correlate of stress. However, as work like Hyman (2006, 2014) argues, stress is canonically defined as a word-level, rather than phrase-level, phenomenon. Tumbuka would, then, be a non-canonical stress language. Further, it would be very unusual for a stress language to maintain contrastive tone in a large corner of the lexicon, namely, in the ideophone vocabulary. Finally, as Gussenhoven (2006) argues, it is unusual for a stress language to have just one intonation melody associated with a stressed syllable. Instead, he argues that languages like Tumbuka, where every stressed (lengthened) syllable is realized with a High tone, are not stress languages with phrasal stress, but rather pivot tone languages with phrasal tone, and the phrasal High tone is distinct from an intonational tone. This is the view we adopt in annotating the pitch tracks in the next sections.

3 Phrasing and intonation in declarative sentences

The traditional Prosodic Hierarchy (Nespor & Vogel 1986; Selkirk 1986) provides two levels of phrasing relevant to the syntax-phonology interface: Phonological Phrase and Intonational Phrase. While there have been proposals to expand the number of levels, I follow Itô & Mester (2012, 2013) in assuming that just these two levels are sufficient to account for attested patterns of prosodic phrasing. As work like Myrberg (2013) notes, prosodic correlates distinguishing these two levels of phrasing are often hard to pin down and are subject to considerable cross-linguistic variation. However, there is wide agreement on the syntactic distinction between the two levels of phrasing: Phonological Phrases roughly align with lexical XPs, while Intonational Phrases roughly align with root clauses, which can contain more than one lexical XP.[6] I adopt this syntactic distinction

---

[6] Work defining and illustrating this sort of syntactically-based distinction between Phonological Phrase and Intonational Phrase includes: An (2007); D'Imperio et al. (2005); Gussenhoven (2004: 167); Kanerva (1990); Kisseberth (2010); Nespor & Vogel (1986); Prieto (2005); Selkirk (1986, 2009, 2011); Truckenbrodt (1995, 1999, 2005); Zerbian (2007). It is not the goal of this paper to argue in detail for a particular prosodic phrasing algorithm, but rather to motivate the relevant levels of phrasing for Tumbuka and Chichewa. See Cheng & Downing (2016) for detailed motivation for the phrasing analysis illustrated here, which refines the syntactic correlate of Intonational Phrases to refer to phases: vP and CP.

in labeling levels of phrasing in this paper. In the next two sections, I motivate the levels of phrasing in Tumbuka and Chichewa, and illustrate the intonation patterns found in Intonational Phrases in both languages.

3.1 Phonological Phrases and Intonational Phrases in Tumbuka

As shown in (6), above, vowel length and a High tone on the first mora of the penult are conditioned by the right edge of XP. The verb plus its first complement generally form a single phrase, and following complements are phrased separately. Subject NPs and Topics are phrased separately from the rest of the sentence. This phrasing pattern is consistent with the definition of the Phonological Phrase, which is conditioned by XP edges (in this case, a right XP edge). Tumbuka also provides evidence for the Intonational Phrase. The Intonational Phrase is aligned, roughly, with a right clause edge. The penult of the Intonational Phrase is extra long, compared to the penult of a clause-internal Phonological Phrase, and the High tone of the sentence-final Phonological Phrase is realized at a lower pitch than the preceding High tones. We see, though, no systematic downstepping pattern lowering the pitch of High tones before the final High tone of the Intonational Phrase. These phenomena are illustrated in the pitch track in (7), which corresponds to the sentence in (6e):

(7)

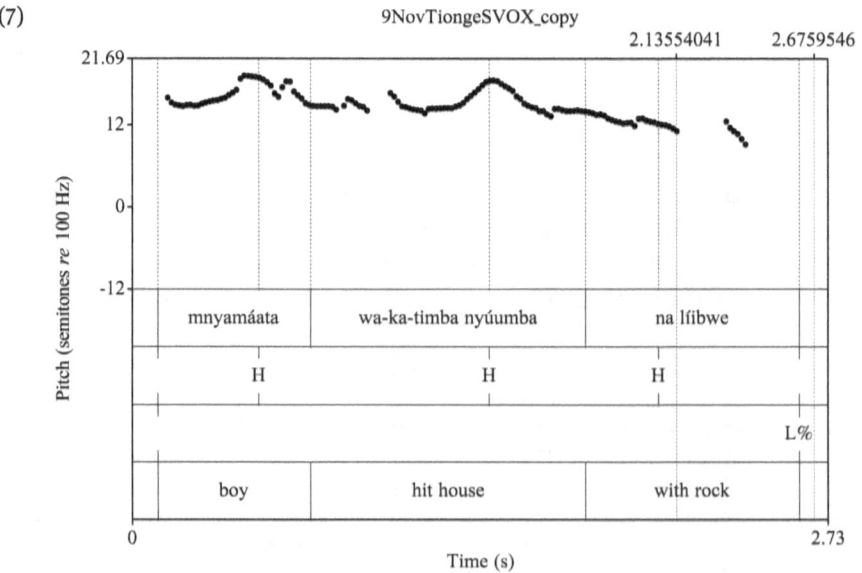

In the above example, the penult vowel durations are: 0.118 secs for *mnyamáata*; 0.120 secs for *nyúumba*; 0.162 secs for *líibwe*. (Short vowels are roughly 0.06 secs long.) Note that the Intonational Phrase-medial penults are similar in length, whereas the penult of the word in Intonational Phrase-final position is significantly longer. This difference is representative.

Intonational Phrase boundaries are also found at the right edges of initial Topics (8), of clefts (9), and of relative clauses or other subordinate clauses (10); '}' indicates the edge of an Intonational Phrase. I propose that these sentence-internal domains are Intonational Phrases rather than Phonological Phrases, as their right edges are typically marked by a continuation rise: i.e., a H% boundary tone, realized as a (super-)High tone on the final syllable of the phrase:

(8) Topics (Downing 2011a)
   Canonical order
   a. {(ŵáana)} {(ŵa-ku-timba bóola)}
      2.child   2SBJ-TAM-kick 9-ball
      'The children are kicking a ball.'

   Sentence initial topic
   b. {(bóola)} {(ŵáana) (ŵa-ku-yi-tíimba)}
      9-ball   2.child   2SBJ-TAM-9OBJ-kick
      '[As for] the ball, the children are kicking it.'
      [Context: Had been talking about the ball.]

(9) Clefts – copula is *ni/ndi-* (Downing 2010b)
   a. Q 'It is which dog that bit the thief?'
        {(Ni ntcheŵe njíi)}   {(iyo yi-ka-luma   mu-nkhúungu)}
         COP 9.dog   9.which   9.REL 9SBJ-TAM-bite 1-thief

      A1 'It is our big dog that bit the thief.'
         {(Ni ntcheŵe y-ithu yi-kúuru)} {(iyo yi-ka-luma   mu-nkhúungu)}
          COP 9.dog   9-our 9-big   9.REL 9sbj-tam-bite 1-thief

   OR A2 'Our big dog is the one that bit the thief.'
         {(Ntcheŵe y-ithu yi-kúuru)} {(ndi-yo yi-ka-luma   mu-nkhúungu)}
          9.dog   9-our 9-big   COP-9   9SBJ-TAM-bite 1-thief

(10) Relative clauses (underlined) (Downing 2010b and elicitation notes)[7]
 a. 'The children who are sitting in the tree are eating bananas.'
    {(ŵ-ana aŵo ŵa-khala mu-khúuni)} ŵa-ku-lya ma-kóombwe)}
    2-child 2.REL 2SBJ.TAM-sit LOC-5.tree 2SBJ-TAM-eat 6-banana

 b. {(n-tcheŵe iyo m-nyamata wa-ka-yi-sáanga)}
    9-dog 9.REL 1-boy 1SBJ-TAM-9.OBJ-find
    yi-ka-zyeŵa mu-ma-thíipa)}
    1SBJ-TAM-be.lost LOC-6-mud
    'The dog which the boy found was lost in the swamp.'

 c. {(mwanalume uyo mwana wáakhe) m-sungwáana) wa-lwáala)}
    1.man 1.REL 1.child 1.his 1-girl 1SBJ.TAM-be.sick
    wa-ku-luta náayo) ku ci-patáala)}
    1SUBJ-TAM-go with.1 LOC 7-hospital
    'The man whose daughter is sick is going with her to the hospital.'

The H% at the right edge of a sentence-initial topic is illustrated by the pitch track on the right in (11b). The two pitch tracks in (11b) show two successive repetitions of the sentence in (11a). As we can see, the subject *amáama* 'woman' is pronounced as a neutral Phonological Phrase in the first repetition, but as a Topic Intonational Phrase, with an H%, in the second repetition. Note that the final Phonological Phrase in the sentence is lowered in pitch in both repetitions:

(11) a. (a-máama) (a-ku-pula ngóoma)
     2-woman 2SBJ-TAM-pound 9.maize
     'A woman is pounding maize.'

 b.

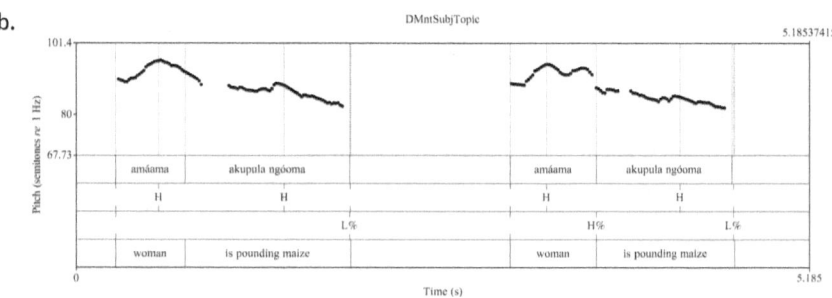

---

[7] Note in (10) that we do not always find the expected Phonological Phrase break following the subject of a relative clause. See Downing (2010b) for more detailed discussion and analysis of the phrasing of relative clauses in Tumbuka.

A continuation rise at the right edge of a relative clause is illustrated in (12) for the sentence given in (10c). Notice in (12) that the entire relative clause preceding the H% boundary tone is realized at a raised pitch register, and the final High tone within the relative clause has a raised pitch. The final Phonological Phrase in the sentence is, as usual, noticeably lowered in pitch.

(12)
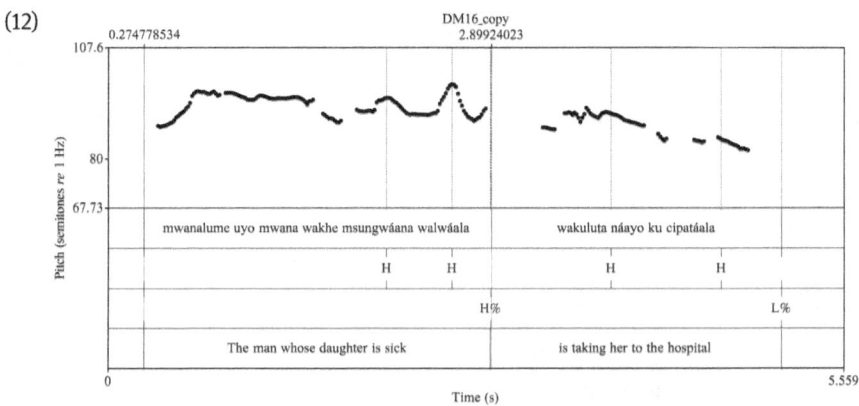

To sum up, Tumbuka prosody provides evidence for both Phononological Phrases and Intonational Phrases. The correlates of the Phonological Phrase are phrase penult lengthening and a High tone on the first mora of the lengthened penult. The correlates of the Intonational Phrase are additional phrase penult lengthening (especially sentence-finally) and boundary tones sentence-finally, as well as at the right edges of Topics, clefts and subordinate clauses. The distinction between Phonological Phrases and Intonational Phrases is nicely illustrated by the pitch track in (12), above. Each penult High tone cues a Phonological Phrase (indicated with parentheses, while the boundary tones cue the Intonational Phrases (indicated with curly brackets):

(13) {{(Mwanalume uyo mwana wakhe msungwáana)
 (wa-lwáala)H% } (wakuluta náayo) (ku cipatáala) L%}
 {{(The man whose daughter)
 (is sick)}(is taking her) (to the hospital) }

One does not find systematic downstepping within the Intonational Phrase. However, raised register in initial Topics and lowering of the final Phonological Phrase leads to a downward trending register within the Intonational Phrase. The fact that an entire phrase can have raised pitch shows that intonation can affect the pitch of more than just a syllable at a phrase boundary. The domain of influence of the boundary tones and other intonational tones in Tumbuka is a topic requiring further study.

3.2 Intonational Phrases in Chichewa

Kanerva's (1990) prosodic analysis of Chichewa also argues for two levels of phrasing in that language: the Phonological Phrase is the domain of penult lengthening and tone processes, as described in section 2.1, above. The Intonational Phrase is the domain of culminative penult lengthening – similar to what we find in Tumbuka – and downstep (= catathesis in Kanerva's terms). Kanerva, as was typical of his time, does not provide phonetic details of these correlates of the Intonational Phrase, but subsequent work confirms his observations. Myers' (1996, 1999a) careful phonetic study provides an analysis of downstep in Chichewa sentences. Downing & Pompino-Marschall's (2013) phonetic analysis demonstrates that the penult vowel of an Intonational Phrase-final word is significantly longer than sentence-internal lengthened penults.

More problematic is the claim that there are two levels of phrasing in Chichewa. If this were so, then we would expect sentences with similar syntactic structure in Chichewa and Tumbuka to be phrased similarly. However, we have seen that this is not the case. Subject noun phrases are always parsed into a prosodic phrase in Tumbuka. However, as shown by the data in (2), subjects only form separate prosodic phrases in Chichewa when they are topicalized. In Tumbuka, if a verb is followed by two complements, only the first one phrases with the verb. The second one phrases separately. However, as shown in Chichewa, both postverbal complements phrase with the verb: compare the Chichewa phrasing in (1d) with the phrasing of the equivalent Tumbuka sentence in (6e). This is the essential problem to be accounted for in any analysis of Chichewa prosodic phrasing: the Phonological Phrase which includes the VP is bigger than we expect because there is no phrase break following the first complement of the verb. The prosodic algorithm must therefore optimize a Phonological Phrase break setting off subject and topic noun phrases, yet it must not optimize a Phonological Phrase break following noun phrases internal to the verb phrase. Truckenbrodt's (1995, 1999) well-known WRAP constraint is a mechanism for achieving this. WRAP penalizes breaking the verb phrase into more than one Phonological Phrase.

Downing & Mtenje (2011a, b) show, however, that WRAP predicts the incorrect phrasing when the first complement of a verb is modified by a relative clause. The verb plus the modified first complement plus a following complement should be WRAP-ed into a single Phonological Phrase. What we find instead is a prosodic phrase break following the relative clause.

(14) Phrasing of relative clauses violates WRAP; relative clause is underlined
(Downing & Mtenje 2011b)
a. ((Ma-kóló a-na-pátsíra mwaná a-méné
   6.parent 6SBJ-TAM-give 1.child 1-REL

   á-ná-wa-chezéera) ndalámá zá mú-longo wáake)
   1SBJ-TAM-6OBJ-visit 10.money 10.of 1-sister 1.her
   'The parents gave [the child who visited them] money for her sister.'

cf.
b. (Ma-kóló a-na-pátsíra mwaná ndalámá zá mú-longo wáake)
   6-parent 6SBJ-PST1-give 1.child 10.money 10.of 1-sister 1.her
   'The parents gave the child money for her sister.'

c. (Ti-ku-gáníza kutí m-nyamatá á-pézá galú
   we-TAM-think that 1-boy 1SBJ.TAM-find 1.dog

   a-méné á-ná-mu-sowéetsa) ku dáambo)
   1-REL 1SBJ-TAM-1OBJ-lose LOC 5.swamp
   'We think the boy will find [the dog which he lost] at the swamp.'

cf.
d. (Subj) (VP) Kanerva (1990: 103, fig (114b))
   (Mwaána) (a-na-pézá galú kú dáambo])
   1.child 1SBJ-PST1-find 1.dog LOC 5.swamp
   'The child found the dog at the swamp.'

Kanerva (1990) and Downing & Mtenje (2011a,b) show that all embedded complement clauses, including *think/say* clauses, phrase with what precedes in Chichewa. A break comes only at the end of the most deeply embedded clause:

(15) Embedded and recursive clauses (underlined) (Downing & Mtenje 2011a,b)
a. (Mu-nthu a-méné á-ná-bweréká búkhú
   1-man 1-REL 1SBJ-TAM-borrow 5.book

   li-méné ndí-ná-gulá ku Liloongwe) w-a-pita ku Mzúuzu)
   5-REL I-TAM-buy LOC Lilongwe 1S BJ-TAM-leave LOC Mzuzu
   'The man who borrowed the book which I bought in Lilongwe has moved to Mzuzu.'

b. (Mu-nthu a-méné á-ná-néná kutí m-balá
   1-man 1-REL 1SBJ-TAM1-say that 9-thief

   i-ná-bá ndaláama) a-ná-thaawa)
   9SBJ-TAM-steal 10.money 2SBJ-TAM-run.away
   'The man who said that the thief stole some money ran away.'

c. (Mu-nthu a-na-néná kutí m-balá i-méné
   1-man 1SBJ-TAM-say that 9-thief 9-REL
   í-ná-bá ndaláama) i-na-tháawa)
   9SBJ-TAM-steal 10.money 9SBJ-TAM-run.away
   'The man said that the thief who stole the money ran away.'

This range of data shows that prosodic phrases can be quite large in Chichewa, as they regularly right-align with clauses (phases), rather than XPs (e.g., noun phrases).

I propose, then, that Chichewa prosodic phrases are best characterized as Intonational Phrases, rather than Phonological Phrases. By definition, this is the level of prosodic phrasing that aligns with the syntactic clause (or the phase). Furthermore, boundary tones often coincide with the right edge of the prosodic phrase, as is expected for Intonational Phrases but not for Phonological Phrases. For example, similar to Tumbuka, we find a continuation rise at the right edge of a relative clause. Note in (16) that the words which end each of the Intonational Phrases – *kusáamba* 'swim' and *mtsíinje* 'river' – have the same tone pattern: a HL on the lengthened penult syllable. But the final vowel of *kusáamba* rises in pitch, while the final vowel of *mtsíinje* falls in pitch. Notice, too, that High tones undergo downdrift, with the final High-toned string considerably lowered in pitch, typically barely rising above the level of a preceding Low tone:

(16)

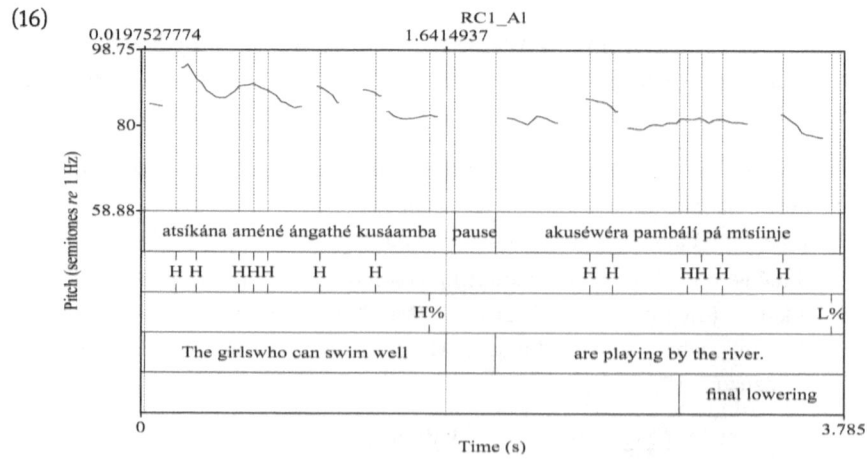

Also similar to Tumbuka, we find a continuation rise following an initial Topic (in this case, a topicalized subject):

(17)
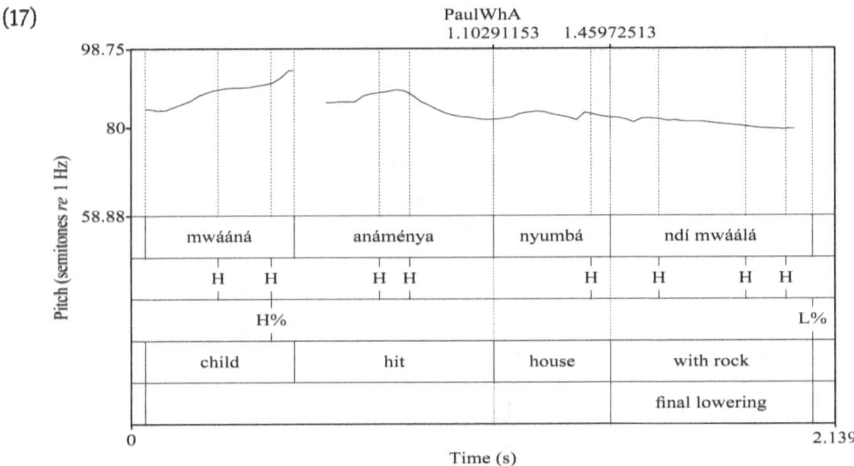

To sum up, we find no strong evidence for a distinction between Intonational Phrase and Phonological Phrase in Chichewa. Prosodic phrasing only seems to motivate an Intonational Phrase level, as phrasing targets clause edges and right edges of initial Topics. (See Connell and Rialland & Aborobongui, this volume, and Zerbian (2006) for discussion of other languages lacking a distinction between Intonational Phrase and Phonological Phrase.) How then, can we define the domain for downstep and culminative penult lengthening, the correlates of Kanerva's (1990) Intonational Phrase? Following work like Itô & Mester (2012, 2013) and Selkirk (2009, 2011), I propose that recursive levels of phrasing can help us avoid multiplying phrase level distinctions in the Prosodic Hierarchy. Adopting this view, Chichewa has recursive Intonational Phrasing and distinguishes a minimal and maximal Intonational Phrase. The maximal Intonational Phrase corresponds to Kanerva's Intonational Phrase, while the minimal Intonational Phrase corresponds to his Phonological Phrase.

4 Intonation of questions and answers

In this section I survey the intonation of both yes-no questions and wh-questions and their answers. Since questions and answers are common contexts for eliciting focus, I briefly take up the (lack) of focus intonation in the final section.

4.1 Yes-no (choice) questions and answers

In both Chichewa and Tumbuka, yes-no questions have the same word order as declaratives. They often begin with a question-signaling word: *kodí* in Chichewa and *kasi* in Tumbuka. These points are illustrated in the examples below:

(18) a. Chichewa yes/no question
 (Koodí) (pali a-lakatuli améne á-ná-takása chidwí mwá íiwe)
 Q LOC-be 2-poet 2.REL 2SBJ-TAM-speed.up 7.motivation in you
 'Are there poets who speeded up your motivation?'

 b. Tumbuka yes/no question
 (Káasi), (ni dokotala péera) (uyo wa-ku-vwira mu-sambíizi) (ku-sukúulúu)
 Q COP 1.doctor only (1.REL 1SBJ-TAM-help 1-teacher LOC-school
 'Does only the doctor help the teacher at the school?'

As Downing (2011b) shows, we find a special intonation prosody for yes-no question in both languages, namely, an obligatory rise-fall over the final two syllables of the Intonational Phrase. This is illustrated in the pitch tracks on the next page. Note that downstep is suspended in Chichewa yes-no questions:

(19) Yes-no question intonation in Chichewa

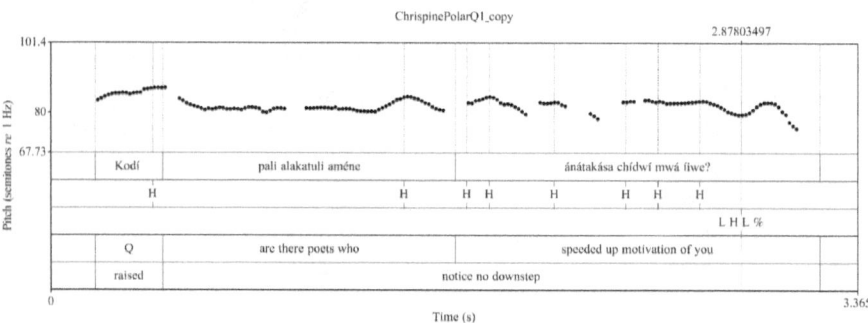

(20) Yes-no question intonation in Tumbuka

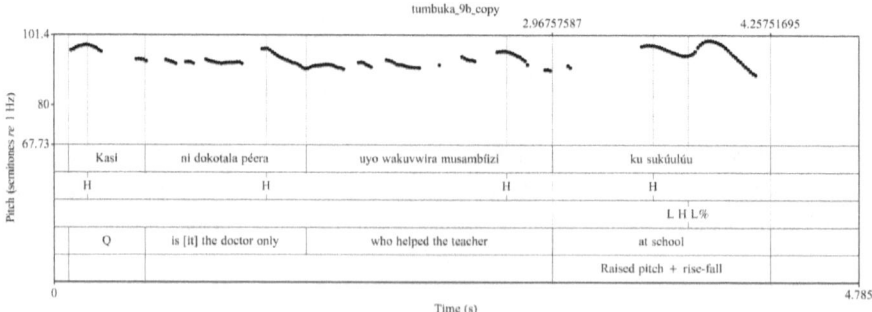

To put these intonation patterns in a wider perspective, a rise-fall melody over the last two syllables of a yes/no question is described for other E. Bantu languages, like Swahili (Ashton 1947). An overall raise in pitch has also been described for yes/no questions in other Bantu languages, like Jita (Downing 1996), as well as N. Sotho (Zerbian 2006) and several other languages discussed in this volume. In fact, cross-linguistically raised pitch is described as common in yes/no questions (Cruttenden 1997; Gussenhoven 2004).

In choice questions, the question prosody is realized only on the first choice in both languages. The rise-fall melody is sometimes truncated in alternate questions in Chichewa, as illustrated in the pitch track on the next page. The second choice undergoes pitch lowering:

(21) a. Chichewa choice question
(Mu-ku-fúná   khóofíí) (kapéná thíiyi)
you.pl-TAM-want coffee   or   tea
'Do you want coffee or tea?'

b. Tumbuka choice question[8]
(M-nyamáta wa-ka-sanga n-chewê ya-ku-zyéewâa)
1-boy   1SBJ-TAM-find 9-dog   9.of-INF-be lost
(panyákhe m-buzi ya-ku-zyéewa) (mu-ma-thíipha)
or   9-goat 9.of-INF-be lost LOC-6-swamp
'Did the boy find a lost dog or a lost goat in the swamp?'

c. Pitch track for Chichewa choice question in (a)

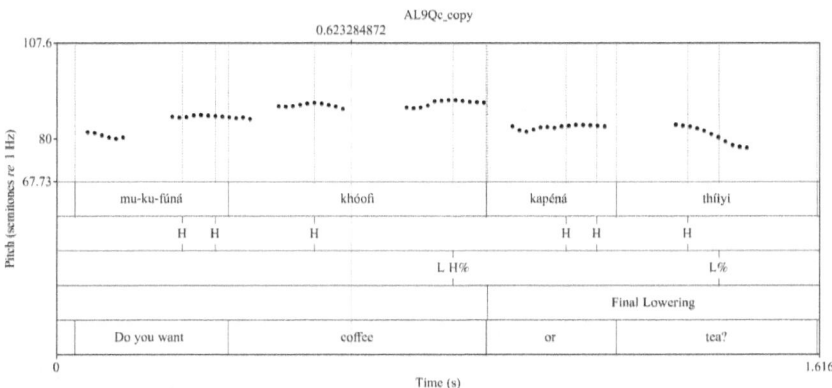

---

8 Strikingly, the phrase break and position of penult lengthening in this choice question does not highlight the words in focus (e.g. the word for 'dog' and the word for 'goat'). Instead, the Phonological Phrase aligns, as usual, with the right edge of XP. See Downing (2008) and Downing & Pompino-Marschall (2013) for detailed discussion of the problems these data pose for theories of focus prosody.

The question arises, for Chichewa, of how the yes-no question intonation melody interacts with lexical tone in the last two syllables. As shown in the examples below, the full rise-fall melody is only realized if the last two syllables of the word are low-toned. If a High tone is found within that two-syllable window, the melody is simplified. This is illustrated the examples below:

(22) Comparison of Intonational Phrase final tone patterns, Affirmative vs. Yes/No Q (Downing 2013)

Affirmative   *Yes/No Q*
a. ... tébuulo   'table'   ... tébuúlóo?
'No, FATHER has made a table.' Answering,
'Have the CHILDREN made a table?'

b. ... mpaando 'chair'   ... mpaándóo?

c. ... aáná   'children' ... áánáa?

d. ... búuku   'book'   ... búukúu?

The contrast transcribed in (22a) is illustrated by the pitch tracks in (23):

(23) ... tébuúlóo?

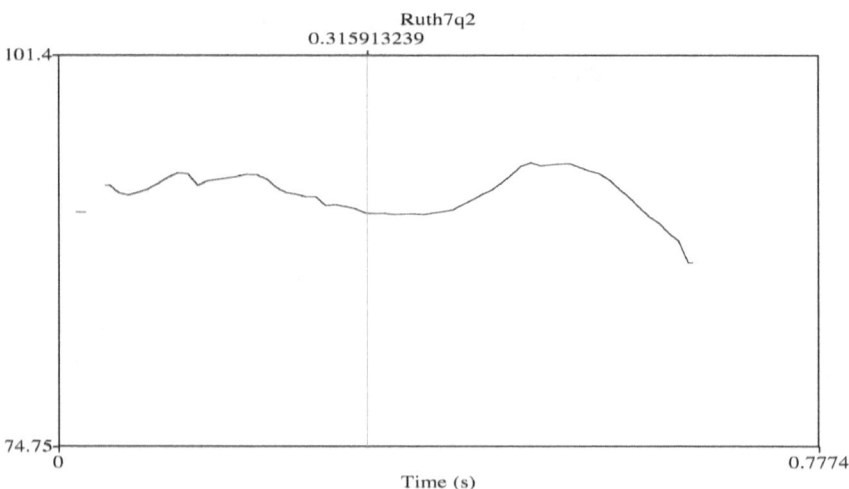

... tébuulo.

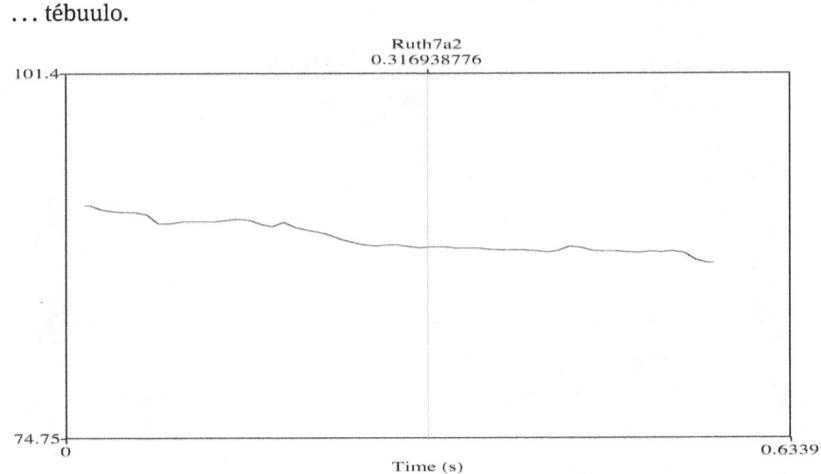

The answers to yes-no questions would, in normal conversation, usually be simple one-word answers. If complete sentence answers are elicited, they have the same intonation as normal declaratives.

4.2 WH-questions (content questions) and answers

In Wh-questions, in contrast, we find no obligatory question melody in either language, though the overall pitch is raised somewhat compared to statements.[9] This is illustrated in the pitch track in (24c) on the next page for Chichewa:

(24) Wh-questions in Tumbuka and Chichewa
    a. Tumbuka Wh-question/answer pair; ')' indicates Phonological Phrase
        Q (U-ka-mu-gulira   njáani)   (mango ya ŵíisi) (ku-gorosáari)
           you-TAM-1OBJ-buy.for 1.who   9.mango 9.of unripe LOC-grocery
          'Who did you buy the green mangoes for at the shop?'

        A (N-kha-mu-gulira   mu-nyáane) (mango ya ŵíisi) (ku-gorosáari)
          I-TAM-1OBJ-buy for   1-my friend 9.mango 9.of unripe LOC-grocery
          'I bought green mangoes for my friend at the shop.'

---

[9] Other languages discussed in this volume also demonstrate no special intonation for constituent-questions. See Myers (1996) for further discussion of Chichewa question intonation, and see Downing 2011b for discussion of the position of Wh-words in both Chichewa and Tumbuka.

b. Chichewa Wh-question/answer pair; '{' indicates Intonational Phrase
Q {mwaáná a-ná-ménya chiyáani} ndí mw-áálá}
   1.child 1SBJ-TAM-hit what   with rock
   'What did s/he hit with the rock?'

A {mwaáná {a-ná-ménya nyumbá ndí mw-áálá}}
   1.child 1SBJ-TAM-hit house   with rock
   'S/he hit the house with the rock.'

c. Pitch track for (b)

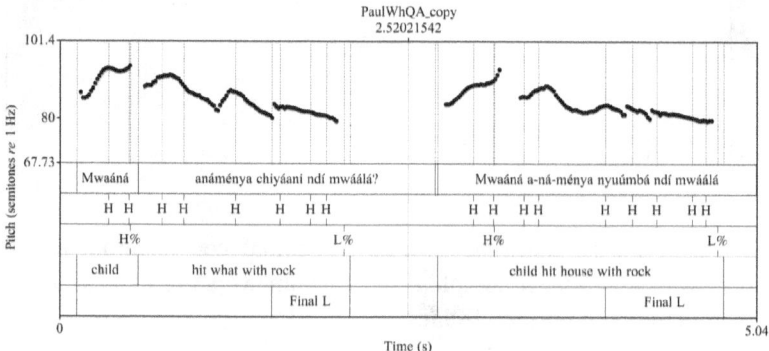

As we can see, we find downstep and final lowering in both wh-questions and in their answers. Non-subject wh-question words are not fronted and do not necessarily have special prosody in either Chichewa or Tumbuka. (Though there is some tendency to put a phrase break after a wh-word in Chichewa. See Downing & Mtenje 2011b for discussion.) In Tumbuka, there is, though, an optional raised (↑) register melody on a wh-question word when it appears in sentence-final (Intonational Phrase-final) position, and the final syllable of the wh-question word is also raised (though not quite as High as the penult syllable). This is illustrated in (25):

(25) a. {(Mu-ku-ŵa-vwira   ŵa-zimáayi) (ku-phika ↑ víí!cíí)}
        you.pl-TAM-2OBJ-help 2-woman   INF-cook 8.what
        'What are you helping the women to cook?'

   b. Pitch track for (a):

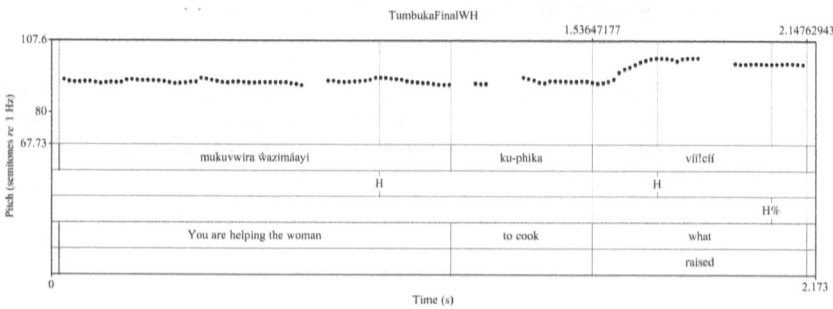

4.3 Focus and emphasis

Neither Tumbuka nor Chichewa has focus prosody, as Downing & Pompino-Marschall (2013) and Downing (2012) have argued in some detail. However, both have what Downing & Pompino-Marschall term 'emphasis' prosody. The register of a word or phrase can be raised to highlight that word. We can see one example of this in (25b), above, where the Tumbuka wh-question word has been emphasized by raising its pitch.

Downing et al. (2004) document emphasis prosody on phrases in focus for one variety of Chichewa, as shown in the data in (26). (The upward arrows in the data indicate register raising on the preceding Phonological Phrase, '||' indicates optional measurable pause.)

(26) Focus and phrasing in one variety of Chichewa (Downing et al. 2004)
    a. /A-ná-meny-a   nyumbá ndí   mw-alá/
       2SBJ-TAM-hit-FV 9.house with 3-rock
       'S/he hit the house with a rock.'

    b. (A-ná-mény-a nyumbá ndí mw-áálá).   (broad VP focus)

    c. Q (A-ná-ménya nyuúmbá) (ndí mw-áálá) (kapéná ndí ndoodo)?
       'Did s/he hit the house with a rock or with a stick?'

       A (A-ná-mény-a nyuúmbá) (ndí mw-áálá) ↑.   (Oblique PP focus)

    d. Q (A-ná-ménya chiyáani) (ndí mw-áálá)?
       'What did s/he hit with the rock?'

       A (A-ná-mény-a nyuúmbá) ↑ || (ndí mw-áálá).   (Object NP focus)

    e. Q (Nyuúmba) (i-ná-táá-ní)?
       'What happened to the house?'

       A (A-ná-méeny-a) ↑ (nyuúmbá) (ndí mwáálá).   (V focus)

As Downing & Pompino-Marschall (2013) argue, the difference between focus and emphasis is that focus is an obligatory grammatical category. Emphasis (prosody) is paralinguistic: gradiently realized in a particular focus context only if the speaker so desires. In both Chichewa and Tumbuka, emphasis prosody is realized with optional prosodic phrasing, and, in addition, with pause and/or pitch span expansion setting off words under emphasis. The pitch tracks in (27) illustrate emphasis intonation for the Chichewa data in (26):

(27)

cf. (26b)

cf. (26c)

cf. (26d)

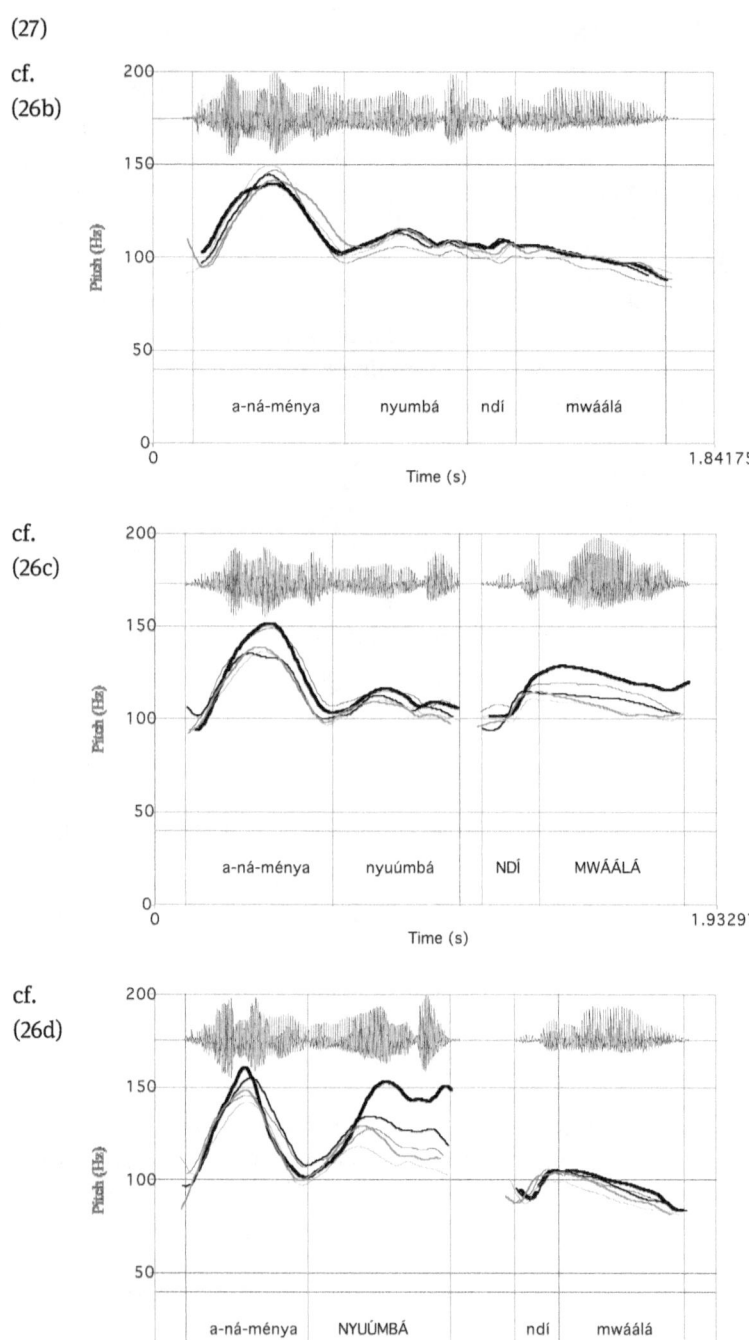

cf.
(26e)

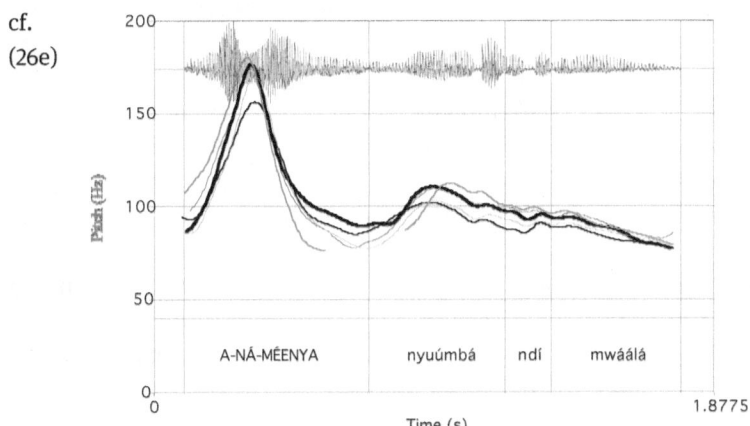

Downing's (2012) recent survey shows that, in fact, focus prosody is not commonly attested in African languages. In this volume, absence of focus prosody is explicitly demonstrated in Makasso et al's study of Basaa. In contrast, the chapters by Kisseberth, Kügler and Patin, this volume, show that focus (and/or emphasis) can affect prosody in some African languages, while Rialland & Aborobongui, this volume, thoughtfully distinguish the effect of focus and emphasis on Embosi prosody.

5 Interaction of tone and intonation: concluding remarks

This chapter has compared the tone and intonation of Chichewa and Tumbuka. The commonalities are striking, since the lexical prosodic systems of the two languages are quite different. This raises the question of whether phenomena like the continuation rise, register raising for emphasis, lowering of a final phrase and question prosody for yes-no questions but not wh-questions are areal phenomena. Is the similar yes-no question prosody in the two languages are more narrow areal phenomena? Further study is needed to shed light on these issues.

To place the languages in a broader typological perspective, Hyman & Monaka (2011) has proposed that three different types of interaction of intonational and lexical tones follow from a sequential model of realization of intonational melodies: *Accommodation*: the two minimally interact, and both are realized.

Submission: intonational tones override lexical tones. *Avoidance*: intonation is minimized. (See Connell, this volume, for an example of a tone language that avoids intonation.) However, other work (e.g., Beckman 1995, Myers 1996, Pierrehumbert & Beckman 1988) proposes that an additional interaction – *Superposition* – is required to account for intonational tones that affect the pitch range or register of other tones in the representation. Intonation is not avoided or minimized in either Chichewa or Tumbuka, nor does intonation override lexical tones. This study of intonation instead has illustrated the importance of *accommodation* and *superposition*. Both languages have H% and L% boundary tones. The H% boundary tone is realized similar to a lexical (Chichewa) or phrasal (Tumbuka) High tone when it can be accommodated. Accommodation is possible when the final syllable of the Intonational Phrase is toneless. The yes-no question melodies also are accommodated: they adapt to the lexical or phrasal tones of the Intonational Phrase-final word, as shown in section 4. In contrast, the L% boundary tone is always superimposed: it has the effect, in both languages, of lowering the register of a final string. The H% can also be superimposed and have the effect of raising the nearest H tones. Register raising of a longer string is used for optional emphasis – of initial Topics, of wh-words (in Tumbuka), to highlight words in focus, and for other reasons of speaker choice. Disentangling the accommodation and superposition realizations of boundary tones must remain a topic of future research.

Acknowledgements

I would first of all like to thank the many native speakers of Chichewa and Tumbuka who have worked with me on their languages since I began in 2004. I am grateful to the Centre for Language Studies at the University of Malawi, and especially Pascal Kishindo and Hilton Madona, for their hospitality and support during my fieldwork. I am grateful to Lisa Cheng, Al Mtenje, Bernd Pompino-Marschall and Annie Rialland for many hours of inspiring discussion and co-operation in analyzing aspects of the data reported on here. I thank Larry Hyman, Shin Ishihara, Tomas Riad and members of the BantuPsyn working group for comments on the work as it has developed over a number of presentations. I thank Caroline Féry and Annie Rialland for a careful reading of this chapter. All remaining errors of fact or interpretation are my responsibility.

References

An, Duk-Ho. 2007. Clauses in noncanonical positions at the syntax-phonology interface. *Syntax* 10, 38–79.
Ashton, E. O. 1947. *Swahili Grammar (including Intonation)*. 2nd edition. London: Longmans.
Beckman, Mary E. 1995. Local shapes and global trends. *Proceedings of ICPhS 95 Stockholm*, vol. 2, pp. 100–107.
Bresnan, Joan & Jonni Kanerva. 1989. Locative inversion in Chichewa: a case study of factorization in grammar. *Linguistic Inquiry* 20, 1–50.
Bresnan, Joan & Sam Mchombo. 1987. Topic, pronoun and agreement in Chichewa. *Language* 63, 741–782.
Cheng, Lisa L.-S. & Laura J. Downing. 2009. Where's the topic in Zulu? In: Helen de Hoop, & Geertje van Bergen, (Eds.), *Special issue on Topics Cross-linguistically, The Linguistic Review* 26, 207–238.
Cheng, Lisa L.-S. & Laura J. Downing. 2016. Phasal syntax = cyclic phonology? *Syntax* 19 (2), 159–191.
D'Imperio, M., G. Elordieta, S. Frota, P. Prieto & M. Vigário. 2005. Intonational Phrasing in Romance: The role of prosodic and syntactic structure. In S. Frota, M. Vigário & M. J. Freitas (eds.), *Prosodies*. Phonetics & Phonology Series. Berlin: Mouton de Gruyter, 59–97.
Doke, Clement M. 1954. *The Southern Bantu Languages*. London: Oxford University Press for the International African Institute.
Downing, Laura J. 1996. *The Tonal Phonology of Jita*. Munich: Lincom Europa.
Downing, Laura J. 2006. The prosody and syntax of focus in Chitumbuka. *ZAS Papers in Linguistics* 43, 51–75.
Downing, Laura J. 2008. Focus and prominence in Chichewa, Chitumbuka and Durban Zulu. *ZAS Papers in Linguistics* 49, 47–65.
Downing, Laura J. 2010a. Accent in African languages. In Rob W.N. Goedemans, Harry G. van der Hulst & Ellen A. van Zanten (eds.), *Word Prosodic Systems in the Languages of the World*. Berlin: Mouton de Gruyter, 381–427.
Downing, Laura J. 2010b. Prosodic Phrasing in Relative Clauses: A Comparative Look at Zulu, Chewa and Tumbuka. In Karsten Legère & Christina Thornell (eds.), *Bantu Languages: Analyses, Description and Theory* (East African Languages and Dialects, 20). Köln: Rüdiger Köppe, 17–29.
Downing, Laura J. 2011a. The prosody of 'dislocation' in selected Bantu languages. In Leston Buell, Kristina Riedel & Jenneke van der Wal (eds.), Special issue on *Movement and Word Order in Bantu, Lingua* 121, 772–786.
Downing, Laura J. 2011b. Wh-questions in Chewa and Tumbuka: positions and prosodies. In Laura J. Downing (ed.), *Questions in Bantu Languages: Prosodies and Positions. ZASPiL* 55.
Downing, Laura J. 2012. On the (non-)congruence of focus and prominence in Tumbuka. In Nikki Adams, Michael Marlo, Tristan Purvis & Michelle Morrison (eds.), *Selected Proceedings of the 42nd Annual Conference on African Linguistics*. Somerville, MA: Cascadilla Proceedings Project, 122–133.
Downing, Laura J. 2013. Rethinking the Universality of the Stress-Focus Correlation. In Karsten Legère (ed.), *Bantu Languages and Linguistics: Papers in Memory of Dr. Rugatiri D. K. Mekacha*. Bayreuth African Studies, vol. 91. Bayreuth: BASS, 47–67.
Downing, Laura J. & Al Mtenje. 2011a. Prosodic phrasing of Chichewa relative clauses. *Journal of African Languages and Linguistics* 32, 65–111.

Downing, Laura J. & Al Mtenje. 2011b. Un-Wrap-ing prosodic phrasing in Chichewa. In Nicole Dehé, Ingo Feldhausen & Shinichiro Ishihara (eds.), Special issue on *The Phonology-Syntax Interface*, *Lingua* 121 (13), 1965–1986.

Downing, L. J., A. Mtenje & B. Pompino-Marschall. 2004. Prosody and information structure in Chichewa. *ZAS Papers in Linguistics* 37, 167–186.

Downing, Laura J. & Bernd Pompino-Marschall. 2013. The focus prosody of Chichewa and the Stress-Focus constraint: a response to Samek-Lodovici (2005). *NLLT* 31, 647–681.

Gussenhoven, Carlos. 2004. *The Phonology of Tone and Intonation*. Cambridge: Cambridge University Press.

Gussenhoven, Carlos. 2006. Between stress and tone in Nubi word prosody. *Phonology* 23, 193–223.

Hyman, Larry M. 2006. Word-prosodic typology. *Phonology* 23, 225–257.

Hyman, Larry M. 2014. Do all languages have word accent? In Harry van der Hulst (ed.), *Word Stress: Theoretica nd Typological Issues*. Cambridge: Cambridge University Press, 56–82.

Hyman, Larry M. & Kemmonye C. Monaka. 2011. Tonal and non-tonal intonation in Shekgalagari. In Sónia Frota, Gorka Elordieta & Pilar Prieto (eds.), *Prosodic Categories: Production, Perception and Comprehension*. Dordrecht: Springer, 267–289.

Hyman, Larry M. & Al Mtenje. 1999. Prosodic Morphology and tone: the case of Chichewa. In René Kager, Harry van der Hulst and Wim Zonneveld, (eds.). *The Prosody-Morphology Interface*. Cambridge: Cambridge University Press, 90–133.

Itô, Junko and Armin Mester. 2012. Recursive prosodic phrasing in Japanese. In T. Borowsky, S. Kawahara, T. Shinya and M. Sugahara (eds.), *Prosody Matters*. Sheffield: Equinox Publishing, 280–303.

Itô, Junko and Armin Mester. 2013. Prosodic subcategories in Japanese. *Lingua* 124, 20–40.

Kanerva, Jonni M. 1990. *Focus and Phrasing in Chichewa Phonology*. New York: Garland.

Kisseberth, Charles W. 2010. Phrasing and relative clauses in Chimwiini. *ZASPiL* 53, 109–144.

Kisseberth, Charles W. & David Odden. 2003. Tone. In Derek Nurse & Gérard Philippson (eds.), *The Bantu Languages*. London: Routledge, 59–70.

Moto, Francis. 1989. *Phonology of the Bantu Lexicon*. Ph.D. dissertation, University College London.

Mtenje, Al. 1986. *Issues in the Nonlinear Phonology of Chichewa*. Ph.D. dissertation, University College London.

Mtenje, Al. 1987. Tone shift principles in the Chichewa verb: a case for a tone lexicon. *Lingua* 72, 169–209.

Myers, Scott. 1996. Boundary tones and the phonetic implementation of tone in Chichewa. *SAL* 25, 29–60.

Myers, Scott. 1998. Surface underspecification of tone in Chichewa. *Phonology* 15, 367–391.

Myers, Scott. 1999a. Downdrift and pitch range in Chichewa intonation. *Proceedings of ICPhS99*, 1981–1984.

Myers, Scott. 1999b. Tone association and f_0 timing in Chichewa. *SAL* 28, 215–239.

Myers, Scott & Troi Carleton. 1996. Tonal transfer in Chichewa. *Phonology* 13, 39–72.

Myrberg, Sara. 2013. Sisterhood in prosodic branching. *Phonology* 30, 73–124.

Nespor, Marina & Irene Vogel. 1986. *Prosodic Phonology*. Dordrecht: Foris.

Odden, David. 1988. Predictable tone systems in Bantu. In Harry van der Hulst & Norval Smith (eds.), *Autosegmental Studies on Pitch Accent*. Dordrecht: Foris, 225–251.

Odden, David. 1999. Typological issues in tone and stress in Bantu. In Shigeki Kaji (ed.), *Cross-linguistic Studies of Tonal Phenomena: Tonogenesis, Typology, and Related Topics*. Tokyo: ILCAA, 187–215.

Philippson, Gérard. 1998. Tone reduction vs. metrical attraction in the evolution of Eastern Bantu tone systems. In Larry M. Hyman & Charles W. Kisseberth (eds.), *Theoretical Aspects of Bantu Tone*. Stanford, Calif.: CSLI, 315–329.

Pierrehumbert, Janet & Mary E. Beckman. 1988. *Japanese Tone Structure*. Cambridge, MA: The MIT Press.

Prieto, Pilar. 2005. Syntactic and eurythmic constraints on phrasing decisions in Catalan. *Studia Linguistica* 52, 194–222.

Schadeberg, Thilo C. 1973. Kinga: a restricted tone system. *Studies in African Linguistics* 4: 23–46.

Selkirk, Elisabeth O. 1986. On derived domains in sentence phonology. *Phonology Yearbook* 3, 371–405.

Selkirk, Elisabeth O. 2009. On clause and intonational phrase in Japanese: the syntactic grounding of prosodic constituent structure. *Gengo Kenkyu* 136, 35–74.

Selkirk, Elisabeth O. 2011. The syntax-phonology interface. In: J. Goldsmith, J. Riggle & A. Yu (eds.), *The Handbook of Phonological Theory*, 2nd edition. Oxford: Wiley-Blackwell, 435–484.

Truckenbrodt, Hubert. 1995. Phonological Phrases: their relation to syntax, focus and prominence. PhD dissertation, MIT.

Truckenbrodt, Hubert. 1999. On the relation between syntactic phrases and phonological phrases. *Linguistic Inquiry* 30, 219–255.

Truckenbrodt, Hubert. 2005. A short report on Intonation Phrase boundaries in German. *Linguistische Berichte* 203, 273–296.

Vail, Hazen Leroy. 1972. *Aspects of the Tumbuka Verb*. Ph.D. dissertation, University of Wisconsin.

Zerbian, Sabine. 2007. Phonological phrasing in Northern Sotho (Bantu). *The Linguistic Review* 24, 233–262.

Sabine Zerbian
Sentence intonation in Tswana (Sotho-Tswana group)

Abstract: The topic of sentence intonation in the languages of the world has received considerable attention in the past years (e.g. Frota & Prieto 2015; Jun 2005, 2014). This chapter presents a first investigation of sentence intonation in Tswana, a Southern Bantu language with two lexical tones. It is based on a review of scholarly sources of the language and its neighbours as well as on own elicitation work with different speakers. The conclusion is reached that penultimate lengthening and overall pitch range modulation are strong cues to sentence mode (declarative versus yes/no-question). Declarative sentences end in a low (L%) or unspecified boundary (0%), sometimes accompanied by devoicing. Furthermore, partial reset occurs at clause and clause-internal boundaries. Lexical high tones are enhanced at certain sentence-internal boundaries, such as paused lists. Other than that, lexical and intonational tones do not interact in this language.

Keywords: downstep, declination, prosodic enhancement, OCP, Phonological Phrase, Intonational Phrase, focus, penultimate lengthening, pitch range expansion, High tone spread, ideophones

1 Introduction

Tswana (S31) is a language of the Southern Bantu Sotho-Tswana group (S30). The languages of this group are spoken in South Africa, Botswana, and Lesotho. They are closely related and mutually intelligible. The group consists of Tswana (S31), Northern Sotho (S32), and Southern Sotho (S33). Lozi (K21), spoken at the border of Zambia and Botswana, is sometimes also counted to this group (Gowlett 2003). Tswana is South Africa's sixth most common home language, spoken by 8% of the total population, or just over 4 million people.

The Sotho-Tswana languages share with the other Bantu languages their rich agglutinative morphology and SVO word order. Like the majority of Bantu languages, the Sotho-Tswana languages are tonal. Their tone systems are relatively well-described (Tswana: Chebanne et al. 1997, Creissels 1998a, 1998b,

Sabine Zerbian, University of Stuttgart and University of the Witwatersrand, Johannesburg

DOI 10.1515/9783110503524-012

1999, 2000, Kisseberth & Mmusi 1990, Lets'eng 1994, Mmusi 1992, Cole & Moncho-Warren 2012; Northern Sotho: Lombard 1976, 1979, Monareng 1992, Zerbian 2006a, 2007a, Zerbian & Barnard 2009, 2010; Sesotho: Clements 1988, Khoali 1991, Kunene 1972).

The intonation system of Sotho-Tswana has received little attention. Single descriptions and studies exist on question intonation in Northern Sotho (Zerbian 2006b), on the effects of focus in Northern Sotho (Zerbian 2006c, 2007b), and most recently on non-tonal intonation in Shekgalagari, a Sotho-Tswana language close to Tswana (Hyman & Monaka 2011).

This chapter brings together the existing sources and enriches them with original research with the aim of presenting a first coherent picture of sentence intonation in Tswana. For the structures under consideration no striking differences were found between Tswana, Northern Sotho and Southern Sotho when working with informants of each of the languages. As only examples for Tswana will be presented, the generalisations illustrated here are only considered to hold for Tswana. Variation in sentence intonation is expected to emerge in cross-dialectal studies within the language group. This, together with quantitative studies on the intonational phenomena reported for Tswana (both from experiments as well as from corpora) remain an area for future research.

Both duration and pitch (comprising local pitch expansion as well as overall pitch range) are relevant acoustic parameters in sentence intonation in Tswana. For pitch, the description and analysis of intonation follows the Autosegmental-Metrical (AM) model of intonation (e.g. Ladd 1996, 2008). The AM theory analyses intonation contours as sequential tonal targets and thereby "provides the basis for describing pitch phonology in all languages in the same terms" (Ladd 2008: 156, 164, using the phrase "unity of pitch phonology"). The Sotho-Tswana languages are tone languages, i.e. that lexical tones already provide sequential tone targets. Therefore, the question is whether sentence intonation provides further tonal targets, and if so, what kinds of tone-intonation interactions are found between lexical and intonational targets.

Ladd (2008: 158) mentions three phenomena that have often been cited as intonational features in tone languages: (i) overall expansion or contraction of pitch range, (ii) modification of specific tones, and (iii) modification of overall contour shapes. The chapter shows that (i) and (ii) occur in Tswana: the pitch range is expanded for both high- and low-toned sequences in order to express the distinction of syntactically identical yes/no-questions versus statements, and clause-final low and high tones are modified by local pitch range expansion to express the distinction of completeness versus incompleteness. Ladd (2008: 158) argues that these two kinds of tone-intonation interaction are compatible with the assumption of sequential tonal phonology that underlies the AM approach. If used for paralinguistic meanings, pitch range expansion works identically in tonal and non-tonal languages. Phrase-final tone modification can be analysed as "the result of associating the final syllable with a sequence of the lexical tone and a [...] boundary tone" (Ladd 2008: 159). It will be shown in how far a modification of this view is necessary to account for the observations in Tswana.

The chapter is structured as follows: Section 2 presents the basic tonal grammar of Tswana, relating to the number of tonal contrasts (section 2.1) and basic tonal processes occurring at the lexical and phrasal level (section 2.2). Section 2.3 provides information concerning the data sources on which the current chapter is based. Section 3 presents the intonation of declarative sentences, its overall declination and downdrift (section 3.1), the marking of sentence-final boundaries (section 3.2) and sentence-internal phrase breaks (section 3.3). Section 4 illustrates the intonation of questions, whereas section 5 addresses intonation used for information structuring in Tswana. Section 6 addresses the occurrence of penultimate lengthening in other contexts than declaratives. Section 7 closes with a discussion of the interplay of tone and intonation in Tswana.

2 Tonal grammar of Tswana

2.1 Number of tonal contrasts and vowel length

Like most of the other Bantu languages, Sotho-Tswana languages are tone languages in which the specification of pitch is part of the lexical representation of at least some morphemes (Hyman 2006: 229). There are two surface level tones in Tswana, namely high (H) and low (L). Tone marks lexical distinctions as well as grammatical distinctions, as illustrated in (1) and (2) respectively. Tone is not marked in the orthography in Sotho-Tswana. Throughout the chapter, lexical high tones are marked by underlining, and surface tones are marked by acute accents. Low tones are left unmarked.[1]

(1) Lexical tone in Tswana (Cole & Moncho-Warren 2012)
    a.   *-bóna* (verb) – 'see'   *boná* (pronoun) – 'they'

    b.   *selopó* (noun) – 'trunk of elephant'   *selópo* (noun) – 'pillow-case'

    c.   *-lora* (verb) – 'burn to ashes'   *-lóra* (verb) – 'dream'

---

[1] All examples are given in Tswana standard orthography (Department of Education 1988), which does not distinguish the different vowel qualities of <e> and <o>. Linguistic resources on Tswana such as Chebanne et al. (1997) and Cole & Moncho-Warren (2012) do provide these distinctions.

Grammatical distinctions marked by tone can be observed e.g. on agreement markers, some of which are low-toned in the main clause but high-toned in subordinate clauses, as *re-* in (2a), or by different tone patterns (HH instead of LH) on the disyllabic verb stem *-reka* marking the same distinction, as in (2b). With low-toned verbs, such as *-dumela* in (2c), a grammatical high tone is inserted in the negative tense in addition to morphemic marking.

(2) Grammatical tone in Tswana (Cole & Moncho-Warren 2012: 122, 126)
    a. *re lema* ... – 'we are ploughing'   *ré̱ lémá* ... – 'we ploughing...'
    b. *ke ré̱ká* ... – 'I am buying'   *ké̱ reká̱* ... – 'I buying...'
    c. *ó dúmela* ... – 'he agrees...'   *ga á dumé̱lá* – 'he does not agree'

The Sotho-Tswana languages do not contrast vowel length. Vowel length is predictable in that long vowels only occur in the penultimate syllable of a phrase-final word (see section 2.2.1). Long syllables can have a falling tone (Cole & Moncho-Warren 2012: 66).

2.2 Basic tonal processes at word- and phrase-level

For many Bantu languages it has been argued that only high tones are underlyingly specified and low tones are inserted late in the derivation of surface tone patterns (Kisseberth & Odden 2003, Myers 1998). The asymmetry is motivated by the observation that high tones actively initiate tonal processes such as spread, shift and deletion, whereas vowels that bear low tones only undergo tonal processes that involve high tones. This section reviews the tonal processes that occur at the word-level (section 2.2.1) and at the phrase-level (section 2.2.2) when morphemes and words are strung together with their respective lexical and grammatical tone specifications.

2.2.1 Tonal processes at the word level

There are three tonal processes applying to high tones in words in Tswana. The first is High Tone Spread (HTS), which refers to the extension of a high tone from its underlying position to immediately adjacent syllables to its right. The exact number of syllables affected by High Tone Spread can differ between varieties of Sotho-Tswana and can also depend on the number of syllables in a verb stem, as shown in (3). For a study on the acoustic realization of High Tone Spread in Northern Sotho, see Zerbian & Barnard (2009).

(3) High Tone Spread in Sotho-Tswana
   a. Tswana: símólola – (to) start (but símólólela)
      (Cole & Moncho-Warren 2012: 101)

   b. Northern Sotho: kólóbetša – (to) baptize (Lombard 1976: 57)

   c. Southern Sotho: khúrúmetsa – (to) cover (Khoali 1991: 38)

At the same time, adjacent underlying high tones are avoided in the Sotho-Tswana varieties. This is known as the Obligatory Contour Principle (OCP; Leben 1973) which originally referred to underlying tone melodies but has later been extended to also refer to surface violations (McCarthy 1986, Yip 1988). It is the latter interpretation that is relevant in Tswana. Depending on the morpho-syntactic context and the variety, the following "repair" strategies can be observed in Tswana: fusion of two high tones or deletion. In (4a) and (4b), the two adjacent underlying high tones (marked by underlining) are both realised. Mmusi (1992) suggests an analysis according to which these separate high tones are fused representationally into one single tone. Note that also the high tones resulting from High Tone Spread are fused with the donor high tone in their tonal representation. In (4c), we observe a deletion of the verbstem-initial high tone. Mmusi's analysis suggests the delinking of the left branch of the spread high tone in order to avoid an OCP violation.

(4) OCP-violations: Tswana (Mmusi 1992: 70, 112, 93)[2]
   a. ó-réká nama (SC1-buy meat)   'S/he is buying meat.'
      H

   b. go-é-rékísa (SC15-OC9-sell)   'to sell it'
      H

   c. ó-ká-reká (SC1-ASP-buy)   'S/he is able to buy.'
      H_1 H_2

---

2 In the glosses, numbers refer to noun classes. Otherwise, the following abbreviations are used:

AGR	agreement,	OC	object concord,	QPART	question particle.		
COP	copula	PL	plural	INF	infinitive		
DEM	demonstrative	POSS	possessive	SC	subject concord	LOC	locative
NEG	negation	PST	past	SG	singular	ASP	aspect

The Obligatory Contour Principle also acts as a rule blocker for the application of High Tone Spread if spread was to create a violation of the OCP, as shown in (5).

(5) Lack of HTS due to OCP in Tswana (Mmusi 1992: 65)

ó-a-réká (SC1-ASP-buy)   *ó-á-réká   'S/he is buying.'
| ⩘
H₁ H₂

An extensive account of word-level tonology in Tswana has been provided by Chebanne et al. (1997) but depending on the theoretical framework further questions remain, e.g. why fusion does not apply in (4c). It does need not to concern us here as the analysis of word-internal tonal processes in Tswana is not of immediate relevance to the central topic of sentence intonation.

2.2.2 Phrasal processes

High Tone Spread does not only occur within words. It also is a phrase-level process in that it is observed to occur across word boundaries too, as in example (6a). In some instances though, it does not occur where it would be predicted, such as on the final syllable of the noun *mosádi* in (6b). One might argue that this is due to tonal context, as a high-toned agreement marker immediately follows the noun (yó). In (6c), however, the same tonal context allows High Tone Spread onto the final syllable of the noun. The alternation in (6b) and (6c) has been accounted for by phrasing (e.g. Khoali 1991 for Southern Sotho). In (6b), but not in (6c), a phrase-boundary has been argued to follow the noun. Phrase boundaries are indicated by parentheses in the examples. High Tone Spread does not apply to phrase-final syllables; they are exempt as targets. It is common in Bantu languages that domain-final syllables are exempt from phonological processes (Kisseberth & Odden 2003: 64).[3] This also accounts for the lack of High Tone Spread to the sentence-final syllable in (6d).

---

[3] An alternative analysis would be that HTS does take place and its result is overridden by a low boundary tone, resulting in a low surface tone. The alternatives need to be carefully weighed against each other. Decisive might be whether prosodic enhancement can be witnessed on the final syllable. A closer examination remains a topic for future research.

(6) High Tone Spread as phrasal process: Tswana (Cole & Moncho-Warren 2012: 93, 88, 89)
   a. (go bóná sétlhare) – to see a tree
   b. (mosádi) (yó móntle) – a beautiful woman
   c. (mosádí ó móntle) – The woman is beautiful.
   d. (Ke kopílé basádí go nthúsa). – I requested the women to help me.

The Obligatory Contour Principle (OCP) can be considered to not only be active in words but also in phrases. In words, it leads to deletion (see (4c) above), whereas in phrases, it leads to downstep. The term downstep describes the lowering of the second in a series of high tones (see also Introduction). Immediately adjacent underlying high tones which occur across word boundaries within a phonological phrase result in downstep (Kunene 1972, Khoali 1991 for Southern Sotho; Zerbian & Kügler 2015 for Tswana), as illustrated in (7a). Downstep is marked by means of an exclamation mark in (7). If high tones occur immediately next to each other across words and across phonological phrase boundaries, however, no downstep occurs (Zerbian & Kügler 2015 for a quantitative study on Tswana, Khoali 1991 for Southern Sotho).

(7) a. Downstep within phrases in Tswana – Parentheses indicate phrases
   (Barwá   !bá-thúsá   balemi)
   2.son   sc2-help   2.farmer
   'The sons help the farmers.'

   b. No downstep across phrases
   (Dinkú)   (tsá-!kgósí   ...)
   10.sheep   poss10-chief
   'The sheep of the chief...'   (*Dinkú) (!tsá ...)

Thus, High Tone Spread emerges as the central tonal rule in Tswana, both at the word- and at the phrase-level. It interacts with phrasing in that phrase-final syllables are exempt from serving as targets for High Tone Spread. Downstep, or rather its absence, is a further indicator for phrase boundaries. The question arises how to capture and characterise where the relevant phrase boundaries occur.

There is conflicting evidence in the Bantu literature on how many levels of phrasing should be assumed, what the phonetic cues to each of these levels are, and how their relation to syntax can be captured (see Zerbian 2007a: 257ff for a brief review; see also Introduction and Downing, this volume). The original proposal of the Prosodic Hierarchy (Nespor & Vogel 1986, Selkirk 1986) proposes two levels, namely the Phonological Phrase and the Intonation Phrase.

So far it seems that there is prosodic evidence for two levels in Tswana: a lower level where the finality restriction occurs and where downstep is absent between immediately adjacent high tones, and a higher level where in addition to the previous two cues boundary tones can occur. Prosodic cues for the lower phrase can be observed e.g. in noun-modifier sequences, whereas prosodic cues for the higher phrase can potentially occur e.g. between left-dislocated objects and a following subject noun (fig. 15), between clauses (figs. 6, 8, 9), and following non-final items in lists (fig. 16).

Indirect reference approaches to phrasing (e.g. Nespor & Vogel 1986, Selkirk 1986, Truckenbrodt 1995) work on the assumption that phrases are not isomorphous to syntactic constituents but can be derived from them: Phonological Phrases roughly correspond to lexical XPs (maximal lexical projections), and Intonation Phrases roughly correspond to root clauses. In most recent direct reference approaches, prosodic domains are defined as syntactic spell-out domains, which serve as a domain for the application of phonological processes (see Downing 2013 for a brief overview; Downing this volume for an analysis within this approach).

First analyses within indirect reference approaches can be found for Northern Sotho in Zerbian (2006c, 2007a) and for Southern Sotho in Khoali (1991). However, they only cover a subset of the contexts given here. Due to a similar phrasal structure in modified noun constructions in the Bantu language Bàsàá, work within the direct reference approach by Hamlaoui et al. (2014) is also relevant. Furthermore, Creissels (2009) suggests a construction-based account to the tonal alternations observed in nouns in Tswana. The development of a coherent analysis for the relation between syntax and Phonological Phrases and Intonation Phrases in Tswana clearly deserves further research.

In the following, all phrase-related prosody will be transcribed even if it is predictable from syntax: the application of the finality restriction is transcribed in the tone labels, and the occurrence of downstep (↓) or its absence (↑; discussed under the term "partial reset" in section 2.3.1) is transcribed in the intonational tier. It needs to be remembered though, that the only real pitch-related intonational features are the boundary tones, as they cannot be derived from syntax.

2.3 Data sources

The analyses provided in this chapter are based on literature on Sotho-Tswana and related languages (references are given where appropriate) as well as on own elicitation work. The speakers consulted were students of African languages and/or Linguistics at the University of the Witwatersrand, Johannesburg. They were 20–25 years old at the time of recording and born in places where the respective variety is the predominant variety (i.e. North-West Province for Tswana, Lesotho for Southern Sotho[4] and Limpopo Province for Sepedi). The speakers only moved to Johannesburg when starting their studies. Their parents' languages were Tswana, Southern Sotho and Sepedi respectively, and these were also the languages spoken at home. They consider themselves speakers of the standard variety of each language.

Sentences were constructed before the elicitation sessions took place, which were controlled for lexical tone. The sentences were discussed with the speakers concerning grammaticality before the speakers read them out from a sheet of paper on which the sentences were given without lexical tone marking as is convention in Sotho-Tswana orthography. In order to avoid confusion concerning intended sentence mode or semantic meaning, appropriate punctuation and an English translation were provided with the examples.

For most of the contexts presented in this section, three different sentences were constructed, which were read out three times (not immediately following each other), yielding nine repetitions per context. Given that the sentences were controlled for lexical tone but not for segmental context, a lot of micro-variation is found in the material, which precludes a quantitative analysis of the data. Only data from Tswana are presented here.

3 Intonation of declarative sentences

The presentation of intonation in Tswana starts out with the intonation in declarative sentences, where aspects of sentence intonation will be presented that apply to other sentence types as well.

3.1 Overall declination and downdrift

Declination is "the gradual, time-dependent downsloping of the fundamental frequency across points that might be expected to be equal" (Gussenhoven

---

[4] It is to be expected that Tswana as spoken in the North-West Province and the Free State as well as Southern Sotho as spoken in the Free State and Lesotho differ from each other, also in sentence intonation. Dialectal variation remains a topic for further investigation.

2004: 98). A distinction is made here between declination, downdrift, and downstep (cf. Introduction).

Declination refers to the realization of adjacent similar tones (either high or low) as gradually falling over the course of an utterance. *Downdrift* refers to the realization of high tones separated by intervening low tones as gradually falling with respect to each other. The absence of downdrift in e.g. Embosi (Rialland & Aborobongui, this volume) shows that it is a language-specific feature. The term *downstep*, introduced in (7) in section 2.2.2, is reserved for the downstepped realization of two immediately adjacent, underlying high tones within a phrase. It is labelled in the pitch tracks with a downward arrow (↓) throughout the chapter. Overall declination and downdrift are not specifically marked beyond this section.

Fig. 1 illustrates how a continuous decline in F0 can be observed for both high and low tones over the course of an utterance in Tswana (see also Cole & Moncho-Warren 2012: 30). Fig. 1 shows an all low-toned sentence (8a), an all high-toned sentence (8b), and a sentence in which high and low tones alternate (8c).[5] F0 decreases over the course of the utterance, most saliently in the case of high tones separated by intervening low tones in (8c). The grey line superimposed on the intonation contour indicates this declination, (8a), or downdrift, (8c). In (8b), the realization of adjacent high tones depends on the domain in which they occur: F0 first rises from the subject concord to the verb, and then drops considerably to the initial high-toned syllable of the following object.

(8) a. *Ke besa nama.*
   1st.SG roast meat
   'I am roasting meat.'

   b. *Bá bóná pódi.*
   3rd.PL see goat
   'They see a goat.'

   c. *Basádí ga sé barúti.*
   women NEG COP teachers
   'The women are not teachers.'

---

[5] Tone marking in all examples has been taken from Cole & Moncho-Warren (2012) unless indicated otherwise.

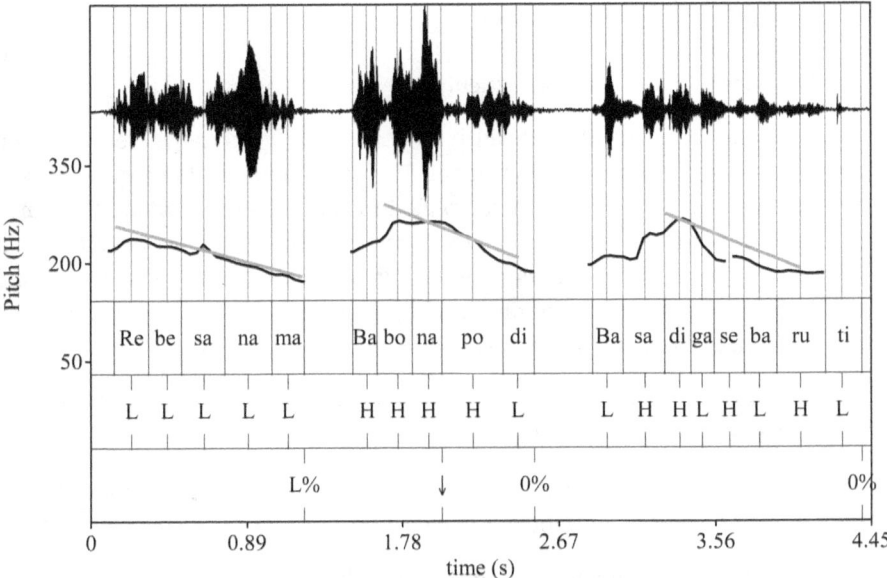

Figure 1: Declination and downdrift in Tswana (speaker LP, female)

The subject agreement marker and the following verb form, though written apart in Tswana orthography, form a phonological constituent, namely the phonological word. Adjacent high tones within this phonological constituent are realised with an increasing F0 (see Zerbian & Barnard 2010 for a controlled study on the acoustic realisation of adjacent high tones in the respective context in Northern Sotho). Verb and object form a prosodic phrase. Adjacent high tones across word boundaries within a phrase undergo downstep, as mentioned in section 2.2.2. Hence, a downstep is transcribed.

To summarize: Declination occurs over the course of an utterance in Tswana with both high and low tones, with the exception of high tones within a word. These rise in pitch in those contexts depicted above. Declination is most salient if low tones intervene between high tones (called downdrift in the Introduction and Rialland & Aborobongui, this volume).

The steepness of declination also depends on the sentence type, as the presentation of yes/no-questions in section 3.1 will show. It is an open question though, whether this is an automatic consequence of the expanded pitch range in these sentence types, or whether declination and downdrift are manipulated independently by the speaker. This seems to be the case in the variety of Chichewa studied in Myers (1996), where yes/no-questions have a less steep declination than statements. Declination and downdrift have received less attention in Bantu languages than they have in e.g. West African languages.

3.2 Sentence-final boundary

3.2.1 Non-tonal: penultimate lengthening

The most salient and best-described boundary cue in declarative sentences in Sotho-Tswana is not tonal but durational: The penultimate syllable of a phrase-final word is lengthened. This is exemplified in (9) for Tswana, where the same noun *malóme* – 'maternal uncle' occurs in sentence-initial subject position (9a), in sentence-medial object position (9b), and in sentence-final object position (9c). In these sentences, the duration of the penultimate syllable of the noun *malóme* changes from 189 ms in (9a), to 158 ms in (9b), to 278 ms in (9c).

(9) a. *Malómé ó rátá ngwaná.* – 'The uncle likes the child.'
    1.uncle sc1 like 1.child

b. *Mosádí ó fá malómé madí.* – 'The woman gives the uncle money.'
    1.woman sc1 give 1.uncle 6.money

c. *Baná bá rátá malómé.* – 'The children like the uncle.'
    2.child sc2 like 1.uncle

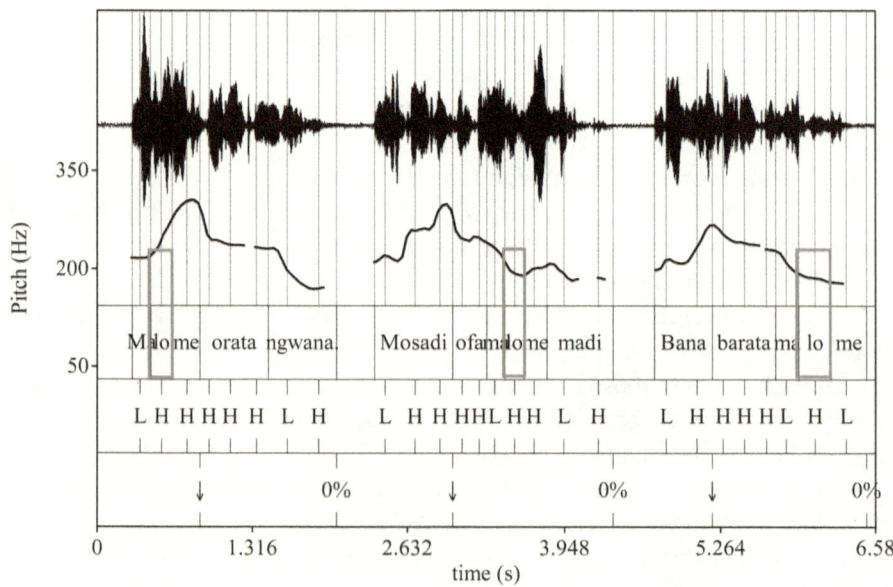

Figure 2: Penultimate lengthening in Tswana (speaker LP, female)

Penultimate lengthening in sentence-final position can be seen particularly clearly both in the measures as well as from the visual display.

Downing & Pompino-Marschall (2013) investigated the effect of focus on tone and penultimate lengthening in Chichewa. For some languages, such as (Nkhotakota) Chichewa and Zulu, penultimate lengthening has been reported to not only occur at the end of declaratives sentences but also sentence-medially (Kanerva 1990: 56; cf. Downing, this volume), at the end of Phonological Phrases following a subject or a left-dislocated constituent. Downing & Pompino-Marschall (2013) measured the penultimate vowels of subjects, non-final objects and final nouns in prepositional phrases. They found clear durational differences between the three positions although the relative ordering according to length was contradictory across the two sentence sets investigated. A carefully controlled study is needed to quantify the durational differences that exist between the penultimate syllables of nouns in these three syntactic positions in Tswana as well as details of their phonetic implementation, e.g. concerning the question whether the entire syllable (as assumed here) or only its vowel (as assumed in Downing & Pompino-Marschall 2013) is lengthened.

The relevance of penultimate lengthening in intonation is undisputed, however (e.g. Hyman & Monaka 2011), especially as vowel length is not contrastive in Tswana otherwise. Penultimate lengthening therefore clearly acts as a non-tonal intonational feature of Tswana and demarcates edges of Intonation Phrases.

Its occurrence also crucially depends on the sentence type. Gowlett (2003: 617) states that penultimate lengthening does not occur in interrogative and exclamatory sentences in the Bantu languages of zone S, among which is Sotho-Tswana. Hyman & Monaka (2011) give a comprehensive overview of the occurrence of penultimate lengthening in Shekgalagari (S311), a variety of the Sotho-Tswana languages spoken in Botswana. They show that penultimate lengthening only occurs at the end of declarative sentences in Shekgalagari but not in questions, ideophones, paused lists, imperatives, hortatives, vocatives, exclamatives and with final monosyllabic words. These contexts are discussed further in section 6 for the Tswana variety under consideration here.

Penultimate lengthening has been interpreted as a stress feature in Bantu languages (see Downing 2010 for review) but stress remains a controversial topic in Bantu phonology.

3.2.2 Tonal: Boundary tone

Language-independent form-function relations have been observed in intonation. These are derived from biologically determined conditions and are exploited by languages to varying degrees. One of these relations is the Production Code that associates final low pitch with ends of speech events (Gussenhoven 2004: 71). Thus, at the end of utterances we can expect to find low or falling intonation.

The pitch track in fig. 3 shows the interaction of lexical tone and intonation at the end of transitive declarative utterances in Tswana. The sentences have been constructed in such a way to show a low-toned verb followed by an object which contains only sonorant segments (to allow an uninterrupted pitch contour) and which differs in the tone of the final two syllables of the noun, being either L-L (10a), H-L (10b), or L-H (10c).[6] The direct comparison reveals that the final vowel is often reduced and/or devoiced when the utterance-final syllable is low-toned, as in (10a) and (10b). Furthermore, final high-toned syllables show less reduction or devoicing so that the final H tone is realised and is often perceivable.

(10) a. *Re batla lobone.* – 'We are looking for light.'
SC1PL search 5.light

b. *Re batla malóme.* – 'We are looking for the maternal uncle.'
SC1PL search 1.uncle

c. *Re batla molamú.* – 'We are looking for a knob-stick.'
SC1PL search 3.knob-stick

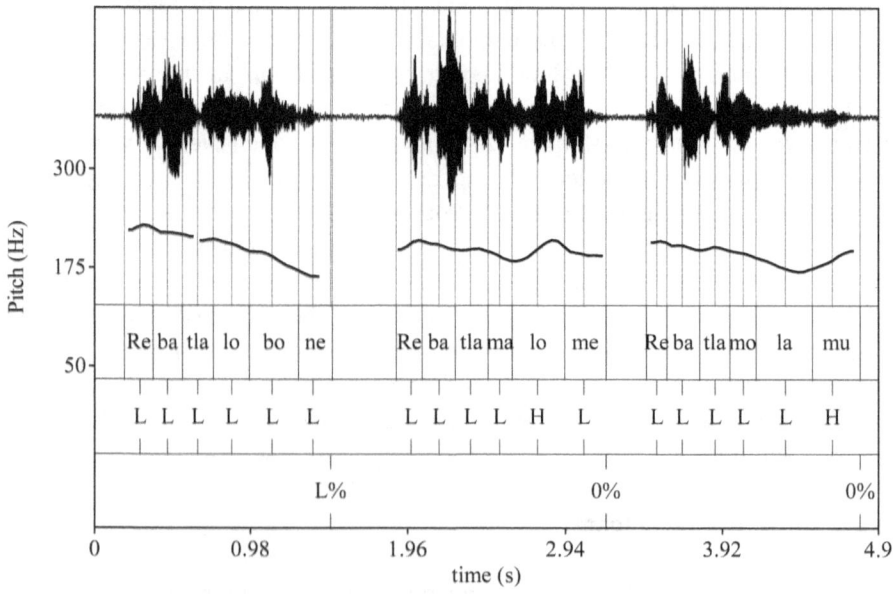

Figure 3: Declarative sentences in Tswana (speaker LP, female)

---

6 Disyllabic noun stems can have an H-L tone pattern (such as *-lépe* – axe) or an H-H tone pattern (such as *-búká* – books) (e.g. Hyman & Monaka 2011, Cole & Mokaila 1981, Cole & Moncho-Warren 2012 for Tswana). The objects used here are listed as showing an HL pattern (Cole & Moncho-Warren 2012).

For the intonation in (10a), an analysis parallel to Embosi is suggested (see Rialland & Aborobongui, this volume), according to which the final pitch lowering is triggered by an L%, which is realised low in the speaker's pitch range (referred to as final lowering in the Introduction). Additionally, devoicing can take place, even spanning the entire final syllable.

For the intonation in the sentences containing final nouns ending in HL and HH no such low target is detectable. In (10b), the pitch of the final syllable is lower than on the preceding high-toned syllable but not as low as if an L% was present (although there is sonorant material to realise a further fall). The observable pitch contour can be captured by the finality restriction, barring High Tone Spread to phrase-final syllables. In (10c), the final underlying H tone is clearly realised, again not suggesting the presence of an L% target. Devoicing is sometimes observed in a final high-toned syllable but the devoicing of the entire syllable is rare if high-toned. Due to the lack of a specific intonational target at the end of the declaratives in (10b) and (10c), an 0% boundary tone is proposed, which refers to a tonally unspecified boundary, comparable to the % tone of the British IViE-system (Grabe et al. 1998).

For the Tswana variety Shekgalagari, Hyman & Monaka (2011) suggest an analysis in which an L% anchors on the second mora of the metrically prominent penultimate syllable if and only if the last two tones are identical, thus in the case of H-H nouns and L-L nouns (which are underlying Ø-Ø). This results in a steep fall on H-H and L-L words (because L is argued to have a lower value than Ø). They do not find evidence for the presence of an L% in the case of H-L and L-H nouns. Analyzing the penultimate syllable as stressed and thereby metrically prominent provides a well-defined anchor point for the boundary tone.

Pending data on the realization of nouns ending in H-H in Tswana, a similar analysis suggests itself here too, where the L% is also only observed with low-toned nouns. A lexical low tone is thus "enhanced" by the boundary tone. Importantly, the anchoring of an L% to the final syllable in Tswana does not lead to any opposite specification of lexical tone and boundary tone and thus to any neutralization of lexical tone contrasts on final syllables. Final syllables are always realised with their lexical tones in Tswana. This is in contrast to the Nkhotakota variety of Chichewa (Kanerva 1990) where the final syllable of an Intonation Phrase is reported to never bear its lexically distinctive tone but an intonational contour (Kanerva 1990: 138), which potentially leads to neutralisation of lexical tonal contrasts on final syllables.

3.3 Sentence-internal phrase breaks

According to Ladd (2008: 289), prosodic domains are not particularly difficult to define and identify. Whether and how they match syntax is a more challenging empirical question, which is beyond the scope of this article (although this interface has been studied in Bantu languages, for Kanerva 1990 on Nkhotakota Chichewa, Downing & Cheng 2009 on Zulu, Khoali 1991 on Southern Sotho, Zerbian 2006c, 2007a on Northern Sotho).

Prosodic phrases are at their clearest when they are set off by audible boundaries in order to fulfill their most basic function, namely to divide the speech stream into chunks. Audible boundaries can be constituted by pauses, by tonal events and/or by durational cues such as the lengthening of a syllable immediately preceding a boundary. It needs to be remembered though that often these cues are gradient and optional.

For Tswana, two processes have been discussed as cues to prosodic boundaries in section 2.2.2: tone sandhi, specifically the lack of High Tone Spread to a phrase-final syllable, and partial reset, introduced as the lack of downstep in a specific instance in (7).

Reset is "the phenomenon in which previous downstep is interrupted, and a return to a higher height is observed" (Truckenbrodt 2002: 85). The initial phonetic value of the second phrase is lower than the initial phonetic value of the first phrase though (depending on the number of intervening syllables), wherefore the phenomenon is referred to as partial. Resets are important indicators of phrasing structure cross-linguistically (Gussenhoven 2004: 113).

As mentioned in the Introduction and section 2.2.2, there is conflicting evidence in the Bantu literature on how many levels of phrasing are needed, what the phonetic cues to each of these levels are and whether the prosodic boundaries differ in type or strength (see Zerbian 2007a: 257ff). The presentation here follows Ladd (2008: 289, 298) by considering prosodic structure flatter than syntactic structure. But it seems to be necessary to make a distinction in type between Phonological Phrase and Intonation Phrase based on the kind of prosodic cues used: the former shows partial reset, whereas the latter shows partial reset together with penultimate lengthening and boundary tones.

3.3.1 Partial reset and tone sandhi at Phonological Phrase boundaries

As seen in fig. 1 and also in the left sentence in fig. 4 below, adjacent high tones across word boundaries are subject to declination in that they are realized at a lower level compared to the high tone on the previous word. If an L tone intervenes, the drop in F0 is stronger than if two high tones are immediately adjacent across word boundaries.

In sentence (11a), shown to the left in fig. 4, we see downdrift over the course of the utterance as expected. In (11b), shown to the right in fig. 4, however, we observe that after the adjectival modifier *moléelé*, the high tone on the following word *ó* is scaled at a *higher* pitch than the previous word, thus crucially not following a declination or downdrift pattern. This is referred to as partial reset, applying the definition by Truckenbrodt (2002), given above. Partial reset is marked by means of an upward arrow in the annotation (for the difference in *moṅná* see section 2.2.2).

(11)   a.   *Moṅná ó̱ díra kwá masímoṅg.* – 'The man is working on the field.'
            1.man SC1 work there 6.field.LOC

      b.   *Moṅna) ó̱ moléelé) ó̱ díra kwá masímoṅg.* – 'The tall man is working on the field.'
            1.man SC1 work there 6.field.LOC

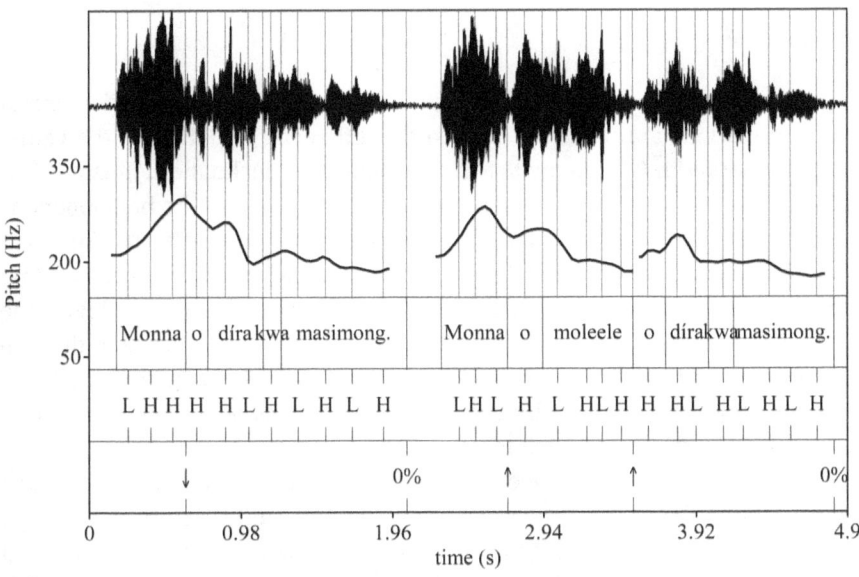

Figure 4: Intonation in sentences without and with internal phrase break

Partial reset partitions the speech stream into chunks and is thus a phenomenon of phrasing. The sentence in (11a) consists of a single phonological phrase across which underlying high tones are realised with a pattern of declination (and downstep as discussed in section 1.2.2). Sentence (11b) has two sentence-internal boundaries, with partial reset marking the beginning of a new phrase.

Fig. 4 also reveals another cue to phrasing in Tswana. The initial noun *mo̱nna* differs in its tone pattern, being H-H when a verb follows directly, and H-L when a modifier follows. The alternation between H-H and H-L has been noted frequently in the literature (e.g. Hyman & Monaka 2011, Cole & Mokaila 1981, Cole & Moncho-Warren 2012, Creissels 2009 for Tswana). Khoali (1991) accounts for a parallel alternation in Southern Sotho by reference to an intervening phrase boundary (as also mentioned in section 1.2.2). If the noun is the subject and is followed immediately by the verb as in (11a), no phrase boundary occurs and the underlying high tone on the penultimate syllable of the noun spreads to the noun-final syllable. If the noun is followed by a modifier, as in (11b), a phrase boundary intervenes and the underlying high tone on the penultimate syllable cannot spread to the final syllable of the noun due to the finality restriction which exempts final syllables as targets of High Tone Spread. The underlying representation is illustrated in (12).

(12) a. *mo̱nna o dira*   b. *mo̱nna) o moleele*
          | ⁄ | | \ |
          H   H   H L H

Different realisations of the high tones on the following verbal and nominal agreement markers are predicted, due to the difference in phrasing: the verbal agreement marker in (12a) is predicted to be subject to declination, thus realised at a lower level compared to the preceding high tone, whereas the homophonous nominal agreement marker in (12b) is predicted to be subject to partial reset, thus to be realised at a higher level than the preceding high tone. The first prediction is borne out in fig. 4, the second prediction is not: The high tone in question is realized at a lower level, similar to (12a). I want to argue that the failure to meet the prediction for (12b) is an issue of implementation: the intervening low tone automatically induces downdrift and, as reset is always partial, it does not reach the initial pitch level.

In cases where no low tone intervenes a clear drop in F0 is predicted between a noun-final high tone and a following high-initial verb in a syntactic context like (12a), and relatively stable pitch between a noun-final high tone and an immediately adjacent high-toned modifier in a syntactic context like (12b). Admittedly, the difference can be expected to be subtle, but empirical evidence supports such a stable and significant difference. In a recent study, Zerbian & Kügler (2015) confirm the described pattern, analysing data of 12 speakers quantitatively (see section 2.2.2 for a specific example).

Partial reset is also found within modified noun phrases in object position, and also if the modification is verbal, as in example (13). Here the object *baná* is followed by a dependent verb form that shows a partial reset on its subject agreement marker *bá* compared to the immediately preceding high-toned syllable of the object noun. Due to the fact that late in the sentence the range available for pitch modulation is narrower, the partial reset is not as salient as if it occurs early in the sentence.

(13)　*Mosádí ó bóná baná) bá léla.*
　　　1.woman SC1 see 2.child SC2 cry
　　　'The woman sees the children crying.'

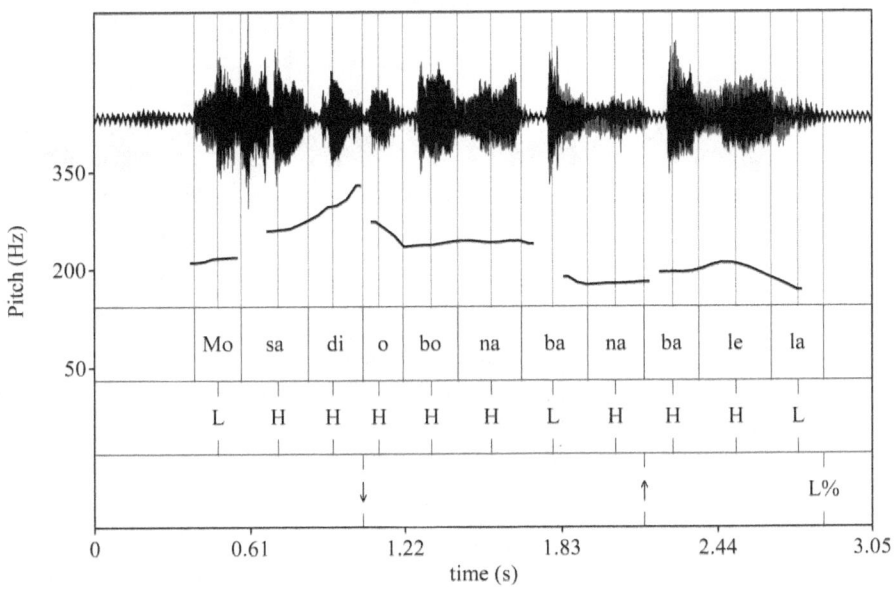

Figure 5: Partial reset in Tswana (speaker LP, female)

3.3.2 Partial reset and boundary tones at Intonation Phrase boundaries

Given that we find partial reset clause-internally within modified noun phrases in Tswana, it is not surprising to also find it between clauses. In addition, a pause can occur at these phrase boundaries. It is important to note, however, that pauses are not obligatory and their occurrence might also depend on the linear order of clauses (see also Kanerva 1990: 146 for Nkhotakota Chichewa).

In fig. 6, we find a partial reset between the two clauses independent of their order. A pause, however, only occurs when the subordinate clause precedes the main clause (14b), not if it follows it (14a). In addition to partial resets and pauses, also boundary tones can occur at these types of phrase edges. Hence they are termed Intonation Phrases. A low boundary tone is postulated at the end of the first clause because it ends as low in the speaker's pitch range as the second clause.

(14) a. *(Taú é ne yá róbala) (fá é fétsa go é já).*
9.lion SC9 PST SC9 sleep when SC9 finish INF OC9 eat
'The lion slept when he finished eating it.'

b. *(Fá é fétsa go é já) (taú é ne yá róbala).*

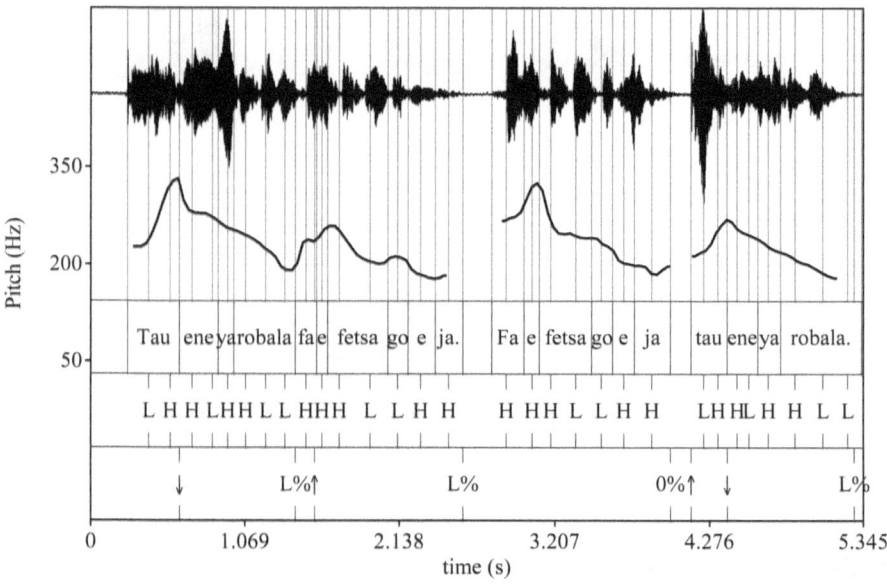

Figure 6: Order of clauses (Tswana, speaker LP, female)

A sentence-internal boundary tone will be annotated using the percentage sign % (0% if tonally not specified; see section 3.2.2), although the reset following it is only partial and not to the initial pitch height, as would be predicted if the beginning of a new utterance was initiated.

The example of self-correction in fig. 7 suggests that clause-internal low boundary tones are actual tonal targets. The speaker corrects herself in the rendition of the tonal realisation of the phrase-final noun: the penultimate syllable is lengthened and realised with a lower tone target at the boundary triggered by the following question tag. Thus, also penultimate lengthening seems to occur at this phrase boundary.

(15) O batla setsẹ́dífatsi⁷) ga gọ́ á nná jạ́lọ́?
      2SG want cold.drink NEG SC17 PST become so
      'You want a cold drink, don't you?'

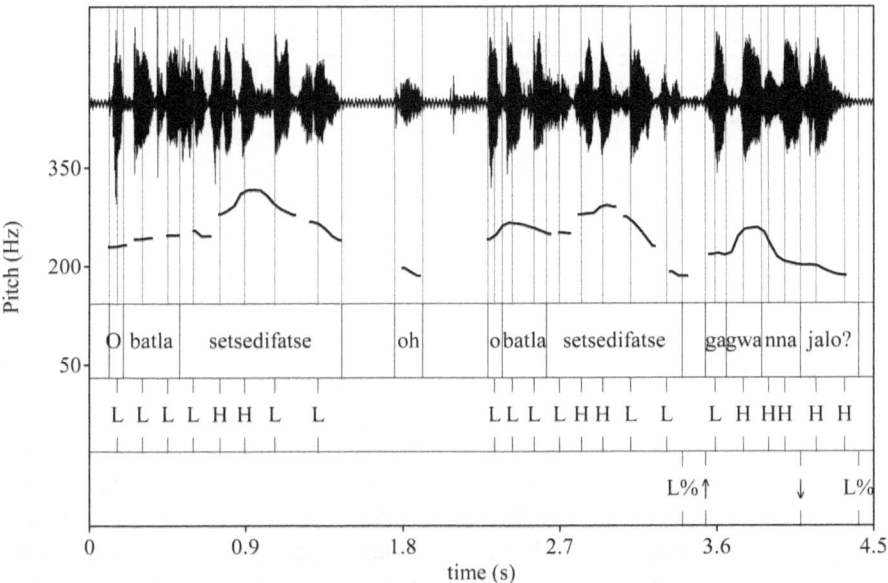

Figure 7: Self-correction concerning clause-internal boundary tone (Tswana, speaker LP, female)

The location of pauses as either preceding or following a conjunction depends on the conjunction. Whereas it occurs preceding the subordinating conjunction *gạ́* – 'if, when' in sentence (16a), it occurs following the subordinate conjunction *gore* – 'that' in (16b), as shown in fig. 8. This might be due to the origin of the conjunction. *Gore* in (16b) is the infinitive of the verb *-re* 'say' (Cole 1955: 384, 391).

(16) a. *Re ne rạ́ tshéga gạ́ ntšwạ́ é éma.*
          1PL PST 1PL laugh when 9.dog SC9 stand_up
          'We laughed when the dog stood up.'

      b. *Re ípọ́tsá gore a re bạ́ léletse gápe.*
          1PL wonder that QPART 1PL OC2 call again
          'We are wondering whether to call them again.'

---

7 Tone pattern not recorded in Cole & Moncho-Warren (2012).

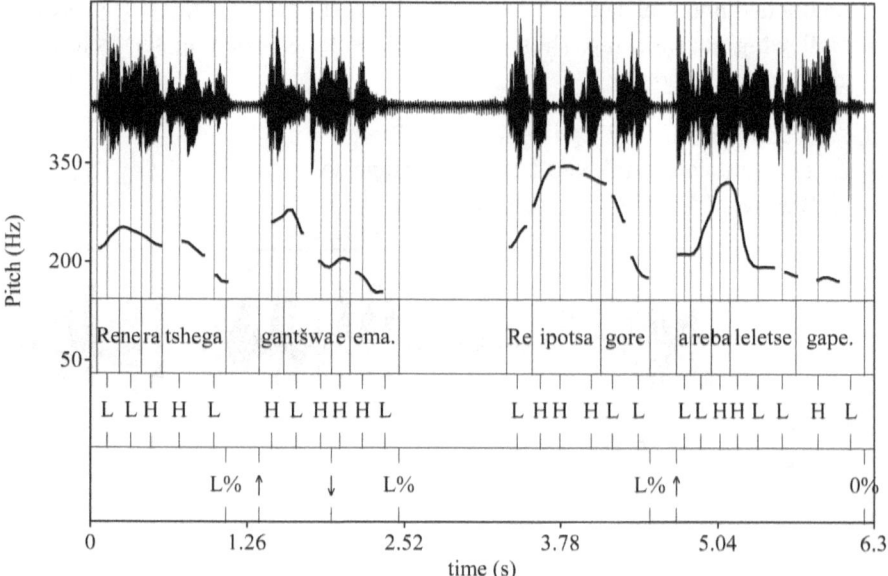

Figure 8: Location of pauses in Tswana (speaker LP, female)

In a complex sentence consisting of two coordinated clauses, the initial clause can be identical to a declarative sentence due to the presence of the L% boundary tone at the clause-internal boundary. Alternatively, a "continuation rise" can be realized at the end of the first clause, an alternation which has not been observed for the subordinated clause in (14b). This is, however, only possible when the final syllable of the first clause has a high tone. The final high is raised, thus making a declarative sentence and a clause coordinated to another clause intonationally different from each other, as shown in fig. 9.

(17) a. *(Basádí bá díraṅg?)* – What are the women doing?
Basádí bá ápaya bojalwá jó bó bogálé.
2.women SC2 cook 14.beer AGR14 AGR14 strong
'The women cook strong beer.'

b. *(Mpólélele ká botshélo jwá kwá motseṅg!)* – Tell me about life in the village!
Basádí bá ápaya bojalwá jó bó bogálé, (baṅná bá ágá ntlo).
2.women SC2 cook 14.beer AGR14 AGR14 strong
'The women cook strong beer, (the men build a house).'

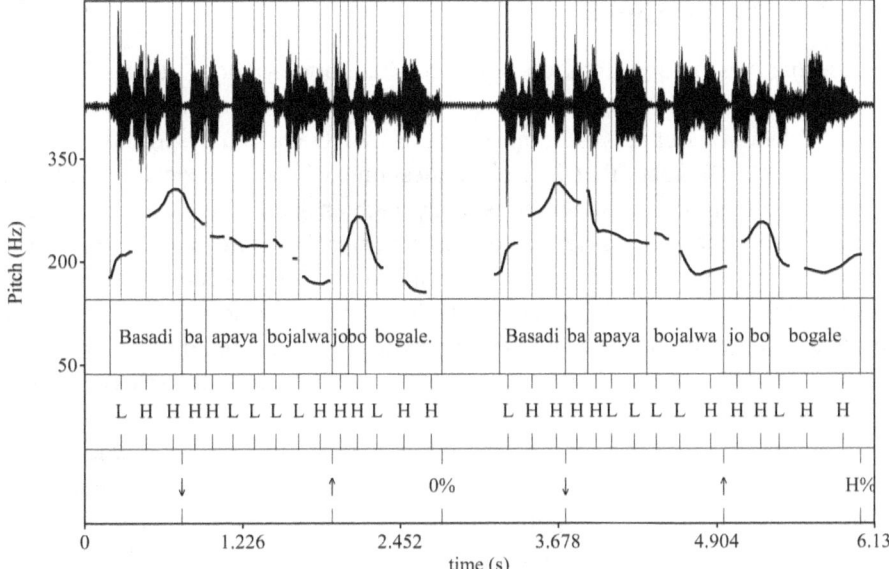

Figure 9: Continuation rises on clause-final high tones in Tswana (speaker LP, female)

Rising intonation is a common marker of continuation cross-linguistically. Though frequent, it cannot be considered a universal, as languages exploit and grammaticalise the phenomenon differently. Tswana is an example of a language where continuation is not grammaticalised as a high boundary tone. A final rise does not seem to be possible with final low tones. Only high lexical tones are found to be enhanced in a way that is expected cross-linguistically.

4 Intonation of questions

Question intonation is another form-function relation that shows common patterns cross-linguistically. The Frequency Code (Ohala 1983, Gussenhoven 2004) relates high pitch to uncertainty. Rialland (2007) shows that many African languages show indeed high-pitched markers in yes/no-questions, such as register expansion, raising of H tones or rising intonation. At the same time, though, there is another group of African languages that shows the opposite, namely final low tones or falling tones (Rialland 2009). In this section, two types of questions are considered and compared to declarative sentences. Yes/no-questions are addressed first, followed by *wh*-questions. It will be shown that Tswana can be assigned to the first group.

4.1 Yes/no-questions

In Tswana, yes/no-questions do not necessitate any syntactic re-organization. The (low-toned) question particle *a* can be used in sentence-initial position but is not obligatory. Hence, yes/no-questions are solely marked by prosody.

Ohala (1983) states that in yes/no-questions, where no lexical or syntactic marker is present to indicate interrogativity, high or rising tone almost invariably signals a question, whereas low or falling pitch signals a statement. In the following, only the intonation of lexically unmarked yes/no-questions is considered. Though a yes/no-question marked with the question particle *a* does not differ in its intonation from yes/no-questions produced without the question particle, neither in sentences containing only high tones nor in sentences containing only low tones.

One participant characterized the intonation of yes/no-questions in Sotho-Tswana as follows: they start high and end fast. The impression concerning speed is due to the fact that penultimate lengthening is clearly absent in these questions, as can be seen from fig. 10. The former impression relates to the fact that there is a salient raised overall pitch as compared to corresponding declaratives. This is also evident in fig. 10. The superimposed grey line demarcates the initial pitch level of the declarative. In low-toned declaratives the initial pitch drops immediately whereas it slightly rises in the case of yes/no-questions. Therefore, not only the average pitch is different but also the pitch dynamics over the course of the utterances differ. Interestingly, the pitch starts and ends on the same level in the declarative and yes/no-question. Therefore, the pitch range is expanded in yes/no-questions, rather than shifted to a higher register.

(18) a. *Re besa nama.* 'We are roasting meat.'
 1PL roast 9.meat

 b. *Le besa nama?* 'Are you roasting meat?'

 c. *Le besa eńg?* 'What are you roasting?'

 d. *Bá bóná pódi.* 'They see a goat.'
 2PL see 9.goat

 e. *Bá bóná pódi?* 'Do they see a goat?'

 f. *Bá bóná eńg?* 'What do they see?'

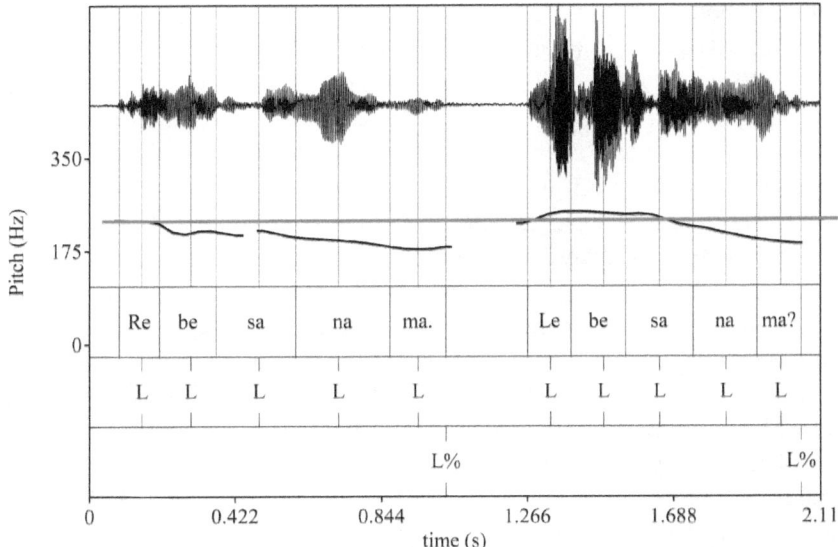

Figure 10: Low-toned utterance as declarative and yes/no-question in Tswana (speaker LP, female)

Fig. 11 shows a high-toned utterance as declarative and yes/no-question. Again, the different pitch dynamics within the utterance are clearly discernible although the lexical tones are identical across declarative and yes/no-question and the start and endpoints of the pitch are roughly the same. Also the shortened penultimate syllable in the yes/no-question is clearly visible in fig. 11.

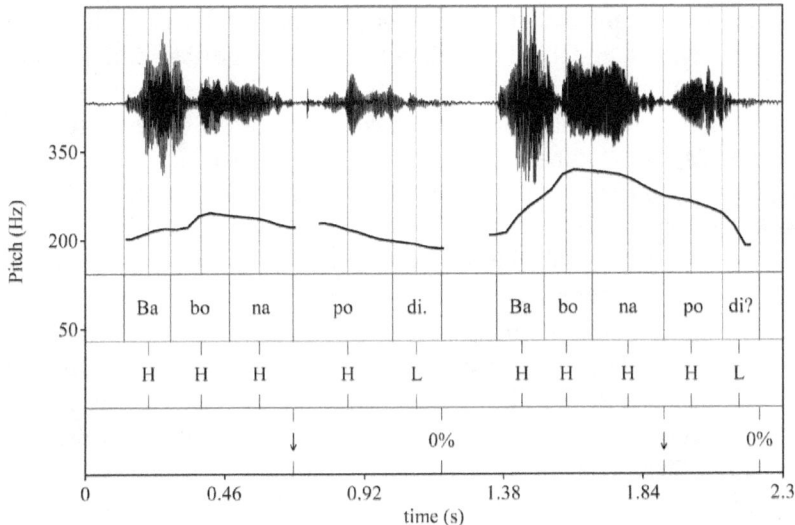

Figure 11: High-toned utterance as declarative and yes/no-question in Tswana (speaker LP, female)

Note that in both low- and high-toned utterances declination can be observed over the course of the yes/no-question. This is in contrast to the Chichewa investigated in Myers (1996), to Hausa (Inkelas & Leben 1990, cited in Ladd 2008: 160), and to Bemba, Chichewa and Shingazidja (this volume). In Chichewa, declination in questions is reported to be less steep than in declaratives, whereas in Hausa downdrift in questions is suspended. If at all, declination is steeper in yes/no-questions in Tswana, given that the pitch range is expanded.

In one of the few quantitative studies on intonation in Bantu languages, Jones et al. (2001a) investigated a comparable intonation pattern in yes/no-questions in Xhosa, a South African Bantu language belonging to the neighbouring Nguni family (S40). Their work is mentioned here, as the prosodic facts seem to be very similar to Tswana. They analysed copulative yes/no-questions produced by 11 speakers of Xhosa acoustically and found, that (i) word duration is considerably longer in statements than in yes/no-questions, (ii) the tempo (syllables per second) is considerably higher in yes/no-questions than in statements, and (iii) the penultimate syllable is longer in statements than in yes/no-questions. All results are highly significant and clearly show that durational aspects and dynamics are extremely important for the prosodic marking of sentence type. For pitch, they found that the average pitch level is higher for all questions than for all statements. Furthermore, their results suggest that some specific relationship between the pitch realisation of the final two syllables might exist because the pitch on the penultimate vowel was found to be a reliable predictor of sentence type in the majority of cases. These cues are also relevant in perception. Jones et al. (2001b) carried out a perception experiment using Xhosa stimuli manipulated for pitch on the initial syllable, pitch on the penultimate syllable, and penultimate duration. They found that duration and pitch on the penultimate syllable are perceptually highly significant features for disambiguation even though listeners make decisions on sentence type as early as the first syllable. If the cues of initial and penultimate syllable are contradictory, however, the cues of the penultimate syllable may override judgments made based on earlier cues.

The intonation pattern of yes/no-questions in the Southern African Bantu languages Tswana and Xhosa are in contrast to what Myers (1996: 30) describes for Chichewa, where yes/no-questions are realised in a raised pitch range, with a sharp rise in F0 on the final syllable and with a less steep downdrift trend across questions as compared to statements. (See, too, Downing, this volume, on the intonation of Chichewa questions.) Myers accounts for the final pitch rises by boundary tones. Given that the rises are rather sharp, he suggests an L%H%, which is aligned to the final syllable of the phrase. In terms of phonological representation, Myers (1996) suggests that boundary tones in Chichewa are interpreted as a property of the whole phrase (in line with Pierrehumbert & Beckman 1988), thus affecting the tone value of every lexical tone within that phrase. This is against the "unity of pitch phonology" as it entails that lexical tones and boundary tones are on distinct tiers (Myers 1996: 53).

Sosa (1999) analyses the overall rising in Spanish yes/no-questions with an initial H%-boundary tone, which triggers upstep and sets the reference line for the remaining intonation contour. As a reviewer points out, a problem with this analysis is that in the AM model, the notation of a left-aligned boundary tone %H is used to indicate a local effect rather than a global effect.

Rialland & Aborobongui (this volume) introduce an H^h tone to account for continuation rises and the raised and expanded register in yes/no-questions. The H^h tone leads to a raised register from the tone to which it is linked. One could thus suggest that H^h links to the first H tone in a yes/no-question in Tswana, resulting in a raised register and expanded pitch range. However, the same effect is witnessed in low-toned sentences, and it remains a topic for further debate whether also L^h tones should be postulated.

4.2 *Wh*-questions

Content questions ask for a specific piece of information and necessarily involve the question word as a lexical marker. In Tswana, the question words are *máng* (who), *-fe* (which), *káe* (where), *léng* (when), *eńg* (what), *jáng* (how) respectively, and occur in their canonical syntactic position. For examples see (18c) and (18e). Thus, there is no inversion in *wh*-questions in Tswana. Due to the lexical marking, they would not be predicted to be marked with high pitch according to Ohala (1983).

The following figures show *wh*-questions in comparison to declaratives for low-toned utterances (fig. 12) and high-toned utterances (fig. 13). Again, a reference line is inserted for ease of comparison. Note that the question word *eńg-* 'what' carries a high tone on the final syllable, thus rendering the two utterances under comparison not identical in terms of lexical tones.

Whereas an expanded pitch register is not always clearly depictable in low-toned *wh*-questions, it is evident for questions containing high tones. Again, the penultimate syllable is not lengthened (the *ń̇g* in *eńg* is syllabic, therefore the vowel *e* constitutes the penultimate syllable of the utterance).

420 — Sabine Zerbian

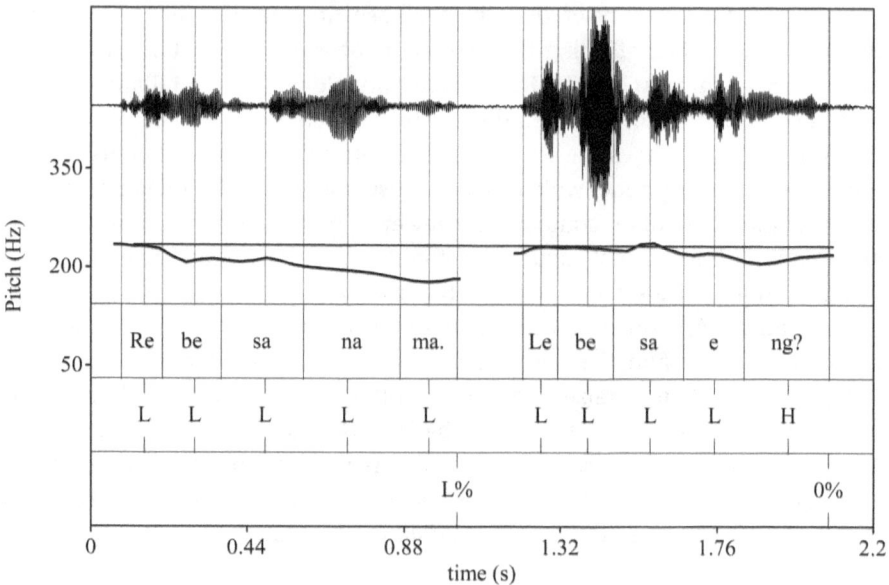

Figure 12: Declarative and *wh*-question containing low tones

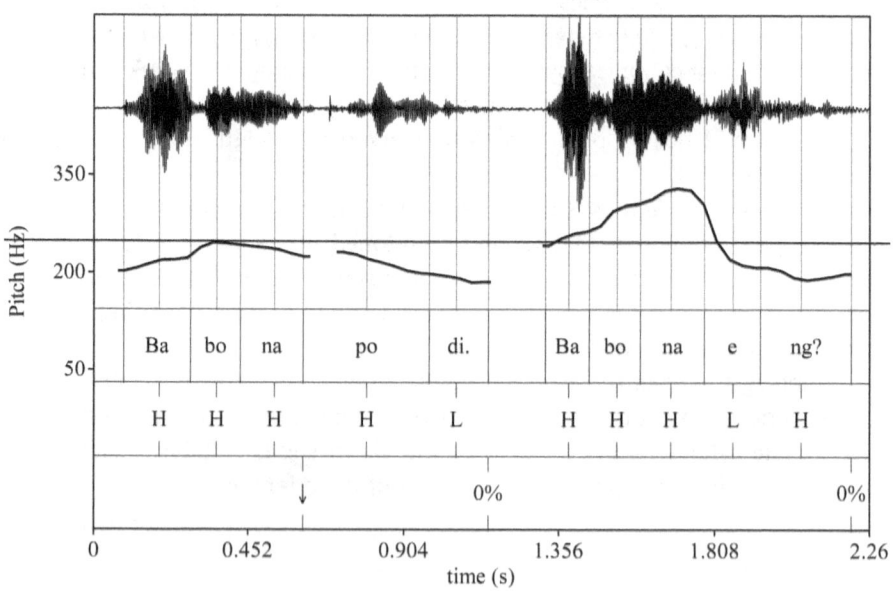

Figure 13: Declarative and *wh*-question containing high tones

4.3 Summary

Both yes/no-questions (with and without the question particle *a*) and *wh*-questions are marked by the absence of penultimate lengthening and an expanded pitch range. The latter effect is –not surprisingly– more evident in utterances containing high tones. It is predicted that controlled acoustic studies will confirm the same effect also for low-toned utterances.

Ladd (2008: 210) explicitly disagrees with Sosa's analysis of raised pitch register by means of boundary tones. Instead, he considers overall pitch range modification a paralinguistic aspect as it is orthogonal to the specification of the string of tones. Particularly the higher overall register in yes/no-questions is a common phenomenon among languages and should be treated as a paralinguistic, extrinsic scaling factor in his view. At the same time, he admits that "the proper treatment of pitch range phenomena in AM intonational phonology is by no means settled" (Ladd 2008: 210).

It seems unsatisfactory to relegate pitch range effects to mere paralinguistic aspects of intonation. The perceptual relevance of initial pitch for sentence type, shown in the study by Jones et al. (2001b) for Xhosa, and the accurate modelling of the phenomenon by Myers (1996) seem to suggest that yes/no-question intonation is both obligatory and highly stable. Also Nolan (2006: 18) states that "in tone languages, where local pitch movements are determined lexically, intonation will heavily rely on such pitch range effects." How the interaction of tone and intonation is modelled in such cases remains a topic for future research. Here, Ladd (2008) will be followed in considering pitch range effects paralinguistic.

5 Intonation used for information structure

5.1 Focus

In Zerbian (2006c, 2007b) it was argued that focus does not have a grammaticalised prosodic effect in Northern Sotho, neither in a systematic extension of pitch range nor in the obligatory insertion of phrase boundaries. An acoustic analysis of pitch in different focus structures showed that focus is not marked systematically through duration or fundamental frequency. An acceptability task of question-answer pairs with native speakers of Northern Sotho confirmed this for perception.

A direct prosodic effect on the focused constituent has also not been found for Tswana when eliciting data for this chapter.

The absence of prosodic focus marking in Northern Sotho was an interesting result at the time for cross-Bantu variation, given that phrasing had been shown to be sensitive to focus in Nkhotakota Chichewa (Kanerva 1990). Grammaticalized prosodic focus marking as known from English seems to be less frequent in the languages of Africa in general (see Güldemann, Zerbian & Zimmermann 2015 for an overview). Even for Chichewa, a recent quantitative study has revealed that prosodic focus marking through phrasing is only optional in this language but that prosodic traces of emphasis can be observed (Downing & Pompino-Marschall 2013; see also Downing, this volume). Kunene (1978: 101) states that emphatic stress in Southern Sotho is primarily carried by consonants whose duration are prolongued.

5.2 Topic

5.2.1 Subject as topic

Sotho-Tswana has SVO word order. If subjects are questioned or focused, they cannot occur in their canonical preverbal position but must occur in a cleft sentence or postverbally instead. This has been attributed to their general discourse function as topic in these languages (Givón 1976; Zerbian 2006c for Northern Sotho).

The status of a subject topic as either new or previously mentioned is sometimes reflected in intonation. In the variety of Tswana spoken by the main informant of the chapter, however, it does not matter whether the subject topic represents a new topic or whether it has previously been mentioned. As the realization of *basádi* in example (17) and fig. 9 above shows, no intonational difference in either penultimate lengthening, tone sandhi on the last syllable or the following tonal realization can be found between subjects that represent given topics, (17a), and subjects that represent new and contrastive clause-topics, (17b).

5.2.2 Object as topic

In contrast to the sentence-initial subject topics presented in the preceding section, left-dislocated objects are set apart from the remainder of the clause through a pause between dislocated object and a following subject constituent, as well as penultimate lengthening on the dislocated object. Due to the clear pause and the observed penultimate lengthening a boundary tone is transcribed. Given that no tonal activity is observed at the boundary it is transcribed as 0%. The following subject constituent is realised with a partial reset.

(19) Leúṅgo lé ngwaná wá gágo ó lé jéle.
 5.fruit DEM5 1.child POSS1 you SC1 OC5 eat.PST
 'This fruit, your child has eaten it.'

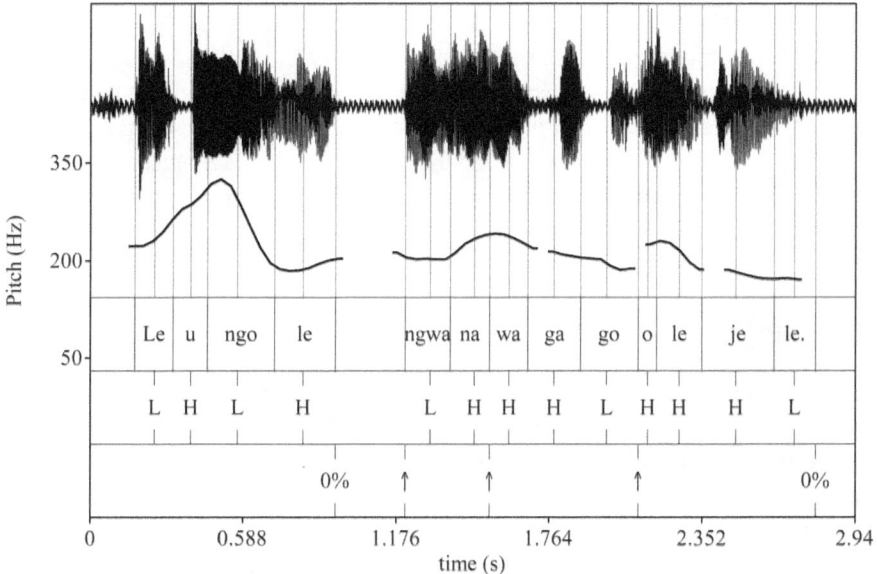

Figure 14: Left-dislocated object in Tswana (speaker LP, female)

The separate phrasing of a dislocated object is encountered frequently across Bantu languages. The phrasing of subjects is less consistent and shows a variety of options, such as being phrased together with or separate from what follows (Zerbian 2007a: 258, Downing 2011).[8]

---

[8] In Zerbian (2007a), I reported that in Northern Sotho left-dislocated subjects, objects and adverbials are phrased together with the following constituent. Evidence for this came from the occurrence of HTS to the final syllable of the dislocated constituent. In all examples in Zerbian (2007a), the dislocated constituent was directly followed by the verb. This is contrary to the example in (19), where the subject noun phrase intervenes. The resulting differences in phrasing might be related to different preverbal subject and topic positions, motivated for Zulu by Downing & Cheng (2009). A closer examination awaits further research.

6 Occurrence of penultimate lengthening in Tswana

Hyman & Monaka (2011) report that in Shekgalagari penultimate lengthening only occurs at the end of declarative sentences and not in questions, ideophones, paused lists, imperatives, hortatives, vocatives, exclamatives or with final monosyllabic words. In contrast, penultimate lengthening occurs in Bantu languages like Chichewa or the Nguni languages in these other contexts. (See overview in Hyman & Monaka). For Southern Sotho, Kunene (1978: 102) reports that penultimate lengthening does not occur in interrogatives, exclamatory sentences and with ideophones. (See also Demuth & Machobane cited in Hyman & Monaka 2011.) It is therefore worthwhile to investigate further sentence types. This section illustrates and highlights some interesting prosodic aspects of these contexts.

6.1 Ideophones

Ideophones constitute a peculiar part of speech in Bantu languages. They can be considered onomatopoetic, although their semantics go beyond the mere sound description and include descriptions of color, smell, manner, appearance, state, action or intensity as well (Cole 1955: 370, Kunene 1978, Dingemanse 2012). Due to their emotional use, they show unusual features, some pertaining to intonation. These features are prolonged lengthening of final sounds, devoicing of vowels, and exaggerated tonal variations. Fig. 15 shows an example in which penultimate lengthening is absent in Tswana (see also Kunene 1978: 102) and an exaggerated high tone is produced on the ideophone.

(20)   Go nó̱ go dídímetse gó̱ ríle tú̱.
       SC17 PST SC17 become_quiet SC17 say.PST IDEOPHONE
       'It was dead quiet.'

The exceptionally high final pitch cannot be accounted for solely by means of a lexical tone as its pitch value lies clearly above the normal tone register of the speaker (in fig. 15 around 450 Hz in a sentence with a general pitch level of around 275 Hz). The label ^H (superhigh) has been chosen as an intonational label (Jun & Fletcher 2014: 517). It is assumed that it attaches to the ideophone rather than to the boundary of the sentence. Because not all ideophones are associated with such a high pitch excursion, a unified account in terms of an

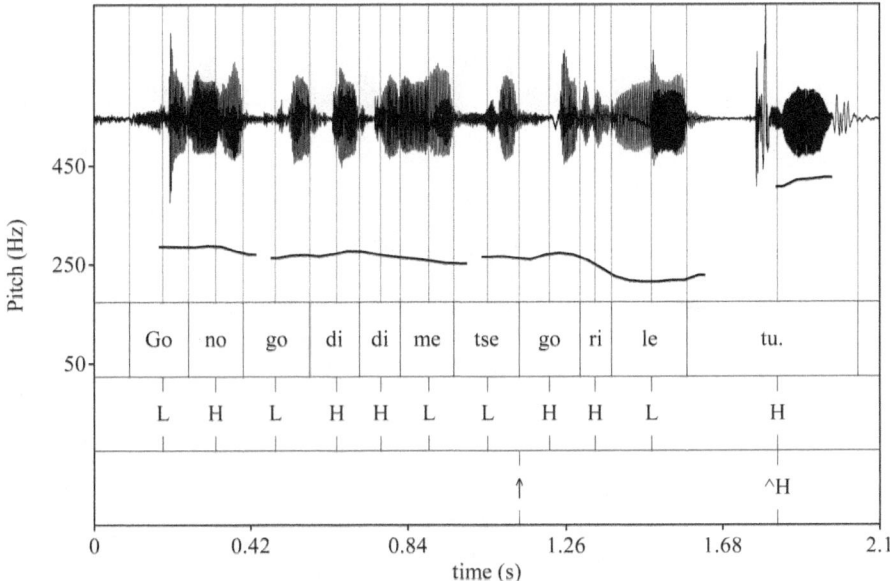

Figure 15: Intonation in a sentence containing an ideophone (Tswana, speaker LP, female)

intonational H tone co-occurring with ideophones does not suggest itself. The special intonation of ideophones remains a rewarding area for further research.

6.2 Paused lists

In paused lists, the penultimate syllable of each item is lengthened. High Tone Spread occurs from the penultimate syllable to the final syllable in words like *dilépe*. Partial reset can be observed after each item of the list. If an item ends on a high tone, this high tone is raised. Words with a final low tone (*nama*), however, do not show a high tone on the final syllable.

(21) *Ó réká dilépé, dibúká, nama, bojalwá lé bogóbe.*
 SC1 buy 10.axe 10.book 9.meat 14.beer and 14.porridge
 'He is buying axes, books, meat, beer and porridge.'

As in coordination structures, it can be observed that final high tones are enhanced on non-final list items when the end of the list has not yet been reached and another constituent is to follow. This intonational enhancement, however, does not interact with lexical tones, in that lexical low tones are not generally raised in non-final list items, they remain low.

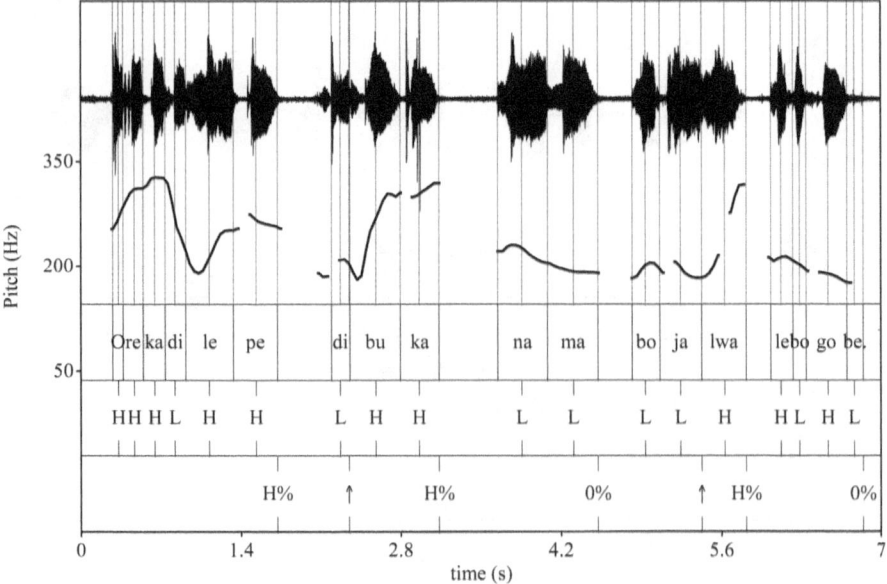

Figure 16: Intonation in paused lists in Tswana (speaker LP, female)

6.3 Imperatives

Imperatives are the only verb forms that can occur without the otherwise obligatory agreement marker in verb stem initial position. The imperative is characterized by a grammatical tone pattern which adds a high tone to the stem-initial syllable of low-toned verbs. Disyllabic high-toned verbs, used in the examples here, remain unchanged. Other than the grammatical tone pattern in low-toned verbs, the intonation of imperatives does not differ categorically from declaratives. The penultimate syllable is lengthened. It does show evidence of emphasis: The final syllable seems shortened, and the pitch range is expanded just as in questions, whereby the start and end point is comparable across declarative and imperative. Also, the initial consonant is produced quite strong, as also explicitly mentioned by one participant. Consonantal strength has been reported by Kunene (1978: 101) as co-occurring with emphatic stress.

(22) a. *(Re) besa nama.* – Roast meat! / We roast meat.

   b. *(Bá) bóná pódi.* – See the goat! / They see the goat.

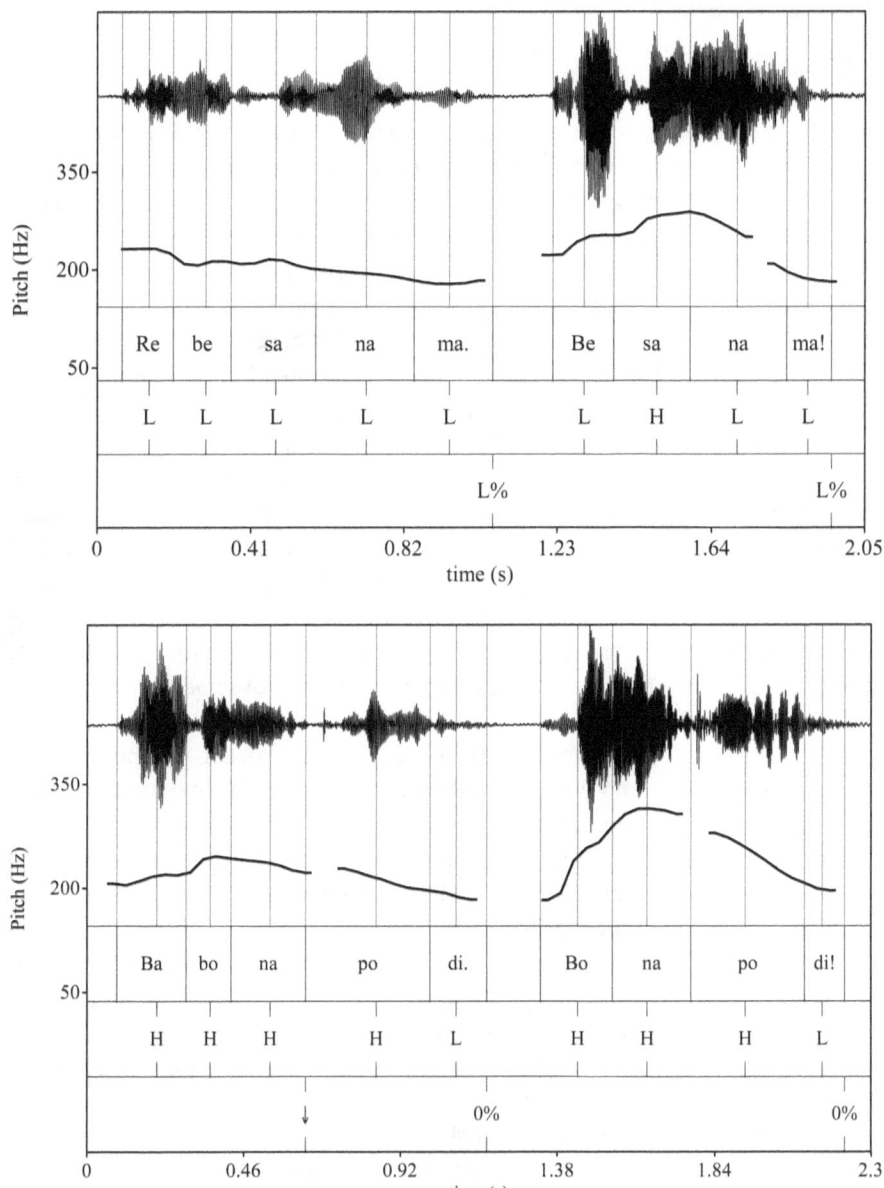

Figure 17 + 18: Intonation in imperatives in Tswana (speaker LP, female)

7 Discussion

7.1 Summary

Intonation in Tswana consists of tonal and non-tonal features. One salient cue to sentence intonation is non-tonal and consists of the presence or absence of penultimate lengthening. Its occurrence at sentence edges is closely associated to pragmatic distinctions of sentence type (and beyond, see Hyman & Monaka 2011). Its absence is clearly perceivable in yes/no-questions in Tswana. The perceptual relevance of the absence of this cue has been confirmed by Jones et al. (2001b) for Xhosa, a South African Bantu language which shows similar cues. Note that cross-dialectal variation has been attested for this feature through the study on Shekgalagari in Hyman & Monaka (2011).

With respect to tonal features of sentence intonation in Tswana, the examples presented in this article show evidence for an L% boundary tone occurring on low-toned constituents e.g. at the end of declaratives and at Intonation Phrase boundaries at clause boundaries. The L% alternates with 0% if the final lexical tone is high. Between non-final items in paused lists and at Intonation Phrase boundaries between coordinated clauses, an H% can be observed that is attracted by lexical H tones. This tone is possibly close to H^h in Rialland & Aborobongui (this volume). Finally, a superhigh tone is observed on some ideophones (^H).

Partial reset (↑) and tonal H-H~H-L alternations occur at phrase edges within clauses (noun and post-nominal modifier) and at clause boundaries, and are thus predictable from syntax.

Given that this is the first description of Tswana sentence intonation, the labels suggested here should be considered "temporary" labels before more detailed analyses confirm the distinctive categories of the language.

The general claim made here is that sentence-level prosody never overrides an underlying lexical tone specification in Tswana. This means that an underlying lexical high tone on a sentence-final syllable is realised, even in declaratives. Whereas final high tones might be enhanced in non-final paused list items, a surface low-toned syllable will not receive high pitch in these contexts. In yes/no-questions where the entire register is raised, lexical pitch relations are maintained. Tonal calculation proceeds as usual, albeit at a higher level. Finally, grammaticalised focus prosody has not been observed in Tswana.

7.2 Relationship between tone and intonation in Tswana

The chapter adopts the approach of "unity of pitch prosody" as inherent in an AM theory of intonation, according to which pitch-related sentence intonation in all languages consists of sequential tonal specification and pitch range modifications. In English, the tonal specification are postlexical pitch accents and boundary tones, in Tswana these are lexical tones and boundary tones. Thus, lexical tones do not constitute a type of phonological specification in addition to intonational tones, a view contrary to the one expressed in Myers (1996) and Hyman & Monaka (2011).

Ladd (2008: 159) argues that pitch range expansion, such as found in yes/no-questions in Tswana, can be attributed to paralinguistic meaning and thus does not need to be modelled in a phonological theory of intonation. He further argues that phrase-final tone modification, such as the enhanced high tone in non-final list items, can be analysed as stemming from the lexical tone in connection with a boundary tone. Following this line of analysis, the presence of a boundary tone would then crucially depend on the presence of a certain kind of lexical tone. An alternative would be to analyse this enhanced high tone as paralinguistic intonation too. It would then be predicted to be optional and less consistent in its realization across speakers and/or contexts.

It remains an open question whether the tonal enhancement of high tones is somehow connected to the fact that only high tones are assumed to be present underlyingly, as suggested by a reviewer.

Hyman & Monaka (2011) differentiate three kinds of interaction between lexical and intonational tones. One might find *accommodation* when lexical tones and intonational tones interact only minimally. Or *submission*, where intonational tones override lexical tones. The last kind is *avoidance*, where "intonation is minimized, perhaps limited to Ladd's [...] "paralinguistic" modulations (pitch range and pitch interval adjustments, etc.)" (Hyman & Monaka 2011: 268).

On the basis of the data presented here it is clear that Tswana intonation cannot be categorized as a case of submission, as intonational tones never override lexical tones. Nor is it true that the two never influence each other. We do find minimal interactions when the intonational tones are superimposed onto the lexical tones and lead to a higher or lower realization of high and low lexical tones. Only a closer examination can reveal whether this minimal interaction constitutes a case of accommodation or avoidance in the system suggested by Hyman & Monaka (2011).

Tswana thus poses an interesting challenge to theories of intonational phonology because it has two salient features which are not yet well-integrated into a coherent theory of sentence intonation: non-tonal features such as penultimate lengthening and systematic pitch range changes.

To conclude, prosodic enhancement is the key word when accounting for sentence intonation in Tswana. Lexical tones are enhanced in line with universal tendencies in the form-function mapping of intonation, such as low pitch in declaratives and high pitch in continuations, if and only if the lexical tone specification points in the same direction.

Acknowledgements

Data for this chapter were elicited from mother tongue speakers of Tswana, Sepedi and Sesotho during September 2014 and 2015 at the University of the Witwatersrand, Johannesburg. I want to thank the School of Language, Literature and Media Studies for hosting me during my research visits, and Lorato Phefo, Malefu Mahloane, Ntombizodwa Muso, and Khutšo Matlou for sharing their languages with me. All errors of analysis and interpretation are my own.

I want to thank the editors and reviewers for helpful feedback on an earlier version. This work is dedicated to the memory of Moruti Dieter Mascher (1937–2015).

References

Chebanne, Andrew M., Creissels, Denis & Nkhwa, H.W. 1997. *Tonal morphology of the Setswana verb*. Munich: LINCOM Europe.
Clements, George Nick. 1988. Tonology of the SeSotho verb. Manuscript.
Cole, Desmond T. 1955. *An Introduction to Tswana Grammar*. Cape Town: Longman.
Cole, Desmond T. & Dingaan M. Mokaila. 1981. *A Course in Tswana*. Goodwood: Via Afrika Limited. 2nd edition.
Cole, Desmond T. & Lally Moncho-Warren. 2012. *Setswana and English Illustrated Dictionary*. Northlands, Gauteng: Macmillan.
Creissels, Denis. 1998a. High tone domains in Setswana. In Larry M. Hyman & Charles W. Kisseberth (eds.), *Theoretical aspects of Bantu tone*, 133–194. Stanford: CSLI Publications.
Creissels, Denis. 1999. The role of tone in the conjugation of Setswana. In JA Blanchon & Denis Creissels (eds.), *Issues in Bantu tonology*, 109–152. Cologne: Rüdiger Köppe.
Creissels Denis. 2000. A domain-based approach to Setswana tone. In Ekkehard Wolff & Orin Gensler (eds.), *Proceedings of the 2nd World Congress of African Linguistics*, 311–321. Cologne: Rüdiger Köppe.
Creissels, Denis. 2009. Construct forms of nouns in African languages. In Peter K. Austin, Oliver Bond, Monik Charette, David Nathan & Peter Sells (eds.), *Proceedings of Conference on Language Documentation & Linguistic Theory 2*, 73–82. London.

Department of Education. 1988. *Setswana. Terminology and orthography, no. 4*. Government Printer Pretoria, South Africa.

Dingemanse, Mark. 2012. Advances in the cross-linguistic study of ideophones. *Language and Linguistics Compass* 6. 654–672.

Downing, Laura J. 2010. Accent in African Languages. In Harry van der Hulst, Rob Goedemans & Ellen van Zanten (eds.), *A Survey of Word Accentual Patterns in the Languages of the World*, 381–428. Berlin: Mouton de Gruyter.

Downing, Laura J. 2011. The prosody of 'dislocation' in selected Bantu languages. *Lingua* 121. 772–786.

Downing, Laura J. 2013. Issues in the Phonology-Syntax Interface in African Languages. In O.O. Orie & Karen W. Sanders (eds.), *Selected Proceedings of the 43rd Annual Conference on African Linguistics*, 26–38. Somerville, MA: Cascadilla Proceedings Project.

Downing, Laura J. & Lisa Cheng. 2009. Where's the topic in Zulu? *The Linguistic Review* 26. 207–238.

Downing, Laura J. & Bernd Pompino-Marschall. 2013. The focus prosody of Chichewa and the Stress-Focus constraint: a response to Samek-Lodovici (2005). *Natural Language and Linguistic Theory* 31. 647–681.

Frota, Sonia & Pilar Prieto (eds.). 2015. *Intonation in Romance Languages*. Oxford: Oxford University Press.

Givón, Talmy. 1976. Topic, pronoun, and grammatical agreement. In Charles N. Li (ed.), *Subject and Topic*, 149–188. New York: Academic Press.

Gowlett, Derek. 2003. Zone S. In Derek Nurse & Gérard Philippson, *The Bantu Languages*, 609–638. London/New York: Routledge.

Grabe, Esther, Francis Nolan & K. Farrar. 1998. IViE – a Comparative transcription system for intonational variation in English. *Proceedings of the 5th Conference on Spoken Language Processing (ICSLP), Sydney, Australia*.

Gussenhoven, Carlos. 2004. *The Phonology of Tone and Intonation*. Cambridge: Cambridge University Press.

Güldemann, Tom, Sabine Zerbian & Malte Zimmermann. 2015. Variation in Information Structure with Special Reference to Africa. *Annual Linguistics Review* 1. 55–78.

Hamlaoui, Fatima, Siri M. Gjersøe & Emmanuel-Moselly Makasso. 2014. High Tone Spreading and Phonological Phrases in Bàsàá. *Proceedings of TAL 2014, Nijmegen, Netherlands*, 27–31. ISCA Archive.

Hyman, Larry M. 2006. Word-prosodic typology. *Phonology* 23. 225–257.

Hyman, Larry M. & Kemmonye C. Monaka. 2011. Tonal and Non-Tonal Intonation in Shekgalagari. In Sónia Frota, Gorka Elordieta & Pilar Prieto (eds.), *Prosodic categories: Production, Perception and Comprehension*, 267–289. Springer.

Inkelas, Sharon & William Leben. 1990. Where phonology and phonetics intersect: the case of Hausa intonation. In John Kingston, & Mary E. Beckman (eds.), *Papers in Laboratory Phonology, vol. 1: Between the grammar and physics of speech*, 17–34. Cambridge University Press.

Jones, Jackie, Louw JA & Justus C. Roux. 2001a. Perceptual experiments on Queclaratives in Xhosa. *SAJAL*, supplement 36. 19–31.

Jones, Jackie, Louw JA & Justus C. Roux. 2001b. Queclaratives in Xhosa: an acoustic analysis. *SAJAL*, supplement 36. 3–18.

Jun, Sun-Ah (ed.). 2005. *Prosodic Typology: The Phonology of Intonation and Phrasing*. Oxford: Oxford University Press.

Jun, Sun-Ah (ed.). 2014. *Prosodic Typology II*. Oxford: Oxford University Press.
Jun, Sun-Ah & Janet Fletcher. Methodology of studying intonation: from data collection to data analysis. In Jun, Sun-Ah (ed.), *Prosodic Typology II*, 493–519. Oxford: Oxford University Press.
Kanerva, Jonni M. 1990. *Focus and phrasing in Chichewa phonology*. New York/London: Garland Publishing.
Khoali, Benjamin. 1991. A Sesotho tonal grammar. Doctoral thesis, University of Illinois.
Kisseberth, Charles W. & Sheila O. Mmusi. 1990. The tonology of the object prefix in Setswana. *Studies in the Linguistic Sciences* 20(1). 151–161.
Kisseberth, Charles W. & David Odden. 2003. Tone. In Derek Nurse & Gérard Philippson (eds.), *The Bantu languages*, 59–70. London/New York: Routledge.
Kunene, Daniel P. 1972. A preliminary study of downstepping in Southern Sotho. *African Studies* 31(1). 1–24.
Kunene, Daniel P. 1978. *The ideophone in Southern Sotho*. Berlin: Dietrich Reimer Verlag.
Ladd, D. Robert. 1996. *Intonational Phonology*. Cambridge: Cambridge University Press. 1st edition.
Ladd, D. Robert. 2008. *Intonational Phonology*. Cambridge: Cambridge University Press. 2nd edition.
Leben, William. 1973. Suprasegmental phonology. Doctoral thesis, MIT.
Lets'eng, M.C. 1994. Les tiroirs verbaux du Sesotho. Manuscript, Grenoble III.
Lombard, Daan P. 1976. Aspekte van toon in Noord-Sotho. Doctoral thesis, University of South Africa.
Lombard, Daan P. 1979. Duur en lengte in Noord-Sotho. *Studies in Bantoetale*. 39–69.
McCarthy, John J. 1986. OCP effects: gemination and antigemination. *Linguistic Inquiry* 17. 207–263.
Mmusi, Sheila O. 1992. Obligatory contour principle effects and violations: the case Setswana verbal tone. Doctoral thesis, University of Illinois.
Monareng, William M. 1992. A domain-based approach to Northern Sotho tonology: a Setswapo dialect. Doctoral thesis, University of Illinois.
Myers, Scott. 1996. Boundary tones and the phonetic implementation of tone in Chichewa. *Studies in African Linguistics* 25(1). 29–60.
Myers, Scott. 1998. Surface underspecification of tone in Chichewa. *Phonology* 15. 367–391.
Myers, Scott. 1999. Tone association and F0 timing in Chichewa. *Studies in African Linguistics* 28(2). 215–239.
Nespor, Irene & Marina Vogel. 1986. *Prosodic Phonology*. Dordrecht: Foris.
Nolan, Francis. 2006. Intonation. In B. Aarts & April McMahon (eds.), *Handbook of English Linguistics*. Oxford: Blackwell.
Ohala, John. 1983. Cross language use of pitch: An ethnological view. *Phonetica* 40. 1–18.
Pierrehumbert, Janet & Mary Beckman. 1988. *Japanese tone structure*. Cambridge: MIT Press.
Rialland, Annie. 2007. Question prosody: An African Perspective. In Carlos Gussenhoven & Tomas Riad (eds.), *Tones and Tunes: Studies in Word and Sentence Prosody*. Berlin: Mouton.
Rialland, Annie. 2009. The African lax question prosody: Its realisation and geographical distribution. *Lingua* 119(6). 928–949.
Selkirk, Elizabeth. 1986. On derived domains in sentence phonology. *Phonology Yearbook* 3. 371–405.
Sosa, Juan Manuel. 1999. *La entonación del español: su estructura fónica, variabilidad y dialectología*. Madrid: Ediciones Cátedra.

Truckenbrodt, Hubert. 2002. Upstep and embedded register levels. *Phonology* 19. 77–120.
Truckenbrodt, Hubert. 1995. Phonological Phrases: their relation to syntax, focus and prominence. PhD dissertation, MIT.
Yip, Moira. 1988. The obligatory contour principle and phonological rules: a loss of identity. *Linguistic Inquiry* 19(1). 65–100.
Zerbian, Sabine. 2006a. Variation in HTS in the Sotho verb. In Mugane J, Huchtinson J, & Worman D (eds.), *Trends in African linguistics*, 147–157. Somerville, MA: Cascadilla Publishing Project.
Zerbian, Sabine. 2006b. Questions in Northern Sotho. *Linguistische Berichte* 208. 385–405.
Zerbian, Sabine. 2006c. Expression of Information Structure in the Bantu Language Northern Sotho. Doctoral dissertation. Humboldt-University Berlin.
Zerbian, Sabine. 2007a. Phonological phrasing in Northern Sotho. *The Linguistic Review* 24: 233–262.
Zerbian, Sabine. 2007b. Investigating prosodic focus marking in Northern Sotho. In Katharina Hartmann, Enoch Aboh & Malte Zimmermann (eds.), *Focus strategies: evidence from African languages*, 55–79. Berlin: Mouton de Gruyter.
Zerbian, Sabine & Etienne Barnard. 2009. Phonetics and phonology of single high tone alignment in Sepedi, *Southern African Linguistics and Applied Language Studies* (SALALS) 27(4). 357–379.
Zerbian, Sabine & Etienne Barnard. 2010. Realization of two adjacent high tones – Acoustic evidence from Northern Sotho, *Southern African Linguistics and Applied Language Studies* 28(2). 101–121.
Zerbian, Sabine & Frank Kügler. 2015. Downstep in Tswana. *Proceedings of the 18th ICPhS, Glasgow*, August 2015.

Notes on contributors

(corresponding authors are marked '*')

*Michael Cahill** is Orthography Services Coordinator for SIL International. His eleven years in Ghana primarily involved working with Kɔnni language speakers in a language development project, often when living on site in the village of Yikpabongo. Since his dissertation on Kɔnni morphology and phonology, he has written on a variety of topics, including translation, endangered languages, orthography issues, and various phonological topics such as tone, intonation, and labial-velars.
Email: mike_cahill@sil.org

*Bruce Connell** teaches in the Linguistics and Language Studies Program at Glendon College, York University, and is a member of the Centre for Research on Language Contact at Glendon. His principal interests are in phonetics, historical linguistics, and language endangerment. His interest in African languages began with a sojourn of nearly four years in the Cross River region of southeastern Nigeria in the 1980s. This was followed by PhD studies at Edinburgh (awarded in 1991). In 1994 he made his first field trip to the Mambila region, which was followed by annual trips over the next several years. His fieldwork continues up to the present, as does his work on Mambila and the Mambiloid languages. Ongoing projects include a dictionary of Ba Mambila, investigations into prosodic aspects of Mambila, and work towards the reconstruction of proto-Mambiloid, including its tone system.
Email: bconnell@yorku.ca

*Laura Downing** is the Professor for African Languages at the University of Gothenburg, Sweden. Since her dissertation, her research has centered on the prosody of Bantu languages, including topics like tone, the syntax-phonology interface and information structure. She has been doing fieldwork in Malawi on issues related to Chichewa and Tumbuka prosody since around 2004 and has written a number of articles on Chichewa and Tumbuka based on her fieldwork. She is currently completing a book on *The Phonology of Chichewa* with Al Mtenje.
Email: laura.downing@sprak.gu.se

Martial Embanga Aborobongui is a junior professor at Marien Ngouabi University (Brazzaville, Republic of Congo). In 2013, he defended his doctoral thesis, entitled "Les processus segmentaux et tonals en mbondzi (variété de la langue εmbɔ́sí. C25)" at Paris 3 University (Sorbonne-Nouvelle). He was a member of the French-German project on the Phonology-Syntax interface in Bantu languages (BANTUPSYN) headed by L. Downing and Annie Rialland (2009–2011). His domains of expertise are: tonology, phonology, Bantu C languages.

Silke Hamann is Universiteit Docent (Associate Professor) at the university of Amsterdam. Her main research interests are in phonology and phonetics and she worked on a wide range of topics including perceptual cues in segmental contrasts, loanword phonology and retroflection. She works on a wide range of languages including Bantu languages.

*****Fatima Hamlaoui** is a Research fellow at the Centre for General Linguistics (ZAS) in Berlin. She does cross-linguistic work on the expression of Information Structure and the Syntax-Phonology Interface. She has been working on Bàsàá since around 2010, has co-authored a number of papers on both syntactic and tonal aspects of the language and is currently leading the elaboration of a reference corpus of Bàsàá within the framework of a French/German cooperative project.
Email: fhaml044@gmail.com

*****Charles W. Kisseberth** is Professor Emeritus at both Tel Aviv University and the University of Illinois at Urbana-Champaign. He is a recognized expert on Bantu tone systems, and has worked, notably, on Makhuwa, Nguni languages like Zulu and Xhosa, and Digo and other Mijikenda languages. He has numerous publications to his credit, and with Larry Hyman, he has edited a volume on *Theoretical Aspects of Bantu Tone*. His work on Chim(w)iini began with Mohammad Abasheikh in the 1970s and has continued more recently under an NSF/NEH grant on Documenting Endangered Languages (PI: Brent Henderson).
Email: kisseber@hotmail.com

*****Frank Kügler** is a researcher and lecturer at the University of Potsdam, Germany. He has just been awarded a Heisenberg fellowship, which will be affiliated with the University of Cologne, Germany. His research centers on tone and intonation from a cross-linguistic and typological perspective, investigating different linguistic factors, such as syntax and information structure, that influence the tonal realization and the phonological representation of tones in tone and non-tone (intonation) languages. His research includes fieldwork on Akan in Ghana.
Email: kuegler@uni-potsdam.de

*Nancy C. Kula is Professor in the department of Language and Linguistics at the University of Essex. Her research focuses on Bantu languages and phonology. She has worked on many aspects of the phonology of Bemba including the interaction between phonology and morphology, the phonology-syntax interface and tone.
Email: nckula@essex.ac.uk

Seunghun J. Lee is Associate Professor of Linguistics at International Christian University in Tokyo, Japan. His research focuses on the phonetics and phonology of Bantu languages, with topics ranging from segments to tone and prosody. He has co-written an illustration of Bàsàá, and is currently working on metathesis, lengthening and vowel syncope with Emmanuel-Moselly Makasso.

Emmanuel-Moselly Makasso is a permanent Senior Researcher at the National Centre for Éducation at the Cameroonian Ministry of Scientific Research and Innovation. He is currently a guest researcher at the Centre for General Linguistics (ZAS) in Berlin. He is interested in the phonology and tonology of Bantu languages. He is a native speaker of Bàsàá and has written a number of research papers on the language.

*Cédric Patin completed his PhD in Linguistics at Université Paris 3 in 2007. His thesis examined the tonal system of Shingazidja. After a post-doctorate at the Laboratoire de Linguistique Formelle (CNRS/Université Paris 7), he accepted the position of "Maître de conférences en phonétique et phonologie du français" at the University of Lille in 2009. His work focuses on the phonology of Bantu languages, with emphasis on the prosody-syntax interface.
Email: cedric.patin@gmail.com

Page Piccinini completed her PhD in Linguistics at the University of California, San Diego in 2016 and is a post-doctoral researcher at the École Normale Supérieure. She has worked on prosody in English and Spanish as produced by monolingual and bilingual speakers. She has also investigated the effects of intonation on tone in Moro in different utterance contexts.

*Annie Rialland is Director of Research emeritus in the Laboratory of Phonetics and Phonology, CNRS (Paris). From the beginning of her career, her scientific approach combined phonetic and phonological perspectives in the investigation of autosegmental phonology, in particular. Her main domains of expertise are phonetics, phonology, prosody, and African languages. Over the years, her work has been concerned with a diverse range of languages, mainly African (from various families: Gur, Mandé, Atlantic, Bantu), but also French and the whistled language of La Gomera.
Email: annie.rialland@univ-paris3.fr

***Sharon Rose** is Professor in the Department of Linguistics at the University of California, San Diego. Her research has centered on long distance harmony and dissimilation, the phonetics and phonology of ejectives and gutturals, and tone. She has conducted research on Ethio-Semitic languages and Moro.
Email: rose@ucsd.edu

***Sabine Zerbian** is Professor for English Linguistics at the University of Stuttgart/ Germany. Her research interests include tone and intonation in Bantu languages and in contact varieties of English. Her dissertation described grammatical aspects of information structure in the Bantu language Northern Sotho. She has worked on Northern Sotho since 2003 and has taken up work on Tswana while being a lecturer at the University of the Witwatersrand, Johannesburg from 2007–2009.
Email: sabine.zerbian@ling.uni-stuttgart.de

Index

Accent 1, 6, 7, 10, 20, 55, 120, 225, 227ff, 230, 234, 238, 279, 286, 290, 295, 297, 305, 306, 318, 322, 342, 350, 357–359, 429
- (see also Final accent, Penult accent, Pitch-accent)
Adverbs (and adverbials) 24, 26, 30, 227, 242, 245, 251, 272ff, 312, 324, 338, 351, 423 (fn8)
Akan 4, 5, 7–10, 12, 89–130, 141, 183, 289, 344, 354
Alternative question 310ff
Associative 54, 57, 61, 62, 95, 96, 97, 138, 255, 256, 259, 269
Automatic downstep 2, 58, 93ff, 133, 177, 195, 326,
Autosegmental-metrical model 285, 394, 419, 421
Avoidance 5, 124, 198, 308, 326, 331, 368, 388, 429

Bantoid 1, 9, 131, 134
Bàsàá 1, 4, 7, 8, 9, 10, 12, 65, 167–193, 215, 387, 400,
Bemba 1, 4, 5, 6, 7, 8, 9, 10, 12, 26, 58, 68, 78, 91, 102, 120, 321–363, 418
Biased questions 312ff
Boundary tone 1, 2, 5, 6, 9, 10, 19, 22, 26, 30, 37–38, 42, 46, 47, 55, 65, 68ff, 71, 80, 89ff, 101, 115, 116, 123, 124, 133, 156, 161, 162, 177, 179, 182, 195, 202, 208, 211–213, 217–219, 285, 290, 292ff, 300ff, 306, 316, 317, 318, 321, 322, 331ff, 334–335, 338, 339, 340, 342, 346, 354, 356–359, 365, 373, 375, 378, 388, 395, 398 (fn), 400, 405, 407, 408, 411ff, 418–419, 421, 423, 428, 429

Canonical word order 227, 373, 422
Canonical sentence 231, 235
Chichewa 1, 3, 4, 5, 7, 8, 9, 10, 12, 102, 103, 104, 120, 133, 161, 162, 171, 176, 183, 195, 196, 199, 215, 332, 335, 344, 356, 365–391, 403, 405, 407, 408, 411, 418, 422, 424

Chimiini 1, 4, 7, 8, 9, 10, 12, 26, 72, 79, 226–284, 308
Choice question 380, 381
Cleft 10, 19, 20, 21 (fn), 32ff, 37, 38, 39ff, 42, 44, 47, 183, 225, 249, 315 (fn), 321, 345, 351, 373, 375, 422
Coarticulation (tonal) 133, 142–149
Complement clause 32, 41, 89, 90, 91, 105, 107, 123, 174, 217, 274–279, 334, 355, 356, 359
- (see also relative clause)
Compound (sentences) 53, 55, 66–70, 72
Compression (register/pitch range) 3, 7, 19, 26, 27, 28, 30, 46, 217, 321, 322, 336, 351, 355, 357, 359
Conjoint/disjoint 336, 352, 353, 357, 358
Constituent question, see wh-question
Content question 1, 72, 74, 131, 132, 156, 157, 160, 161, 163, 315, 316, 317, 419
- (see also wh-question)
Continuation 11, 19, 20, 41–47, 68, 209, 334, 335, 339, 342, 355, 359, 365, 373, 375, 378, 379, 387, 414, 415, 419, 430
Contour tone 55, 62 (fn), 77, 132, 135, 137, 138, 139, 140, 169, 171, 197, 323
Contrastive topic 300, 303, 304, 313, 314, 338–342, 355, 356, 357 (fn)
- (see also Topic/topicalization)
Coordinate structures 44, 106, 107, 108, 289, 300, 414, 428

Declarative (sentences) 1, 19, 23ff, 41, 42, 44, 46, 47, 55, 64, 80, 89, 97ff, 100–104, 105–112, 114, 116, 119, 123, 124, 131, 132, 133, 141ff, 150, 154, 156, 161, 163, 167, 177ff, 189, 285, 290ff, 300–304, 306, 307, 308, 311, 322, 331–342, 344, 346, 347, 352, 355, 356, 358, 365, 371ff, 383, 393, 395, 401–415, 416, 418, 419, 424, 426, 428, 430
Declination 2, 3, 4, 26, 30, 38, 133, 142, 143, 144, 146, 148, 150, 154, 155, 161, 162, 165, 179, 332, 341, 344, 346, 350, 401, 418

Devoicing 6, 208, 292, 406, 407, 424
Discourse 72–74, 85, 163, 182, 183, 217, 241, 270, 339, 357, 359
Dislocation 1, 10, 218, 225, 231, 263, 270ff, 336ff, 355
– (see also Left dislocation, Right dislocation)
Doubling (tonal) 169, 325–327, 328, 329, 331, 358, 368 (see also Spread/spreading (tonal))
Downdrift 2, 3, 4, 8, 9, 10, 54, 60, 65, 74, 85, 91, 93, 133, 143, 147, 148, 149, 165, 195, 196, 200, 201, 202, 204, 206, 207, 208, 219, 402, 403, 409
Downstep 1, 2, 3, 4, 7, 9, 15, 16, 19, 22, 28, 38, 89, 90, 91, 93, 94, 95, 102, 103, 104, 116, 123, 133, 142, 165, 169, 227, 232, 235, 237, 243, 245, 249, 260, 263, 267, 272, 279, 287, 290, 291, 301, 303, 306, 322, 325, 326, 330, 331, 335, 337, 338, 341, 342, 343, 344, 346, 347, 348, 357, 359, 372, 375, 379, 380, 384, 400, 402, 403, 408
Downtrend 2, 3, 4, 6, 131, 132, 141, 142, 144, 146, 148, 149, 155, 160, 164
Dschang Bamileke 2, 326, 342

Echo question 313, 314
Edge (tone) 133, 162
Embosi 1, 4, 5, 6, 7, 8, 9, 10, 12, 26, 62, 102, 176, 177, 195–222, 332, 335, 362, 387, 402, 407
Emotion 54, 65, 81, 84, 85
Emphasis 53, 72, 75, 81, 91, 116, 121, 140, 195, 196, 202, 216–219, 225, 239, 243ff, 272, 274, 276, 277, 279, 304, 385ff, 422, 426
English 25, 69, 70, 76, 104, 133, 150, 174, 207, 208, 209, 428, 429,
Expansion (register/pitch range, pitch) 2, 3, 6, 8, 9, 19, 26, 27, 46, 120, 154, 162, 182, 195, 206, 216–219, 313, 314, 315, 321, 322, 336 (fn), 342, 343, 344, 346, 347, 348, 350, 351, 354, 355, 357, 359, 385, 394, 419, 426

F0 scaling 132, 150, 163, 165

Final accent 225, 227, 229, 233, 234, 241, 243, 246, 249, 253, 255, 261, 264, 273, 274, 275, 276, 278, 279, 281
Final lowering 2, 3, 4, 6, 41, 65, 80, 101, 102, 115, 119, 123, 133, 142–149, 161, 163, 179, 182, 202, 204, 205, 207, 208, 215, 292, 321, 322, 332, 333, 334, 341, 344, 346, 350, 355, 357, 359, 365, 372, 375, 384, 387, 407
Floating tone 3, 57, 58, 60, 61, 62, 96, 169
Focus 1, 3, 6, 7, 19, 39ff, 47, 72, 81, 91, 99, 100, 116, 120ff, 157, 167, 183ff, 196, 202, 215, 216, 217, 225, 227, 231, 232, 236, 239–242, 243, 244, 245–252, 253, 256, 258, 260ff, 268, 271, 273, 274, 276, 277, 279, 289, 321, 322, 327 (fn), 329, 336 (fn), 342, 348, 351–354, 355, 357, 358, 359, 381 (fn), 385ff, 394, 405, 421ff, 428
French 76, 142, 218,
Fronted (element/constituent) 10, 19, 25, 47, 53, 55, 72ff, 99, 108, 115, 175, 303, 317, 321, 329, 334, 335, 338, 339, 340, 359, 384

Grammatical tone 92, 93, 96, 131, 132, 137, 138, 161, 323, 324, 396, 426
– (see also Melodic tone)

Hausa 76, 150, 165, 188, 215, 342, 344

Ideophones 424
Igbo 3, 141, 195
Imperative 91, 97, 118, 119
Interrogative 74, 112ff, 117, 124, 141, 157, 163, 213, 262, 315, 405, 424
– (see also echo question, polar question, surprise question, wh-question, yes-no question)
Intonational enhancement 425
Intonational phrase/Intonation phrase (i-phrase) 11ff, 90ff, 97, 100, 101, 116, 140, 161, 167, 174, 176, 189, 199, 209, 218, 219, 264, 286, 288, 289, 290, 294, 297, 301, 302–305, 308, 318, 322, 329, 333, 340, 342, 354–359, 365, 366, 371, 372, 373, 374, 375, 376, 378, 379, 380, 388, 399, 400, 405, 408, 411

Kɔnni 1, 4, 7, 8, 9, 10, 12, 53–88, 216, 344,
Kwa 2, 82, 89, 121, 129, 348

Lax question prosody 9, 76, 113, 163, 177, 182
Left dislocation 89, 108ff, 114, 123, 218, 227, 268ff, 423
– (see also Dislocation)
Lexical tone 6, 19, 24, 27, 28, 35, 39, 42, 46, 63, 89, 91, 92, 93, 97, 101, 124, 131, 132, 133, 135, 136, 161ff, 177, 195, 219, 285, 286ff, 292, 294, 296, 298, 301, 304, 308ff, 314, 316, 318, 321, 323, 324–326, 328, 331, 332, 352, 366ff, 368, 382, 387, 393, 394, 395–401, 406, 415, 417, 428, 429, 430
Lowering (register/pitch range/pitch) 2, 3, 4, 6, 7, 10, 91, 120, 121

Mambila 1, 4, 5, 7, 8, 9, 10, 12, 102, 131–166, 216
Mambiloid 134, 164
Melodic tone 323, 326
– (see also grammatical tone)
Moro 1, 4, 7, 8, 9, 10, 12, 19–52, 58, 62, 214, 215, 326
Multiple questions 348–350
– (see also wh-questions, content questions)

Negative (verbs) 95, 96, 138, 161, 225, 229, 260–263, 266, 282, 396
Neutralization (tonal) 89, 101, 103, 111, 113, 118, 123
Niger-Congo 24, 89, 93, 129, 222, 321
Northern Sotho 393, 394, 400, 408, 427

OCP (Obligatory Contour Principle) 3, 4, 53, 58, 62, 198, 316, 323, 325ff, 328, 331, 393, 397, 398, 399

Paragraph 74, 85
Paralinguistic 3, 6, 54, 81, 84, 85, 86, 385, 394, 421, 429
Penult tone 287, 288, 289, 290, 292, 293, 295, 296, 298, 303, 305, 306, 307, 308, 309, 310, 311, 312, 313, 314, 318, 375
Penult accent 225–231

Penult lengthening 6, 9, 171 (fn), 183, 226, 295, 333, 365, 367, 368, 369, 370, 375, 376, 379, 381 (fn), 393, 395, 404, 405, 413, 416, 418, 419, 421, 422, 423, 424, 425, 426, 428, 430
Phonological word 135, 195, 199, 200, 225, 403
Phonological Phrase 11, 12, 13, 171, 199, 200, 219, 286, 288, 289, 290, 291, 292, 295, 296, 297, 298, 299, 307, 312, 320, 327, 329, 352, 358, 368, 372, 374, 376, 378, 399, 400, 405, 409
Phrasing (prosodic) 7, 10, 12, 44, 89, 95, 97, 98, 104, 105, 108, 111, 120, 122, 179, 225, 263, 274, 286, 288, 289, 322, 327, 331, 336, 338, 354, 358
– (See also Intonational Phrase, Phonological Phrase)
Pitch-accent 299, 318
Pivot lengthening 371
Plateauing (tonal) 368
Polar question 1, 8, 9,19, 20, 23, 24,25, 26, 27, 28, 29, 30, 33, 34, 35, 41, 46, 47, 54, 76, 77, 78, 79, 89, 90, 91, 102, 112, 113, 114, 115, 116, 118, 124, 131, 132, 141, 154, 156, 160, 161, 163, 196, 305, 308, 309, 311, 342, 343, 344, 345, 355
– (See also yes-no questions)
Polarity (tonal) 59, 60
Prosodic constituent 11, 226, 227, 231, 240, 243, 245, 264, 266
– (see also Intonation Phrase, Phonological Word, Phonological Phrase, Recursive)
Pseudo-relative/relativization 245, 249, 252, 255, 256, 257, 268, 276, 277, 278

Question marker 154, 156, 157, 161, 163
Quote (direct/indirect) 70

Raising (register, pitch range/pitch) 2, 3, 6, 7, 8, 9, 15, 27, 30, 37, 43, 46, 47, 322, 340, 341, 351, 354, 355, 357, 359, 375, 384, 418
Range (pitch) 2, 5, 20, 41, 65, 68, 85, 133, 134, 159, 165, 206, 208, 312, 313, 355, 388, 393
– (see also Compression, Expansion, Lowering, Raising)

Recursive (prosodic constituency/phrasing) 12, 98, 100, 108, 111, 127, 179, 218, 225, 234, 241, 354–356, 359, 379
Register 2, 3, 6, 9, 16, 36, 79, 90, 100, 103, 107, 118, 121, 130, 154, 162, 169, 195, 206, 211, 219, 237, 245, 311, 315, 322, 331, 332, 341, 375, 385, 388, 415, 419, 421, 428
– (see also Compression, Expansion, Lowering, Raising, Register tones, Register tier theory)
Register tones 130, 162
Register tier theory 162, 164, 165
Relative clause 22, 32, 215, 218, 227, 229, 246ff, 256, 283, 335, 336 (fn), 345, 355, 356, 359, 373, 374, 376, 377, 378
– (See also Pseudo-relative)
Replacement (tonal) 89, 93, 96, 97, 118
Reset (pitch) 100, 107, 409, 411, 412, 423, 425
Right dislocated/dislocation 10, 218, 263–266, 268, 271, 279, 336, 338, 355, 357
– (see also Dislocation)

Sepedi 401
Shekgalagari 163, 394, 405, 407, 424, 428
Shift (tonal) 287, 288, 329, 330
Shingazidja 1, 4, 7, 8, 9, 10, 12, 26, 62, 72, 91, 120, 183, 197, 285–320, 418
Simplification (tonal) 168
Sotho-Tswana 394, 400, 405, 416, 422
Southern Sotho 393, 394, 400, 401, 408, 410, 421, 422, 424
Spread/spreading (tonal) 19, 21, 22, 37, 38, 40, 44, 56, 60, 61, 63, 65, 89, 91, 93, 94, 95, 96, 98, 168, 169–171, 189, 323, 324–331, 352, 357, 358, 396–398, 399, 407, 410, 425
– (See also Doubling (tonal))
Stress 7, 91 (fn), 229, 229–230, 267, 290, 295, 305, 306, 318, 322, 368ff, 371, 405, 407, 422, 426
Subordinate clause, see Complement clause

Super-high tone 305, 307, 308, 309, 310, 311, 312, 318
Superimposition/superposition (of boundary tones) 6, 196, 208, 219, 388
Surprise question 314
Swahili 2, 225, 290, 381

Terraced-level (tone languages) 90, 93
Topic/topicalization 10, 99, 100, 108, 112, 321, 329, 334, 338, 339, 340, 341, 355, 356, 357, 359, 366, 367, 372, 373, 374, 376, 379, 422
– (See also Contrastive topic)
Tumbuka 1, 4, 7, 8, 9, 10, 12, 91, 215, 292, 305, 365–391
Turkish 351, 354 (fn)
Tswana 1, 4, 7, 8, 9, 10, 12, 13, 26, 58, 62, 91, 123, 326, 399–433

Utterance phrase 294

Vowel length(ening) 9, 10, 19, 41, 42, 44, 46, 76, 79, 80, 81, 89, 90, 91, 105, 113–116, 123, 169, 198, 225, 226, 229, 230, 238, 318, 329, 371, 396
– (see also Penult lengthening)

Wh-questions 19, 32–41, 97, 112, 115–118, 122, 183ff, 195, 196, 213–215, 217, 239, 256ff, 285, 291, 313, 315, 316 (fn), 317, 345–354, 383–384, 385, 415, 419–420
– (See also Content question)

Yes-no questions 76, 167, 177, 180ff, 189, 195, 196, 209, 211–213, 219, 227, 233, 235–238, 241, 243, 244, 261, 264, 266, 267, 269, 270, 271, 273, 279–280, 286, 305–310, 312, 314, 318, 342, 379–383, 387, 416–419, 421, 429
– (See also Polar questions)
Yoruba 3, 5, 14, 93, 102, 161, 162, 165, 195, 206, 207, 214, 343

www.ingramcontent.com/pod-product-compliance
Lightning Source LLC
Chambersburg PA
CBHW022103290426

44112CB00008B/527